Derek Van den Bogaerde in Calcutta, November 1945

Dirk Bogarde

Dirk Bogarde
The authorised biography

JOHN COLDSTREAM

'I don't like myself as I am, I suppose, so I've had to invent another person. It's not so harmful, really. We've all got daydreams. Mine have gone a step further than most people's – that's all. Quite often I've even managed to believe in the Major myself.'

MAJOR POLLOCK, IN *SEPARATE TABLES* BY
TERENCE RATTIGAN, 1954

Weidenfeld & Nicolson
LONDON

For Sue
– 'Force of life'

First published in Great Britain in 2004
by Weidenfeld & Nicolson

A CIP catalogue record for this book
is available from the British Library.

ISBN 0 297 60730 8

Typeset and printed in Great Britain by
Butler and Tanner Ltd,
Frome and London

Weidenfeld & Nicolson

The Orion Publishing Group Ltd
Orion House
5 Upper Saint Martin's Lane
London, WC2H 9EA

Contents

List of Illustrations ix

Family Tree x

Prologue 1

Introduction 5

PART ONE: DEREK

1   'Constant dripping wears away the stone' 23

2   '. . . life is not all cushions and barley sugar' 40

3   'Christ Almighty! Now I know there's a war on: they've started to ration the Talent!' 64

4   'I'll end up by being a good manager, you see!' 85

5   'I imagined it all so completely, and in such detail, that finally I almost came to believe it had actually taken place' 106

6   'Full of complexes I am' 127

PART TWO: DIRK

7   'He can toss us a pancake any day!' 153

8   'It's all perfectly normal. If you wait until tonight, you'll see the rape and buggery set in' 173

9   'You, what's the bleeding time?' 'Ten past ten, Sir' 193

10   'I suppose they prefer to put me to bed than to take me to bed' 211

11   'To have news value is to have a tin can tied to one's tail' 233

12   'Il faut le voir pour le croire' 252

13   'It is comforting to think that perhaps a million men are no longer living in fear' 270

14 'I'm a gentleman's gentleman. And you're no bloody gentleman!' 289

15 'I have never felt quite so abandoned and destroyed as I do today' 310

16 'FORCE memory!' 327

17 'I did a great look' 347

18 'There is a movement afoot to take Dirk Bogarde seriously!' 364

19 'You felt you were in the same room with him' 382

20 'The world is full of dotty people' 404

21 'Would you call camouflage deceit, lying, or merely a means of survival?' 427

22 'You are very good indeed at saying an interesting bookful without in fact saying anything *really* personal at all' 446

23 'But I'm still in the shell, and you haven't cracked it yet, honey' 465

24 'Stuff this!' 485

25 'I just love to be asked to talk about *me*' 507

26 'DO remember it is *not* what we really did' 527

Epilogue 541

Acknowledgements 550
Sources 555
Appendices 579
Index 589

List of Illustrations

Sections of photographs appear between pages 116–117; 244–245, 372–373 and 500–501

Endpapers
(front) The three ages of Dirk[1 and 31]
(back) Drawing by Richard Cole

Frontispiece
Derek Van den Bogaerde in Calcutta, November 1945.[7]

Between pages 116 *and* 117
Derek's paternal grandfather, Aimé Van den Bogaerde, 1899.[1] • Local newspaper report on the death of Aimé's cousin, Valère.[1] • Derek's grandmother, Grace.[1] • His father, Ulric, aged about seven.[1] • His maternal grandfather, Forrest Niven.[1] • Grandmother Jane's 1886 Christmas card.[1] • Derek's mother Margaret, 'waiting for the Wolf'.[1] • Margaret, wartime entertainer.[1] • The newly-commissioned Ulric.[1] • Ulric at *The Times*, 1920.[2] • Ulric and Margaret, 1920.[1] • The infant Derek and his parents, 1921.[1] • Derek in his first year.[1] • Father and son, c. 1926.[1] • Derek and Lu.[1] • Lullington from the air.[1] • The Church of the Good Shepherd.[1] • The Cottage.[1] • Family day out.[1] • Margaret and Lally at the Cottage.[1] • Ulric and Margaret on the Downs.[1] • 30 Winton Street, Alfriston, painted by Derek.[1] • University College School report.[1] • Class 1a at Allan Glen's.[3] • Margaret.[1] • Sarah Murray (Aunt Sadie).[4] • William Murray (Uncle Murray).[4] Hester McClellan with her daughter Nickie and Derek.[4] • Derek's study of the Queen Mary, 1934.[1] • Drawings by Derek in his Allan Glen's exercise-book.[3]

Between pages 244 *and* 245
Guy Fawkes Night at Newick, 1938.[5] • Nerine Cox.[5] • Derek's poster for *Journey's End*.[5] • Derek and Lionel Cox in *Journey's End*.[5] • Margaret and Gareth.[1] • In *You Never Can Tell*, Amersham, November 1940.[1] • William Wightman.[1] • Derek's 'fiancée', Anne Deans, in Clemence Dane's *Granite*.[6] • E. L. L. (Anthony) Forwood.[1] • Gitta Alpar.[1] • Derek's dressing-room at Wyndham's Theatre, 1941.[1] • With Vida Hope, Joan Sterndale Bennett and Peter Ustinov in *Diversion No. 2.*[1] • At Catterick, June 1941.[1] • Jack ('Tony') Jones with Margaret, Elizabeth and Derek at Clayton.[7] • Derek by Ulric.[7] • Kenneth Costin, Christopher Greaves, Derek and Sydney Allen in Normandy, 1944.[8] • Derek in his mobile office.[7] • Falaise Gap, August 1944.[7] • Derek and Chris with the 'family' at Eindhoven, 1945.[7] • With Eve Holiday, 1945.[7] • With Bert Garthoff and 'Milly' at Radio Batavia, December 1945.[7] • Major-General Douglas Hawthorn, Bandoeng, 1946.[1] • Dorothy Fells.[1] • At Tandjoengpriok, July 1946.[7] • With Hugh Jolly in Singapore, August 1946.[9] • With Maureen Pook in *Power Without Glory*, 1947.[1] • On location with Kathleen Ryan for *Esther Waters*.[1] • With Gareth at Pinewood.[1] • With Jack in London, 1948.[7] • Tony Forwood and Glynis Johns on their wedding day in 1942, with Beatrice Lillie.[1] • Dirk with Glynis.[1] • 44 Chester Row.[1]

• Tony and Gareth Forwood.[1] • Mary Dodd (née Forwood).[1] • Tony as Will Scarlet.[1] • Dirk as Tom Riley in *The Blue Lamp*.[10] • As Captain Molineux in *The Shaughraun*.[11]

Between pages 372 and 373
Earl St John.[1] • Olive Dodds.[1] • John Davis.[1] • In *Doctor in the House*.[12] • With Ralph Thomas.[1] • With Betty Box.[12] • Theo Cowan at Cannes.[13] • With Agnes and Hans Zwickl.[12] • Jean Simmons.[1] • Dirk's favourite still.[12] • Irene Howard.[1] • With Noël Coward.[1] • Arnold Schulkes.[14] • With Kay Kendall, Rex Harrison and Margaret Leighton.[1] • 'Idol of the Odeons'.[12] • 'The price of fame?'[12] • Meeting the Queen.[1] • In *Mirabelle* magazine.[1] • With Rock Hudson, 1957.[12] • With George Cukor.[15] • Victor Aller on *Song Without End*.[1] • On location for *The Singer Not the Song*.[12] • As Melville Farr in *Victim*.[12] • Basil Dearden.[1] • As Barrett in *The Servant*.[16] • With Joseph Losey on *King and Country*.[1] • In *Darling*, with Julie Christie.[1] • With John Schlesinger.[1] • At Bendrose with Jon Whiteley.[12] • At Beel House, with Elizabeth and her son Mark.[1] • At Drummers Yard.[1] • Capucine and Judy Garland, Christmas 1960.[1] • At Nore.[1] • Gareth Forwood and Kay Young at Adam's Farm.[1] • With Annie.[17] • Villa Berti.[1] • With Labo.[18] • As Gabriel in *Modesty Blaise*.[1] • With Jacqueline Sassard and Michael York in *Accident*.[1] • With Jack Clayton on *Our Mother's House*.[1] • With Ingrid Thulin in *The Damned*.[1]

Between pages 500 and 501
With Luchino Visconti.[1] • Le Haut Clermont, by Dirk.[1] • 'Erecting defences'.[1] • With Capucine.[1] • Clermont from above.[1] • With Charlotte Rampling.[1] • In *The Night Porter*.[19] • Liliana Cavani.[20] • With Glenda Jackson, 1983.[1] • With Alain Resnais.[1] • With Rainer Werner Fassbinder.[21] • With Sean Connery.[22] • With Jane Birkin.[23] • Bertrand Tavernier.[1] • The 'Long Room' at Clermont.[1] • Dorothy Gordon by Mervyn Peake.[24] • With Norah Smallwood.[1] • Hélène Bordes.[1] • Nicholas Shakespeare.[1] • The writer at work.[25] • In the Pond.[1] • With Lucilla and Gareth Van den Bogaerde, 1981.[1] • With Brock, 1977.[1] • The Bowlbys, 1986.[1] • With Sheila Attenborough.[1] • At the National Theatre in the early Nineties.[26] • With Helena Bonham Carter.[27] • With Molly Daubeny.[27] • With Elizabeth after being knighted.[28] • With Tony and Alma Cogan, 1964.[1] • Sheila MacLean.[29] • Portrait by Bruce Weber.[30]

The author and the publishers are grateful to the following for permission to reproduce the photographs listed above:

1 Estate of Dirk Bogarde	18 Tom Murray
2 Derek Heath	19 Warner Brothers
3 William Lockie	20 Trevor Humphries
4 Forrest McClellan	21 Karl-Heinz Vogelmann
5 Estate of Nerine Selwood	22 United Artists Pictures
6 Jason Barnes	23 UGC Cinemas
7 John Beech	24 Estate of Mervyn Peake/Rebecca Harrison
8 Times Newspapers Ltd	25 Carlos Freire
9 Caryl Roberts	26 Julian Calder
10 Carlton/Rank/Ealing Films	27 Doug McKenzie/Professional Photographic Services
11 G. Scott Bushe/Richard Johnson Archive	28 The Daily Telegraph (© Copyright of Telegraph Group Limited)
12 Carlton International Media/Rank	29 Sheila MacLean
13 Laurie Bellew	30 Bruce Weber (© Bruce Weber, All Rights Reserved)
14 Arnold Schulkes	31 Dmitri Kasterine
15 Gerald Hill	
16 Warner-Pathé	
17 Roddy McDowall	

Niven tree

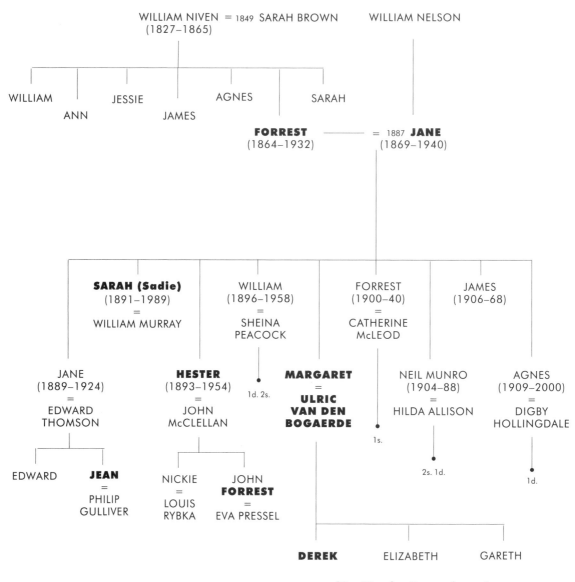

WILLIAM NIVEN = 1849 SARAH BROWN
(1827–1865)

WILLIAM NELSON

WILLIAM

ANN

JESSIE

JAMES

AGNES

SARAH

FORREST ——— = 1887 **JANE**
(1864–1932)   (1869–1940)

SARAH (Sadie)
(1891–1989)
=
WILLIAM MURRAY

WILLIAM
(1896–1958)
=
SHEINA
PEACOCK

FORREST
(1900–40)
=
CATHERINE
McLEOD

JAMES
(1906–68)

JANE
(1889–1924)
=
EDWARD
THOMSON

HESTER
(1893–1954)
=
JOHN
McCLELLAN

1d. 2s.

MARGARET
=
**ULRIC
VAN DEN
BOGAERDE**

NEIL MUNRO
(1904–88)
=
HILDA ALLISON

AGNES
(1909–2000)
=
DIGBY
HOLLINGDALE

EDWARD

JEAN
=
PHILIP
GULLIVER

NICKIE
=
LOUIS
RYBKA

JOHN
FORREST
=
EVA PRESSEL

1s.

2s. 1d.

1d.

DEREK

ELIZABETH

GARETH

[See Van den Bogaerde tree]

Van den Bogaerde tree

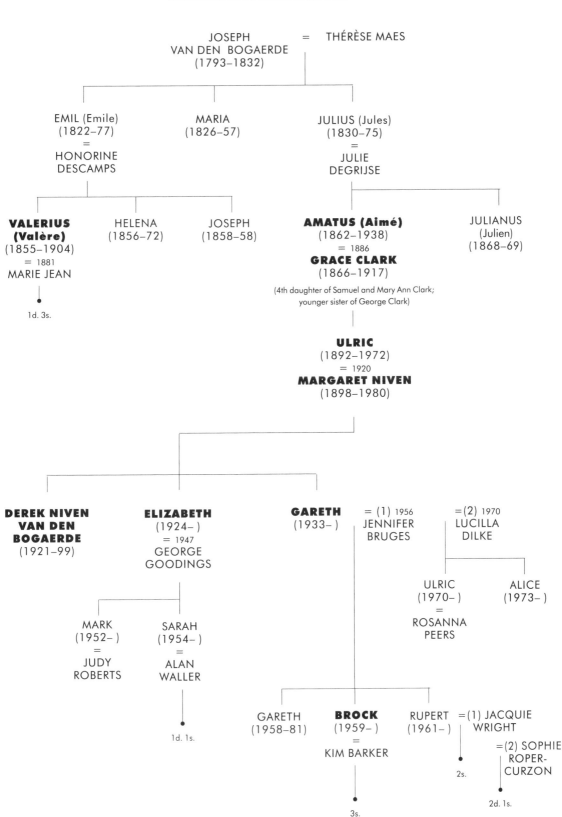

JOSEPH
VAN DEN BOGAERDE
(1793–1832)
= THÉRÈSE MAES

EMIL (Emile)
(1822–77)
=
HONORINE
DESCAMPS

MARIA
(1826–57)

JULIUS (Jules)
(1830–75)
=
JULIE
DEGRIJSE

VALERIUS
(Valère)
(1855–1904)
= 1881
MARIE JEAN

1d. 3s.

HELENA
(1856–72)

JOSEPH
(1858–58)

AMATUS (Aimé)
(1862–1938)
= 1886
GRACE CLARK
(1866–1917)

(4th daughter of Samuel and Mary Ann Clark;
younger sister of George Clark)

JULIANUS
(Julien)
(1868–69)

ULRIC
(1892–1972)
= 1920
MARGARET NIVEN
(1898–1980)

DEREK NIVEN
VAN DEN
BOGAERDE
(1921–99)

ELIZABETH
(1924–)
= 1947
GEORGE
GOODINGS

GARETH
(1933–)

= (1) 1956
JENNIFER
BRUGES

=(2) 1970
LUCILLA
DILKE

ULRIC
(1970–)
=
ROSANNA
PEERS

ALICE
(1973–)

MARK
(1952–)
=
JUDY
ROBERTS

SARAH
(1954–)
=
ALAN
WALLER

1d. 1s.

GARETH
(1958–81)

BROCK
(1959–)
=
KIM BARKER

3s.

RUPERT
(1961–)

=(1) JACQUIE
WRIGHT

2s.

=(2) SOPHIE
ROPER-
CURZON

2d. 1s.

Prologue

'I think you and I have the measure of each other'

At about noon on Saturday, 8 May 1999, Sheila MacLean, holding a glass of white wine, took the few paces from the kitchen to the drawing-room window of the fourth-floor apartment in Chelsea where she had been living for a little over two years. On the way she placed the glass, as usual, on a table next to a wheelchair which, for most of the day, rested just inside the open doorway and faced towards a slim, neglected balcony, then south across a tidy communal garden with its tall trees, to the upper reaches of the reddish-brown buildings 150 yards away, and to the Light. The all-important Light.

For the moment, however, the Light was not a priority. At this time of day the occupant of the chair liked to watch the television news, no matter how lowering its content. In a way, the more ghastly the better: the mess man is making of the world was always a stimulus for a decent argument at the lunch table. Sheila switched on the set – a large device, out of proportion with its surroundings – and tweaked the curtains across to shade the screen. As she did so, the man in the chair began to cough. 'You've choked yourself on that sweetie,' Sheila said, with a hint of the scold. She had in mind the chocolate bonbon which a visitor had brought at teatime the previous day. She turned round to see the man, still coughing slightly and with the triumphant look of a schoolboy who had scored a point against his teacher, holding between his outstretched right forefinger and thumb a small object. It was the sweet. Sheila laughed and returned to the kitchen, leaving her charge to his Frascati and his baleful news. The coughing ceased.

'I swear to God I was in there no longer than 20, 30 seconds, max, and something came into my head,' Sheila would recall, much later. ' "Something's gone wrong." ' She went back into the drawing-room and found the figure slumped in his chair. 'He was gone. That first cough must have been the beginning of an embolism in the chest – no pain, nothing, just a little cough. You couldn't ask for a better death.' Despite what she knew in her heart, and despite his instruction from the outset that he was not to be resuscitated, the instinct of the skilled nurse compelled Sheila to go to work. She put him on the floor and checked that nothing was lodged in the throat. Then, with the head back, ready for mouth-to-mouth, she began pulmonary resuscitation:

> At the first couple of major pushes on the chest, there was a big influx, a noise
> of breath going into the lungs, and an attempt to inspire, to inflate them. All
> the time I'm doing this, I'm saying, 'Not like this. It's too much for everybody.
> For *me* – it's too sudden for me, too.' I kept going for about twenty minutes.
> For a while I felt like he was trying to come back. Then that stopped, and this
> communication came to me, almost as if he spoke directly into my ear. It said,
> 'That's enough, Sheila, stop now. I'm out. It's OK, it's not as bad as you think.
> It's OK.' I swear to God, I stopped like that – as if somebody had taken my
> hands off him.

She stepped towards the telephone in the hall. 'I was sort of communicating
then to him myself, "OK, if you're out, make it go right. Don't get stuck. Keep
moving."' On the one hand, her own distress and the implications of what had
happened were hitting her hard. On the other, 'It was all calm, completely calm.
Really, really easy.' She had the presence of mind not to dial 999, with the
attendant risk of publicity. Instead she called the owner of the nursing agency,
Angela Hamlin, and said, 'Come quickly, he's gone.' Then she rang the doctor,
Peter Wheeler, who immediately abandoned the weekend chores which had
taken him to his attic in south London. Finally, weighted with apprehension,
she contacted the family. As her fellow professionals took over, Sheila packed her
belongings in the smaller of the two modest bedrooms, summoned the lift, and
left 2 Cadogan Gardens for ever.

Not for the first time she had been present as a life ended. However, the
conclusion to this one was a severe shock, both because of its suddenness and
because the relationship with the man in her care had assumed an intensity
and significance more powerful than that of a love affair. Sheila MacLean, a
straightforward, plain-speaking, no-nonsense, humorous woman from County
Donegal, believes that in some unfathomable way she was sent to prepare Dirk
Bogarde for what, in the circumstances, would be the best possible death.

When they met in the spring of 1997, Sheila had returned recently to nursing
after six years working on the rehabilitation of prisoners with drug and alcohol
problems. She was reluctant to take on a long-term residential commitment, but
agreed that she would if necessary spend six weeks living-in before going 'non-
residential'. After about a week with a patient, she was told by Angela Hamlin:
'There is somebody else, a celebrity who lives close to Sloane Square. We've been
trying to find placements for him, but I suppose the delicate way of saying it is
that he is difficult to suit up with people.' Sheila, who guessed the identity
immediately, was unenthusiastic; she had admired some of Dirk Bogarde's best
and most serious films, but was wary of 'celebrities'. The portents were not
favourable when she and her employer visited the flat.

She found, in effect, another prisoner: at that point, Bogarde used the word about himself. A man who for most of his seventy-six years had zealously fostered his independence was now trapped by physical incapacity and was wholly dependent. A public figure famed for an impenetrable privacy was reliant on others in his most intimate moments. A seemingly self-assured, controlling, even manipulative, and above all supremely competent human being had been reduced by a stroke to acute vulnerability. He was depressed and resentful. His left side was paralysed. He required physical support. 'She's quite small,' said Angela Hamlin when she saw him appraising the new arrival, 'but she's very strong!' The patient needed that reassurance.

Sheila knew right away that here was somebody with whom she could empathise. 'He was quite irascible. But what struck me more than anything was that his character was really obvious, over and above the physical problems. Illnesses operate on all kinds of different levels. People can use illness, sometimes quite obviously, sometimes much more covertly, to control situations. And I have to say that right from the start I didn't feel that about Dirk. Because of that, that level of empathy was really strong from the start.' She established quickly that although Bogarde was depressed by his predicament, the essence of what he was had survived:

The big thing was a sort of old-fashioned, gentlemanly good manners – integrity, old English values, things that people don't consider to be of any moment really. I saw those in Dirk in a way that I'd never seen in anybody else. I know all that is to some extent a contrivance, but it was so much part of what he *really was* that one couldn't help but identify with it and feel that it was something really important. The other aspect was that he was unique and had contributed a lot and he still had something to say and do. And that is when it became clear to me that I should stay longer than six weeks. I thought: 'To hell with this, I'm not going to be able to walk away.'

Once or twice, Bogarde asked what Sheila's plans were, and received a non-committal reply. During lunch one day he again broached the subject. 'He said, "You know, it is getting close to the six weeks. What is it that you want to do? Because it is really important to me." And I said, "Well, I think I could stay on a wee bit longer." I didn't want to overdo it. And he said, "You have no idea how much of a relief that is to me. Because in all honesty I think you and I have the measure of each other." And I understood exactly what he meant. Because I did think that was true – that we did have the measure of each other.'

The importance of this association so late in Bogarde's life cannot be exaggerated. The following pages will demonstrate that until Sheila MacLean moved in to take care of his needs, he had only ever had one sustained involvement with another person living at close quarters. All the other, deepest friendships were at a remove; perhaps out of necessity, as in the war – and usually at a considerable geographical distance – but almost invariably out of preference. It was safer that way. Yet this unexpected meeting of minds in the late nineties was to prove profoundly salutary.

Mercifully, the stroke had not impaired his intelligence and wit. He was handicapped, but not in pain. There was no progressive, wasting illness, his greatest dread. He could carry on a sort of life. Conversation, company, even a little written work, were still possible. More important, however, was the gift of time, to enable a 'Coming to Terms' – the title of a chapter in his final volume of memoirs. 'Those last two years,' says Sheila, 'were valuable for whatever a human being has to do – to contemplate who and what he was. He didn't have to pretend anything. He didn't have to affect a certain way of being.' So he stripped away all artifice, all performance. He divested himself of those who sapped rather than revitalised him. Just as in the sixties he had come to relish the challenge of young co-stars with nothing to lose, so he continued to revel in a verbal joust on equal terms. He told Sheila that he needed her 'energy'. He was referring not solely to the physical drive which resulted in him standing, even walking a few steps, when his faithful physiotherapist of many years had tried without success; no, he also required Sheila's capacity to take it and to dish it out. His sense of mischief was unabated. At the table in the hall where they had their meals the politically correct received short shrift and his provocative sallies about race, the clergy, even friends of long standing, were answered with equal force. There was electricity in the conversation and he enjoyed being wound up as much as being the winder-up.

So, against the odds, spirits were high when Lauren Bacall came to call on the Friday afternoon of that fateful weekend; it was she who gave him the sweet. Bogarde was in a more positive mood than at any time since the stroke. He had begun to read another book for review. He had even talked of sitting for a photographer friend. The American actress stayed for more than an hour and, as she left in a taxi, commented to Sheila on what 'great shape' he had been in. Less than forty-eight hours later she was telling *The Daily Telegraph*'s arts correspondent how she had found Bogarde 'in terrific form and feeling very sharp'. By now she was talking about her late friend.

Sheila had no premonition, but in retrospect realised that she had seen in others a 'big surge' of optimism just before they died. This patient, with whom she had made a conscious decision to become involved, to help beyond the normal constraints of her occupation, had become reconciled with himself. His business was done. Thanks in large measure to the woman with whom he found himself sharing his life for the last two years, he could leave painlessly and peacefully by the door at the far end of his own private corridor.

Introduction

Chaff – sb. 6. b. Strips of metal foil or similar material released in the atmosphere to interfere with radar detection (Oxford English Dictionary, *2nd edition, 1989*)

It was the American military which first coined the term at the end of the Second World War. The radarscope operator's screen would glitter with the promise of targets in the air, but the purpose was only to distract and confuse. By the time the word came into general currency during the Falklands conflict of 1982, Dirk Bogarde had been releasing his own variety of chaff onto the printed page for several years. He would tell interviewers, with an unmistakable finality: 'It's all there in the books, if you know where to look. The lines are wide enough to read between.' He once said something of the kind to me, and I knew that if ever there were a case for quoting Evelyn Waugh's foreign editor in *Scoop* – 'Up to a point, Lord Copper' – this was it. There are fifteen volumes aglow with brilliant description, wisdom, self-analysis, poignancy and humour. Seven are what you might call memoirs, and they inspire confidence with their directness, their simplicity, their unpretentiousness. A collection of letters and another of journalism complete the non-fiction and make the same crisp, honest sound. However, there are those who say that to approach the beating heart, one needs to go to the six novels. At the beginning of this strange quest, I agreed. Now I am not so sure. For Dirk was a writer whose entire *oeuvre* became a fiction, thanks in large part to his hyperactive imagination and his fantasies – fantasies so vivid and powerful that they were, for him, a reality. When Sheila Attenborough said succinctly that 'Dirk imagined his life',[1] she was not talking merely of his writing. She and her husband Richard knew him for fifty years and realised at an early stage that he was a fantasist, a romanticist; that he spun elaborate, mischievous, sometimes cruel, tales to a point where he convinced himself they were true. The Attenboroughs and others chuckle at the memory of being led to believe that Dirk was on three different continents simultaneously, at the centre of great happenings in each. This is why a number of those who worked with him, even some who were related to him, could not persevere with his autobiographies. It became, for them, exasperating to find distorted not only events in which they had been involved, but also people whom they knew in common. For Joseph Losey's widow Patricia, for example, it was all too much. On the flyleaf of a heavily annotated copy of her husband's biography by David Caute,[2] in which Dirk is much quoted, she wrote: 're Dirk Bogarde: anything goes as he strings together his anecdotes – he'll literally say anything. At the beginning of his writing career, he advised me NOT to read his biog. stuff as it would "just annoy me". Yes, his perfect disregard for what went on does.' A conversation among friends round a table at La Colombe d'Or is one thing; a gossipy throwaway on a chat-show, fair enough. But for the record? One might just as well take the characters he created on the screen as life studies.

The fifteen books and more than sixty films as a 'name above the title' secured for Dirk Bogarde a unique place in the world of the arts. His account of how it happened is proof of the axiom that all autobiography is merely a version of a life. In the hands of the born writer that Dirk was, it became a highly coloured tapestry in which often mundane events were embroidered, sometimes dramatically enough to achieve the impact made at Bayeux by the severed limbs and the arrow in Harold's eye. But heaven help the reader who tries to establish such an uncomplicated narrative from the Bogarde memoirs. I did, at the outset, by rereading them all in straight succession. Immensely entertaining they were still, but several times I had to lie down in a darkened room. At one point I resolved to dismember the seven books, plus the volume of letters to 'Mrs X', and reassemble them in a coherent chronology. I could not live with such a heresy, however, so the bindings remained intact. In any case, I knew the exercise would be fruitless.

In Noël Coward's play *A Song at Twilight*, Hugo Latymer is accused of producing an autobiography that was 'the most superlative example of sustained camouflage'; Dirk's ran it a close second. There is a delightful logic in the fact that his wartime job as an interpreter of aerial reconnaissance photographs was to penetrate the camouflage of the German armed forces. He was then in his early twenties and in the first stages of fashioning the web of protective material and colouring to cover a tough outer skin which he had begun to develop in his teens; and which, by the time he began to write for a wide public, had hardened into a formidable carapace. 'I'm still in the shell, and you haven't cracked it yet, honey,' he said scornfully to Russell Harty after inviting the latter to throw him some trickier questions during their famous filmed interview in 1986.[3] Nor in the next thirteen years was anyone else to succeed where Harty failed. In a sense there was little point in trying. As many in the same milieu have managed with varying degrees of success, Dirk constructed a persona for public consumption. His was impregnable. In private, he sometimes gave the illusion of relaxing his guard, but, as the director Alan Strachan said of Alec Guinness, 'there was a finally untouchable core to him'.[4] The similarities between Dirk and Guinness – the name of the former's favourite drink, by the way – are notable. 'I do like to withdraw and back-pedal and watch,' said Guinness, 'and I enjoy being elusive.' He, too, began to act from a very young age, as a release from loneliness and insecurity; he called it 'latching on to make-believe and pretending'.[5] Dirk, too, was a great observer, a great pretender, a great latcher-on to make-believe, and as elusive as it is possible to be. No wonder he harboured such a respect for the watchful, darting, disappearing frog. And yet, compared with Guinness, who seldom talked publicly about himself, Dirk was positively gregarious, submitting to countless interviews and playing each of them as a psychological game: the more intelligent and sophisticated the questioner, the greater the challenge and the keener his stimulus.

Three books appeared about this fugitive figure in his lifetime: two were substantially about his films; the third, by Sheridan Morley, was, as the author freely states, an extended and liberally illustrated essay. The first,[6] by Margaret Hinxman and Susan d'Arcy, had its subject's help; the second,[7] by Robert Tanitch, was tolerated from a distance until the moment of publication, when it had to be withdrawn, for the amendment of a single sentence to which Dirk took exception. Sheridan Morley had no co-operation – rather, a legal warning – but, after sending Dirk an early copy of *Dirk Bogarde: Rank Outsider*,[8] received a note saying: 'Could have been worse, I suppose.' Dirk knew full well that, following his death, attempts would be made to prise open the shell. At one point he seemed to welcome the idea, for after delivering his second and longest volume of autobiography, *Snakes and Ladders*, he wrote to his publisher, Norah Small-wood: 'I adore writing, and write I shall ... but perhaps this is not the way ... too many people to hurt, distress and make angry ... for no good reason at all beyond the obvious one of self-pleasure. I might just as well give a series of interviews to the "Express" as continue. All this would be much better left to someone else, after I have gone. It is too soon.'[9] Nine years later, however, he told Russell Harty: 'I don't see any point in somebody, a long time later, riffling through the memorabilia and the debris of my life.'[10] He added: 'Those who know me will understand what I have written. What there is of me is what I have chosen to show you.'[11] And so to the chaff and the camouflage he added a scorched-earth policy, whereby a mass of his papers was consigned either, in true Byronic fashion, to the flames, or to the shredder. He had at one time kept journals, but only one of these, covering a tiny period early in the war, survives.

Most of the letters he received were destroyed, but a few he kept or sent to Boston University, where a modest collection – mainly of his typescripts – is housed in the mighty Mugar Memorial Library. On some of the letters which he preserved at home he scribbled the surname of the correspondent where only the given name appears; for whose benefit, it is hard to fathom. Fortunately, in many cases his side of the traffic still exists: the recipients of Dirk's letters knew that they were far too precious to throw away, not because of any financial value but because they were so damned *good*. The essence of his appeal as a writer was that he made his reader believe that they were having a private conversation; in his letters the conversation became that much more confidential, even confessional. Many of them ran to two densely typed sides or more of A4 paper and were essays in all but name. Inevitably, they were at their most prolific between the late sixties and the mid-eighties, when he was living abroad, and meetings with his correspondents were rare. In the case of 'Mrs X', as readers of *A Particular Friendship* know, a meeting never happened at all, because it would have broken 'the spell'. It is worth noting that the majority of the extensive exchanges were with women, usually older than Dirk, invariably with forceful personalities and often with a social or intellectual cachet. Remoteness allows a special kind of intimacy – one that is safe and controllable, and therefore entirely suited to Dirk, who described the relationship with 'Mrs X' as 'a love affair without carnality'. Hers appears to have been the only one at that time, but others were to follow, sometimes concurrently; sometimes even provoking a twinge of jealousy.

My belief is that these correspondences were Dirk's journal. They coincided with his second career, when he graduated from writer to published author, and, in simple terms, the output of words for both individual and general absorption was so immense that any further regular setting-down of private thoughts seems improbable, if not superhuman. There was, after all, some land to work, and, let us not forget, the occasional film to make. There was also the Diary. It exists only from 1955, seven years after Anthony Forwood moved in with Dirk, and it was in the main kept by the former. Yet if Tony lopped off the tip of a finger in a gardening accident, or was confined in hospital, Dirk would take over. There are some prolonged periods when no entries are made by either – for example, in the watershed year of 1961 and towards the end of Tony's life; the volume for 1956 is missing. The Diary is at its fullest from the mid-sixties to the early eighties, and it has proved of incalculable worth in the preparation of this book. Apart from providing a record of the 'who, what, when and where', it gives indications of the 'how' and the 'why'. Every now and then, too, like a lighthouse beam momentarily picking out a white sail, it reveals the strength of the bond which united these two men in a relationship that was admired by their friends and by the most casual of acquaintances as more secure than many a marriage. Indeed that word has been used by several of those friends to convey the constancy and the particular air exuded by complementary and equal partners. In later years, at home, and only in front of the most deeply trusted, Dirk would sometimes address Tony as 'wifey'. It meant little: he had nicknames for everyone. It simply testified to the affection between them.

In a spiral-bound notebook containing a few of Dirk's random jottings is an extract – characteristically not wholly accurate – from the journals of Edith Olivier, the novelist, eccentric and cousin of Laurence. She befriended and inspired Cecil Beaton, Siegfried Sassoon, Lord David Cecil, Stephen Tennant and, above all, Rex Whistler, with whom Dirk had more than a little in common. When Whistler was killed in action in July 1944 Edith wrote that, since the death of her beloved sister Mildred, 'he has been the whole happiness of my life. Such companionship, sharing of interests, sense of humour in common. Everything which I like to do he likes. Everything that I would like to do he can do. He creates enjoyment of life wherever he is.'[12] In a world of few certainties there is no doubt whatever why Dirk should have made that extract. Nothing in the three and a half years since I began this journey has moved me more than discovering, imprecisely copied in his own hand, Edith Olivier's declaration of devotion.

The pity is that he felt unable to celebrate his good fortune in his own lifetime. The nearest he came to doing so was in his penultimate volume of autobiography, *A Short Walk from Harrods*, where the poignancy of their illness-dictated return from France, and of Tony's subsequent death, is so acute that the reader has neither the need nor the inclination to search between its lines; Dirk's robust language fails to disguise the pain. Yet, what has stayed as prominently in the minds of some of their friends, heterosexual and homosexual alike, is the legacy from previous books in which Forwood – as Dirk referred to him with a nod towards school and the Army – is either treated as subservient or written out completely. An early reviewer noted that Tony came across as a kind of handyman; in one of the long, private correspondences, he appears only at a late stage; in the published version of *A Particular Friendship*, he is not mentioned at all. He fared better than Perry Sheldon, Hugo Latymer's amanuensis in Coward's play: 'He loved you, looked after you and waited on you hand and foot. For years he travelled the wide world with you. And yet in your book you dismiss him in a few lines as an "adequate secretary".'[13] And yet, and yet … Dirk's denial had the most understandable of origins, but it became more and more regrettable as the years went by, and as the social climate warmed. It is for this reason that John Fraser, who appeared with Dirk in *The Wind Cannot Read* and who has written about him in a volume of memoirs, asks: 'And what use is talent, or even genius, for God's sake, if you have to live a lie and deny love?'[14]

The novelist and essayist Philip Hensher wrote recently that homosexuality acquired 'a sort of social history, because it was rarely allowed to rest as simply a biological variation, but was turned into a sin, a disease or a crime by society at large'; he added that 'nobody much cares any longer'.[15] Alas, people do: even in these early years of a new millennium one has only to look at the turmoil in the Anglican Church over the appointment of an openly homosexual bishop to see how long is the course which that social history still has to run. At an entirely personal level and in the context of this book, it is perhaps worth saying that in the eight years I knew Dirk, the question most frequently asked about him was: 'Is he homosexual?' I would answer, in all truth: 'I don't know – and I don't care.' With some regret I now have to care. I hope, therefore, that the reader will be patient as I deal with this matter and dispose of it before getting on with the story. After all, it informs Dirk's life, some of his most important work in the cinema and – even if by omission – his writing. Laurence Harbottle, Dirk's solicitor from the early fifties, puts it unequivocally: 'It is not given to many people to know themselves thoroughly. Even less can our observers, friends and acquaintances achieve a complete picture, especially because they are usually deprived of the knowledge of what we do on the streets or in bed. Nevertheless I shared the view of every friend of his I have ever known that Dirk's nature was entirely homosexual in orientation.'[16] He finds in Dirk certain common traits underlying that orientation: 'lust and insecurity informed by a possessory instinct'; petty bitterness, which can be a manifestation of that lust; and 'minor cruelty', which is often a release from sadistic images:

> I think Dirk both recognised and demonstrated a great deal of this but relaxed into its manifestation as he became more famous and more frightened both of his instincts and his position. The word 'frightened' is much too strong, but the fact that he regretted or even despised his nature alone explains his jealousy of people who were no threat to him, his often malicious speech and his paradoxical avoidance of ordinary action.

Only once in all the years that they knew each other did he talk openly about his own sexuality to Laurence Harbottle, when during a conversation sparked by stills of Dirk in his knee-weakening eighteenth-century costume for *A Tale of Two Cities*, he spoke of his sexual sadistic fancies. 'Fancies or fantasies,' recalls his lawyer and friend, 'there was no suggestion of any practice or reality and that precisely fitted my picture of him.'

As L. P. Hartley wrote in his prologue to *The Go-Between*, the past is a foreign country where they do things differently. But it is not that far away. It is a place where, as recently as the 1960s, to grow up as a homosexual was to live in a very real fear of state-initiated disgrace. A certain leniency seemed to apply towards the arts, and especially the West End theatre where, from the inter-war period through to the late fifties, the power and influence wielded by a homosexual Mafia, with Hugh 'Binkie' Beaumont of H. M. Tennent as its *capo di tutti capi*, were formidable. Yet there was an ever-present threat of either prosecution or blackmail. Bryan Forbes, a fervent admirer of the elegance and discretion with which Dirk and Tony lived their lives, wrote in his memoirs that Terence Rattigan 'was well aware that if any whiff of scandal about his private life escaped, the whole pack of cards would come tumbling down. Just as we were warned during the war that careless talk cost lives, careless talk cost careers.'[17] It was, as Laurence Harbottle says, 'a more formal time'.

At least some of the reason for that fear was removed by a change in the law, but no legislator can affect personal prejudice, and in the course of researching this book I have met middle-aged men who, even now, are unable to admit to a parent the truth about themselves. Again, Noël Coward proved both sage and seer in *A Song at Twilight*, which opened fifteen months before the Sexual Offences Bill received the Royal Assent. When the law ceases to exist, says Hugo Latymer, 'there will still be a stigma attached to "the love that dare not speak its name" in the minds of millions of people for generations to come. It takes more than a few outspoken books and plays and speeches in Parliament to uproot moral prejudice from the Anglo-Saxon mind.'[18] If blackmail became far less of a danger than it once was, the stigma remained, for some, a potent worry. The clumsy rigour of a bad law gave way to a strident, militant, tendency which aims – in that crude expression – to 'out' the prominent, who for their own sound reasons choose to live their lives quietly and discreetly. This, coupled to a prurience, an obsession with celebrity and an unprecedented appetite for the humiliation of the famous, has led to an atmosphere which can be every bit as venomous. I shall not forget the moment during one of my visits to Dirk's flat when he flicked at a broadsheet newspaper carrying a story about the public disclosure of Nigel Hawthorne's seventeen-year relationship with Trevor Bentham. 'Poor Nigel,' was all he said, and the empathy was palpable. In 1983 Dirk was on the point of suing a magazine that left its readers in no doubt as to his orientation, but he wisely refrained. Fifteen years later he did not bat an eyelid when Matthew Parris, the writer and former politician, expressed his 'unfashionable regard' for 'famous men who were gay, never quite said so, may never have joined the early campaigns, but lived and worked as openly as they dared'. He bracketed Dirk with Noël Coward, Liberace and Oscar Wilde. 'Some (not all) of these would look upon homosexuality as a *cause* with horror,' wrote Parris. 'But they served the cause by an inner honesty, a disposition to be themselves, which is greater than the honesty of words.'[19] Dirk never commented on this gratifying tribute, not even to express his indignation at being grouped with the dead. What could he say? The point, surely, is that he constructed the outer shell for his own personality in an era when he had to do so; but the 'house of cards' in which he then lived and worked was altogether more vulnerable. If Terence Rattigan, a shy playwright creating his brilliantly perceptive chamber pieces from the seclusion of his home, felt threatened, how much more fragile was the structure assembled around a matinée idol, his image magnified to vast proportions on screens throughout the land, who had to go out and 'flog the product'? So the shell became harder and harder, until it was impossible not only for any outsider to 'crack', but also, I believe, for Dirk himself to shed.

With studied remorse he told the director Stanley Donen, who was on Dirk's 1984 Cannes Film Festival jury, that he himself had simply not found the right girl. Whether the remark was for effect or the genuine product of self-delusion, no one knew, but either way it was embarrassing. Helena Bonham Carter, who appeared as the daughter of Dirk's character in *The Vision*, the last of his few films for television, found herself being flirted with off-set in a way that was at once complimentary and disconcerting. He felt it necessary to reassure her 'hand on heart, that I am NOT Charlie Dodgson'. She has a fascinating and highly plausible theory: that Dirk had to stay in denial because if at some stage he had decided to be true to himself he might have found it impossible to live with his regret at not having done so sooner – at missing the 'what might have been'.[20] This accords with Ian McKellen's reflection on the moment when in a radio discussion he admitted his homosexuality:

Coming out was a big thing. It wasn't just, oh, here we go. But it was the best thing I did. And why, why, why didn't I do it earlier? Well because I was too busy acting. And why was I too busy acting? Covering up the fact that I was gay. Because as an actor you're always pretending to be somebody else; you're drawing attention to yourself in a story-telling way because you can't draw attention to yourself as a gay man. And I think that's why a lot of gay men become actors – because they can't draw attention to themselves as being gay. Well, they can, but there's a cost to that.[21]

McKellen, eighteen years Dirk's junior, was nearly thirty when the law changed, and fifty when he 'came out': even for the generation after Dirk, it was far from easy. At the time, McKellen was known much better for his work on the stage, so a closer parallel can be drawn between Dirk and Richard Chamberlain, who, thanks to working extensively on both large and small screen, achieved far greater international fame as a *jeune premier*. Nor are the similarities confined to the fact that both men had stardom bestowed on them when they donned a white coat and stethoscope to play Doctors Sparrow and Kildare respectively.

Chamberlain was 'outed' in 1990, but said nothing until he published a memoir thirteen years later, when he wrote that 'it's difficult for those who weren't around in the forties and fifties to appreciate how deeply terrifying it was to imagine being labelled a faggot, a pansy, a pervert. It seemed to me then that even traitors and murderers were generally held in higher esteem than I would be if anyone ever found out the truth about me. I remember walking home from school one day solemnly swearing to myself over and over that I would never ever reveal my loathsome secret in any way to anyone.'[22] Like Dirk, Chamberlain, who was born in Beverly Hills, suffered from what he calls 'scholastic paralysis', which subtracted further from his self-worth. Like Dirk, he took easily and enthusiastically to painting – a solitary activity, in which the empty canvas is filled 'with no one but yourself', but which is similar to acting, in that it too works with shape, line, colour and rhythm. Like Dirk, he worked hard to hide any trace of effeminacy, and to be 'an acceptable male'. Chamberlain lost his virginity under agreeable, even fragrant, circumstances to a Japanese woman while on military service in Korea; Dirk writes of being deflowered against his will in a grotty Chelsea basement. Each man learned how to act his life.

Richard Chamberlain admits that his easy tenancy in Hollywood society was in large measure thanks to a practised charm, a commodity which everyone attributed to Dirk, too, from an early age. But whereas Chamberlain made no bones about wishing to be liked, and ingratiating himself, Dirk appears to have had less need and less patience. One of the most crucial aspects of Dirk's career is that Hollywood never took him to its ice-cold heart. Research suggests that there are four main reasons for this. First, the vehicle for his potential break-through was a flop; and the foetid whiff of failure tends to cling in Tinseltown. Second, his qualities at that time were not recognised as being sufficiently different from those of, in particular, Montgomery Clift, John Cassavetes and Anthony Perkins; nor could he possibly compete as a light-comedy lead in the manner of Cary Grant and Rock Hudson. Third – and I have heard this several times – he was 'too intelligent' for Hollywood. And fourth, the dark, cigar-chomping forces who arranged marriages for homosexual stars, who encouraged them to have children, who even turned a blind eye to Hudson's promiscuous antics, did not welcome the idea of an uncompromising dude from across the Pond and his inseparable male companion. Apart from a dent to his pride and his ambitions, Dirk had little time for that sink of hypocrisy; whatever might be said about the camouflage, the embroidery, the deceptions, he never committed the ultimate act of self-betrayal: to marry for the sake of appearances only; to parade wife and family as a screen.

Dirk's relatives, friends and acquaintances are in no doubt that any so-called engagement was a non-starter. One of the newspaper gossip columns was quick to knock on the head a rumour about him and the French-born actress Capucine going to live together abroad – or anywhere else. 'Forget that one,' it said flatly.[23] My contention is that he had only two truly serious love affairs, with or without 'carnality', in his life, and both were with older men. The first was relatively short, but intense; the second, with Tony, lasted for more than half of Dirk's seventy-eight years. Nevertheless, many believe that he would have liked to have children, and that their lack was his deepest sadness. One of the unresolved mysteries surrounding Dirk is that he said to at least two of his friends he had fathered a child. None of those best placed to corroborate him knows anything about this. The general feeling is that it was Dirk's ultimate fantasy. For there should be no underestimating the power of his imagination. Frederic Raphael, who wrote the screenplay of *Darling*, said that Dirk convinced himself he was almost English, almost a star – in a global sense – and almost a heterosexual.[24] At least five people to whom I have talked in the past year – among them a publisher, an agent and a distinguished actress – have told me, again without being asked, that Dirk for no apparent reason chose to inform them that he was not a homosexual. All of them felt they did not need to know, and in any case disbelieved him. To Sheridan Morley and to Nicholas Shakespeare he also issued flat denials. And after a piece appeared in a French magazine in 1991, he wrote to his niece, Alice Van den Bogaerde: 'I do hope that seeing me slammed as a homo has not upset you? It is actually quite untrue anyway . . . and what about the ones who *are* and don't get onto the elegant list!'

It is another of the quirks in this story that Dirk should first be published by Chatto & Windus, on whose impressive list was Laurens van der Post, the Afrikaner who became a bestselling author, inspiration to multitudes and guru to royalty. He, too, was a fantasist of the first water; as his biographer, J. D. F. Jones, said: 'Laurens was an enchanter.'[25] Van der Post and Dirk were in Java at the same time and, given that they were both in military intelligence, it seems extremely unlikely that they never met. Yet neither refers to having done so. Dirk must, later, have recognised a master at work, someone whose 'act' was more impressive even than his own, because it was accepted consistently at the highest level of English society, and without that licence which the performing arts afford. The same applies to a lesser extent in the case of the novelist and translator Patrick O'Brian, like Dirk an exile to southern France, whose persona was a deception but who wrote little about himself. His stepson, Count Nikolai Tolstoy, rationalised O'Brian's untruths as 'harmless fantasies or perhaps, because he was very shy, just the responses he came up with when pushed. Patrick had a terrible childhood, so he built up an outer shell to protect himself and created a personality within it.'[26] I suspect that Dirk believed more strongly than either O'Brian or van der Post in the truth of his own imaginings.

For this reason above all Dirk is a nightmare to pin down. When I have said that my principal aim in writing this book is to try to understand him, the reply on several occasions has been: 'You'll never do that.' It is my greatest regret that I never met Tony, or 'Tote', because among all those to whom I have spoken or written there has not been a single dissenting voice; he was, clearly, the life-enhancer that Edith Olivier found in Rex Whistler. Laurence Harbottle says that 'whether because of his bisexuality or something more he was a naturally affectionate being who devoted his life to Dirk. He was a strong, generous and remarkably certain person. He was, in my view, Dirk's manager in every sense except that in which Dirk portrayed him in his books.' Sometimes I had the feeling that Dirk and Tony, happily reunited on some south-facing, vine-trellised, heavenly terrace, were looking down and smiling – the one sardonically, the other sympathetically – as I toiled through the undergrowth at the foot of the hill, with a little red notebook rather than a net. I was convinced of it when my wife and I drove to their fabled house in Provence. First, a handsome woodpecker swooped in welcome in front of the car. Then a dragonfly danced above the bonnet as we crept up the path. But with Dirk around, even in spirit, it was never a good idea to be complacent. When I began, innocently enough, to take photographs, the newly serviced camera jammed after the first frame. A rather darker moment occurred on Sunset Boulevard in Los Angeles, when a 'crazy', as they call them there, wrote off the car I had hired twenty minutes earlier, and, had it not been for a seat-belt and an air-bag, this book would be in other hands. When I was delivered eventually to my rendezvous by the Los Angeles Police Department, Michael York rationalised the position by saying that Dirk was putting me to the test but obviously wanted me to carry on. Not even Dirk the author, though, would have dared to plot that day's series of coincidences. As I arrived, Michael York's wife Pat told me that their housekeeper, who would normally have been with them on a Saturday, had telephoned to say that her husband had been in a bad car smash on the freeway. My primary reason for going to see Michael York was to talk about *Accident*, the film he made with Dirk that began and ended with a fatal crash. Most bizarre of all, a little while after I had telephoned my wife in London to let her know what had occurred, she took her supper in front of the television, switched on the set and, without changing channels, found Michael York standing in his garden in the Hollywood Hills, talking about his early career.

Mercifully, the bulk of the research for this biography has been carried out under less dramatic conditions. Even so, it has often proved astonishingly frustrating. Trails repeatedly led to dead-ends. Memories wobbled, clouded and flatly contradicted. Archive material, where it existed, was often startlingly limited: at least two sources had been destroyed by fire; a vital file in an American library had been weeded out as early as the 1960s; another, in Sussex, had been ruined by mould. Even so, a good deal exists and, wherever I went, its custodians would usually do their best, and sometimes more, to help. The same applies to the many interviewees, a majority of whom wrestled with the fact that even if they had spent a good deal of time with Dirk they did not really *know* him. He was a great compartmentaliser, so that his friends from the cinema seldom coincided with those from publishing, and only a handful with members of his family. When his nephew Brock held a small party shortly after Dirk's death, to toast his memory, most of the names but few of the faces were familiar; all had been close to him in one way or another. A further curiosity is that Dirk seems to have been little talked-about, and even less written-about, in his profession. Of those who worked with him, Michael York is an exception in having devoted several passages of his autobiography to Dirk. It became something of a ritual for me to turn to the index of books by his contemporaries, and to find almost invariably Humphrey Bogart, but only on rare occasions the near namesake, and then in a glancing reference. Dirk's is an amazingly anecdote-free zone. This cannot be simply because he spent so much of his working life abroad, and so became out of mind as well as out of sight. It has more to do with that other distance – the one which he kept by staying in his trailer between set-ups and by going straight home after the day's filming; by eschewing as many of the countless invitations as he decently could and entertaining at home; by just being private and leading a tidy, organised, *orderly* existence, free of scandal. And of course he applied a subconscious deterrent to anyone thinking of writing about him even briefly, let alone at length, by publishing well over two thousand bound pages about himself. It was, in its way, a power, and an extraordinarily effective one, for although he made often preposterous, sometimes wounding, assertions and claims, he was seldom challenged seriously about anything he had written or said.

This biography attempts to construct, not – as I said earlier – to dismantle, or, worse, to deconstruct. If it were possible, nothing would be more tedious than systematically toiling through Dirk's books and trying to work out where the contents match and depart from a verifiable reality; even where they themselves are in conflict. As Peter Ustinov said not long before he died:

In an autobiography it's not that you don't tell the truth, but you distort what actually happened by playing with time. Something which actually took a week, in a book has to take a sentence or so. Everything becomes slightly distorted, although not in spirit. I've always been very much opposed to the courts of law where you are asked to tell the truth, the whole truth and nothing but the truth, because I think that's impossible. If I was forced to do that, I should refuse because I'm willing to tell *my* truth, but I can't guarantee that it's the whole truth, and certainly not that it's *nothing but* the truth. The truth is like a chandelier in the courtroom, which everybody sees, but from a different angle – because they're different people and can't occupy the same seat.[27]

Ustinov offered another persuasive apology for the autobiographer who might be cavalier with his or her own facts. 'What is writing?' he asked. 'It's thinking aloud, really. Referring is like being interrupted the whole time.' Suzanne Lowry, after interviewing Dirk at a particularly sensitive time, wrote that 'no one will ever be able to rearrange his story, for whatever reason'; autobiography, she added, 'is the art of ordering your own past'.[28] She was right: Dirk's account of his life, with all its contradictions, conceits and colours, is set in type as indelibly as if it were in stone; yet there is, as always, an alternative. In trying to achieve it, I have reproduced short extracts from his books, usually without comment. However, there are two purported wartime incidents – visiting Belsen and a fatal accident in India – that perplex even friends of long standing. Some of the people acknowledged later in these pages have asked, unprompted and doubting, about those two events, to both of which, especially the first, he attributed much importance in later life; I have attempted to arrive at a truth. Speculation can aggravate, so I have avoided it where possible; but given the paucity, in some areas, of both documentary material and of memory there are inevitable gaps, especially so in the war years. Dirk would always say that his Army service was the making of him. There is little doubt about that. It also scarred him, as it did so many others, once he had embarked on active service. Because of his behind-the-front-line job he was, effectively, a non-combatant; and my belief is that he suffered later, to a significant degree, from war guilt. On a BBC Radio programme in April 1986, Enoch Powell, who had been a brigadier in the Army, was asked how he would like to be remembered. His reply was both shocking and intensely moving: 'I should like to have been killed in the war.'[29] Powell broke down during the recording, as did Dirk at least once on both radio and television when recalling his experiences in Europe in 1944–5. He was never as explicit as Powell, but there are hints in the autobiographies that Dirk felt similarly, if not equally. He admitted that his was, compared with so many, a relatively easy war. However, its contribution to the emotional baggage which he carried around with him should not be underestimated.

What follows is a sincere effort to net this fleeting figure, but only to hold and examine him, and then to let him fly. To subject him to any kind of sustained academic or psychological analysis would be suffocating. Far better to send readers back to his own words and to encourage those who have not read him to do so. At the time of writing, Dirk's books are lamentably out of print: only random copies of the non-fiction are to be found; the novels seem to have disappeared completely. If nothing else, I would like to think that this volume might help to reawaken interest in the name of Bogarde the author. As far as Bogarde the actor is concerned, I never thought his reputation would fade. Yet in a 2001 survey of the one hundred greatest films, none of Dirk's was mentioned, and in 2003 he was missing from a similar poll to find the one hundred greatest film stars; that said, so too were Guinness, Tracy, Peck and Fonda – four more quiet men of the cinema, men who cherished the value of stillness, men for whom less was almost invariably more, as it was for Dirk.

Histrionics should never be mistaken for commitment. Jonathan Miller told a cast which he was directing in a Los Angeles production of *Richard II* that when members of the audience went backstage afterwards, they ought to find in the dressing-room nothing but a pile of ash.[30] There are examples in Dirk's story of him achieving just such a level of commitment: nervous breakdowns; an inability to put away the clothes worn by Stephen, his character in *Accident*; an involvement with Gustav von Aschenbach which, when he spoke and wrote about it later, prompted one or two fellow actors to mutter among themselves: 'For goodness's sake – get a life!' Few directors ever felt let down by Dirk: he would give of his best, even when working with poor material. If there were occasions when he was not especially popular on a set, I heard only one account of him behaving unprofessionally. Usually he was not only impeccable, but also generous with his colleagues, even when the work was allowing him to sublimate some of the tormenting imagery inside his head; to relieve the repression. When he did, it was our turn as spectators to be disturbed. In considering the dressing-room of his own life the pile of ash is every bit as apt. His brother, Gareth, believes that the 'terror' which both beset and fuelled Dirk was not so much a fear of anything specific, as of fear itself; that below the surface complexities and the skilfully woven camouflage netting, deep inside the shell, there was not just an emptiness but a nothingness. I am, now, not so sure. 'Terror lurks not very far beneath this apparently cool facade,' Dirk wrote to a friend in 1988. 'I'm as cool as a microwave oven really.'[31] This reflection was prompted by a young woman, in the next seat at a cinema, offering him a Malteser. A terror, then, born of shyness. 'You're shy, aren't you?' he said, recognising it in my wife. 'It's such a waste of time, isn't it.' We can add to that a terror of losing control. In discarded notes for his first book – their spelling corrected here – he wrote of this dangerous, detestable, thread in his make-up which might one day do him harm. 'I judged it to be a form of weakness, femininity, softness. Abhorrent. I therefore cultivated enough layers of camouflage to hide a battleship. Not always successfully, but effectively. This control I knew, instinctively, probably was essential to my work as an actor. An actor must conceal his art from the public eye. Never indulge it or let it give him away.'[32]

Linked closely was the terror of letting himself, or his audience, down – with the attendant risk of derision. And finally, consider the terror for the country's foremost matinée idol of possible exposure by, say, a blackmailing acquaintance of a former homosexual lover; the kind of fear which, as Gielgud's recently published letters make clear, reduced Sir John to helplessness.[33] That Dirk was able every now and then to turn his jangling nerves to advantage was a release for him and a benefit to us, and stands, surely, to his credit. Nevertheless, there was more at his centre than rampant feelings. Many people in the last three years have described him to me as 'complex', 'enigmatic', 'a puzzle'. In trying to piece together the jigsaw I have come to believe that he was essentially a simple soul, at his happiest with nature and beauty. Indeed, life as a naturalist, with a sketchpad and an unlimited supply of writing-paper, might have suited him admirably; it is easy to see why he found common ground with John Fowles, to whom plants and flowers are as vital a passion as were butterflies to Nabokov. Instead, Dirk escaped into acting, using his fierce intelligence to put his self-control endlessly at risk. The complexities were part of the construct: the shell and the camouflage.

Sheridan Morley, when considering Dirk's relationship with Tony, thought it possible that when 'that particular closet' was eventually opened, all anyone would find would be 'Dirk's old gardening clothes'.[34] After he died, his nephew Brock Van den Bogaerde opened a small hanging cupboard in Dirk's bedroom and found two incongruities among the few suits: one, tailored by Huntsman, from his first starring role in *Esther Waters*; the other, the tails he wore as Franz Liszt in *Song Without End*. In the waistcoat pocket of the latter was one of the tiny coloured sweets he would suck to calm his nerves; in the breast pocket was a handkerchief embroidered with the letter 'C' – Capucine. Sometimes, while rummaging in Dirk's cupboards both metaphorically and literally, I have been troubled by Oscar Wilde's aphorism, 'Every great man nowadays has his disciples, and it is always Judas who writes the biography.'[35] Pinned alongside it above my desk is a postcard reproduction of David Tindle's 1986 canvas showing Dirk in casual clothes, almost dwarfed by his wing chair and looking pensively away from the artist; and next to it, Thomas Carlyle's observation that he 'often found a Portrait superior in real instruction to half-a-dozen written Biographies'. With these salutary reminders, and with the authority of those acknowledged at the end of this book, I set about the task of trying to establish a truthful *version* of Dirk's life. I hope the reader will not be irritated if questions remain unanswered, holes unplugged, because the ultimate truth has gone with Dirk and others to the grave.

He told interviewers that at the end of the fifties and the beginning of the sixties – the 'hinge' of his career – he had been persuaded to reconsider where he was going, in part because of the new generation: Courtenay, Finney, Bates and others; but not only actors. When during research I have drawn a parallel with Cliff Richard, the name has been met with the occasional derisive snort: 'How can he be considered in the same breath?' Well, on more than one occasion Dirk mentioned him as a pretender to the crown. Sir Cliff, as he now is, looked at twenty remarkably like Dirk at twenty-five or even thirty. In 1959 the Mirabelle Pop, Film and TV Star Library of pocket-sized magazines dedicated itself to 'the film world's most thrilling love-stories', and featured Dirk, 'Britain's most eligible bachelor', on its cover; with the promise of Cliff to adorn its next issue. Both men failed to make a mark in America. Both refused to compromise. Both ploughed their own furrow – in Dirk's case, two distinct furrows – with sustained success. Both refused to be drawn any further than they wished. And both would seem to have settled for the celibate life of the true solitary. In a 2003 television profile, Sir Cliff said that when he first started, 'they tried to make me out to be some kind of heterosexual sex maniac. When that didn't really catch on, they turned on to the gay thing. And now I find it really rather *fun*. You know, I'm an *enigma*. Once I'd looked that word up, I thought, I *like* this. They don't *understand* me. Long may it reign.' He enjoyed, he added, 'being slightly with a question mark above my head'.[36] So, too, did Dirk. But it would seem that he became a puzzle to himself. When I told Glynis Johns that I was having trouble working him out, she replied: 'Dirk couldn't work it out for himself, so don't worry if you can't.'[37]

I trust that Wilde's dictum will not apply here. I have neither the inclination nor, I believe, the wherewithal to carry out an act of treachery. In any case it is arguable whether Dirk was a 'great' man. I believe he was, at heart, good. The Dirk I knew for regrettably few years, from 1991 to 1999, was the one whom Michael Gough knew for half a century and whom he described in a letter to me as 'a kind generous wise and comical friend'.[38] When the IRA wrought havoc in London's docklands one Friday evening, at about the time of my weekly call to him, the first person who telephoned my wife with an offer to help in any sensible way was Dirk. He *was* generous, and supremely – sometimes uncannily – thoughtful. And he was much else besides, not all of it admirable, as he was the first to acknowledge; it is healthier when the narcissist recognises his own flaws. In an interview in the seventies he was asked why he called Ava Gardner 'Snowdrop'. Because, he said, anything less likely was hard to imagine. 'What flower would you say *you* most resemble?' was the next question. Like lightning came the reply: 'I? Holly.' His pointed edges, as I had particular cause to celebrate, helped to make him a joyously incisive critic, who once described a collection of short stories by Doris Lessing, no less, as a 'limp lettuce'.[39] That, too, has been for me a spur.

London
May 2004

Part One
DEREK

One

'Constant dripping wears away the stone'

The 1921 Easter Bank Holiday fell on 28 March. It was what editors now call a slow news day. 'Nobody could say it was a nice Easter Monday,' reported *The Times*, 'and yet great numbers of people insisted on enjoying the holidays ... Excursion trains during the morning were crowded and the strings of motor charabancs which left London for Brighton and other resorts had no vacant seats.' The King and Queen travelled to Aldershot to watch the Army football cup final. There was greater excitement at Brooklands Automobile Racing Club, where Count Zborowski introduced his six-cylinder 'Chitty-Bang-Bang'. This mighty beast, propelled by the same 600 horsepower engine as used in Zeppelin aircraft, thrilled the crowds by reaching an average speed of 103 miles per hour. Back in the capital the sky was overcast, and those who decided to forgo the seaside took to the streets in mackintoshes and overcoats to protect themselves against a chill wind and intermittent showers. The Zoological Gardens in the Regent's Park received 48,428 visitors; the Victoria and Albert Museum, 23,471; and the British Museum, 9,994. In the evening every place of entertainment was packed, and long queues formed for the cheaper tickets to see Fay Compton in *The Circle*, Gladys Cooper in *The Betrothal* and Gerald du Maurier in *Bulldog Drummond*, as well as Charles B. Cochran's latest revue, *League of Notions*, and *Chu Chin Chow*, now in its fifth year.

Two mornings later the front page of *The Times* carried twenty-nine birth announcements, one of which read: 'Van den Bogaerde – On the 28th March, at West Hampstead, the wife of U. Van den Bogaerde, of a son.' While other Londoners had been dodging the rain and seeking cheer from a big screen, an Elgin marble or a new recruit to the reptile house, the Misses Annie and Kate Weeks were doing their best to ensure that at their nursing home in a Hampstead terrace, four miles from the West End, Margaret Van den Bogaerde, an attractive twenty-two-year-old former actress, would be as comfortable as possible while labouring to produce her first child. She and her husband had walked the short distance from their house when she knew her time was near, but only after she had applied her make-up and mascara, and arranged her hat. This procedure – essential for one who had been 'always applauded' – was interrupted by the pains, which her husband helped to dull by administering a slug of whisky. She arrived on his arm at number 12 Hemstal Road, perspiring freely, with her mascara running, her lipstick smudged, her hat askew and a perceptible whiff of alcohol on her breath. Nevertheless, the Misses Weeks did their duty. Two months later, formal notice was given of the boy's full name, which the Registrar of Births for the district of Hampstead recorded as Derek Niven Van den Bogaerde. Not for the first or last time the family caused officialdom's clerks a slight headache: on the certificate an attempt at the father's given name resulted in 'Ubric' and had to be amended to Ulric. Clerks – and clerics too: on 30 October, when the baby was baptised at St Mary's Church, Kilburn, the Reverend H. E. Noyes, who managed easily enough that day with Atkinson and Campbell, evidently struggled to spell Bogaerde. Even in a part of London which was being colonised to an extent by artists, writers and thinkers, many of them from abroad, there was a touch of the exotic about the new parents: he with his Germanic-sounding roots and his reserve; she with her thick Glaswegian accent and flamboyance. It is easy to imagine them exciting curiosity.

The telephone directories of Belgium and Holland give ample proof that Van den Bogaerde and its several variants – meaning of, or from, the orchards – are as common in the Low Countries as Dujardin and Desjardins are in France. There have, for instance, been Van den Bogaerdes in Bruges since the fifteenth century; eleven are listed today. The family tree which interests us – at the risk of bringing down on the reader a grey mist – has at its head Joseph Van den Bogaerde, a lawyer and merchant who in 1830 was rewarded for his upright citizenship of Izegem by being elected its first Mayor. This small town in West Flanders, close to Bruges and to the French border, built a reputation in the Middle Ages on the production of linen, then on the manufacture of brushes and shoes.[1]

Joseph received 101 votes out of 102, largely as a result of his local leadership in the economic and political upheaval, 'a salon revolution', which saw off the Dutch in 1830. According to Michel van der Haert, whose mother was a Van den Bogaerde, Joseph was 'a bourgeois who took the situation in hand to protect the interest of the bourgeoisie. He didn't care about *les petits gens*. He just knew how the wind blew, and he was voted in by all the richest people in Izegem.' In 1832, while still in office, he died in an accident in his nearby native town of Kortrijk, leaving his widow, Thérèse, who was extremely rich in her own right; a daughter, Maria; and two sons, the younger of whom, Jules, is Derek's great-grandfather.

Joseph's elder son, Emil, emulated his father by siring two boys and a girl, but the younger of *his* two boys died in infancy and the daughter at the age of fifteen. Emil's surviving son, Valerius Julius Emilius (Valère), plays a significant role in our story, for in 1900 he became the seventh Mayor of Izegem and, although only a cousin twice removed, would one day be claimed by Derek in a family letter as his paternal grandfather and garlanded, preposterously, with the title of Baron. It certainly sounded good, as did a wholly unsubstantiated assertion that there is a direct line of descent from Anne of Cleves. There is a strain of Van den Bogaerdes who were reinstated to the Belgian nobility in 1726 and whose involvement with botanical work entitled them to include on their coat of arms a chevron and three trees; but they have no known connection with Izegem. The arms found above a fireplace at Château Wolvenhof ('Wolves' Lair'), which is one of two fine early-twentieth-century houses on the outskirts of the town that belonged to members of Derek's Belgian family, depict two deer, two stars and a man in the moon. They are fantasy arms: less noble, perhaps, but more colourful and certainly more apposite.

No, the blood flowing into the infant Derek's veins from across the North Sea was not exactly blue, but some of his relatives were prominent at a certain level. Burgemeester Vandenbogaerdelaan, one of the more impressive streets leading out of Izegem towards the family's former properties, is named after Valère. Great-grandfather Jules, however, was less honoured. Born in the town five months before the momentous events of November 1830, he lost his father when he was two. He was the apple of his mother's eye, and she spoiled him. He dabbled in the drapery trade, wrote a history of the town and was a founding member of its Jockey Club. He was also a major in the local military reserve and a crack shot. But just before his twenty-fifth birthday his unstructured life tottered when his mother died. He fared worse than his elder brother and sister, and became very much the poor relation. Three years later he was in the neighbouring town of Ingelmunster, unemployed and living near the railway station at a hotel owned by the Degrijse family. Happiness and tragedy followed in fairly rapid order. In 1861, eight days after his thirty-first birthday, he married the second of the widowed innkeeper's four daughters, Julie. A year to the month later, a son was born and was given the ultimate parental blessing by being named Amatus (Aimé). Another son, Julianus, followed in 1868, but within a year Julie was dead and, eight weeks later, so too was baby Julianus. Aimé might have been greatly loved, but by the time he was eight he had lost his mother and his brother. At thirteen he would be an orphan.

The story of Aimé Van den Bogaerde is as bizarre as it is incomplete. An indication of its potency came as recently as a Sunday morning in May 2002, when under an azure sky and in a stiff breeze Gareth Van den Bogaerde unveiled a headstone on an unmarked grave at a cemetery in the hills above Brighton. With some difficulty and perseverance he had traced the spot where his, and Derek's, grandfather was buried in 1938. The inscription read *Vir aenigmaticus* – man of mystery – and no one could take issue with that. Against the gleaming white stone Gareth placed a posy of orchids, a further symbolic gesture to reinforce the reclaiming of an ancestor exiled from his own family.

When his father died in 1875 Aimé was taken under the wing of his uncle and aunt, Emil and Honorine. Their son Valère, seven years Aimé's senior, was to be both friend and guardian. After leaving school Aimé spent four years studying art in Paris. He became keen on photography and acquired a considerable knowledge of plants. However, a rackety lifestyle and a disdain for economy did not endear him to his relatives back in Izegem – especially not to Valère, who would soon be fathering his own four children and, the essence of probity, heading towards the mayor's parlour. The next recorded sighting, in the mid-1880s, places Aimé in the Hertfordshire cathedral town of St Albans, working and studying at a firm of orchid importers called Sanders Ltd. Among the employees was a Gérard Noyelle, also an orphan, who by an odd coincidence came from Joseph Van den Bogaerde's birthplace, Kortrijk. It was his keenness to travel to South America in search of orchids that led both men into the kind of adventures that were red meat for Conan Doyle and Rider Haggard. Indeed, much of the detail of Aimé's exploits is contained in a work-in-progress by Gareth Van den Bogaerde which is drawn mainly from a brief period of extensive letter-writing and journal-keeping, and which, whatever its final form, is likely to read more as a novel than a biography. Aimé left no formal memoir. His only known published writing is a collaboration with one Robert A. Newill in translating from the French a novella by Ludovic Halévy called *A Marriage of Love*.[2] The story was published in 1885, at Stamford in the Midlands, where the following year, just like his father, he would fall in love with a hotelkeeper's daughter.

Derek's paternal grandmother was born in 1866 in the village of Empingham, near Stamford, and christened Grace Lizzie Clark. Her father, Samuel Cope Clark, kept an inn and farmed 282 acres, with a total workforce of fifteen. Grace, the fourth of five daughters, had an elder brother, George. By the time she met Aimé the family had moved the five miles east to the main town, and Samuel, who had fathered two more sons, was the proprietor of the Stamford Hotel. In Gareth's account Aimé caught Grace's eye while he was on a visit to an orchid grower. She was captivated by his looks, his charm, his stories and his painting. When she became pregnant Aimé, who would not marry without proper means, went back to Belgium to see his guardian, Valère, in the hope of securing the inheritance which would be coming his way in 1887, on his twenty-fifth birthday. Valère agreed to give written permission, but only if presented with the relevant certificate. On 6 November 1886 Aimé and Grace were married by a Roman Catholic priest, Henry Van Doorne, at Bethel House in Lambeth, south London, near the bridegroom's present lodgings. The certificate, witnessed by Grace's father and mother, gave Aimé's rank or profession as 'Gentleman', as it did those of his late father and his father-in-law. The document permitted him to obtain his inheritance; however, according to Gareth, Grace miscarried.

By 1891 Grace and Aimé had moved up in the world. They were living on the outskirts of Birmingham, in Perry Barr, with a housekeeper of their own. Aimé's business was doing well. A snapshot survives from 1890 showing Grace in profile, elegant in full riding habit, holding a crop, and at her feet a hound staring fascinatedly at the photographer. On the face of it, there is no reason to doubt that the house in Walsall Road was a place of contentment. The arrival on 14 June 1892 of a baby boy, delivered at home and registered not quite accurately as 'Ulrich [Ulric] Gontran [Gontron] Jules Van den Bogaerde', surely set the seal on 'a marriage of love'. But no, according to Gareth, The Woodlands had been riven by rows as the temperamental, pleasure-seeking, spendthrift, restless Aimé refused to be reined in by his prudent wife. At least Ulric's birth had one immediate beneficial effect: the father was besotted.

Aimé also considered himself to have graduated from 'gentleman' to 'land-owner'. His 1896 Christmas card, bearing in capital letters 'Best Greetings from Mr and Mrs Aimé Van den Bogaerde' and a new address, was skilfully drawn, and signed with his initials inside a heart. It showed a handsome pile set in extensive lawns, with a fountain in the foreground and smoke wafting from one of several chimneys. This was Perry Villa, in Perry Barr, and the evidence suggests that its occupation by Aimé, his wife and their child owed less to affordability than to *folie de grandeur*. The present state of the orchid business, while healthy, could not support this kind of lifestyle. Aimé and Gérard Noyelle, the kindred spirit he had met in St Albans, decided to raise their game: instead of relying on plants found and despatched by others, they would seek out the rarest specimens for themselves.

In January 1897 Gérard sailed for Colombia and within a few months their fortunes began to improve significantly. To give some idea of the potential rewards: in Europe and America customers would pay up to £50 for a single bulb, when a few pence would secure a dozen 'on the ground'. Not surprisingly, with stakes as high as that, collection was a dangerous undertaking. So when Gérard was forced by illness to return home, his debriefing to Aimé ensured the latter fully understood that the gains to be made had to be balanced against the perils presented not only by the jungle but also by rival collectors. Nothing daunted, and in defiance of his wife, Aimé set off in 1898 for Barranquilla.

The subsequent events are properly left for Gareth's text, pieced together from the existing writings of Aimé and Gérard. Suffice to say that Aimé had reckoned without a revolution, banditry and a great deal of skulduggery, from all of which he was lucky to escape with his life. He returned to England, dangerously ill and fleeced of his money, in August 1901, by which time Grace had abandoned Perry Villa and a life of some opulence. On a visit to her Belgian relatives Grace told Valère – by now Izegem's first citizen – of the wretched lot that had befallen her and the nine-year-old boy. To make matters a hundred times worse, there had been a scandal, unspecified to this day, which resulted in Aimé being declared *persona non grata* in the family: his name was not to be spoken. For Grace a concentrated dose of religion was prescribed. She returned to England, deter-mined to do the best for her son, but would never again live under the same roof as her husband, choosing instead to stay on the south coast with her sister Edith and brother-in-law George Nutt.

Aimé spent three months in hospital, returned to Perry Villa and with Gérard and two financiers set about resuscitating the business. They did enough to sell it as a going concern, then Aimé moved south to start again, with the newly married Gérard, in the Brighton area. Whether it was he or his wife who effectively took charge of the teenage Ulric is unclear. Grace was leading an austere existence about a hundred miles to the west; Aimé, always a stranger to responsibility, had fallen on harder times. Yet in 1905 Ulric was enrolled at Brighton Grammar School, founded in 1859 'to provide a Liberal Education at a Moderate Cost',[3] and stayed there until 1908, the year the Orchid Trading Company was wound up. His pupil record card, the briefest of documents, gives no fewer than four addresses for his father.[4] The extent of the contact at this time between parent and son is unknown. It was thought inside the family that they never saw each other from 1898 until February 1931, when a friend of Aimé sent the thirty-eight-year-old Ulric a letter explaining that his father was seriously ill in Brighton General Hospital. Given what we now know about Ulric's schooling, that period is probably shorter, by as much as ten years.

What is certain is that when the letter reached Ulric and his young family in Golders Green, he had not heard anything of or from his father for a very long time indeed. Only later did it emerge that Aimé had been living a hand-to-mouth existence, painting to commission, bedecking wooden chests with images of the countryside and distressing them to look antique, paying with paintings for food and drink, and decorating with hunting scenes the leather-panelled walls of a local pub. When it came, Ulric's reunion with his father was not particularly welcome; but its aftermath had a powerful effect on his own son. Just think, a grandfather, apparently non-existent, suddenly enters your life with saddlebags that have straddled the backs of mules in the rainforest; who sleeps in a bed fashioned from a giant swan that once graced the scenery dock at the Theatre Royal, Brighton; and who has a torrent of tales to tell, with 'a vague not-quite-true-but-could-be quality about them which in no way diminished their delight'. No wonder that when he was introduced to this 'vague shadow lost in the distance of a time unknown to us' the ten-year-old Derek Van den Bogaerde was mesmerised.[5] They had more in common than a surname, Hispanic features, and the same dark brown, unfathomable eyes.

From Derek's father there will have been no show of emotion. For he was a man who kept his own counsel, and his distance, in a way that could be mistaken for aloofness. Nor did he write down his thoughts about even this dramatic turn of events. The pocket diaries, which he kept far from methodically in a spidery, pencilled hand, contain brusque, allusive references. The entry for 11 February 1931 reads, 'Letter from Hove.' There is no reference to the fact that Aimé wished to come to live with the family; nor that he told Margaret, 'And then I can teach you to cook'; nor that Ulric resisted the proposal, preferring instead to help financially towards his father's lodgings. As the years passed, the visits to Brighton were infrequent and irregular, usually following word that Aimé was unwell. On 13 March 1937, Ulric found 'F looking much older. Stooping & frail.' In January

1938, he took Margaret and Gareth to see Aimé. 'Father very feeble,' he noted; 'Not recognized.' A month later, 'Knew me & M, but mind gone. Unable to talk about anything.' And then, on Thursday, 14 April 1938: 'F. died 1.15 p.m. Brighton 4 p.m.' A simple 'On' indicates that for Ulric the Friday was a normal working day. On the 16th: 'Funeral.' One thing is certain: the atmosphere at Woodvale cemetery will have been in stark contrast to that sixty-four years later, when Ulric's younger son, three of his grandchildren and a smattering of great-grandchildren went some way towards rehabilitating his family's 'black sheep'. A black sheep, moreover, about whom so little was known that a note in the back of Ulric's 1938 diary gave the wrong day, the wrong month and the wrong year for his father's birth.

The difficulties in Ulric Van den Bogaerde's own life had made him withdrawn, but he was a good and honest man whose achievements were not acknowledged vehemently enough in his lifetime. Admittedly he did not excel as a pupil in Brighton. The school magazine makes no mention of him among the prize-winners either in the classroom or on the playing-field. However, he will have been comfortable at art, which was well taught, despite poor equipment and a 'bad smell' in the passage leading to the poorly ventilated basement room where modelling classes were held.[6] From Brighton Ulric went to St Martin's School of Art in London. His first paid job was at a stained-glass business in Endell Street, Covent Garden. In July 1912, he was taken on as a black-and-white artist at *The Times*, and rapidly proved his worth. At that time the only illustrations appearing regularly in the newspaper were line drawings for advertisements, and Ulric, aware of how keen the proprietor, Lord Northcliffe, was on the visual content, began to experiment with grained paper. Shortly after war broke out in 1914, Robert Porter, the first editor of Special Numbers (supplements), wrote to a senior member of management:

> I feel it is my duty to call attention to Mr U. V. Bogaerde. He came into *The Times* Office over two years ago at a salary of £2 per week, and was promised that in the event of his proving satisfactory, this should be increased. I first had to do with Mr Bogaerde about a year and a half ago, when I found him most useful in making the line drawings for the Special Supplements. He did nearly all of these drawings, and I think his work was admirable. He has also helped us in this way in such Numbers as the Russian Supplements, the Spanish Supplement, and so forth and did some very good work in all of these [...] I do not know of any young man in the Office who gives more constant attention to his work than Mr Bogaerde [...]
>
> His work on the History of the War began about four weeks ago, and he now has charge of the thousands of photographs which come into this Office from thirty-five or forty different sources. He also helps me with the make-up of the 'History' [...] Mr Bogaerde's hours of work are at times very long, as

not infrequently we have been obliged to stay at the Office from 9.30 or 10 in the morning until 12 or 12.30 p.m. [*sic*], and he has often had to come to the Office on Saturdays and Sundays [. . .]

Under these circumstances I think you ought to give him a substantial increase in pay, as I do not know what I should do just now should we lose him, and I feel that he has not only worked very hard, but is doing work of considerable value for the paper.[7]

Three days later, the salary was £3 a week. It was Northcliffe himself who had asked Ulric to take over the make-up and illustrations for the *History of the War*, which would eventually run to twenty-two volumes. When German cruisers carried out a lightning raid on Scarborough, Whitby and other coastal towns, Ulric was despatched to Yorkshire to take pictures of the damage. As a result he became in effect the newspaper's first staff photographer. He also knew how to give a good account of himself. He told Northcliffe that the paper being used for the *History* was inferior. The proprietor was livid, because he had bought the stuff himself at a bargain price and had enormous stocks of it at Greenwich. He sacked Ulric, telling him that the cashier would be given instructions to pay the whippersnapper a month's salary. No order ever reached the cashier. And when a few days later Northcliffe sent for Ulric on a mundane matter, there was no mention of the sacking.

In March 1915, Porter was writing again, this time asking that his protégé should receive a one-off payment for a drawing that had been done in his own time:

Before the History of the War absorbed all his energies, Bogaerde was able to give lessons in drawing and so forth at home, and in this way he added to his income. Since he has been working on the History he has been obliged to abandon the work, as he cannot possibly leave the Office some nights until 7 or 8 o'clock, or even later.[8]

The pressure paid off. A file copy of the Russian Supplement from April that year shows that Ulric was given 15s 6d for his impression of the Georgian city of Tiflis. One of Ulric's most powerful cover illustrations – for which there was no additional fee – was carried on a Recruiting Supplement published with *The Times* on 3 November 1915. A signed letter from Buckingham Palace, in which the King appealed to 'men of all classes, to come forward voluntarily and take your share in the fight', was superimposed on a mounted St George in full armour, banner unfurled against a blazing sun. Five weeks later, Ulric enlisted. For the past year he had been a cadet with the Officer Training Corps at the University of London, from which he resigned only after he had joined up and – oddly – 'for family reasons'. It would appear that his allegiance was now firmly with his mother, because she was living in Clapham, and so too, according to the official documents which he signed at the nearby recruiting office, was he.

Whatever the reasons for his resignation from the OTC, 140251 Gunner Van den Bogaerde of the Royal Horse Artillery was placed in reserve on a net daily pay of 10d. He continued to draw for *The Times*: striking images of an ice-breaker at work off Archangel, two Japanese women chasing fireflies, and a Russian in gala costume adorned supplements until as late as June 1916. However, in July he was called up. The Army Medical Board at Kingston on Thames found the slight figure – he was five foot, seven and a half inches tall and weighed 113 pounds – to be in good health, and he was posted to the RHA depot at Woolwich, then to St John's Wood. With character references from Robert Porter and from his Brighton headmaster, Thomas Read, he applied successfully for officer training and by the end of January 1917 was a second lieutenant. Three months later his war began in earnest.

If there is a single defining characteristic of men who have seen conflict it is that they seldom, if ever, talk about it to those who were not there. Little is known about Ulric's experiences in France and then in Italy, but what he witnessed in the mud and the noise and the terror made it impossible for him in later years to remain in a kitchen while eggs or potatoes were boiling. He is believed to have opened the door to a church and found the building full of bodies – an image which dealt a hammer-blow to any belief in the existence of God. Like so many who toiled with, and felt the impact of, the guns, he was to a degree shell-shocked. On 17 April 1917 he joined 106 Battery of 22nd Brigade, Royal Field Artillery, at Croisilles, and spent three months in the hell of the Somme, with occasional breaks for gunnery training.

Hardly had he arrived in France when, on 3 May, his mother died of tuber-culosis. Grace was just fifty. Under the heading 'occupation' on her death certificate is the unusual and poignant entry:

> 22 The Chase
> Clapham
> Wife of
> Aime
> Van den Bogaerde
> Artist
> (water colors)

For their differing reasons neither her husband nor her son could be by her side when she ended her days among the nuns at the Hostel of God in Clapham.

The close of 1917 found Ulric's brigade in Italy, where he would spend the next fourteen months. It had been a chaotic theatre, with the Italian Second Army routed by the Austro-German force and with alliances wobbling. The first half of the following year was relatively quiet, on this front at least. Ulric spent much of his time on sketching duties. In July, as serious fighting began again, he was promoted to lieutenant, but by the end of the year principal hostilities were over; the Italian campaign had cost the Gunners twenty-six officers and 205 other ranks. In January 1919 Ulric was home – or whatever passed for home. When the War Office wrote to the most recent address he had supplied, thanking him for his service and informing him that he could retain the rank of lieutenant, the letter was returned, 'Not Known'.

They should have tried *The Times*. With effect from 3 February, Ulric had rejoined his old newspaper as a draughtsman in the advertising department at £5 per week. Not for long. Northcliffe set him to work on half-tone and photogravure reproduction. The research, carried out in top-secret conditions, behind the bars of an iron birdcage in the basement of Printing House Square, resulted in an issue on 25 July that was a landmark. Despite the occasional dismissal, he evidently pleased The Chief. On the anniversary of the historic edition, the latter wrote to congratulate him. Shortly afterwards Northcliffe wrote again, asking for a film to be brought to his home. The memo was addressed to W. Bogearde Esq:

> My dear Bogearde,
>   Among bad writers in the office you at present hold the championship!
>   Please type your signature in future, for the sake of my overworked Secretaries . . .
>   Chief [9]

At this point Ulric had been promoted to art editor of the *Weekly Edition*'s picture section, with an annual salary of £624. Early one morning Northcliffe telephoned him and demanded that a fully captioned proof of a page of half-tone news photographs should be brought to his house by noon. Taxis were deployed to wrest etchers and process-operators from their homes. At midday Ulric arrived at number 1 Carlton Gardens to find a room full of people:

> They were all asked what they thought of the page. Thank God they liked it and so did he. He then turned to me and said 'It will do – except for one picture I don't like – put in something else and it is to go into the paper to-night for to-morrow – and from then on a page of pictures every week-day!' That was March 1922.
>   It was a staggering order, for we were hardly prepared, but we managed somehow. On the third or fourth morning he rang me up at about ten at the office. 'Chief speaking. Can you keep it up six days a week? It wants doing you know.' I forget my reply. He then said 'Go and see Campbell Stuart about your pay' – which I did. I was put up to £800. [10]

Events were moving fast. Ulric established an art department and remained its editor for the next thirty-five years. In the General Strike of 1926, when emergency editions of the newspaper were produced by management and heads of department, he worked on alternate nights for two weeks in the machine room and as a driver. For this he was rewarded with 'special gratuities' totalling £34 and a silver matchbox engraved with the legend *Ictus Meus Utilis Esto* ('May my strike be useful'). During his tenure as art editor he was responsible for several innovations which, in terms of newspaper photography, were revolutionary. Disliking flashlight as much as the artists did, he sought the best technical help from manufacturers of film and lenses, and took his camera to Covent Garden where Thomas Beecham was conducting *The Perfect Fool*. Previous attempts to capture ballet in performance had never been satisfactory; Ulric's results were startling. His subsequent photographs of Pavlova fascinated both the ballerina and Diaghilev alike. Stark entries in his diary such as 'Infra-red $\frac{1}{2}$ page' on 9 and 11 August 1932, and 'First Aerial Infra-red photographs' on 3 August belie the momentousness of his experiments. The use of colour and – after various mishaps – underwater photography were other areas in which Ulric and his colleagues led the way.

Evidently, theirs was a happy ship. In the middle of preparations for coverage of the 1937 Coronation his department, by now thirty-strong, sprung on him a presentation to mark the twenty-fifth anniversary of his joining the newspaper. He was described as 'a Chief who has the knack of getting the best out of his staff in the nicest possible way'. Indeed, he was known affectionately in some quarters as 'CD' or 'The Dripper' because of his good-mannered persistence – 'constant dripping wears away the stone'. And there was more: frequent expressions of gratitude from Buckingham Palace and Windsor Castle for the newspaper's portraits of royalty; numerous applauded exhibitions; quiet satisfaction for the planning and execution of photography on the 1953 Everest expedition, to which *The Times* had exclusive rights. The expedition leader, John (later Lord) Hunt, remarked to his fellow team members that the 'object of the other newspapers is to break into this copyright as much and as often as possible';[11] Ulric was just the man to protect the scoop.

Recognition came on two levels. The Royal Photographic Society awarded him a Fellowship in 1943; and on Ulric's somewhat reluctant retirement from *The Times* in the summer of 1957, the acting Editor, Maurice Green, said:

When he first came here he was an artist drawing the pictures with his own hands. They were very good pictures and he has put the imprint of a real artist on everything he has touched. Mr Bogaerde has made an imprint on some departments of newspaper work which I think will be noticeable as long as newspapers go on, because he has really been a pioneer of the technical advances of newspaper photography, particularly those he established. Through him we have had pictures which by their form and content have made good news. But if he is an artist, he is the last person in the world to have an artist's temperament.

Nobody, concluded Green, had made such a distinguished contribution to the newspaper and 'there is nobody who has been better liked by the staff all over PHS [Printing House Square]'.[12] Ulric was given a cheque for £68, raised by all departments, and a further £162 10s by management.

There is an odd postscript to Ulric's career at *The Times*. In April 1969 the newspaper published an obituary of Arthur Hickman, who for forty years had been an assistant in the art department. It said he had invariably been entrusted with the task of choosing for reproduction pictures from the Royal Academy Summer Exhibition. Ulric took great exception, writing to the letters editor, Geoffrey Woolley: 'He never did. I made the selection entirely myself, from the earliest days, when I persuaded Geoffrey Dawson [the Editor] to let me have a whole page, and sometimes two pages for display.' He added: 'The selection of the RA pictures was one of my most trying jobs, not only to reflect the trend of the current exhibition, but to balance the pictures on the page.' This letter was not published, and the affair seems to have been only partially resolved by the then Editor, William (later Lord) Rees-Mogg, writing to Ulric's elder son, who mentioned in reply his father's 'distress over the Hickman thing'.[13]

It is hard to imagine such a strong reaction nowadays, when 'the record' is treated with disdain. But for the fastidious Ulric it mattered greatly. After all, he had given his working life to the newspaper. At the presentation in 1937, when he received from his staff a silver cigar box, his wife was given a cigarette case, in partial compensation for being 'deprived of many hours of her husband's company by the calls of the Department'.[14] His son put it more floridly forty-seven years later, in a tribute commissioned for the newspaper's bicentenary:

'Your father has sacrificed us all on that damned red-brick altar of his in Printing House Square!' my mother would cry in despair as another lovingly prepared supper was burnt or left to go cold by his delayed arrival home.

My mother was an ex-actress and, as such, prone to mild exaggeration. The red-brick altar to which she referred was *The Times*. It was not our father's property in any way: it belonged at that time to the Hon. John Jacob Astor, and we weren't sacrificed. Very much.[15]

Maybe not sacrificed – but, in Margaret Van den Bogaerde's case, cuckolded. For the article concluded with Ulric's description of *The Times* as his mistress: 'I loved her very, very much. I can't forget her, you see.'[16]

The wife who so frequently took second place to that demanding, older woman in Printing House Square was born Margaret Niven on 26 April 1898 in Glasgow. Like her husband, she came from an unconventional family.

In August 1865 *The Scotsman* carried a brief report of an accident at Lockerbie in which a railway employee, William Neavin, was crushed between the buffers of two engines and fell beneath the wheels. He died on his way to hospital in

Carlisle.[17] William Niven – apparently even *his* name could cause confusion – was an engine driver on the Caledonian Railway. He was thirty-eight and the father of three boys and four girls, aged between fifteen and eight months, of whom the eldest two were already working. In October his widow, Sarah, who earned one shilling a week by working her mangle, applied for poor relief, but did not go to court to pursue the claim; the inspector who visited her noted that of the £50 she had been given in compensation by the railway company and by others, £30 still remained. At the time of the tragedy her sixth child was three years old. His name was Forrest, and he would be Derek's other grandfather.

Forrest Niven's two elder brothers were William and James. The latter became a diamond-setter who would boast among his clients the Tsar of Russia. William chose a less sedentary but related occupation, mineralogy, which led eventually to archaeology. Doubtless inspired by David Livingstone, a family friend, he set off at twenty-nine for America, where he spent the next fifty years unearthing treasures and, in doing so, throwing light on the continent's earliest civilisations. His finds helped to enrich the world's public collections and his exploits earned him not only a Fellowship of the Royal Society of Arts but also front-page billing in the *Houston Press* when he turned eighty. After all, he had met Billy the Kid, survived fever, earthquake and raging torrents, discovered three new minerals while on an expedition for Thomas Edison, located a lost city in Mexico called Quechomictlipán – which, he said, means 'what a lot of bones on top' – established a private museum with 20,000 exhibits, produced nine children and narrowly avoided being executed by firing squad for having had cordial relations with Emil Zapata.[18] Here was a figure who could have matched Aimé tale for tale.

While William was accumulating nine tons of ore samples for a trade fair in New Orleans, his youngest brother was moving in a different direction. In December 1883 a Glasgow publication called *The Chiel* noticed an amateur double-bill at the Langham Halls in which Forrest Niven acquitted himself well, although 'scarcely any one spoke correctly, and for this blemish there can be no excuse'.[19] Before the month was out the same newspaper had advised readers of its 'Wheel World' column that the same Mr Niven, who had designed the ladies' invitation for the Paisley Victoria Bicycle Club, was 'hard at work on matter for his own club's dance. Something choice may be expected from this rising young sketchist.'[20] The columnist had a nose for talent. By May 1886, when Forrest announced that he was leaving the Glasgow firm of Mackenzie & Co., 'theatrical artists and lithographers', for a similar job in Belfast, he had made his mark on Clydeside as a newspaper caricaturist, competitive cyclist and actor. The critic from *The Stage* who attended the inaugural production of the First Lanarkshire Rifle Volunteers Dramatic Society declared that in Private Forrest Niven the company has 'an amateur whose services are now in great request, and who is rapidly coming to the front rank in social theatricals'.[21] His departure for Ireland moved the *Scottish Athletic Journal* to print a portrait and tribute to 'one of the most popular of our local wheelmen':

> His popularity is not due to his merits as a rider; it is due solely to the geniality of his disposition, the kindliness of his nature and the versatility of his accomplishments. A man having his qualities could not be other than a popular man [. . .] He has left a host of very attached and devoted friends, who will be glad to welcome him back, should he ever make Glasgow his home again.[22]

They did not have to wait long, for by August he had returned, and established himself in an office in the centre of the city as a 'lithographic artist'. No one knows why his stay across the Irish Sea was so short-lived, but a matter of the heart might have had something to do with it. The previous December he had attended the Bellahouston Bicycle Club Ball, at which another of the guests was a Miss J. Nelson. On 1 July 1887 Forrest Niven married Jane Nelson, the daughter of a master baker from Stranraer.

It was a happy time for the young couple. Work was plentiful for Forrest and he was taken on by the *Glasgow Evening News*, which gave increasing prominence to his political and social cartoons. He resumed his acting. In December 1887 he appeared at the Theatre Royal in a production of *Guy Mannering* and, to the delight of audiences and critics alike, played the role of the smuggler Dirk Hatteraick, 'his Dutch accent being almost to the manner born'.[23] The next year, in Dion Boucicault's *The Shaughraun*, his portrayal of Corry Kinchela was described by the *Glasgow Herald* as 'loud-voiced and generally offensive, as became the character',[24] while the *News* considered that the abandon with which he seized the role 'must have infused confidence into even the most timid member of the company'.[25] He was also receiving rave reviews for his antics at cycle meetings. His impersonation in several 'character races' of Ally Sloper, the hero of a long-running comic strip who specialised in staying one step ahead of the law and the rent-collector, was hailed as 'screamingly funny' and won him a number of trophies.

Domestically, too, this was a fertile period. Two weeks after Forrest's success in *The Shaughraun* Jane produced a daughter, who was also christened Jane. Two more girls, Sarah and Hester, followed swiftly; then a son, William; and then a fourth daughter, Margaret. By 1911 Forrest and his wife would have nine children, five of them girls. If the principal figure in our story is Margaret, at least two of her siblings, Sarah and Hester, have important parts to play. The family moved four times, to ever-larger tenements, while Forrest took over one of several rooms on the sixth floor of an office building in Hope Street, close to the Central Station and to the *News*.

His work had brought him into contact with the Celtic writer Neil Munro, to whom we owe a few sparse insights into Forrest's doings. He endeared himself to Forrest with his whimsy and pronounced sense of fun. They were clearly staunch friends: when Forrest's third son was born in 1904 he was christened Neil Munro Niven. There was loyalty too. Munro's surviving 'diary', which he compiled many years later, has an entry for 29 June 1896 which reads: 'Forrest Niven, artist, dismissed and A. Stewart taken on in his place again.' Then, on 20 July, 'Niven resumed on News on my pleading.'[26]

They went shooting together on the island of Little Cumbrae and in 1897 travelled to Iona. Shortly before his death, Munro recalled in a column written under the pseudonym of Mr Incognito how he, Forrest and two colleagues took indoor riding lessons at Hillhead, then ventured out and 'spent one hectic, alarming and dangerous afternoon in leaping hurdles'.[27] More hazardous still were the celebrations to launch an offshoot to the News called St Mungo. Munro described how at noon on 3 December 1896, the eve of publication, two six-inch mortars mounted on the roof of the News office fired a fusillade of papier-mâché bombs which were supposed to detonate in the air some distance away and scatter leaflets all over the neighbouring streets. The first bomb went off almost as soon as it had left the muzzle, snowing the area with circulars meant for further afield. The discharge shook the entire city centre, and a large crowd gathered at the Central Station, believing that the boiler of a locomotive had exploded. 'Before the police turned up, the second mortar shook the welkin, and strewed Argyle Street, Union Street, and Renfield Street with the most unholy litter of fly-sheets. Forrest Niven, whose idea it was thus to arouse immediate interest in St Mungo, promptly remembered an engagement elsewhere, and disappeared.'[28]

At the turn of the century, Forrest was becoming known outside Glasgow. Contributing to Strand Magazine gave him a platform alongside the likes of Conan Doyle. In the theatre he had already made at least one foray south of the border: in 1892 he was to be found acting at Toole's Theatre near Charing Cross Station in London and assisting with the stage management of J. M. Barrie's first hit, Walker London, which the company took on tour. According to family legend, he went on to set up his own troupe of strolling players, but Scotland's main theatrical library at Glasgow University has no records to back this up. What we do know is that after the birth of his last child he was in England again, this time with his daughter Margaret, the only member of his family who showed any enthusiasm to follow him on to the stage. There is a 1913 photograph of Madge Niven, taken by a Colchester photographer, showing her in a production of Graham Moffat's Bunty Pulls the Strings. Her son would write one day that Margaret's career reached its apogee when she was in the cast of this frothy comedy at the Theatre Royal, Haymarket in 1911. Alas, the evidence suggests that the closest she came to the West End was East Anglia and, perhaps, Golders Green. None the less she was, and continued to be, determined to lift spirits. Another photograph, published by the Scots Pictorial on 21 December 1918, in a column otherwise dedicated to the activities of the Royal Family, had Madge Niven in Army uniform, sleeves rolled up and cap at a jaunty angle. The caption declared her 'an excellent entertainer' who 'has delighted thousands of our wounded soldiers with her readings and naïve children's impersonations'. Her repertoire included poems of derring-do and of Service life; Kipling's 'Gunga Din' was a firm favourite.

The same caption described Madge as the 'daughter of Glasgow's erstwhile well-known cartoonist, Forrest Niven'. That 'erstwhile' is both strange and poignant. For the heady days of the 1890s and early 1900s, when Forrest's illustrations sprang from broadsheet pages of otherwise solid grey print, when his watercolours were given space by the Royal Glasgow Institute of the Fine Arts, and when he 'swaggered about Glasgow in cloak and highland bonnet',[29] were over. He took to the bottle and fell into obscurity – in which order is hard to determine. He died on 4 January 1932 in the Eastern District Hospital, which cared for the destitute. The newspapers were kind, but not exactly lavish, in paying their respects. His former employers gave him five brief and somewhat careless paragraphs:

> Mr Forest [sic] Niven, who died in Glasgow yesterday, was in the early 'nineties one of the most familiar figures in Press life in Glasgow.
>
> He was a very clever cartoonist, and his black and white sketches for The Evening News, more especially when there was a breeze on at a meeting of the Town Council, were decidedly clever, and a feature of the paper.
>
> 'Forest,' as he was called, was a clever actor, and in 'Rob Roy' he played the part of Captain Thornton with much credit.
>
> He was greatly in evidence eat [sic] all big Corporation functions, and could draw at lightning speed striking caricatures of prominent Bailies and Councillors, including 'Benburb,' the late Bailie John Ferguson.
>
> Mr Niven retired from The Evening News a good many years ago, but did a considerable amount of work in his home, including etchings.[30]

The Scotsman noted that 'Mr Niven's best work was achieved about the time of the 1901 Glasgow Exhibition' and the Herald added with a flourish that, like many other artists of the period, 'Mr Niven wore the Highland cloak and was a kenspeckle figure in the city'.[31] It is not known how many members of his family attended the funeral; one suspects, very few. The diary of his son-in-law, Ulric, is blank for the first two weeks in January, but it would be no surprise if he had stayed away. Ulric was incompatible with the family into which he had married, and he had an aversion to Scotland itself; when he and his wife went on a camping holiday shortly after their wedding, it rained constantly and he was attacked mercilessly by midges.

Family lore has it that Ulric Van den Bogaerde met Margaret Niven when he arrived home unexpectedly from Paris, riddled with flu, to find her in his bed, sleeping off the effects of the Chelsea Arts Ball at the Albert Hall. He turfed her out. She spent the rest of the night beyond his bedroom door, but forgave him, nursed him and in a trice married him. Margaret's address at the time was 24 West End Lane, Kilburn, which is just two streets away from where Ulric was living, so the detail of their first encounter probably owes more to Goldilocks and the Three Bears than to reality. Nevertheless on 7 January 1920 the twenty-seven-year-old journalist and the twenty-one-year-old 'theatrical artist' were pronounced man and wife by the Hampstead Registrar. The witnesses were Ulric's loyal aunt Edith and her husband, George Nutt. No parent was present, but the respective fathers appear on the marriage certificate as being, in Aimé's case, 'of independent means' and, in Forrest's, an 'Artist (painter)'.

The house to which Ulric returned with his vivacious young bride was a substantial three-storey building at the end of a terrace, backing on to a stable yard. He had moved in to 39 St George's Road on 10 September 1919, and the council registered its new occupier for rating purposes as 'Hugh Bogaerd'. Because there is no Hugh on the Van den Bogaerde family tree, the only logical explanation is that the council official who came to collect the biannual payment was so flummoxed by the impenetrable Christian and family names that Ulric must have said something along the lines of, 'Oh, don't worry – just write down "U"'. For a short while after he arrived, he shared the house with a couple called Pigott, but by the autumn of 1920 they had been supplanted by Cecil Godfrey and Prebble Rayner, artist friends of Ulric's, who took rooms and helped him with the £75 a year rent. At this point, he was earning £12 a week in his illustrious new post as art editor of the *Times Weekly Edition*. And his wife was pregnant. It was a moment of truth, for any ambition Margaret might have had to make a career in the theatre, or even in the excitingly nascent cinema, was now at an end. Ulric had, it was said, refused to allow her to travel to Hollywood and take up an invitation to join Famous Players-Lasky, the studio which would become Paramount. Given his unsettled background and its surfeit of wandering, it is no surprise that he should put his foot down. Yet his decision, born of possessiveness and a yearning for stability, would always be resented. Such stability seems to have been confined to Ulric's work; by the end of the decade he and his wife would have moved house no fewer than three times. However, thanks to the child she was about to bring into the world, Margaret would be able in due course to live some of her dreams – albeit vicariously.

Two

'. . . life is not all cushions and barley sugar'

There are two photographs in the Van den Bogaerde family archive which show Margaret in her bedroom at St George's Road and in a condition which might today be described as 'sultry' or 'smouldering'. A third image, of the same high quality and evidently taken with the help of a delayed shutter release, has a dressing-gowned Ulric tenderly lighting a cigarette for his wife, who is wearing a pinafore – perhaps a maternity – dress. The story-in-pictures continues with a sketch of mother and baby. Unsigned, it is believed to be the work of a close family friend, J. H. Dowd, the *Punch* artist who illustrated the first version of what was to become *Winnie-the-Pooh* and whose pre-eminence in capturing the essence of children was celebrated by, among others, *Strand Magazine*.[1] Sixty-five years later, Dowd's drawing was used as the frontispiece to *Backcloth*, with Derek captured at eight months, dummy plugged firmly in mouth.

Ulric and Margaret did not stay long at their first home, with its reek of turpentine and linseed oil, the mixed scent of which left a lasting impression as 'the one that I remember best and with which, anywhere I go, if I smell it, I am instantly at ease, familiar and secure'.[2] By the time the compilers of the October 1922 London telephone directory recorded 'Bogkerde U.V.' as one of a rapidly growing body of subscribers, the family had already moved, to another tall house, at 173 Goldhurst Terrace. It was only ten minutes' walk away, but – somewhat less important then than later – it was properly in Hampstead, not Kilburn. The Van den Bogaerdes occupied the ground floor and basement; there was a fair amount of coming and going upstairs. A few doors along the road lived a relative, Kathleen Nutt – perhaps the 'Aunt Kitty' whose living-quarters enchanted the infant Derek as 'a vague, shadowy place, filled with sweet scents and the trembling shapes of feathers and handkerchiefs flickering high on the ceiling', not to mention a polar-bearskin rug on the floor, a gold-and-black striped divan and a gramophone.[3]

Within a year of moving, Margaret was pregnant again. She and Ulric travelled to the Continent and called at Izegem, in the hope of meeting his father's relatives. They arrived at Wolvenhof to find a large lunch party in progress, with everyone speaking French and their cousins too preoccupied to take notice of the visitors from London. In any case, any reminder of 'the Scandal' was unpalatable. They were given the cold shoulder. As far as his Belgian family was concerned, that, for Ulric, was the end of that. The baby who arrived on 2 April 1924 was born at home and baptised in the same church as her brother, where she was given the names Margaret Elizabeth Marie. Only the second of these was used, and then formally. From the beginning she was known to all as 'Lu'. She still is. In an *aide-mémoire* provided in 1960 to his son for a series of autobiographical articles, Ulric explained that the inspiration was the tall younger sister of Thomas Hardy's Tess of the d'Urbervilles, Eliza-Louisa. ' 'Liza-Lu is so gentle and sweet, and she is growing so beautiful,' says the mortally ill Tess. 'She has all the best of me without the bad of me.' In Ulric's words, she was the 'odd man out'. Lu was not introduced immediately to her three-year-old sibling. Before the birth, Derek had been fetched by his grandmother, Jane Niven, and shipped off to Glasgow. When he returned, there was 'an enormous pram, with wheels like dustbin lids',[4] and a sister. For now at least, the family was complete – but not rooted.

Its next stop was near the Thames. Ulric bought number 14 Cross Deep Gardens, a modest house in a new terrace a short stroll from the river at Twickenham and some eleven miles from his office. The area is known as Strawberry Hill, reputedly because in 1747 the essayist Horace Walpole took the understandable decision to rename his newly acquired home after Strawberry Hill Shot, a plot of land included in the property, instead of Chopped Straw Hall. More influential on the suburb's topography, however, was another, even greater, man of letters – the poet Alexander Pope, who moved to Twickenham with his mother in 1719, when he was thirty-one. He remodelled a house beside the river as a Palladian villa, and laid out an elegant garden on the opposite side of the busy road, connected by a tunnel known to this day as Pope's Grotto.[5] Much had changed to both house and garden by 22 May 1925, when the Van den Bogaerdes moved in, two streets away. Pope's villa itself had become a private girls' school, St Catherine's, which was to prove convenient, and there were other attractions nearby: the riverside lawns of Radnor Gardens; the frisky marble nudes in York House Gardens; above all, the Aladdin's cave at 42 Church Street, where Mrs Brand, whose dolls were reputed to be Twickenham's finest, sold 'superior toys':[6]

[...] every Saturday I went there with my 'Saturday penny' (actually I was given two) to buy a celluloid animal from a huge cardboard box to add to my growing 'zoo'. I [...] thieved one or two occasionally when the elderly woman who ran the shop was not looking. Twopence only bought one creature. Sometimes the desire to have another was too great and wickedness overcame me. With horrifying facility.[7]

Mrs Brand also had to keep an eye on the confectionery she dispensed as a sideline. In short, for a four-year-old boy with a baby sister, this was altogether a more alluring environment than boring old West Hampstead. However, there was a downside: school.

Derek began his formal education at a kindergarten on Twickenham Green, run by two sisters, Mrs Chapman and Miss Harris, the latter of whom was also secretary of the Young Women's Christian Association. All he could remember of it in later years was a long tin shed, painted dark red, a blackboard, a large iron stove and tables. Lessons were spent thinking about Minnehaha, the cat he had rescued from a rubbish tip; how to build an aquarium; and the next expedition to fish for minnows at Teddington Lock: 'I simply didn't bother with Miss Harris and her silly kindergarten; my brain absolutely refused to see the connection between "CAT" and "MAT" and I frankly didn't give a damn which sat on which. As far as I was concerned it was a wasted morning.'[8] There was something else that kept him brooding and distracted: a green-eyed monster which for most of his life would never be far away. Derek had begun to realise that his sister was 'far more cosseted and fussed over because she was younger. And prettier. Jealousy started to sprout like a bean shoot in the darkness of my heart – it also began to show.'[9]

Miss Harris's best endeavours came to nothing. Ulric and Margaret tried another tack. They sent Derek to join the girls at St Catherine's, in the hope that the nuns might do better. 'I was captivated by their swirling grey habits, by the glitter and splendour of the modest, but theatrically ravishing, chapel, the flickering lamps beneath the statues of the Virgin Mary and Joseph. It went to my head in a trice and I fell passionately in love with convent life.'[10] His parents must have thought it was working. With the zeal of the convert, Derek built an altar in the nursery at home and decided that his destiny was the priesthood. He was too young to understand how and why his father, who went to war a staunch Roman Catholic, had his faith destroyed in France and Italy. No, even in the 'vaguely ambiguous atmosphere' at Cross Deep Gardens, Derek thought he had identified in Catholicism his inamorata: 'Without, of course, realizing that what I had *actually* fallen in love with was the Theatre. Not religion at all. The ritual, the singing, the light, the mystery, the glowing candles: all these were Theatre, and Theatre emerged from these things and engulfed me for the rest of my life. Learning my catechism was, after all, merely the prelude to learning my "lines".'[11]

Just as his hours away from home were now governed by a strict regime, so too at Cross Deep Gardens a new discipline began to apply. Derek's capacity to explore forbidden and dangerous territory, to indulge in petty larceny, to swallow poisonous fluids at random, and all in all to find trouble, was not easy for his mother to cope with when she already had her hands full with a baby daughter; nor was his father over-tolerant when released from the ever-increasing demands of the Mistress in Printing House Square. They sought help. What they found was an absolute authority, based on robust common sense, practicality, decency and unflappability, underlain with dedication and a gentle sense of humour. All this in someone not yet out of her teens.

Ellen Searle lived half a mile from the Van den Bogaerdes in a semi-detached house at number 14 Second Cross Road. Her father, George Searle, was a builder, whose expertise in minute brickwork took him on occasion to Hampton Court Palace. His wife, Jane, had been a highly proficient nanny and was full of encouragement when their daughter left school to follow suit. Ellen was seeking a reference for a position a bicycle-ride away in Teddington when a friend of her mother's, who had helped every now and then with Derek and Lu, suggested she might be ideal for a permanent job at Cross Deep Gardens, living in with the Van den Bogaerdes. She arrived for 'interview' in her Girl Guides uniform and immediately hit it off with Margaret: 'We got on famously together. We just took to one another.'[12] She returned shortly afterwards, to meet Ulric, and passed the test. Derek was wary: he suspected curtailment. And to Lu goes the credit for solving the problem of how this new member of the family should be addressed. At her home and at school, Ellen was called Nellie; here at Cross Deep Gardens she was the Nanny. Both caused difficulties for the little girl, who, according to Derek, settled for Lally. Which is how Ellen Searle has been known ever since among the Van den Bogaerdes, and, more recently, to a much wider circle of intimates whom she has never met. For she has been a principal player in, and dedicatee of, two non-fiction bestselling books.

Lally moved in. Initially, Derek, who was just under ten years her junior, responded with fascination to the new rules about table manners, personal hygiene and, in particular, the need for regular reports on the morning visit to the lavatory. Before long, they began to pall somewhat and it would not be fanciful to suggest that his relationship with Lally was the first of a series in which a will as strong as his own presented a stimulating challenge, leading to great affection. In those days when summary justice was the norm, she would not hesitate to back up a threat of 'I'll box your ears'; and if behaviour went really beyond the pale, there was always in the background the fearsome prospect of her brother – a real-life policeman. But from the start Lally regarded Derek as 'such a grown-up little boy. He must have been about six then, but you thought of him as being older than he really was.'[13] If he had reservations about the new regime, there was none as far as Lally's parents were concerned. Both children adored visiting the house in Second Cross Road, and continued to do so after they had left the area. Lu would stand behind George Searle's wing-chair and sing in his ear. Derek divided his time between the linnets and canaries which George bred in an adapted greenhouse and the chickens kept by Jane Searle at the bottom of the garden. Several years later, just after Mrs Searle's death, Derek and Lu went to stay with Lally and her father. They found the chicken population depleted – it was thought that they had pined for their keeper. During the visit one of the fowl turned up its toes, moving Derek to create a headstone bearing the lines:

> This is the grave of Selina Hen
> Who died of a disease unknown to men.

Not exactly in the Alexander Pope class, it was nevertheless Derek's first recorded verse.

The bond between Lally and the Van den Bogaerdes was special indeed. She was struck by the contrasting characters of Margaret and Ulric – the former, outgoing, exuberant, stopping to talk to duchess and dustman alike; the latter, withdrawn but always gentlemanly, and all too frequently unwell. When Lally first met him, 'he was very, very poorly'. She soon learned how badly affected he had been by the war: 'He suffered terribly with his nerves. It was a sort of shell shock and there were times when he was really, really ill. He would look terrible. Mrs Bogaerde was marvellous with him. She used to sit with him and talk to him quietly. It would pass, but he would have to fight it. Twickenham didn't suit him. It is low-lying and they say it is bad for people with nerves.'[14]

The Van den Bogaerdes did not stay. Apart from the problems with Ulric's health, there was a hostile factor which would recur in Derek's life: encroachment. No sooner had the family arrived than the trucks, the diggers, the saws and the hammers set to work on translating the nearby trees and fields into the 'bricks and pebbledash' of seventy-six new dwellings. In 1929 the house was sold and on 5 October the family moved 'away from the river-mud of beloved Twickenham, to the gravel hills of Hampstead, which I hated'.[15] In fact, their passage back to the relative heights of north London took them not to Hampstead but to another growing suburb: Golders Green, a part of the capital synonymous with Jewish settlement. The three-storey, unprepossessing end-of-terrace house in Highfield Avenue was at right-angles to a small parade of shops on Golders Green Road, which included Grodzinski, a long-established Jewish bakery, and the essential sweetshop. It was also, like Cross Deep Gardens, conveniently close to a convent school, La Sagesse. No less crucially to Ulric, there was accommodation for his beloved motor car, an OM. This was the Lancia or Alfa Romeo of its day, a sports car rather than a tourer, made in Brescia, Italy, by Officine Meccaniche; and Ulric had two of them in succession, one blue, one silver. More expensive than its British equivalents, such as the Riley, it was unquestionably a status symbol, and an indication that, for all his prudence, Ulric could indulge in at least one overt luxury. The only occasion on which Lally knew of him raising a hand to either of the children was when one of them accidentally scratched the car on their way from house to garden. Neither knew who had done it, so both were smacked. Derek would not take the responsibility, but accepted his punishment and left Lu to hers. She did not speak to her father for several days afterwards. It was, says Lally, one of those small things that showed how different from each other were brother and sister.

One of the first steps Ulric had taken on moving to Twickenham was to apply to the council for permission to erect a wooden garage. Here in Golders Green he already had the garage, but access was a problem: the path to it was owned by the shops. For six and a half weeks the Van den Bogaerdes were in limbo while Ulric's uncle, Arthur Nutt, applied a legal mind to sorting out the potential awkwardness. The furniture was put into storage; Ulric and Margaret lodged with close friends, the Hatfields; Lu and Lally stayed with the Searles in Twickenham; and Derek was again despatched to Glasgow. Not until 19 November could they be reunited with each other and with their belongings in their new home, where they would stay for six years. By now, however, they had the use of a second property which was to assume a far greater significance in all of their lives; and for Derek and Lu the OM was their transport from 'gravel hills' to chalky downland. To them it was a magic carpet.

The hamlet of Lullington – originally Lulla's Farm – lies a dozen miles east of Brighton, and four from the coast, in spectacular and largely unspoiled countryside. From separate vantage points are visible in the distance a white horse and a long man, carved to a gigantic scale out of the hillside to the south-west and the north-east respectively. There is no shop, no post office, no pub and no more than a scatter of houses. But there is a church, and, close by, two cottages, one of which was rented during the 1920s by a colleague of Ulric's at *The Times*, William Salmon. Ulric and Margaret would visit him at weekends. At the turn of the decade, 'Uncle Salmon' gave up his tenancy and Ulric took it over. In the past, the Van den Bogaerdes had spent holidays on the Normandy coast, at resorts such as Wimereux and Deauville, or in the West Country: in 1927 they took the children to Cornwall and in 1929, with Lally, they shared a house in Swanage with the Hatfields. Now they had a fixed point within easy access from London, and although it was a part of their lives for only three years or so, the investment of less than one pound a week paid rich and rare dividends – not just for the family, which established a relationship with rural Sussex that has lasted for three-quarters of a century. The many who have read *A Postillion Struck by Lightning* and *Great Meadow* will be in no doubt that, however coloured the anecdotes, however skewed the portraits, both books are an elegy to a lost and irrecoverable time, characterised by a simplicity, an innocence and a oneness with nature.

The Church of the Good Shepherd is an extraordinary building, just sixteen feet square and with a seating capacity of twenty-three. It is, wrote Derek, 'the Smallest Church in Sussex'.[16] Some claim it to be the smallest in England. In fact it is a portion of the chancel of a larger church believed to have been destroyed by fire in Cromwell's day. Restored in 1894, it stands alone and proud, its spire, supported by a white weather-boarded belfry, poking above the encircling trees. The larger of the two cottages one hundred yards away has been known variously as the Old Rectory and Little Chapel, but when the Van den Bogaerdes moved in their furniture at the end of July 1931 the church had recently united with its much bigger companion at the bottom of the hill, St Andrew's, Alfriston, and any formal connection with the neighbouring houses had ceased. Even so, an informal relationship continued: '. . . all we had to do was change the water and the flowers in the vases once or twice a week. On the altar. Well, they weren't vases for the flowers. Jam jars. But we put white and blue crêpe paper round them so they looked rather pretty. And my sister always picked the flowers and arranged them herself. Sitting in the sun on a gravestone singing a hymn-sounding song.'[17]

The cottage itself was built of brick and dressed flint, with a tiled roof. At some point it had been divided into two, but the family had both sets of living-quarters to itself. Forty-six years later Derek would write to the then occupant:

In our day, [it] was very primitive indeed. As you have gathered. Lamps, privvy, pump . . . the road from Lullington Court was a chalk road . . . the path up to the cottage just a chalky track. Very slippery in the rain and dangerous with heavy baskets! Inside it was a warren of rooms each leading out of the other, as far as I remember . . . and the North End was fearfully damp and rather gloomy . . . we spent most of our time in the big room on the south looking down to Lullington Court and Littlington [sic].* Lullington Court was a working Farm. Vast dairies with bowls of cream, and all kinds of milk, plus great blocks of yellow butter standing on slate slabs. It was very cool, covered in ivy, and sweet smelling. After the pig-sty, our favourite place . . . apart from the great barn, where the Stallion lived . . . at the far corner of Great Meadow which was, I believe, converted into a chic house sometime just before the war. There was no one living nearer than the Axfords (as they were really called.) at the Court . . . I believe there are two cottages down at the bottom of the road now . . . but they were not there in our time.

It was, he concluded, 'pretty isolated'.[18]

Life at the cottage, for those few precious weeks in each year, was bliss. The children were on their own a good deal: Ulric and Margaret would confidently leave Lally *in loco parentis* while they travelled elsewhere. Once or twice her own parents came to hold the fort. If Ulric could not take the whole period off work

---

* Author's note: Derek's eccentric spelling and punctuation have been preserved throughout this book wherever quotations are used from his own writings.

he would commute, a tortuous journey which for him meant even longer days than usual. Sometimes there would be guests, such as Angela Hatfield – Angelica Chesterfield in the books, where she is treated not altogether flatteringly – or a cousin from Scotland. But there is little doubt that Derek regarded such visitors as intruders on a private idyll. His own invited guests were a different matter. As Lally, Lu and he clambered into the back seat of the loaded car, donning their helmets if the weather permitted the roof to be down, he would smuggle under their protective rug a favourite tortoise or hedgehog. When they had reached a point in the journey where he considered it too far for his father to turn back, he would triumphantly unveil the stowaway, to the irritation of the driver and the poorly concealed amusement of Margaret.

Derek had already established more cordial relations with the other members of the animal kingdom than with his fellow man. Despite their companionship, even Lu – especially Lu, because of the constant proximity – would be on the receiving end of petty spite and cruelty; he once abandoned her at the head of the Long Man of Wilmington and listened with glee to her screams. There is a passage in *Postillion* where he writes that 'a glimmer of liking flickered in me for her' and, two lines later, 'hate glowed deep in the coals of my heart'. More often, however, they would, as Mark Daniel noted in a 1986 article, join forces against a common foe:

> He and his sister defended 'their land' with the utmost savagery from their chief enemies, hikers, who were already infesting the countryside ... [They] would mix a brew of the deadliest weeds they could find, colour it with berries, and leave it in squash bottles in the overgrown lane near their home, hopefully to be found and consumed by thirsty hikers on their way to the smallest church. No successes were ever recorded. On other occasions they hid from the hikers, or, if taken unawares, insulted them with out-thrust tongues, crossed eyes and screeches.[19]

Ulric had called it 'the most beautiful place in all England'. Now, for Derek and Lu, it was 'our world' and its boundary, 'fixed by the weakness or strength of our legs', was Alfriston to the west, Wilmington to the north, Jevington to the east, and Litlington to the south. 'Within that frame all belonged to us. Or so we steadfastly believed for we shared it with few others.'[20]

Only a little further afield, there were the cliffs and beaches of the English Channel; inlets such as Cuckmere Haven and Birling Gap, close to Beachy Head, where Derek would haunt the rock pools with his shrimping net. Swimming was not on his agenda: he had once found himself unexpectedly out of his depth and for ever afterwards he loathed immersion. No, it was nature itself that preoccupied him. For all the exhilaration of hurtling from top to toe down the Long Man on a tin-tray, the greatest delight was in the moments after clambering back up again to allow Lu her turn: 'You could just lie there in the grasses and listen to the wind wuthering gently above your head, the larks singing high in the blue intensity of the sky, the bleat of lambs and the clonkle-clankle of the sheep bells. There was no other sound.'[21]

Whether they slithered, jumped, skittered or flew; grunted, cheeped, hooted or neighed, God's other creatures held him in thrall. Many years later he was to itemise four tests which would have to be met by anyone wishing to mourn at his funeral – a list which must have struck some of his acquaintances as curious and which, in the event, proved academic. A fondness for children; a refusal to patronise, ignore, or belittle; and 'the vitally important qualities of humour and, above all, laughter' were the first three:

> They must also like animals: if they couldn't quite *adore* them as I did, then they had to show, at least, a warm interest and not, as some, pale with terror at the sight of a harvest mouse, or cry out in horror at the presence of a cheerful old toad or even, silliest of all, a harmless bat.
>
> People like that simply couldn't pass. It was not essential, but of course greatly to be desired, for them to come fishing for efts or sticklebacks, or even to assist at the delivery of a family of white rats or a litter of rabbits, but it was perfectly all right if they merely showed interest in the business, and more so if they offered (as many did rather than actually look at the messy business) a piece of silver money with which to defray the cost of feeding them, or for the purchase of a larger cage or a better aquarium in which to house them.[22]

Outside the cottage frogs would be carefully trapped and carried in a box to Lally, whose shriek of horror could probably be heard a quarter of a mile away at Plonk Barn. Both she and Lu remember how Derek would sit for an eternity on one of the three seats in the privy, watching the birds through its open door. Early in *Postillion* there is an account of his quest to acquire a canary at the fair held annually in Alfriston. He had been told that the birds were actually sparrows dyed yellow, but he would not be swayed. 'I wanted one very badly. Basically because they were birds, and I worshipped birds, and also because the cages were so terribly small.'[23] Those are the words of a free spirit, and here in Lullington there was more freedom than at any other time in his life.

There were also excellent opportunities to practise his budding skills as a playwright, staging mini-dramas with Lu in the nearby barn or in the garden, to a critical audience sometimes comprising their next-door neighbour and near-contemporary Ronnie Diplock, alias 'Reg Fluke', and any passing bird or beast. But soon the scene had to shift. In 1933, the Lullington Court estate, which consisted of the entire parish with its population of seventeen, was put up for sale. The farmer, Thomas Axford, was relinquishing his tenancy, and the owner, Lieutenant-Colonel R. V. Gwynne, decided to break up the property. The 'big house', Plonk Barn, the Great Meadow, two smaller houses and the two cottages all came under the hammer on 14 June at the Corn Exchange in Hailsham, and although Ulric could not be there – he was working on the first experiments with underwater cameras – he was keen to bid. He was prepared to go up to £700, but the cottage, with its three acres of land, its privy, its rainwater tank and its rotary pump, fetched £900. The idyll was almost over. Ulric's fondness for the cottage and all it meant can be gauged from the fact that he appears – as 'Alec Bogarde' – in the parish electoral register for 1932, and again – correctly this time, and with Margaret – in 1933; it was, after all, not their principal residence. But leave they must, after one final month's holiday. At least Major Pothecary, the new owner, wanted some of the furniture.

Shortly after Ulric's disappointment at the auction, Derek acquired a brother. Since Lu's arrival, Margaret had suffered two miscarriages – the second, at the cottage, where Lally comforted her. On Wednesday, 19 July the doctor and nurse who had been called early that morning to Highfield Avenue announced that she had given birth to a son. 'Boy born 2.30 p.m.,' wrote Ulric in his diary. The next day: 'Very hot. Took Baby's photograph.' And on the Thursday: 'Very hot. Bought fan.' Lu had been sent to the Glasgow relatives, but Derek was at home. On the previous Sunday he and his father had visited the British Museum, and he is mentioned in his father's diary on the Tuesday. He was already racked with unease, because of the upheaval: 'I just sensed that someone had turned my egg-timer upside down and that the sand had started to run the other way.'[24] Lally remembers that on the fateful day itself Derek was round at the house of an Italian family, the Govonis, whose daughter Giovanna had befriended Lu at school. When he returned, the spirit in which he greeted his new sibling was far from welcoming – in retrospect, anyway: 'It looked, from my point of view, like rabbit-offal wrapped in a shawl. I was silent with shock at the sight of this living stranger in our midst. This was the bulge in my mother's belly. This the cause of the vastly disturbed household. [...] Small fists beat helplessly in slow motion at a bloated, scarlet, screwed-up, old man's face. The head weighed tons, the neck seemed delightfully frail.'[25] Note the 'delightfully' – as if the link from head to torso was eminently snappable.

The birth was registered on 15 August, and the baby's name given simply as Ulric, amended later to Gareth Ulric. There had already been a scare, because he seemed to be having difficulties with his circulation, but the family's holiday went ahead as planned. For a month they revelled in fine weather, with swimming expeditions to several of the beaches between Brighton and Pevensey. And there was good news. Halfway through the holiday Ulric arranged to rent, for 10s a week, another cottage, on the western fringe of Alfriston, at number 30 Winton Street. Despite an even more ravishing outlook, it could not cast quite the same spell as Lullington, but the Van den Bogaerdes could at least keep a foothold in the landscape they had grown to love. On 17 September they left the Old Rectory, or Little Chapel, for good, with Lally doing her best to boost morale by pointing out its defects: the lack of sanitation, the wobbly flooring which had once given way under Margaret's foot, the dicey roof. Derek remembered his nanny had told them: 'You can't have a summer without a good winter.'[26] He was about to pay dearly for his own exquisite 'summer', and he would learn that it was wiser to keep the best experiences in the memory, not to attempt to relive them. In the letter to the much later occupant of the cottage he wrote: 'You must NEVER go back, must you?' He had, he said, just once, in the autumn of 1960, and although he found his and Lu's World 'nearly all the same', it, and he, had grown older.

He did, however, have to go back to school. By the time the family had moved back to north London from Twickenham, Derek's academic hopelessness was apparent to all. He failed the entrance examination for University College School in Hampstead, so, on 10 April 1931 – just after the shock of Aimé's sudden re-emergence – Ulric took him to meet Bernard Thompson, who gave private tuition at his home, number 1 Kemplay Road in Hampstead. Three days later the ten-year-old boy began being 'crammed'. He would recall how he 'drifted in a haze of happy, and determined, ignorance through the veined hands of a black-booted and wing-collared tutor. In a stifling room in a mouldering villa in Willow Road. To no avail.'[27] Dennis Rendell, five months his senior, was there at the same time; he, too, had failed to pass into UCS: 'We were both pretty thick.' He remembers Thompson as 'a terrifying man, and his wife, Ethel, who had nothing to do with the teaching, was even more terrifying.' The house was early Victorian:

> We used to do our work in the drawing-room which had French windows onto a garden. We had lunch with the Thompsons, and had to go into the kitchen for that. At about 2 p.m. we had some time of our own – about half an hour before we went back to work. In that half hour we used to go to the house next door, which was very much more modern than the Thompsons'. Its garden was full of dock leaves, and laurel, and there were thousands of snails. We used to have snail races along the laurel.[28]

Derek might have considered the formalities 'lethal, dull, boring',[29] but the period with the Thompsons succeeded well enough. Four months later, both boys were enrolled into the Junior Branch of University College School, with Derek, now in his maroon-and-black-striped blazer, assigned to Campbell House and Form 4B. If he had feared something out of *Tom Brown's Schooldays*, he was to be agreeably surprised. The founding headmaster of the junior school, Charles Simmons, took as his philosophy Shakespeare's 'No profit grows where is no pleasure ta'en'. Just as important to him as fractions, dates, syntax and declension were handicrafts, plays, the school's luxuriant garden and its magazine. According to a history published for the 150th anniversary of UCS in 1988, Simmons was 'well aware that small boys are seldom happier or better employed than when they are making something'.[30] Fortunately, his successor, Dr Bernard ('Bunny') Lake, was of the same mind. Other preparatory schools attached undue import-ance to Latin and Greek; here on Holly Hill priority was given to the 'Conversazione', an occasional festival at which the boys could show off their training in 'Aesthetic Appreciation' and 'Manipulative Skill'. Art was taught by an inspirational figure named C. E. F. 'Smaggie' Smaggasgale, who took over Campbell House during Derek's time; he looked like the Prince of Wales. There was a high standard of drama, and no little eccentricity. The benign, bespectacled, golf- and cricket-loving Dr Lake was reputed to carry about with him an assegai, which he called his *hasta sacra* (holy spear); this would be pointed at the boy of the moment with a cry of either 'Pax!' or 'Bellum!' In such unconventional ways might a little of the Classics be absorbed. Breaches of discipline would result in an early morning parade on the playground, reviewed by the headmaster from the balcony of his third-floor flat; satisfied that justice had been done, he would go back inside and finish his breakfast.

This was the far from hostile environment in which Derek began his studies on 16 September 1931. Dr Lake's daughter, Jennifer Hiley, describes it as 'almost a family atmosphere', where the staff turnover was minimal.[31] Ian McGregor, headmaster from 1976 to 1991, regarded Holly Hill as a place where 'there were always sympathetic characters among the boys and among the parents', where 'life was never dull', and where 'you would develop a natural exploration'.[32] Dennis Rendell recalls:

> Half the staff was female. The Second Master was Miss Fuller – she was a magnificent creature, a huge woman, very masculine, with masculine-type hair, but a jolly good teacher. She and one of the other women teachers took a close interest in the communal bath which we took after soccer. We would play against other forms in the Junior School, but Derek wasn't very good at games. He didn't like soccer. He was slightly effeminate on the field, and didn't like barging into people.[33]

Richard Rubinstein, another almost exact contemporary, agrees; but, although great store was set by those boys who seemed to be on their way to the rugger fifteen or to the first eleven at football or cricket, few thought the worse of Derek for preferring more solitary pursuits: 'He was a bit of a loner, but he was always cheerful and popular. He was interested in model aircraft and there was even some schoolboy talk about a possible career in aeronautics.'[34] Lally tells how she and Margaret attended an end-of-summer-term sports day, excited that Derek was to be in several races. When they arrived, they found him ill-prepared: 'He was helping Mrs Lake, seeing the teas were all ready, administering anything. He had somehow got around the Head Master. He was not a boy for racing; if he could get out of it, he would. Mrs Bogaerde was so disappointed, because she thought that at least he was going to be doing something other than acting.'[35] And it was clear to everyone that what mattered most to Derek were theatricals. Ian McGregor recalls a correspondence in 1976, in the course of which the former pupil confirmed that during lunch breaks he would dragoon anyone in sight, boys and staff alike, to watch his 'productions', mounted with whatever props were available: 'He said that nobody ever seemed to put any undue pressure on him at school, but it was possible that he put more pressure on others. In fact, he said he could be a perishing nuisance.'[36] He revelled in performing to 'a trapped audience of Masters and Mistresses' but, strangely enough, there is no record of Derek taking part in any official productions, either on or behind the stage. He preferred to do his own thing, and this was refined at home.

Thanks to their shared experience at Mr Thompson's, Dennis Rendell was one of the very few friends to be invited back to the Van den Bogaerde house. He would cycle there from Edgware once a week for tea and remembers well the sweetshop and tobacconist's on the corner of Golders Green Road:

> They would throw out a lot of cardboard boxes which Derek would use for his toy theatre. It was made of wood, and all the props out of the cardboard. The stage was about three foot wide, and had curtains which he would open with a piece of string. The figures were made of cardboard, which he painted and moved around the stage with little sticks from the back, where he was hidden. I thought they were quite lifelike. He painted them and made little chairs and tables. There were quite a few parts in these things; Derek would take not only the leading role but also quite a few others. I can remember one about Roman soldiers where someone had to rush up with a message and a spear in his hand. Elizabeth appeared in his productions, but I was not good enough. Sometimes I was somewhat grudgingly given a bit part.[37]

What did the authorities make of Derek? At the end of that first Michaelmas Term he was marked sixteenth in his class of twenty-two. In English he came fifteenth; his apprehension was 'fair' and his diligence 'very fair', but the overall judgment was 'terribly inaccurate'. In Mathematics he was placed last: 'Has *very* little aptitude for the subject'; in French, tenth: 'Will improve on this, I think'; in History, equal ninth: 'Could do very well but will not take pains'. However, as Ulric read on, not all was gloom. In Geography Derek was equal sixth and 'Quietly studious'; in Nature Study, equal third: 'A good start'. Drawing found him equal eighth, but hampered by being 'Slapdash at present'. In Music, Handwork and even Physical Exercise he was applauded for his efforts. Interestingly, he had been absent on eleven mornings and on six afternoons, but had never once been late. His house mistress, Miss E. Polimeni, who drove a bull-nosed two-seater Morris and sometimes gave the boys lifts to the Underground station, came to this conclusion: 'Too self-satisfied & rather plausible, but promising in many respects.' To which Dr Lake added: 'Not a bad beginning but should note carefully what his House Mistress says.' He also observed that Derek's age-height-weight ratio of minus fifteen per cent 'needs watching'.

By the end of the Lent Term 1934, the staff had given up awarding marks and class positions, so his overall performance was not calculated. Derek's English teacher found that 'Promise – in the way of oral work – is always so much better than performance of written work'. In History: 'I cannot understand why he finds it so difficult to transfer his ideas to paper successfully'; and in Mathematics: 'Seems to try but results poor'. His achievement in Geography was satisfactory, but in Nature Study he 'Should try to write & draw more accurately'. However, in Drawing itself, he was 'Very promising'. The attendance record shows that he was off school on twenty-eight mornings and seventeen afternoons; but even when he was there his mind seems to have been elsewhere. Lally remembers how the headmaster called him in for a ticking-off. Derek stood in front of him without saying a word and with eyes averted; then, when the Head stopped to draw breath, said: 'That's a lovely picture, Dr Lake. Is it a masterpiece?' Any other boy would probably have incurred a clip round the ear, even a beating, but the good Doctor realised no insolence was intended. It was 'just Derek'. No wonder Bernard Lake signed off the report by saying: 'He makes me impatient but I am trying to be more philosophical about him – time will show.'

Three weeks into the following term, Ulric wrote to the headmaster, to say that Derek would not be returning for the next academic year. This was the reply:

Dear Mr Bogarde
    I have just received your letter & am sorry to learn your son is to leave UCS. But it is not unlikely that a boarding school life will suit him better.
    I cannot give you any intelligence quota as we do not indulge in these things here.
    But I can say that your boy has the makings of a very intelligent man & when once he has found his feet & has learned to concentrate on the ordinary work of the School he will do very well. It is of course conceivable that his development in the practical side of things will be very late, but I am convinced that much excellent material is lurking about somewhere.
    He is a very nice fellow & an amusing companion. I wish him the best of luck.
    Yours sincerely
    Bernard Lake

In the Lent Term report the master of Campbell House, 'Smaggie', had been no less perceptive about his thirteen-year-old charge: 'Has still to learn that life is not all cushions and barley sugar.'

The boarding school life, in its strictly residential sense, might well have suited Derek, but that is not what his father and, to a lesser extent, his mother had in mind. The impact of Gareth's arrival, nine years after that of Lu, was felt in obvious ways in the small house at Highfield Avenue, where the baby needed its own accommodation and where the adolescent Derek could no longer share a bedroom with his sister. Derek had noticed that his father had become more distant and there were no more jokes between them. Lally said that Ulric was 'disappointed' in him. There were also worries about Derek's relationship with his mother, whom he idolised. If Margaret was out late or away from home Derek would keep one of her belongings – sometimes even a shoe – under his pillow. Elizabeth, who believes that 'deep down, he simply worshipped her', recalls an embroidered birthday card which he inscribed with lines of poetry addressed to 'Darling Margaret'. No one factor led to the decision that Derek should go to stay with his mother's family in Glasgow and have 'a Scottish education'; it was cumulative, or, as Lally is believed to have put it, just the need for a 'pull on the reins'.[38] It turned out, rather, to be 'a crack on the backside which shot me into reality so fast I was almost unable to catch my breath for the pain and disillusions which were to follow'.[39]

There is little doubt that it was a relieved father who drove south from Glasgow on the morning of 1 September. The baby had recently had a temperature of 105 degrees; his wife had been ill for four days, Aimé was 'not too well' in Brighton and he himself had experienced colonic pain. In Alfriston, Elsie Brooks, who lived in the cottage next door and had taken over as nanny from Lally, developed scarlet fever, and Derek had burned his hands when Lu's dress caught fire. And all the time, belying her vivacity in public, Margaret sought solace from her own resentment – often in the bottle. At least the eldest child would be off their hands for a while. Ulric ensured Derek had £7 for various expenses, including £2 12s 6d for school fees, and 14s 2d for books. A further £5, for the first month's lodging, was left, along with the boy, at number 42 Springfield Square, in the rapidly expanding suburb of Bishopbriggs. This was the home of William Murray and his wife Sarah, the second of Margaret's three elder sisters. They were known in the family as Uncle Murray – Margaret's elder brother William already had the title of 'Uncle Willie' – and Aunt Sadie, but would achieve a strange notoriety as 'Uncle Duff' and 'Aunt Belle'. They lived five minutes' walk from the railway station in one of the new 'four-to-a-block' houses that were springing up as a semi-rural alternative to the city's tenements, but which were in effect two pairs of apartments. There was a small sloping garden, but the view from the Murrays' rooms on the ground floor was unexciting: to the back, an almost identical building at the bottom of the garden; to the front, across the road, another one. Little has changed. It is a dispiriting, claustrophobic place – one where it is easy to see how quickly a free spirit would suffocate.

William Murray was an engineer who had fallen on hard times in the Depression, but was re-establishing himself as an agent with an office in St Vincent Street. Forrest McClellan, one of Derek's cousins, remembers their uncle as clever, hard-working, very gruff-looking, with a 'neat, fussy and aggressive temperament'. He drove a Morris 8 with much pride but little competence. Politically he was an idealist. His background was inferior to that of his wife, who 'clearly regarded it as her mission in life to civilise the brainy but socially gauche young man whom she had married'. Sadie, in her turn, was 'a deft and competent house-wife and needlewoman', handsome, well-dressed, witty, gregarious, anti-Semitic and slavishly dedicated to keeping up appearances: *never* must one approach a boiled egg by slicing off its top with a knife – it must always be battered with the spoon.[40] William had married her at the end of the war. Now she was in her mid-forties, and knew she would never be a parent – unlike all but one of her eight siblings. Forrest McClellan sums up the Murrays' predicament:

> They were a complex and tragic couple. They wanted to have children, but children didn't come. In cases like that it was assumed that the woman was barren, so my aunt carried this stigma. Your heart breaks when you think of the other members of the family being so fecund. So she held a bitterness against Uncle Murray. He was tormented too. He found fulfilment in material success, but there were layers of deep, sad loss and deprivation.[41]

Into this situation came Derek with whom, on the previous occasions when they had met, relations had always been warm. Brief exposure was one thing, however; prolonged cohabitation, quite another – especially when the boy's circumstances had changed so fundamentally. The Murrays were looking forward to having a surrogate son about the place, not to mention a helpful injection of pound notes from the father. What they acquired, in their tiny flat, was 'a bolshy, obstreperous, strange, solitary, strong-willed thirteen-year-old',[42] wrenched from his adored and preoccupied mother – Sadie's own sister – and with a satchel full of problems. Or, perhaps, a sack full. For this was the start of a period which he would come to recall as 'The Anthracite Years'.[43]

Glasgow in the 1930s hid its welcome rather better than it does today. In his *Scottish Journey* Edwin Muir wrote:

> Scraps of newspaper, cigarette ends, rims of bowler hats, car tickets, orange peel, boot soles, chocolate paper, fish-and-chip paper, sixpences, broken bottles, pawn tickets, and various human excretions: these several things, clean and dirty, liquid and solid, make up a sort of pudding or soup which is an image of the life of an industrial town. To this soup must be added an ubiquitous dry synthetic dust, the siftings of the factories, which is capable under rain of turning into a greasy paste resembling mud, but has no other likeness to the natural mire of a country road . . . Sometimes this compost is thickened still more by a brown fog permeated by the same manufactured dirt, with a smell which is neither clean nor obnoxious but is simply the generalised smell of factories.[44]

The train from Bishopbriggs took only a few minutes to reach 'the compost' – at Queen Street Station which, to Derek, was 'an enormous inverted iron colander. Black and sooty, rife with pigeons and the smell of urine.'[45] Uncle Murray headed for his office while Derek, 'like snail', crept unwillingly up Cathedral Street to Allan Glen's School: 'Standing isolated in the centre of a vast asphalted playground, surrounded by high iron spikes, its red sandstone blocks rotting in the filth from the city, it resembled a cross between a lunatic asylum and a cotton mill [. . .] Cold, unloving, unloved. A Technical School for Technical People. What on earth was I doing here?'[46]

Allan Glen's was founded in 1853 in memory of a joiner, property owner and philanthropist who left the bulk of his fortune to establish 'a School for giving a good practical education to, and for preparing for trades or businesses from 40 to 50 boys, sons of tradesmen or persons in the Industrial classes of society'.[47] Its motto was *Cum Scientia Humanitas* ('With knowledge, culture'). Eight decades on, it counted among its alumni a preponderance of shipbuilders and engineers, but it had also produced physicians, academics, diplomats and architects – most notably, Charles Rennie Mackintosh. When P. A. Grimley, a writer from the *Scottish Daily Express*, visited the school's second, recently built home in Montrose Street, he remarked on two stipulations by the founder that were not generally known: Allan Glen had forbidden the teaching of Greek and the giving of religious instruction. Grimley was evidently impressed by the equally practical policy of the headmaster, James Steel, whose belief in the development of individuality and originality ensured, first, that in English classes the boys were encouraged in speech-making to make them more confident and less frightened at the sound of their own voices; second, that every pupil went through a course of training in the workshops 'which seem to be the favourite classrooms': 'Here boys were standing at forges or sitting at tables forming chunks of copper and brass into beautiful ash trays, bowls, candlesticks, and sugar basins ... In the section devoted to art-craft, where the greatest advance has been made in recent years in the school, pupils were shaping clay into various designs ranging from insipid inkwells to glossy simpering shepherdesses.'

Grimley finished his tour at the bookbinding and printing section, where 'originality seems to reach its highest point'. He found the boys producing elaborate illustrated volumes, one of them bound in morocco, and took away with him another entitled *Delights as High* which carried the printed inscription: 'This book is dedicated to you in the hope that, when the dark days come, and you feel the emptiness of disenchantment, you will look on the grass in bloom and know that all is well.'[48] Perhaps William Murray was genuinely optimistic in commending Allan Glen's to Ulric and Margaret for their son. The contemporary evidence suggests that life at the school was nothing like as bleak or harsh as he would paint it forty years later.

Among the parents were a blacksmith, fishmonger, watchmaker, shipwright, newsagent, master mariner, upholsterer, plumber, cabinetmaker, fruiterer, retired police officer and a lavatory attendant. None could afford the school fees and their boys were awarded scholarships – as was William Lockie, the twelve-year-old son of a Paisley tailor, who entered Class 1A at the same time as Derek. Dr Lockie, now retired as a much respected general practitioner, recalls him as 'completely charming' and relatively well-off: 'He was always much better dressed than the rest of us. He had several suits, which most of us were impressed by. I remember a light-brown suit, with a handkerchief hanging out of the pocket. He was often in suede shoes, which were unknown at the time.'[49] Whereas most of the boys brought their own sandwiches each day and ate them at benches in a wooden shelter where drinks and pies were sold, Derek was one of the handful who every Monday would buy five tickets at 1s 6d for a week's lunches of soup, a main course and a pudding, served by waitresses in the school restaurant. Even so, he would go to the hut afterwards and join his classmates. Bill soon learned about Derek's 'idyllic life in Sussex – and I envied it'. He also heard enough about Lu to make him think she was almost part of his own family. 'And Lally – I hadn't met anyone before who had a nanny.' Impressive, too, were the 'aristocratic connections in Holland' and an apparently authentic French accent: 'He had been to France, which was amazing for a boy of thirteen in those days.' How curious, then, that 'when it came to the first term exam, the teacher read out the marks and Derek came near the bottom. That's when I started to think he might need help.'

There is no question but that life could be uncomfortable for such an obvious outsider with his awkward name, 'posh' accent, thin voice and aversion to sport. However, it came as a complete surprise to Bill Lockie when he read many years later that his chum had been upended into a lavatory bowl while the chain was pulled, and had been one of the two principals in a bloody lunchtime brawl that resulted in a bully missing school for three weeks with a bandaged eye. The Derek he knew was retiring and shy – giving the lie to the somewhat pugnacious-looking figure in the back row of a form photograph from that first term – and, like Bill himself, physically unscathed:

He didn't have an air of authority, but he certainly felt a cut above everybody else. When we talked about things at school, it was almost as though there was an understanding that he didn't need to be involved. In classes – chemistry, physics, science in general – he gave the impression that he knew all about it and it wasn't worthy of his attention. This was based on the fact that he knew nothing about it. He didn't participate in school activities. We had plenty of societies and clubs, but no. For him, as soon as the ordeal was over, he was going back down to Sussex to resume the life he had left.

The non-participation was skilfully managed. On Wednesdays, classes ended early so that the boys could go out to the Allan Glen's School Club at Bishopbriggs to play rugger. Bill Lockie remembers Derek boarding the tram-car but somehow never arriving: 'I could not understand why he never went to the Club, which was just around the corner from where he was living. But at the end of games there was a communal bath. That would not have appealed to him at all. He avoided like the plague manly activities.'

He might not have exuded authority, but Derek gave the impression to Bill Lockie – or 'Tom', as he would become in *Postillion* – and to others that his family had means. So when Bill and another boy were asked home by Derek on a reciprocal visit, they were surprised by what they found:

It was a house with a garden, which made it a respectable place, but I expected it to be bigger and to have better furnishings. He had told me of his room, where all his treasures from Sussex would be, but he had very few possessions, and we all had to sit with his aunt and try to make conversation. She was old-fashioned, her hair braided over the top of her head, severe-looking, starchy, with lace collar and dark clothes. She looked *ordinary*, which I had not expected. The house was cold – there was no family feeling about it. She had no children and I don't think she knew how to talk to boys. I was amazed, uncomfortable, and couldn't understand how this boy came from that home. He seemed to be upper-class, and it turned out that he wasn't. He had delusions of grandeur, which I thought were legitimate, and which turned out not to be. I felt sorry for him.

The Murrays, initially at least, tried hard. William took Derek to Ibrox to watch the football; Sadie chose better with the cinema. There were hazardous excursions, with William at the wheel of his car, to the sensational countryside that was within easy reach. Of Loch Lomond Derek wrote to Lu: 'It was lovely & I am sure you would have liked it – it is just like the Sea side only it is a great big Lake with lovely wee island in the middle of it – on the Shore there were to Moorhens building a nest – they had 3 wee Chicks.' Even the two-mile walk on Sunday to Cadder was worthwhile, if not for the activity inside the church, at least for its sinister history; almost hidden in woods, it stands next to the Forth and Clyde Canal, where boats fetched bodies that had been snatched from the graveyard and conveyed them to doctors for dissection. But it would take more than these romances to banish the 'emptiness of disenchantment'. Towards the end of the first term, Derek wrote home:

My Dear Mummy:-

I am afraid I do not know what to say – as you have not written to me latley, but of course if Lu has not been well I can reason why you'd not write.

Uncle and Auntie took me to St Andrews Hall on Thursday to hear the Orpheus Choir, oh what a hall is yon! and O! what a choir! I know two men in it who are teachers in my School, and who have actually (tried to) teach me. you'd hardly believe it. Eh?

Talking about School – Auntie and I went to a Cinema Show in The New

Savoy in Hope Street. it was in aid of the Necessitous Childrens Holiday
camp fund. The School always goes and gives 6d. It was quite good. When it
was over, we had din, in town!! This afternoon, I am going, as I said last
week, to the Munich Marionettes, I am being taken by a Mr McKell. My
Chemistry Master, who seem's to delight in the things that I delight in for
instance:- Films, plays, models, and drawing! After which I go to Grannies
for the night. We are all well up here, touch Wood! Althoug Auntie has a
nasty cold on her lip – and I have had a beast of a boil on my arm – but owing
to Aunties careful doctoring it is much better. It hurt like ... (a word of 4
letters signifying heat!) I am writing a play for Broadcasting,!!! I'ts called 'Black
Adder'! And though I say it my self – its quite the best I have ever done! And;
please take note – for Christmas I want (1). A wrist watch, (2). Fur lined
gloves, (3). One of those miniture Michrophones, one can get one in Gamages
for 2/11 or 3/-. You connect them to the wireless – talk from the scullery into
the mike' – and you have the fat stock prices at any time you want!! Well
dear my very best love to you and all
   Love from
   Derek. xxx
      xxx xxx
      xxx xxx

His letters, a mélange of the childish and the sophisticated, were, he maintained, monitored by Uncle Murray to put the best gloss on life at Springfield
Square. Nevertheless it is clear that the creative juices were still flowing. The fate
of 'Black Adder' is not recorded, but Derek excelled in the workshop, where his
mark of seventy-nine per cent for the Michaelmas Term was way above the class
average. Bill Lockie has to this day one of the many frogs which Derek made in
pottery sessions; a miniature bird-table and its two birds were fashioned in wood
as a gift for Sadie. Unsigned illustrations appeared in the handsomely printed
school magazine, and a single copy survives of an unofficial four-page 'newspaper',
The 2C Chronicle, produced entirely in pen-and-ink, and published on 28 March
1935, Derek's fourteenth birthday. Its jokes are feeble: 'Books Received for
Review – The Bus Conductor by Miles Standing'; but the headlines arresting:
' "LIVE" BOMB SCARE IN 2C – LEITCH BRINGS HAND GRENADE'; 'Gailey
Narrowly Escapes Soaking'; and there is a persuasive 'Hobbies' column about
the axolotl, a Mexican salamander at the tadpole stage, which is 'not a pretty
creature' and is tipped to be an also-ran when the Loch Ness Monster eventually
emerges to compete in the Deep-Sea Denizens Beauty Competition. For his
sister Derek devised a serial fairy tale, impeccably realised in primary colours,
and mailed from Bishopbriggs in regular instalments. His letters to Lu were
embellished with elaborate drawings of the family's life in Sussex and with
puzzles. Of his desolation she had no clue. Neither, at first, did his uncle and
aunt. Nor his parents. Nor 'Tom', or anyone else at school. He would one day

recall that his first conscious piece of 'acting' was as a four- or five-year-old, wrapped in a blue velvet curtain and 'wearing a hat with a bunch of pheasants' tails'.[50] He had continued performing ever since. Now, however, the act became a survival suit, beneath which the skin had begun to thicken.

Bill Lockie noticed that as time went on Derek gave an impression of being more self-assured and confident, 'especially in the Art Department where he obviously felt most secure'. He began to wear a pork-pie hat. There was also the suggestion of 'a special relationship with the staff, a sort of unexpressed confidence that he could be immune from punishment or penalty, should he not conform'. To an extent this is borne out by Derek's letter to his mother, in which he referred to the Chemistry teacher who was taking him that afternoon to a marionette show and who 'seems to delight in the things that I delight in'. Robert McKell was one of a group of young men, recently recruited to the teaching staff by Dr Steel, who were 'sometimes barely to be distinguished from the senior boys'.[51] He was a prime mover in the new Dramatic Club and, evidently, the butt of his pupils' humour. The school magazine reprinted an item from *The 2C Chronicle* headlined 'Our Tame Bobbie', which stated that 'Mr McRobert McKell our "fairy polis-man", gave a brilliant display of "polising" in a film on view at the New Savoy last Friday, entitled "The Goal". In the film he arrived when a fitba' match was in progress and as he was in full plumage the game was abandoned in order that the players might evade the limb of the Law. How nice to know that you can/Act like a bobby too/If we could walk like you can/We'd all be bobbies too.' Bill Lockie was not taught by McKell, but remembers him as 'a thick-set, fair-haired, authoritative man' – imposing, too, to judge by a 1932 staff photograph in which he is by some margin the tallest of the ten in his row. If, as the letter implies, there were extra-mural outings with McKell, and Derek had 'found a friend at Court', this would, says Dr Lockie, have been 'sensational stuff if it had been known at the time!'

Derek's life outside school began increasingly to be dominated by the cinema. The school was conveniently close to the city centre, and by his own account he would play truant, slinking twice a week into afternoon showings and wallowing in 'the glamour, the glory, the guns and the chases'. Life was '*never* to be dull and drab again'. Not that he saw his destiny unfold at the end of a twitching beam of light. No, he was there as 'the Original Audience for which these films were made. The refugee from worry, humdrum life, anxiety or despair.'[52] The Paramount, which opened on Renfield Street in 1934, had swiftly established an unwanted reputation as the kind of place where young women should not venture alone, in case they fell victim to white slavery. Young men had to be on their guard, too. According to *Postillion*, it was here, at a matinée of *The Mummy*, that Derek was befriended by one 'Alec Dodd'. They arranged to meet later in the week to see the film again before its run ended and, after tea, Mr Dodd, a medical student, took Derek back to his flat nearby, and, cheerfully inspired by what they had seen on screen, swathed him from crown to toe in bandages: 'I was wound tightly into a cocoon as a spider rolls a grasshopper.'[53] Manoeuvred by his captor into an upright position in front of the wardrobe mirror, Derek saw that 'Boris Karloff wasn't half as convincing'. The only blemishes in his envelopment were the tiny slits that had been left for each eye, the small hole for his nostrils and, horror of horrors, 'pathetically thrusting through the swaddling rags, my genitals, naked and as pink and vulnerable as a sugar mouse'. Swung, rigid, onto the bed, he resorted to prayer as Mr Dodd, wielding a pair of scissors, made reassuring noises about the joys of masturbation: 'The anxious, firm, slippery fingers caressing and annointing me splintered my whole being into a billion jagged fragments. I was only aware that if they didn't stop something terrible and horrifying would happen. Which it did. And I knew.'

Even if 'it' did not happen in such an extravagantly shocking way – and spare a thought for a blameless namesake, the Van den Bogaerdes' GP in Sussex, Dr Dodd – there can be little doubt that at some point during the 'Anthracite Years' Derek discovered the truth about his sexuality. Bill Lockie believes that Derek arrived at Allan Glen's the product of weak parents – Lally's was the firm hand – who had brought him up 'more or less as a girl' and on whom he could not now fully depend: 'He thought as a girl, and this added to his charm. He was colourful.' His visits to the cinema were part of the process of finding out about himself, 'to experience a frisson of excitement'. The 'mummification', the ducking in the lavatory – both redolent of passivity – and the victory over the bully are all in keeping with an attempt to explain the changes he was going through, and the adjustments he had to make in order to come to terms with his sexual development, which, inevitably, had to be repressed. He was discovering his ambivalence and, as he did so, learning that he had something to conceal.

Although he would deny that a wartime nickname, 'Pip', had anything to do with the narrator of *Great Expectations*, it is possible to see parallels in the way that Derek overrode his disadvantages, and later recounted his life. Take, for example, his spelling. 'I struggled through the alphabet as if it had been a bramble-bush,' said Dickens's hero. Derek knew all about those brambles, and eventually gave up the struggle, leaving them for others to negotiate. With the benefit of today's knowledge and his own experience, Dr Lockie suspects that he was slightly dyslexic – a trait that runs in the family – and possibly even autistic: 'Autistic children are self-centred and have difficulty with relationships. An inability to fit in. They are also amazing for the amount of detail that they can absorb. Derek's descriptions, all those years later, of the school, the canteen, how the tables were arranged, and so on, were uncanny. They were examples of that kind of observation, that kind of mental thinking.' In the thirties, however, none of this wisdom was available. Dr Steel knew only that the boy was lagging behind: his June 1935 report showed him twenty-fourth out of thirty-two in a lower class than the one to which he should have progressed, with dismal marks in French and, even more surprisingly, in technical drawing. But no one truly knew why. Least of all his Scottish family.

Derek endured the best part of two years in Bishopbriggs, at the height of a period which was to be immortalised by two local historians as its 'Golden Years'.[54] Initially, the Murrays gave him their bedroom with its impoverished view down the garden. Then they relegated him to a put-you-up in the drawing-room. The austere regime – Uncle Murray would on returning home touch the wireless to discover whether it was warm from illicit listening – was in excruciating contrast to the openness, tactility and laughter of home. No filial embrace last thing at night; a stifling of enjoyment at the piano; no unselfconscious wandering about in the nude. On the contrary, there is a strong suggestion in *Postillion* that William took an unhealthy interest in Derek's Friday night 'ablutions', but this – and its logical extension, that the uncle subjected him to some kind of abuse – is dismissed as 'nonsense' by Forrest McClellan, who later found himself, too, living with the Murrays and treated to a far greater degree as a substitute son: 'Never, ever, was I conscious, even once, of paedophilia or anything sexual.'

Life among the wider Niven family was not all grim. Forrest Niven had died in 1932 and his widow Jane now presided as matriarch over large Sunday gatherings at her third-floor tenement in Ibrox. Even without Margaret, there were four aunts, four uncles – three of whom were unmarried and had not yet left home – and an assortment of cousins from whom the cast could be drawn: 'My uncles were, without exception, handsome, dark and jolly. My aunts pleasant and kind and knitted. The cousins quiet and gently smiling.'[55] None of the cousins smiled more, or was more glamorous, than Jean, whose mother, the senior aunt, Jane, had died in her mid-thirties; the teenaged Jean, her father and two brothers had moved in with Granny Niven. None of the uncles was more flamboyant than the youngest, Jimmy, then an engineering salesman in his early thirties, homosexual, alcoholic, and something of a wide-boy. And none of the aunts was more pleasant and kind than the third eldest, Hester McClellan, who supplied a lifeline by putting up Derek for his last year at Allan Glen's.

Whether this initiative resulted from a plea by the Murrays, or by Ulric and Margaret, is not known, but it was a fillip for the troubled boy. John and Hester McClellan were toiling on a government clerk's salary to give a decent start in life to their teenaged daughter, Nickie, and their son, Forrest, who was then about four. The family lived in a recently built 'four-to-a-block house', but in King's Park, a respectable area of the city much favoured by young parents. To Derek's delight, the first-floor flat was unusually furnished, with wicker firescreens and other trophies from Africa, where Nickie had been born. There were cinemas within walking distance, and an ice-rink a bus ride away, on which Derek could flail about, supported by the highly competent Jean. She and Nickie would be recruited into Derek's improvised plays. 'I genuinely liked him,' recalls Jean Gulliver. 'He was fun. He had a nice sense of humour. He was good company. I used to enjoy it when he came through the door. He was always smartly turned out, arrogant, a bit of a snob.'[56] And although she always felt that 'he wanted in a way to wash his hands of us lot up in Scotland', and yearned to return to the place where he was most happy, she had no idea of the depth of his misery. He used to declare his love for her, but she never took him seriously: 'That was just part of his everyday speech.' One day, however, he wrote home that he intended to marry his cousin Jean. 'Ulric', she said, 'took one look at the letter and carted him off back to England!' It was, quite likely, the final straw. A brisk note from Dr Steel on 22 December 1937 thanked Ulric for letting him know that Derek was leaving the school and wished the boy 'the best of luck'. There was an emotional farewell at the Central Station as 'Aunt Hester, tall, worried, continually harassed, loving, gentle as a dove, merely held me just that little bit longer in her arms', before hurrying away into the crowd. 'I settled back into my compartment, lit a Black Cat, and felt the train rumble over the Broomielaw Bridge. Looking out of the scummy window I watched the cranes and tugs and hulks of ships lining the sullen waters of the Clyde. I hoped never ever to see it again. And I never have.'[57]

In October 1955 he held court in his dressing-room at the King's Theatre, where eighteen years earlier he had proudly escorted Bill Lockie and a few others to meet a friend of Margaret's, Yvonne Arnaud, then starring in *Laughter in Court*. He was interviewed by two boys who wrote and edited an unofficial newssheet called *The Glenallan*. Harry Marsh and Gordon Hunter asked what he recalled of his time at the school. After a long pause, he said: 'Well, I remember there were very good pies sold in the canteen.'[58]

Three

'Christ Almighty! Now I know there's a war on:
they've started to ration the Talent!'

B ill Lockie would never meet Derek again; a letter proposing a reunion drink during that same week at the King's in 1955 went unanswered. They had, however, kept briefly in touch. Derek sent him a sheet of striking caricatures in pencil, depicting Laurel and Hardy, Garbo and Mickey Rooney – a reminder to Bill more of how 'inspirational' his companion could be in their art classes than of a budding cinephile. Another lasting memento of their friendship is the good doctor's ability to raise a single, quizzical eyebrow – a technique taught him by Derek, who would himself deploy it to great profit. But no, the door marked 'Glasgow' had closed; in fact it had been slammed shut. Derek was seldom to cross the border again, and certainly not purely for pleasure. The paradox is that Ulric's initiative had in one sense been a disaster, with dismal school results and irreparable damage within the family, although the latter was largely concealed at the time; yet in another, it had been almost too successful – that is, if one of his intentions had been to toughen up the boy. As Derek would recall:

They were, I know, the three most important years of my life, the horseshoe-on-the anvil ones. I could not have done without them. In that time I was forced to reconsider who and what I was. I had never, to be sure, given it much thought: only that I was a pleasant enough fellow, happy, obliging and fond of everyone, or nearly everyone, I met. Causing no trouble that I knew of, and wishing none. It was a simple pattern.

But in the bosom of my real kith and kin I began to realize that to survive I must alter the pattern of behaviour drastically. Being happy and obliging and fond of everyone was a sign of weakness. It was, in fact, considered 'cissie' to behave like that. A boy had to be strong, play games, speak when spoken to, and never idle around with poetry or books, keep frogs and tadpoles, or play the piano. Having a personal opinion was considered impolite, and to ask questions would only make one 'impertinent' or imply disrespect for one's elders.

So I began to construct a private world of my own.[1]

The 'sheer, unadulterated loneliness and misery'[2] could be turned to advantage. Solitude, he decided, became desirable, and he sought it:

I started to isolate myself from people, and to build a strong protecting shell against loneliness and despair, both of which could have been my constant companions had I been weak enough to allow them to come too close. I sometimes felt, cheerfully, that I was rather like a hermit crab. Tight in his borrowed shell, like the ones I had scrabbled about for in rock-pools at Cuckmere Haven in the happier days, I was safe from predators; and by predators I meant everyone I met.[3]

He also began to follow the urging of his father, and of his paternal grandfather, that he should always pay the closest attention to his surroundings. 'Observe. Notice. Above all, *look* at life,' Ulric had told him and Lu.[4] Aimé, apparently, had put it more forcibly still: 'You must be Observant, boy. Always Observe. If you do not understand what you see, ask someone to tell you what it is . . . if they don't know, you must take books and find out. Always seek, always question, always be Interested, otherwise you will perish.'[5] The alien life he saw in Scotland had sharpened Derek's perception: 'I, who had heeded little around me before, was now suddenly obsessed with storing up sights and sounds, and people too, for that matter.'[6]

So the sixteen-year-old who returned finally to England at the end of 1937 was altogether warier, less carefree, more capable of petty cruelties. The little brother whom, at a distance, he had sketched affectionately in his letters to Lu as 'Gags' – after a character called Gagnunc from the *Daily Mirror* comic strip, 'Pip, Squeak and Wilfred' – was in his company a creature more than ever to be despised. On one occasion, as Gareth leant out of a sash-window Derek came up behind him and brought it down on his fingers. Their mother heard the scream and asked Derek what he was doing to the boy. 'It's all right, I'm just squeezing a thorn out of his finger,' was the reply. Margaret believed him. The incident is Gareth's earliest memory of his brother. Whereas Lu had been the target of spasmodic acts of beastliness – the new doll's house which Derek set alight before attempting to extinguish the flames with his own new fire-engine; the ritual humiliations; even a bread knife between the shoulder-blades – the hatred towards Gareth ran far deeper. 'I would never forgive that stinking, smelly, shrieking, little beast who had burst, unwelcome, into my perfect Two Pivot and Centre Life. And I didn't for over twenty years.'[7] The sooner, then, that Derek left home, the better for everyone.

Home, by this time, was exclusively Sussex. In August 1935, during the annual holiday at Alfriston, Ulric had made an offer on a three-storey, gabled, Edwardian house called Milnthorpe at Chailey, six miles north of Lewes. The family moved in the following March, and for a while had to subsidise two premises, because Highfield Avenue was not sold until October. Milnthorpe, with its dark brick-work and hints of the Gothic, looked unwelcoming in the winter months, but in the spring and summer came into its own. The large garden had an untended orchard, a silted-up pond, a rotting punt and even a tiny island. Derek and Lu established a hideaway in a wooden shed which they named 'Trees'. Wildlife teemed both at home and on the neighbouring common. Hedgehogs, baby birds, above all frogs, were given names such as Squinch and Mickey, their every move studied as if by professional naturalists, with Lu having to hold the fort during Derek's long absences. 'Are my tadpols still OK & my pond?' he asked in a letter from Bishopbriggs. 'You *do* seem to be working hard at "Trees",' he commented in another, from King's Park; 'Fancy you making a cupboard! How perfectly splendid! You might try a Piano next time you decide to use Daddies tools!! I think a Piano would be rather nice in "Trees" dont you – we would be able to get it in *so* easily.' The dog, a terrier called Rogan, was in seventh heaven. Indoors, two goldfish, George and Gertie, fought less than they had done and cruised contentedly in their tank. Elsie Brooks, the 'Rubens shepherdess' who briefly became the object of Derek's 'muddled fantasies', proved an acceptable successor to Lally, even if the last could never be replaced in the household's affections. All in all, Milnthorpe had an air of permanence about it, and despite Margaret's hankering for the bright lights, the Van den Bogaerdes were committing them-selves to a country existence. Never again would they return as a family to live in London.

Ulric had to travel there, however, every working day – often on a Sunday. He commuted from Haywards Heath, usually after the main rush in the morning and invariably after that in the evening. It was a hectic period at *The Times*, not least because of the newspaper's special relationship with Buckingham Palace. The death of George V, the Abdication, the Coronation of George VI – all required and received elaborate treatment, some of it using innovatory colour. 'The King Crisis' was the terse entry in Ulric's diary for 2 December 1936; the next day, 'Mirror Scoop on Mrs Simpson.' On Tuesday, 11 May 1937 it was 'To bed at office 1.15 a.m.' On the Wednesday, Coronation Day, 'Slept Office – called 4 a.m.' In the wider world, there was much to preoccupy him and his staff, above all as Europe moved inexorably towards another war. In the narrower, his father's decline was causing concern, and so was the future of his elder son, the height of whose ambition was 'to construct a cage from garden-bamboo for a pet linnet'.[8] Ulric had hopes for Derek either in his own profession or in diplomacy, but although a flair for writing had become apparent, there were serious problems with spelling and syntax, quite apart from the patience and application needed for a start on the bottom rung of the journalistic ladder. Nor, despite his charm, would Derek have fared well under the scrutiny of the Foreign Office examiners. Art school looked an altogether safer bet. It had, after all, led to unexpected rewards for Ulric himself.

On 10 January 1938 Derek arrived at the Chelsea Polytechnic, a rust-coloured Victorian building in Manresa Road which was founded in 1891 to provide a first-class technical and art education 'for the benefit of the poorer classes'.⁹ Just as its student population had begun to reflect a broader cross-section of society, so too the School of Art had extended its remit from a predominant concern with the fine arts to courses of craft training. Enrolment was at a record level, and Derek found he was one of some 350 day students, with the females outnumbering the males by five to one. Jean Thomson, who as Jean Winterbottom was studying commercial art and was a year his senior, recalls how the Polytechnic was better known for its science side than for its art, which meant that there was far less scrutiny: 'Some of the people who were at the Art School were frightfully classy – Lady This and Lady That – and the rest of us were fairly ordinary. But we had two incredible teachers – Henry Moore and Graham Sutherland.'¹⁰ Quite how incredible was not realised at the time: 'They were just staff.' Derek studied under both, and absorbed elements of their respective styles. Sutherland he found 'the kindest and most encouraging of all the teachers at the School. He was rather frightening too, because he smiled often, spoke very little; one was never certain of what he exactly thought.'¹¹ Jean Thomson agrees: 'He would go round the world and, by the time he'd finished, you realised he didn't like what you'd done. He was a nice man.' Moore, whose later 'Shelter Drawings' of cocooned figures Derek would emulate, took the students for Life and Perspective. Derek had difficulties with the former: 'Although, up until then, I had never seen an entirely naked woman, I was completely unmoved. I only remember being saddened by the sight of so much ugly flesh humped so dejectedly in a bent-wood chair. I found drawing their ugliness far harder to cope with than anything else.'¹² He was happier with Perspective and when he said that his preferred field was stage design Moore encouraged him; 'Which is why, to this day, I can still do a remarkably good bird's eye view of the Piazza San Marco, Times Square or even Kennington Oval looking as if they had been struck by bubonic plague. My perspectives are empty. However I am very good at people leaning out of windows.'¹³

In the short term, however, the most important influence was Graham Sutherland's wife, Kathleen, who, although not a prominent figure in the school, taught fashion design. In her classes Derek could bring his eye for the theatrical to bear on the practical, and on one occasion – possibly the only one – he saw a creation through, to the delight of a fellow student. Jean Thomson asked him if he would design for her an evening dress, suitable for dancing. He produced a royal-blue chiffon number, fitted to the waist, then full, with a sea-green coat, again in chiffon, slit at the sides. 'It was beautiful,' she recalls. 'I was always the belle of the ball when I wore that dress.' Yet he never partnered her on the dance floor. To Jean Thomson, Derek's social life was a mystery. At lunchtime in warm weather, sometimes with another student, Christine Clegg, they would buy a sandwich at the refectory, take it to the river and sit at the bottom of the steps, talking about little of substance: 'It was all light-hearted rubbish, really. We never got very deep into anything. Strange.' She says she 'never thought of him as particularly good-looking. He was just a nice bloke and he used to laugh a lot. He wasn't very sociable with the other students, really. He wasn't friends with any of the boys – they didn't seem to interest him in the least.' Only once did she ever see him away from Chelsea, when Ulric invited Derek to bring a friend to watch the Lord Mayor's Show pass the *Times* office. Otherwise, at the end of the day Derek would simply disappear.

For part of the time he was at the School of Art, Derek lodged in London with his parents' friends, the Hatfields. For the rest, he commuted, like his father. Perhaps he did glimpse the more sordid side of a student existence in west London, but almost certainly from a safe distance. It has to be remembered that this was an innocent time for all but the leisured class, to whom he did not belong. He described being deflowered by 'an avid girl with earphones and breasts like filled hot-water bottles, who raped me expertly on the floor of her studio in front of the gas fire and sent me reeling on my way',[14] but this smacks more of the fifties than the thirties. If ever. In any case there were excitements of a less turbulent kind much closer to home.

Early in 1938 his mother struck up a conversation with a fellow bus passenger called Winifred Cox. She, too, had been an actress. Now she was living with her husband and their three children at Newick, a couple of miles from Milnthorpe. Lionel Cox's business was a nursery, which he ran from their home, Chez Nous. Successful as his trade in bulbs was, however, he regarded it as an often irritating distraction from his true love – the theatre, on both a large and a miniature scale. To mark the birth in 1932 of his only son, Derek, he had built for the village a hall, equipping its stage with 'state-of-the-art' lighting, cloud effects, a tray to produce rain, a trap-door and other features which would be the envy of many a professional house. In an annexe to the Derek Hall, he installed his Toy Theatre, an immaculate model of a proscenium, with a stage six feet wide and nine feet deep, another intricate system of overhead lamps and footlights, and a repertory company of about 15,000 'Tumps', electronically controlled marionettes, on whom he could draw for productions to enthral the local children. 'Robinson Crusoe', 'The Siege of Troy', even 'The Battle of Waterloo', were re-enacted at the hands of Mr Cox and his dutiful family, before audiences numbering up to fifty, with proceeds going to needy youngsters. On 24 April he noted in his diary that he, his wife, their younger daughter Heather and Derek caught the bus to Chailey 'to meet Win's new-found friends the Van der Beaugarde's. They con-sisted of the mother, eldest son Derek aged 17, daughter Elizabeth 14, & small boy Gareth 5. This family seemed to have a great lot in common with ours, love of reptiles & animals, toy theatres, acting, painting etc.' Small wonder that our Derek immediately recognised in Lionel a kindred spirit and, when the elder daughter Nerine arrived a little later from teaching at Sunday School, another, of almost exactly his own age.

I can remember exactly meeting him at the Milnthorpe gate. He said, 'Hello, you must be Nerine. I'm Derek. All the others have gone in and are all talking together. They have looked around the garden and the orchard and it's such a lovely afternoon perhaps you would like to look round the orchard too?' There was a little garden shed and he said, 'Would you like to see my lizards?' We went into the shed and here were these very ordinary greyish lizards, just two or three, which he had caught on the Common. I told him that I too used to keep these ordinary lizards, but *I* had a fanned lizard which I caught and brought back from Switzerland. I also had two wall lizards and even a long green lizard. I felt immensely superior. It was the only time in my life that I ever felt superior to him.[15]

A month later – the day after a Special Correspondent for the *Sunday Dispatch* gave Lionel Cox national prominence to his 'Tumps' – Derek and Lu were shown 'behind scenes' at the two theatres. By July, Derek was inviting Lionel to see *his* marionettes in performance, albeit on a more modest scale. A firm and important friendship was sealed.

Just before that first meeting with the Coxes, the burial of Aimé had taken place at Brighton. Behind the single word 'Funeral' in Ulric's diary for 16 April lay goodness knows what emotions, but the death of the 'Faker', as Derek would eventually refer to him – with no little affection – removed at least one lingering burden from Ulric's shoulders. If only his son's future could look a little more promising. Hardly had Derek started at Chelsea than Ulric went to see P. H. Jowett, the Principal of the Royal College of Art. They arranged that Derek should come for an interview in the summer. On 20 July he duly did so, but nothing came of his talk with Jowett, certainly not the scholarship mentioned in biographical material a decade or so later. Nor did Ulric have much luck when he arranged for Derek to spend some of the holiday at the Sun Engraving Company, the mighty printing plant on the outskirts of Watford, where he could be shown every stage of magazine production. He learned 'absolutely nothing'; Ulric's consuming passion 'was not being transmitted to the son'.[16]

Margaret's was, however – both in Newick and in Chelsea. In the autumn Lionel Cox began work on two new productions for his main house: *Alf's Button*, a comedy by W. A. Darlington, the drama critic of *The Daily Telegraph*; and a Christmas pantomime, *Babes in the Wood*. Derek was recruited for both, and committed himself to the somewhat haphazard rehearsal schedule, with both plays being prepared simultaneously. In the meantime, back in Manresa Road, the students were devising their end-of-term 'Stunt', in which Derek was to be a leading player. So, too, was Christine Clegg, a prize-winning designer who joined him and Jean Thomson on their riverside picnics and seemed to be his only other close friend. She, at least, saw something of Derek outside School hours. On 17 September he took her to the Coxes for the first read-through of *Babes in the Wood*, stayed for tea and then engaged in a 'long debate on religion'.

On Bonfire Night – a spectacular occasion in the villages surrounding Lewes, where, historically, anti-Papist feelings ran as high as the flames from the gigantic fires – the Van den Bogaerdes and the Coxes formed a tableau as Snow White and the Seven Dwarfs. Christine was the Prince; Margaret, the Queen; Lu, the Witch; and the Coxes were the dwarfs. Snow White was 'played' by Derek. Ulric's photograph of the group on the village green, waiting to join a procession lit by 2,000 torches, is a unique document: it shows his elder son in drag.

At the end of November the Newick Amateur Dramatic Society (NADS) gave the first of its two performances of *Alf's Button*. It was, for one of the local newspapers, a triumph, which 'kept a large audience in uncontrollable laughter'.[17] The portrayal of Lance-Corporal Greenstock by Derek Bogaerde was not singled out for mention, but this was hardly surprising, given the extent of the role:

> [...] all that was required of me was to stand perfectly still, for rather a long time, in an arch-way wearing a fez, a curley stuck-on moustache, a weskit, and a pair of transparent, saggy, orange bloomers.
>
> The transparency caused a certain amount of trouble, which we managed in the end to overcome, but I never got over the cold. The stage was freezing, and I had been firmly instructed 'Not To Move A Muscle'.
>
> Harder to do than I thought under the circumstances. I 'acted' standing still with commendable effort.[18]

It had been, as he noted when the NADS celebrated their golden jubilee in 1982, 'a start'; 'I knew, without a shadow of a doubt, baggy transparent bloomers and all, that I had found my metier.'

The second and final performance three nights later was even more successful; according to Lionel Cox, it 'went swimmingly'. But there was no time to rest on laurels. That afternoon, the company had rehearsed *Babes in the Wood*, and over tea Derek and his mentor discussed the possibility of staging R. C. Sherriff's First World War drama, *Journey's End*. There was also the little matter of *Gulliver's Travels*, to be staged in the Toy Theatre with a cast of about a thousand and with Derek pulling the strings of the Gulliver he was himself fashioning in wood. At the same time, the 'Stunt' was taking shape in Chelsea. A programme shows that on Wednesday, 21 December, Derek Bogaerde wrote and appeared in the opening sketch, 'Much Twittering Rehearses', an 'interlude with Mrs Murgatroyd's Gals (all ages) in the Village Reading Room. "Macbeth" is the victim.' This was produced by Roger de Grey, a future President of the Royal Academy of Arts, and evidently involved a further outbreak of cross-dressing, because Mrs Murgatroyd was played by Derek himself, and Little Arthur by Christine Clegg. Derek took part in two of the night's other offerings, notably as one half of a 'Sweet English Couple' in a 'monstrous patriotic spectacle' entitled 'Rule Brittania [*sic*] or Right Triumphant', which promised 'moral and instructive entertainment for young and old'. There is no further record of him taking to the stage during his time at the School of Art, but it would be surprising if he had not seized every chance to indulge in a 'Stunt'; the School's official magazine mentioned one such performance in the Polytechnic's main hall, 'where we by suitable camouflage maintained the atmosphere on which we pride ourselves'.[19]

Derek's next engagement, *Babes in the Wood*, provided his first opportunity for villainy when, as Sir Maltravers Goodman, he hired two miscreants, played by the Cox sisters, to bump off the eponymous children, played by their parents. As the scene shifted to Sherwood Forest in the third act, Lu was to be found impersonating Little John. It was that sort of show. The two performances on 7 January 1939 were replete with slapstick, 'chestnuts', topical quips, a spluttering machine-gun and a 'clever burlesque of popular wireless programmes'. Again, the reviewer's eye was not particularly drawn to Derek, nor the ear to any above-average hiss-and-boo quotient for his wicked Uncle Maltravers, but the *Express & Herald* described the proceedings as 'altogether a remarkable village effort', which raised £32 16s 2d for children's hospitals, and reflected the greatest credit on Mr and Mrs Cox 'and all associated with them'.[20] And no one was more associated with them at this time than Derek, who came calling at Chez Nous with the utmost regularity. Lionel Cox's diaries for the period are studded with references to the eager young man – one or two hinting at irritation, most of them reflecting some joint purpose. It is clear that although Derek was spending a good deal of time with Nerine on cycling expeditions to Rotherfield Woods, playing parlour games, visiting Brighton by bus and occasionally going to dances, his primary interest was in the happenings on the Derek Hall's two stages.

'NADS PRESENT A PLAY THE RISING GENERATION MUST SEE!' announced the poster which Derek drew for the single performance of *Journey's End* on Saturday, 15 April 1939. Set in a dugout on the British front line in March 1918, the play, which starred Laurence Olivier at its première in 1928, was a thought-provoking choice for a village that might soon be losing its young men to another dreadful conflict: conscription was announced within the fortnight. Derek took the role of eighteen-year-old James Raleigh, in his smart new uniform as a second lieutenant, who finds a family friend and sporting idol from 'Barford' public school, Dennis Stanhope, now two ranks as well as three years his senior and much changed by war. Shell-shocked and drinking heavily, the company commander shows no favours to the new arrival, who brightly thinks it is 'a frightful bit of luck' that they should be reunited and only latterly comes to understand that Stanhope's behaviour is a result of, and defence mechanism against, the horrors. The part allowed for plenty of 'Righto!'s and 'How topping!'s, especially in two-handed scenes with Lionel Cox as the ostensibly 'hard as nails' Lieutenant Osborne who encourages Raleigh's awe at the Very lights bobbing up and down in the night sky over the serpentine trench system. 'There's something rather romantic about it all,' he says. 'Yes. I thought that, too,' Raleigh replies keenly. 'You must always think of it like that if you can,' adds Osborne. 'Think of it all as – as romantic. It helps.'

The diligent *Express & Herald* found that 'The right amount of shyness and deference was contributed by Derek V. D. Bogaerde', as he was now billed – twice, in fact, because he was also credited as assistant stage manager.[21] Margaret complimented him on covering up for a mistake when a plate he slammed onto a table flew into the audience, which believed it was deliberate: 'That's what acting is all about,' she is supposed to have said. 'Convince yourself and convince them.'[22] Derek himself described the experience as 'my very first crack at acting' and 'I knew that nothing would deflect me from my path as an Actor. And nothing did.'[23] He showed his gratitude at the time by inscribing one of the photographs taken by Ulric of the production, 'To Uncle Osbourn with love from "Raleigh".' For 'Uncle', read father figure. Much later he would write to Nerine about her parents: 'So many people in the years to follow claimed the doubtful responsibility of "discovering" me! But the fact was that had it not been for Uncle and Erm (And how those silly names stick after 40 years . . .) I would never have got my first try at the theater.'[24]

The relationship with Nerine was, for a time, close – but in truth somewhat lop-sided. She fell for 'those beautiful brown eyes' and the 'lovely speaking voice' which she saw he had inherited from Margaret and Ulric respectively. He recalled her as 'soft, blonde, gentle and deeply interested in all my theories'.[25] They spent a lot of time together, writing poetry, discussing plays and talking of his future: 'We never, it seemed, ever got around to hers.' In February 1939 Derek took her to a Caledonian Society dance at Cuckfield, where he was much in demand and she was a wallflower. In the car hired by Margaret to take them home, Nerine said, 'I was supposed to be your partner for the evening.' He replied, 'Come on, be matey.' She did not expect to be asked again, but two weeks later he invited her to a party he had organised with other Polytechnic students in Holland Park. He said it would be held in three adjoining attics and that he and she must not be separated in case she was raped; some of the students were 'rather wild'. In the event he picked her up from a friend of Margaret's in Pimlico and after walking for miles through London, carrying their supplies of beer and ginger beer, arrived at the 'rather tame' basement of a local school:

> We sat on benches talking, and the students seemed quite mild. We danced to records played on a gramophone. A young man and a girl sat immobile behind a blue curtain in an alcove, with only their legs protruding for most of the evening. Derek said they couldn't be dead because we would have heard a death-rattle. Eventually he and a girl student called Rivka Black went off to pay the caretaker, leaving me to talk to Rivka's fiancé, an architect. He said we were the only two sane people there that evening.[26]

The following morning, after visiting the ducks and the statue of Peter Pan in Kensington Gardens, Derek and Nerine took the train back to Sussex. A day or two later he told her: 'You didn't really fit in the other night. Rivka said it was like bringing a wild flower and putting her into a hot house.' Despite the blows to Nerine's confidence, and to her hopes, the friendship continued. On her eighteenth birthday in March, Derek presented her with a Chatto & Windus edition of *The Lyrics & Shorter Poems of William Shakespeare*, inscribed:

> To Nerine
> In youth when I did love
> > Hamlet
>
> With all my love
> Derek xx
> 24 March 1939

The signals were conflicting indeed. Only later did she realise fully the futility of 'trying to capture a bit of his free spirit'.

Following the success of *Journey's End*, Nerine's father took the bus with Derek to Uckfield, where an elderly and determined woman called Elissa Thorburn had built a theatre as a 'rival' to the opera house at nearby Glyndebourne. Her motto was *Vivimus in spe*. The first event was a demonstration of 'Rudolf Steiner's Eurythmy', and the Thorburn Playhouse opened for serious business on Wednesday, 2 November 1938 with a matinée performance of André Obey's *Noah*, using a core of professional actors to play the principal characters and some unpaid NADS stalwarts as the animals – among them Lionel as the Bear and his daughter Heather as the Monkey. The good people of Uckfield were bewildered, but Miss Thorburn's withers were unwrung: she was not going to put on fare simply to please *hoi polloi*. For her second production she chose *Glorious Morning*, a drama by Norman Macowan, about the invasion of a European democracy, Zagnira, by a fascist neighbour. Perhaps, thought Lionel, she might find a part for his young protégé in this topical piece. She might indeed. Derek was engaged, allegedly at 5s for each of the four performances, as Leman, a council member in the provincial town of Burglitz, and began rehearsals forthwith:

> The theater was approached down a cinder path immediately behind the coach station. It was set backing onto the buttercup meadows and the river. There were some splendid oak trees under which we (the company) used to sit in the heat of the summer and eat our picnics. The theater had a decent kitchen and provided coffee and tea. But we had to bring our own food. There was nowhere, apart from the pubs, where you could eat, in those days.[27]

On 28 June 1939 Derek gave his first paid performance. The fact that he was twenty years too young for the role worried neither him nor Miss Thorburn, he recalled, 'however I did agree that a black leather coat, a hat and a heavy moustache, would assist me in my "performance" '.[28] He was also assisted by the presence alongside him of two fellow councillors – Rutzstein, played by Lionel, and still more so, Buloff, by William Wightman.

Bill Wightman, the thirty-two-year-old son of a Yorkshire timber merchant, was one of the 'proper' actors engaged by Miss Thorburn for *Noah*, in which he had played Ham. Now he was back at Uckfield, 'looking oddly out of place in the buttercups dressed, as he was, in a double-breasted suit, brown suede shoes, long white cuffs with gold links and a rather faded carnation in his buttonhole'.[29] He was a 'tall, calm gentleman, with a private income and an immaculate sense of good grooming'.[30] He was also a homosexual. Naturally, no specific reference to that fact appears in Lionel Cox's diaries, but a subtle shift in allegiance is detectable. Early in rehearsals, Lionel writes of staying behind in the lunch break to have his sandwiches with Derek; two days later he is alone, as 'Derek had invitation to lunch with one of others'; on the eve of the first performance 'Buloff' gave both of them a lift home; but after the matinée, when one would expect the company to be united, if only in self-appraisal, 'Derek disappeared'. On the other hand he did make an effort in the middle of all this to visit the Coxes by bicycle, but fell off and had to complete the journey by bus. The emergence in Derek's life of another avuncular, but more sympathetic, figure was significant: 'My first counsellor and adviser had arrived.' And he could drive!

> Quite apart from his own considerable personal charm, warmth and wisdom, Bill's car was the Pipe in Hamelin, if he could be called, as he was, the Piper. But he was as much sought after for his advice and counsel as any of the more obvious pleasures which he could give. Every young Actor, or Actress, is plagued by the most appalling doubts and fears and only another actor can really share or understand them.[31]

Unfortunately Miss Thorburn had an 'unerring way of upsetting anyone in "authority" '[32] and her uncompromising policy divided the community. One day on the way home to her cottage at Nutley she was badly injured when some stone-throwing children forced her off her bicycle: 'She got badly cut,' recalled Derek, 'had to lie up for a while, and I visited her there to try and comfort her. No one else did!'[33] Although she struggled on for as long as she could with plans for future productions her Playhouse would never stage another show. When an Evacuation Committee was established to prepare for the now inevitable emergency, her theatre was summarily closed, the seats taken out and accommodation made ready for evacuee mothers and children. In due course this brave venture became a granary co-operative. Back in Newick, Lionel Cox was preoccupied with the fate of his business and had to scale down activities at the Hall. For Derek, who had caught a whiff of the professionals' greasepaint, the Toy Theatre and even the NADS itself were losing their allure. He continued to visit the family and to devise one-act plays with Nerine; occasionally he would stand alone on the stage and deliver a favourite scene as the tormented Danny from Emlyn Williams's *Night Must Fall*, to his audience of one. On 2 September, the day before Neville Chamberlain declared that the country was at war, the Coxes called at Milnthorpe and found no sign of Ulric and Margaret. Nerine stayed behind to talk to Derek. On the 3rd, he went to have tea with them, and helped prepare Chez Nous against a possible gas attack. Nerine never forgot how 'very down' he was at this time; and how fearful that he might be blinded or mutilated: 'If you are killed outright, you are killed outright,' he told her, with the resignation of one who felt he could not possibly survive a war unscathed.

Two poems survive from this period, both written for Nerine:

'The Sleepless Night'

Sleep said the Woman, Sleep
How can I sleep ...
A shattered tree, a broken stone
Mangled flesh, a splintered bone
Mud and Foulness as I creep
And you say softly, sleep O! sleep.
Sleep said the Woman, sleep
How can I sleep ...
Tottering houses, a rotting smell
A candle gleaming in this Hell
Beams and Bodies in a heap,
And you say softly, sleep O! sleep.
Sleep said the Woman, sleep
How can I sleep ...
Buttons turning Green in Gas,
And on the Wire, a stinking mass.
Death walks the Mud, I see him Reap,
Then I too wait for sleep.

'To Thepval [*sic*] Wood'

I saw you first beneath an Azure
sky, the simplest form of beauty,
We were alone the girl and I,
Then I was called to Duty.

We lingered here that last sad day
Amongst the whispering bracken,
Among the rooty earth we lay,
Our love we'd never slacken.

We left your canopy of green, the
late sun burning Golden,
She was the dearest thing I'd seen
My true love I'd beholden.

I see you now beneath a Crimson sky,
A shattered twisted copse
A place where men may creep to die
The Graveyard of their Hopes.

Your twisted trunks are stripped of
bark ... Somewhere a big Gun mutters
The mud is thick,
And through the dark ...
A Wild Machine-Gun stutters.

By the end of September his morale had lifted somewhat, but Nerine's father had discovered that immediately after *Glorious Morning* Derek had returned secretly to the Playhouse and since then had been helping Miss Thorburn with her abortive plans. Lionel and some of his NADS team felt deserted – to the extent that he wrote a long, disapproving letter in which he took Derek to task for disloyalty towards those who had given him his first break. That afternoon Derek was on the doorstep. He had not yet received the letter, but evidently charmed his way out of trouble because he continued to be welcome at Chez Nous. Nerine, too, tackled him on his attitude, but understood his explanation that he had to take every opportunity of experience in theatre work as he was determined to pursue an acting career; she, after all, had taken drama lessons in Brighton. Together, they settled down again to write a two-hander called 'Dark Comfort', about a young man, Robert Kemp, meeting a girl of easy virtue called Gladys Mangle on a bench in a London park; she realises he is blind only when he walks away, leaving behind his white stick. Described as 'a comedy with pathos', it was to receive just one performance, opening a quadruple-bill mounted for the Red Cross on 6 January 1940. The cast of the evening's third play, *Shall We Join the Ladies?*, with 'Costumes by Derek V. Den Bogaerde', included all but the youngest of the Coxes, plus Derek, Lu and Margaret. It was the only time that mother and son formally shared a stage. They might have done so again in February 1940, when the NADS presented *The Two Mrs Carrolls*, but Derek had to pull out. It was probably for the best; the producer, Elise Passavant, who herself had to step into one of the roles at short notice, came off-stage after a scene with Margaret, spluttering: 'Maggie, you completely buggered my entrance!' Not only that. The 'very artistic', violin-playing and married Elise Passavant had taken a shine to Derek; he had emerged from rehearsal with his heart pounding in terror. For some time afterwards, his name was unspoken, but one day Nerine

Cox mentioned him. 'Oh, he's nothing but a prattling child,' said Elise Passavant. Years later, in an old people's home, she had one photograph by her bed – not of her husband, but of Derek.

Nevertheless, the reasons for his withdrawal were professional. A year earlier it had become obvious to all concerned that his heart was set on the theatre as a career. On 4 April 1938, H. S. Williamson, the Head Master at Chelsea School of Art, wrote to Ulric:

> I was very interested to see your son's collected work last week and to hear of his present problem. It seems to be clear in his mind that a career connected with the stage is definitely his first choice, which is always a help in coming to a decision in these matters, but on the other hand, lack of promise in art does not help to confirm this, because I was very struck indeed by the promise of your son's work and his unusual facility of invention.
>
> On promise such as this, which is well above the average, I should not normally hesitate to encourage him to go forward.
>
> I feel bound, therefore, to let you know of my good opinion of his capacity in art in order that you should know all the facts involved while you are helping him to come to a decision.

With Ulric's help – relations between *The Times* and the leading theatres were good – Derek was offered an audition at the Old Vic. Its Dramatic School had been founded in 1933 by Lilian Baylis, manager of that fabled house from 1912 until her death in 1937. At 11.30 a.m. on 8 August, Derek presented himself at the Vic, with the single instruction that the passages he chose should be 'short and well contrasted in style'.

> [...] I walked up and down the Waterloo Road mumbling away at 'Is This A Dagger?' from 'Macbeth', the whole of Blunden's 'Forefathers' which begins: '*Here they went with smock and crook,/Toiled in the sun, lolled in the shade,/Here they mudded out the brook ...*' which I found moving, referring as it did to the last War, and the country life I loved; and also a frightful chunk of my monologue from the play I had written for the NADS about the poor blind man on his bench.[34]

He recalled the 'glittering cold eyes' of the Vic's director, Tyrone Guthrie, as more frightening than anything he had ever encountered: 'They were, to paraphrase a description of Aldous Huxley's, "pale blue and triangular, like the eyes peering from the mask of a Siamese cat".'[35] What Guthrie thought of him is not recorded, but Esmé Church, one of the producers, was impressed enough for the theatre's acting secretary to write to Ulric that 'Miss Church thinks your boy's work most promising, and we should very much like the opportunity of training him here.'[36] At the audition, they had not realised that Derek wished to be a candidate for a scholarship; nevertheless he was offered a place at half-fees of £50 for the first-year course and £25 for the second-year. The School would be reopening for its new season on 4 September. It never did.

Bill Wightman's connections with rural theatre extended to the picturesque Surrey village of Shere, near Godalming, where a company called the Otherwise Club, comprising mainly Cambridge undergraduates, staged a summer season of plays in a barn behind the parish church at High House Farm. The Barn Theatre's 200 seats on raked flooring were invariably filled to capacity by audiences keen to feast on the kind of highbrow fare that Miss Thorburn was championing with less success in Uckfield; the 1938 season, for example, had contained work by Racine, Lorca and Chekhov. A feeling of 'family' was heightened by the fact that members of the company either took rooms in the village or slept under canvas in the field next door. Barbed wire surrounded the girls' tents – a wise, if not always successful precaution: Constantine Fitzgibbon, translator of Racine's *Britannicus*, referred to a 'retinue of young men and quite a whiff of decadence', while one of the villagers who had wandered off-course said, 'I can understand girls in bed with boys, but *boys* in bed with boys!'[37] The atmosphere Derek found when he went to visit his new 'counsellor' was a novel combination of camaraderie and intellectual rigour. Bill was appearing in three of the 1939 season's four productions, two of them – *The House in Dormer Forest* and a fantasy by the Russian poet Alexander Blok, *The Rose and the Cross* – with an eighteen-year-old showing evidence of a formidably precocious talent: Peter Ustinov. The latter had, with his mother Nadia Benois, translated and adapted the Russian play; he was its producer; and he gave himself the part of a fisherman. Ustinov, who remembered Bill as 'a very solid, white-haired, middle-aged man, balding, and very genial, laughing all the time',[38] was nineteen days younger than Derek, who in turn recalled the 'rough-haired, scatty boy in wrinkled tights covered with grass' responding to the visitor's stated intention to be an actor with 'All that counts is dedication, total dedication' – before 'lumbering off to do his play'. For Derek, Ustinov, with his 'blinding ambition and this all-consuming passion for his work at the theatre, and for writing, and for music', was 'streets ahead of anything I'd ever come across'.[39] No wonder the undisputed 'Belle of the Barn', Joan Thomas, retains as her single image of Derek's visit to the Otherwise Club his 'lively, smiling' face as he talked to Ustinov in the barnyard.[40]

At about the same time, Derek had his first insight into how a film is made when he appeared as an extra in a George Formby comedy, *Come on George!*, written and directed by Anthony Kimmins, whose mother, Grace Kimmins, had founded the Chailey Heritage for handicapped children, close to Milnthorpe, and was an acquaintance of Margaret. Unfortunately Derek's barely perceptible debut was in a crowd scene at the races, and no still photograph survives. Little did he know it, but two other members of the crew would resurface in his life: the assistant director, Basil Dearden, and the director of photography, Ronald

Neame. For the moment, though, it led to nothing. A year too young to enlist, his ties severed with Chelsea, his chance at the Dramatic School wrecked by its closure, he was in limbo. Then another theatrical contact of Ulric's came to the rescue. T. J. (Tom) Kealy, who had already given a nudge to the careers of Olivier, Charles Laughton and Sybil Thorndike among others, had been told incessantly of the son's urge to work in some capacity and offered to help. He took Derek to meet the impresario Bronson Albery, who was casting a play at his New Theatre in St Martin's Lane. Albery was 'quite agreeable, but the play's producer had other ideas – he already had someone in mind'. The West End would have to wait, but Tom Kealy then tried the next best thing: 'I went to Jack de Leon of the Q Theatre, with whom I was then also working. I told him of Derek's abilities both at acting and designing and painting scenery. De Leon agreed to take him. I consulted Derek's father, telling him there would be little, if any, money. He said that did not matter, for the time being, and so Derek settled in at the Q.'[41]

The Q Theatre was opened in 1924 by Jack and Beatrice de Leon in a shed which had been variously a beer garden, a swimming-pool, a roller-skating rink, a dance hall, a cinema and a film studio. Jack, like Derek a former pupil at University College School, had trained as a lawyer; Beatie had won a scholarship to, and the Silver Medal at, the Royal Academy of Dramatic Art. By the time Derek arrived at their unattractive but businesslike building near Kew Bridge it had established a formidable reputation as a showcase for new writing and for transferring productions. There was no permanent company of actors, and the plays ran for just six days, usually moving for a second week to the Embassy in Swiss Cottage, which Jack had bought in 1938 with Sir Charles Hawtrey's son, Tony. Through the Q stage door had passed Anthony Quayle, Trevor Howard, Vivien Leigh, Margaret Lockwood, James Mason, Michael Wilding and Bernard Miles, the two Hermiones – Baddeley and Gingold, in the same show for the first time – and even the redoubtable Mrs Patrick Campbell. Through its foyer came all the leading producers and critics. The de Leons were respected and persuasive: 'Never more than £5 a week' was Beatie's watchword, even when in search of the finest talent. Peter Saunders, who would one day produce *The Mousetrap*, recalled that on his first visit to 'this extraordinary set-up' he was backstage on the opening night and heard Beatie say to 'a fairly well-known actress': 'You're not on during the last ten minutes of the first act and you don't come back until half way through the second so you won't mind helping us out in the coffee bar during the interval?' Of course the actress did not mind.[42]

The first person Derek met when he came to see the de Leons was Tanya Moiseiwitsch, painting a set in the yard. Then in her mid-twenties and destined to be one of the finest stage designers of the century, she remembered 'an attractive young man who wanted to be a painter and artist and thought this would be a stepping-stone'. She said she could not help because she was only the assistant scenic artist, but that he should go inside and find Mrs de Leon. 'He disappeared through the door and never appeared again. I think he got a job as an actor immediately.'[43] When he first set eyes on Beatie de Leon, 'she was coming down a corridor eating a cheese roll'. She was 'small, intense, hair lightly greying, eyes bright with interest',[44] and she took him on – for either 7s or 7s 6d a week – as a 'dog's-body', 'sweeping the stage, cleaning out the gents and waiting at table in the club room. There was a promise that if I showed that I was capable I might just get a part in one of the plays one day.'[45] From then on Beatie 'always reminded me of a bright-eyed wren or robin; eager, alert, determined. She never fussed, was always direct, to the point and completely on the ball. In this amazing partnership she was the heavy, she took up the gun, the knife, even the hangman's rope, protecting Jack at all times, leaving him to concentrate on the business side of things, the choice of plays, the whimpers and boasts of writers.'[46] Jack, Derek found, was 'a silver haired, handsome man, as beautiful as a Persian, immaculately dressed always, tired, often'.[47] Although the war was putting him under strain both in casting and at the box-office, 'his elegance, his perfect manners, his kindness never suffered. He was a truly beautiful man, groomed, tall, softly spoken, extremely warm-hearted towards those who, like myself, were prepared to die for that squat little theatre near Kew Bridge.'[48]

The chance to 'go on' came soon enough. Derek had acquitted himself well enough to earn a credit as assistant stage manager in the programme for *When We Are Married*, J. B. Priestley's 'Yorkshire Farcical Comedy', when one of the cast fell ill just before the dress rehearsal. Beatie told Derek to step in. In some panic, he went off to report for duty: to the director, Basil Dearden no less, 'a red-haired young man in a wrap-around camel hair coat' who was 'assiduously modelling himself, with considerable success, on Basil Dean, a director noted for his brilliance, sarcasm, acidity, and apparent abhorrence of actors'. 'Christ Almighty!' he said as Derek approached. 'Now I know there's a war on: they've started to ration the Talent!'[49] Nevertheless, on Monday, 15 January 1940, just over a week after he had been playing his own blind man on a park bench at the NADS, Derek V. Bogaerde spoke his first lines on a truly professional stage as Fred Dyson, Priestley's 'cheerful, rather cheeky youngish reporter' on the *Yorkshire Argus*, who is sent with a colleague to cover the silver wedding celebrations of Alderman Helliwell: 'Evening, Miss Holmes. How-d'you-do? This is Mr Henry Ormonroyd, our photographer.' He had two scenes, the second of which called for him to have had some drinks and to be 'pleased with himself'.

Three weeks later, by now firmly out front and free of any responsibility for stage management, he appeared in another comedy, *Little Ladyship*, without attracting undue attention either way; the cast of twenty-one 'contains no weak points', declared the *Brentford & Chiswick Times*.[50] For a second Priestley, *Cornelius*, which the author described in a programme note as 'a study of the relation between a not untypical middle-class Englishman and an economic system in a state of rapid decay', Derek was given a more substantial role as Lawrence. He also continued to trim his stage name. The anonymous reviewer for *The Stage* drew its readers' notice to 'two neat studies', one of which was by 'Derek Bogaerde as the cheeky office boy'.[51] The North Country playwright and insolence seemed to suit him. Next, the de Leons lent him to Bernard Miles for a thriller called *Murder by Night-Light* at the Richmond Theatre. The following week he was back at Q, for Frank Harvey's comedy, *Saloon Bar*. Looking back on his progress Beatie de Leon remembered how when playing a telegraph boy he left the stage and 'surreptitiously he put out his hand behind him for a tip. It was his own business. It got a laugh and impressed me. I remember thinking "that boy is good". From then on I gave him parts – small roles, whenever there was an opportunity.'[52] The several coins that constituted his weekly wage had become just one, plus a pound note; he was excited at the recognition implied in the raise. Yet the parts were not plentiful, the progress seemed to stall, and he was reluctant to revert to menial backstage duties while waiting. Bill Wightman 'knew of a woman who was running a Rep Company in the country and who might be willing to give me a job'.[53] Her name was Sally Latimer.

Like Miss Thorburn in Uckfield, Sally Latimer was a doughty evangelist for good theatre. She had established her company in 1936 at the Amersham Play-house in south-east Buckinghamshire, the very heart of what had become known – largely thanks to John Betjeman – as Metroland because of its rapid growth as a London dormitory and the frequent rail service into the capital. The growth of new housing in this part of the Chiltern Hills meant that Miss Latimer had an ever-expanding potential audience for her 240-seat auditorium, but she had twice narrowly averted closure: in 1939, the day was saved by Robert Donat who wrote a powerful letter to the local newspapers and ensured full houses for a production of Ibsen's *The Master Builder*. For the first year of the war, Miss Latimer and her co-producer, Caryl Jenner, managed to keep going, principally by including in their programme suitable fare for the increasing population of evacuees and a season of revues for troops stationed locally; but by the summer of 1940, the position looked hopeless. A group of local supporters had formed 'a non profit-making group to continue the theatre's educative and cultural policy', thus cleverly avoiding tax on any play considered to be of 'educational and cultural value',[54] but the outcome was far from certain. It was at this time, towards the end of the company's seventh season and with an eighth in the balance, that Derek presented himself to the resourceful Miss Latimer and, having falsely reassured her that he could 'do an American accent', was taken on at 'twenty-two shillings a week'.[55] An expected eruption from the Q never came: 'All right, dear, good luck,' Beatie said. 'Remember, if you ever want to come back we'll see what we can find for you. I'm busy now dear, so let me get on with it, will you?'[56] He would no longer have to seek lodgings with the Hatfields in Kensington or the Searles in Twickenham. Now he took digs for himself. He really had flown the nest and its various annexes.

Luckily Derek had been primed for a fast turnover of parts, and for weekly rep in its literal sense. The American accent and he were first deployed in a comedy by N. C. Hunter, *Grouse in June*; the next Monday he was having a love affair in a melodrama about the actor's life; and forty-eight hours after the final curtain he was giving one of 'a series of amusing character studies linked together by a thread of interest and family ties' in Dodie Smith's *Call It a Day*.[57] Just as he was settling into the rhythm, however, a summons came from Q. *Cornelius* was to make a belated transfer into the West End, with a partially changed cast under the direction of Henry Cass. On 24 August Derek resumed the role of Lawrence, this time in the company of Max Adrian and Stephen Murray, and once again *The Stage* considered him 'a sulky true-to-life office boy' in a 'finely acted and brilliantly produced' revival.[58] He did not, however, stand out for the national newspaper critics, led by James Agate of *The Sunday Times*, who applauded the revival but disapproved of the play. Worse, it seems that within the cast there was a feeling that the inventiveness which had appealed to Beatie de Leon was now a little out of control and that Derek needed to be taught a lesson: 'One matinee, unable to bear my behaviour any longer, Max, who played a humbled, timid little clerk, took up a great leather ledger and brought it crashing down on my totally unsuspecting head with an infuriated cry of "Never do that again, I say!"'[59]

Paul Scofield, who as a student at the London Mask Theatre School was given a walk-on role in the production, remembers no such incident. He got on well with Derek, who was, even then, 'clearly a very talented actor'. Somewhat surprised to be described in *Postillion* as 'a pale, tall, blond boy with anxious blue eyes', whose shyness led to his eventual replacement by an irritable Cass, Scofield thinks he may be the victim of mistaken identity: 'My hair was a fairish brown, which maybe sometimes looked blond but my eyes are brown.' Moreover, as he was in such a lowly role and joined the cast only at the dress rehearsal stage, he had virtually no contact with Henry Cass and remained with the play until it closed. Of Derek's ledger episode he says: 'Perhaps his self-deprecation grew with time & his own natural modesty encouraged him to embellish.'[60] The closure came soon: the theatre was uncomfortably near the Houses of Parliament, Downing Street and other tempting targets for the Luftwaffe. A duly humbled, but not necessarily timid, Derek was on his way back to the Chilterns and the revitalised Playhouse.

His first engagement was *The Painted Veil*, Somerset Maugham's adaptation of his own novel set in Hong Kong – a 'steamy tale concerning the high contagion of passion and cholera'.[61] Derek played Charles Townsend, a dashing and dangerous fellow whose affair with the wife of a bacteriologist leads remorselessly to disaster. With him in the cast for the first time was Anne Deans, a perky, auburn-haired, twenty-one-year-old Glaswegian who had earned a teaching diploma in elocution from the Royal Academy of Music. Already established as a firm favourite with the Amersham audience, she had just returned from a brief stint at Basingstoke Rep, and the following week she and Derek appeared opposite each other again, this time in a domestic comedy by Harry Delf, *The Family*

Upstairs, with Anne playing a doting parent. 'By the way,' noted the *Bucks Examiner*, 'Anne was "mother" to Derek: it is rumoured that the pair are engaged, and the mother and son part therefore had piquancy.'[62]

> With a stunning lack of timeliness I announced our engagement to the aston-ished company during a coffee break in the Green Room on the very day that the shattered British Army started its desperate withdrawal to Dunkirk. I seem to remember that Annie was about as astonished as the Company, but was carried away by my eloquence and passion and needed, as she said, cheering up.[63]
>
> I was never absolutely certain how this happened. Where did my hermit crab shell go? How could I have been tempted from it for long enough to be, literally, caught? I have no idea.
>
> [...] Did I lose my cool and control simply because of war hysteria? It is impossible, all these years later, to remember. Perhaps, and it is quite possible, I was simply in love with her, and with the army looming at my side, so to speak, military service was beyond avoidance. (I had tried to be a conscientious objector, at her suggestion, but found that the questions which were asked at a tribunal at High Wycombe were so idiotic that I simply had to abandon her idea.) With the beckoning terror before me, I suppose that I decided, as so many did, to marry before I was thrust into oblivion.[64]

When word of this development reached the Van den Bogaerdes, none of them took it too seriously. 'That won't last,' said Margaret, with the authority of one who truly knows. And by now she did: there had, after all, been sexual confusion in her own generation of Nivens. Her instinct and experience, coupled with Ulric's acute observation, meant that, although the matter could not be discussed openly, it was recognised – with all the attendant feelings of concern, regret, even guilt. At Chez Nous the news caused astonishment, with Lionel Cox noting in his diary for 9 October that 'Derek B had gone & engaged himself to some girl called Ann at Amersham!!!' Nerine, who had been 'very "down" ' about him earlier in the year, appeared to take it in her stride. Derek introduced them in November and three days later took Anne to meet the family. She 'seemed quite a nice natural sort of girl,' noted Lionel. 'If he did buy her a ring,' said Nerine many years later, 'it might have come out of a Christmas cracker.'[65]

Derek and Anne Deans would act together just half a dozen times, and it was always she who came away with the better notice. An ambitious production of *Jane Eyre*, in which neither appeared, had a 'scenic design by Derek Bogaerde' which 'meets the case admirably'[66] – the only time any backstage endeavour of his was recognised. The following week Bill Wightman himself came to play the wise waiter in Shaw's *You Never Can Tell*, with Derek as Finch McComus, 'a nice innocent family solicitor'. Anne Deans was 'indisposed'.[67] For the final straight play before Christmas, Derek was given the title role in a Kenneth Horne comedy,

The Good Young Man. The unnamed local newspaper critic, who so assiduously followed the Players' fortunes from his regular seat in the stalls that he sometimes referred to them by their first names only, decided: 'High praise must go to Derek Bogaerde as the good young man. It is, perhaps, his best part so far, and he rises to the occasion and makes a success of a funny role – the role of a seeming innocent amongst blasé and plausible people, who proves not so innocent.'[68]

The review was a valediction. Ten days later Derek was taking his bow from a stage at the very centre of the West End, and the next time Buckinghamshire readers saw the name in print he was reported as having left the company. By coincidence, Anne Deans returned to it that same week. Derek had more or less shut the door on the Playhouse – he would contribute a sketch for a revue at Easter – but not on Amersham itself. For an encounter had taken place which was not only to bring him back as a prominent resident, but was also to prove the most momentous of his professional and his personal life.

Four

'I'll end up by being a good manager, you see!'

The Forwood family – motto: *Fide virtute et labore* – came originally from Kent, but made its reputation and its fortune as shipowners in Liverpool. Of six brothers two, Arthur and William, became Mayor in the late nineteenth century; the former was Tory MP for Ormskirk and a founding father of the city's Anglican cathedral; the latter was High Sheriff of Lancashire in 1910. The fifth brother, Ernest, moved south to represent the firm in London and helped to start the Baltic Exchange. In the early 1900s the family business, which had also flourished for a time in smaller harbours on the south-west coast, foundered; but Ernest did not return to his Liverpudlian roots. He had moved from Hampstead to Buckinghamshire, where he bought from a farmer, one Annie Clark, a fine old house called Bendrose in a cherry orchard, and built others nearby for his family, establishing a significant Forwood presence on the edge of Amersham with his second wife, Margaret Maud Lockton. By 1940, Ernest was twice a widower. Two of the sons from his second marriage, Philip and Langton, were living within hailing distance of him and next door to each other, with their own families; he himself was being looked after at Bendrose House by an unmarried granddaughter, Phyllis. At about the time of his ninetieth birthday on 15 October, one of his grandsons brought to meet them a nineteen-year-old actor appearing at the Playhouse in a melodrama by Merton Hodge called *Grief Goes Over*. The old man was introduced as 'Pip'. Derek felt 'immediately at my ease'.[1]

The grandson, then a lieutenant in the Royal Artillery, was Ernest Lytton Langton Forwood, although everyone knew him professionally and socially as Anthony or Tony. His father, Leslie Langton Forwood, was Ernest's middle son and had himself been a lieutenant – in the Oxfordshire and Buckinghamshire Light Infantry – when on the last day of March 1915, a fortnight after his twenty-second birthday, he married Edith Westing, an engineer's daughter, at St Mark's in Surbiton. It was not only the demanding rumble of heavy weapons across the English Channel that caused the wedding to be arranged in haste; one might also have heard the more immediate report from a shotgun. Their son was born on 3 October at Melcombe Regis in Dorset – and not to everyone's delight.

Although in civilian life Leslie became a shipbroker, it seems to be accepted in the family that he was something of a wastrel, and certainly no use as a father. Nor much of a husband, although that might have been by mutual agreement: he and Edith, whom everyone knew as Esmé, occupied separate floors of their house on the Thames – she downstairs, so that the piano at which she taught would not be in danger of crashing through the ceiling. Anthony was sent to private schools; his headmaster at Canford in Dorset said at the end of the summer term in 1930 that the fourteen-year-old was a 'very pleasant companion' and hoped that he would return from holiday with 'plenty of sketches & more concentrative power!' Otherwise, he was more or less brought up by the grandparents, uncles, aunts and cousins clustered at Bendrose. The end product was a young man of astounding looks, impeccable manners, abundant charm, immense good humour and a rare generosity of spirit.

The school medical officer at Canford found that the young Forwood responded poorly to exertion tests and concluded: 'This boy's heart is far from strong.' Evidently that condition improved, but what is undeniable is that the amalgam of qualities listed above put the hearts of the opposite sex under the severest strain. One photograph album from the late thirties is littered with portraits of strikingly glamorous women, most of them prominent in the theatre, who signed their pictures with an endearment to Tony in terms of genuine affection, not simply as star-towards-fan. There is also a succession of fast and handsome cars – his other great passion and, for sure, no handicap to his allure. In 1936, billed as Tony Forwood, he appeared at London's Saville Theatre in a Herbert Farjeon revue, *Spread It Abroad,* which put him among an extraordinarily lustrous cast including Nelson Keys, Ivy St Helier, Cyril Ritchard, Madge Elliott, Michael Wilding and Hermione Gingold. Some firm friendships were made, notably with Wilding and his first wife, Kay Young. The following year, a Hungarian singer and actress, Gitta Alpar, came to Britain to appear with Nelson Keys in *Home and Beauty,* a 'Coronation Revue' presented by C. B. 'Cockie' Cochran and written by A. P. Herbert. Cochran had seen the soprano in *Rosenkavalier* at Covent Garden, and the 'magnificence of her singing raised such a tempest of enthusiasm' in him that he pursued her to Berlin and to Budapest, where he saw audiences refusing to leave the theatre 'until she had given several encores of her solo numbers'.[2] Now, after several years, he had an appropriate showcase for her. The revue opened in Manchester on Christmas Eve, and the Alpar voice again worked its magic, but 'some obscure, debilitating malaise', which would require surgery, meant that her remaining performances in Manchester and subsequent run at the Adelphi in the West End were 'indifferent'.[3] Nevertheless, there was some consolation. Tony Forwood met and was smitten by the 'Hungarian nightingale' and, despite an age difference of twelve years and the presence of a child from her marriage to the star of Fritz Lang's *Metropolis,* Gustav Fröhlich, they began an affair and a business partnership, with Tony acting as her personal representative.

During just seven months in 1938 the couple travelled to Paris, to South America and to Zagreb. In the French capital Tony wrote to Ernest that there was to be 'Big business here for both of us today'; from Rio de Janeiro he told his Uncle Carl and Aunt Gwen in Bournemouth: 'If you don't come here you will never really know why you were born'; and, back in Brazil from Buenos Aires, he sent his grandfather a view of Sugar Loaf Mountain: 'Very hot & wonderful here. Swim in the sea in the morning & work in the afternoon when it is cooler. Have arranged for Gitta to sing at the Opera here if she approves of the terms. I haven't heard yet, & also perhaps the radio too. I'll end up by being a good manager, you see!' Tony was without Gitta when he wrote the card, waiting for her to join him from the Argentinian capital. He was staying at the Riviera on Copacabana Beach, 'a nice hotel with full board & very good food for 10/-a day' but felt he might have to move to a cheaper one. 'I've some Italian & American friends here, & my dog so I'm not quite alone, tho' I miss someone much too much & am very underweight in consequence! But I'm so brown I look fine!' A month later, he was on the *Augustus*, returning from Argentina, again without Gitta, who had another two weeks to sing in Buenos Aires. He described the liner, the most luxurious on the Europe–South American route, as 'just a little too much "Ritz Hotel" but that is just personal!' Gitta had 'travelled out on this ship & I can see left a big impression'. A fortnight later, Gitta was still in Buenos Aires. Plans remained 'a bit indefinite', he wrote, wanly, to Aunt Gwen, adding: 'How awful things are in Europe.' The managerial life, even in a cradle of hedonism, left something to be desired. Gitta never returned to him.

Tony resumed his acting, in a half-hearted way. A thinly fictionalised memoir, written in 1981 under the title 'The Last Summer' and never intended for publication, gives an impression of the life he was leading at this period on the fringe of the *jeunesse dorée*. He tells of a holiday in August 1939, when, despite the ever-increasing 'awfulness' in Europe, he and a chum, Derek Hall Caine, set off in the latter's Rolls-Royce for Antibes. Hall Caine's father – son of the novelist – put a stop to the joint adventure before they had even boarded the ferry because the lad was supposed to join the family's printing firm in Watford, so Tony went alone by train to the Riviera, principally to ensure that Derek's girlfriend, a pretty young actress who had gone on ahead, did not get up to mischief. The cast of characters swirling around the Hôtel du Cap included Marlene Dietrich, Noël Coward, Norma Shearer, Elsa Maxwell, Douglas Fairbanks, Beatrice Lillie, the odd title and even 'a rather silent fair haired boy called Prince Phillip of Greece'. Tony's looks, congeniality and growing sophistication enabled him to pass inconspicuously among them while not being wholly of them. For him money was tight, as it had been in Rio, and moderate success at the roulette table was not enough to deliver real ease. The band played on, but the cast was depleting. The Germans were about to mass on Poland's border. It was time for him, too, to leave for home – in something of a hurry.

Tony's short tale, which contains almost as many makes of top-of-the-market automobile as it does familiar faces, places him, as narrator, in that milieu extensively documented by the social historians, novelists and playwrights of the inter-war period; one of extravagance, elegance, somewhat nervous gaiety and, at one remove, loucheness. It ends with him at Bea Lillie's Regency house just outside London, raising the possibility of becoming a conscientious objector, to which his hostess replies coolly: 'One could always be that among other things. And one could always get one's yellow little ass out of my house and go and fight for one's country.' The next day, Friday, 1 September, he enlists at Uxbridge and by the following night, with Poland overrun and the world waiting to see if Hitler will take notice of the British and French ultimatum, he is on sentry duty, itching in his new khaki.

One Saturday night a little over a year later – as Derek would tell it – the fine, uniformed figure of Lieutenant Anthony Forwood, on leave from his battery at Hornchurch, failed to get into the cinema, so strolled to the Amersham Playhouse and took one of the many empty seats for the last two acts of *Grief Goes Over*. In his semi-official role as a 'scout' for H. M. Tennent he sent his card backstage and waited. Derek emerged to find him sitting uncomfortably at one end of the front row of the stalls:

> I was quite unprepared for the elegant splendour reclining in the too-small seat before me. Booted, breeched, tunic'd, buttons and badges glittering brightly in the meagre light of the dim auditorium, his hair shining like a halo, he extended an indifferent hand, told me his name and said that he had been in Front and thought I was 'interesting'. I sat nervously in the empty seat beside him. 'Far too young, of course, but a very strong – Quality?'[4]

There was a set to be struck and a new one rigged for the next production, so Tony suggested they talk further over cocoa at his grandfather's house. He might be able to secure a part for Derek as a glorified chorus boy in a London revue, and, if so, would Derek agree to be represented by him when the war ended? 'We shook hands, I remember, which was the only form of contract we have ever had'.[5] Anne Deans was, apparently, none too impressed when Derek rejoined the members of the cast later that evening: 'Agents from the West End, she pointed out, were pretty sharp people, who seldom kept their words, and a Revue didn't seem the best place for a straight actor to begin his attempt on the West End. And if I did get the job, she asked pointedly, what would happen to her?'[6] The answer was that she would quietly disappear from the scene.

The Revue was *Diversion No. 2*, the logically entitled successor to a well-received 'Mixture' by Herbert Farjeon which had opened in October at Wyndham's. The company, headed by Edith Evans, included Joyce Grenfell, Dorothy Dickson and Peter Ustinov, whose creation of a washed-up, ugly Austrian diva, Madame Lizelotte Beethoven-Finck, had infallibly brought the house down. Now the 'scatty boy in wrinkled tights' was performing a routine, 'Producing

King Lear', in which he impersonated several distinguished theatre directors, and using every spare moment backstage to fill school exercise-books in pencil with the draft of his first play, *House of Regrets*. Derek was assigned to Ustinov's dressing-room, number four, and found him 'always playing Bach or Beethoven. He was far ahead intellectually, whereas I was so abysmally *un*-intellectual. He scared the shit out of me. While I was whistling things from "Babes in Arms", he would be whistling Vivaldi.'[7] According to Derek, Ustinov established a 'small salon', often thrumming with the babel of foreign visitors and Russian gramophone records, where he would hand his nascent play 'sheet by sheet, to an enraptured Joyce Grenfell who sat at his feet on the cramped floor in blue velvet',[8] and nursed the pages 'as if they were the Holy Grail or the Turin Shroud'.[9] As for his room-mate, 'Peter must have thought me terribly boring. I know he hated my whistling. It was very shrill and it went against the intellectual grain.' Sir Peter had no recollection of the whistling, 'but I developed a kind of concentration where if I was writing a play I couldn't hear anything. In fact I nearly missed my entrance on several occasions because I was right in the middle of a line.'[10] He found Derek a likeable companion, 'very studious and nice'. He particularly appreciated the fact that 'silence didn't embarrass him very much – which is a wonderful thing in anybody, especially when you are sharing a dressing-room'.

Derek's opening night on 1 January 1941 was in fact an opening afternoon; the bombs and the blackouts had restricted performances to matinées. *Diversion No. 2* comprised two dozen sketches, of which he appeared in five, including 'In for a Dip', and 'I Simply Adore My Dentist'. The former was a musical scene described by Ustinov as an Edwardian bathing party, in which 'two mashers attempted to seduce a couple of beauties by discreetly splashing them'.[11] He and Derek played a 'moustachioed gallant' apiece – the only time, apart from the finale, when they shared the stage. Derek's trickiest moment came at the opening of the second half of the show, in 'Nanty Puts Her Hair Up', a Farjeon sketch about a girl growing up, for which he was obliged to wear the kilt. The actor James Cairncross, who had studied with Ustinov at Michel Saint-Denis's theatre studio and was now passing through London on home leave to Scotland, could not get a seat in the packed theatre but, because he was in uniform, was allowed to watch from the wings. At one point he discovered standing next to him Derek, who, conscious of his own pending call-up to the Army, exchanged 'a few whispered words' before proceeding to the stage to deliver himself of the immortal line: 'Nanty! ma Nanty! whit are ye daein' therr?'[12] Joanna Horder, who was in the routine with him, remembers that he carried it off, but 'couldn't manage the accent at all!'[13]

Their theatre was one of a handful still functioning. Air-raid sirens moaned constantly. Three nights before the show opened, the Luftwaffe had carried out their most fearsome raid on the City, an event captured in the now iconic photograph showing the dome of St Paul's Cathedral defiant above the smoke and flames. The company's final run-through before the dress rehearsal had been cut short by the bombing which destroyed the Hippodrome on the opposite side of St Martin's Lane. In March the Café de Paris was demolished, with terrible loss of life. Ustinov recalled that he and Derek fire-watched together, 'on the roof of Wyndham's, wearing tin hats. I felt we were playing in an Ealing film – one of those where Jack Hawkins and Dickie Attenborough appear together and the dialogue goes as follows: "That'll be all, Murray." "Yessir. Thank you, Sir. And Sir?" "Yes." "Nothing, Sir." '[14] Derek remembered that as they regained their feet inside the theatre after the Hippodrome bomb, a small disc of paper came floating into Ustinov's outstretched hand. It read: 'Do Not Accept This Pro-gramme Unless The Seal Is Unbroken.'[15] A somewhat larger document came by more conventional means to Derek himself – his summons for an Army medical examination in Brighton. He emerged from this ritual humiliation fit and healthy, and duly signed up. There was a short deferment, because *Diversion No. 2* was deemed a morale-booster, and then an even shorter interlude when in mid-April he was released for the show to be recast. It had been an instructive engagement; not least for its opportunity to scrutinise time and again the polished poise of Dorothy Dickson 'walking through' her dance routines; to witness Edith Evans, in all her glory, declaiming Elizabeth I's speech before the Navy took on the Armada; and to absorb some of the creative energy emanating from Ustinov. However, it was the influence of a lowlier cast member which made the greatest impression.

Vida Hope was only three years older than Derek, but had a wise head on young shoulders. Born into a Liverpudlian family which claimed to have been in showbusiness of one kind or another for three centuries, she started as a journalist and copywriter. However, on the strength of a performance in an amateur show, Farjeon booked her for his *Little Revue* in 1939. She went on to become a regular at the Players' Theatre behind Charing Cross Station, 'where her slyly droll renderings of Cockney laments from the Victorian music hall were especially appreciated'.[16] Ustinov stretched a point perhaps in describing her as one of the 'beauties' in 'In for a Dip', for she was no beach belle, but her vivacity and warmth, and her readiness with encouragement endeared her to Derek from the start. Vida's principal advice was that once in the Army he should not give up his writing or his drawing. She had seen the slim sketchbook he acquired on 7 February, and which he began to fill with watercolour and pen-and-ink images of striking vividness and fluidity – capturing the bleakness of bomb damage, a Moore-like huddle in the depths of Oxford Circus Underground station, a set for an imaginary ballet called 'Carnage'; repeatedly, the grace of high fashion; in a few strokes, a suggestion of Marlene Dietrich, a Can-Can girl, an unidentified woman on a train, and a lithe creature called Jean at the Nightlight, the cellar club where actors retired after their shows and where Ustinov, among others, did 'a turn'. Between the green covers were signs of further experiment: few drawings carried a signature, but when they did, the most frequent was 'EREK'. What Vida had seen of his writing is hard to gauge. The verse about Thiepval, composed in his melancholy at the forthcoming war, had been for the eyes of Nerine Cox alone. Just as the latter had been urging him since they met to read the Lakeland poets, Keats and the Classics, and to write, write, write, so now Vida too told him that to keep his mind going in the Army he should write anywhere and everywhere and not 'just flop about cleaning your equipment or whatever they do in their free time'.[17]

Between March and May Derek paid his final visits home as a civilian. Twice he took with him, not Anne Deans, but a companion described by Lionel Cox as 'an airman friend named Eugene'. On Tuesday, 6 May he went, alone, to say *au revoir* to Chez Nous and its occupants, before spending his last day amid his family at Milnthorpe and its deceptive tranquillity. Margaret was occupied with her sewing, her vegetable garden and her wider responsibility for air-raid precautions. Lu and Rogan hunted rats by the pond. Gareth asked Derek for 'a German helmet or a coconut, depending on where I got sent'.[18] Ulric was philosophical, believing the war was so different from the one in which he had been involved that it would swiftly be over. In common with every household touched directly or indirectly by the conflict, the atmosphere was underlain with apprehension. The air-raid shelter which Derek and his father had dug together filled with water the first time it rained. Even 'Trees' was showing signs of neglect.

A small, blue, worse-for-wear exercise-book which, with the single volume of sketches, has somehow survived the travels, the flames and the shredder, is headed on its first right-hand page 'THE DIARY OF DEREK BOGAERDE', and begins:

THURSDAY MAY 8TH 1941
Awakened by Elsie, our maid, at 7.30. Had uneasy feeling inside, realized with a start, today I start life in the Army. Feel Sick. Rush about packing etc. Family all unnaturally cheerful, me included. Leave the house at 8.45. Rather grim, wonder when I'll be back again. Next time I come back it'll be Winter. Bade farewell to Mother. Beastly. Reach London with Daddy at 10. Say cheero! to him – rush up to Wyndhams leave case at Stage door – say goodbye to Doris Stagedoor Girl. Meet Vida Hope outside Warner Cinema – Coffee in Lyons Piccadilly, all very dull, both trying to be extremely Gay and Clever. Feel like character from Noel Coward.

Vida Sees me off at Kings Cross – very teary. Train Crowded – Soldiers, old women, Conscripts like self. Journey awful – gaze out at receding Country – wonder if I'll die, and never see London again, hope not. Awful old Bitch in Compartment says she'll vomit if I smoke – have to stand in Corridor – feel like going back to School.

Arrive Richmond Yorks at 6.45. Bundled into Army Lorry with 22 others. Arrive at Camp – bleak, barren and horrible – have awful supper – Sausages. Get Shown to bunk-room – sleep on floor on Straw Buiscuits – 4 blankets – lights out at 10.30. 25 of us here, all homesick dead tired – feel life has ceased for ever – weep four bitter tears under my blankets. Feel much better when find my neighbours doing same – fall into a troubled sleep, full of train journeys – Soldiers – Far-East all mixed up with pathetic glimpses of home! *DB.*

For reasons best known to themselves – perhaps they took too seriously his three years at Allan Glen's – the authorities had assigned Derek to the Royal Corps of Signals: 'I who had the co-ordination of a bursting dam and the technical intelligence of an eft'.[19] So it was as Signalman 2371461 that he ended his first day in the embodied Territorial Army at Catterick Camp. The doctors who subjected him to another inspection reported that he was five foot eight and a half inches tall, weighed 127 pounds, had hazel eyes, brown hair and a sallow complexion, and could expand his chest to thirty-three and a half inches. He had a mole two inches above the left edge of his rib-cage and had a papilloma on his left buttock. Medically, he was A1.

FRIDAY MAY 9TH 1941

Up at 6. God its cold. Clear up beds, clean out barrackroom and fire places etc. Breakfast at 7.15. Mugs of tea. Sausages again! Exam at 8. Mental Arith – English Composition – Maths was awful!! Lecture by Captain Someone on how to Kill Germans quickly. Issued with Gas-Mask – Tin Hat – Great Coat – Boots, 2 pairs – Caps and badges – Then lunch. Lots of it – *very* filling. Another lecture by very Yorkshire Yorkshire man on Veneral desease – hope to goodness I havent got it – must have a look. Wrote letters, to all my friends. Acute shortage of cigarettes – Made friends with two boys of own age – George and Bernard – George a Clerk from Lewisham – Fair haired, clean and plesant. Bernard – dark, worked in Post Office. One topic of conversation here, Women and their bodies, rather revolting, however. BG and I go over to NAAFI have Coffee and Bun – buy cleaning things Dusters – Polish etc. Que up for 15 minutes for 5 woodbines – then over to the YMCA – awful barn like place. This settling in is the worst part of all – cleaning boots until lights out – creep into pujamas – bed very welcome and quite comfortable. Feel cheerful and depressed every 10 minutes, very annoying. No leave for 20 weeks! Chaps here range from Bakers assistants to office clerks, but all pretty decent – Think I shall be OK when I settle in. wish London was'nt 260 miles away. This camp is like a prison – right in the middle of a Moor. Get used to it; like Sailors and the drowning. *DB*

Sadly, the diary ends after those two days in May. Derek made a heading for the Saturday, but the rest of the folio is given over to a peculiar juxtaposition of Shakespeare – 'Shall I compare thee to a summer day – Thou art more lovely and more temperate than the breeze that shakes the darling buds of May' – and two drawings, one of a rifle, the other of telegraph poles reaching towards a distant cluster of buildings, beneath which is written: 'Many Marry The Woman'. He was heeding Vida's advice, for the following hundred pages are busy with ideas and sketches for concert parties, lecture notes ('Aids to good shooting'; 'Four types' of gas), lists of duties ('Friday June 6th. Boots. Sew flashes on jacket [...] Blanco puttees, and Sling'); notes for a production of Patrick Hamilton's *Rope*; several poems; numerous doodles; and a playlet entitled 'Reunion at a Price'. Set in a Lyons tea shop 'somewhere in London', this involves a chance meeting between Donald, a soldier on leave, and his former girlfriend, Agnes, who says: 'You broke my heart you did, Donald, broke it proper, not just chipped it, or anything, broke it – you did.' All, apparently, because of his parsimony, which comes to the surface again when he suggests they go to a newsreel at the Regal about the Scout Movement in Japan and she would 'much rather see Michael Redgrave at the Odeon'. This brief, edgy encounter, which ends with Agnes calling Donald 'a frustrated soldier' and suggesting he go to the YMCA for a meal – 'its cheaper there' – was written in the NAAFI reading room on 25 May 1941, Derek's third week at Catterick.

A few days later, he filled in the necessary application for officer cadet training. Asked in which Arm or Corps he would like to be commissioned, he gave as his first choice 'RE [Royal Engineers] Camouflage only', citing as his technical qualifications '$3\frac{1}{2}$ years Chelsea Polytechnic, & Royal College of Art. Also stage Decor experience and Commercial Art.' Under 'Civil occupation' he wrote: 'Actor, Artist, Stage designer.' A barrister at *The Times* certified as to his 'good moral character for the past four years', and the wheels were set in motion. Meanwhile, after one month at Catterick he was posted to the 1st Operators Training Battalion and the 'settling in' appeared to be going well. He sent home to his mother a postcard showing a formal 'team photograph' of the Signals' 524 Squad. Formal, that is, as far as his twenty-two colleagues are concerned. On closer inspection one sees that Derek, standing in the back row, has his right arm round the shoulder of the signalman next to him and his left hand on that of the one sitting in front. 'Guess who that is in the back row!' he wrote. 'God dont I look a sight! Ive got my hat on all wrong. Loved hearing you on the phone today. If you dont mind Ill always phone when I get depressed. Got a dreadful ache for some Sussex air – Love Derek. Excuse cocoa stains!' He considered himself to excel at drill and to be the squad's sharpest shot with his heavy Lee Enfield. As the best boot-polisher and no mean stitcher-on of badges, flashes and buttons, he bartered his services for cigarettes, while his companions 'lay disconsolately on their beds reading *Health and Strength, Tit-Bits*, or just staring into space'.[20] He also scored plus-points with the less literate by composing letters to their loved ones, while confiding his own thoughts to his notebook. On 20 May, in a 'Sonnet to Gusto', he wrote of being told 'by many men' that love is 'an elusive and bitter thing', to be tasted and then spat out; however, 'My love it is no bitter tea./Rather it is like a Chopin etude on a summer evening –/like the green of the greenest meadow'. It is, he concluded, 'the lovliest thing possible – because principally it is you'. The name 'Martine' is written twice, in the margin.

The regime suited him, with its mixture of square-bashing, mundane duty and enough free time to keep the creative spirit alive. By the end of June he had been promoted to Lance-Corporal. The 1st Operators Training Battalion Dramatic Society was involved in productions not only of *Rope* but also of Elmer Rice's *Judgment Day*. He found enough confidence in his verse to allow one of the notebook poems, 'The Sniper', to reach an audience. Based on an incident in which he had 'shot' one of his comrades during an exercise with dummy ammunition, it was published, as 'Man in the Bush',* on 30 August in *The Times Literary Supplement* – no small achievement for a twenty-year-old whose schooling in English prose and poetry had little to do with the classroom. His self-esteem was boosted further still in October when his Commanding Officer, Lieutenant-Colonel R. R. A. Darling, reported that he was suited both 'by personality and intelligence' for officer training, that his 'power of leadership' was 'good' and that his 'military character' was 'V. good'. The high-powered interviewing board which saw him on the 22nd agreed, noting that he 'Wants to be employed on camouflage work if possible', failing which he would like to join the anti-aircraft arm of the Royal Artillery. So keen was Derek on his preferred choice that Ulric had asked Colin Coote, a former MP and now senior leader writer on *The Times*, if he could bring any influence to bear. Coote, who had a desk at the War Office, wrote to the head of the Camouflage Development and Training Centre at Farnham, and was told that although there were no vacancies at present Derek should try to be interviewed towards the end of his OCTU course when there might be a chance. There was a second interview, in January 1942, by which time the prospects had faded, because Derek was recommended for light anti-aircraft training. The Royal Corps of Signals, 'delighted with my theatrical ventures, distressed by my lack of any technical knowledge whatsoever, even after almost half a year under their very careful eyes, bundled me off, unexpected and unwanted, like a plastic netsuke in a packet of cornflakes, to the unaware Royal Artillery';[21] it was not a good idea. He joined the Gunners on 20 February and for the next seven months rode a rollercoaster of approval. His company commander at 133rd Officer Cadet Training Group reported after his first full month: 'This Cadet is very young and at present has a childish outlook. He has little natural ability for things Military and has not absorbed enough knowledge to go on with his present Course Serial. He needs to acquire balance of mind and strength of personality.'

It is hard to believe that Major A. F. J. Forsyth was reflecting on the same young soldier whom Lieutenant-Colonel Darling had commended so warmly six months earlier. Derek was relegated, and almost immediately disappointed

---

* 'Man in the Bush' is reprinted in *Snakes and Ladders*.

in his examination results. 'He appears unable to absorb the elements of military knowledge in spite of very willing efforts to make good,' wrote Forsyth in May. 'He puts plenty of life into outdoor work which is now reasonably good. A pleasant but not very forceful personality. Officer material if and when he can acquire the necessary knowledge.' A hint of a smile from the Major? By June it had become a beneficent grin: 'His work has improved in quality and is now satisfactory. His outdoor work is good and now that he appears to have overcome his teething troubles he should gain self confidence and go ahead. He has a good word of command – is keen and willing.' Then everything went awry again. In mid-August another Major, C. E. Lumb, offered this verdict on Derek's technical training: 'Young in years in manner. No self confidence or power of command. Continues to make innumerable elementary mistakes. Knowledge poor. A likeable cadet who has tried hard.' On 22 September the Commanding Officer, Lieutenant-Colonel V. H. Seymer, summed up with the following mixed review: 'This cadet is without any mechanical aptitude and himself feels unable to cope with technical training. He is young, active, and enthusiastic. He seems intelligent and of the type who should make a useful officer if trained for an arm of less technical difficulty than RA (AA). Infantry, Parachutists or Airborne Division are suggested.' Infantry – fair enough. But Parachutists? Airborne Division? Suppose he came down in the water!

Derek had been defeated, 'once again, by machines, which I came to dread and loathe for the rest of my life'.[22] For a couple of months he was attached to 148 Independent Brigade Group, and evidently had absorbed some lessons from the AA: his notebook has a page, dated 2 November, which is given over to aircraft recognition. Then, at the beginning of December, he was despatched to 161 OCTU, which would normally have been based at the Royal Military College, Sandhurst, but, as part of the infantry wing, had moved to Mons Barracks in Aldershot. Here, he decided that if granted a commission he would like it to be with the Queen's Royal Regiment, the Royal Fusiliers or the East Surreys, in that order. His platoon commander, Captain C. P. Whitehead, believed after the first month that Derek would 'develop considerable prowess as a leader', but after two that 'he is taking life rather too easily'; and at the end of the third, 'I still think he could do better than he does'. The company commander, Major P. V. Makins, reported that he had 'done well but he must realise that to be a good officer he must always do his utmost and must never relax'; and the Commanding Officer, Lieutenant-Colonel P. L. Bowers, grading him Category C, remarked: 'Has it in him to be a good officer if he will take himself in hand and realize his responsibilities. Will need firm handling at first if he is to make proper use of his natural advantages. Could have been graded higher if he had extended himself more.' Derek and his fellow members of D Company passed out on 1 April 1943, and had the privilege of doing so at Sandhurst on what is believed to be the last occasion at which infantry cadets marched up the steps to Old College. That night, at one minute past midnight, he became officer number

269237, 2nd Lieutenant Derek Van den Bogaerde of the Queen's Royals, and was now, in principle at least, a leader of men.

He had been commissioned into his first choice of regiment and could proudly wear its badge. He did so for the rest of his service, but the Queen's Royals saw little of Derek. First he was sent to a 'holding battalion' in Lancashire, where he spent several weeks in the officers' mess at a deserted mill, 'reading old copies of *The Field* and *Everybody's*. No one seemed to know what to do with me.'[23] It was the beginning of a rum existence as 'a draft of one' – someone who belonged to a body with which he spent no time and who passed the remainder of his military service on attachment to outfits that had no proprietorial, let alone paternal, interest in him. In a way, however, the arrangement suited Derek admirably. He was part of successive teams without ever feeling owned by them; he could observe from the perimeter, where the shell is less vulnerable to unwanted probing. By the middle of June he had been posted to the 7th Battalion of the Somerset Light Infantry in Redruth, Cornwall, and on the 17th was appointed to Headquarters 214 Independent Infantry Brigade as a liaison officer, which 'meant that I should be used to send messages of a private and personal nature, rather like a pigeon, only that instead of using wings I would be required to ride a motorcycle'.[24] Making much of his problems with co-ordination and his well-founded antipathy towards machines, he later gave a highly coloured account of arriving at the Brigade's base, a large country house near Truro; of falling off his bike into the rhododendrons lining the drive; and of meeting in disarray the Commanding Officer, who had nipped outside to answer a call of nature and who showed remarkable tolerance. As usual the reality was less interesting: why on earth would a brigadier leave a comfortable, well-appointed billet to have a pee? Yet if Hubert Essame did observe the new member of his small staff making erratic progress up the long drive he might well have wondered what he was being saddled with.

Brigadier Essame was himself unconventional. Short, dapper, sandy-haired, with 'brilliant blue eyes and a tongue like a whip',[25] he had fought on the Somme, was awarded the MC in 1918, and spent most of the inter-war years in India. He was known as 'Twinkle Toes' because of the rapid steps made by his small feet and because of what his son Robin describes as a 'rather unusual gait'.[26] He believed in keeping his officers alert by leading them at mealtimes in smart conversation, quizzes and parlour games. In action, he was to prove a formidable leader from the front. Initially the Brigade's duties were 'stationary', guarding vulnerable points such as radio and power stations and airfields, and Derek settled easily into this 'semi-wartime existence'. So much so that he later claimed to have been made the Brigadier's unofficial ADC. Having to move about by motorbike was the sole drawback. John Denison, Essame's Staff Captain, recalls Derek as 'always biddable, wanting to play his part in whatever was going on. He played the role of the young subaltern charmingly. Everybody said "What a charming man". And he was willing to do whatever he was expected to do. But he was never anything other than an actor playing a part – incurably so.' When Denison sent him off to check on a nearby unit, Derek reported his findings. 'But what about so-and-so-and-so?' asked Denison, waiting for the most important information of all. Back came the reply. 'Do you know, Sir, I quite forgot to ask.'[27] There was no question of favouring Derek; indeed, had any such treatment been on offer, it would have been more likely to go towards Richard Wollheim, another of the liaison officers and subsequently a much honoured philosopher. But Essame did not work in that way. All officers should be of equal merit, and if one was not quite up to scratch, there were plenty of courses on which he could be sent – to everyone's profit.

First, however, there was some serious business to be dealt with. The Brigade was sent to Inverary in Argyllshire, for 'Operation Lifebelt', a top-secret plan using combined services to invade the Azores. The operation never took place because the Portuguese finally agreed to allow the Allies to use the facilities that they intended to take by force, but the preparations had reached an advanced stage. Essame was concerned that his troops had no experience of battle. In the brief time that they were in Scotland, working with the Navy and the Royal Marines, they underwent the next best thing. Stan Procter, Essame's wireless operator in Britain and in Europe, was reminded by his journal entry for 14 July that the Brigade 'had just come off a week's training in assault landing with live ammunition flying all over the place, some from fighter planes and some ricocheting off the hills. Eight men had been killed. A 1% fatal casualty rate was acceptable. They were exhausted, the weather had been appalling, as it was today, raining stair rods.'[28] How Derek and his fellow junior officers dealt with the specific hazards and with the 'general mumble that on no account were [the men] going on parade that morning' is not recorded. The Brigade moved south of the border, to Wooler, and to a few weeks of uncertainty. Derek managed to keep his hand in theatrically. On 11 September the *Little Revue* was staged at the Corn Exchange, produced and designed by 'Lieut Van den Bogaerde', with 'Rick Bogaerde' starring in three of its sketches. Stan Procter noted 'a young and very good looking officer, Lt Rikki van den Bogaerde who acted as an impressario' with 'mainly "rookie" performers'. Derek also had a further literary success when a second piece of verse, 'Steel Cathedrals' by D. Van den Bogaerde, was published as one of the 'More Poems from the Forces' in the September–December issue of *The Poetry Review*. It would be reprinted in at least three anthologies of war poetry:

> It seems to me, I spend my life in stations.
> Going, coming, standing, waiting.
> Paddington, Darlington, Shrewsbury, York.
> I know them all most bitterly.
> Dawn stations, with a steel light, and waxen figures.
> Dust, stone, and clanking sounds, hiss of weary steam.

Night stations, shaded light, fading pools of colour.
Shadows and the shuffling of a million feet.
Khaki, blue, and bulky kitbags, rifles gleaming dull.
Metal sound of army boots, and smoker's coughs.
Titter of harlots in their silver foxes.
Cases, casks, and coffins, clanging of the trolleys.
Tea urns tarnished, and the greasy white of cups.
Dry buns, Woodbines, Picture Post and Penguins,
and the blaze of magazines.
Grinding sound of trains, and rattle of the platform gates.
Running feet and sudden shouts, clink of glasses from the buffet.
Smell of drains, tar, fish and chips and sweaty scent, honk of taxis,
and the gleam of cigarettes.
Iron pillars, cupolas of glass, girders messed by pigeons,
the lazy singing of a drunk.
Sailors going to Chatham, soldiers going to Crewe,
Aching bulk of kit and packs, tin hats swinging.
The station clock with staggering hands and callous face,
says twenty-five-to-nine,
A cigarette, a cup of tea, a bun,
and my train goes at ten.

He left the north without making much of an impression militarily, but he was doing well enough to secure the promotion assumed by the cover of the *Little Revue* programme; on 2 October he was made a full (War Substantive) Lieutenant. 'Operation Lifebelt' had been completely hush-hush at the time, and, as far as Derek's later writings are concerned, remained so. This has nothing to do with official secrecy; everything to do with his own. For on that achingly beautiful coastline in the west of Scotland, which was standing in for the Azores as the combined forces rehearsed their landings, he either met for the first time, or consolidated a brief acquaintance with, his first unqualified love. The uncertainty – caused by conflicting dates on the reverse of a photograph and in a letter – is of little concern to us. However, it mattered very much indeed to Derek that among the complement based in the Duke of Argyll's castle grounds at Inverary in July 1943 was one Jack Jones – a man fortunate to be anywhere at all.

John Francis Jones, the second of three sons, was born on 16 July 1915 at home in Suffolk. His father, Hugh, was a farm manager who, with his wife Edith Maud, brought up their boys comfortably enough. They moved twice before settling in Witnesham, some eight miles from the River Deben, where Jack and his younger brother George discovered the particular pleasures of life both on and beside the water. Hugh Jones had the inspired idea of transporting a small farm hut to the riverside at Waldringfield, a village which was to assume a singular importance in Derek's life. Here, Jack and George were entrusted to a former barge-skipper, Jimmy Quantrill, who taught them at first the rudiments and then the finer points of sailing. It was a carefree idyll similar to that described in the books of Arthur Ransome – whose yacht Jack was to acquire – and one not far removed from that lived by Derek and Elizabeth in Sussex. Hugh Jones died in an accident on the farm when George and Jack were still in their teens. Jack, whose intelligence matched his ability, had his heart set on becoming a doctor, but there were insufficient funds to give him the education necessary for that profession or any equivalent requiring years of formal training. He turned to design, and secured his first job at a brass foundry which made marine hardware. In his spare time he began to make drawings of yachts. One of these, innovatory because of its unfashionable approach to theories about the centre of buoyancy, was published in *Yachting Monthly*, followed swiftly by a second. The editor liked his contentious approach and gave him a column called 'You Needn't Agree . . .' which he wrote under the pen name of Canvas.

At the outbreak of war, Jack volunteered inevitably for the Navy. He started on the lower deck of a destroyer, and had to swim for his life when the ship was divebombed in Dover harbour. In late 1940 he passed out third of one hundred in the Drake Class at the King Alfred training establishment and came first in the Commanding Officers' course. By the end of May 1941, he had his first command: Harbour Defence Motor Launch 1024, based at Sheerness in the Thames Estuary, from where she would carry out her principal task of mine-spotting at night. The ensuing months were eventful. Jones was at the centre of three courts of inquiry, prompting him to observe many years later that 'if one's a good-all-round but otherwise un-spectacular officer, you're more than likely to *stay in your rank* throughout service life. Get a Court of Inquiry, or better still a Court Martial (for something in which you've been *justified*. . . that I'd emphasise) and some-one up at Admiralty wakes up and notices you . . . so promotion!'

In the early hours of a January day in 1942 Jones was making his way down from the bridge to the wheelhouse when an underwater explosion caused his ship to lurch. The fall resulted in injuries to his back and, internally, to his groin. The bigger problem for Jones was that later in the day he was to take on board his superior officer, Captain E. C. Cordeaux, another charismatic figure, who won the DSO at Dunkirk and was now senior officer of the sixty-seven-strong Thames Local Defence Flotilla. The task was to sink a fort off Harwich, one of several which still dot the estuary. Shrugging off his injuries as best he could, Jones set out again. By the second day, he confided in Cordeaux, a doctor in civilian life, that he was in a bad way. The latter examined him, said that he should try to stick it out until their mission was accomplished and added reassuringly that at least there was no trace of venereal disease. On their return to harbour at Sheerness, Cordeaux telephoned for an ambulance and Jack spent the next four months in hospital.

By the summer he was back at sea. In 'Operation Jubilee', the disastrous

Dieppe Raid on 19 August 1942, he commanded one of the supporting ships, Rescue Motor Launch 513. When the flotilla was set upon by some twenty Focke-Wolf 190 fighters, two of her fellow rescue vessels were set alight, but RML 513 and another craft managed to save forty-seven RAF personnel and bring them home. In the attack either a bullet or shrapnel had gone through Jones's neck, severing or damaging half his left-side cranial nerves. Despite this third and most severe of his wartime wounds, he remained in charge of his ship – filling with his blood the voice-pipe from the bridge as he issued orders to the coxswain – until she docked at Newhaven. On the way to the ambulance, he asked a colleague, Lieutenant-Commander Alan Villiers, who was waiting on the quay-side, to take over command. Villiers' new charge, his first, had 209 missile holes in her hull and decks; all the rubber-covered fuel tanks were, as Jones put it, 'bulging from bullets or (mercifully unexploded) cannon shells'; and another seventeen missiles were embedded in the vessel's depth-charges. How she and her crew had made it back across the Channel was little short of miraculous. What gave Jones lasting cause for pride, however, was the fact that none of his men, aged in the main between eighteen and twenty, had been hurt. For them, Jack Jones was a skipper to respect, if not revere.

His were the kind of exploits about which morale-boosting films were made. Their protagonist was dashing, handsome and cultivated. The photograph which half a century later would accompany his obituaries was enlarged from a shot of RML 513's crew. In it he wears his cap at a rakish angle and his smile betokens adventure. Jack Jones was aware of the impact he made. As his sister-in-law, June Jones, observed, 'If you look like that, you don't wrap yourself up in a mackintosh.'[29] Yet it was not for the derring-do that on his death he was afforded a significant quota of column inches in the national newspapers, but for his more sedate accomplishments as one of the country's most prominent and influential yacht designers in the 1950s and 1960s. No mention was made of any association with the young Derek, let alone one of real importance. However, once again Derek had found a confidant, almost exactly the same age as Tony Forwood, and every bit as full of worldly wisdom. It was Jack Jones whom Derek's family met first. Oddly, they were introduced to him, too, as Tony.

Ulric and Margaret, who had quietly been making a further contribution to the war effort by offering temporary accommodation to child refugees from Europe, left Milnthorpe in the autumn of 1941 and moved to a substantial house in Burgess Hill called The Poplars, which Ulric, with some distaste, swiftly renamed Winton House in memory of their happy times at Alfriston. 'Uncle Bogey' was as usual at his desk in Printing House Square when the Coxes came to call and, after a 'special lunch with 2 glasses of port', were given a guided tour of the house by Margaret. Lionel recorded: 'Didn't think much of it. Lou's dog [a mastiff puppy called Sheba] left it's card everywhere.' The occupants were none too keen either. By the spring of 1943 they had moved again, to the more cosy Hillside Cottage at Clayton, another small downland village, dominated at a distance by two windmills known as Jack and Jill. The house was next to the Church of St John the Baptist, dating in part from Saxon times and renowned for its eleventh-century frescoes; its rector was the father of Derek's Staff Captain, John Denison. Nearby lived the 'Forces' Sweetheart', Vera Lynn. Apart from spasmodic dogfights and the drone of bombers in the skies above, and the night-time rumble and clatter from the railway as it carried tanks and other matériel to the coast, there was little to remind the villagers of the grim, threatened outside world. It was here that Derek introduced his parents, sister and brother to 'Tony' Jones. Why 'Tony'? No one in his own family called him that. The Van den Bogaerdes were never to know him as Jack. To add to the confusion, a framed snapshot of a smiling Derek, dating from shortly after the Scottish adventure, is inscribed 'To Tony – Remembering a few days of July – Peter '43'. A year later Derek was signing himself 'Pip', 'PP' or 'Pippin'. In *Cleared for Take-Off* he would write:

> My name was Pip in those days. There was no pixie-like reason for this. It was not a diminutive of 'Phillip' or 'Paul' or 'Peter', and nothing whatever to do with *Great Expectations*. It was just brutally slung at me by an exhausted instructor in Le Cateau Lines, Catterick [...] Maddened by my calm, bovine, agreeable incomprehension of anything whatsoever to do with valves, wires, wireless, frequencies, transmissions or the total absurdity of Morse code, indeed anything remotely connected to the business of my becoming a little Signaller, the unhappy man suddenly hurled his piece of chalk, the book of instructions, a duster and, finally, his cap at me and roared for quick delivery from my numb bewilderment. 'You bloody give me the *pip*!' he yelled.[30]

If that account is true, why would he call himself, for however brief a period, 'Peter'? Certainly, to those at 214 Independent Infantry Brigade, he was known simply as Derek, Rick, or, as Stan Procter had it, 'Rikki'. The flat denial so many years later of a connection with the Dickens novel makes one wonder whether in fact the well-read Jack Jones *did* make the comparison with its narrator; or with the cabin-boy Pippin in Melville's *Moby-Dick*. Or perhaps there was a link with those same cartoon characters Pip, Squeak and Wilfred, who, as Ulric well knew, gave their names to three First World War service medals. It matters little. What counts is that Jack/Tony Jones was in Derek's life and was to stay there for some while. Lu did not take to him at first, but Gareth was captivated by the scarred action hero: 'He was very good-looking and grizzled. He wore a Naval captain's uniform and he brought me a lifebelt and a signalling lamp.' Particularly enthralling for the young boy, who would develop a lifelong love of the sea, was the occasion when Jack accepted a commission to design a yacht for two neighbours, Eustace and Sylvia Cleary. Enlisting the help of Ulric, Derek and Eustace, Jack laid out its pattern in rope and string on the Clearys' large, immaculate lawn. The boat was never built, but its phantom elegance remains with Gareth to this day. As for the relationship between its designer and his brother, Gareth thought no more of it than he did of that between his increasingly attractive sister and her suitors. In those days, nothing was spoken, especially not in front of ten-year-old boys. In any case, the visits, which could be made only during home leave, were necessarily short.

Those to Chez Nous had already assumed a lower priority; indeed it is somewhat remarkable that contact with the Coxes continued at all, given the extraordinary entry in Lionel's diary for 14 November 1941 – the day news came through that the *Ark Royal* had been sunk: 'For first part of morning we sat up in Nerine's room & all discussed Derek Bogaerde's delinquencies.' Whatever these unexplained lapses were, Nerine herself was characteristically forgiving. To mark their respective twenty-first birthdays in March 1942 she wrote to Derek, who replied from his OCTU course at Shrivenham that 'in spite of quarrels and fights and general tantrums – we still know each other, write to each other, and love each other in our odd way'. He told her that he had built the set for, and was about to reprise the role of Raleigh in, *Journey's End*; reminisced about a recent trip they had made together to see *Blithe Spirit* – 'another lovely memory was imprisoned in my mind'; and concluded: 'One day Nair, we shall look back to this day, our 21st, and sigh softly, and say – "we were happy then – and life was good – but we are happier now – and life is lots better!" '

There is affection in the letter, to be sure, but a careful lack of commitment: any looking-back would be a common rather than a shared experience. Nerine was as naïve as most of her contemporaries, but she knew that their relationship was more like that of siblings than of lovers. She thought little of it at the time, but in retrospect realised the significance of a conversation they had had about a chance encounter between Derek and a man in the pub closest to Milnthorpe: 'The man – I think he was a schoolmaster – had suggested that they meet up and go out for a meal. Derek said, "I like him, but I thought, 'I don't know'. I decided I didn't think I ought to go." He would say quite a lot of things to me without being completely explicit. I would only ask a question if I thought it was really, really relevant.'[31] In any case, the chances were that such a question in this case would be given short shrift. Since his baptism as a soldier his personal life had become intricate. One of the early entries in the journal he started in May 1941 is a list of ten names, headed by Bill [Wightman], and including Tony [Forwood], Vida [Hope], Anne and Mrs Deans, his aunt Hester and – bizarrely, given his apparent unhappiness under her roof – Sadie [Murray]. Fourth on the list is Lusia [Parry, a friend of the Forwoods]. Completed by 'Maggie' and Lu, this is clearly a roll-call of significance. All but two are women, but there is no mention of Nerine. At the barracks, Derek befriended Peter Ewing, who was born on the same day in 1921, appeared with him in *Judgment Day* and was to receive letters from him as the war progressed. Another relationship, closer to home, had developed with John Nelson – almost certainly the schoolmaster of Nerine's memory – who would cut a dash at the Van den Bogaerde household by sweeping Lu off on his motorcycle; yet his primary interest was her elder brother. All very complicated. Compared with the turbulence of human relationships, the confused Derek found the ordered passage of military service quite straightforward.

'So intent was the Brigadier on bettering his unofficial ADC that he sent me off on various courses all over the country,' Derek would write.[32] That is how it might have seemed to the newly promoted Lieutenant at the end of October 1943, but there is every reason to believe that Essame's strategy was not quite so positive. According to his family, in later years the Brigadier was uncharacteristically reticent if Derek's name was mentioned. Essame's daughter Primrose remembers him remarking that Van den Bogaerde 'was the sort of chap who used to like getting out of uniform and sitting around the mess in a silk shirt. My father did not have a high opinion of actors, regarding them as unstable personalities, not a good bet.' Her brother Peter had the impression that the Brigadier had 'felt let down' in some way, and a family friend who had long conversations with Essame a few years after the war formed the distinct opinion that the latter believed Derek had 'tried to secure a less perilous posting'.[33] John Denison believes that Essame sent a note upstairs, recommending that Derek could be 'more usefully employed in other tactics'. Whatever the motivation, the next five months found Derek steeping himself in the detail of a more sedentary kind of warfare.

Smedley's Hydro at Matlock had been requisitioned by the Army as an Intelligence training centre. On 26 October Derek began a War Intelligence Course from which he emerged five weeks later as a Brigade Intelligence Officer. A brief exploration of 'Enemy Documents' followed in December, and in mid-February 1944 he returned to the Derbyshire spa town for a further seven weeks, during which he was briefed in the speciality that was to become his job: the interpretation of aerial photographs. How ironic that after rejecting any suggestion of following in his father's footsteps he should find himself qualified in an area so close to home. The urgings of Aimé and Ulric to 'Observe, observe, observe!', and the 'apparently witless game which my father made us play as children'[34] when they had to memorise what they had seen in shop windows, on the Underground and at the breakfast table, had borne fruit in an unexpected way. Derek might not have succeeded with his original request to be involved in camouflage, but he was now involved in the next best thing – its penetration. A training booklet noted that 'the enemy can do a great deal by well planned concealment and camouflage. Nevertheless there is little he can hide from the prying eye of the air camera – the Mata Hari of this war.'[35] Constance Babington Smith, who founded and ran the Allied Central Interpretation Unit, described the work as 'a new kind of photographic reconnaissance, strategic as well as tactical', which resulted in a new intelligence that 'gave answers of a rapidity, scope and accuracy which had never before been envisaged'. In certain pictures items of military interest could be recognised by anyone: 'But the vast majority of the war's aerial photographs were taken from great heights and from immediately above, and the wealth of information they hold has meaning only for the initiated. Indeed, their secret language may be compared to the language of X-ray photographs, which can be fully understood only by an eye which is experienced and a mind that has been specially trained.'[36]

Secret language, Mata Hari ... this was more like it. No wonder Derek set to work with a will:

> I loved the detail, the intense concentration, the working out of problems, the searching for clues and above all the memorising. It was, after all, a very theatrical business. How many haystacks had there been in that field three weeks ago? Look back and check. Six. Now there were sixteen ... did the tracks lead *to* them and not *away* from them? Were they made by tracked vehicles or wheeled ones? Guns, tanks or radar maybe? Or were they, after all, only haystacks, it was June...[37]

The principal laboratory for the new science was a ludicrous, pseudo-Tudor Buckinghamshire mansion called Danesfield, built by a grocery millionaire on a magnificent site looking down on the Thames between Marlow and Henley. The Air Ministry changed its name to RAF Station Medmenham, after the small village nearby, where in the eighteenth century a ruined abbey had played host to the black magic ritual and 'obscene cavortings' by Sir Francis Dashwood's 'Mad Monks of Medmenham', the Hell-Fire Club.[38] The house on the hill was known by its temporary inmates as 'The Wedding Cake' and by the time Derek went there in the spring of 1944 – no longer under Brigadier Essame's command but as an intelligence officer with General Bernard Montgomery's 21st Army Group headquarters – a number of immense Nissen huts had sprouted in the grounds for the personnel needed to cope with the demands of 'Operation Overlord', the Allies' imminent invasion of Europe. According to Sarah Churchill, the Prime Minister's daughter, who spent much of the war at Medmenham, conditions were 'to say the least, strange': the house was given over to the work and the huts were the living-quarters for an odd assortment of the professional, the amateur and the unwelcome – mice and wood-spiders abounded. 'Puzzling and tedious as it often was, there were moments of terrific excitement and discovery.'[39] Derek wrote many years later that 'we were clever little fellows planning D-Day and were all BIGOTS. A splendid code name for "top secret".'[40] He was not there long: 'I was shoved off to join the Canadien Airforce at Odiham (I was VERY good at my job, you see!) and that was the end, almost, of my stay at Med.'[41]

RAF Odiham, near Basingstoke in Hampshire, was the base for 39 (Reconnaissance) Wing of the Royal Canadian Air Force, part of 83 Group under the umbrella of the 2nd Tactical Air Force. Derek was to be attached to the Wing for much of the coming twelve months. And with his new qualification had come a further connection to the Intelligence Corps, whose badge is fondly described as 'a pansy resting on its laurels'. His relationship with the regiment into which he had been commissioned, the Queen's Royal, had always been remote; now it became more distant than ever, as he was 'shoved off' to work not only with the Canadians but also with another arm of the Services. He had begun his new existence as the 'Draft of One' – engaged with, but never properly belonging to, a cohesive group. It was to suit him down to the ground.

Five

'I imagined it all so completely, and in such detail, that finally I almost came to believe it had actually taken place'

As D-Day approached, and life became 'conducted at top pitch',[1] leave was the more precious. A photograph taken on 19 May shows Jack Jones and Derek walking in uniform along Coventry Street in the West End. Eleven days later, Derek completed a 'Form of Will' in his Officer's Record of Service, which appointed his father as executor and stipulated that after his just debts and funeral expenses had been paid all his estate and effects should go to his parents, apart from 'THE PICTURE IN MY ROOM OF THE CLOTH TOWER, YPRES, AND MY SILVER RING – FROM MY LEFT HAND.' These he left to his 'Friend', named as Lieutenant J. d'Enfer Jones, of 'Sandringham', Llandrindod Wells, Flintshire. The address is that of Jack's widowed mother, who had moved – provisionally at least – from Suffolk to the attractive town in north Wales. The 'd'Enfer' is harder to explain. Family lore has it that Jack came across the name of Felix Denifer among his antecedents and both adopted and adapted it unofficially, as an affectation. His version was d'Enever or d'Enifer. For once it is hard to tell whether Derek's effort was careless, ignorant or mischievous; whichever, the result made Jack a beneficiary 'from Hell'.

The knowledge of imminent momentous events was just as certain at Hillside Cottage, not merely because of Ulric's status in the 'need-to-know' hierarchy. Elizabeth had joined the WRNS and was stationed a few miles away at HMS *Lizard* in Hove. The ten-year-old Gareth marvelled as the fields around them filled with American soldiers: 'I woke up one morning to find a sea of khaki, with tanks and jeeps all over the place.' Ulric and Margaret had always gone out of their way to make servicemen welcome; Nigel Kingscote, who was with 214 Infantry Brigade, remembers being mightily impressed by Ulric's home-made stereophonic sound system when Derek had taken home a small group from their temporary station at Battle. Now, the Van den Bogaerdes had a full-scale fighting force on their hands and they invited as many as they could onto their lawn. Margaret would cook for hours and heap the soldiers' proffered mess trays. Ulric would direct the twelve-inch roller speaker of his gramophone towards the open window and play his extensive collection of classical records, so that the warm evening air was filled with Wagner, Beethoven and Debussy. 'All the boys were silent,' remembers Gareth, 'thinking of home and knowing they were about to be thrown onto the beaches in France.' There is a poignant contrast in the respective and characteristic approaches of his parents. 'My mother was in her element. She loved it – it was her stage again. She used to gee them up and do her Scottish pieces for them. They thought they had found someone who was larger than life.' Ulric, meanwhile, spent as much time as he could with the officers, taking every one of their names and addresses, and knowing full well that many would be killed on the first two or three days of the invasion. Using the resources of *The Times* to find out who they were, he wrote to their parents and loved ones, to tell them that at least they had been with him and his family in pleasant surroundings before leaving to fight.

At Odiham, meanwhile, as the pressure intensified Derek had found himself working alongside a congenial colleague, who was to become a trusted companion, if not exactly a brother-in-arms. Flight Lieutenant Christopher Greaves was a thirty-one-year-old freelance commercial artist and photographer who had studied at the Central School of Art and Design and, like Derek, kept his sketchbook to hand. When war broke out he had been publicity manager for a bus company in Hull. He was stationed in Malta during the siege and contracted a mild form of polio, which left him with a slight limp. He had also witnessed, and would never forget, an appalling accident on an airfield in Britain when a pilot walked into a propeller. Of about the same height, but with thinning brown hair and 'granny glasses', he was, to Derek, 'calm, quiet, wry, funny'.[2] He could also use his words evocatively. Among Christopher Greaves's few surviving papers is a handwritten essay entitled 'Briefing', which describes the events of 5 June when all officers were summoned to the 'Ops room' at 6 p.m. For three months they had prepared feverishly and rehearsed every conceivable emergency, 'yet somehow I suppose most of us worked with the thought that "It can't really happen" in the backs of our minds – The whole adventure seemed too colossal to bear contemplation':

> The tent was crammed to capacity and I had a great desire to paint the scene – The weird light of the evening sun trying to seep through the canvas – soft yellow – the hushed murmur – the occasional remark of the type behind or in front – Everybody trying to look as if 'This doesn't matter a damn' – everybody deeply excited.
>
> [. . .] The CO came in and everybody became very quiet – I shall never forget that quietness – all that could be heard was the flapping of the canvas – I began to think of home and loved people as one does in those moments and I drifted away – Suddenly the CO said in a small voice – 'Well gentlemen – I have called you together to tell you that the invasion of the continent has started – the ships are leaving the ports at this moment – they will rendezvous here.' He indicated a spot in mid-Channel on the map 'and the first assault

parties will storm the beaches at 6-o-clock in the morning. The moment we have all been waiting for has come [. . .] If this thing fails it will be the greatest disaster ever to befall mankind – It can't fail' and he told us of the staggering forces that were to be thrown into the battle.

The Group Captain called for the maximum effort and said 'good luck chaps'.

We wandered out into the evening light and I was somehow surprised and reassured to find that the world outside was just the same – the summer evening light was just as lovely and the curve of the downs just as delicious as it was last night – as it had always been. I wandered over to my tent and had started to undress slowly and thoughtfully – 'I wonder what they'll say at home when they here [*sic*] the news in the morning – How awful it is to know this and not be able to tell anybody –' Then slowly I was conscious of the soft roaring of engines in the sky – so slow that I couldn't remember when I had first heard it. I went out – it was dark now and and [*sic*] I looked out over the downs in the direction from which I thought the sound was coming – and saw hundreds of little pink lights in the sky – travelling slowly oh! so slowly in groups towards me – The gliders – Slowly they came on – so slowly that I wondered how they could hang like that in the sky – and in about a quarter of an hour they were over my head – they did not look to be more than a thousand feet up but all one could see was the pinkish light each one carried – The sky was full of them and the roaring of the engines of the 'tugs' – it seemed to come up out of the earth –. 'Good luck' – I found myself whispering – 'Oh good luck' – All night long they went over – sleep was impossible – I could not understand how I was living so calmly and so safely through such a night.

At the foot of this piece is a pencilled annotation: 'I *love* the stuff of this, and, maybe, because I remember how it all happened, and it was so like this, I get a lump in my throat in the last 4 lines! – PP'[3]

Derek had added his endorsement. He, too, would describe that night, but in doing so would give the impression that he was alone in a long and empty dormitory because the remainder of the Wing had 'taken off for war' and he had been left to analyse some photographs which might supply worrying proof that the 21st Panzer Division had moved 'East of Caen': 'Everyone in the world it seemed was airborne except me,' he wrote. Hearing 'the distant roar of a thousand thousand planes begin to fill the sky', he crawled out of bed and stood by the windows until their frames began to rattle, the wooden floor started to tremble and the entire sky became 'darker than night with the enormity of the massed planes, thundering, wave after wave after wave, unceasingly, towards France'. Forced to his knees by 'the terror and magnitude of the noise above', he 'started to pray unthinkingly, something that was *not* a part of my being', his tears ran into his mouth as 'thin, diluted salt, like blood' and 'still the floor shook and trembled, the windows rattled and clattered and the air was sucked out of the room, roared back in, burst my eardrums and sent me crouching, burrowing into my bedroll'.[4] In truth his experience of that night must have been common to most of his colleagues. The main body of 39 Wing left Odiham on the 14th, 'D+8', and passed through camps near Salisbury and Winchester before embarking for Normandy from Gosport on the 25th. Derek was to follow one week later.

Jack Jones, on the other hand, was in the thick of it from the start. Having been invalided out of Light Coastal Forces, he was now in command of a landing-craft tank flotilla – a potentially far more hazardous posting. As the Normandy landings began he led the flotilla to Sword Beach, the most easterly of those in the British sector. The vessels to each side of him were blown up, but he managed to land all his payload of tanks and guns before discovering that his LCT, 593, had been badly holed. He could have abandoned her, but decided to try to effect repairs. He and his crew stayed on the beach for the next fortnight, under constant shelling from the heavy German artillery at Le Havre, but eventually managed to limp back to Portsmouth in a violent gale. The loss of one man, and the wounding of two others, would haunt him for years to come. He brought home a postcard of a more frivolous scene, yachts racing off the French coast. On the reverse Derek wrote that it had been ' "captured" by Tony' at La Brèche d'Hermanville on 15 June. Despite its modesty, a small cluster of pinholes indicates that it was an especially, if not uniquely, prized possession. And the traffic in gifts was not one-way. On arrival in England Jack will have found waiting for him some portraits of Derek, one of which would appear in *For the Time Being* above the caption: 'This reprehensible photograph was taken by my father on my last 48-hour leave, just before D-Day. I am wearing his boots and breeches from the Royal Artillery in the First World War, and my own tunic from the Queen's Royal Regiment. The disgraceful mix of uniforms I cannot explain. Maybe I had been riding that morning on the Downs?' An unlikely proposition, it must be said. Of much greater significance, however, is the inscription on the back of a second picture, showing Derek perched on a table and reading a map. Dated 17 June 1944, it reads: 'PP – to Tony, who shares my life'.

The Dakota carrying Derek landed on 1 July at Sommervieu, three miles from Bayeux, where in less than a fortnight the Royal Engineers had bulldozed farmland belonging to the Yvetot and Le Bret families, felled some 400 apple trees, and created for the British and Canadian forces B8 – an airstrip 1,200 metres long and eighty metres wide, with the necessary access routes, parking and service areas. Until D-Day the principal task of 39 Wing had been to provide the material from which the interpreters could evaluate bombing damage and assess the German defences at the Normandy beaches. The heavily armed, single-seater Mustangs had also carried out low-level sorties called 'rhubarbs' against supply trains and convoys. According to Richard Rohmer, one of the RCAF pilots based at B8, the planes of the RCAF's 430 and 414 Squadrons, and those of the RAF, were now deployed 'solely to tactical, photographic and artillery reconnaissance in support of the British and Canadian armies in their assault against the German fortifications on the Normandy coast. We became the eyes of the army, watching and reporting the enemy's every move in the area of the battlefield and the approaches to the front lines [...] we were all-seeing hawks scouring the ground for prey. However the Germans called us not "hawks" but "bloodhounds".'[5] What Rohmer and his fellow pilots spotted, and what Derek and Chris interpreted in their specially equipped truck on the edge of the airfield, indicated that 'our stay would be long and that the risks ahead would be high'.[6] Montgomery had failed to take Caen and there was vicious fighting in the twenty-mile stretch of what was to become known as the Falaise Gap. Yet, apart from isolated incidents when a lone Focke-Wolf sprayed B8 with Bofors fire and a Messerschmitt was chased across the airstrip by Spitfires, the most common threat to those now encamped outside the Yvetots' St Sulpice farmhouse came from the shrapnel hurtling earthwards as the Allies' anti-aircraft guns defended the Mulberry Harbour at Arromanches.

Derek put up his tent in the orchard, dug his slit trench and reconciled himself to the ten-seater latrine separated from the world by a burlap. Two days after landing, he drew the 'View from my tent', a modest sketch which would before long join the British Museum's collection of modern prints and drawings. On Sunday, 16 July, at 11.15 p.m., he began typing Elizabeth 'a delayed letter from your erring brother', saying he had nearly missed the plane – 'Typical of me; I miss everything, and anything these days' – but that he was at long last in France. 'Lots of it would bore you to death,' he wrote. 'Lots of it would excite you. There seems to be no limit to the make-up, scent, and stockings, tho' silk ones are getting rare these days.' He promised to bring, or send, her what he could 'as soon as the mail business clears itself up a bit. I'd hate to trust anything valuable in the post these days.' Then he added some fashion notes:

> The hats here are really very odd, immensely tall, sometimes two or two and a half feet high. Enormous affairs of lace and feathers and flowers ... whole seagulls perched, with open wings, on top of the head. Awful in a gale, I should think ... and in the nesting season. Shoes are all wedge type, and very high off the ground ... almost like stilts ... and as there is no leather, they are made of pink plated paper! Which goes soggy in wet weather ... the soles are made of wood ... but they look nice, and are all kinds of odd colors. Earings are the great thing ... whopping big ones too. Made from Glass, wood, or beads. Hope this is not boring you to death? What else can I tell you about ... you'd hate to be told the war bits ... any way you get enough of that at home. Things are fairly quiet at the moment, we have some noisy nights and things go up, and a few come down ... it's very beautiful to watch ... if you feel like watching, that is.

He bewailed the lack of mail – but 'Tony writes every day, and I get them in bundles of 8 or 9 twice a week' – and asked for her news, 'any old thing which will bring a memory of Brighton, Clayton, or Home into this smelly French Orchard':

> Yes, my dear, we are living in an orchard, rather like the one at Milnthorpe … full of trees. We also have a cow, tied to a post all day, called Marie. She loves us all devotedly, because we feed her Biscuits and odd pieces of chocolate … she also has a yen for Gin! And will jig happily all over the place if given a little glass.
>
> Dear Marie. Quite soon she is to go to the butchers, I hear … well she ought to make good meat … she's bung full of biscuits, chocolate, and gin … ought to be tasty. I'v been doing a bit of painting recently … ruins and things, not bad. I'm sending them to Daddy … so you ought to see them if they ever arrive.
>
> Out of the corner of my eye, I see the work for the night has come in … I must fly.

The 'war bits' he confided to his father and to his drawing-paper. He sketched in the ruins at Tilly-sur-Seulles, a village on a crucial crossroads, which in eleven June days had changed hands twenty-three times and where seventy of its inhabitants had been killed; at Villers-Bocage, where the 7th Armoured Division had been beaten back by Rommel's Panzers; and at Carpiquet and Caen, finally liberated in early July. The destruction and the loss of life affected him profoundly, as did the awful ironies of war: none more so than the wind bearing away leaflets dropped by the Allies to warn inhabitants that their village or town was to be targeted. 'Death', he would write forty years later, 'was monarch of that summer landscape'.[7] As for 'the work', conditions contrasted greatly with those he had found at Medmenham, RAF Benson and Southwick Park, where manpower was backed by immense technical resources; here, quite literally in the field, immediacy was the key. On 1 August, in fading light, Richard Rohmer was heading back to Sommervieu in his Mustang when the flash of a gun caught his attention: 'I went into a gentle bank to see what was firing. To my astonishment I found I was sitting over dozens of tanks, probably the greatest number I had ever seen in one place in a battle situation.' It was 'an incredible sight, one extremely exciting for a young bloodhound. The long guns hanging way out over the front of the tanks signalled only one thing to me. They were German Tigers!'[8] They were in an area over which radio silence was the rule, but Rohmer called his control and, before turning for home, snapped off a few pictures. When he landed he was given a severe roasting because he had broken silence and given away vital intelligence: needlessly, too, because the position of the tanks 'inside our bomb-line' meant that they had to be British. There was only one escape from a probable court martial: the photographs. He took the wet prints from the

developing unit and headed for the Army Photographic Interpretation Section
truck:

> Bursting in on the startled APIS duty officer, who was unaccustomed to seeing
> a pilot in his place of business at that time of night, I quickly explained the
> situation, produced my photographs and asked him to make a judgment. What
> were those tanks?
>
> With no great haste he took the films, put them together in front of him,
> picked up the main tool of his trade, a pair of stereo lenses which when placed
> over two in-line photographs gave him a three-dimensional view of the objects
> in the photographs. By this time I was in a terrible state of anxiety. But still he
> was in no hurry. Studying the images below him he emitted two or three
> contemplative grunts. Then, laconically, and without even looking up, he said,
> 'They're Tigers.'
>
> Thank Christ! I could have kissed him.[9]

They never met again, but in 1980 Major-General Rohmer picked up a copy
of *Snakes and Ladders*, read that the twenty-three-year-old Derek had been at B8
and wrote to ask whether he had been the duty APIS officer that August night
when the photographs Rohmer was enclosing were interpreted. Back came the
reply: 'Right off I KNEW the Sortie-Snap.'[10] A brief correspondence ensued,
and convinced the Major-General that Derek had been his saviour.

As Monty's 2nd Army, led by General Sir Miles Dempsey, began to prevail,
the lulls increased. One of Ulric's photographers, Bill Warhurst, arrived at
Sommervieu and took a series of pictures showing 39 Wing's four APIS officers –
Derek, Chris, Captain Kenneth Costin and Derek's boss, Captain Sydney Allen –
taking 'A Rest from the Line'. One of the prints features Marie the cow, evidently
still worth more for her milk and her company than for her flesh. On 5 August
Derek wrote to Elizabeth, commiserating over a romantic disaster with a solicitor – 'there are tons of fish in the sea' – and making in her favour disparaging
remarks about Nerine and Angela Hatfield:

> The bloke you will have to marry, wont be a blond major, or yet a simpering
> subaltern ... no, you must get yourself a worthwhile person. And you will.
> Dont take any notice of these War-time affairs ... such as they are, they are all
> phoney ... I know too many of the blokes. Out for a day or an evenings fun.
> You and I wont get married for ages and ages, we'll write, or paint, and have
> lots of charming and amusing love affairs, and be terribly interesting all the
> time. You bet you will.
>
> And when I do come home, which wont be long now, I think, you and I
> shall do things in a big way ... I'll make you so bloody Ritzy and sophisticated
> and gay, that you wont know youself.

He said he had more soap than he would ever need, likewise cigarettes, but appealed for 'a bundle of old Magazines' once in a while – 'not the new ones, just a few back copies of the Tatler or Sketch or Theatre world'. In reply to Elizabeth's suggestion that her fellow Wrens might correspond with the lads of 39 Wing, he wrote:

> About this Pen pal business ... What about it indeed! Are'nt there enough glam. Naval types for all your sex starved little things; surely there are! But if they want to write tell 'em all to! We'd love it out here, we dont get much mail at all ... and there are one or two good looking blokes with me.
>
> [...] Its wet again today, and life is pretty well hell, however there is a war on, or so they say. And things are pretty exciting these days one way and another, and I feel that I sahll be home very much sooner than I expected. Unless I land up in Japan! which is a little unlikely ... By the way, for God's sake pull that awful photo of me down, its Hell. Warhurst took some very amusing ones last week, take the best of them. Those pansy ones stink ... I look as if I was pregnant or something awful.
>
> I'll send you one that I had taken here in my very Glamorous breeches and shirt, looking ever such a soldier, and so dashing. then you can have copies made and hung in all the WREN Lavs ... such fun ... until they run short of Izal!
>
> Sorry, I forgot you dont like me to be rude, but I just am, so there you are.

He concluded by advising his sister to 'keep away from Buzz bombs and things ... they are almost as dangerous as Blond majors ... or pilot officers with little black whiskers under their noses'.

A week later 39 Wing was on the move, to Ste Honorine de Ducy. The weather and morale improved. By the end of the month the battle for the Falaise Gap was won and the Allies were in Paris. As the Wing moved again, to Evreux, it passed the devastation at Villers-Bocage, Condé, Falaise itself and the nearby fields of Chambois where, as the unit's own magazine recorded, 'entire German convoys had been caught by the "Eyes of the Army" and then came the rocket Typhoons and dive bombers to sow death and chaos amongst them. In lanes, on open fields, under hedges they lay dead in groups. These men had died for Adolf Hitler. It was a terrible sight and yet more sorrow was expressed for the poor horses that lay dead by the hundreds in this carnage.'[11]

Derek and Chris, like many of their colleagues, carried out their own unofficial liberation of the French capital. Maybe the Germans were still 'banging away' so that their bullets 'whined and zinged all about us like mad hornets'.[12] More certain is that near Pontoise, about eighteen miles from the city, they arrived in their jeep outside a large country house just as the Germans were leaving. A woman flung her arms in joy around Chris's neck and said: 'It *had* to be you!' They had stumbled on a family with whom Chris and his sister had been on exchange visits during the thirties. If their reception in and around Paris was enthusiastic, they encountered unbridled ecstasy when 39 Wing followed in the wake of 2nd Army's hell-for-leather push north and crossed the border into Belgium. Lieutenant-General Brian Horrocks, Commander of 30 Corps, recalled that as they entered Brussels:

> From every house people poured into the empty streets, until it was almost impossible for the tanks to get through. There were flowers, fruit, champagne, girls on the vehicles and such kissing as has probably never been seen before or since! By now we had all become connoisseurs of liberation ceremonies, which had been going on in every town and village since we had crossed the Seine; but everyone agreed that the welcome by the citizens of Brussels had never been equalled.[13]

That was on Sunday, 3 September, and by the time the main body of the Wing reached the city a week or ten days later, the welcome was just as warm. It would seem, however, that Derek and Chris, with the latter's batman-driver, had gone on ahead, because the account which opens *Cleared for Take-Off* has their jeep meandering through the 'screaming, delirious population' on Monday the 4th. Again, it is of little consequence, but for the fact that on a card to Elizabeth dated the 22nd, and posted from Belgium, Derek hopes she has received a handkerchief he sent her from Paris, and makes no mention of visiting Brussels; on a second card, dated the 30th, he says in a low-key way: 'I spent a day here recently, and also a lot of money! Got you some bits and pieces which I'll give you when we meet, soon I hope.' Little sign of a brush with hysteria there. A further omission is any visit to Izegem or Kortrijk. In *Cleared for Take-Off* Derek adopts the 'fearfully romantic' idea 'of swanning up to the family château and liberating them all'; but when they arrive at 'Courtelle' they find a town decidedly not *en fête* and 'no sign of life anywhere' at the Van den Bogaerdes' house. Just an old boy with 'oyster-dead eyes', wearing wooden clogs and a cap from the 'Palace Hotel', who hobbles out of a doorway with a sack over his shoulders and in a brief exchange claims to have been Aimé's groom as a boy. 'The old man shrugged, and asked if I was part of the family. And I said again that I was, and he just said everyone was away, they would not welcome strangers.' Chris and Derek speed off.

> Somehow I had had a lyrical, theatrical vision of it all being very different indeed. I had imagined (in those drifting moments just before sleep) that we would have been received with enthralled rapture by a flag-bedecked town, that all the dignitaries would have hastened to welcome us: the mayor, the mayor's wife even, my long-lost family – I didn't know how many, but masses of them – the priests, and perhaps even the bishop or someone tremendously grand, with a crozier and pointed hat, acres of lace and flowing vestments.

We'd have been taken in a procession (I was certain it would have been a formal procession) all the way to the great church with the high spire where all my relatives would have been laid to rest (after all, they ran the town). Then after a solemn mass, with censers and altar boys flying about, we'd be led down into the huge tombs under the altar: arches and pillars and flaming torches, and under the most enormous and elaborate tomb, perhaps with my great-great-great-great-grandparents, lying side by side in stone, with ruffs, clasped hands, and their pointed feet lying on little stone dogs, would be marvellous family treasure! Then the bishop, or maybe the senior member of the family, would give a signal to four strong townsmen, and I would be brought respectfully to the side of the tomb as the great stone lid was jemmied open, so that I could pay my respects to the dusty relics of my ancestors and their fortunes. But instead of dusty relics from the Middle Ages, all there would be in the tomb would be the *entire* contents of all the town's wine cellars hidden during the German Occupation! Bottles and bottles of Krug, Lafite, Château-Yquem and so on (I was, at that time, a bit hazy about my wines, and these were the ones which most loudly beckoned). My 'imagining' continued with a tremendous kind of bacchanalia under the soaring arches in the flickering light of the fires. But, of course, it wasn't ever like that, and perhaps just as well. I imagined it all so completely, and in such detail, that finally I almost came to believe it had actually taken place, the bishop, the Krug and all.[14]

This extract belongs on the wilder shores even of *his* fancy. Izegem was no different from any other Belgian town, in that for months after the liberation anyone in an Allied uniform was treated like visiting royalty. Madeleine Phillips, one of Derek's distant cousins, was living in the family's other château at the time and remembers how they would stop Army trucks at random and invite the soldiers to lunch. Furthermore, Wolvenhof was never empty; of course the Van den Bogaerdes would have been at home.[15] Perhaps Derek *needed* to believe that he and Chris had been there. For this same Flanders where Ulric had fought, and which he himself had now helped to free, exerted no pull on his heart; just the occasional tweak on his curiosity.

The latest airstrip for 39 Wing had been laid in an open field on the crest of a hill near Diest, some thirty miles north-east of Brussels. Derek and his colleagues arrived there in the same week that Eisenhower and Montgomery had begun 'Market-Garden', their audacious initiative to end the war by deploying virtually the entire First Allied Airborne Army of American, British and Polish troops to seize and hold all the most important bridges on the Lower Rhine so that they could be joined by ground forces to liberate Holland, capture the Ruhr and press on to Berlin. The weather collapsed and for ten days, while the operation foundered, the Canadians' fighter aircraft stood impotently in a quagmire. 'At this very moment when the Army needed us desperately we were condemned to agonizing idleness,' wrote the Wing's historian.[16] The order finally came to leave, and 'Like a great prehistoric monster that slowly stirs in its bed of mud, 39 Wing strained and pulled to lift itself from that bog in Belgium.' The next stop was Eindhoven in Holland. Little did they know it, but it would be a long time before they would move again.

On 1 October Derek was promoted Acting Captain. Two days later, after nearly twenty-four hours on duty, he wrote to Elizabeth, keener to celebrate a no less coveted honour:

> You'll never guess where I am now at this moment! I am lying full length in a wonderful bed with feather matress and 2 fat pillows, in my own little room, right under the roof, in a Dutch cottage! Yes – we have left our tents and are now billited in Cottages with wonderful people whome I cant understand, and who cant understand a word I say! So refreshing. This is a great joy for me, to be in a real bed, in a real room again! But I dont suppose it will last for long.

It did for a while. On the 17th he wrote again, saying the bundle of magazines she had sent were a big success, 'and we all adored having them in the Mess, need I say that the film mag has been cut to ribbons, and all the "glam" women now adorne the bare walls of the School Room which we use as a mess, its a bit trying to have so much female beauty, undressed, about the place, especially at breakfast!' Four days later his mood was much changed. He had been given a new posting, with (Main HQ) 50 Northumbrian Division, part of 30 Corps, which was stationed in an area known as 'the island', between the Waal and Nederrijn bridges at Nijmegen and Arnhem respectively. Suddenly he was back with the Army, and he was none too happy: '[. . .] Ive been in this bloody country for a month now – and loath it more than I can say – rain and mist – a howling gale, mud and the eternal guns all day and all night. And having left, temporarily, the old crowd, I hate it worse than ever. I hope to get back to the old crowd as soon as possible – This job is rotten – I am worth more than this, and I've let them know at HQ!' His card crossed with a letter from Elizabeth and on the 23rd he wrote again: 'I'm working hard, and hating life here at the moment, just a mood, but I've got a new job – wot I dont like.' He had some cause for cheer: 'I'm so glad you like Anthony now – its grand to know you do – and that you have accepted him as your half-brother! Cos thats what he's going to be from now on chum!'

On the 28th he typed a long letter to his parents, lamenting the fact that he was away from his 'trusted and devoted friends' at the Wing, but saying he had managed the day before to 'get down to the old place', where 'they miss me as I miss them':

> [. . .] Sydney, my boss, has flown to England today on a very special job . . . cant tell you what it is . . . but it's a feather in his cap . . . Tonight, an hour ago,

Derek's paternal grandfather, Aimé Van den Bogaerde (centre), in the Colombian jungle, 1899. Propped against the wall above the table are the photographs (right and below right) of Grace and Ulric.

Derek's paternal grandmother, Grace.

The local newspaper announces the death of Aimé's cousin, Valère, aged 49.

His father, Ulric, aged about seven.

Derek's maternal grandfather,
Forrest Niven.

Grandmother Jane's 1886 Christmas card,
drawn by Forrest; they were married seven
months later.

A family photograph of
Margaret, inscribed on
the reverse: 'Forrest says
Madge is waiting for the
Wolf'.

Derek's mother, Margaret,
praised as 'an excellent
entertainer'.

December 21, 1918   The Scots Pictorial

The Onlooker

THE COURT

The Queen's Varied Afternoon

THE Queen, of necessity, has many and varied experiences, but even she can seldom have had an afternoon's engagements so piquantly contrasted as happened one day last week. First, she put in an appearance at the private view of a doll show and sale at the Duchess of Marlborough's house in aid of the Children's Jewel Fund. Then she went, practically on the spur of the moment, to the West Ham Central Mission Women's meeting, where over 1000 women of the very humblest class were being entertained to tea in celebration of the coming of peace. Dressed as she had come from the ducal mansion, where the most celebrated of actresses, in gloss of satin and glimmer of pearls, exquisitely furred, scented, and deferential, surrounded her, the Queen sat down among the women of West Ham and drank tea with them. It was an occasion they will never forget, and it is not drawing upon imagination, but upon what one really knows of the Queen, to say that probably she enjoyed the assemblage in "darkest London" considerably more than the gathering in Mayfair.

The King at Home Again

THE King returned from France last week after a fortnight which contained some of the most thrilling experiences of his life. He was very tired on arrival, but lost no time in taking up the routine of State business. Prince Albert returned with his father, but they parted from the Prince of Wales in Belgium, and he went on to Brussels. It is not yet known whether the Heir-apparent will be home for Christmas, ... will be spent by the Court at York ... allowed ...

planning a happy domestic reunion at Sandringham, at which the King and Queen, her three daughters, all her grandchildren, and her great-grandson will be present. Queen Maud, by the way, has not yet seen her great-nephew, the son of Prince and Princess Arthur of Connaught, as he was born after the

Miss MADGE NIVEN, daughter of Glasgow's erstwhile well-known cartoonist, is an excellent entertainer. She has delighted thousands of our wounded soldiers with her readings and mimic impersonations.

outbreak of war, and she will be surprised to find him such a well-grown sturdy boy. The Royalties ... on the other hand, have no less ... surprise at ...

Popular Queen Maud

THE welcome extended to the daughter of King Edward and Alexandra would be sufficient ... dial on her own account, since was extremely popular in her land always, and its warmth is cert... not diminished by the remembrance all that Norway has done for us during the war. Comparisons ... odious, but it seems no more than justice to describe her as the best friend we have had among the neutral nations. Queen Maud still retains her home at Appleton Hall, near Sandringham, and it has been put in readiness for her, but probably she will spend a good deal of time with her mother. In the old days the Queen of Norway came to England for the celebration of her own birthday, and that of her mother a week later, returning to Christiania for Christmas, but the arrangement was not found possible this year. King Haakon may come from Norway for a few days later, ...

A Scottish Diary
December 18, 1918

Princess Louise, Duchess of Argyll, returned to her residence at Kensington Palace last week after her visit to Edinburgh, where she fulfilled philanthropic and charitable engagements. She is very fond of Edinburgh, as she is, indeed, of Glasgow and Scotland generally.

It may safely be said that Princess Louise is fonder of Scotland than is any other member of the Royal Family, with the possible exception of the Princess Royal. But the younger Princess's heart is mainly centred in the Highlands, in and about Mar Lodge, to be quite accurate. She has never moved about its cities as freely as does her aunt.

The newly-commissioned Ulric.

Ulric in his office at *The Times*, 1920; a self-portrait drawn for his secretary, Ivy Heath.

The couple captured on camera in 1920 at St George's Road, Kilburn, using Ulric's expertise as a photographer.

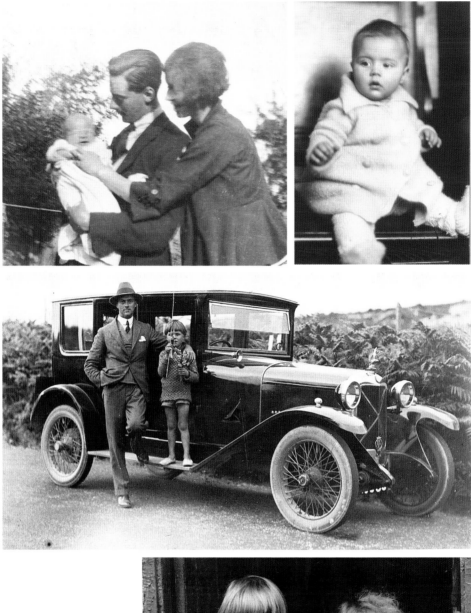

Clockwide from top left
The proud parents, 1921;
Derek in his first year;
Derek and Ulric with one
of the latter's fine motors -
a Salmson; the siblings, 1927.

Top The Cottage, the church, the Diplocks' house and (far left) the privy in an aerial photograph arranged by the resourceful, ever-experimenting Ulric; *Inset (left)* the Church of the Good Shepherd in a sketch sent by Ulric to his elder son at Christmas, 1971; *(right)* the Cottage, Lullington.

Above (left) A day out, probably with 'Uncle Salmon' behind the camera, at Lullington; *(centre)* Margaret and Lally at the Cottage; *(right)* Ulric and Margaret on the Sussex Downs - the caption in Derek's album reads 'Lovers' Lane'.

UNIVERSITY COLLEGE SCHOOL
JUNIOR BRANCH

Lent Term. Session 1933-34

Name van Bogaerde, D.N. House Campbell Form VIb

Age on July 31st, 1933 12.4 Average age of Form 12:0 Age—Height—Weight—Ratio ___ %

SUBJECT	Place	% of Marks	Form av. Marks	Apprehension	Diligence	REMARKS
English (counts double)				v.f	v.f	Promise - in this way of oral work - is always so much better than performance in written work.
Mathematics (counts double)				g.	r.g	Seems to try but results poor.
French				v.f	v.f	Good at translation, work in composition.
History				v.f	improved	I cannot understand why he finds it so difficult to transfer his ideas to paper successfully.
Geography						Satisfactory
Nature Study				f.g	f.g	Should try to write & draw more accurately
Drawing				g.	g.	
Latin				g	g	Very promising.
Music (counts half)				v.f	v.f	average
Handwork						fair.
Physical Exercise						

Marks obtained ___ %   Position in Form no places

No. of times absent { M. 28 A. 14 }   No. of times late { M. .... A. .... }

House Report   Head Master's Report

Has still to learn that   He makes me impatient but
life is not all cushions I am trying to be more
& barley sugar. C.G.7.S philosophical about him -
                          time will show   Bernard Lake
Beginning of next Term May 2nd at 9.10 a.m.

Parents are expected to inform the Head Master at once of any case of infectious illness occurring in their homes.

Above Class 1a at Allan Glen's, with a pugnacious Derek at the back and William Lockie in the next row.

Right A picture of his mother which Derek kept with him during the 'Anthracite Years'.

Below (left and centre) Sarah and William Murray (Aunt Sadie and Uncle Murray), photographed a few years before Derek came to stay in Bishopbriggs; *(right)* Hester McClellan (née Niven), the aunt with whom he found refuge for his third year in Glasgow, photographed in about 1930 with her daughter, Nickie, and a visiting Derek.

A study by Derek of the Queen Mary four days before her launching on the Clyde in 1934.

Drawings made by Derek in his exercise-book during the final year at Allan Glen's and given to Bill Lockie.

I got the *most* wonderful letter from him, saying that it was only my influence, and my spirits which inspired him to do the job as well as he has done!! said that I was to take as much credit for it as he . . . because 'If it had not been for you, Pip, nothing would ever have happened'.

Was'nt that a wonderful thing to read about yourself in a letter? Especially as Sydney is a very controlled man . . . not by any means an emotionalist like me . . . and writing that must have cost him a good deal. Needless to say it has made me awfully happy myself. Not often your boss says such tremendous things.

And it's all because Maggie gave me her stupid sense of humour . . . is'nt it funny, I'm able to laugh, and make others laugh, in a spot of bother . . . much more than when life is being staid and normal. Whooo!! But are'nt I a conceited sod? Dont worry, I'm only telling you both . . . and Tony [. . .]

He went on to describe the new conditions:

I've got the usual cold, it's all this mud and rain and living in a shell pocked attic. Did I tell you that I am sleeping in the attic of a house with 9 old men, 2 old women, a boy of 10, and the milk-maid . . . (A comley bit) . . . they are all refugees from the village up the road which is now in the front line, and about 2 inches high . . . But to return to my Ark like existance . . . it is quite, quite wonderful . . . no one is embarressed, except me!! The Milk maid, Yannie, Slips into her nighty nightly, with giggles of maidenly joy, and ever such a come-and-be-allied look in her eye. And I could'nt care less.

I tactfully put a curtain up the first night . . . so she moved her matress . . . so trying. And one of the old men snores just exactly like the sound of a falling shell, so that one wakes up in the night and positively ducks . . . incase the thing bursts in the room . . . then you see it's only him . . . and go back to sleep again.

Poor beggars . . . lost all they have, except their matresses and a couple of pots and pans . . . and, as usual, the odd dog and canary.

I forgot to say that immediately below our 'Room' there are 20 or 30 chickens, a large sow, and a gaggle of geese . . . wont I ever get away from geese . . . awful things [. . .]

This drab period was described by the Divisional historians as one of 'static warfare',[17] but the work had its lighter moments. The War Diary for 50 Division on 23 October noted that a deserter who brought information of a planned German attack at Nijmegen had been an ex-music-hall artist, called up at the end of July after Goebbels had closed all theatres and places of entertainment. He had been dropped by his wife during their act and broke his knee, 'thus qualifying him for 41 Fortress Bn'.[18] Derek's letter explains further:

Was talking today with another prisoner ... spoke a little English ... stood about 4 foot high. Told me he was a cabaret artist in Leipzig ... one of a team who called themselves 'Viola unt Pardner' Viola being his wife ... and what a wife! Massive piece of Brunhilda ... with flaming red hair and a mouth like a closed rat trap ... she used to wear sequins and roller skates and chuck poor old dad all over the music halls of Europe ... one day she chucked the poor little blighter too far ... into the orchestra, and broke his knee, which act, caused him to be exempt from the army until Gobbles called him up in July ... Viola was shoved into the German ATS ... and, as he said, is playing hell with the SS brigade. I can well believe it ... all very Wagner and Tutonic ... so one night Dad, lying out in his little hole, got fed to the teeth with life, and walked over to our lines singing 'Roll out the Barrel' of ALL things to sing! And he proved a very useful chap God knows where he is now ... but he has asked me to look Viola up if I ever go to Essen ... and to tell her that he is alright and with the Tommies. I only hope to God I never go to Essen ... next to Total War I can think of nothing more unpleasant than Viola [...]

Oddly enough, Derek *would* go to Essen, but not for twenty-four years, by which time looking Viola up had receded as a priority.

At the end of November he told Elizabeth he was 'back at my old address at last, thank God'. It was not only the shells and the mud that had depressed him. Neville Beale, an RAF aircraftman who had been working with 39 Wing as a meteorologist since before D-Day, remembers how much less 'stuffy' the Canadians were than their English counterparts, and how they numbered fewer 'bullshitters' than the Americans – partly, he thinks, because all had volunteered to fight in Europe: no Canadian conscript could be sent unwillingly abroad.[19] Certainly Derek's reception on returning to 39 Wing was in sharp contrast to that from 214 Independent Infantry Brigade, on which he had recently called. Hubert Essame's brigade, which had played an active role in 'Overlord' since D-Day, had been involved in sustained and bitter fighting, with many casualties, and were holed up at Elst, on the road from Nijmegen to Arnhem, when Derek arrived:

There was no one I knew in the Mess in the shell-pocked red-brick château which his Brigade occupied. They were polite, if evasive, all looked rather young and new. Eventually he came into the room – we were having tea – glanced at me, sat down, crossed his shining little booted feet, milked his tea and asked me if I had enjoyed, what he called, 'your cushy job'. There was no forgiveness. He had lost too many since the Normandy landings, and made it clear. 'Won't find anyone you used to know here now; all gone. We lost more than half the Brigade. Bloody lucky for you that you got out when you did.'

There was nothing to say. Useless to try and explain that he had been my catalyst, and that even though I was still alive and in his Mess, there had been times … useless. I left very shortly afterwards; he was reading and didn't look up.[20]

John Denison, who was otherwise engaged, recalls that no one who missed Derek's visit had been particularly sad. At times like that, with wounds being licked, the 'poor bloody infantry' took a rather dim view of 'swanning about' by someone who they did, indeed, believe was in a 'cushy job'.[21] The atmosphere at the former primary school building in Eindhoven where 2nd Army had based its APIS operations was altogether more tolerant. Geoffrey Stone, who joined the section in November, described it as 'a fluctuating population – quite academic or sub-academic'. Before being introduced, he was told 'by someone with his tongue slightly in his cheek' about 'this young actor – wait till you see him!' Stone, who was to work alongside Derek for some weeks, had never met anyone quite like him before:

> He was extremely amiable and could turn on the charm. He was inclined to be not frightfully punctual, and was quite prepared to get someone else to do a bit of work for him if they were willing. My impression was that he was a bit of a dilettante, a bit of a poseur. He liked to play the young actor. He reminded me of Bunthorne, the aesthete in [Gilbert and Sullivan's] 'Patience' – I could just imagine him with a daffodil or a lily. I didn't regard him as someone who would carry much weight with hard-bitten soldiers. He struck me as effeminate, effete, but we wouldn't have talked of him as a homosexual – if it was thought, it was never spoken. He was acting the whole time. He defined a role for himself and played it for all it was worth. But no one held it against him.[22]

To his immediate colleagues, then, Derek was in both senses an 'acting captain'. Major E. W. (Ted) Espenhahn was in command of the photographic interpreters from 21 Army Group and 2nd Army – about sixty in all – and would visit the latter every two or three weeks. He found Derek 'on a par with the others, some of whom I had known for a year or more. He certainly wasn't one of those for whom one had been asked to find other jobs. 2nd Army seemed to be a particularly happy bunch of people and very effective, as far as one knew. Looking back on it, one wonders what one did all the time!'[23] Geoffrey Stone, who inevitably saw much more of him, said Derek 'was quite different from everyone else, and they were prepared to indulge him. Some even regarded him as a bit of a pet – like his puppy.' For, yes, Derek had acquired a young hound, whom he called variously 'Chug' or 'Peewee' – the latter for obvious reasons. 'In the peacetime Army,' recalls Stone, 'dogs were fairly common. But not in war. Everyone thought it was typical of Derek that he had adopted this puppy. No one else would have kept it, but he did. It was quite a small dog, but it grew to be a large one. He had been misled about it.' Derek sent both Elizabeth and Jack photographs of himself cradling the four-legged refugee, but common sense prevailed. On 9 January 1945, he wrote to Elizabeth that 'he is now living with a local Baroness – much better than with me – he is an awful pest!'

Despite some dire weather, life at Eindhoven was none too tough. Photographs show Derek, Chris and Sydney Allen relaxed and well. Derek went to the cinema twice a week and 'got well in' with the forces' theatre companies – 'all very good for me after the war'. For a week, in an ENSA performance of *The Merry Widow*, Cyril Ritchard and Madge Elliott 'burst into our delighted, amazed, deprived lives'.[24] At one point Derek himself was writing a play, but its fate is not known. There was time, too, for portraits to be taken at a photographic studio in the town; 'glam' pictures which he sent home to Margaret and to Jack. She was worried about Derek, and sought reassurance from the pleasant family with whom he was now lodging. A photograph shows a cheerful group of adults and children surrounding Derek and Chris at the mother's birthday party; and in a letter sent just before Christmas the parents tell Margaret that 'it is a real satisfaction to us, to be able to do something, by which our common unpleasantness of being separated from our sons may be relieved a little'. They sign off:

So long dear Madam, and not disturbing the romantic feelings of your son we remain his temporary

Papa & Mama

At its foot Derek adds: 'I think "papa" wrote this with the help of a Grammer Book, he does'nt speak a word of English himself – it must have taken weeks!' Yet despite the levity, his mother's need for reassurance was not misplaced. Northern Holland was still occupied by the Germans and, as the weather became harsher by the week, the population was suffering dreadful privations. At Eindhoven blizzards and freezing fog all but closed the Army's 'eyes'. On New Year's Day – which brought Derek another promotion, to Temporary Captain – about twenty Luftwaffe fighters caught the Wing on the ground, destroyed nine of its aircraft and damaged another thirteen; fifteen personnel were wounded. Even a good way behind the front line danger was ever-present.

Chris's sketchbook contains one short piece of writing, which seems to date from this period. He, Derek and Sydney Allen are sitting by the stove in the mess, which has pale oak chairs and a long low divan looted from the Germans; a cupboard turned on its side as a bar; another containing glasses, cutlery and a barrel of beer and the bottle of white wine from Normandy 'which is ceremoniously opened at 6.30 every night' by Driver Bell; a blackboard bearing the orders for the day and urgent appeals for mess bills to be paid; and 'bare walls covered with lewd drawings in high colour done by Pip and myself'. Pip is reading a novel called *Dusty Answer*; Sydney, *The Argosy*, 'Some inexpressibly lovely thing is coming over the radio', and they have the place to themselves:

[. . .] we are never all here together – which is a good thing – it is far too small –
There are always three or four of us out on jobs – usually delivery runs up to
the line – we have ceased to worry about whether they will come back – They
always do – except once – incredible that in all this we have only lost one
officer and two men – all in the same incident – he was an objectionable
fellow – the officer – but we were all very upset at the time – though nobody
said anything.

The 'delivery runs up to the line' took Derek over the Waal at Nijmegen. In
mid-January he sent Elizabeth a picture postcard, saying: 'I thought you would
be interested to have a look at this! Its going to be one of the most famous bridges
in history.' Little did he know how generally and personally prophetic that
remark would prove. 'I used to cross there 2 times a day, and they were always
shelling it! It was definately not a very nice ride – but, oddly enough, they did'nt
ever hit me and my jeep, tho' they came very near to it more than once!'
As the weather improved, the Allies pressed on. By the end of March, with
Derek now in his twenty-fifth year, the battles of the Bulge and the Rhineland
were won. With the crossing of the river itself, 'the curtain went up on the
terrors'.[25] The Wing was now in Lower Saxony and until the end of the war
would remain in the area. It was one that had no monopoly on the sites of
concentration and extermination camps – the entire map of Germany was
blistered with them, as if with a pox – but thirty miles north of Hanover lay the
two villages which gave their names to the ultimate symbol of Nazi excess:
Bergen-Belsen. There were a reported 45,000 internees and 1,500 cases of typhoid
when the camp was entered on 15 April by Lieutenant-Colonel Bob Daniell, of
the Royal Horse Artillery. Like those who were to follow him in the next few
days, he found himself as close as he would ever be to hell on earth.
    That same day 39 Wing reached Wunstorf, due west of the city. It would move
again on the 26th, to Reinsehlen near Soltau; and finally, on 6 May, to Lüneburg.
The route of that second leg, from Wunstorf to Reinsehlen, passed relatively
close to Bergen-Belsen.

Only during really bad thunderstorms would I remember Belsen, and the girl,
shorn head covered in scabs, face cracked with running sores from which she
carelessly waved away the April flies, who grabbed my hand and stumbled with
me along the sandy tracks amongst the filth, talking, crying, singing all at the
same time, pointing me out proudly as we went, her filthy striped skirt flapping,
breasts swinging like empty pockets against her rib-lined chest. A Corporal,
red-faced and gentle, took her from me and pulled us apart, thrusting her
away. She stood appalled for a moment, and then with cascading tears pressed
both hands to her lips and threw me kisses until I had gone from her sight.
    'Sorry, Sir,' apologetic, careful. 'Typhoid. The place is full of it . . . I reckon
they'll all go.'[26]

In *A Short Walk from Harrods* he would write of 'blundering into the unspeakable agony of Belsen, watching bulldozers shovel bloodied carnage into open graves';[27] and in *Backcloth*: 'In April, as the last of the snows melted in the larch forests like strips of soiled bandage, we came to Belsen and the first concentration camp: a hideous "liberation" this time which erased for ever the erroneous idea we had had that "Jerry is really just the same as us". No way was he.'[28] Then, from *An Orderly Man*, in 'Vught Camp, or perhaps in Belsen, I can't remember exactly which now (both were as terrible) I had wandered through huts piled high with the relics of human life';[29] and in *Cleared for Take-Off* he and Chris 'gratefully followed the black and yellow signs to Bergen-Belsen. Where we lost our boyish laughter for ever.'[30] In a 1991 letter he would ask rhetorically of the Roman Catholics who opposed the legalisation of voluntary euthanasia 'just *where* their God, or Jesus, was on the 13th–16th of April, '45 when I was standing among 60,000 dead and dying at Belsen'.[31] Most oddly, in a book review, his recollection was that he remembered that on a clear, cold, April morning – 'The 17th or 18th, not certain of the date, one seldom was in the war' – a report that the Germans had pulled back a few kilometres, abandoning a large concentration camp, prompted him to have a look.

> I was anxious, I recall, to acquire a pair of German boots . . . better than ours, and I had no more in my mind than that. I had known for some time that the camps existed – we saw them on our aerial photographs often enough – but it didn't really occur to me that through the greening larches and under a clear, hard, blue sky, the last traces of snow melting in the woods, I would be entering a hell which I should never forget and about which, for many years, I would be unable to speak.[32]

There is confusion here. There is also an extraordinary, indeed perplexing, contrast between these vivid accounts of being a witness to atrocity and the card he sent to Elizabeth on 21 April, hoping she was having a 'gay time' with her current beau, asking for her news, and reporting: 'We have been having the most beautiful weather here – I've actually been sunbathing, and got quite brown.' Nor was there a noticeable change of mood by 2 May, when he sent a card of Mount Ortler: 'I wish all Germany looked like this – It does'nt – looks like Hampstead Heath really.'

Perhaps this was another act – a total denial to others, if not to himself, of what he had seen; but given the exclusion zone around Bergen-Belsen in those early days after 2nd Army took it in hand; given the warnings about typhus; given the prohibition on access against all but essential personnel and a few accredited correspondents including, most famously, Richard Dimbleby – given all that, what would Derek have been doing even at the gates, let alone inside them? There can be no doubt that he encountered some of the consequences of the Holocaust. He wrote of a wood outside Soltau where in the dark pines 'tent-pegs driven in slid into slime. The stench then, and the massed grave . . .'.[33] There *was* a mass grave at Soltau, but in the town's cemetery, where some eighty unknown dead – thought to have been concentration camp inmates who had died or were murdered during one of the 'death marches' in April – were buried. In Holland he had been stationed not far from Vught, an internment camp for Gestapo prisoners and a transit camp for Jews, south-east of 's-Hertogenbosch. And as the Allies pushed north and east, the Wing passed within striking distance of several others. One of his few extant albums of photographs contains three tiny snapshots which are uniquely indistinct; the first shows Derek leaning on a small bridge in a thickly wooded area, with buildings in the background; the second is so blurred that it might be a double exposure; and the third has two tall, thin structures – possibly chimneys – on the edge of a smouldering forest. Why did he bother to fix them carefully in a book unless they had a special meaning? Expert eyes at the Wiener Library's Holocaust archive confirm that they might well have been taken in Lower Saxony; and Helen Bamber, who as a twenty-year-old member of the Jewish Relief Unit went to work at Belsen with its survivors, says that the third picture, with the twin structures, 'has an atmosphere for me' – one that is evocative, if not of Belsen itself, at least of another camp not far away called Kaunitz.[34] Nothing is certain. The safest conclusion is that the images are distilled in part from what Derek saw; in part from what he learned at second hand thanks to the unsparing newsreels and photographs of the time; and in part from what was conjured in that ever-active imagination. Some of those interviewed for this book said that received images were so vivid that soldiers serving in the vicinity of events became convinced that they had seen them for themselves. If that is what happened in Derek's case, there is, as we shall see, ample justification. After all, as the writer Frederic Raphael said: 'Belsen stood for something much worse even than Belsen itself.'[35]

On 4 May, at 2nd Army headquarters on Lüneburg Heath, Montgomery accepted the verbal surrender of the German forces, and hostilities formally ceased on the 6th. That day the Wing moved to Lüneburg. On the 7th, VE Day, Derek heard the reports that in Rheims General Jodl had signed Germany's capitulation. A letter to Ulric, reproduced in part in *Backcloth*, reads:

[. . .] if that is so, that's that. I don't know quite what will happen to me now, it's a bit sudden in some ways, but I expect I'll be given UK leave and then get shipped off to the Far East. There is still a war there. One sometimes forgets! It'll suit me in a way. I think I'll have a serious try at staying on with the Army: if I survive the next lot of course! I've enjoyed the companionship and the unexpected lack of responsibility. The Army, as far as it can, DOES take care of you, and I'm not at all certain now that I would ever be able to settle down among civilians again.[36]

One week later he had said farewell to the Canadians and to his 2nd Army colleagues. Their job was done. He was on his way back to England and, almost immediately, to his first brush with celebrity.

The show which had its private view on 17 May at the Batsford Gallery in North Audley Street, Mayfair, was entitled ' "With the BLA" 1944–1945' and according to the catalogue:

> The works shown in this exhibition, from the battlefields over the water, represent the impressions gained by two young artists who, in common with the flower of our race, forsook the constructive paths of peace to engage in the grim business of war. Captain Derek Van den Bogaerde and Flight Lieut. Christopher Greaves already had shown great promise in the arts before they became soldiers. So when they took to battledress and D-Day dawned, they carried to the great adventure something more than Army equipment.
>
> [. . .] From their first landing these two soldier-artists kept pencils and colours going. Amid rigorous routine, quick action, and weariness, they snatched every possible chance to express in their own way the day-to-day scenes around them in the passage through France and Belgium. They saw stark realism, and strange contrasts of brilliance, beauty, horror and devastation alternating in quick succession. They worked from jeeps and shell-holes, in dust and rain, among unexploded bombs, booby-traps, and the smell of dead things, with the sound of gunfire never absent . . .

On the gallery walls were forty-seven watercolour drawings, of which twenty-seven were signed by Derek. Two had already been 'sold' – one, of the beach at Asnelles, was reserved for Jack. Red spots proliferated during the private view. 'Tents in Orchard, 1944' – the drawing he made two days after arriving at Sommervieu – was bought by the Contemporary Art Society and given to the British Museum. More important still was the review a few days later in *The Times*, contrasting the technique of Chris – 'primarily a pen draughtsman' – with that of Derek, who 'seems to think primarily in water-colour, which he uses very effectively. He has the gift of suggesting the character of a scene, and he brings the physical nature of the campaign vividly before the eye.' The anonymous critic found the influence of Sir Muirhead Bone and Edward Ardizzone in Derek's work; 'But Captain Bogaerde has talent on his own account, and he and his companion-in arms and in arts – have provided an interesting record of things seen and experienced by those who went to France to fight.'[37] Socially, too, the event was enjoyable. Chris's brother remembers Ulric hosting a celebratory lunch at the Cumberland Hotel, where John Greaves noted another contrast: that between the quiet Ulric and his wife. 'Margaret was an extremely glamorous and striking woman. I remember she was wearing a black two-piece in stiff silk. She was gregarious, open, charming and relaxed.' In other words, in her element, even if not quite top of the bill.

The exhibition ran until 9 June. The partnership with Chris was over and, although there would be spasmodic contact in years to come, their new worlds would have little in common. Chris resumed his career as a commercial artist, taught at the London School of Printing and became art director of three London advertising agencies before being made redundant by an American pharmaceutical company. With his pay-off he and his wife Margaret opened a craft shop on the harbour at Mousehole, one of the most beautiful coves in Cornwall, where they sold pottery, jewellery and a certain amount of what he called 'trippers' trash'. They had two sons and two daughters, but lost the second son to cancer at the age of seven – a tragedy from which Chris never recovered. When Margaret, too, died of cancer in 1985 his own life 'seemed to fall away from him'. His former comrade in arms and in arts told John Greaves: 'I did try, on two long occasions, to get him to try and write notes down for me of the things which he remembered us doing together in the war, but though he sounded excited [...] nothing, of course, came of it.' The end came on 30 October 1986:

> On a vicious winter's day, with the sea raging and a force nine gale battering the harbour, he was seen to stagger along the jetty carrying what appeared to be a package of books.
> His body was washed up a day or two later, weighted down with heavy stones. Finding life intolerable without her, in his quiet, deliberate, determined way, I imagine he had gone to join his wife.[38]

The reality was less dramatic and more poignant. Chris, by now alcoholic, depressed and helpless, had been taken into care in Penzance. He walked from the old people's home to the harbour at high tide, evidently intending to clean his soiled bedding, but slipped and fell into the water, where his floating body was seen by a holidaymaker. One of the witnesses at the inquest told the coroner that about three weeks before his death she had found Chris sitting, 'worse for wear', by the harbour, and he had said he was going to walk into the sea. She liked to think she had talked him out of it.[39]

The Far East was indeed to be Derek's next wartime theatre. In preparation, he was sent to the Intelligence Corps depot at Wentworth Woodhouse, a stately home near Sheffield that had been stripped of its furniture. The photographic interpreters were lodged in the lower servants' bedrooms at the top of the house. A bugle was the summons to lunch in a Nissen hut. Derek was there for only a few days, before a final snatched leave. He had a boat to catch; Jack had to go back into hospital for more operations on the neck wound that was to plague him for the rest of his life. Their time together was treasured. Jack's mother had returned from Wales to Suffolk and had bought a large house on the River Deben at Waldringfield, where he and his brother George started their respective yachting businesses in the loft above the garage – Jack as a designer, George as a broker. A friend of theirs, David East, said many years later that the Jack who had come through the war alive, 'albeit the worse for wear', was good-looking, a snappy dresser, and full of style and charm. He was also 'an ace communicator' and no mean hustler for business; if he saw the chance of a commission he would whip up to London and be at his table in Wheeler's, 'wining and dining and chatting up the client – and he was *very* good at it!' He loved the good life, and spent money like water; the bank was always on his tail. The smart restaurants, the hand-made shoes, the powerful motorbike – Jack had panache.[40] Around him at Waldringfield and, later, at Woodbridge congregated not only some of the most promising young designers, but also some of the good-looking young men who belonged or were drawn to the secluded yachting community. Derek, already averse to water, had little interest in anything that travelled through it, but he loved the riparian atmosphere. And he loved Jack, as Jack loved him. The voracious reader encouraged Derek to expand his knowledge of literature and, to a far lesser extent, his understanding of serious music. It should also be noted that they shared a fetish, which bonded them further, for leather and rubber; the mere sight of a diving suit was profoundly arousing and as for the motorcyclist's standard garb . . .

At the end of June they had a final holiday in Sussex, visiting another yachting idyll, Birdham Pool, and staying at Clayton, where photographs taken on Ulric's camera – showing Jack very much one of the family as they picked raspberries and relaxed in the sun – indicate how the relationship was now taken for granted, even if its true nature was not fully understood, let alone discussed, by all the occupants of Hillside Cottage. The 'shared life' had been unimpaired by prolonged absences and other less obvious strains. Yes, things had turned out surprisingly well for the Draft of One, as he packed his kitbag again.

Six

The SS *Carthage* steamed out of the Clyde from Glasgow on 1 July, with a little under 1,200 troops on board. The seventeen-day journey took them through the Suez Canal and across the Indian Ocean to Bombay. A fellow APIS officer, John Young, recalls a 'rather pleasant voyage, apart from the living accommodation, which wasn't very nice'. The junior officers were on a troop deck, little better than the hold, with tiers of fold-down bunks and noxious lavatories. 'We spent most of the time on deck.'[1] Young, who, unlike Derek, failed his audition for the ship's concert party, remembers to this day one of its songs:

A thousand thirsty soldiers a-sailing on the sea
A thousand thirsty soldiers, they're as thirsty as can be
A thousand thirsty soldiers, do they pine for love?
A thousand pints of Foaming Glory's all they're thinking of.
Soon they'll be in Bombay
Spending rupee notes
Pouring pints of Foaming Glory
Down their thirsty throats.

In Bombay, they were herded straight onto a troop train in a monsoon and spent the next three days rattling towards Calcutta. Although they were in a carriage reserved for officers, conditions were pretty primitive: slatted wooden seats, more fold-down bunks and, at each end of the carriage, a squat-plate lavatory which became increasingly noisome as the passengers succumbed in turn to 'traveller's joy'. They would eat at halts, in the station restaurant, where the air-conditioning was usually provided by a lazy ceiling fan. In one, however, they dined, unforgettably, under punkahs made of royal-blue velvet and edged in silver braid scrolling. Otherwise the journey, in the main through unexpectedly barren landscape, was enlivened by occasional glimpses of jungle and a leaping monkey. Calcutta was both a relief from the tedium and, as it has been to every Western visitor before and since, a culture shock.

Derek had been posted to 347 (Reconnaissance) Wing of the RAF, whose primary role was to provide intelligence for 'Operation Zipper', the planned amphibious invasion of Malaya. The PI (Photographic Interpretation) Section was stationed at Bally, off the Barrackpore trunk road, in premises with echoes of Medmenham: a palace belonging to the Maharajah of Tagore, and messes in Nissen huts nearby. The officers lived in 'bashers': palm-thatched mud huts with two rooms apiece and a small veranda. By the time Derek and John Young arrived, the monsoon had washed out virtually all flying and, as the latter put it, 'I don't remember anybody doing very much work there. In fact, I don't remember doing any work at all.' Derek had surely fallen on his feet. His posting appears to have been dominated by cinema-going, amateur theatricals and socialising, interrupted every now and then by some tedious administration. Latterly, he found an outlet for his drawing by contributing cartoons to an Army Command weekly, *Victory*; he sent Jack a contents page on which his surname had been spelt correctly, with the note: 'It *can* be done!' He established a rapport with the poet, bibliographer and considerable eccentric John Gawsworth, then a thirty-three-year-old RAF officer but later editor of *Poetry Review* and inheritor of Redonda, a tiny, guano-encrusted Caribbean island, to the throne of which he was to succeed as King Juan I. The most exciting military event in the city during Derek's time was caused by a screening of *Objective, Burma!* at which the returning Royal Inniskilling Fusiliers took exception to Errol Flynn freeing the country single-handed, and registered a protest by setting fire to the cinema.

There was some surprise that Derek secured temporary membership of the Saturday Club, a Calcutta institution snooty enough to turn up its nose at all but the most senior Army officers, unless, of course, the candidate was a polo player. John Young detected a 'strange influence' exerted by Derek – a capacity to pull strings, or to have them pulled for him. He remembers that from their first acquaintance on the voyage out Derek 'always tended to be a little remote and aloof'. When he deigned to join his colleagues in the mess bar, he was usually flanked by two women, one of whom, the senior WAAF interpreter at Bally, was in effect his superior. In the hierarchical world of the Services, it was unusual, if not ill-advised, to fraternise too closely with a woman senior officer, especially one nearly fourteen years older. But then, this relationship was to prove altogether out of the ordinary.

Edna Flavelle Holiday was born in Yorkshire on 1 June 1907 to Roslyn Holiday, a colliery agent, and his wife, Amélie Eva Boitel. The family lived in some style in the village of Featherstone, near Pontefract. Understandably, Edna adapted her mother's second name and became known to all as Eve. When war broke out she joined up immediately and, after nine months in the lowest form of RAF life as an Aircraftwoman 2nd Class, on cooking and clerical duties, she was promoted. By December 1940 she was showing enough initiative and skill to be appointed Assistant Section Officer at Wembley, where one of the embryonic PI units was based. Here, Eve and four other WAAFs, including Constance Babington Smith, listened enthralled as a 'farouche Flight Lieutenant' called Michael Spender – brother of the poet Stephen and the artist Humphrey – taught them how to interpret shipping. He defined their task in general as 'rather like that of a motorist driving through a town, who suddenly sees a rubber ball bouncing across the road from a side street. He can't *see* any children playing, but he knows in a flash they are there and his brake is on. You must know what is normal, but you must also know the significance of what you see when you see it.'[2] Constance Babington Smith recalled that at the end of the course they sat an oral examination 'on which our fate depended'. It was conducted by a demanding Squadron Leader, Peter Riddell, who fired questions at the students: 'How do you tell the difference between a naval unit and a merchant vessel?' he asked Constance Babington Smith. No answer. He turned to an eagerly waiting Eve: 'Do *you* know?' 'A merchant vessel is like an oblong box with pointed ends, and a naval unit is a very elongated oval – *cigar-shaped*.' In the end all five WAAFs passed the course, but it was Eve who had shone in the oral.

In the early summer of 1941 Assistant Section Officer Holiday was stationed on a remote clifftop airfield at Wick, in northernmost Scotland, where she had helped a brilliant geographer, David Linton, to build up the Photographic Reconnaissance Unit, dedicated to monitoring the movements of the German Navy's cruisers, pocket-battleships, battle-cruisers and, mightiest of them all, the battleship *Bismarck*. These capital ships were a deadly menace to the Allies' Atlantic convoys. On the morning of 21 May – while Derek was undergoing his Army baptism at Catterick – Pilot Officer Michael Suckling, known as 'Babe' because of his youthful looks, took off from Wick in his Spitfire to check out the Norwegian coast near Bergen. Three and a half hours later he returned in a state of high excitement, having spotted and photographed two large ships and eleven supporting vessels anchored in two separate fjords. His pictures were examined by Eve and Linton, and their confirmation of what Suckling had found led to an epic pursuit that ended six days later with the *Bismarck*, shattered by torpedoes, lying on the seabed. Eve's involvement in this momentous episode was a feather in her cap professionally. She was already popular with her colleagues: Constance Babington Smith noted how 'Eve, in her cheerful easygoing way, took a special interest in caring for their needs, and always had a hot cup of tea ready when a pilot returned cold and exhausted after hours of solitary flying.'[3]

After two years at Medmenham, she was posted to Delhi and then to Bally. When the Governor of Bengal, R. G. Casey, called on 347 Wing early in June, it was the senior WAAF interpreter, Squadron Officer Eve Holiday, who was singled out for an invitation to dinner at Government House the next Saturday. Derek met her a few weeks later: 'She arrived suddenly through the doors flowing in long white chiffon, her hair tonight tumbling about her shoulders, in one hand a slim cigarette holder, in the other a book; the only completely un-feminine thing about her was the big Service watch on her wrist. She came straight to the bar and slid on to the stool beside me and ordered a Gin Sling.'[4]

This was 'Nan Baildon' – a name playfully constructed from a palindrome and from Bill Wightman's birthplace near Bradford, little more than twenty miles from Eve's at Featherstone.

> She was older than I by about six years, tall, grey eyes, good hands, a generous figure. 'Ample', she used to call it, or, in a kinder manner, 'my Edwardian body'. Which it was. She wore her hair in a plait bound round her head, and had an ever ready capacity for tremendous laughter and a surge for living. She was like a crested wave, always about to tumble, full of excitement, cool, grey-green, poised, crest tilted towards whatever shore. Never quite breaking.[5]

Although John Young never had much to do with Eve, he remembers her as 'an unusual looking woman' – her hair, in particular, with a kiss curl looping onto her forehead, and, in one photograph, twin curls like slipped headphones. He would often see her occupying Derek's attention with one of her colleagues, Margo. They all had a good deal of time on their hands.

Until 6 August, when the Atom Bomb was dropped on Hiroshima, 'Operation Zipper' was still a reality; 347 Wing was planning to move forward to Rangoon. Six days later, hostilities ended, and on the 15th President Truman announced the unconditional surrender by the Japanese. Flying operations were now concentrated on identifying POW camps for the rescue of the wretched captives. Derek had mixed feelings:

> If I had felt absolutely useless when Germany had surrendered, I felt worse now. There wasn't a war to fight and I wanted to stay on in the army: I was deeply thankful that I would not have to face the Japanese in battle [...] but I consoled myself further by my awareness that there would be much to do in the areas which they had occupied and ravaged and in which they had spread their dreadful gospel of hate and vengeance.
>
> Someday someone would send for me.
>
> But they didn't: I was forgotten for the time being.[6]

It was in this atmosphere 'of euphoria and exotic laziness, among the sights and sounds and scents', that he claimed to have 'drifted into an affair' with Eve, who was 'no starry-eyed girl. Quite the opposite: she knew very well, instinctively, that I was cautious, evasive, unwilling to be trapped. Afraid of possession.'[7] He would write of her offering to teach him 'how to enjoy Poetry' and of learning blocks of verse on the cool of her veranda.[8] He seems to have been adopted by another literary mentor. More than that: 'At nights, lying in the noisy darkness beneath my mosquito net, her body heavy in sleep beside me, the scent of "Je Reviens" on her throat and shoulders, I felt a wrench of panic that I was entering a maze from which there could, decently, be no escape.'[9] And again:

Crushed against her on her wide charpoy, the mosquito net like a much-mended wedding veil, I was pretty well preoccupied one afternoon and not performing very well. This alerted her instantly. 'Oh! Pippin! Floating off into your dream world? Thinking of one of your plots? Nothing *wrong* is there?'

[. . .] Afterwards we'd slide stickily apart, the heavy scent of our sweaty bodies and her stale 'Je Reviens' sour in the wet heat.[10]

It was, he came to believe, a 'gentle web of love and affection which was surreptitiously being woven about me'.[11]

According to *Snakes and Ladders* they spent VJ Night – officially 15 August, but the festivities went on for four days – celebrating at the Saturday Club:

We drove home in torrential rain and struck a group of soldiers somewhere along the Barrackpore road. We turned over twice I seem to recall: Nan had a cut head, I was unhurt. There were two or three men sprawled in the muddy, roaring waters of the street. People came and took Nan back to barracks. I knew that two must be dead; but remembered, and remember now, very little. They were members of a gang of American GI deserters, known in the area, who high-jacked cars at nights. We spent weeks of misery in Court, and finally were exonerated, because witnesses had seen them link arms across the road and form a line to halt us. I had not seen them in the dark and the rain. I have never driven since.[12]

The operations record book for 347 Wing, an accurate summary of all noteworthy events involving its personnel, mentions an 'Unfortunate incident on the 16th', when 'LAC (Leading Aircraftman) Hodgkinson drowned while bathing at Mt Lavinia'[13] and in October the death of an Army liaison officer. Otherwise the most interesting occurrences in the period leading up to disbandment were the equipping of the rest-room with armchairs and a library, the setting-aside of two rooms in the palace for a badminton court and table-tennis, and the acquisition of a supply of gramophone records. The Wing's cinema had increased its pro-grammes to four each week. Nowhere is there a record of a fatal accident involving two British officers. The most sensational of the English-language Calcutta newspapers, *Amrita Bazar Patrika*, carried reports almost daily of pedestrians being mown down by military vehicles, but there were few fatalities, and no suggestion of any incident involving British officers or American casualties. Nor was there a report of a current or pending court case or court martial. John Young recalls hearing about an accident of some kind, but without any detail, or concrete knowledge of who was concerned: 'I can't remember Eve appearing in the mess with a bandage round her head or anything like that.' If there was an incident, it was skilfully and comprehensively hushed up, otherwise the halls and corridors of Tagore Palace would have been alive with gossip. In fact the only whisperings about Derek came John Young's way from the shower block, where it was reported that in the battle against prickly heat the Captain had acquired a powder-puff.

Certainly one would never guess from the scant surviving correspondence that anything untoward had happened. On 27 August, less than two weeks after VJ Day, Derek was writing to Elizabeth of his 'dull, but fairly social life out here. I dine at my club, dance with the tatty women, and drink with tattier men.' The cinemas were always packed – 'Some of them are air cooled, and you actually manage to shiver in them' – and he was hoping to go next week 'and see "Blith Spirit" It was such a good play, I want to see the film.' That afternoon he was off to ENSA 'to try and get another job'. There appeared to be just two blots on his landscape: 'I am doing Administration now, and you can guess how I adore, but ADORE, that. Fart it.' And, in contrast to some of his recent thoughts about remaining with the Army: 'I am glad to hear that you will be out by October! God you lucky bitch! I shall be here until March '47 I think. Unless something absolutely wonderful happens . . . and you never know.'

With air operations now minimal and PI effectively redundant, there was the chance to explore. On 21 September, he and Eve obtained a pass from the Sikkim authorities granting permission to cross the frontier into Tibet. By the beginning of October they were in Darjeeling which, he wrote to Elizabeth, was '*the* most beautiful place I've seen'. Snapshots sent back to Jack show Kanchenjanga at dawn and Derek stretched out on the ground in a deodar forest; another, published in *Backcloth*, has 'Nan' in the far distance dominated by the trees. A small wartime album, partly given over to the trip, makes it plain that this was no 'activity holiday' – no riding into Sikkim on a three-week trek; indeed there is not a mule in sight. It was the most relaxed kind of tourism, and clearly a happy time. Nor were they entirely alone. 'It was decided that we should both go away on leave,' states *Snakes and Ladders*. 'To clear our minds. Whatever that meant.'[14] The implication is that Derek and Eve set off to prepare themselves for the impending ordeal of a court case. How odd, then, that they should take with them a colleague, Lawrence Hutchinson, known as 'Hutch'.

Back in Bally after their fortnight in the Himalayas, Derek found a letter from Elizabeth waiting for him with news of romantic developments. In reply he wrote:

[. . .] For the first time you will be knowing what Hell it is to be in love; you will be writing the most outrageous nonsense to your beloved in penny envelopes, and will be waiting with beating heart for his . . . you will realize that being in love has two sides to it; one of complete and bewildering beauty, and the other of angry pain and soul tearing misery.

When you meet you feel that your hearts will burst for joy, when you part you find that steel bands have encircled your throat and that your voice wont keep still, but insists on wobbling aboit it a most disgraceful way. I know! Too bloody well. I too have been in love.

Not, though, with Eve, who is unmentioned in his letters. 'My love for her was provisional only. I hadn't the remotest idea how to escape from an intense affair which I had helped create only to ease the tedium of my boredom and idleness, and which was now beginning to overwhelm me.'[15] Yet the friendship was honest enough for Derek to send Jack a snapshot dated 3 November, showing him and Eve sitting on his veranda, examining the occupants of a birdcage who were apparently known as 'Evie' and 'Tits'. On the reverse Derek wrote: 'I look a bit as if I was pre-natal' – a theme he continued in a second photograph taken on the same day at the Dakhineswar Fair, where he, Eve, two colleagues and his bearer, Abdul, are posed in front of a 'gay backcloth': 'My right breast is a little low – I was feeding my young just before.' A third picture, a startling Romanesque studio portrait, is inscribed to Jack 'With all my love – Pippin'. There is little doubt where his true affections lay. Whatever Eve's hopes, the Army was about to part her from Derek; yet they were to meet again under different, stranger circumstances. John Young remembers Derek disappearing from Bally 'in a bit of a hurry', but no one thought much of it. He also recalls a conversation reported by another officer, Austin Coates, son of the composer Eric, in which the former asked Derek what he intended to do after the war. 'I think Rank wants me for something,' came the reply, 'but whether it's on the production or acting side I don't know.' 'Of course he hasn't the slightest hope,' Coates told Young. 'He has no training.'

The Draft of One had been despatched to Java, via Singapore. Derek crossed the Equator on 25 November 1945, and arrived on a tank-landing ship at Tandjoengpriok in Batavia Bay during the first week of December. His new posting was to 23rd Indian Division, whose task was to deal with a situation that a Reuter special correspondent felt moved to describe – even after Hiroshima and Nagasaki – as 'atomic'. Nationalists, extremists, the Dutch, the British and to some extent the surrendered Japanese had conflicting interests and although the war itself had ended, the beautiful Indonesian island was a tinder-box igniting in sporadic acts of terrorism. 'Merdeka!' – 'Freedom!' – was splattered on walls in blood-red paint. Caught in the middle were many thousands of Allied POWs and internees, mainly Dutch and Eurasian women and children, in camps scattered throughout the country. For the RAPWI – as they were known, after the organisation set up to care for them: Repatriation of Allied Prisoners of War and Internees – the ordeal under the Japanese was theoretically over, but in practice it continued because they were now held virtually as hostages, with surrendered Japanese as their protectors rather than their oppressors. In charge of this bizarre redeployment was Laurens van der Post, who had himself been a prisoner of war for more than three years.

In simple terms, the Dutch felt that the British had let them down. The British saw the powers back in the Hague as Rip Van Winkles, 'unaware that while they have been asleep their old colonial theories have become as extinct as the dodo'.[16]

The Nationalists felt they needed no lessons in government from either; the Antara press agency declared: 'Indonesia was already a civilized country at the time that the British the Dutch and other European nations were still roaming the forests, clad in bark.'[17] The 23rd Indian Division, which had earned distinction in Burma, found itself entrusted with the role of military policing rather than of fighting a campaign, and was, to put it mildly, uncomfortable. During two and a half months of admirable restraint, it had seen the country steadily deteriorate into a guerrilla war. At one point the Indonesians called on the people to use against the Dutch every weapon at their disposal – 'all kinds of poison, blow-pipes, arrows, knives, spears, wild animals like poisonous snakes, petrol and other incendiary materials'.[18] On 15 December, shortly after Derek's arrival, the Division's war diary recorded: 'The Indonesian leaders have shown themselves incapable of controlling the Terrorist elements, who continue to foster unrest, prevent the flow of food to markets, indulge in kidnapping & murder of civilians, & cause loss of life to our forces.'[19] That loss of life included the murder of a Brigadier, A. W. S. Mallaby; the butchery of all crew and passengers on a troop-carrying Dakota which had been forced down by bad weather; and the loss of twenty-four men in an attack on an ambulance convoy. No wonder Lieutenant-Colonel A. J. F. Doulton, Assistant Adjutant and Quartermaster-General, noted in his diary for 20 October 1945: 'God, we've come into a place! Human nature run amok'; two days later, 'This is a filthy, filthy business'; and on 21 November, 'This is war.'[20] In its official history, he would look back on the Division's involvement in Java, with 1,377 dead, wounded and missing, as 'a story of deep tragedy and surpassing courage'.[21]

The unfortunate CO charged with trying to sort out the mess was forty-eight-year-old Major-General Douglas Hawthorn, who had been decorated for his inspiring leadership in Burma and Malaya. Six foot two inches tall, and strongly built, he was a calm, firm, kindly man, whose slightly austere manner disguised a delicate sense of humour. He had, wrote Doulton, 'the mind of a soldier who had made a deep study of his art'.[22] Hawthorn later summed up his responsibilities on the island as 'administering a foreign territory the size of England and Wales; rescuing and caring for over 50,000 Dutch refugees – men, women and children; taking the surrender of 75,000 Japanese troops; maintaining the morale and welfare of my own troops which at one time with six brigades and ancillary troops under my command amounted to over 60,000 men'. In addition he had reluctantly to become involved in 'a most difficult international political situation', negotiating 'on the highest level with the Dutch, Americans, Indo-nesians and Japanese'. It was, he concluded, 'a very onerous assignment'.[23] He and his fellow officers had a lot on their plate when the Draft of One turned up in Batavia. The lack of an effusive greeting disappointed Derek:

> There is a profound difference between being 'alone' and 'lonely'.
>   I was both for the first few days after my arrival in the Division, stuck in

one or other of the three bleak little villas which constituted 'A' Mess. My brother officers were perfectly civil at all times, but there was a clear feeling that I was an outsider among a group of people who had fought together, and suffered heavy casualties doing so, in bitter and costly battles up on the Assam–Burma border.

[...] So really it was little wonder that I wandered about feeling like a leper with his bell. I didn't fit, had not been expected, no one knew what to do with me, and quite frankly had neither the interest nor inclination to suggest anything I could do; they were much too preoccupied with the bloody job in hand, which had taken them by surprise as much as it had taken me.[24]

If there had been little to tax his PI skills in Bally, there was even less in Batavia, where political intelligence and security were of far greater importance than aerial reconnaissance. Derek had installed himself in an office at Divisional Headquarters and put an 'APIS' plate on the door with his name underneath. In the next room was the office of a daily newspaper, *The Fighting Cock*, which had been founded in October by Hawthorn and took its name from the Division's emblem. The General's brief had been that it should not only keep the widely scattered units informed about the Division's activities and more general news, but also 'give us interesting and perhaps amusing leisure minutes when we sit back from our exacting duties of keeping law and order'.[25] A good portion was printed in Urdu, and the newspaper swiftly became 'one of those rare concerns in which British, Dutch and Indonesians co-operated in a friendly spirit'.[26] The first of its two or four pages was usually bare of illustration, but on 4 December, sitting somewhat incongruously above the day's 'splash' headline, 'BANDOENG UNDER CONTROL – Evacuation Continues', was a photograph of the Seven Sisters cliffs in Sussex. In the next few days others, of Inverary and Alfriston, followed. On the 10th, a full column was given over to an essay, entitled 'I REMEMBER ...', in which the author strolled through his memories of fish and chip shops, coster barrows in Kilburn and Coventry Street, plane trees in Green Park, the 'softness of Chanctonbury Ring, with the breast like Downs swelling up from the Weald', the Yorkshire moors, a fairground, Brighton Rock and the slot machines on the Palace Pier, a railway porter yelling the familiar stations, Myrna Loy or Betty Grable at the Regal, a 'quick one' at the Prince of Wales ... It was a reverie he highly recommended, because 'remembering things, little things, you get rather rested in the mind'.[27] It was signed 'D.V.d.B.' A week or so later Derek wrote a cheeky piece under the heading 'New Bod', which consisted entirely of a dialogue between a young officer and the Colonel on to whose staff he had been posted by a distant HQ. The Colonel, 'looking like something out of "Punch", only not nearly so intelligent', asks the 'new bod' to explain himself:

'They told me I was on an urgent Posting...'
'First I've heard of it' said the Colonel belligerently... 'Who told you?'

'We got a Signal,' I said

'Signal!' exploded the Colonel as if someone had told him Labour had stopped Fox Hunting [...]

After listening to a volley of abuse about the 'hopeless bunch' far away – 'remember I saw their Rugger Team get absolutely torn to bits' and 'as a HQ they are just the same' – the new arrival pleads, without success, to be sent back to his former posting: 'I was happy there once upon a time...'.[28]

If this was a none-too-subtle protest at being under-appreciated and under-employed, it worked. There would never be many calls on him to use his stereoscope to identify pictures from the air, but in the newspaper there was always space to fill. In the coming months he would contribute news stories, essays, quiz questions, cartoons and morsels of whimsy to occupy a down-page corner under the title 'Bran Mash', for which he used the *nom de plume* 'The Bantam'. He developed a particularly keen following with his short stories, which appeared under the byline 'Icarius'. We must give Derek the benefit of the doubt and assume this was not a misspelling of the high-flying young man who reckoned without the effect of the sun on his waxen wings. It was, surely, a deliberate homage to Odysseus's father-in-law, the first mortal wine-maker. He too, however, met an untimely end. He gave a sample jar of his wine to some shepherds, but they ignored advice to dilute it, and believing their double vision had more to do with witchcraft than with drunkenness, bumped him off. Whatever the inspiration, Derek's Icarius was the principal player in his one-man journalistic band. Back home to Jack would go the printed stories, usually carrying a scribble from 'Pippin': 'Don't know if I like this or not. The end is a bit wonkey!'; 'A collection of bitchy remarks about people I wot of! Alas!; Not good writing'; 'Rubbish!!' He might have been unsure that his work would satisfy a stern critic, but at least idleness was no longer an issue. He was happier by the day. And his responsibilities, both unofficial and official, grew.

'A' Mess was a group of villas in a suburb of Batavia. It was here that Derek had his quarters, in 'a prim, almost empty little room with sun-rotted lace curtains at the bay window' and 'a rusty tin garden table'. He had been welcomed by 'a silent, but grinning, Gurkha with an embarrassment of gold teeth' who 'unpacked my kit, erected my camp bed and mosquito net and indicated that his name was Goa'.[29] The Gurkha is famous for having perfect teeth – he avoids sugar – and has far better things to do with any gold that might come his way than place it in his mouth; he would send it home to his family. No one interviewed for this book remembers Derek's domestic arrangements in Batavia nor any personnel who assisted him. As always, he kept his own counsel while socialising as much as was both expected and useful. He made friends at Radio Batavia, where one of its most prominent pre-war presenters, Bert Garthoff, had returned from captivity under the Japanese and was helping to put the station back on its feet. Jack was sent a snapshot dated 27 December, showing Derek and Bert outside the studios with a striking woman identified only as Milly. The programme listings for New Year's Eve included at 7.40 p.m. ' "Evening Star", presented by Pip Bogaerde'.[30] In English, of course. Journalist, radio announcer, whatever next? Strangely enough, not producer, performer or even set designer. For although the Division staged an elaborate revue early in January at the Opera House, there is no sign of Derek among the credits for 'Cock Tales of 1946' – a show which Doulton described as 'superior to all but one of the Ensa efforts I've seen. And there's a glorious sense of a return to civilisation & peace in being inside a theatre again.'[31] Derek probably did not have time to become involved; as he noted to Jack, he was being rushed off his feet.

Across the road from 'A' Mess was the Box Club, an establishment that had expanded its original civilian membership to include all British officers stationed in the city, and had proved so popular that its large ground-floor rooms were overcrowded and its supplies of alcohol unable to keep up with demand. A notice went out that in the evenings, when the stone floors proved ideal for dancing, no one could bring more than one guest, 'either male or female'. It was here, just after midnight on 1 January, that an incident described by Doulton as 'the disgrace' began. A group of well-oiled officers pulled out their revolvers and heralded the New Year by firing them into the air, at which 'the whole of Batavia took up the tune'. It took about half an hour for calm to return, and General Hawthorn had to be taken home under strong escort. No one was hurt, but the Division's impeccable reputation had been 'smirched'. Nevertheless his officers remained welcome at the Club. On 14 January the Division held a regimental dance, attended by the military and diplomatic great and good, including the Commander-in-Chief, Sir Philip Christison. A 'Special Correspondent' began his report in the next day's *Fighting Cock*:

> The social life for which Batavia was famed before the war returned in a blaze of flowers, laughter and soft lights when 23 Indian Division threw its tremendous party last night at the Box Club. It has been many days since Batavia saw such a gathering, and would have seriously confounded our critics abroad who imagine the place to be a dark shadow in the land filled with shots in the night and murder at every turn.

On he went:

> Out on the terrace people sat at their tables gaily decorated with flowers and brightly coloured cloths, the moon was thinly veiled behind soft clouds, the evening air warm and still ... lights gleamed from the roof above, and the music from the ballroom came softly through the great windows.[32]

The cutting reached Jack in England with the note: 'This is hell, too Patience Strong for words, but just what they wanted! I laughed myself sick writing it! P.' It was not quite what 'they' wanted. Doulton recorded in his diary: 'The Fighting Cock gave a lush & very flowery report on the evening's activities – foul journalese. I gather Master Pip Bougerd, the Gen's newly appointed ADC is responsible. I'll sift him tomorrow.'[33] It was true: Derek had officially been assigned the role that he liked to think he had fulfilled three years earlier for Brigadier Essame.

Hawthorn had commandeered a large house near Divisional HQ and, after lonely early days, was now surrounded by a group of females who caused disquiet among some of his staff. The calculated charm of one in particular, a Marushka Petit, who ran a shop in the city, led Lieutenant-Colonel Doulton to confide to his diary that she was the cleverest woman he had ever met, 'in the feminine sense'. In other words, trouble with a capital T, and the sooner the General was free of her clutches the better. A week after taking Derek to task for his report on the regimental dance, Doulton wrote:

> The Petit sacked! This is tremendous news! This new ADC is a man of parts. When he took over, Marushka told him that his duties in the General's house were confined to the ground floor (I don't think this implied what one might take it to mean) & their paths have crossed on a number of points where Pip considered he was being thwarted in his duty. He followed up before the General & said it was either Marushka or him. The General thanked him for having the courage to speak & the woman has been cast out into the wilderness.[34]

A 'man of parts' indeed. If he was making that kind of impression on his seniors, Derek's credit rating was truly on the up. There was more to come. In mid-February, with order more or less restored in Batavia, the Division moved to Bandoeng, where some 45,000 RAPWI were still interned. In one way the attractive town in the hills brought welcome relief: it was cooler here than in muggy Batavia. However, the dangers were more evident. The road from the coast was constantly vulnerable to attack from extremists; on a Sunday in March a convoy was ambushed and the Division lost eight of its men, with another twenty-five wounded. Bandoeng itself was divided by the railway, and the Allies took over the northern part. South of the line terrorism was rife, and on several occasions mortars sailed over into the British sector, one of them landing on the printworks which *The Fighting Cock* was to use. All such incidents were duly reported in the newspaper, which, with the move, had 'gone tabloid', or 'compact'. It also had a new editor. At Divisional Headquarters, the offices of APIS and *Fighting Cock* editorial were one and the same. Derek now had three official jobs and for him the latest was no sinecure. Editorials, written under the heading 'Cock Crow', joined the steady flow from his typewriter.

Several witnesses from that period saw a fair amount of Derek, but none knew him well. Lieutenant-Colonel Bryan Hunt, the Division's senior intelligence officer, 'bumped into him frequently, and we got on well. He was always polite, and he seemed to get on all right with the Dutch. He was also a very good organiser of a show.'[35] The show in question was *Curtain Up*, staged at the Concordia Club as a kind of 'joint ops' between the Division and talent hunted from among the local population. Hetty van Winsen, who with her sister Barbara had been freed after three years of internment, remembers his flair as a producer and how sensitive he was to the predicament of those who had been so degraded and for so long: 'To us, he was a brilliant, elegant man who knew what he was doing and was really busy *directing* us. It gave us great pleasure. He was very good looking, in a special way; very *soigné*, a real gentleman.'[36] She also saw him 'always going about with a half-Indonesian girl', who to an extent fitted the description in *Backcloth* of 'Harri', the 'ravishingly beautiful', Modigliani-like interpreter-secretary with long legs, long hair, long neck, three languages and an antipathy to housework, who metamorphoses into the mandolin-playing 'Emmie' in *A Gentle Occupation*. Her real name, Dirk told a friend many years later, was Nini. Mrs van Winsen says she and her friends speculated, as was natural, about the relationship: 'We never saw them kissing or anything like that. So we wondered. We didn't know about homosexuality in those days, but I did think that she was a sort of camouflage.'

There was speculation, too, about the goings-on at the General's house. For himself and his mess he had acquired a huge hilltop pile with, as Derek would put it, 'a striking resemblance to the Hoover factory on the Western Avenue'.[37] Derek, who had been assigned a substantial bungalow in its grounds, was much engaged with Hawthorn's essential comforts. Donald Lee, who was in intelligence but whose duties at this point included supplying furniture from a Japanese warehouse, remembers Derek – or Pip, as he knew him – turning up and saying, 'I've got to find a big bed for the General, up on the heights of Bandoeng.' The mission was accomplished.[38] Lee remarks on the contrast between Hawthorn, 'a brusque robust soldier', and the diffident Derek, 'who could be quite elusive', but found the latter pleasant company. When he went to the *Fighting Cock* office to place an announcement of his engagement to Hetty van Winsen's sister, Derek asked him: 'Are you sure you want to go ahead with this?' Both laughed. Bryan Hunt believed that Derek was doing 'a perfectly good job' and confirms that he satisfied the vital criterion for an ADC of being able to 'sit a table'. Hunt held Hawthorn in lower regard than had the now-departed Lieutenant-Colonel Doulton: 'He was not a bad general, but he was a bore.' According to Hunt's diaries, the General's parties were a strain: 'He is so formal. Lots of people turn down the invitation.' On one occasion a game of tennis was followed by an 'awful film and dancing'. It was the hangers-on whom Hunt could not stand. 'Damn the general's women!'

he noted – and with good reason, because it seems that Miss Petit, the multilingual, Tarot-reading, Belgian shopkeeper who had been seen off by Derek, was back in favour. Hunt recalls a scandal connected with the General's house, as a result of which a senior member of the Divisional staff was arrested by the Military Police and sent back to Britain. 'I thought at the time that it might have had something to do with homosexuality, but I never knew for sure.' There were other scandals – including arrests for looting – and at least one court martial of a senior officer. All of which lends credence to *A Gentle Occupation* as a historically and atmospherically based account of life in a hybrid of Batavia and Bandoeng during a period which would come to be known as a 'forgotten war'.

The General attracted attention not only among those under his command. Sadao Oba, a twenty-three-year-old officer cadet in the Japanese Army, noted how Hawthorn 'used to drive round the city in a convertible car every evening with a beautiful young blonde girlfriend and a dog'.[39] Unfortunately there are no recorded sightings of Derek in similar vein, wafting through the city in the back of a jeep with 'Harri' and the male, 'lynx-like' creature – a feral cat – which he adopted and christened Ursula.[40] Nor did either of them feature in the snapshots which drifted back to Hillside Cottage and to Jack, several of which were taken on the beach at Tandjoengpriok, where the officers swam; in one, his companion bears a striking resemblance to Tony Forwood. If there were involvements, they did not distract Derek from keeping Jack informed of his well-being, physique and wardrobe; 'Not *too* skinny am I? Like the trunks? I do.'

As the weeks went by, Derek maintained his input at the newspaper, concentrating on short stories and on his page-one editorials. In July it was unquestionably his hand, as 'Cock Crow', behind a plea for tolerance, saying that without it 'you just can't get along in life – well, not very far anyway', and regretting that when the Americans arrived in Britain in 1942 not enough was done to try to understand them: 'Intolerance of each other bred suspicion. We lived together in a state of discreet discourtesy ... a pity; because we *could* have done well in the future Peace. Really well, not diplomatically well. There is a parallel just round the next corner, just across the street, in the house next door. Why not think about it a little?'[41] More and more he was looking ahead to an uncertain future. Its job done in Bandoeng, Divisional Headquarters had moved back to Batavia on the first small leg of a much longer journey. Hawthorn would be in Java until October, some of his men until the end of November, but repatriation from the unhappy paradise was under way. In *Backcloth* Derek writes to his father that 'there won't be any need of the Army because there won't be an Empire to run' and that he dreads coming home: 'God knows what I'll do in UK. It's a gloomy prospect, but there is no point in trying to hang on in the Army as I thought. But what do ex-Officers DO?'[42] A fortnight later his 'Cock Crow' began:

Someone said the other evening, 'You know I dread going home on Demobb … I'll never get a job,' and we have probably heard that remark about fifty times a week from people out here in the Army [. . .] During the war years they learned a good deal about life, which should help them, they also learned a lot about themselves, which should also help them a bit … they learned about their fellow men, and were faced with heavier responsibilities than they had ever had to cope with during the years of their civilian life. They are faced with the prospect of going back to a world of civilians, all pushing and striving to get jobs, food, houses and clothes [. . .] Most of them know only how 'to manage men' and admit, in the Agony Columns, that they have 'a knowledge of office work'. Neither of which are a great deal of use, we know. Most of them dread the thought of going back to a Shine-Seat Existence and a dull routine; one can hardly blame them after their years of war. But surely courage is needed to face up to these realities? Courage of a kind comparable with the type they have had to show for the last seven years?

   [. . .] If a man has personality there is little that he can not do. That has been proven over and over again. If he is aware of himself, and aware of what he can and can not do … and will take the trouble to learn from people, he has made a start. We have all striven for our Freedom, and now, when so many of us have it within our grasp, we baulk at it, and are afraid to go forward and take our opportunities with open hands. The world is as full of Jobs as it is of fools … there are a thousand chances waiting if you have the courage enough to seek them out; courage, hardness, determination, and personality. If you say 'I will!' who's to stop you? If you mean 'I will' sincerely enough.[43]

Thus his filial thoughts and his clarion call from a public platform. However, the most telling insight into his real feelings at this unsettling period came – as it would again – in letters to a complete stranger called Dorothy.

In February *The Fighting Cock* had run a column in which Dorothy Fells, an Army wife living in a Buckinghamshire village, wrote of the weather, the cigarette shortage, the commuting to life imprisonment of the death sentence on a Nazi war criminal, a new type of boarding school, and the arrival at Liverpool of 1,600 tons of bananas. Exactly who first established this important contact is unclear, but 'Letter from Home', with its charming mixture of the portentous and mundane, became a regular feature; one that Derek, as editor, knew was read avidly. Eventually he and its author began a brief correspondence, seemingly initiated by something exceptionable in the newspaper, for on 4 June he wrote from Bandoeng to reassure her that he was not, as she seemed to think, a 'Squarehead':

In honest to God fact I am as English as yourself, and can often be seen at social functions with a Union Jack in my pocket, and tears in my eyes when they play 'Rule Britannia' … fact!

The point is that I am really and truly an Internationalist, having a Dutch father and a Scots-Spanish Mamma ... both of whom I adore, and neither of whom I revile for breeding in me such a strange mixture. Your mistake, if it was that, was perfectly justified; my name is unforgivable and has caused me more anguish than anything else in life ... but, and I hasten to say this, I am proud of me name! It originated with the 'Flemish Mare' who seems to have so many olde worlde cottages dotted about the softer counties of England ... Anne of Cleeves. I'm afraid a lot of her failings are often evident in the members of this generation. Fun.

Derek expressed the wish to get to know Dorothy Fells because she led 'the kind of life that I so admire, a good humoured existence with a wealth of dry humour to season'. He declared himself a polyglot and offered her a 'short cigarette-card biography' of himself:

Ran away from home at the age of 15. Got a job painting scenery at 'Q' Theatre, and the 'Embassy'. Got a small part in Priestley's 'When We Are Married' and went into the Theatre for good. (My mother, being an actress herself, one of the Nivens.) From there I went on in the world, did the Rep grind, got to the West End, stayed there in comparative sin and comfort until the war started, when I was forced to abandon a perfectly good career by joining up in '40. When I left the stage I was appearing with Edith Evans and Dorothy Dixon in the big Farjeron show 'Diversion' at Windhams.

I paint, moderately, and write, badly. I am quite the worst soldier in the world, refusing, as I do, to cut my hair or wear uniform after seven in the evenings. In 1943 I joined Monty's staff as a Photographic Interpreter and helped plan the Second Front in which I also played a part from June to June. The most tremendous and wildly exciting twelve months of my life. And there you rather have me in a nutshell.

The romanticised biography was taking shape nicely.

I am now awaiting my demob, which 'Please God' will be at the end of this month, and then I can come home to a civilised existence once more. These last six years have been wonderful, I would not have missed a moment of them; I have learned manners, comradeship, fear, and how to laugh. I have learned people and values, have realised that youth is an overdone expression and that one is either 'Young' or 'Old' only, whatever your age.

I loved your paragraphs from the [D. H. Lawrence] letters to a Mother. I have not read them myself, but I have tried to rustle through as many of his works as I could. I must confess that 'Sons and Lovers' while I appreciated the beauty of his technique and the theme of it, bored me a little. I find that I do get a little weary of frail women with wilful sons and cancer somewhere around the corner. Is that very wrong of me? I am, I agree, a Philistine I'm afraid, liking things which are not normally admired, and hating things which send the intellectual-from-provincial-universities into shivers of delight.

Those frantic people who try to read messages into Shakespeare, Picasso and Olivier! I had an exhibition of paintings at Batsfords last June, of pictures I had done in BLA. They were done solely to amuse me and to take my mind off the hurts which battle and blood can give. I painted exactly what I saw and exactly as I saw it. On sheets of blotting paper, notepaper, and, in one instance, on a sheet of the 'Daily Express'. At the private view I wandered round listening to the comments. At one small picture, of which I was fond, I came across two young men of the Hairy-Tweed-Walter-Scott-Tie School. They stood for a long time in raptures. One of them presently turned to the other and said.

'My dear. He *definitely* has got it there.'

'You mean the *line?*'

'But of course! And form. *Acres* of form. Look at the emotion in that penline there ... the wild sweep skywards, that exquisite blend of misery and joy in the shape of that hand, you see what I mean? And the *agony* of that purple!'

'I always think purple is sort of *agony*, don't you?'

'Or sin. He was definitely following the Topolski technique. You can see how he has suffered. So clever.'

Now that sort of thing I just can not tolerate, Mrs F. Not for a moment. There was no emotion in the penline, it was just a squiggle with a poor nib; I can't see misery or joy in a hand which took two minutes to draw and was wrong (two fingers short) anyway ... and as for being influenced by Topolski ... well I give up. Silly, idiot young men. And the Theatre, Art and Literary worlds are full of them.

He wondered why he had 'nattered for so long ... can you tell me? Is it that I feel I may have found a kindred boooosom!' – and suggested they meet in September: 'We'll have Martini's at Claridges, or a pleasant little lunch at Kettners, which I adore for its "Lobster Newburg" and excellent Chablis, and the clean towels in the Gents.' The response does not survive, but it must have been positive because three weeks later back in Batavia, Derek wrote to 'My dearest Dorothy':

What an adorable woman you are! Your charming and revealing letter arrived here last night and filled my heart with a warm feeling; rather like red flannel. And how very much I want you for a boooosom friend! More than ever before in fact.

Tho' in your last wise paragraph you did your best to wrap me gently across the knuckles, and suggested that I was a second 'Young Woodley' in that I had invited you to join me in town merely because I was, at the moment, bored with my environment and uniform ... believe you me, a life in the Theatre with strange people and stranger morals has made me wery (Christ! how do you spell it? ... warey (Still looks cock) ... of casual or impetuous invitations. I have read your carefully pruned writings every week, and from the banal phrases and between the written-for-the-soldiers lines I have imagined a You. A you which, I may say, I wanted to meet for a variety of reasons.

I suppose you will glibly pin the label 'naïve' to this as usual, but I have a very small regard for woman as a whole, considering most of them to have but one purpose which even then they don't often fulfill very well. I think it was Coward who said Women should be beaten like gongs ... regularly. And I do so endorse that. If one is unable to do it physically one can do it mentally, and that, to my Sade mind, is a great deal of fun.

But there are the few women who, to my mind, are worth knowing, from whom one can learn a great deal and gain a great deal of mental happiness ... You, I felt, were one of them. I know now that you are.

Poppet I AM a child, and an absurdly foolish one at times, and then again I get all 'worried' because life appears to be too adult and people plaster me with their troubles and imagine that I am thirty six ... it's all very confusing sometimes, and I'd so much rather lead a sandles-on-the-feet-wind-in-hair-existence. Life could be far more amusing than the continual round of hectic gaiety in smart bars and doubtful hotels.

I have the Army to thank for a great deal; for making me wise and a little hard, for making me see that the tinsel glitter of the proscenium arch was really a most insubstantial thing, and not the life for me. I like People; I am never bored, for even the dullest person has some hidden streak of something under the dross of humdrumity. And they are delightful when you find that streak, and surprised too.

How I go on, sorry.

Do believe me, my sweet, that I meant September sincerely. Don't delve too deeply into your knowledge of the world and 'my sex' for you must admit, and will be the first to admit, that you can always learn, and life is bung full of surprises.

I *am* in uniform, I am *not* bored, and I do *not* write charming letters in moments of nostalgia ... whatever else I do, sweetie ... I don't do that. Nuff said on the subject, we shall now consider that I have re-established my Adulthood (!) and proceed.

He stated his intention to take her to dinner in Soho, not at Kettners, but at 'Lion D'Or' in Frith Street, where they would share not a Chablis but a 'very good Chianti … if you like that sort of wine. Personally the straw round the bottle is, to my mind, the best part of the wine.' And then he expanded on the 'thumbnail' of the previous letter:

I am Anglo-Saxon and Spanish. My mother being half Scots half Spanish. In temperament very Spanish. Hysterical, passionate, and with a love of violent contrasts and colours, both in my life and in my clothes. I have a capacity for making women fall in love with me, not from a sexual desire, or not often, but usually from the Mothering complex which every woman seems to retain right through their lives. I adore being rude, and cruel at times. I have but one weapon which is sarcasm, and I use it to the full. It is often a double-bladed weapon, but one can always thrust first. I am a rank sentimentalist, keeping idiot things like Hotel bills, bus tickets, and pressed primroses to remind me of dusty love affairs … I love people I like; literally I'm afraid, and loathe with seething hatred the people I dislike. I have more enemies than friends, and a million acquaintances. Which is fun, for the friends are friends, and the enemies salt in the meal of life. I am supposed to be vain, I suppose I am, altho' I excuse it as being fastidious in my clothes and making the most of a God-awful figure. I am conceited too. Which is fun, because people without conceit are seldom very lucky in their ambitions, and I am very ambitious. I try to be hard and bored very often, to cover my weak spot … sensitivity. I love making sweeping entrances into hotels and restaurants to cover my extremely stupid inferiority complex (which my parents insist is conceit again!) La! But this is a bad impression I'm giving. So what.

I love being blase in the Bagatelle, and laughing secretly at the frightful people who are so very overbred and dreary. I'm desperately sincere about Dignity, with a large begilded capital letter … I refused to lie down in the street during the blitz because I could consider nothing more ridiculous and undignified as lying down full length in a gutter to escape one's fate … which one seldom did even if one did lye … lie down.

I loathe concentration, and I hate being tied in one place. I abhor the middle classes, Suburbia, small villages, bowler hats, and men who wear wing collars and try to be pompous, and all forms of politics. (Dreadful young men with red ties and corduroys who bleat about Russia and Capitalists and wag pamphlets about with a vague idea as to their meaning; and awful young women with fat legs and high ideals who strive for better things, and seldom get them). One thing you may have noticed. I also talk far too much.

Dee darling, you must forgive all this. I know that I am giving myself away wholesale, not by what I say but what you are reading between the lines of what I say! Which is far more subtle and dangerous for me. However, you can choose now about September.

There was more. He had just finished reading Christopher Isherwood's *Mr Norris Changes Trains* for the third time – 'I adore the man's writing' – but *Forever Amber* left him feeling he had seldom been so bored with a book:

> Beds and miscarriages do begin to pall after every chapter, and the whole thing was a blatant copy of 'GWTW', that annoyed me into the bargain. However that is neither here nor there. I read it because everyone had read it and I had been offered a part in the film which is shortly to be made in America. But I could see nothing that I could play, and if it's being made in America that wouldn't do for me. Next to the Dutch I loathe Americans with a fierce loathing. And, I nearly forgot, Australians as well.
>
> Full of complexes I am.
>
> Dearest I have gone on for ages, far too long for you anyway. Forgive me, but it is so pleasant to get these things onto paper, then one can realise what a sod one really is. How you will read all this I dread to think.

On his return he intended to spend some time in Sussex with his parents, 'and then I hope to have a week in Normandy, and back to my house which I share with my brother in Suffolk'. He hoped they might meet before he went 'Francewards'. Yet Dorothy Fells was clearly apprehensive. On 16 July, he told her in a postcard: 'If you work yourself into a lather about things you'll mist your glasses and see me all crookedly anyhow. I want to see you a great deal . . . and I am determined to present ME to you as opposed to the other me that tries to be wot it aint.' In this amalgam of candour, self-analysis and skewed facts – delivered directly and as a confidence to someone older, remote, disinterested and again, above all, *safe* – she was a married mother – lies the embryonic author. Not so much the *writer*; he was always there, scribbling for his own pleasure and largely for private consumption. No, this was the way in which Derek the *author*, the professional working with a faceless reader in mind, would set about his Life.

That, however, was a long way off. Immediately, there were the farewells from a battered island, now a good deal safer than it had been eight months previously when, as Bryan Hunt noted in his diary, the Division felt as if 'we really are on the edge of a volcano'.[44] Derek made a final appearance as an announcer on Radio Batavia. There was a mess party, and a parting – without 'goodbyes': 'Harri was a loner in every way. Something which I understood perfectly. "You tell me that you do not like to be possessed, or to possess! Neither do I. So that is why we are beautifully matched." '[45] Unlike 'Nan', 'Harri' 'never, at any time, spoke of a future', yet 'I was quietly convinced that when the time came, the ultimate moment of choice, to stay or to come away, she would come with me. I may have a modest ego, but it has a loud voice.'[46]

Yet there is no mistaking the generous send-off given to him by his newspaper. Derek's replacement as Fighting Cockerel crowed in a prophetic editorial:

> We will not say that you have read the last of Icarius; we may still cherish the hope that perhaps our most popular contributor may still send us the odd jotting, and it is more than likely that, elsewhere than in the columns of this newspaper, the products of his pen, the offspring of his imaginative genius, will be read and enjoyed by us and many others in the wide world, to whom now 'Fighting Cock' probably suggests the name of a public house, and 'Icarius' some obscure mythological god.[47]

Derek sailed on 25 July, equipped to reflect fifty years later, in a letter to another Java hand, that his time with 23rd Indian Division had provided 'a lot of good things for a young man!'[48] He had gone there believing Java was 'a long tropical country too far away to bother about and probably too full of bugs and cholera to want to bother about', only to discover that it had 'an air' which 'grew on one like a second skin' and left him with an aching heart.[49]

Like most of those returning from the furthest reaches of the Far East theatre, he was held in one of the transit camps in Singapore until he could take his turn on a troopship back to Britain. At Nee Soong he was delighted to find good company:

> The first thing that I noticed about Hugh was his feet. Hardly surprising really, because they were almost ten inches from my face, sticking out of his mosquito net. White, bony, slim and sinewy as skate wings [...] He was, like his feet, amazingly long, like a very elegant crane. Even his nose looked like a probing beak. He had tumbled, sandy hair, a cliff of teeth, bright, clear, all-seeing eyes (he was a psychologist) and an enormous Adam's apple which rode up and down his throat like a lift when he laughed; and Hugh laughed a great deal of the time: big, roaring belly-laughs. We became friends.[50]

Hugh Jolly was a twenty-eight-year-old captain in the Royal Army Medical Corps, and they had met once before, in Bandoeng, where his primary responsibility was to examine and treat the soldiers' skins rather than their minds: indeed he was, at that stage, not a psychologist at all. Although he was to become one of the world's leading paediatricians, and to be called 'Britain's Dr Spock', it was as a dermatologist that he was working in the Dutch East Indies. The following year, when Derek attended as godfather the christening of Hugh's daughter Caryl, he introduced himself to the baby's aunt Cynthia with the words: 'Your brother painted me purple in Indonesia.'[51] Derek suggested that Hugh take the spare bed in the room which he was already sharing with two others. The fortnight or so at Nee Soong would be made infinitely more bearable by this clever and dedicated man who, in one of the scores of letters he sent home to his wife Geraldine, wrote that the brief acquaintance in Java had been renewed:

> His name is van den Boegarde his father being Dutch & his mother Scottish. He is in the Intelligence Corps & is certainly very well placed. He is called Pip & his father is Art Editor to the Times while his mother was on the stage. He seems to have combined the talents for both in no uncertain terms & now is going to take up journalism & is to work for the Express when he gets back. Before he was called up in 1941 he was on the stage in several of Priestley's & was beginning to make a considerable name for himself (he is only about 26 now) when the blitz began & everything snarled.[52]

A Dutch father; 'in' the Intelligence Corps; the *Express*; 'several' Priestleys – Derek was off again. No matter. Hugh, more than anyone, would know the score. According to *Cleared for Take-Off*, they discussed Derek's vague plans, which no longer included the stage because 'it's a pretty silly job for a man', seemed to ignore journalism and now inched towards preparatory schoolteaching. Hugh apparently felt Derek would be 'misapplied'.[53] One suspects Derek did too, because there is a telling memento of their stay in Singapore: a copy of a book published that year, called *The Siege of London*, by Robert Henrey, which Derek bought and passed on to Hugh. On the endpapers, next to what reads like a packing inventory – '3 pairs slacks/3 pyjamas/5 shirts/6 sox/2 puppets/2 pair bathing trunks' and so on – Derek wrote:

> DEREK
>
> DIRK
>
> DEREK

Was he trying to decide which looked better in a byline? Or outside a theatre? Or even on a cinema marquee? Not, surely, on a schoolboy's report.

He sent two postcards back to Hillside Cottage, on one of which he judged Singapore 'expensive, smelly, and British', then announced that because he had only been able to draw a quarter of his month's pay Ulric and Margaret would have to forgo silk and gold: 'All I can possibly bring back as a present is myself!' On the other he declared: 'This is the Raffles! Need I say more! When I get home, and have my letters published (!) I shall use this as an illustration.' He reported that the weather was 'torrid and dull, I am hotter than a snowball in hell – must away for a shower', and hoped his father would be able to take a week off in mid-September 'to show me round the pubs again!' To Jack went a snapshot of Derek outside a restaurant with one of his room mates. One week later he was at sea, on the Furness Withy liner *Monarch of Bermuda* and the largest complement to date of returning Service personnel. Barbara Lee, whose engagement announcement Derek had seen into *The Fighting Cock*, was among the passengers and recalls that Derek arranged the inevitable concert party; he also managed with remarkable ease to persuade various nurses to keep his shirts ironed.[54] The *Monarch* arrived at Liverpool on 4 September, and docked in the early hours of the 5th, when she began to disgorge the 2,666 of her passengers destined for 'demob'.[55] It is a safe bet that none was dressed more snappily than the Draft of One.

Part Two

DIRK

Seven

'He can toss us a pancake any day!'

Margaret Van den Bogaerde sent the thirteen-year-old Gareth to meet the lunchtime train from London at the quiet little station in Hassocks. 'I walked the two miles along the cinder track from Clayton,' he recalls. 'Soon after I arrived, the train pulled in and two or three people stepped onto the platform. One of them was an Indian. I didn't recognise him at all, but he seemed to recognise me. It was my brother, and he was absolutely black.' They walked home to Hillside Cottage, Derek carrying a round canvas duffel bag. Among its contents were gifts: 'a bayonet or something' and the marching compass that had travelled through Europe, to India and to Java – 'a huge treasure'. Just the thing to impress the other boys at Hurstpierpoint, where Gareth was now a boarder. Derek would be staying in his brother's room, among unfamiliar belongings and enveloped by the particular affection of his parents. The palaces and pavilions of the East, the messes full of joshing fellow officers, the enormity of events – after all that, and despite the beauty of the rolling downland beyond the garden, everything here seemed so *small*. It is not a large step from warmth and comfort to suffocation. Similar homecomings were happening throughout the country hundreds, even thousands of times a day, as men and women returned to their families, older, wiser, grown-up. And as in the previous, so-called 'Great', war many harboured images and memories of which they would never speak. All experienced in varying degrees a sense of dislocation. Some wondered who on earth they now were.

Derek had been 'demobbed' at Guildford and was now officially on eighty-one days' leave. Unofficially, his military service was over. There are a few pieces of writing from this period, and all are steeped in melancholy. Even the weather was no help to morale:

In the country the harvests are, alas, almost ruined by the rains of last month. Since I have been home there have been but two fine days ... and it always rained in the evenings. The seaside places are full to the brim with hearty British holiday makers, intent on their week by the sea, even if it does mean goloshes and a rain coat and ration books in a boarding house. Brighton is

selling Rock and dirty postcards, Eastbourne has a Classical band concert twice
a day in the Marine Hall ... the Pier at Hastings is golden and glittering
through the rains and sleet, and you can still have a ride on the 'Dodgems' for
sixpence. All in all, it isn't so bad here, just at first anyway. It's later on that you
will start to feel it all. When the joy of being back with your family, with your
friends, and among your mothbally slacks and shirts, has worn off ... as indeed
it will eventually.

And remember, the Standard Way of Life in England has changed since you
were away. Not apparently at first, but more and more obviously so as you
become used to the fact that you are now no longer a man of the Battles but a
man of the People.[1]

The article, written ten days after his arrival at Liverpool, was published in
Batavia above his essayist's byline and with the heading 'Demob Despair'. It had
been triggered by the problems he was having with a landlady in Chelsea, a
'Fallen Gentlewoman' from whom he had rented 'two rooms with a sink in the
corner' for '£4 15s' a week. Derek and she had fallen out somewhat rapidly, not
because she was 'fat, Irish, and rather drunk very often ... and played Chopin
on a Broadwood with an amazing amount of verve and a staggering lack of
melody'; no, it was because she refused to allow a telephone to be installed in
her house. The veracity of Icarius's story is undermined by the 'weeks of hellish
hunting from one loathsome district of London to another' that had brought
him to this 'Refined' Chelsea square. Nevertheless, the importance to Derek of
the telephone is beyond question. His Army gratuity was not going to last long
and he had to find work. 'How do you, at twenty-six, green as a frog, join the
team with all the years since nineteen missing?'[2] He had evidently gone right off
the idea of being a preparatory schoolmaster – if he had ever sincerely been on
it, which is unlikely, given his antipathy to anything academic. *Snakes and Ladders*
has him destined, *faute de mieux*, for the Surrey village of Windlesham, where
Woodcote House, a long-established boarding school, might have had an opening
for him thanks to his friend from the early Army days, the motorcycle-mad John
Nelson, who was now teaching there. Mark Paterson, son of the school's founder
and formerly its headmaster, remembers that his father interviewed a potential
member of staff at the relevant time, and turned him down. If that was Derek,
it was probably for the best, all round. Journalism was a more suitable option,
even if it was notoriously insecure – for the freelance, anyway. In this respect,
Derek would say repeatedly, he had been a dismal failure to Ulric, whose dream
had been from day one that his elder son should 'be trained, and trained hard,
to follow him into the sanctity and majesty' of *The Times*. Alas, even extremity
was not going to persuade Derek to 'climb upon that red brick altar'.[3] So,
according to another despatch back to his comrades, he was writing, 'not for a
warm and critical reading public as I did in Java, but for a wider and more cruel
public. I keep on getting "Editor Regrets" notices, and occasional "We Are Glad

To Accept" billets which make my bank balance fluctuate rather alarmingly.'[4] In truth, however, he knew where he wanted to be: on a stage and, maybe, on a screen.

Here, Jack Jones could not help him directly. Invalided out of the Navy, he was embarked fully on the career that was to bring him renown as the creator of more than a hundred individual yacht designs. However, he could offer sanctuary to Derek:

> London being what it is at the moment, a great cauldron of vicious, shabby, money-grabbing people, lacking hotels, food, flats or jobs ... I have cleared out to a small village on the Deben in Suffolk. This village is a huddle of cottages on the river bank with a pub called 'The Maybush' as its centre point, and a charming red brick Church set amid Ash and Pine trees.
>
> The river here is wide, flat and salt, the sea being but a few miles down. Riding at anchor, straining gently against the tide, float hundreds of little boats. Yachts, dinghies, sharpies, cruisers and punts, canoes and prams ... the sky is raked by a hundred empty masts; booms and tillers waggle gently, and weed-grown buoys bobble and bounce under the force of the running current. This village is a yachting village – a haven for the men from the City who have sailed boats in their dreams, their baths, and their imaginations all their lives, until they have managed, at last, to purchase a real one of their own. In the evenings the Public of the 'Maybush' is filled with the jargon of a yachting community. People talk of their day's work, their sails, their masts and booms, charts and caulking ... if you like this sort of conversation you join in, for they are the friendliest of people; if you do not – then you sit back over the fire and enjoy your Old and Mild, which is what I do.
>
> The peace of this place, the damp smells of mud and October mist, the rust and slate colours all around, and the cronk! cronk! of the Heron wading his solitary way across the marshes, is a breath of heaven after London. I regret that I shall have to go back in a day or two.[5]

Of greater interest to Derek than the charts and the caulking was the coincidental visit to the village of a film company, 'one of the Rank affairs', on location for *Captain Boycott*: 'I watched them all for a bit today, and had a long conversation with Stewart Granger, who is, as usual, the star.'[6] Derek's affections lay in Waldringfield, but not his future. Both Jack and he knew that. Likewise, Jack needed only occasionally to indulge himself in the bright lights. It was not long before Derek insisted that Jack sit for some studio photographs, with a view to his taking a screen test; the portraits were embarrassing and the test, wrote Jack, was a dismal failure, 'quite as much because I'm *not* photogenic as because I wanted to design small craft, yachts &c.' Geographically, he and Derek were now so much closer; in their ambitions, a gap was widening, as it would in their emotions. Not that Dorothy Fells had anything to do with it. She and Derek finally met in London for their much anticipated lunch, when, according to Derek, 'we seemed to each other to be very old friends indeed, and our Gins went down easily and in good spirits. We talked of all the days which had gone past . . . of Editors, of the archaic presses, the Indonesians who set us up, and the Japs who cut our sheets ready for delivery to the Units. We talked easily, and with nostalgia, about "Our Paper".'[7] Mrs Fells, a petite and colourful character, remembered it differently, telling friends many years later that the rendezvous had been a complete failure because both were over-excited and behaved foolishly. To meet is sometimes to break a spell.

There was a friend who might be able to help. No one knows how much contact, if any, there had been during the past six years between Derek and Tony Forwood. The latter had spent his war alternating between active service – including a period with Monty's 8th Army in the Desert Campaign – and keeping the troops at home entertained through ENSA ('Every Night Something Awful'). Thanks to friends such as Beatrice Lillie, Cicely Courtneidge and Jessie Matthews, he had in a modest way become an impresario, boosting morale and raising money for charity. In 1942, while on leave, he went backstage at Wyndham's Theatre to see his friend Michael Wilding, then playing in *Quiet Weekend*, and met his young co-star, Glynis Johns, the daughter of the character actor Mervyn Johns and with musical genes on her mother's side. Born in South Africa, she had made her London stage debut in 1935 as a child ballerina – strangely enough, named Ursula – in a piece called 'Buckie's Bears'. She was put under contract by Alexander Korda, and was now one of the most sought-after actresses, with five West End appearances and three films to her name. And she was only eighteen. She was smitten by the six-foot-one-inch-tall Lieutenant, with his fine looks, his twinkling eye and his courtesy. Her mother had told her, 'Just remember, always, that good manners are a form of love for your fellow man', and Glynis had never met anyone with manners as impeccable as Tony Forwood's. Nor anyone as good-looking: 'He was the most handsome thing around.' Although, as she jokingly admits, she had a crush on Wilding, 'he was married, so I thought I'd better concentrate on the next best thing!'[8] On 29 August 1942, at Caxton Hall register office in Westminster, they married. Shortly afterwards, Tony was given enough time off for the couple to do a brisk tour with her in an ENSA production of *Peg o' My Heart*, but the demands from their respective masters – the military and the moguls – meant that their time together was always limited. The following year, while Tony continued to make the best of mingling the Army and entertainment in the Home Counties, Glynis's career took on an even greater momentum, despite some of the screen vehicles she was given. Reviewing *The Adventures of Tartu*, James Agate noted that 'if our film directors had the intelligence of a weevil – which they haven't – they would put Glynis under contract and give her £20,000 to do nothing for three years. She is not quite old enough to star, and the time could be occupied in looking round for the proper material. Or getting it written. Directors are always complaining that this country has no

Bette Davis. Well, here's a Bette Davis in the making.'[9] On Christmas Eve she opened at the Cambridge Theatre as Peter Pan and, in today's jargon, blew the critics away.

Despite a great love, the marriage was always under strain. Until the spring of 1944, when Tony was stationed in London for the first time, they were unable to share a home for any sustained period. Their hopes that a baby would, in Glynis's words, 'give substance to our marriage', were not realised. When Gareth Forwood was born in The London Clinic on 14 October 1945, his parents were still together but leading separate lives. Glynis Johns talks of Tony with immense affection, citing him as 'the epitome of the word gentleman': 'I never saw or heard Tony do or say a vulgar thing.' Ever candid, she adds: 'He was the best lover I ever had.' He was, she says, 'initially homosexual', but, after being 'inducted by an older woman', had had a succession of heterosexual affairs, with, among others, Margaret Leighton and, probably, Hermione Baddeley. Ken Annakin, who directed Glynis in her most famous screen role from that period, as the eponymous mermaid Miranda, gives an entertaining account of how he became besotted with her during the filming. It was, he reminds us, 'the story of a sexy lady being in a position to tempt three men. And Glynis was a very sexy lady.'[10] Late one night she summonsed him urgently to the flat she was still sharing with Tony, ostensibly to tell Annakin that she had broken a tooth and would be unable to work the next day, but in fact, as she put it, to 'get it over and done with!' With great reluctance Annakin, who realised that a fling with his leading lady would compromise his authority on the set, made his excuses and left. As he let himself out of the front door, Tony emerged from the lift:

> 'So that's why she wanted me to stay out late,' he said in an emotionless sort of way.
>   'Don't worry, Tony, we've been having a little professional discussion about goldfish. I'm the one who got away.' I gave him a wink and hurried off.

The next day, back on set, Glynis took Annakin's arm and whispered: 'I should have told you, darling, Tony's gone gay!' He wouldn't, she added, 'have cared a damn'.[11]

A return to acting by Tony could easily bring his and Glynis's careers into conflict. They were never going to achieve a professional partnership of equals, like those of Michael Denison and Dulcie Gray, or of Googie Withers and John McCallum, let alone the combustible and shorter-lived one of Olivier and Vivien Leigh. Glynis was the high-flyer. There was a baby to look after, but that was the nanny's job; Tony was no pioneering househusband. He had no one to manage professionally; the agency world was not really for him. He needed to do something, if only for his self-esteem. Proud as he was of his wife's accomplishments and celebrity, there had to be more to life than standing on the edge of a set at Islington Studios and watching her jitterbug with her fellow players in a replica of a Canadian Army canteen. Glynis, however, knew what it took to make a success, knew her husband's limitations, and issued a blunt warning: 'I told him that I would lose respect for him if he wanted to continue with trying to be an actor. He was *such* a bad one. I said, "Be an agent, be a producer, be a road-sweeper, but don't come on to my ground unless you know what you're doing." But his love for acting was such that he couldn't give it up.' He had a brief attempt at working for the Al Parker agency, but it came to nothing, and in the summer of 1946 he secured a part in a new play by the out-of-fashion Frederick Lonsdale, *But for the Grace of God*, which was to tour extensively before coming to the St James's Theatre. Glynis went to see the out-of-town dress rehearsal, sat making notes for him, and afterwards travelled home: 'He saw me off, and as the train pulled out he was waving to me with the tears rolling down his face. Because it was the end.' As was the way in those more clumsy days, their divorce would not be finalised until the summer of 1948, but the union had broken down irretrievably. Yet they would always remain good friends – and not only at a distance. Glynis would come to stay, and she enjoyed the company of the young man to whom Tony introduced her one evening backstage.

'Hazy' is probably the best description of the events in late 1946 which led to Derek and Tony pursuing that handshake at Amersham in 1940. The auto-biographies paint a picture of desolation as Derek trudges to 'Q', where Beatie de Leon greets him with: 'Hello dear. Been away?' – but no work;[12] of being discouraged by a genial, successful Ustinov; of making fruitless telephone calls from 'a small bedroom on the Strand side of the Savoy' – by which he surely meant the Savoy side of the Strand – which he occupied with an Oxo tin containing his financial assets.[13] Having decided to give up and go home to live with his parents, he went to the Savoy Grill 'to spend the last of my slender means in a final burst of epicurian delight', and was spotted by the Forwoods' friend, Lusia Parry, whose name appeared in the list he had compiled at Catterick. She asked whether he had an agent: 'I had ... Tony Forwood,' replied Derek, 'but apparently he has given it up, now he's an actor himself.' Lusia explained that after seven years in the Army he could not go back to an office, that he had grown fed up with 'getting jobs for total idiots at twice his salary' and had taken up the stage again:

'He got married, you know, to Glynis Johns.'
'Yes, I knew; he wrote to me years ago.'
'But they've broken up. It's sad because there is a baby, a boy, did you know?'
'No. Lost touch in 1942.'

Lusia said Tony was in a play, but was 'wretched and ill'. Derek should go to see him: 'He doesn't see anyone much now. It was a big blow, the marriage breaking up.' Whereupon Derek set off for Chesham Mews, and found him, seemingly with little to offer but a dose of flu.

Something like that happened: an entry in the Diary many years later confirms so. Incontrovertibly, Derek went to visit Tony at the St James's, where, after its encouraging tour, *But for the Grace of God* had opened on 3 September. Its producer was Peter Daubeny, before the war an actor in repertory at the Liverpool Playhouse and now making his way as an impresario after fighting through North Africa and on to Salerno, where he lost an arm. Daubeny agreed with the critics that his fifth production was in some respects 'an old-fashioned play, with a touch of 1880s melodrama under its fashionable jokes', but the piece, about blackmail and murder in a Scottish baronial hall, was lifted by a superlative cast, which included A. E. Matthews and Mary Jerrold; Robert Douglas, whose performance won him a Hollywood contract; and Michael Gough and Hugh McDermott, who took part every night in 'one of the most realistic stage fights ever seen on the London stage'.[14] Tony, in a small role, was perfectly at home with the 'aristocratic style' demanded if the play was to work. It did, and it ran for seven months, 'well into the coldest winter for years, and then, in spite of fuel shortages, floods and deepening post-war austerity, for another three or four months touring the provinces'. Perhaps, reflected Daubeny, the austerity helped: 'Audiences seemed to find a positive comfort in escaping into Lonsdale's eternal pre-war world.' During the run Daubeny became good friends with Tony and, much later, gave him a memorable notice of his own: 'His unvarying affability towards everyone always reminded me of a great blond horse in a sunny meadow, nosing towards you for a piece of sugar.'

Daubeny recounted how one day Tony asked if he would see 'a young friend of his who had had very little luck in the theatre'. The producer agreed, but said that at present he was not casting a play: 'When I met him in Tony's dressing-room I gathered that he was a young out-of-work actor doing some scene-painting at the Queen's Theatre, and that his theatrical experience was practically nil. He made no impression on me at all, except that his face, with its Spanish black eyes, reminded me of Eddie Cantor.' It was hardly a breakthrough for the downhearted Derek; but the introduction to this happy company would lead before too long to professional associations and firm personal friendships with 'Matty' Matthews, Michael Gough and Daubeny himself. Where to turn? There was this outfit called the Reunion Theatre Association. The idea had been conceived three years earlier in, of all places, Baghdad, when William Fox, an actor then serving as a major in the Army, had a conversation with the son of a governor of the Shakespeare Memorial Theatre in Stratford about how to cope with the 1,200-plus actors and actresses who would be returning to 'civvy street' and a theatreland which had nothing like enough jobs for them all. It had become a reality in March 1946 when the RTA presented *And No Birds Sing* at the Comedy Theatre under the auspices of the Greenroom Rags Society, and earned royal approval when the Princesses Elizabeth and Margaret attended a matinée of *1066 – And All That* at the Palace Theatre in May, which raised £5,000. Again, none of the principal theatrical archives can corroborate the account in *Snakes and Ladders*, which has Derek turning up for an audition at the Duke of York's, where, on the set of the Ralph Lynn farce *Is Your Honeymoon Really Necessary?*, the Australian director Allan Davis was casting a one-act play called *The Man in the Street*. He had found a 'Mary Magdalene' and a 'Joseph', and was searching the aisles for his 'Jesus' when he tripped over Derek's feet:

> We rehearsed in the Dress Circle Bar for a week or so [...] Mr Davis was very particular and gave the whole horrid little playlet the importance of 'Tosca'. I can't for the life of me remember what it was all about, save that it was a play for children and had a religious flavour if not much religious fervour [...] We opened one morning, at the deathly hour of eleven [...] before a sparse audience of Agents, Managers' Assistants, Casting Directors and what were called, in those days, Talent Scouts [...] and to my intense surprise I was a great success as Jesus; and after the play was over found myself jammed into a corner of the Stage Box surrounded by excited, complimentary, quacking people handing me telephone numbers and begging that I call them, all, it appeared, immediately.[15]

Confusingly, the first professional portrait in the Derek scrapbook gave as his agent Vivienne Black, who had an office in St James's. The list of credits on the reverse was up to date as far as *A* [*sic*] *Man in the Street*. It also told any prospective producer that the client was twenty-five, and five feet eleven inches tall [!], that his colouring was dark and that he could manage all dialects. He had under his belt fifteen months [*sic*] at Amersham and one year [also *sic*] at Q and the Embassy. Vivienne Black vanished from the picture pretty rapidly, because by the middle of December Derek was represented by Frederick Joachim, who was unlikely to have been part of any 'quacking' mêlée at the Duke of York's or anywhere else. The forty-one-year-old son of an immigrant Jewish stockbroker, he had worked briefly in a theatrical agency run by Herbert de Leon, brother of the Q Theatre's Jack, and had now set up on his own. With an acute inferiority complex – largely the result of his parents' undisguised preference for his musician brother – Freddy was an improbable agent, but his small roster of clients, including Eric Pohlman and Thora Hird, were devoted to him. The late Denis Quilley described him as:

> shortish, square-ish, beautifully spoken, modest and quiet. He had silvery hair and looked like a very reliable bank manager, or a businessman of a respectable nature. He was unflashy, untheatrical, charming. He was a *gent* – not a word you can use often about agents. He used to say that the best publicity an actor can have is good notices – everything else is superficial. He expected his artists to be *asked for*; they didn't need to be promoted. If you had acquired a sufficient reputation, managers would ring up for you.[16]

Donald Sinden, too, had a high regard for him, saying that Freddy's only serious shortcoming was a narrow horizon: America was beyond his reach and his ken – which would come to matter in the case of his new client. The agency was on an upper floor at Remo House in Regent Street, a short step from Shaftesbury Avenue and the Strand. The location was prime; the facilities modest. There was just – but only just – enough room for Freddy, his secretary and a visitor. Presumably recognising that there was no future with Miss Black, Derek went to see Freddy, then called at another, larger, agency, only to return to Remo House. 'I've decided to come to you,' he told Freddy, 'because you've got such a bloody awful office that I feel you'll work like stink to get out of it!'[17]

The new client was called Dirk Bogarde. It said so on the back of the photograph issued by Vivienne Black, and that was the name Freddy now began to tout around, if not exactly to promote. The partial experiment on the endpaper of the book given to Hugh Jolly in Singapore showed that Derek had almost resolved the problem by the time he came home. According to *Snakes and Ladders* the matter was finalised over lunch at Peter Jones, the Chelsea department store, when Tony dismissed 'D. v.d. Bogaerde' as out of the question; 'Simon Garde' as 'Simple Simon. And dull'; and 'Dirk Niven' as potentially leading to confusion. 'I'm going to be Dirk Bogarde, and that's it; that's my new name, no one else is called that, for God's sake.' Possible worries about the great Humphrey were swatted away: 'He's in America and anyway he's the same family and it ends in "t".'[18] So that was that. If Freddy preferred the idea of 'Dick' – as 'friendly' – he did not try anything sneaky. It was emphatically for Dirk Bogarde that he began to 'work like stink' by arranging an appointment in early December with the BBC's recently arrived infant – television. The start was unpromising: Dirk turned up a week late to meet the senior clerk in the booking section, Mrs M. C. Burch.

The following Wednesday he made no mistake. It was the first rehearsal at St Hilda's Convent in Maida Vale for Patrick Hamilton's *Rope*, which Dirk already knew well from Catterick, and in which he had now been engaged to play Charles Granillo. The author describes the character as slim, expensively and rather ornately dressed in a grey suit: 'He is dark. A Spaniard. He is enormously courteous – something between a dancing-master and a stage villain. He speaks English perfectly. To those who know him fairly well, and are not subject to Anglo-Saxon prejudices, he seems a thoroughly good sort.' The neurotic killer was a plum part. Rehearsals spanned Christmas and the New Year. On 4 January 1947 the *Star* printed the meagre list of television programmes for the following day – less than three hours in all, beginning with a spot by the fourteen-year-old singer and actress Petula Clark. Sandwiched between 'Starlight: Carroll Gibbons (piano)' and 'News (sound only)' was 'Rope, play by Patrick Hamilton, with David Markham, Dirk Bogarde'. For Dirk, travelling home on the train to Haywards Heath, it was the first time he had seen his new name in print and, he noted in his scrapbook, he 'went pink in the face'. There were two transmissions from Alexandra Palace – one on Sunday evening, the second on the Tuesday, and both, of course, live. Afterwards, the producer, Stephen Harrison, sent a report on his cast to the manager of the television booking section, S. E. Holland Bennett. Having praised David Markham, with the single reservation that he was 'possibly a little too nice' for the part of Wyndham Brandon, he wrote of Dirk: 'I think he has possibilities. Although he is rather inexperienced, he was good from the start in the more emotional scenes, and eventually sustained his performance consistently in the duller connecting links. He, too, was possibly too charming a type for the part of Granillo.'[19] Dirk, with a favourable notice among the hierarchy and twenty-seven guineas better off, wrote immediately to Mrs Burch from Hillside Cottage:

> I came along to see you one wednesday afternoon, a week later than you had arranged, and, if you remember, you sent me up to see Mr Holland Bennet on 'the spur of the moment' as you put it.
>   I landed a job of work within ten minutes of being in the room.
>   The job was 'Rope' and we finished yesterday.
>   Stephen Harrison seemed pleased with what I did and has promised me more parts in the future, and altogether life has been grand fun for me!
>   I want to thank you, very sincerely, for you help and kindness ... and for having the thought to send me up to see Bennet!
>   It was terrific experience, and excellent for a somewhat jaded moral!
>   Once more, thank you Very Much ...
>   Dirk Bogarde[20]

It was, as he put it, 'a beginning again'. Little did he know. Six months would elapse before he acted in another 'telly', but by that time life had become grander fun still.

Accounts differ, but whether it was the result of a farcical mix-up, or a nerve-racking but formal audition, Dirk found himself in the cast of Michael Clayton Hutton's *Power Without Glory* at the New Lindsey Theatre Club in Notting Hill, 'London's most intimate little theatre', which prided itself on 'presenting vital plays'. The twenty-nine-year-old playwright was a newcomer to the London theatre. So too – at least as a director – was Chloë Gibson, a forty-six-year-old actress who had run a drama school in Devon and whose first impression on Dirk was that of a chain-smoking 'hysterical virago' with a straggle of rope-like reddish hair and a tongue which would not have been out of place on the barrack-square. In her infinitely more reliable account she had heard scores of young actors and almost made up her mind when someone whose judgment she respected – probably Freddy, or one of the BBC producers – telephoned to say she ought 'to see this boy' because he was quite exceptional. She agreed, provided he paid his own expenses to come up from Sussex: 'Then I saw him for the first time as he slipped through the door into the studio; looking very small, very shy and very young. He hadn't a script, hadn't even read the play; but even then there was a magnetism about him, something different. I told him a little about it, and there he stood, in a duffel coat and looking absurdly boyish, reading a scene from the play.'[21]

He had, she said, the nervous tension she wanted, 'but a tremendous tenderness as well'. The play, billed as 'A Tragedy', is a portrait of the impact on a working-class London family when Eddie, a soldier returning from the war after six years, finds his girlfriend involved with his younger brother, Cliff, who has a 'guilty secret'. Kenneth More was cast as the elder brother, Beatrice Varley as their mother, Dandy Nichols as their aunt and Maureen Pook as the girlfriend. Dirk had the star part – and for the second time in succession had murder in mind. Kenneth More wrote in his memoirs that he shared a dressing-room with Dirk:

My first impression of him was of a very shy, dark, reserved young man who tended to gravitate towards corners, where he would sit, saying nothing. He had to be persuaded to go anywhere.

He was, in fact, rather unsure of himself. Few people know it, but he was so conscious of what he considered to be his lack of acting experience – he had been with the Amersham rep for a short while – that when the first audition for *Power Without Glory* was held, and he saw experienced professionals waiting in the room, he was overcome with doubts. He hesitated while his hand was on the doorknob and very nearly chucked the whole idea by going home.[22]

More recalled that during rehearsals Dirk had lunch with Chloë Gibson one day and offered to give up the part if there was any danger of letting her down. But his hard streak – the one 'that's got to be in anyone who tries the rough and tumble of show business' – was not far from the surface. Both men were taken to the East End for their costume-fittings, where Chloë Gibson decided that Cliff should have a 'coat with a cut up the back'. Dirk asked the youth behind the counter if he had such a garment. No reply. Dirk tried again. Still nothing: 'Dirk was roused. Despite his look of bland, youthful innocence he had held the rank of staff-major in the Army and was used to authority. In a firm loud voice he snapped: "I've asked you twice for the coat. NOW GET IT!" The boy practically leapt up in the air in surprise. So did we.'

Opening night was 25 February. Ulric and Margaret sent a telegram: 'ALL THE BEST FOR TONIGHT DONT BE FRIGHT – MAG AND DADDY'. If some of the critics had their reservations about the play – one said it was evident that it had been written in five days – most agreed with *The Observer* that it was 'compact, exciting and sharply-acted'.[23] *The Times* judged Dirk 'an excellent casual murderer, all egotism and nerves'; the *Daily Express* considered his performance 'as a weak, vain and handsome murderer was the best of a brilliant company';[24] and *Cavalcade* pronounced: 'More will be heard of Dirk Bogarde. His portrait of a

slack-jawed youth under pressure is hauntingly memorable.'[25] Elizabeth Frank
went further in the *News Chronicle* by heading her column 'Man With a Future'
and naming Dirk personality of the week: 'I am prepared to lay 100 to 1 with
anyone that this young man will make a big future for himself, and I have reason
to believe that at least two substantial film contracts will soon come his way.' He
was, she added, 'an unusual actor of great sensitivity and intelligence'. So the
perceptive Elizabeth Frank may be forgiven for swallowing the fact that: 'Faced
with family opposition he ran away from home when he was 17 and took a job
as jack-of-all-trades at the "Q" Theatre.'[26] The cuttings were encouraging, even
head-turning, but during rehearsals there had been an even more important
development. Peter Daubeny, the producer who had seen in Dirk a likeness to
Eddie Cantor and nothing else, was told that the New Lindsey's backers had
pulled out and Chloë Gibson's company was 'stranded'. It would cost £250 to
come to the rescue. Daubeny set off reluctantly to Notting Hill, with a cheque
in his pocket, because he 'felt too much of a coward to pass a death-sentence on
these young actors, whose whole future might well depend on outside good
will'.[27] As he went in, he felt the tiny auditorium 'vibrating with nervous tension'.
The play began, and he found himself caught up with the characters and their
background of 'cockney attitudes and brutal humour which possessed real drama
and plausibility'. His interest was engaged:

> Suddenly there rushed on to the stage a breathless figure, half choking with
> emotion: a slight, dark youth, radiating a curious, almost hypnotic power;
> every movement, every inflection of his voice, uncannily suggesting the poetry
> of the gutter, of a lost soul. Beyond any doubt, here was an actor of the first
> quality. It turned out to be the young man with whom I had been so unim-
> pressed shortly before and his name was Dirk Bogarde.

As he handed his cheque to the director, Chloë Gibson, Daubeny felt 'that on
the strength of Bogarde's performance alone it would be money well spent'.

During the run Dirk and Tony became the best of friends with the impresario,
spending time with him at his parents' house and in Bournemouth with Tony's
Aunt Gwen and Uncle Carl. Daubeny had an option to transfer *Power Without
Glory* if the circumstances were right, and when the play closed at the New
Lindsey the seven actors and actresses, now out of work, waited in hope. During
this 'melancholy interim' the producer's telephone would often ring in the night.
Even if they had just had dinner together, it would always be Dirk, asking
how he was and adding 'Any news?' 'I imagined him,' wrote Daubeny, 'as the
spokesman of a stranded ship's company in a Somerset Maugham novelette'.
Then, out of the blue, came the day he was able to tell Dirk: 'It's all fixed.' A
haven had been found at the Fortune Theatre, across the road from the stage
door of the Theatre Royal Drury Lane, where Noël Coward's *Pacific 1860*, with
Mary Martin, was coming to the end of its run. Coward had seen *Power Without*

Glory at the New Lindsey, and afterwards, like royalty, addressed the paraded cast. According to *Snakes and Ladders* he complimented them effusively, but told Maureen Pook that her name was 'a disaster, change it immediately' and, moving on to Dirk, said, with wagging finger: 'Never, ever, ever take a pill, not even an aspirin before a show, and never, ever drink until after curtain-fall.' As they wandered off the stage, Coward caught Dirk's elbow: 'And never, ever, go near the cinema!'[28]

Daubeny invited Coward to the dress rehearsal of *Power Without Glory* on 4 April, and 'The Master', even more impressed, said he would do his utmost to make the production a hit. He was as good as his word, sending Daubeny on a postcard a note which could be used on posters all over town: 'Anyone in London who really cares for vital, true and exciting acting, must see – "POWER WITHOUT GLORY" – a most moving and finely written play and on all counts an enthralling evening in the theatre.' He also sent Dirk a first-night telegram: 'I HOPE YOUR BRILLIANT PERFORMANCE HAS THE TRUE SUCCESS IT SO RICHLY DESERVES – NOEL COWARD.' The reviewers were even more enthused than they had been at the New Lindsey, and Dirk was again singled out. The *Evening News* said that he 'gives a brilliant study of the "mamma's darling" whose cheap good looks and easy success with women pitch him suddenly and inevitably into crime';[29] the *Star*, that as the 'spiv' brother he 'gives a superb performance of nervous tensity';[30] and the *Evening Standard* described him as 'the most convincing neurotic murderer ever seen outside the Old Bailey'.[31] Yet despite the critical tide running in its favour, the play struggled. It was never more than a *succès d'estime*. The arrival of *Oklahoma!* across the road at Drury Lane did not help: ' "Oh What a Beautiful Morning!" became, alas, our requiem.'[32] After eight weeks, *Power Without Glory* closed, with Daubeny £6,000 poorer, but legitimately proud of his ' "artistic" flutter' which had given a nudge to several careers, including those of the playwright and the director. Coward continued to champion the young company by taking them all into his new production, *Peace in Our Time* – all, that is, but one. By now Dirk had other plans.

Joe Mendoza and Tony Skene, scriptwriters working for the dynamic producer Sydney Box – whom the J. Arthur Rank Organisation had put in charge of its Gainsborough arm – went to see the play while it was still at the New Lindsey. Mendoza remembers how they were struck both by the quizzical, humorous More and by the actor playing the 'misfit', who, although a physical lightweight, had an 'extraordinary strength of character and total charisma that swept everybody in the cast – and the audience – away and before him into his own complete "world" '.[33] They reported back the next morning to Box, who said: 'We'll test the one with the charisma. Write me a scene for him.' Mendoza and Skene were already working on an idea of Box's based on a recent incident involving a crashed American Army Dakota and the passengers' plight as they waited in hope for rescue. The hero was to be a famous athlete, stricken by polio and travelling in an iron lung for treatment, who offers to sacrifice his own air supply in order that there should be enough power for the aircraft's radio to signal their position. A tear-jerker, or what? On 17 March Dirk, accompanied by Peter Daubeny, took a screen test at the Gainsborough Studios in Shepherds Bush. A photograph shows him supine under blankets, with a concerned Jane Barrett leaning over him. Neither she nor Dirk was asked to appear in the finished film, which began as 'We Want to Live!', went into production under Ken Annakin's direction as 'Rescue', and was released as *Broken Journey*. Nor did Sydney Box have anything to offer immediately in the remainder of his hectic programme. However, Dirk had been noticed. Mendoza, who directed the test, said Dirk 'transformed what could have been sentimental melodrama into something understated yet truly noble, totally believable and moving beyond words'.

Which was more than could be said for the tiny role which Dirk claimed that Tony Forwood secured for him. But it was a speaking part. Dirk had spent a day at Cromwell Studios in Southall, uttering his first words in front of the camera in an unpretentious thriller called *Dancing with Crime*. Directed by John Paddy Carstairs, it starred Richard Attenborough, in his first 'tough' role, as a cab-driver, back from the war and trying to make an honest living; and Sheila Sim, his wife in real life, as the chorus girl he wishes to marry. Dirk's contribution comes right at the end of the film, when he is heard calling somewhat frenziedly into a police despatcher's microphone: 'HM3 from M257. Message number one zero seven. Ridley and Masterman. Shop premises. Number nine zero seven Oxford Street. Broken into. Pick up call Baker.' That was it – and the moment was no more memorable in vision, because Dirk was shot in medium close-up from over his left shoulder; his family would have been hard-pressed to recognise him. And the part was too small to earn a credit in the closing titles. No stars were involved in the scene, so he did not even meet the Attenboroughs. 'But it was a start, and for that one day's work I earned double my week's salary in the theatre. [...] I vaguely thought how simple it was, and how much better paid, and how I could, in a very short time indeed, fill the Oxo tin and move to a larger flat'.[34]

Even as *Power Without Glory* opened at the Fortune Theatre, it looked increasingly as if Dirk was about to break the last of Coward's three commandments. Leonard Mosley in the *Daily Express* reported that 'Mr Bogarde has already had offers from three film studios'.[35] The director Henry Kendall wrote congratulating Dirk on his performance as Cliff and hoped that they could work together, 'Before you become a film star – which I'm afraid is inevitable!'[36] On 23 April, less than three weeks after the Fortune opening, Olive Dodds, of Rank's contract artists department, sent an internal memo reporting that the company was taking an option on Dirk's services for six months, during which time it would 'try and find him a part in a film, which he wishes to do, but he shall not unreasonably refuse to do the part offered him'. From 1 May he would be paid £25 a week, set off against the £2,500 for the film, if one materialised. Thirty days after he completed his part in the film, the company would be entitled to exercise its right to put him under a contract, starting at £5,000 and rising in the seventh year to £20,000.[37] The die was cast. When Noël Coward came to rescue Daubeny's little liferaft full of protégés for *Peace in Our Time*, Dirk had to own up. In *Snakes and Ladders* he tells of shyly following Coward to the latter's home in Gerald Road and of being reassured that he would not be jumped on because, said Coward, 'I'm not the type'; of listening intently to the 'considered, wise, careful' advice; and, finally, of having to be told: 'I think you are being a cunt. And I am very, very angry indeed.'[38] In a letter to Coward's biographer, Philip Hoare, Dirk gave a more measured account, saying that, yes, Coward, 'like most theater people', felt that the cinema was 'a piffling business. You don't have to act, it's all technicians.' However, the reproof was based not so much on any prejudice, or personal slight – he was 'more astounded really than angry' that Dirk had turned down the part in his new play – but, rather, on his fear that the theatre was moribund, and 'was screaming out for new blood': 'Every old tabby with a varicose vein has been playing the Juvenile since '39. We need new guts, a new breath, new wind.' Dirk explained that 'after six weary years on a Captain's Pay', the security of the cinema was a comforting and enticing prospect. 'He eventually, reluctantly, saw my point. He was sad, but understanding. "It was bound to happen" was all he could finally say.'[39] One suspects that Coward, the shrewdest of players both on and off the stage, understood very well where Dirk's decision might lead, and why, precisely, comfort and security were not only desirable but also necessary.

The principal price of being an actor, albeit in a small house and with a 'heavy' piece, began to be paid almost from the start. Four days after the screen test, the *West London Times* gave the first newspaper profile to the 'Actor, artist, soldier and journalist', who said he was not particularly proud of his versatility:

> 'Perhaps I've too many irons in the fire,' he says ruefully. But one feels the only difficulty is for him to decide which he shall work upon; most people would advise acting, and that is his choice too. 'Even,' he says, 'If I'm not very handsome.' But wax-model beauty is no longer a requisite for stage success and popularity, the 'bobby soxers' are already storming Dirk's dressing room, finding plenty of attraction in this over six foot, slim, dark-eyed young man.[40]

His bedazzled, anonymous interviewer found Dirk 'friendly, well endowed with a sense of humour, and entirely free from airs and graces'. He was living in Hasker Street, 'a row of quaint and attractive cottages, in the artists-quarter of Knightsbridge', managing his rations 'with the typical haphazard bewilderment of a demobbed bachelor, and returning at intervals to his parents' house in the country, for carefree life and food free of the mysteries of cooking it'. All too soon, *Woman's Own* was to print a reader's letter about the helplessness of men in the kitchen, and place alongside it a gratuitous photograph of Dirk, holding a spoon and a pudding bowl. An editorial hand would add: 'He can toss us a pancake any day!'[41] Hasker Street, in the hinterland between Knightsbridge and Chelsea, and equidistant from Harrods and Peter Jones, comprised small Georgian workmen's cottages – 'two up, two down and two in the basement'. Laurence Harbottle, who would become Dirk's solicitor, lived there when he first came to London in 1952 and recalls: 'It was an interesting street in those days; it had all sorts of funny people in it – a mixture of down-on-your-luck nobility and sleaze. A lot of the houses were occupied by elderly relics of noble families, with the old butler and his wife, for whom there was *just* room. There were two lesbians further up the road from us, one of whom had a wooden leg. She used to get very drunk on Saturday nights and throw the wooden leg through the window.'[42] As it turned out, Dirk and his Oxo tin were really passing through. Nothing to do with the neighbours; everything to do with new-found wealth. He was trading up.

Dirk had already received seven £25 retainers when on 7 June Freddy witnessed his signature on an agreement with Production Facilities (Films) Limited, the centralised operation working on behalf of – and often making life difficult for – Rank's disparate group of companies. This heavy-handed bureaucracy was known among producers and directors as 'Piffle'.[43] The contract bound Dirk from his first day of shooting – or 1 September, whichever was the sooner – for seven years. His services were to be entirely exclusive, although he could be lent, for a fee, to other companies. He was obliged to attend tests, rehearsals, costume fittings and conferences; to have still photographs taken as required, and to make personal appearances. Under one extremely long clause he undertook to pass to the company all his fan-mail, which would be handled on his behalf, provided that he paid £100 towards the cost, signed photographs whenever 'Piffle' asked him to do so, and helped to deal with it 'expeditiously'. The company was entitled to set up, or authorise, a 'Fan-mail Club'; it could also publish or approve 'a Fan Magazine or Fan Magazines'. Under other clauses he had to remain a British subject ordinarily resident in the United Kingdom and to undergo 'such massage treatment as the Company may from time to time consider necessary or desirable'. He was forbidden from making without prior consent any public statement about the company's business, policy, personnel or artists; and he could be suspended for 'committing or permitting in his private or professional life any act or thing which in the opinion of the Company would cause scandal or prejudice the public against' him. Further sub-clauses made him liable to possible suspension in case of fourteen days' illness during a production; 'suffering any facial or physical disability or disfigurement' which might detract from his appearance on the screen; and his voice becoming 'unsatisfactory in quality or tone or otherwise unsuitable for any part he is taking'. The company, in its turn, agreed that for the first three years he would not be required to take anything less than a 'feature' part and in subsequent years anything less than a 'leading' part in 'major' productions. His £5,000 salary for the first year would be paid by the week. And he was allowed four weeks' annual holiday.[44] This 'marriage' was triggered because a film had been found for Dirk – in fact, there were two. Its Cupid was one of the many practitioners who had been to see the play: Ian Dalrymple, known as 'one of the quiet personalities of our industry who says little but obviously thinks much'.[45] As executive producer of the Crown Film Unit during the war, 'Dal' had been responsible for several classic, morale-boosting documentaries, including *Western Approaches* and *Target for Tonight.* Now he had turned to making features for Rank with his own company, Wessex Films, one of the four independent groups based at Pinewood Studios. Among his projects in the pipeline were two adaptations: George Moore's splendidly miserable 1894 novel, *Esther Waters*, and a Montagu Slater story about a ruthlessly social-climbing speedway rider. On 25 May Dalrymple wrote to Dirk, suggesting that they have dinner together once *Power Without Glory* had finished at the Fortune, and expressing his delight that Dirk had 'fallen to my lot': 'I will try hard to put you on the Map, the celluloid one, with the little I know of my medium: and God knows *you* have something to give! But it all depends on our close co-operation together & complete trust in each other. Let's try.'[46]

In the meantime, Freddy had been busy doing his best for his client. Capitalising on the success of *Power Without Glory,* he spent a good part of May writing to various drama producers at BBC Radio; to each of them he stressed Dirk's 'unusual facility for dialects'. The controller of the Fortune, Frederick Lloyd, added his ha'p'orth by asking the Director of Drama, Val Gielgud, to consider broadcasting the play. A producer, Peter Watts, was despatched to the Fortune and reported back that the work was only just above average, needed drastic cutting and most of the accents were phoney; there was, however, an outstanding performance from Dirk Bogarde, 'who should be well worth using.'[47] Another member of the drama department, Hugh Stewart, promised to add Dirk's name to his list for the next audition in about a month's time. There was better luck at Television where, on 22 July, Dirk appeared in *The Case of Helvig Delbo*, a reconstruction of an incident in 1943 when twelve Danish patriots who had been helping downed aircrew to escape back to Britain were betrayed to the Gestapo. On the day after the broadcast the producer and writer, Robert Barr, wrote to Dirk, apologising for having to kill him off in the middle of the show, 'but I am sure you will agree that it is pleasant to go out in a blaze of glory – particularly when it is only a play'. He added that a number of people at Alexandra Palace 'were most intrigued by your scene in the night club – very nonchalant'.[48] He could afford a little nonchalance off the set, too. Ian Dalrymple had written again to him following tests at Pinewood from which 'one or two things emerged' but 'far, far the most important was, that if we all keep calm, you will rocket into the Firmament. So, when you're a Big Shot, remember that your celluloid birthplace lay in Wessex! But I wonder, will you! Or are you as hard as the rest?' The generous 'Dal' continued:

One thing I can tell you now. I shan't be telling you what to do much, for I think you know far better than I do. But this I will say from the start: you register so strongly, you are so photogenic, you are so easy & natural, that you won't need any tricks, however subtle. We must both bear this in mind & be sparing for you need so little that is calculated, however nicely, when you yourself *live* your rôle so vitally, and the Camera is so fond of you.

'Dal' wished Dirk a 'blazing success with your first 2 films which should land you at the top by 1949. Not bad going! But, keep all this under your hat, be sincere & modest. Let's work hard – and you're *there*.'[49] Dirk had found another mentor.

He had also found somewhere else to live, somewhere more fitting for a star-in-the-making. Chester Row was half a mile from Hasker Street, close to Sloane Square, but in Belgravia as opposed to Chelsea, with diplomats heavily out-numbering wooden-legged lesbians, and Noël Coward one street away. From a Mrs Gwendoline Watson of Sussex, Dirk rented, furnished, number 44 which, like his previous lodging, was in an attractive terrace, but which had an extra storey. Instead of a single room he now had three floors, a basement and a garden, all to himself and a rescued cat whom he had christened Cliff. When the electoral register for 1947 was compiled in the summer, four names were recorded: Dirk; two other men, Alfred Beloe and Kenneth Leather; and a woman – one Edna F. Holiday. It was 'Nan Baildon', or, rather, Eve, who had been released from the RAF in March the previous year and was now installed at number 44 as a glorified housekeeper and house-sitter. Without putting too fine a point on it, the superior officer was now the servant.

When he came to write about this period thirty years later, Dirk admitted that he was undergoing some kind of internal crisis: 'My adventure had begun and I really rather liked it all. There was one gentle, worrying doubt, however. Just one. Who the hell was I? More important still, what was I? Like people of an immigrant race, I was searching for my identity, although I was not at all sure what I'd do with it when, if, I found it.'[50] He was, quite suddenly, 'hot' – and Rank was going to do its damnedest to ensure that he justified its investment by keeping him that way. The heat was fierce enough to dissolve some of his existing relationships. 'Old friends, such as I had, began to fall away,' he wrote. Some had the door closed on them pretty smartly. Denis Thomas, who met Dirk on the voyage home from Singapore and hit it off so well that there was a possibility of their sharing a flat, told a colleague that Dirk had taken him out to lunch shortly after signing with Rank and said: 'I'll be mixing and dealing with people you wouldn't even want to sit down with. I'm telling all my other friends the same, and also saying goodbye to each of them. You'll never see me again.' And Thomas – who became deputy editor of Independent Television News in the fifties – never did.[51] With others, the parting was more drawn-out. John Greaves, who at the time was sharing a flat in Primrose Hill with his brother Chris, recalls how Dirk, just after being spotted by Rank, rang up out of the blue, needing a bed for the night, and deeply concerned for the welfare of the clothes he had bought. 'He arrived in a taxi from the tailor's, with this very fragile, rather flamboyant suit. It was some sort of mohair mix, and off-white, so it would very easily get dirty.' Unlike Chris, whose bed was sprung on four bricks, John had a cupboard, and looked after the suit.[52] Their sister, Sylvia, was struck by the fact that Dirk always wore white socks. When he volunteered to become godfather to her daughter, Sylvia's husband put his foot down, saying that actors were 'unreliable'.[53] They all met again for a lunch at Kettners to celebrate the Rank contract, and that would be the last time – apart from a visit by the brothers to the theatre, when they were 'appalled at the fawning women'. It was clear, says John Greaves, that Dirk 'had got out of our orbit, our social scene. Chris, particularly, felt that.'[54] Hugh Jolly's was a slightly different case, as we shall see. And Jack? Just after *Power Without Glory* opened at the New Lindsey, he visited Dirk in Chelsea and they spent two days together before Dirk saw him off to Suffolk. 'I was awfully worried about you being without food – or dough – and probably hours on a snowbound train,' wrote Dirk late that night. Another tiny snapshot exists, showing the two men, smartly dressed and on the town, apparently in 1948; but their meetings, never frequent, were now at best sporadic, and for old times' sake. There was never any question of Jack being part of the Belgravia household; as we have seen, his life and his work lay properly in Suffolk. He, more than anyone, had now to encourage from a distance as Dirk took on what he described as 'my new inheritance' and played host at Chester Row to professionals from his new milieu.

Cornel Lucas was the first of the Rank portrait photographers to work extensively with Dirk – 'I always thought he looked like Frank Sinatra' – and had a productive session at the house: Dirk showing off one of his paintings; pretending to read a magazine; dispensing tea for two ladies seen only from behind; spooning liquid from the pudding basin – the 'toss us a pancake' image which would feature in *Woman's Own*; and, no less memorably, with the camera on the ground, Dirk lighting a cigarette while he took a break from mopping the floor. Lucas's job was 'star promotion'. 'They were putting people under long-term contract, and at one point they had forty-nine artists. The idea was to emulate Hollywood – in the style of photography too. They were keen to keep the continuity going. If an artist was not needed on a film, they would say, "Give him, or her, to Cornel Lucas to do a portrait. Keep 'em busy".' From their first meeting, which he believes was in Hasker Street, Lucas could tell that Dirk had an unusually acute sense of image: 'He was living in this tiny little one-room bachelor flat, but the important thing was that he was in a very important area and at a good address!' He was, says Lucas, 'a bit of a snob, and it must have started early'. He was also 'tremendously publicity-minded. It was quite an inspiration to see an actor so keen on that side of things. He was interested in the photography too – and that undoubtedly came from his father.' As the years went by, recalls Lucas, 'the photographs became as important to Dirk as the film. Apart from Marlene Dietrich he was the only artist I knew who had a contract that gave him control over his photographs.'[55] But that came much later.

For the moment, all the public could see as the promotion machine whirred effortlessly into action on Dirk's, and the Studio's, behalf were still photographs, usually attached to a brief piece of copy about this brightest of new prospects. On 15 October the *Sketch* magazine reminded readers that, as occasion arose, 'it is our policy to seize the psychological moment when a young man, hitherto unknown or hardly known to the public, rises from his surroundings and shows himself to be something out of the ordinary'. Under the heading 'In Politics, Films, the Stage – Four Young Men of Mark' it printed a page of pictures, showing J. Harold Wilson, the thirty-one-year-old newly appointed President of the Board of Trade; Kieron Moore, 'a new British screen discovery of the first magnitude'; Peter Daubeny, 'London's youngest actor-manager'; and, at his kitchen stove, spoon and saucepan in hand, 'another British actor fresh to stardom' – the laughing, tee-shirted Dirk.[56] Even when, with his greater authority, Sydney Box chose him as one of 'The Ten British Stars of To-morrow' – and how fortuitous that the accident of alphabet put Bogarde at the top of the list, above Michael Denison, Christopher Lee, Margaret Leighton and the others[57] – many months were to elapse before a cinema audience would actually be able to see Dirk Bogarde move.

Eight

'It's all perfectly normal. If you wait until tonight,
you'll see the rape and buggery set in'

The working life of Dirk Bogarde as a 'name above the title' began effectively on 6 September 1947 on Epsom Downs, where, in a pale bowler hat and a hideously checked three-piece suit, he heard Ian Dalrymple's cry of 'Action!' It was Derby Day in 1881 and, with his neat moustache and laughable tailoring, Dirk looked every inch the 'King of the Turf' that his character, William Latch, had become at this point in George Moore's story. The special logic of the cinema meant that this would not be the opening sequence in the finished film, nor did Dirk have to do more than sit in the back of a carriage while it pelted through swarming crowds, but it was, as he would say, 'a beginning'. As shooting progressed on the heart-rending tale of a young servant made pregnant by an aspirational groom who cannot get the racing game out of his system, locations for Dirk and his co-star Kathleen Ryan included Jevington and Folkington, uncannily close to his beloved Great Meadow. The interiors were shot at Pinewood, where the fourteen-year-old Gareth had his first experience of a film studio, playing Esther's illegitimate teenage son: 'The son had to look like his father, so my mother was instrumental in getting Dirk to let me do it. I got five pounds for about three days. I remember it very well. I wore a naval uniform and they put Vaseline all over my hair. I remember walking down the corridors at Pinewood. Dirk was not there when I was filming.' Nor did the star offer his brother lodgings at Chester Row: 'He wouldn't have me in the house, so I stayed with Ian Dalrymple at Iver.'

Esther Waters, Dirk's first 'epic', was a happy enough production for the large cast and crew, although it became quickly apparent to him why Stewart Granger had turned down the role. Ever afterwards, too, Dirk would profess to having received no direction from Ian Dalrymple, which, in light of the latter's encouraging letter, seems a trifle unjust. Fortunately, the verdict of the critics would not be decided until late the following year, and in the meantime Dirk was kept reasonably busy. First he narrated a radio programme about the Ku Klux Klan, then, just before fulfilling his speedway commitment for 'Dal', he was given the leading role in one of the four Somerset Maugham stories which R. C. (*Journey's*

End) Sherriff had adapted for the screen as *Quartet*. Dirk's segment, directed by Harold French, was 'The Alien Corn', in which he played the heir to a great estate who feels his true destiny lies as a concert pianist and is fatefully disabused by his teacher, played by Françoise Rosay. He was shrewdly cast, as the script called for 'a good-looking, normal young man: quiet in manner, with a deceptive hesitancy and shyness that conceals a very firm determination'.[1] He battered away quite convincingly at a piano with a dummy keyboard while the real notes were played on a recording by Eileen Joyce – an experience which would stand him in good stead a decade later. However, his most enduring memory was of having to wear 'a thick make-up and lipstick'; once it was over, he 'rebelled' and 'refused ever after'.[2] Maugham had already made his contributions to the film, so Dirk and the other members of the cast missed the famous day at Shepherds Bush when, on an exact replica of his study in the south of France, the nervous author stammered his way even more than usual through an introduction and epilogue. The floor crew were on his side. When the shout came for a 'take' and Maugham hesitantly pushed his beaker of coffee out of shot, a camera assistant said: 'Go on – have a sip, Somerset – it'll do you good!', a prescription which swiftly entered cinema legend.[3]

Dirk went straight from 'The Alien Corn' to *Once a Jolly Swagman*. Apart from heavyweight boxing it is difficult to think of a milieu more foreign to Dirk's natural abilities than speedway. After all, this was a man who used to fall off his pedal bike on his way to the Coxes, and who alleged he was fighting a losing battle with his motorcycle when he first met the Brigadier in Cornwall. According to *Snakes and Ladders* there was a solution: 'The director, standing beside a quite enormous copper and chromium bike, told me softly that he would like me to take it home, stand it in my bedroom, and love it as I would a woman.'[4] More prosaically, Dirk was given one or two lessons. Elisabeth Holbrook, whose husband Owen was on the staff of the Army Motorcycle Training School at Bordon in Hampshire, remembers that Dirk was 'pretty hopeless at first'; he 'took off with an enormous "wheelie" and fell off backwards'.[5] Studio trickery and stuntmen took care of the problem, but Dirk still had to look convincing in his mud-bespattered white leathers while being towed at high speed round the circuit at New Cross – 'as near as I had been to sudden death since the freedom struggles in Java'.[6]

The film, directed by Jack Lee, caused a rumpus in the sport, which had half a million regular followers, because, as one of its champions, 'Split' Waterman, said after a private screening: 'It stamps the riders as a bunch of spivs.' He predicted that speedway fans would 'tear the cinemas apart' when they saw it.[7] The threatened riots never materialised, but it was all excellent publicity, with Dirk expanding his fan base in an unexpected direction. Yet *Once a Jolly Swagman* was not *about* the sport. Its uneasy mixture of themes included trade unionism, the dismal lot of the working classes, the Spanish Civil War, celebrity – with Thora Hird as Dirk's mother having plenty to say about that – and blind ambition. 'To the victor the spoils,' muttered one of the characters into his glass of beer; 'there's only one trouble, though, they sometimes spoil the victor.' It even had a drunken rider declaiming Walt Whitman: 'O Captain! my Captain! Our fearful trip is done'. It was all too much for that great poet's fellow countrymen, who retitled this worthy enterprise *Maniacs on Wheels*.

Once a Jolly Swagman was safely in the can when *Esther Waters* finally had its press showing at the Gaumont in the Haymarket. Dirk made a dramatic arrival on the big screen by vaulting over a post-and-rail fence, but his subsequent antics made little impact. On the first page of notices in his scrapbook he wrote 'PANNED! (Naturally!)'. A. E. Wilson, in the *Evening Standard*, was one of the first to plunge the dagger: 'There is nothing so pathetic as a comedy that doesn't make you laugh – unless it is a tragedy that doesn't make you weep.'[8] Dirk emerged relatively unscathed, although – despite the suit – another writer said he lacked entirely William Latch's loud vulgarity. Dirk could afford to be sanguine about this unfortunate start. He had his contract, and he had two other films already behind him, with a fourth going into production shortly. Unlike the theatre, where the consequences of a critical hammering have to be lived with the next night, and the next, and the next, the cinema allows its practitioners rapidly to consign their work to history. In this respect it can be harder on the director than the star: the ever-generous 'Dal' wrote apologetically to Dirk, saying it was 'my one big reverse in 21 years', and telling him that with *Swagman* on its way 'thank heaven you have so little time to wait for your compensation'.[9] Yet Dirk was troubled. In November, an article appeared under his name, in which he reflected on the events of the past two years since the Reunion Theatre audition: 'Now all this, I believe, is supposed to be rocketing to stardom ... but I have never felt less like a rocket and more like a damp squib in all my life.'

> You see, none of my carefully planned effects seemed to 'come off' on the screen. At first, in ignorance, I worked on the theory that by underplaying, stage technique could be transformed into film technique. As an example, where I would have raised my left eyebrow half an inch on the stage I raised it only a quarter of an inch ... then I found that nothing had happened on the screen at all ... just a rather odd sort of flicker from me. I thought that you only projected on the stage; that on the screen you didn't have to do anything but 'think' your part. And I tried that. I thought like mad and still nothing came over. And then it was, after a very long time, that I realised 'You have to project on the screen too. You must act.' It isn't enough to just be natural.
>
> [...] Every week I go off to the local cinema and watch our top stars doing their stuff. I watch enraptured and often in awe ... not their big emotional scenes, or the passionate love that goes on. I want to know how they handle those little moments on the screen that matter ... the crossing of a room in a long shot; taking off a pair of gloves; the raising of an eyebrow ... the

commonplace actions which all add up to that tremendously important thing –
'Coming Off The Screen.'

These are things which reveal a technique that is born only of experience
and knowledge; they prove once more that there are no short cuts . . . no quick
rockets to the stars. You have to work. You have to know how. And you have
to want to succeed. I do.[10]

He had been set thinking by a brief return to the theatre. Rank had allowed
him to go back to the de Leons at Q, where he appeared for the customary one
week in *For Better, For Worse*, a domestic comedy by Arthur Watkyn about the
difficulties for a young couple of starting married life in post-war Britain. It was
received warmly – 'A nice, cosy little play in a nice, cosy little theatre'[11] – but
counted for nothing, except as a reminder to Dirk of how to connect directly
with audiences. Not that much encouragement was needed on *their* part. The
problem lay with him, and, as we have seen, his self-questioning about identity.
Just as pressing as any concerns about acting technique was the matter of exactly
who he was becoming, in the public's eyes as well as in his own. Laying out his
difficulties and dilemmas in an uncommonly frank way was an effective means
of engaging the sympathy of magazine readers; at the same time he was colluding
in the distortion of his own history, as presented by the Studio publicists. The
following brief profile is compiled entirely from two biographical notes issued to
the press:

Derek Jules Gaspard Ulric Niven Van den Bogarde was born in 1920, to an old
Dutch family. His father, a direct descendant of Anne of Cleves, came to
Britain at an early age and married an English actress. Dirk spent a nomadic
childhood, mostly on the Continent. His education was a 'travelling' one, as
he went to school wherever his father happened to be at the time, and that
meant in a good many countries. He went to Allan Glens College, Glasgow,
and University College School, London, where he studied literature, art,
sculpture and languages. At fifteen he went to Chelsea Polytechnic to take a
course in stage and film décor, and won a scholarship to the Royal College of
Art at the age of sixteen. After two years at the RCA he decided to go on the
stage. Passing the 'Q' Theatre in a bus, he suddenly alighted, went inside and
asked for a job. Speaking several languages fluently, he was trained for the
Diplomatic Corps. In March 1941, he joined the Army and was commissioned
the following year. He landed in France on D-Day. Two of his wartime
drawings, one on blotting paper, were bought by the British Museum. A few
days after the end of the war in Europe he was flown to Burma. On the fall of
Singapore, he went to Java where he became chief British announcer for the
country's radio network. He returned to Britain in October 1946 with the rank
of Major. Five feet ten inches tall, he enjoys such outdoor recreations as riding
and squash.

Added to the 'official' record, of which almost every factual statement is incorrect, was the gossip. One unsourced cutting in Dirk's scrapbook expresses relief that the nation was in no danger of losing him:

> A long time ago the Hollywood moguls propositioned him with honeyed words and a high-figure salary, and Dirk was all set to go – until he read the contract. A formidable document. It told him the number of his bungalow and who his neighbours were to be. It told him he would have to grow side-whiskers, change his name to Ricardo and play Spanish parts indefinitely. After a few months he would have to marry a studio starlet (for publicity purposes), although he was under no obligation to live with her. Dirk took one look at the list – and decided to stay here.

It was all good fun, as were the poses in a Fair Isle pullover, or in a MacQueen hat; or on the cover of *Spivs' Gazette*, 'Britain's "Comic-paper for Grown-ups" '. And when Jean Simmons began to be seen on his arm at premières and jointly handing out trophies to speedway riders, the Studio revelled in its match-making: its handsome discovery, and the entrancing young actress who had recently appeared in David Lean's *Great Expectations*. When they met, she was working at Pinewood on *The Blue Lagoon*, Dirk on *Swagman*. There were eight years between them, but they clicked immediately, mainly because they shared a heightened sense of the ridiculous. 'Jean is about the sweetest girl you could wish to meet,' wrote Dirk; 'and all you read about her being natural and unsophisticated is absolutely true. She has a great sense of fun, and one of these days I would like to do a comedy with her.'[12] They did not manage a comedy, just a 1949 melodramatic mystery, *So Long at the Fair*, their only film together.

Reflecting today on a period that seems 'three lifetimes away', she says: 'I thought of him as a gorgeous young man, but not really as a *man*. He was such fun – a great giggler. I loved Dirk, and was hoping that perhaps we would be married one day; but I was dreaming, I was fantasising.' Stewart Granger put an end to the fantasy by whisking her off to America and marrying her the following year. 'Dirk and I were very close friends for a while,' she says, 'but I never really *knew* him. I didn't realise he was gay – in those days people didn't talk about it.'[13] Dirk recalled that he did not like the film, 'but I had to do it, and, at that point, I was very much in love with Jean Simmons. Rank thought it was a great idea to encourage their two juvenile stars and we were given this film which was supposed to launch our engagement. Unfortunately, by the time the film was finished Jean had fallen in love with Stewart Granger, thereby ruining the publicity effort.' The 'kids', he added, 'went to see it because Jean and I were pretty'.[14]

The 'publicity effort' was in the hands of Rank's efficient, overworked, but good-humoured team which not only fed the many insatiable newspapers, magazines and specialist publications, but also dealt with the thousands of requests from the public for signed photographs and the 350 applications every month for stars to make personal appearances ('PAs'). At the head of this operation were Derek Coyte and Theo Cowan; the latter, initially because of his position in charge of the PA department, was to become Dirk's staunchest ally in the industry. Cowan had fought with the Royal Artillery in Burma, achieving the rank of colonel, and now he was involved in manoeuvres only marginally less intricate and hazardous. Fêtes, flower shows, garden parties, cricket matches, the Master Bakers' Ball and, naturally, screenings and premières – all came under the heading of 'personals' and at peak periods his headquarters might plot seven or eight a day. When he and his charges – or 'chicks' – arrived in a town at the end of a cross-country rail journey, it needed only one over-excited, unrequited member of the waiting crowd to cause a problem; en masse they were dangerous – and that was just the press. The fans could terrify. Cowan's imposing presence and calm authority would reassure the stars. Donald Sinden recalls how Cowan could defuse the most volatile situation with a quip, causing him to be likened to Groucho Marx. An actress having hysterics in his office at the prospect of travelling by aeroplane was told: 'But there is nothing safer than flying – it's crashing that is dangerous.'[15] A tall, bespectacled, genial figure, Cowan was never separated from his pipe and seldom from food; he would sign letters 'Beau Nosh'. Dirk, three years his junior, came to know him as 'Thumper' and would one day write openly to honour this shrewd, alert, sympathetic man, recalling that when they first met in 1947 Cowan, who was used to working with 'more rugged types', such as Stewart Granger, David Farrar and James Mason, had found him 'a bit of a shock'.[16] But for forty-four years Cowan would be '*always* there', ready to remind him, whenever it turned out that the kindly-looking person to whom Dirk had been talking could not be trusted 'with a fly-swat or a feather duster', let alone a pen: 'What they write today you'll eat your chips from tomorrow. Remember that through your tears.' Another mentor, for sure. Another with whom a handshake would be an understanding for life.

It is, perhaps, worth pausing here to consider the organisation for which Dirk and 'Thumper' were working. J. Arthur Rank was a Yorkshire-born, Methodist flour-miller, whose missionary zeal led him in the early thirties to supply film projectors to church halls and Sunday Schools, and then, when the supply of films dried up, to make them himself under the banner of the Religious Film Society. By 1946 this philanthropic initiative had grown into a mighty commercial concern, with five studios, a disparate group of production companies turning out features, documentaries, newsreels and cartoons, for screening in nearly 650 cinemas.[17] When he made his first visit to Hollywood in 1945, one of the 'big noises' asked Rank why he had entered the film business. 'Well,' he replied, 'I want a fair share of the playing time of the screens of the world for British pictures.' 'Do you know anything about making pictures?' persisted the mogul. 'No,' said Rank, 'but I know how to blend wheat, and I know how to get a good sack of flour from it.'[18] And he could afford to buy the brains to make the pictures. His principal 'mill' was a splendid country house at Iver Heath in Buckinghamshire, which, as Heatherden Hall, had once been owned by the cricketing Jam Saheb of Nawanagar, K. S. Ranjitsinhji; was the site for the signing of the Irish Free State treaty in 1921; and had become a country club under the ownership of Charles Boot – of Boots the Chemists – who had a dream of building a film-making complex to rival those in Hollywood. He and Rank joined forces, and Pinewood Studios opened on 30 September 1936, with five sound stages, an administration block of sixty-five offices and separate accommodation for feature players and up to 1,500 extras. At its heart was the house itself, with a seventy-six-foot by thirty-foot sprung ballroom which was now the restaurant and would be the scene of many private dramas as well as countless grand, and not-so-grand, entrances on the four stairs at one end.[19]

Rank's managing director was based elsewhere, which was no bad thing. John Davis, an accountant by training, is remembered by Donald Sinden as 'a terrifying figure: a tycoon who ruled his empire from an office in South Street, Mayfair. Heads rolled – important heads – when he was displeased.'[20] Next in the chain was Earl St John, originally from Baton Rouge in Louisiana, who fought in the First World War, stayed in England, joined Rank in 1939 and was now running Pinewood as executive producer. The same age as Ulric, he had, said Sinden, 'a lined, florid face and silvery hair' and a reputation for finding scripts difficult to read; he would take them to the lavatory, where, as Ken Annakin puts it, 'he clearly felt more comfortable concentrating'.[21] St John and Dirk did not hit it off:

> 'Head's too small, kid,' said Earl St John from behind his cigar. He threw a scatter of glossy photographs across the partners' desk. 'We're looking for people like that!' he said proudly indicating Stewart Granger, James Mason, Dennis Price and a sundry collection of retouched, lipsticked, hair-creamed gods.
>
> 'Nice of you to come . . . but your head's too small for the camera, you are too thin, and the neck isn't right. I don't know what it is, exactly, about the neck . . .' he squinted through money-box eyes, 'but it's not right.'[22]

That was in the days before Dirk had been signed up. Now they had to get on as best they could. It is one of the quirks of this story that, unlike most of his contemporaries, Dirk should find the tyrannical Davis more congenial than the showmanlike St John. But in the end he would have cause to be grateful to both.

If neither St John nor Theo Cowan was especially enthusiastic about the company's new signing, it was hardly surprising. Their male stars usually had a straightforward appeal: the craggy masculinity of Granger, Jack Hawkins and Stanley Baker; the military bearing of Richard Todd; the endearing decency of Kenneth More; the cleft-chinned glamour of Anthony Steel; the fresh-faced innocence of Richard Attenborough, so brilliantly contorted for Graham Greene's character, Pinkie, in *Brighton Rock* – a role Dirk coveted. Dirk, with the dark looks, edgy attitude and unspectacular physique, his voice closer to tenor than baritone, was altogether more ambiguous. There was about him more of James Mason – feline, sibilant and fully as capable of menace as of charm – who had already established a nice line in 'sexy sadism'.[23] Dirk looked younger than his age, which, for the purposes of publicity material and reference books, he increased by a derisory and peculiar single year. There was a hidden disadvantage, too. If Dirk had been just three or four years older he might have established himself before the war, as had Mason, Alec Guinness, John Mills, David Niven and Michael Redgrave. Nevertheless, as it turned out his timing was not too unfortunate. After the best part of a decade of unabashed patriotism, there was now a genre of film to run parallel with the eternal escapism: a cinema of disenchantment, which – in crude terms – asked the questions 'What have we come back to, and what do we do now?' A third, in the voice of the individual, was 'What sort of a life is this?' As the social commentator Simon Heffer puts it: 'The war years and the Attlee Government that followed them were the most centralised, socially controlled and over-regulated of our history.'[24] There were, therefore, stories to be told about self-expression and, of course, about class. So much so that the President of the Board of Trade, Sir Stafford Cripps, felt it necessary to issue a cautionary word when he spoke to a gathering of Rank executives in January 1947:

> It is the primary function of films to entertain and not to teach. It is not propaganda that we want in our films but a natural interpretation of what is good and interesting, amusing and tragic in our cultural and historical heritage. British films internationally are not only one of our contributions to inter-national culture but are also inevitably taken to be an interpretation of our character as a people.[25]

The prospect of English society being 'interpreted' for foreign consumption through the prism of *Maniacs on Wheels* must have been fairly unpalatable. Yet the stories were there and the studios made them. It was astute of Rank to recognise that, despite the officer credentials Dirk had acquired during the war, he possessed the qualities to be persuasive as a working-class anti-hero or petty villain: a nervous energy, a chippiness, a suggestion of straining against a social or emotional ball and chain. *Boys in Brown*, made in 1949, was set in a Borstal – the reform system said at the time to benefit eighty per cent of offenders. The inmates, in their brown uniform of shirt and shorts, were played by adults, including Richard Attenborough and Michael Medwin.* Dirk's character, Alfie

---

* Richard Attenborough, Michael Medwin and the other 'boys' in the cast seem to have had trouble reverting to their real age during the film. Barbara Murray recalls, and Lord Attenborough confirms, that at one point they locked the director in a room at the end of a long Pinewood corridor. Dirk was not involved in the prank.

Rawlings, was seen by the film's writer and director, Montgomery Tully, as 'a strange type; "smooth" best describes him. He has blue eyes, an angel face and an ingratiating manner. There is a sinister quality of sadism about him'.[26] 'Blue eyes', no; 'angel face', debatable; but for the rest Dirk managed very well indeed, subtly assuming a Welsh accent. He strutted about the place wearing 'his usual half-smile'. He gave the impression of being immune from punishment under the institution's rules: 'I'm the smartest one here . . . They'll learn that someday.' Above all, he invested with an almost lyrical grace a speech about the crushing effect of imprisonment on the spirit. Hearing late-summer evening laughter from outside as people walk, talk, have a smoke and think about what they will do next, while all you can do is lie there knowing that for you there is no freedom of action or choice – 'you know it'll be the same tomorrow and the next night and as many nights as you can bear to think of . . . That's what breaks your heart.' Dirk alleged that he had a lifelong phobia of any confined space because he had been shut in a drawer when a child; maybe he simply sympathised with the bird in too small a cage; or maybe it was a lot more complicated – whatever the impulse, Dirk found it easy to play a caged bird. Within a fortnight of completing the role he began work on becoming Public Enemy Number One.

The Blue Lamp was made at Ealing Studios, one of Rank's 'satellites', as a homage to the police forces in Britain which, as its commentary said, were fighting in the aftermath of war 'a nationwide wave of crime which threatens the property and sometimes even the lives of many citizens'.[27] Michael Relph and Basil Dearden had formed a producer-director partnership determined to wrap urgent social questions inside a compelling narrative. *The Blue Lamp* was their attempt to show as realistically as possible how the police were in increasing danger as they tried to hold the line against a new breed of delinquent born from a 'restless and ill-adjusted' youth – a kind which graduated with bravado to serious crime. They were a class apart from the genuine underworld and regular thieves, and 'all the more dangerous for their immaturity'. T. E. B. Clarke, the scriptwriter, stipulated that Tom Riley, the yob who shoots the avuncular neighbourhood Police Constable George Dixon, should be a lean, 'neurotic type'. Basil Dearden knew just the man. The film was, said Dirk, 'the first of what we would call today *cinéma vérité*: the first true, on-location movie we had ever made'.[28] Certainly it was impressively documentary in its portrayal of police work on mean city streets, but some of the characterisation was thin. Dirk was exempt from the criticism. *The Times*, while speculating that 'some hard-working, tax-paying members of the audience may feel a little aggrieved by the film's insistence that bookmakers and tic-tac men at greyhound-racing meetings are an example to everyone and pillars of society', praised Dirk who, 'as a representative of the new type of criminal, the reckless youth with a kink in his mind, gives an admirable performance'.[29] Simon Heffer believes it was Dirk's best film – one 'where an undercurrent in society says, "Sod this, I wish to express my individuality." Admittedly, becoming a criminal and shooting a policeman is an extreme way of doing so, and *The Blue Lamp* caused great shock, but it is a crucial film in that it delineates the destruction of innocence in a supposedly ordered society.'[30] Jack Warner, who had appeared with Dirk in *Boys in Brown* and was also under contract with Rank, would resuscitate Dixon for BBC Television and would stand under the blue lamp for eight years, saying 'Evenin' All' to as many as fifteen million viewers. Dirk, his murderer, became for a while the man you love to hate, especially as he appeared to take singular pleasure in scaring the living daylights out of his girlfriend while manipulating his gun – 'the thump of her heartbeat amuses and excites him'.[31] Andy Medhurst, in an essay on Dirk, saw his performance as not only a personal breakthrough but, in its 'compelling, thrilling and above all erotic' way, innovative as well: 'Erotic cruelty was not new to British films; in the 1940s it had been the property of James Mason. Yet where Mason's successes had been mostly in historical or aristocratic roles, Bogarde's appropriation of the thrilling sadist persona is urban, contemporary and working-class. It is, then, less distanced and more radical, more of a challenge to the norms of British screen masculinity.'[32]

Dirk himself was aware that, with or without the erotic cruelty, playing Tom Riley had been some kind of watershed:

Dearden pointed me in the right direction with his illuminating, over-simplified, approach to the camera. It was the first time I came near to giving a cinema performance in any kind of depth: I think it had some light and shade, whereas the work which had gone before was cardboard and one dimensional. I have never been an extrovert actor, always an introvert; instinctive rather than histrionic, and in this semi-documentary method of working I discovered, to my amazement and lasting delight, that the camera actually photographed the mind process however hesitant it was, however awkward. It had never, of course, occurred to me before, since I had very little mind of my own; but the people I played had minds, of some sort or another, and I became completely absorbed in trying to find those minds and offer them up to the camera. I was never to be satisfied again with a one-dimension performance. And neither was the camera, which now became the centre of my whole endeavour.[33]

Curiously enough, when *Quartet* had been released, Jessie Matthews wrote to Dirk – the first time she had sent a 'fan letter' – saying that he had 'everything it takes to make a really great star' and that she had been reduced to tears by his long close-up as Françoise Rosay played the piano; also, offering to discuss the way he was photographed in future: 'I feel I may be able to help you with camera angles.'[34]

In Cornel Lucas's cigarette-and-mop photograph, there had been a hint of someone on the margins, someone sullen; but in general the off-screen personality which Rank and Dirk were presenting to the world was benign, almost homely. There he is in his scrapbook modelling a sleeveless sweater, next to the headline:

'He'll like this HE-MAN pullover'; in his cravat, nudging up to a horse with a bag of oats; judging the National Hair Beauty Contest; accepting the 'Freedom of the Ted Mor Boys' Club'; above all, looking utterly content with Jean Simmons. Yet the Studio had no patsy on its hands. 'Save me from SPIVS' was the heading on an article in which he said that 'personally, I'm a little tired of spivs, wide boys and junior crooks, however they come and in whatever period. I found *So Long at the Fair* a refreshing change after all these excursions into the shady nooks of petty crooks. For once I wasn't sharp and sly, or imbued with the reckless daring which springs from cowardice.'[35] Typecasting was its own form of imprisonment. And then he issued a challenge to the nation's young women, laying down his ideas about the perfect wife in an open letter to 'Miss Exwye' on the pretence that she had applied to 'fill the vacancy in my household'. Even to stand a chance of being interviewed she would have to satisfy some essential qualifications:

- Do not smoke in public.
- Do not wear high heels with slacks.
- Wear a little skilful make-up.
- Treat all waiters, maids, bus-conductors, etc., with charm and the utmost courtesy at all times, and under all sorts of provocation.
- Never draw attention to yourself in public places by loud laughter, conversation or clothing.
- NEVER try to order a meal from a menu when I am with you.
- Never laugh at me in front of my friends. Laugh with me ... laugh for me ... but remember, lady ... never at me. There will probably be many moments of temptation.
- Never welcome me back in the evening with a smutty face, the smell of cooking in your hair, broken nails, and a whine about the day's trials and difficulties.
- Be a perfect hostess for me with all my friends ... even the ones who bore you ... and even the ones whom you hate.
- Want children, but don't be hysterical about them. Two are fine, three I can cope with ... more than that – definitely no!

As if that were not enough, Miss Exwye would have to be between five foot four and five foot nine – 'I am five eleven'; should look 'like a composite blend of Joan Greenwood-Glynis Johns-June Allyson'; be able to dance and not scowl when he kicked her shins; be able to cook – '*really* cook ... with spices and oil and garlic, and a dash of cooking sherry here and there', not 'pie crust like the cover of an old library book'; must love the countryside; and must be prepared for a bigamous marriage because he was wedded already to his profession, 'The World of Stage, Screen and Heartbreak', and 'there won't ever be a divorce'. After all that, he told Miss Exwye, 'I feel that you will think that you'd be much happier in another situation ... and you're probably right', but 'miracles do happen ... especially in Love!' Back came the replies, including one from Evelyn S. Kerr in Gidea Park, Essex: 'After reading Dirk Bogarde's article, I find that I am his ideal woman. The only snag is, I breathe. Do you think it matters?'[36]

Bucking convention by expressing dissatisfaction with the work his masters were giving him, and by inviting his fans to think him pretty obnoxious, had its risks: it was, after all, early days. Dirk was certainly doing a good job of disguising his shyness and insecurity, while at the same time warning everyone not to come too close.

Tony Forwood had moved out of his flat in Chesham Mews and into Chester Row on 26 May 1948, a month before he and Glynis were granted their decree nisi. To read Dirk's autobiographies, one would think that Tony's acting career had again come to an abrupt halt with the end of the six-month run of *But for the Grace of God*; but no. In the summer of 1947 he was given one of the leads in *We Proudly Present*, a play about two naïve young impresarios who set to work on a highbrow subject but are reduced to transforming it into a farce. The piece, which presaged Mel Brooks's *The Producers*, was written by Ivor Novello for, and partially about, Peter Daubeny, and when after two months Tony was needed elsewhere Daubeny himself took over the role; the press were fascinated by the idea of a theatrical manager being seen in one of his own productions caricaturing a theatrical manager. Tony went into an 'unashamedly vulgar' farce, starring Frances Day, called *Separate Rooms* which stayed for three months at the Strand, and then, in the new year, appeared in three productions for the de Leons at Q, and, at the New Lindsey, in *Paulette*, a gentle little period piece about which W. A. Darlington felt he had not 'the heart to be unkind or the incentive to be enthusiastic'.[37] It was shortly after the third play at Q that he joined Dirk and Eve Holiday in Belgravia. In the literal sense it was now a *ménage à trois*; in the accepted meaning, it was not.

With *Esther Waters* behind them both, Dirk's brother was no longer either a potential embarrassment or an immediate threat. Margaret persuaded Dirk to put Gareth up in the house while, still only fifteen, he took drawing lessons at the Regent Street Polytechnic. He was given one of the two basement rooms. Eve Holiday had the other. He remembers a strange and uncomfortable atmosphere. Eve was just forty-one and, says Gareth, 'terribly shocked by her situation':

> She had gone there thinking she was going to be a sort of social secretary, housekeeper, confidante and even a kind of manager. All Dirk wanted was someone in the kitchen. He was terribly rude to her. I remember one day she made an amazing salad – it had radishes all over it and looked wonderful. She made a piquant tomato sauce which she poured on to it. Dirk looked at it in disgust and said, 'What's this – sanipad ketchup?' Eve burst into tears. He turned a perfectly ordinary and pleasant lunch into something graphic and

horrifying. She went down into her bedroom, next to the one I had, and sobbed. I went down too, to see her. We could hear Dirk arguing with Tony upstairs.

Eve would prepare breakfast, but refused to take it to the top of the house, because – at that time – Dirk and Tony shared a room. Gareth would mount the stairs with the tray, and on one early occasion opened the door to find them in bed. From then on he left the tray outside. 'I understood that there was something going on,' he recalls, 'but at that age and at that time I didn't really know what it was about.' Gareth himself was on the receiving end a good deal. He recalls one night when Dirk, 'in a dreadful state', was particularly beastly to him. Gareth waited until he and Tony were alone, then asked why Dirk was being so awful. 'Tony said, "Have you ever seen anybody eat the carpet, dear?" I said, no, I hadn't. Tony said, "Well, your brother's doing it now. He's having a very bad time, but don't worry about him, he'll be all right." And he was.' There were, says Gareth with classic understatement, 'undercurrents'. Glynis Johns, who saw a lot of both Tony and Dirk at this time, remembers how the latter was 'spoilt, very egotistical and to an extent quite selfish'. Added to which were 'an explosive, dramatic temperament, inherited from his mother, along with her dark looks; you usually saw it only when you knew him well'; and an inability to suffer fools: 'That's why we got on so well! Like him, I had a problem with tolerance and impatience: Dirk put it into words many times.' Small wonder that Dirk was bringing so successfully to his work the part of his character that his brother had known from the time the sash-window was brought down on his tot's fingers – the part of Dirk which relished 'pulling the wings off flies', or, rather, off his fellow human beings. Small wonder that as his star ascended he needed a moderating influence in his life; someone to keep him under control. Because, as Gareth reflects, in those days, and for many years to come, the loss of control was Dirk's greatest dread. The unflappable Tony – and, frequently, his ex-wife – managed to keep a lid on things, at least in public.

At the end of the year Dirk found himself acting with Glynis in an adaptation of Arnold Bennett's *Dear Mr Prohack*, a sadism-free comedy – unless you count a scene in which she hurls him over a sofa before flinging at him every inanimate object in sight. Then, after another week's visit by Tony to Q – in Arthur Miller's *All My Sons* – he and Dirk made the first of their rare joint appearances on a stage. *Foxhole in the Parlor* meant a return for Dirk to the New Lindsey, and to his 'discoverer', Chloë Gibson. Elsa Shelley's play was about an American soldier released from a mental hospital who tries to deliver mankind a message about the futility of war and, when he cannot put his idealism into acceptable words, goes irrevocably mad. The praise for Dirk was a little faint – 'gives his familiar supercharged performance'; 'a telling impression of tension and cracking nerves'; 'goes out of his mind, thereby distinguishing himself from the other characters who have no minds to go out of'. Interestingly, the play's original production had made audiences and critics in the United States sit up and take notice of

Montgomery Clift, the American actor most often mentioned in the same breath as Dirk. In May, as shooting finished on *Boys in Brown*, Dirk had a further reunion, with Michael Clayton Hutton, whose new piece, *Sleep on My Shoulder*, was given its première at Q. Dirk played a blinded airman – shades, one might say, of 'Dark Comfort' with Nerine – and Tony a successful architect with Casanova tendencies. The so-called fantasy was described as 'a meretricious meringue', and its cast pitied, but the public flocked to see Dirk and once again his reputation was untarnished. Playing a frothy actress was Faith Brook, who remembers the production with pleasure rather than with pain, and tells how Dirk was both supportive and complimentary: she had talent and was photogenic, so why had she not been signed up? He said he would talk to Olive Dodds at Rank.

> One evening he came in, very long-faced, and told me, 'I don't believe this, but Olive said the reason you won't figure more in movies, and you haven't been signed up, is that your nose is too straight.' Can you beat that one! You can't have *too straight a nose* for movies! Anyway I was eventually signed up by Alex Korda. Whether Dirk made it up, or whether it was true that Olive said it, that was the end of that. He did try for me.[38]

For the week at Q, Dirk received 14 guineas; Tony, £10. They could afford to be charitable. On 19 July Dirk signed the agreement with Rank for his second year, at £7,000. And the new house he and Tony had found was available at a concessionary rent. Not that it was exactly new: it had stood since at least the 1700s. Nor was it unfamiliar: since his childhood, Tony had spent a lot of time at Bendrose House, where his grandfather had lived and, in 1942, died at the age of ninety-one. It had been empty for some time and needed to be occupied. The Forwood family, with whom Dirk felt at ease, were grouped around it. There would always be help on hand to look after young Gareth when he was not with his mother. Pinewood was ten miles away, and access to London simple. There was privacy and there was space. It was time to leave Chester Row, and by the end of the summer of 1949 they had done so. It was also time to leave Eve, who in April had rejoined the Air Force as a volunteer. She stayed on for another year at number 44, but just as unhappily. Mary Dodd, Tony's first cousin, remembers how Eve – 'no sex-kitten' – had 'read more into the relationship than was ever there. She thought it was something that was going to have a future. But that was obviously a non-starter. The sad thing is that she thought Tony was usurping her. It became impossible.'[39] The conclusion to Eve Holiday's part in Dirk's life has an extra poignancy: when she filled in an official form that summer, she named her brother her next of kin, and also asked that in the event of her death the other person to be notified should be Dirk Bogarde, c/o the J. Arthur Rank Organisation.

Dirk could now begin to live the life of a squire – a translation that pleased him and satisfied his masters: 'the move from the shabby canyon of Chester Row to the elysian fields of Amersham Common was pounced upon with alacrity. I could now be given a Country Background; rolling fields, sunsets, a man of the earth, brooding solitude in the sombre plough of the Home Counties. A kind of anaemic Heathcliff.'[40] The public were informed that the house was 500 years old, had once been the home of Oliver Cromwell, and came complete with a ghost, probably a soldier slain in the Wars of the Roses, who made it impossible for Googie Withers to sleep a wink when she came to stay. This led in due course to a 'psychic investigation', during which Dirk, Glynis, Kay Kendall, Michael Gough and others were photographed in full evening dress, stalking the corridors in the hope of running the spook to ground. It filled four pages of *Illustrated* magazine in a harmless way.[41] There were dogs – a mastiff called Rosie and a basset hound, Chug; a fine, rambling garden, a cherry orchard and the Chiltern hills. A copper-bronze Sunbeam Talbot, bought with a £750 advance from Rank, stood in the driveway. He told one newspaper that he had seven acres of land, two pigs and three goats; was on the way to fulfilling his ambition to be a farmer; and would not be worried if he never earned another penny from the screen. Even in his fresh incarnation, Rank's loose cannon would not be silent.

The films were irregular, but Dirk kept busy. He was now in demand at BBC Radio, making guest appearances in series such as *The Piddingtons, Clay's College – the Fun and Games Academy* and a quiz show, *Ignorance is Bliss*. He appeared opposite Jean Simmons and Cecil Parker – his co-star in *Dear Mr Prohack* – in *A Suit for Christmas*, a radio play about a successful young writer from a humble background. His voice was heard abroad. He wrote a talk for listeners to the Far Eastern Service about his time in Java, and delivered it under the assertive title, 'I Speak for Myself':

> I got caught by the Eastern Island because I was captivated by the colour, the sun, and the slowness of living. I fell in love with people with lovely names and lovelier faces . . . with the evening winds, heady with frangipani blossoms which came down from the mountains after the heat of the day [. . .] I gave my heart, and my body, to the long golden beaches arcing round the edge of that sapphire sea . . .[42]

He told disbelieving readers of *Picturegoer* that because of his many disadvantages, such as 'a face like the back of a rather ancient cab' and 'sparrow legs', he was hard to cast.[43] That was why he found himself back in the theatre, playing the dashing Captain Molineux in Boucicault's *The Shaughraun* at the Bedford in Camden Town. One of the critics noted that he was 'taking a stage holiday from screen spivery';[44] another, gratifyingly, thought that 'the part could afford a touch more *bravura*, but it responds effectively enough to Mr Bogarde's deliberate quietism'.[45] It was here that the Greaves brothers were appalled by the 'fawning women'. Richard Johnson, who was in the cast, remembers that Dirk was 'very affable, though he must have wondered what he had got himself into!'[46] Dirk was billed in the programme as star of the Bedford's next production, *The Leopard*, a new play which had nothing to do with Sicilian politics and was set in a Norwegian whaling station; but, for reasons never properly explained, he withdrew at the last moment, and was replaced by another Rank artist, Albert Lieven. It was the first tremor in the stage career. Shortly afterwards, but not soon enough to explain the sudden departure, he started work at Pinewood with Anthony 'Puffin' Asquith on *The Woman in Question*, a mediocre psychological thriller in which he was called upon to affect an American accent as 'Bob' Baker, a Liverpudlian musical-hall artist who had never been further west than Bristol, and was a 'type that might be dangerous in a mean, underhand fashion'. The film ended with a shot of a parrot's overturned cage, the occupant fluttering helplessly and frightened inside its prison.

Apart from any symbolic reference to Dirk's life we might find in that closing image, there was a more obvious twist. On 8 April 1950 he returned home to Bendrose at about 9.30 in the evening and found the house locked and barred, with no sign of Harold Quigley, the thirty-six-year-old housekeeper he had engaged from an agency the week before. After breaking in through a window, Dirk found that clothing and other possessions worth £184 9s were missing. Quigley was arrested in Exeter, and at the end of May appeared at Amersham Magistrates Court, where it turned out that his real name was Norman Billington and he had a string of convictions spanning thirteen years. Dirk gave his evidence and, after listening to the constable who had arrested Billington, asked to return to the witness box, where he said: 'He was a most excellent servant in every respect. His record sounds very bad, but I should like to make one plea to be able to assist him in some way.' The magistrates handed down a sentence of six months, but Dirk was permitted to visit Billington in the cells. 'He does not seem to want much help,' he told the waiting press, 'but he told me that he wants to get into the Merchant Navy and if I can do anything to help him achieve that object, I will do so.' One of the press reports concluded with a note: 'Dirk Bogarde played the part of the young criminal who shot a policeman in the British film, "The Blue Lamp".'[47] There was no escape.

From the day Tony had moved in to Chester Row he and Dirk were, in the eyes of those who knew them best, inseparable. Once or twice, early on, work kept them apart – ironically, Tony's. He had appeared as a bewildered lover in a French comedy translated as *Gooseberry Fool* which opened in Glasgow before an undistinguished West End run at the Duchess, and although *The Philadelphia Story* at the same address – with Wilfred Hyde-White, Robert Beatty and his beloved Margaret Leighton – had not taken him away, he was forced to leave Bendrose temporarily when he landed a small part in Raoul Walsh's film *Captain Horatio Hornblower RN*, some of which was shot on location in the south of France. A pair of connected postcards to Dirk from Villefranche indicate how tight the currency restrictions made it for the English members of the unit;

Gregory Peck was ensconced at the Réserve de Beaulieu – 'supposedly one of the de luxe hotels of the world and certainly it is pretty magnificent'. The Pecks were hospitable to Tony, and he clearly liked them, but confided to Dirk that 'being with even nice people one doesn't know well is a strain'. In traditional fashion he concluded: 'How I wish you were here!' It is hard to tell whether he signed the second card 'Toto' – as in Judy Garland's faithful cairn terrier from *The Wizard of Oz* – or 'Tote'; certainly, the latter was a name that stuck. As a small boy he had been known as 'Trot'.

'The Bendrose days', Dirk would recall, 'were the happiest; although there would be grander houses, greater riches, finer views, it is always to Bendrose that I look with nostalgia and happiness.'[48] An extraordinary procession of beautiful women came to picnic on its lawns or loll in the deliberately pint-sized swimming-pool: Jean Simmons, Elizabeth Taylor, Kay Young, Anouk Aimée, Kay Kendall – all, and especially the last, with their problems at one time or another; all benefiting from a balm, patented by Dirk and Tony, the principal ingredients of which were plain-speaking and laughter. Glynis Johns says that Dirk was – as she herself is – at his best when he was *needed*, and had to set aside his own worries: 'He was a wonderful *friend*.' For Kay Kendall, Bendrose became a permanent refuge, even though on her first visit she insisted on calling Dirk 'wifey'. Her biographer, Eve Golden, recorded: 'Before Bogarde or Forwood quite realized what had happened, Kay had talked herself into one of the guest bedrooms. The following weekend, she piled some suitcases, a white fox rug, and her anaemia medications ("wretched blood capsules") into her room – Bogarde adds that "There had never been a happier decision ever made".'[49]

It was a lively association – and one very much part of Dirk, not Derek. When Nerine Cox dropped in with her husband, son and dog on the way back from a camping holiday, Tony answered the door. She apologised for their rudeness in arriving without warning. Tony said: 'He's in bed. He's had rather a lot of pain in a tooth.' Gareth Bogaerde remembers how – astonishingly, if not perversely – Dirk invited their uncle and aunt to stay, presumably on their way to or from home in Bishopbriggs:

> My parents and I were going to drive across and meet them at Bendrose. When we arrived, there were no Murray and Sadie. Mother was dreadfully upset. Apparently they had arrived at 11 a.m., Dirk had put their things in the house and they went outside to find Anouk Aimée in the swimming pool with no top on, and somebody else lying on the grass with not much on either. Sadie was terribly prudish and said, 'Is this the sort of thing that happens here, Dirk?' He replied 'It's all perfectly normal. If you wait until tonight, you'll see the rape and buggery set in.' They turned and left.

On a less volatile level were the associations with the neighbouring Forwoods – above all with Mary and with a younger cousin, Jane, who spent a good deal of her childhood in Gareth Forwood's company. She remembers how she and Tony's son were invariably the only children when guests descended for the weekend, 'but we were never made to feel in the way or a nuisance. We would try very hard!'[50] In the late summer of 1950 Dirk, Tony and Kay Young went on a long holiday together in the West Country, taking Mary with them. She was to become a cherished companion, wholly discreet and unaffected by any prejudice in her parents' generation against Tony for deciding to take up the stage and to share his life with a fellow actor.

With just two films made in 1950, bits and pieces on the radio and nothing on the horizon, the 'fellow actor' took on a serious piece of theatre. Kitty Black, a key member of Hugh ('Binkie') Beaumont's team at the omnipotent production house of H. M. Tennent, had translated Jean Anouilh's play *Eurydice* and engaged Mai Zetterling to take the title role. She and Dirk had recently made a weak thriller, *Blackmailed*, together. Peter Brook was to direct, and he and Kitty Black decided that Dirk, as Orpheus, would be the perfect foil to the blonde Swede. In the event, the play, by now entitled *Point of Departure*, was directed by Peter Ashmore and spent a week at the Theatre Royal in Brighton before opening at the Lyric Hammersmith. In her memoirs Kitty Black recalled:

> The chemistry between Mai and Dirk flamed into the most perfect fusion and on the first night at Hammersmith it seemed as though everyone in the audience was enjoying a good cry. Mai herself was so overcome with emotion that during the last scene Dirk found his espadrilles were soaking wet with her tears and set to work to console her under cover of the dialogue. A transfer was immediately arranged, we opened at the Duke of York's Theatre on Boxing Day and when Queen Mary was among the visitors who came to enjoy it, we felt sure we were set for a long run.[51]

The reviews were uniformly excellent, not only on a cerebral level but also in drawing attention to 'the frankest bed scene ever shown in the London theatre'. Dirk and Mai Zetterling were praised to the skies. Alas, however, the forecast of a long run was misplaced. Leonard White, Dirk's understudy, says that the styles of the two principals made for a superb contrast, but that Dirk's was to prove his downfall:

> They were chalk and cheese. Dirk was working on his nerves, working for reality, all the time. Mai was much more technically attuned and, in rehearsal, always ahead of him. Not in any sense *better*, not at all. It worked extremely well – what came over was marvellous. But Dirk lived it to the point where I had to go on in the middle of the show to take over. He worked himself up to such an extent that he made himself ill. You think of acting as a technique – of being able to perform night after night, night after night, because you are relying on your technique. You are not using your own personal emotions as

such: you are re-creating, over and over again, something which you *have* created through rehearsal. It was that element that I thought Dirk was short of. It's almost like an early example of the Method – he had to do it for *real* all the time, and it affected him.[52]

It reached the point where Dirk was physically sick, throwing up into a bucket in the dressing-room, and incapable of going on. Leonard White was kept busy. After eight weeks in the West End, Dirk told Kitty Black that he was pulling out on medical advice. John Moffatt, playing a sinister hotel waiter, noted in his diary for Saturday 3 March: 'Dirk off. Nervous breakdown. Has left cast.' The following day, Peter Finch began rehearsing the part. John Moffatt remembers how in the original rehearsals Mai Zetterling had been 'fairly remote and very intense', whereas Dirk had been light-hearted and friendly: 'I remember him coming in one day and telling us about going round Lillywhite's and what he had bought there.' On stage his performance had been 'very swift and light, full of nervous energy, but it was a very emotional role and he found re-engendering all that emotion eight times a week a great strain'.[53] Kitty Black agrees, saying: 'He had a magical presence on the stage. But he lacked the technique that comes from long experience. He acted on his nerves the whole time.' She also identified a rare quality in Dirk – an insolence, which she had only otherwise come across in French actors such as Gérard Philipe and Jean-Louis Barrault: 'He looked down the nose at you as if you were a nasty smell.'[54] Dirk returned to the play, but 'the original impetus had been spent' and the curtain came down finally on 12 May.

Dirk's involvement would have been considerably shorter had it not been for Hugh Jolly, who was now working at the London Hospital and with the children at Great Ormond Street. Theatrical in temperament and stage-struck by inclination, he made frequent visits to see Dirk at the Duke of York's. In *Cleared for Take-Off* Dirk writes that when he feared he was losing his mind, the walls of his dressing-room were moving in while he was on the stage, and the bed he shared with Mai Zetterling 'began to sway and bounce like a dinghy in flood', he appealed for Hugh to help him through. The latter said he had a pill, wrapped in tinfoil, which he had taken secretly from a hospital cupboard. It could be used only if absolutely essential. After several nights, with Hugh standing reassuringly in the wings, Dirk gave in and begged to be given the pill. It seemed to work for a while, until the 'strain of suddenly becoming a "pop idol", of crowds screaming and crowding the stage door, of police to help me to my car – all these idiotic things, and also Mai's clear irritation with my selfish behaviour, did, eventually, bring me down and after a year I had a very modest breakdown'. Long afterwards, when both men were famous, Hugh admitted to Dirk that the pill had been an aspirin.[55] By the time Dirk told this story, Hugh had died of cancer; his wife Geraldine, in a car smash. His sister Cynthia remembers how Hugh, like Dirk a late developer, had always been 'drawn towards the vulnerable'.[56]

None of the four people involved in *Point of Departure* and interviewed for this book remembers the fan worship for Dirk as anything unusual, although it was not always as discreet as that of the two anonymous women who left a package for him at the stage door; Dirk opened it to find a watercolour landscape by his grandfather, Forrest. Rather less respectful was the character who, between the matinée and evening shows, would entertain playgoers mustered at the gallery door with a repertoire adapted according to the fare on offer inside the theatre. In this case he chose a variant on Rodgers and Hart's 'Bewitched, Bothered and Bewildered', where the second word became an act of gross indecency. A further substitution – that of the male star's surname – was, alas, all too tempting. Yet the most curious incident connected remotely with this significant production is also the most seemingly mundane. Leonard White lived, as he does now, near Brighton, where the play first opened. One morning, as he walked along the main road, a car drew up on the opposite side. 'It was Dirk, surprised to see me there. He had no airs and graces – it wasn't like the star from London, driving through Newhaven and wanting to get the hell out as soon as he could. Not at all. He seemed at home, and in a sense he was, as he had been in the area so many times. We had a perfectly ordinary conversation and off he went.' There is nothing remarkable about this chance encounter – apart from the fact that Leonard White is absolutely certain no one else was in the car.

Nine

'You, what's the bleeding time?' 'Ten past ten, Sir'

Tony Forwood continued to disregard his former wife's advice, although his stage career was almost at an end. Like Glynis and Dirk he, too, was now concentrating on films. His fine features were in no way impaired by the natty goatee he sported as Will Scarlet in Walt Disney's *The Story of Robin Hood and His Merrie Men*, and he looked a good deal more comfortable on a horse than Dirk ever would. Ken Annakin said that it was indeed a merrie production, and that Tony, although in a smaller role than those of Richard Todd and James Robertson Justice, was very much part of the team. Annakin remembers Tony as 'completely pliable' and looks back with amusement at his cry of 'Off with your curtals and on with your rags!', which he uttered in 'a wonderfully camp way that I never questioned at the time – it seemed to suit that group of people!'[1] As Tony strolled about Denham Studios in a forest of Lincoln green and tights, so Dirk was with some reluctance fishing out his mackintosh and growing a new stubble. *Hunted*, directed by Charles Crichton, was an unpretentious drama about a killer on the run with an adopted boy who had seen too much. Shot at Pinewood and on location in the south-west of Scotland, it was notable for its understatement and for the relationship between the fugitive, Chris Lloyd, and the boy, Robbie, played by Jon Whiteley. The blond son of an Aberdeen headmaster, Whiteley was exactly the right age – six – for the part, which he secured after being heard on the radio reciting 'The Owl and the Pussy-Cat' in his school playground. He says that his parents, especially his father, were 'not at all keen that this should lead to a career in acting, but they thought that the cinema might be a way of instilling discipline, because there was no room for tantrums, or breaking off when you felt like it and going your own way'.[2] They agreed that he could do *Hunted*, and if it led to anything he would be restricted to one film a year until he was eleven; then it would be back to proper work. For his screen test, with another actor taking Dirk's part, he performed the scene where Lloyd catches Robbie in the wrong place at the wrong time, and grabs him round the neck: 'I remember the other actor didn't put his heart into it. Unlike Dirk.' Jon Whiteley has nothing but happy memories of the production and of working with Dirk: 'He treated me as if he was an older brother – we had a marvellous time together. He used to take me to toyshops. He was a jolly and generous companion, and he had a nice instinct for buying the right presents. He was always very good-natured, endlessly laughing. He had a good range of jokes.' While they were shooting on a bombsite in central London, Dirk spotted lice in the boy's hair, to general alarm; 'Dirk just laughed.' A charming photograph of star dispensing tea to novice on the Bendrose lawns bears witness to a happy experience, at the end of which Dirk asked Jon what he would like as a parting gift. 'I proposed a monkey from Harrods' pet shop, but he wisely passed this suggestion before my mother and I'm glad to say that it did not go any further. He gave me instead a handsome Tri-ang tractor and trailer.' They would meet again, but not for five years.

Dirk's next film, *Penny Princess*, was, he wrote, 'as funny as a baby's coffin'.[3] He had been given the role after Montgomery Clift and Cary Grant had turned it down. The film's director and writer, Val Guest, then offered it to Frank Sinatra, whose career was at a low ebb, but Earl St John was not impressed. He suggested Dirk. Guest said that Dirk was not exactly known for light comedy. 'So you can lighten him up,' said St John. 'Get him a good tailor, give him some square shoulders.'[4] The need for 'square shoulders' was lost on Guest, and the tailor was fairly redundant as Dirk's character was to spend most of the ninety minutes in pyjamas. Nevertheless there was a good company spirit and the locations in Spain afforded a pleasant opportunity for Dirk, Tony and Mary Forwood to drive slowly through France in a new Lagonda. On his return Dirk was given a pay rise, as Rank exercised its option for a fifth year – at £8,000. But he was not happy. The raincoat would be coming out again all too soon, and so would some unorthodox vowel sounds, for the impersonation of an IRA bomber in *The Gentle Gunman* opposite John Mills; not even Basil Dearden could rescue a script which reduced Gilbert Harding to saying: 'You're a bunch of pig-headed, bog-trotting rapscallions!' A few weeks playing Nicky Lancaster in a revival of *The Vortex* – the work which put Noël Coward on the map – provided some solace. Coward himself cast Tony alongside Dirk as Tom Veryan, described by the playwright as 'athletic and good looking. One feels he is good at games and extremely bad at everything else.' Coward's diary for 30 January 1952 records: 'Rehearsal of *The Vortex*, extremely good, well directed and played. Dirk Bogarde a little floppy but a fine actor.'[5] As Dirk wrote to Philip Hoare, Coward was a hard taskmaster:

> [...] we had to be word perfect after the first (agonizing) read-through. Remember only he and John G. [Gielgud] had had a bash at Nicky before. I was not about to do a replica of them. This he sensed at the read-through. I think he was alarmed. Never said so, just went off to Jamaica and sent me a telegram on the first night which simply said 'DONT WORRY DEAR BOY IT ALL DEPENDS ON YOU'.[6]

The first night was not without incident. Dirk recalled shaking Isabel Jeans – who played his mother – so violently that her wig fell off, after which she resorted to glue. The notices were mixed, but the Lyric Hammersmith enjoyed a success. For Dirk, it was an exhausting period, filming *The Gentle Gunman* by day and giving vent to Nicky Lancaster's neuroses by night; fortunately his run in the play was limited because he had to travel to County Wicklow for location work. *The Vortex* would be his last appearance in a theatre for three years, and the last time he and Tony shared a stage. However, there was a part for Tony in the next film – as a brisk navigation officer at a pre-flight briefing.

Appointment in London was written by John Wooldridge, an RAF pilot who had flown so many missions – 108 – that when he based a script on his experiences he had to reduce the figure because no one would have believed it possible. His purpose was to convey what it was really like to be a Bomber Command pilot, and to take part in an eight-hour raid on Germany. With the film in preparation, he recorded in his diary for 29 May 1952: 'Went to Berman's to meet Dirk Bogarde. He was charming, & said mine is the best script he had ever read.' Dirk, who had been disappointed not to secure a role in the Rank production of Nicholas Monsarrat's *The Cruel Sea*, was happy to be rented out to a small company, Mayflower Pictures, to play a Wing-Commander determined to fly three more missions and reach a personal tally of ninety. Tim Mason was, wrote Dirk, 'an upper-class Wing Commander at that; never wore a raincoat and never saw a Copper'.[7] It was 'the first time that I actually made any kind of impression for good on the screen', and Philip Leacock 'made me more aware than any director up till then that it was the thought which counted more than the looks'.[8] Dinah Sheridan, who played the Wingco's disputed girlfriend, found that Dirk was pleased to be given something different to do and 'relaxed into the part'. She also recalls that Leacock was 'shy, and difficult to talk to about any aspect of the script, or any emotions, with other actors'.[9] The atmosphere on location at an airfield near Peterborough inspired a degree of laddishness among some of the cast, entertainingly described in his first volume of memoirs by Bryan Forbes,[10] who was then twenty-five. Dirk was not involved. 'I was the third lead,' Forbes recalls today, 'and Dirk was the star. He seemed to have everything I wanted for myself – his name on a chair, and all that. But he was very kind to me.'[11] Forbes, who would later direct with great distinction, noticed how Dirk was 'undoubtedly a *jeune premier*, incredibly good looking. It's not so important nowadays but, then, you had to *look* a leading man, as well as be one. He did. He also knew what was going on in terms of lighting, and how he should react. He was a very good *re-actor*. He knew the quality of stillness.' Dinah Sheridan, too, remarked on Dirk's selflessness towards his fellow players. She was apprehensive because she had not worked with him before, 'but I certainly need not have worried. He was kind, helpful and charming. And at the end of the shooting gave me a mohair rug to keep me warm in "Genevieve", my next film.'[12] Leacock's effort was received well enough locally, but bombed in the United States, where the producer André Hakim reported that 'we have in Appointment in London a dud on our hands. I cannot even give it away.'[13]

As he set off for Berlin, for yet another thriller, and for a reunion with Mai Zetterling that briefly interested the press for non-artistic reasons, Dirk's latent urge to write had been reawakened. He recorded someone else's short story for the Light Programme, heard its transmission on a battery-set in a field near Peterborough, and found it 'perfectly dreadful [...] the dullest thing I had ever heard and quite embarrassingly read!!' He informed the producer that he had for some time been working on 'little stories, in a biographical vein', which he had grouped under the heading 'Never Again Like This' and which he thought might make a radio series: 'They are all shorties, about 2,000–3,000 words and are mainly highlights in my life, from seeing my first snowstorm, through to knifing my sister at ten, on through the early days at the Theatre and Art School, the war, Belsan, Berlin etc., and up to date.' He proposed telling them, rather than reading them, 'as if to a friend after coffee round a fire'.[14] Inexplicably, although the BBC expressed an interest in the idea, it came to nothing. Dirk's literary output was confined to pieces for the film and women's magazines, which sometimes carried his signature but which more often than not were the work of other hands, using his spoken words. However, he did feel moved to write at length when he was taken to task from an unexpected quarter. In an interview during the shooting of *Desperate Moment* he said that Rank had been worried about his physique and had equipped him with a full set of barbells, chest-expanders, rowing machines, Indian clubs and other 'instruments of torture'. When the Studio next saw footage of him as a tattered but burlier fugitive, he received hearty congratulations. Rashly he confided to his interviewer that he had achieved the new look by donning extra sweaters under a windcheater and a 'double ration of trousers'. The packages of gymnastic apparatus lay unopened in the garage at Bendrose. According to the editor of the august fitness magazine *Health and Strength* – founded in 1892 and still going very strong – several of its readers had 'gone up in the air' about Dirk's disclosure: 'They want me to point out to their once-favourite film star that unless he gets down to it and puts some real beefcake on that lean frame they are going to give *Desperate Moments* [*sic*] (now in the making) a miss when it comes round! They want me to tell him what he is missing. They want me to invite Dirk to their clubs, to show him what two-evenings-a-week will do for him.' The editorial was headed 'Beefcake for Bogarde'.[15] A troubled Dirk wrote back:

> I have been an ardent reader of your publication ever since I was a schoolboy way back in the early thirties, and except for the six war years, when I only managed to sneak an odd copy in France, Burma or Java, I have remained so ever since.
>
> The last four years have provided me with a handsome set of *H & S* bound in red leather, and proud possessors of space on my bookshelves.

It was therefore with a good deal of distress that I found the whole editorial of the current issue devoted to an inaccurate account of my doings.

I should like to apologise to any readers who were annoyed by the newspaper article in question, and hasten to state here and now, that *I have the greatest admiration in the world for bodybuilding*. Also I have *never* in the whole of my career, ever worn two pullovers – or two pairs of pants – or padded my shoulders. That is utter rot! I have fortunately never had to resort to such a silly deception.

The newspaper story was, he said, meant only to be 'a bit of a lark' and came about because the 'Front Office', worried about his loss of avoirdupois from overwork and illness, had decided that 'pushing the weights about for a couple of weeks would give me a body like [Steve] Reeves'. It would never work, because 'I am a thoracic type.' However, as a joke he 'dressed up in a multitude of thick garments and told them with pride that the exercises had been successful' and the reporter duly reported. In the films Dirk made, 'I just *have* to be fit: You can't jump through plate glass windows five or six times a day, fall under moving cars, jump off a moving train or fight a fight down a flight of stone steps, unless you *are* fit.' Somewhat contradictorily, he then took pride in the fact that he had 'never used a double (unless it was for falling off a five storey building, or crashing a car, when I might have been cut about and held up a costly production) and that I have always been fit enough to play in the movies which I like best – action and pace'. He added: 'Not all film actors run about with padded shoulders and spindle shanks. In just the same way, we don't drink only champagne and eat only caviar. Those days are over. The public demands more these days – and so much the better.' Finally he wished good luck to 'the men and women who have the sense to protect and cherish the bodies God has given them'. The editor headed the letter, 'Sorry, Dirk, we take it all back!'[16]

Unlike the steadily widening row of leather volumes containing his bound scripts, *Health and Strength* failed to attract the attention of the women's magazine which, after a visit to Bendrose, featured Dirk's 'design for living'. He took great satisfaction in pointing out that almost every ornament and item of furniture had been a bargain: a walnut and ebony Regency bookcase – £20; two red damask, wing-backed chairs – 30s and 45s respectively; the 1840 Broadwood spinet – £9; the Zuccarelli painting – £3; the platoon of model soldiers – a souvenir from the set of *Esther Waters*. The harmony of colour and décor throughout the house was not only warm but also the mark of someone with a natural flair. His lampshade and chair-covers were even the subject of a do-it-yourself pattern. And then there were the animate occupants: the cats, the dogs, the birds, the tree frogs and the tropical fish. In the aquarium was a two-foot spectacled cayman, called Amy – or maybe Aimé? – which even Dirk found too hot to handle, so he presented it to London Zoo, where an official said that it had turned out to be not as biddable as its owner had hoped: 'Caymans do not tame so readily as alligators; few of them make good pets.'[17] Even so, it did not stop Dirk having another one. In his new home.

At the end of 1953, Coronation year, Dirk was fifth in the *Motion Picture Herald* annual poll of the most popular British draws at the box-office, after Jack Hawkins, Alec Guinness, Ronald Shiner and Alastair Sim.[18] Readers of the *Daily Mirror*, asked to decide in its Teen Queen contest which of all the men in the world they would like as their escort for the evening, chose Dirk at number two, ahead of Max Bygraves, Tony Curtis, Gregory Peck, Dickie Valentine, Rock Hudson, Anthony Steel, Richard Todd and Alan Ladd. At number one was Prince Philip.[19] The Teen Queen – a shorthand typist from Ashford in Kent called Olwen Evans – won a 'date' with Dirk. Goodness knows what agonies he went through on these occasions, but he was usually stoic and sometimes generous to a fault. It was not always easy for either party. John Wooldridge's daughter, the actress Susan, tells how her father once arranged for her much younger Aunt June to visit the set of *Appointment in London*. It meant taking the day off school. On the morning of the meeting with her idol, she woke up with 'the worst stye ever visited on a human being'. When Susan Wooldridge reminded Dirk of this many years later, he told her of the young woman who won just such a competition as the Teen Queen – her prize, a date for lunch at somewhere like the Ritz or the Savoy. Dirk was not exactly looking forward to it, when the girl arrived, 'her hair done to death, and quaking with fear'. A photographer and reporter were on hand to record the meeting. After about twenty minutes of chattering away, trying to make her feel more comfortable than he did, Dirk looked at the speechless prizewinner, and said to the journalists, 'Now, we want to be on our own.' He waited for them to disappear, then said, 'Come with me', and led the wretched girl through a side door to the lavatories, where he stood guard while she was violently sick. He helped her to wash her face and waited while she pulled herself together, then took her gently back into the dining-room, where the press returned to find them all smiles.[20]

He had made sixteen films as a leading player, of which the last but one had been *They Who Dare*, the story of a Special Boat Service raid at a German airfield on Rhodes. For Dirk its principal allure was not so much the script – it had arrived without an ending – or the locations on Cyprus, but the chance to work with Lewis ('Milly') Milestone, director of the First World War masterpiece, *All Quiet on the Western Front*. If Noël Coward was demanding, Milestone was an irresistible force. 'If he gives me an ulcer I'll keep it as a pet and a keepsake,' said Robert Westerby, the screenwriter summoned to the rescue.[21] Dirk and the other members of a crack commando squad – Denholm Elliott and Akim Tamiroff among them – were fitted out by Milestone with ninety-pound packs: 'The first time we all struggled into them we fell flat on our faces before him; Moslems in Mecca.'[22] At the end of the ordeal Westerby summed up the unit's experience: 'I wouldn't have missed making this film with him for five years off my life ...

which it's probably cost me anyway.'[23] The reviewer who retitled the movie 'How Dare They?' was a little unkind. It had left Dirk with good memories – and with a Milestone maxim of fundamental soundness: 'You can make a good script bad, but you can't ever make a bad script good.' The next script to come his way, about a group of trainee doctors, was pleasant enough, but surely not a life-changer?

Much has been written about the social and sexual climate in Britain during the 1950s. Sheridan Morley noted in his Life of John Gielgud, who was arrested for soliciting in a public lavatory in Chelsea, that

> historians of the period still seem divided as to whether what was happening in 1953 was the result of a co-ordinated police crackdown, or whether it was just the last, vicious, gasp of official puritanism. For Philip Larkin, sex may have started with the Beatles in 1963, but ten years earlier it was certainly stopping for a lot of people suddenly aware of a witch-hunt as potent as the one being contemporaneously waged on supposed Hollywood communists by the McCarthy tribunals in the USA.[24]

Hugh David, in his study of homosexuality in Britain from 1895 to 1995, says of the fifties:

> Partly in response to public 'concern' when scant but sufficient details of the lifestyles of Guy Burgess and Donald Maclean became known after their defection in May 1951, all manifestations of homosexuality had been included in a crackdown on law and order instituted by Sir David Maxwell Fyfe, a prosecutor at the Nuremberg trials who became Home Secretary that year.[25]

Maxwell Fyfe left no one in any doubt about his personal feelings on the subject. In December 1953 he told his fellow MPs that homosexuals in general were exhibitionists and proselytisers, and were a danger to others, especially the young. If there had been a less draconian atmosphere during the war, when thoughts were otherwise engaged, the clock now seemed to have sprung back to the mid-1890s and Oscar Wilde's trial. A graph showing buggery and related offences as a percentage of all recorded crime in England and Wales during the twentieth century begins with a gentle incline from 0.2 per cent in 1900 to 0.4 in 1945, then soars to a peak of 1.5 per cent in 1955, before dropping almost as rapidly and tailing away from the late 1960s.[26] The number of prosecutions for homosexual offences had risen from 1,276 in 1939 to 5,443 in 1952.[27] Nothing represented the climate of the time more forcefully than the successive trials of Edward, Lord Montagu of Beaulieu, who was charged initially in the summer of 1953 with indecent assault, and jailed the following year for separate offences. In October 1953 Rupert Croft-Cooke, the biographer of Oscar Wilde's 'Bosie', Lord

Alfred Douglas, was sentenced to nine months for offences involving two sailors. The scandals, fomented by the press, were so intense that it led in part to Maxwell Fyfe asking Lord Wolfenden to chair a committee which would examine the existing law on prostitution and homosexual behaviour between men. In the case of the latter, it was a law which led to the conviction in 1952 of the brilliant scientist Alan Turing, who invented the 'Bombe' – the machine that helped to break the Enigma codes in the Second World War – and who in June 1954 swallowed half an apple containing cyanide rather than live with the stripping of his security clearance and his shame. It was a law which, because of its susceptibility to the *agent provocateur* and the blackmailer, placed countless men in constant jeopardy. It was, in short, a law which Wolfenden found to be 'in rather a mess'. As he wrote in his memoirs, the vulnerability of men had been widened by 'an extraordinary legislative accident' in 1885, during the passage through Parliament of a Bill designed to protect women and girls by raising the age of consent and suppressing brothels. Henry Labouchère, an MP and newspaper editor, introduced an amendment in the Commons which made any act of gross indecency between men an offence. The clause was passed 'without any discussion of its substance', the amendment became law and that was how it stood when Wolfenden and Maxwell Fyfe had their first discussion on an overnight train from Liverpool.[28]

While Hugh David identified 'an officially sanctioned intensification of the police harassment which had developed since the war',[29] Sheridan Morley believes the increase in prosecution was 'not an especially organised or even sinister affair, merely the British in one of their periodic fits of hypocrisy'. A number of senior policemen, magistrates and civil servants 'had decided that in this Coronation year, certain barriers did have to be repositioned if the country was not going to go to the dogs'.[30] Any complacency about a degree of tolerance towards the world of the arts was summarily shattered by the Gielgud prosecution for 'cottaging'. Even though he emerged from the magistrates' court with a 'standard fine' of £10 and an instruction to see his doctor, the newspapers did not let him off so lightly. Luckily Dame Sybil Thorndike was on hand at a rehearsal that afternoon and broke the ice for Gielgud and for everyone else by saying: 'Well, John, what a very silly bugger you've been.' He had, between being charged and tried, for the first and only time in his life contemplated suicide.[31] Donald Sinden recalls that when the reports of the conviction reached Pinewood, a form was distributed, addressed to the Prime Minister and calling for the withdrawal of the knighthood that Gielgud had been awarded in the Coronation honours list four months earlier; not a single actor or actress would sign it. The fact that such a document should have existed in the broad-minded ambience of the Studio indicates how opinion on the issue was polarised between some in the corridors of power and those working on the floor.

No one will ever know what the relationship was between Dirk and Tony at this point. Citing her mother and proving that candour is a family trait, Glynis

Johns asks rhetorically: 'Were you under the bed, dear?' For her, 'never once was I shown, or led to believe, that they were sharing a bed, or that theirs was anything other than a close friendship with everything in common. I was never made embarrassed by it, and neither was anybody else.'[32] Whatever their situation, it was not even a topic of conversation in the business. Everyone simply accepted that with Dirk came Tony. The latter had now given up his own career completely: in his penultimate film, *Knights of the Round Table*, he was by some strange quirk cast as Gareth. Now, fifteen years after making his prediction on a postcard to his grandfather, he was indeed beginning to be 'a good manager'. Their association attracted nothing but respect from those working most closely with them. Dinah Sheridan, who married Dirk's ultimate boss, John Davis, in 1954, says that her husband was 'antagonistic to homosexuals'; but Dirk would not have been made directly aware of that. Everyone agrees that he and Tony were then, as they would be for the rest of their lives, the model of discretion. Yet in an industry which exists by the image, and in the prevailing atmosphere, there were hazards for a star who, at the same time that his eligibility was being presented as an overriding asset, shared his house and his life with another man. With all this in mind, it might not be coincidence that Dirk's scrapbook came to an abrupt end, in mid-volume, in 1953; that, thirty years later, it should have been necessary for Jack Jones to reassure him that 'all pre-1954 letters are *destroyed*'; and that no volume of the Diary exists before 1955. It is far more likely that this erasure resulted from a general unease than from some event directly involving either Dirk or Tony, or both. Then again, in the case of the scrapbook, the most probable cause is laziness: an awful lot of material required pasting.

If there seemed to be a disorganised sexual witch-hunt in Britain, the political one under way in Hollywood against alleged communists was highly systematic. Yet Dirk owed the House Un-American Activities Committee a favour. Without the blacklist, it is extremely unlikely that he would ever have met, let alone established the most creatively fruitful partnership of his career with, Joseph Losey. 'A large shy man, with a remarkable sculptured face'[33] is Michael York's description of Losey, who came to England as a permanent exile in January 1953. He had directed twelve Broadway plays, five films in Hollywood and a number of documentaries for the government when the witch-finders began to close in on him. He arrived in Britain, his career in tatters, but thanks to two others on the list, Carl Foreman and Harold Buchman, he was able to set up *The Sleeping Tiger*, which he described as 'a lousy cheap story, as bad as James Hadley Chase's *Eve*, worse maybe. A sort of bedtime reading for senile stags.'[34] Losey had never heard of Dirk when his name was suggested, but after seeing *Hunted* said, 'I'm going to do this picture with Dirk Bogarde and nobody else.' Losey was told that under no circumstances would Dirk take on a film with a minuscule budget under a blacklisted director, but telephoned him none the less. A screening of Losey's *The Prowler* was set up at Pinewood by Olive Dodds and, after twenty minutes, Dirk knew who would be directing his next film – 'Victor Hanbury', a pseudonym borrowed by Losey for £100 from a production manager with a bad heart condition.[35] To give some idea of the pressure Losey was under: when he and Dirk's co-star, Alexis Smith, were having dinner at their small, discreet hotel in Shepperton, Ginger Rogers and/or her mother – there is confusion in the collective memory here – walked in. To Losey, Ginger Rogers was 'one of the worst, red-baiting, terrifying reactionaries in Hollywood'[36] and she knew both Alexis Smith and him. Dirk recalled 'a scream of horror': 'I got him smuggled, literally, into an hotel at Windsor. We got him two rooms, one they turned into a private sitting room for him at great effort. And when we proudly took him there, hidden in the back of my car under a rug (can you believe!) he complained bitterly about the noise.' The noise was from a 'gentle weir in the Thames some distance across the gardens'. It was then, wrote Dirk, 'that I knew I'd got a problem for a friend.'[37]

The film was made at Nettlefold, a studio so run-down that according to Dirk 'we had to fire a gun to frighten away the sparrows from the Sound Stage before every Take'.[38] Dirk's character, Frank Clements, is a young hoodlum, with 'great physical magnetism leavened by a boyish quality that gives him charm', whom a psychiatrist believes he can reform by taking him into his home for six months' therapy. After all, says the doctor, he is 'immature and unhappy and, I think, frightened, under that hard shell of his'.[39] Even at thirty-two Dirk was able to convince as the 'tough little cookie' from a broken family, who seduces the shrink's wife but then becomes so changed for the better that he prefers to go fishing with her husband. The consequences are tragic. The film was taken to task for its psychobabble, but Dirk seemed comfortable enough being dangerously cynical towards women and brooding in his riding gear. He and Tony struck up a fast friendship with Alexis Smith – described in the publicity as 'the girl with a laugh in her voice'. Above all, he had found in Joe, twelve years his senior, something of a kindred spirit:

> I will always remember the first time I really fell 'in love' with Jo was in the bar of the Pier Hotel pub on Cheyne Walk one night on 'sleeping Tiger'. He was wearing a full blue denim suit ... (we had'nt seen one before that. Not the bum freezer as well ...) and boots and a red spotted handkerchief at his throat. His hair was longish ... and he was very brown ... and he looked enormously tall and exactly like a Red Indian. And proud. Naturally. And was rather grotty when I said so and hastened to grumble that he was of Scots descent ...[40]

Here was someone who knew exactly what it was to be an outsider. Here, too, was someone for whom Dirk was 'prepared to dig in and use certain aspects of his own life and his own character that he had never used before in films'.[41]

As he and Losey made their modest start together under difficult conditions, Dirk was attracting attention from Hollywood. Its offshoots in Britain had been nibbling. There was talk of him starring with Greer Garson and Walter Pidgeon in MGM's sequel to *Mrs Miniver*, and he was approached by Twentieth Century-Fox to appear with Richard Widmark in Jules Dassin's *Night and the City*. Both were to be made in England, but for Dirk neither came to anything. Then, as work finished on *The Sleeping Tiger*, Darryl Zanuck at Fox asked him to replace Marlon Brando, who had fled to New York after a read-through of the pyramids-and-sandals epic, *The Egyptian*. Dirk had already been offered a subsidiary role, and turned it down. Now he was interested. Hedda Hopper became excited at the news: 'Dirk is tall (6 feet), dark, handsome and 32 years old', she wrote under the sub-heading, 'Another Burton'.[42] Dirk was about to sign on the dotted line when Fox asked to insert a clause that would have bound him to make a film annually for the next five years, regardless of whether he liked the scripts. He and Rank put their feet down. 'I refuse absolutely to commit myself in Hollywood without having the right to manage my own career by being able to say no to a part I don't like,' he announced.[43] Hedda Hopper was silent. And not everyone at home was impressed. A correspondent to *Picturegoer* won 2 guineas for a letter suggesting that experience in Hollywood might benefit Dirk by adding to their credentials 'two things in which our players are not over-abundant – warmth and self-assurance.'[44] After much scrabbling about with the likes of Rock Hudson, José Ferrer and John Cassavetes, Fox finally cast Edmund Purdom as the physician Sinuhe – 'He who is alone'. It was a pity only in the sense that Dirk and Tony would have enjoyed the company of some good friends: Michael Wilding and Jean Simmons were in the cast. Everyone had high hopes, because the film was to be directed by Michael Curtiz, who had made *Casablanca*. In the event it was a disaster. 'He was awful,' says Jean Simmons. 'I remember I had to be shot with an arrow and poor Ed Purdom had to carry me round the arena. I was giggling all the way. And my brother spotted it when the film came out.'[45] Dirk had a neat way of celebrating his narrow escape: he christened one of his corgis Sinuhe.

Had he gone to America, Dirk would have missed the moment that signalled the 'absolute turning point' in his career to date. Betty Box, sister of Sydney and producer of *So Long at the Fair*, had been on a visit to Wales and the West Country to promote her thriller, *Venetian Bird*, directed by Ralph Thomas. While they waited at Bristol Temple Meads Station for the train back to London, John Troke, who ran the Special Services Division of Rank Theatres, bought from the bookstall a new title that a colleague had mentioned: *Doctor in the House*. He handed it to Betty Box. Every now and then, she would turn to Ralph Thomas and read him a passage that had particularly amused her. At one point she said: 'This is a picture for Dirk.' Troke recalls: 'I don't think she could get back to Pinewood quickly enough, to tell Earl St John about it.'[46] History does not relate whether this was one for contemplation on the St John throne, but he gave the project the go-ahead. However, he was strongly opposed to the casting of Dirk, doubting his capacity for comedy. Dirk, when he read the script, was not that enthused either: 'It all seemed a bit light, the role a bit dim-witted, and every other character had funnier things to say and do. I was to be the simple Juvenile.'[47] Tony, however, understood exactly why Betty Box's idea was so inspired. Not just because it was a break from spivs and uniforms, but also because Dirk could be a still centre in the middle of chaos. Dirk telephoned Betty Box to say yes, subject to the small matter of Kenneth More – his co-star from *Power Without Glory* – who seemed to have more than his fair share of screen time. A similar conversation followed between Betty Box and More.

The filming, at Pinewood and University College London, was a delight for all concerned, but no one was conscious of anything exceptional in the wind. The director lived up to his reputation as 'Five Minute Thomas', who would shoot in one day practically double the amount of eventually shown footage than anyone else in the business. Donald Sinden, who with Donald Houston completed the quartet of trainee doctors at the centre of the story, remembers it as being 'just another Rank film. There was no buzz around it.'[48] Richard Gordon, the Oxford anaesthetist who wrote and adapted the novel, had already been told by another production company that it would not work. But he was having a good time anyway, as he had been retained by Betty Box to advise the cast on hospital procedure, how to handle a stethoscope and the like. He also had the first of a series of walk-on roles, as an anaesthetist. For him, filming at Pinewood was like being at a country club, with the 'baronial hall' as its social centre. As shooting progressed, he saw how Dirk was 'invaluable in his excellent playing of the butt'; the film 'depended on him being charming and bemused and getting all the laughs'. Richard Gordon felt that Dirk's aptitude for the part was 'a case of pure professionalism', and joked: 'I don't think there was any soul being dipped into my script.'[49] He remembered Dirk as being more reserved than the others, and that the camera crew would sometimes call out 'Oh, he's Ginger, inne?' – as in 'Ginger Beer', Cockney rhyming slang for 'queer'. Donald Sinden, who had not worked with Dirk before, was struck by his insularity. Whereas More, Houston and Sinden would spend their breaks at the University College location sitting on the steps of the fountain, swapping anecdotes with no shortage of ribaldry, Dirk would retreat to his Rolls-Royce – 'his first status symbol' – and sit by himself. 'We used to say, "What's wrong with him?" It was very much the chaps together, and the feeling came around that he was the only homosexual among us. But nobody bothered him. It was a very happy unit – as was always the case with Ralph Thomas and Betty Box.'

Films about hospitals were considered to be toxic at the box-office, and the Studio had been far from confident about its future. Sinden recalls how for the first publicity photographs the cast had to wear sports jackets instead of white coats. No one knew whether Betty Box's various hunches had paid off until she, Thomas and members of the unit attended a sneak preview of the film in public performance at a cinema in the Edgware Road. The reception was cordial from the start, but the moment of truth came when James Robertson Justice as the orotund surgeon Sir Lancelot Spratt barked at an inattentive Simon Sparrow, 'You, what's the bleeding time?' and received the reply, 'Ten past ten, Sir.' Donald Sinden remembers: 'That line got such an enormous laugh that it went right through the next scene. So the next day we went back into the studio to film me doing something with chrysanthemums – no dialogue – just to cover the laugh.' When the film went on release three weeks later, it was greeted with rapture. In its first year, an unprecedented 17 million tickets were sold, prompting the producer William MacQuitty to calculate that there were 34 million people of cinema-going age in the country, so 'why didn't the other 17 million go?' Dirk's performance was welcomed with delight as a departure from 'heroic desperadoes' and 'neurotic coshboys', but what really swept him into the affections of those millions was one of the film's *sotto* sequences, based on a wartime experience of Richard Gordon's: a house call, when, in the absence of a midwife, a terrified Simon Sparrow has to deliver a baby. He might be completely out of his depth, but so exquisite is his bedside manner that the mother decides there and then to christen her son Simon. Sobbing was heard throughout the land. Many lands, in fact.

From those most unassuming beginnings, it had been 'the absolute turning point' – one which, Dirk admitted later, 'secured me in my profession'. Shortly after filming was finished, Dirk wrote to Betty Box and Ralph Thomas, saying that he had never been so happy or felt more confident in his director and producer, and that he had done 'my very best to show you my appreciation in my work'. He added: 'Please let me work with you again. Couldn't I possibly be a pine tree in "Campbell's Kingdom"? I wouldn't want any lines . . .'.[50]

On 16 February 1954 Dirk signed a contract with Tony's family to buy Beel House. The previous owner, William Lowndes – 'Good sportsman: good citizen: good friend'[51] – had moved from the area and wanted to develop some of his parkland for housing, but was thwarted by stiff opposition from councils and neighbours alike. The Forwoods acquired the estate and simultaneously sold Dirk the house and seven acres of land for £4,000. Part of the building had its origins in the seventeenth century, when it was the home of Mary Pennington, a prominent Quaker whose daughter married William Penn. Since then it had been much altered and extended, so that one of Dirk's first actions was to engage a local builder to demolish 'a wing of eleven ugly rooms', gut the house and 'start from scratch'.[52] At the end of the work there were still fifteen rooms, the pride and joy of which was a thirty-foot conservatory, with Doric columns leading on to a south-facing terrace. This room, which Dirk filled with a jungle of plants, was promptly dubbed by Kay Kendall 'the Out-Patients Department'. Other wildlife were housed in a vivarium, and an aviary of thirty-four tropical birds, dominated by a parrot called Annie, named after Michael Gough's actress wife, Anne Leon. There were the dogs, Chug and Rosie, soon to be replaced by 'He who is alone' and another corgi, Bogie. There were four cats, including a chinchilla called George; and a Siamese, Missy, which Dirk had saved from being put down by the vet. There were a hamster, a hedgehog, a squirrel, another prudence-defying cayman called Ludwig, and a heated pond containing several dozen fish. And there were staff – to begin with, a French husband and wife, Thomas and Yvonne, whom Dirk later accused of racial prejudice but whose real offence may have lain in the kitchen where Yvonne tended to cook too richly; and then an incomparable Austrian couple, Hans and Agnes Zwickl, who came with added value because a friend from their home town near Vienna was an expert gardener. Florian stoically put up with many an attack by Annie; but he was not alone. As Tony's cousin Mary recalls, 'it was a one-person bird' – and that person was Dirk.

It was quite a set-up; one where a young man might easily allow free rein to his *folie de grandeur*. Most of Rank's leading male contract artists were married, and had families to keep their feet on the ground. What is more, they had made their way into films via drama school and the theatre, with its own levelling disciplines. In America there was more of a separation; of course the two met, but, to put it crudely, the theatre was on the East Coast and the cinema on the West, where the Hollywood Star was its own discrete breed. As Rank tried to compete with America, it had in Dirk someone who would play to the hilt a version of the Hollywood game. On the one hand he guarded his privacy – better, his mystery – as zealously as Ludwig would defend his tank; on the other he would invite his favoured stills photographer George Courtney Ward to capture him strutting about his acres in tweed jacket and jodhpurs, snuggling up to horses he never rode, leaning against the Bentley he never drove, and needlessly exercising Florian's lawnmower. Much capital was made out of the luminous casts who would assemble for his Sunday lunch parties, often including those very American actors and actresses whose lifestyle he was emulating. Magazines printed extensively illustrated articles about 'Squire Bogarde' and his mansion. With the house he had inherited a horse show and gymkhana, held each September in Beel House Park. The local newspaper noted with commendable balance that the first such event over which he presided was attended by 'what can almost be termed as a galaxy of stars' – Kay Kendall, Glynis Johns and Denholm Elliott – who for most of the time were confined to an enclosure, while two twenty-year-olds from Cheshire who had spent half the day waiting for a close-up glimpse of Dirk were prevented by a steward from taking his photo-graph.[53] He admitted twenty years later that the 'Country Squire was fast in danger of believing his own image and changing to Lord of the Manor. It is an insidious business.'[54]

In private, however, Agnes Zwickl, the cook-housekeeper for five years, knew Dirk as someone far less self-conscious. She and her husband had arrived to be interviewed by Tony, not knowing that their employer would be Dirk. When Tony told them, an image flashed through her mind of a scene in *The Sleeping Tiger* when Frank Clements hurls a tray of tea to the ground. 'He did it so realistically that I wondered if he was a person like that,' she recalls. 'Mr Forwood said, "If there are any problems, it would be better to bring them to me".'[55] She had little cause to do so:

> Mr Bogarde was such a kind and nice man. I can't find words to say what a lovely person he was. He had a great heart for people who were not so well off as he was. He lived a very quiet life, and did not like to be in the public eye. He always looked happy, never depressed. And he did not seem to me to be lonely. Sometimes on a Sunday morning he would go into the garden on his own and think. In the evenings he would study. It was a very correct life – there were no scandals. I never, in all those years, saw him have too much to drink. I don't think he would have had much time to fool around in those days, even if he had wanted to.

As for Tony: 'He was awfully good-looking, very charming. All the women fell around him like crazy. He seemed to me to be a person to whom you could tell anything. He did everything for Mr Bogarde. Whatever he touched came out right, whatever he arranged for Mr Bogarde came out right too. I never heard an argument between them.' The only nagging problem was the fans: 'Some of them were so stupid. Even in the snow and ice, they would come and sit in the hedges. One girl came with her father from Holland just to get an autograph.' Some went further still:

> One day there was a tea party. I think Michael Wilding was there. My husband took in the tea, and the doorbell rang. I went to answer it, and there was this attractive woman. A Rolls-Royce was in the drive. I thought she must be another guest. In she came, and she said she had not been invited but that Mr Bogarde was the father of her child. He went straight up to his room and she became hysterical, telling everyone that they had met in Salzburg and she had had his baby. Eventually they managed to calm her down and get rid of her.

Tony noted in the Diary that Freddy Joachim had helped to see off the premises 'a demented Austrian woman' claiming paternity, and added: 'She was one of many!'

The Beel years were those in which Dirk achieved a success far beyond anyone's expectations – his own included. At the end of 1955 the 4,358 cinema managers who contributed to the annual *Motion Picture Herald* poll named him 'the World's Greatest Money-Drawing Star'.[56] Simon Sparrow had provided the impetus, but Dirk had been doing all in his power to keep the momentum going. In the seventeen months after the release of *Doctor in the House* five more of his films opened. Among them was *The Sea Shall Not Have Them*, Lewis Gilbert's portrait of 'stiff upper lips in a dinghy', in which Michael Redgrave, Bonar Colleano, Jack Watling and Dirk spend twenty-four hours hoping to be picked up by the Air-Sea Rescue Service. The director recalled how his two stars did not get on too well. On the first day Dirk, who was genuinely in some awe of Redgrave, attempted a compliment along the lines of 'You know, Michael, I'm so happy to be acting with you.' Back came the reply: 'This is not acting; this is just reacting.'[57] Alas, the film is now known less for any merit than for the remark made by Noël Coward as he crossed Leicester Square and saw:

Michael Redgrave   Dirk Bogarde
THE SEA SHALL NOT HAVE THEM

'I don't see why not,' he said. 'Everyone else has.'[58]

Barely had the film opened than Dirk was back on the water, for *Doctor at Sea*, the rights to which Betty Box had optioned from Richard Gordon while their first collaboration was still in production. It was based on Gordon's experience as a ship's doctor, a post he filled as a break from hospital work, and one he put doubly to good use: during that period he wrote *Doctor in the House*. For the female lead Rank put up a twenty-one-year-old contract artist called Joan Collins, whose roles to date had found her pigeonholed as a 'naughty girl', labelled in the press as 'The Coffee-bar Jezebel' and 'The Esses Girl – She's sultry! She's sexy! She's a Siren!' She was delighted to be asked to do a test at Pinewood opposite 'the "Idol of the Odeons", the gorgeous, sensitive Dirk Bogarde'. 'We slithered around self-consciously on creamy satin sheets, I wearing a pink baby-doll nightgown, he a bemused expression. We attempted to look as though we were made for each other but we were seriously ill-matched and this time the part went to Brigitte Bardot.'[59]

Dirk was to claim that he had discovered Bardot, after being despatched to Paris by Betty Box and Ralph Thomas with a list of three possible candidates. There was, he wrote, no need to see the other two: 'From where I sat in the cramped little dressing-room, this amazingly glowing child – she was seventeen at the time – wrestling furiously with a vast lurcher-type of dog called Clown, was all I needed for my duties as a valiant young doctor at sea.'[60] Betty Box's husband, Peter Rogers – producer of the *Carry On* series and himself a pillar of Pinewood – says his wife was puzzled by the claim: 'Where did Dirk get that from? Betty and I saw Brigitte Bardot in her first film, in the south of France. It was called "Le Trou normand", with Bourvil. Betty remembered her and got in touch with Olga Horstig-Primuz, her agent, and didn't even go over to Paris herself. So why should she send Dirk? A producer doesn't send another artist to pick up an artist. What an extraordinary aberration.'[61] Dirk did meet the twenty-year-old in Paris, but only after she had already been cast. 'Wait an hour for her – she's taking a bath,' he wrote in a 'diary' published under his name in *Picturegoer*. 'Worth waiting for. She's captivating.'[62] Of more significance to him, however, was Bardot's agent, who would represent him in France for the rest of his career.

The *Doctor at Sea* locations involved sailing on a Greek liner, the *Achilleus*, to

Piraeus, Alexandria and Athens. The ship was leaving from Venice, so Dirk and Tony went by train. It was Dirk's first sight of 'La Serenissima' and Betty Box wanted to see his reaction. She set off with Ralph Thomas in a motor-launch to fetch him from the station:

> Halfway there along the Grand Canal we saw a large boat coming towards us and, standing like a statue in the prow, the wind ruffling his hair, his eyes showing his admiration for the grandeur of the city, stood Dirk, taking in all the beauty of his surroundings. As we drew nearer we bellowed at him, but Dirk's thoughts were obviously elsewhere (perhaps with Lord Byron, whose palace we were just passing).[63]

The filming went crisply, but not without incident – 'Man overboard during shooting', noted Tony one Sunday. The Parthenon was visited in the rain. The unit was fêted wherever it went: the popular British Ambassador to Greece, Sir Charles Peake, led a multi-national platoon of diplomats, among them a relative of Tony's, on board the *Achilleus*'s sister ship, the *Agamemnon*, to add authenticity for a party sequence. Locals working in the fields beside the Corinth Canal gazed in awe as the *Achilleus* passed, bearing the massive, bearded figure of James Robertson Justice, resplendent in his summer whites. He was playing the ship's captain, an unashamed misogynist: 'I don't approve of women, you understand. They're unseamanlike and unnecessary.' In life, it was a different matter. Poly-lingual, disarming, he seemed as delighted to be in Bardot's company as she in his. An early guru to the Prince of Wales, Justice took him on to the set at Pinewood and introduced him to the mesmerising French actress. Prince Charles was duly impressed; but he was only six.

Dirk spoke and wrote fondly of Bardot. Forty years later he remembered her as 'huge fun' to work with: 'She was wise, funny, and far in advance of anything we had at that time in the UK and, of course, we didn't know how to handle her'.[64] How true.

Tony organised flowers – '£5' – to be sent to her room at the Dorchester, but there was little rapport with her co-star. According to Peter Rogers, another member of the cast took her to dinner in London and when she told Dirk on set the next day, he said: 'What did you want to go out with *him* for?' She replied: 'Well, *you* nevair asked me.' It was clear to Betty Box that, in Dirk, Bardot sensed there was 'a neuter'. He made no mention of the startling moment when, after trying in the usual flesh-coloured garments to appear convincingly nude behind a shower curtain, she stood in the briefest of briefs and said to Ralph Thomas, 'You can tell me, Ralph, when I goes in the shower, when I am to take off my knickairs, OK?' Off they duly came, the crew somehow pulled itself together, and she was the talk of Pinewood – reputedly the first completely naked actress in a British studio. It was nothing to her. The British press went mildly potty about the discovery of a 'Sex Kitten', and she was justified in describing *Doctor at Sea* as her 'conquête de l'Angleterre', but the experience left little impression on her. In her compendious memoirs, published in 1996, she devoted a page and a half to the film, which she judged 'no masterpiece, but charming'. The separation from her husband Roger Vadim and her equally beloved 'Cocker Spaniard', Clown, made her feel as if she had been left like a child at a boarding school. Alone and miserable at the Dorchester, exhausted by the five o'clock starts to each working day, falling asleep into her room-service 'pudding', she took comfort in the fact that the whole thing was 'an excellent linguistic exercise', because no one on the set spoke a word of French. One Sunday, she wrote, she was invited to lunch at Dirk's 'cottage', a 'two-hour' drive from the hotel, where she found herself in a crowd of 'regular guests who all knew each other'. Their talk gave her a migraine: 'I would have swapped my birthright for a phrase in French.' She was rescued by the London correspondent of Agence France Presse, who, with his wife, took her under their wing for the rest of her stay.[65] In fact she went to Beel twice in three days – the first time for an 'Athens re-union' with many of the others in the cast; the second, for a quiet lunch with Dirk, Tony and Geoffrey Keen and his wife. The *entente* can not have been entirely as strained as she made out. But about Dirk she made no comment at all.

There is, said Bardot ever afterwards, only one word which it is essential to know in English: 'No'. Dirk, in his 1994 paean, gave her credit for teaching him the effectiveness of that 'one killer word, administered always with a charming smile'.[66] In the same article he gave a peculiar description of the nightclub dress which Bardot wore for her 'big number': 'She proved, before my eyes that she could turn her body all the way round within the scarlet-sequinned, crimson-beaded gown, so that it remained absolutely rigid and nailed to the floor.'[67] Oddly enough, just before the piece appeared, the costume designer, Joan Ellacott – who worked on three of Dirk's films and created Elizabeth Taylor's unforgettable white swimsuit for *Suddenly Last Summer* – had put the original drawing up for auction. Hiding her hurt at his description of her handiwork, she wrote to Dirk, saying that by attracting attention to the dress he might help to bring up the price. He wrote back: 'I fear that both Brigitte and I, frankly, would fill the bodice plentifully! Sadly ... ah well ... it was fun at the time.'[68] The drawing fetched £143.

Ten

'I suppose they prefer to put me to bed than to take me to bed'

On New Year's Eve 1955, with his name now dominating the polls, Dirk wrote to John Davis. The letter has not survived, but a draft in Tony's hand, while admittedly a little clumsy, gives a telling insight into Dirk's thoughts about his attachment to 'the Rankery':

> I do feel badly the necessity of trying to prove what I feel to be untapped resources in my ability. It seems to be almost impossible to find in this country the type of role which has made actors of the Brando & James Dean style, with whose school of acting mine has I think some affinity which hitherto I have only been able to employ in the theatre. I am of course happy to have found the 'Simon Sparrow' type of comedy role but am anxious that this should be balanced with some really solid dramatic work and even perhaps with some 'Tony Curtis' stuff which I think might prove amusing & rewarding, & for which I would gladly undergo the necessary forms of PT!'

The letter was prompted by a state of near-limbo. In two years nine of his films had been released. Now he was looking at a calendar with only one project inked-in; one which was causing him enough concern at the script stage to make him doubtful that it would help to 'consolidate & improve my position'. Apart from the *Doctor* films, he had made a screen adaptation of *For Better, For Worse* and stepped at a late stage into *Simba*, a story set against the background of the Mau Mau troubles in Kenya, for which the producer, Peter de Sarigny, and director, Brian Desmond Hurst, had been hoping to secure Jack Hawkins. So much so, that they had been to Kenya and, using a double who looked vaguely like Hawkins, shot 'miles of footage' which could be married up with the latter's performance in the studio. Alas, Hawkins proved unavailable. You do not need to look too closely to see the discrepancies as the film cuts from double to Dirk, who was about six inches shorter than Jack Hawkins. Again, Donald Sinden was Dirk's co-star, as a police inspector. In Kenya, Hurst and de Sarigny had recruited as their double a real, blond, athletic police inspector. Back in Pinewood they could find no one at Rank who looked anything like him. As the disconsolate pair sat drowning their sorrows amid general hilarity, Sinden walked in. He was preparing for the role of a fisherman in *Mad About Men*, and Betty Box had suggested he convey the great outdoors by having his hair streaked, or 'sun-kissed'. Hurst and de Sarigny looked up at the apparition. De Sarigny did 'a perfect double-take' and said: 'Would you bleach it all over?' Of course he would. And did. Once more Sinden was amused by Dirk's tricks, especially the manoeuvres he used in order to avoid being shown in right profile:

> The lighting cameramen were aware of this, and they would line a shot up so that it was the right way round for him. But sometimes it couldn't be helped. I've seen Dirk perform the most astonishing contortions to make sure that his left side was the one in shot. If in one shot he had to go through a door and the next be behind a desk, he would find a good excuse for a move – 'I'll put my hat down over there' – and come back so that all you would see would be the left. He would almost climb over the desk if necessary! We all thought it was farcical.[2]

Dirk's next leading lady, after *Simba* with Virginia McKenna and *Doctor at Sea* with Bardot, was Margaret Lockwood, making the most of a screen adaptation of Janet Green's play, *Cast a Dark Shadow*. In this second of three films with the director Lewis Gilbert, Dirk portrayed Edward Bare, a ruthless predator with a high-pitched laugh whose bait is 'charm, just charm'. He says he has had 'the old psycho routine for years', but is unable to escape himself: 'I think I'm a sort of little Napoleon or something. Highly strung, and emotional. I know it all! But there's not a doctor I can't beat at his own game.' Dirk marked out that passage in his copy of the script.[3] *Cast a Dark Shadow* was to prove Margaret Lockwood's last film for nearly twenty years; and when they finished shooting, Dirk's expect-ations looked not much brighter. He had, however, added a string to his bow, as a radio presenter – shades of Batavia 1946. In the week that Alistair Cooke surprised followers of his *Letter from America* by singing jazz numbers to his own piano accompaniment in a special recording for the Home Service, Dirk displayed his own taste in music on the Light Programme. For six weeks he was invited to take over Eamonn Andrews's show, *Pied Piper*. Dirk had his own ideas and called it 'I Play What I Like', prompting *Radio Times* to label the title 'uncompromising'. At least 120 pieces of music would be required to fill the six hours, so Tony and he plundered their own substantial collection, and records were shipped from America that had not been broadcast in Britain before. The result was a splendidly eclectic series, in which Kathleen Ferrier and Arthur Rubinstein jockeyed for position with Sinatra and Caruso, Richard Tauber with Carmen Miranda, and Mario Lanza with Jimmy Young. There was a heavy emphasis on show tunes, and exposure for friends such as Jessie Matthews, Noël Coward and Glynis Johns. Layton and Johnstone were featured in almost every programme, and even Anthony Steel had his moment, singing 'West of Zanzibar' with the Radio

Revellers. Dirk was paid 42 guineas a show and the BBC were delighted, once they had found a way round the particular problem posed by his chosen title. As the producer, Michael Bell, wrote to him: 'It is always difficult when the announcer has to give out a title which includes "I" unless it is something like "I play what I like, and here is Dirk Bogarde to carry out his threat"!'[4] Dirk struck a chord with the listeners: 'It never occurred to me that anyone would bother to write,' he said, 'and when more than four thousand letters came in it threw me into a panic. And, you can believe this or not, but only twenty letters were anti.'[5]

There was something else to fill the gap. After a holiday in the south of France with Tony and Elizabeth, Dirk went back on to the stage for the first time in three and a half years. The producer Toby Rowland asked the twenty-four-year-old director of the Arts Theatre, Peter Hall, who had just staged a bewildering piece entitled *Waiting for Godot*, to find a vehicle. While still a student at Cambridge, Hall had seen *Point of Departure* and thought it 'funny and haunting and sexy';[6] Dirk was 'wonderful in that play – he had such simplicity. There was no sense of an actor *working*.'[7] Hall found *Summertime*, a frothy confection by Ugo Betti, for whom there was 'a fever for a short time'. An excellent supporting cast was assembled, including Geraldine McEwan, Gwen Ffrangcon Davies, Michael Gwynn and, as a farmer in the third act, Ronald [sic] Barker. Dirk wrote to Sylvia and Kathleen Withersby, theatre-loving followers of his:

I was so determined not to come back to the theatre in a black-neurotic-looking-after-God part that I have waited a long time for what I hope will be a complete change for me. The play is about nothing at all, and as the title suggests is good and bright and full of hot sunshine which should be splendid in November fogs. So there you have it! And I only *hope* to God that I have made the right decision![8]

The play, set in the Italian Alps, opened in – of all places – Glasgow, for which Dirk managed, publicly at least, to suppress any latent hatred. The reviews were 'mixed', the *Herald* saying he 'makes an agreeable nincompoop, and his curious air of suffering from intermittent abdominal cramp does not seriously hinder the portrayal of so very backward a suitor'.[9] The three-week tour that followed attracted full houses all the way, so much so that Peter Hall, on his small percentage, walked into a garage in Manchester and bought his first new car, a blue Ford Prefect. 'The fans stormed the theatres in each town,' noted Tony in the Diary, 'and it became a nightmare for Dirk.' There are references to mounted police being brought in to control the crowds in Manchester, and to an invasion via the scene dock in Cardiff. In *Snakes and Ladders* Dirk wrote:

The audiences in the main, however, came to see the Film Star and not the Play, something which had never remotely occurred to me, and each performance became an exhausting, and extended, Personal Appearance, during which every entrance and exit was greeted by the hysterical screams and moans reserved today for pop singers; and the alarming chants, during the performance, of 'We love you, Dirk!' or, if I was unwise enough to let exasperation show, even more threateningly, 'We put you where you are!', destroyed the play, dismayed my fellow actors, and distressed me to such an unforeseen extent that every theatrical appearance became an ordeal.[10]

Peter Hall recalls: 'There were huge crowds of people at the stage door, and I remember Dirk telling me that he couldn't walk down the street without being stopped, which was true, but there was no direct effect on the actual performances. He's making an exaggerated image of the truth, because the fans in that sense were in his head when he walked onto the stage, even if they weren't in the audience.' For the twenty-three-year-old Geraldine McEwan the scenes outside the stage door were 'amazing – all those people calling Dirk's name. When I was very young anything which I hadn't experienced before was a surprise, but although this was very big, strangely I accepted it.' She was unaware of any disturbance inside the theatres during the run but 'maybe I sensed from him that he was finding it a burden and maybe it interfered with the job in hand'.[11] The play moved in to the Apollo on Shaftesbury Avenue, where it was welcomed as 'a comedy spun out of treacle and thin air'. On the morning after the first night Dirk told a journalist that he had stood in the wings before each entrance, saying to himself that no one could be quite as terrified and still go on living; now, he said, he felt as if all his teeth had been pulled out.[12] Nevertheless he seemed at ease enough to tell Frank Granville Barker how much he had enjoyed tackling the play, which was so light, so fragile, that it placed special demands on 'careful timing and complete confidence'.[13] After three weeks in the West End, he was taken ill. The press reported that he had jaundice. Tony in the Diary called it infective hepatitis, possibly 'from a doctor in Manchester who gave him a B12 injection from an unsterilised needle'. Nigel Stock took over as Alberto until Dirk's return which, as in *Point of Departure*, was short-lived.

Once again, Dirk's ambition to do well as a stage actor had been overwhelmed by the nerves which both drove his performance and made it impossible for him to sustain week in week out. 'Dirk was enchanting to work with,' says Peter Hall, 'not at all, in any sense, difficult. Perfectionist, yes, but there is nothing wrong with that. His problem in the theatre was that he never found a way to quieten his nerves. He was too considerate and professional to take them out on other people, so he suffered in silence very acutely. I think he did in front of the camera too, but for briefer periods, of course, than eight times a week. The camera can be more forgiving.' Geraldine McEwan, remembering how generous Dirk was in his encouragement to her as a young actress, said he confided in her about his affliction. She saw for herself how the fans were making the problem worse:

If you can't go on stage and love it, and feel that your audience is just *one* person, that they are all making up one group who have come to see a play with a number of actors and actresses; if you feel that there are people out in front who are there only because you are a film star, it is no good. It's a different kind of audience from one which is going to *see plays*; it's a film-star-struck group of people. It is frightening if anyone gets a fixation on you. It's all a bit unhinged. It happened to me at the National: there was a woman who used to come to every performance and sit in the front row. You are aware she is there, and at the end you even look to see that she is still there. It becomes a nasty, horrible situation. There were probably people in the audience who saw every one of Dirk's performances, and because he was obviously a very feeling, and sensitive, creature, he wouldn't like that.

When she saw what was happening at the stage doors, 'I did feel, "Oh my God, I'm glad I haven't got all that." ' She has never forgotten how he told her that he did not want to go through the agonies of it all any more. 'He said, "I'm never going to do the theatre again. It's too nerve-racking, and that's it." ' He was almost as good as his word.

On the credit side, Dirk's appearance in *Summertime* attracted – in the provinces in particular – a young minority who had never set foot in a theatre before. He told how he asked a girl in one of the stage-door crushes whether she had enjoyed the play. 'Lovely,' she said. 'When the curtain went up, it was just like fairyland. I'm glad I saved up to come.'[14] On the debit side was the kind of treatment which resulted in a *Picturegoer* headline: 'BOGARDE GETS THE RAY MOB PLUS' – a reference to the astonishing scenes provoked in Britain two years earlier by the visit of the half-deaf crooner Johnnie Ray, billed variously as 'The Nabob of Sob', 'Mr Emotion' and 'the Prince of Wails'. Noël Coward had been to see Ray at the London Palladium and noted, with more restraint: 'He was really remarkable and had the whole place in an uproar.'[15] Dirk was now in that odd and, in those days, rare position of someone revelling in the renown for his achievements, while at the same time detesting – even being terrified by – what that renown carried with it. You might say, he enjoyed fame but hated celebrity. The Rank publicists knew all too well that in Dirk they had the least pliant of their artists. Donald Sinden recalls how on one occasion at a screening Dirk was introduced to the audience by a nervously gushing cinema manager, who kept on referring to 'this up and coming star'. When Dirk was given the microphone he said: 'I've never been up and coming so often in two minutes.' It did not go down well with the powers that be. Nor did his opening remark to serried ranks of filmgoers in Bristol about his journey via the Severn Tunnel: 'I've just come through the longest lavatory in the world.' Nor did his *hauteur* at trade and press shows; still less his remarks to journalists about the confines of his contractual obligations and the shortage of worthwhile material; and this characteristic combination of honesty and disingenuousness: 'I act in films and I'm glad to take the money, but I'm not a *film star*, and never have been.' Naturally, the newspapers and magazines revelled in his openness; some drew attention to the expletives with which he peppered his interviews when no women were present. Theo Cowan, as Rank's most skilful bomb disposal officer, and his team had to be on their mettle. Soon their role would change slightly – for the benefit of both parties. As Laurie Bellew, Cowan's right-hand man for many years, puts it: 'Our skill was being able to say to the press that Dirk would like to oblige, but, alas, on this occasion he can't; and to leave both press and public believing he was a smashing bloke.'[16]

As he composed his letter to John Davis, the BBC Light Programme was preparing a radio portrait of Dirk, which went out as 'Reluctant Star'.[17] It is a rare treasure, because of the cast of characters assembled to pay homage in their contrasting ways. Olive Dodds said she could not blame the BBC for using the 'quite amusing' title, but added, 'believe me, there's nothing very reluctant about the film star I know. Dirk may not approve of all the trimmings involved in stardom, but from the beginning I'm certain he looked on this business of making films as a challenge. I'm not saying that he isn't rebellious; but he is a constructive rebel.' Chloë Gibson, whom Dirk described as 'a Greek coin' because of her fearsome aspect when they first met, recounted a more credible version than his of how she came to cast him in *Power Without Glory* and how he had two sides: a 'strange Peter Pan-like quality, his refusal, as it were, to grow up'; and 'a certain ruthlessness mixed with the charm. It's a quality he shared with the late James Dean, a sort of vehement sensitivity. Real tears come into his eyes; there's no need for the glycerine.' Kenneth More and James Robertson Justice reminisced joshingly with Dirk himself; and the Withersby sisters explained – with Dirk's blessing – why they had been to see *Point of Departure* thirty times. There was also a contribution, surely unique, from Tony, who explained how he had first seen Dirk at the Amersham Playhouse in 1939 [*sic*], when the play 'wasn't particularly interesting, except for the performance of a young man heavily bewhiskered in a vain endeavour to look middle aged. I won't say the performance was a brilliant one, but the actor seemed to have a strain of that – that un-definable magnetism that we call "star quality".' Tony explained how he helped to obtain the engagement in *Diversion No. 2*, and how Dirk 'had progressed at such a rate after the war that he asked me to take some of the strain off his agent and himself by becoming his personal manager'. It had, said Tony, 'been fascinating to watch him develop his career':

> Freddy and I find him very receptive to advice, but it's always himself alone who makes any final decision, and stands or falls by it. I wouldn't really say that he's stubborn, but many of us have found that the amount of different inflections that he can wring out of the word 'No' would do credit to a United Nations delegate. As a man, he's inclined much towards shyness, in the way

that many artists are; and the quality of gentleness that C. A. Lejeune* referred
to recently is very much there. But it's a gentleness that can turn quickly to
ice, if anyone takes unfair advantage of it. I've heard him accused of being
reactionary in his approach to life, but [...] I think this is because he really
does prefer the quiet pursuits of country life, and a way of living that goes with
them. Ideally, I think he would like to have lived in the nineteenth century
with a television set.

In the hour-long profile, presented by Brian Matthew and punctuated with
laughter from all quarters, Dirk did not go as far as he had in an associated
interview, when he said: 'I never wanted to be a film star. In a strange way I
rather resent it.'[18] The programme ended with him announcing that his ambition
was to play Romeo on the stage.

Dirk was well into the second term of his contract – now worth a basic
£20,000 a year for two Rank films. In 1955 he and Tony had set up a company
called Bendrose Film Productions Ltd, principally to buy rights for film, television
and theatre presentation, to 'carry on the business of theatre and cinema pro-
prietors and managers', and generally to produce and exploit work in film and
television. An additional clause enabled Dirk to enter into agreements which
would benefit the company by his endeavouring 'at all times to maintain and
increase his reputation as a first class Star Artist'. Thus the *Summertime* contract
was made with Bendrose, and in mid-1956 Rank began to divide his payments –
increased to a basic £22,500 – so that half went to Bendrose, which paid him a
salary of £1,800 a year; and half directly to Dirk himself. In March 1956 Laurence
Harbottle was appointed a director. He had recently left the firm of Langton and
Passmore to set up on his own as Harbottle and Lewis. Dirk went with him,
having first written to the partners with the explanation that 'my manager and
my agent have established an easy and pleasant understanding with him and we
all feel that for this reason and the sake of continuity in the handling of my
affairs, it would really be more satisfactory if he could continue to do so'. The
letter was a formality. Laurence Harbottle recalls: 'When I told my boss that
Dirk Bogarde wanted to come with me, he said "Who's Dirk Bogarde?".' Dirk
was the first client – and his was the first file, labelled 'H1'. A lot of traffic was to
flow between them in the next forty-three years.

First, there were films to be made, the salary to be earned. It had been nearly
a year since Dirk had worked in front of a camera when he, Tony, Ulric and
Margaret set off for the Costa Brava. They drove through France, stopping for
one night at Uzerche, near Limoges, where, as Tony noted twenty-one years
later, 'it was so bitter that D & I shared a bed to keep warm'. The next day they
were in S'Agaro, near Barcelona, where Dirk was to make *The Spanish Gardener*,

---

* C.(aroline) A. Lejeune (1897–1973), film critic.

an adaptation of A. J. Cronin's 1950 novel about a priggish failed diplomat, whose delicate, over-protected, nine-year-old son befriends a local youth of nineteen engaged to tend their luxuriant flowerbeds. Dirk was to play the sensitive man of the soil who in his spare time goes fishing or thrills the populace with his prowess on the *pelota* court. It was in part his worries about the script that had prompted Dirk to write to John Davis. He felt dubious about returning from a long absence in a weak role compared with those of the other main characters. He had approached the producer, John Bryan, who promised to try to 'improve the character', but Dirk was worried that it would be difficult to do so without upsetting the balance of the story. He was correct, but not only for that reason. Cronin's novel made no bones about it: as the Consul, Brande, looked out of his window into the garden, 'the flame sprang out in his heart again, nearly suffocating him'. Why?

> The gardener stood on the edge of the bright lawn, naked to the waist, young thighs planted well apart, his golden-skinned torso gleaming in the sunlight, swinging the scythe with easy strokes. Fascinated, scarcely breathing, Brande watched the splendid rhythm, every sweep cutting into his flesh. In a sweat of hatred, his fingers twitched and clenched upon the pen, snapping it off short. But he did not notice. Lost in a swirling lust, he still watched, with dilated pupils and throbbing eardrums, that clean, glittering blade, sweeping and sweeping in a perfect arc, sweeping like a scimitar, against the faraway blue mountains.[19]

It is doubtful whether the average moviegoer was conscious of swirling lust. None the less Stephen Bourne, in his study of homosexuality in the British cinema, found: 'All through the film there is a homoerotic undercurrent, especially when Bogarde appears. He looks absolutely gorgeous with his suntan, bare chest and deep, soulful eyes. But *The Spanish Gardener* is Michael Hordern's film.'[20] Hordern was splendid as the starched, deluded, jealously possessive Brande, 'bent double with the chips on his shoulder', who is told by his superior that his academic qualifications have never been questioned, but, 'It is as a man – as a human being – that you have failed'; while Dirk pottered about sympathetically with a wheelbarrow, saying: 'This work is nothing. You know I am as strong as an Andalusian donkey.'[21] He looked back on the film as 'a travesty': 'Some of it's quite good, I suppose, but I saw it and was heartbroken because it just wasn't true.'[22]

The Consul's son was played by Jon Whiteley, by now eleven and with an extraordinary c.v. from his ration of one film per year. He had won a special Academy Award for his part in *The Kidnappers*, and in his most recent film, *Moonfleet*, had been directed by Fritz Lang, an experience he describes as 'like working with Michelangelo'. When he was offered the part of Nicholas, his mother was reassured by Philip Leacock – who had directed *The Kidnappers* –

and John Bryan that 'the darker side of Cronin's story would be omitted and the film designed for family consumption'. The boy and Dirk had not met since the release of *Hunted,* and their reunion took place in the restaurant at Pinewood during pre-production. 'Before I saw him I heard his voice,' remembers Jon Whiteley.[23] 'He was complaining about the garlic in his lamb. From the start there was a slight reserve; it stayed right through the making of the film. I remembered him as a friend with whom I had lost contact, but there was never quite the rapport we had had before.' On the location at S'Agaro, Whiteley, his mother and eight-year-old sister Marsali stayed in a hotel. Dirk had a villa round a point on the coast, where he and Tony were joined not only by Ulric and Margaret but also by Glynis and by Gareth Forwood, who became great friends with his close contemporary Marsali. Jon Whiteley is the first to admit that he himself had probably altered somewhat – and not only in height – since their happy time working on *Hunted*: 'At the age of six I was a young anarchist – a rebel, who didn't do anything he was told. Eleven-year-olds are stiff and priggish. I guess that was true of me too.' That said, he found 'Dirk had become more self-regarding than he had been in 1951. His sense of humour had become more unkind, a tiny bit acid. I didn't care for it when he made remarks against the people with whom he was working.' The stills photography which had been a minor irritant to Whiteley on *Hunted* was now a pest as Dirk and he were captured off-set at every turn.

There were personal tensions, too: 'Dirk sometimes tried to decide what I should do. He said he wanted to take me to the seaside, when my mother had other plans.' Christine Whiteley would go to see Tony, who always understood her position and for whom she developed a great liking. Tony's special oil would be applied to the troubled waters. For Jon Whiteley these were signs of a new high-handedness in Dirk. 'He was very professional, but he was terribly miscast as a Spanish gardener. I remember hearing unkind comments about him on the set. And of course there was a huge contrast between him and the actual Spanish gardeners – with Dirk in his tight jeans and cut English accent. He was supposed to be a peasant, but he stood out. The film could have been done with someone else, and it might have worked.' Christine Whiteley puts some of the problems down to jealousy. 'Dirk seemed to be more worried than he had been about his position as a film star. A child in a film is always – well, not exactly a menace, but ... I remember a publicity girl asking about Jon. He had been to America, got an Oscar, met Princess Margaret, all that sort of thing. We duly told the Rank person, but Dirk squashed it – it wouldn't do to have a child in the film outshine him. It showed how anxious he was to preserve his position. He was quite different.'[24]

All of this was to have the oddest of sequels. For Jon Whiteley *The Spanish Gardener* was his last film: he took his eleven-plus exam, finished his education and became a distinguished art historian. He never met Dirk again, or had any contact with him, or read any of his books. Over the years, in interviews, Dirk would claim several times that not only had he wanted to adopt the boy; he had also had the papers drawn up to do so. Word of this never reached Jon Whiteley: the first he knew of it was in the nineties when he was visiting his mother at home in Scotland and Channel Four broadcast two hour-long documentary films made by Lucida Productions, 'Dirk Bogarde – By Myself'. He was only half-watching. Fortunately his mother was neither watching nor listening. Jon Whiteley heard himself being described as the child of elderly parents, one who had come late in the marriage and was unwanted, so Dirk planned to adopt him, but friends had advised him against it. 'It was mind-boggling rubbish,' says Jon Whiteley. 'I thought he must have been talking about somebody else, and the BBC had put the wrong picture up on the screen. There was no bearing on reality at all. Apart from anything else, we were a particularly close-knit family, and my younger sister was with me right through the making of both films. I found the whole account very bizarre.' He mentioned nothing to his mother, who learned about Dirk's claim only during the preparation of this book. 'What a nerve!' was her crisp reaction. 'It is totally untrue, and degrading to the family to suggest such a thing.' After a moment's reflection, she added: 'That is such a disturbing memory. I wonder if he really had a happy life.'

Dirk and Tony returned to Beel, where all was well, under the care of Hans, Agnes and Florian. The more hazardous task of dealing with the fine cedars was in other capable hands – those of George Goodings, once a member of the RAF 'Dam Busters' squadron, who had married Elizabeth in 1947 and who was now an expert tree surgeon. However, the longer-term prospects did not look so good: there were plans to build a girls' school less than two hundred yards away, between the house and the main road. Dirk and Tony thought of selling up immediately, reckoning that Beel would probably fetch about £10,000, but they decided to stay for the present. In July they were travelling again, this time taking Elizabeth to the south of France for a holiday before work started on the next film. *Ill Met by Moonlight* was the story of Patrick Leigh Fermor's exploit in occupied Crete in April 1944, when he organised and led a band of islanders in the abduction of the German General, Heinrich Kreipe. Dirk was to play Leigh Fermor – 'I like them to think me a sort of duke . . . a latter-day Lord Byron' – with David Oxley at his right hand as Captain W. Stanley (Billy) Moss. Michael Powell, the pugnacious genius whose partnership with Emeric Pressburger had yielded *49th Parallel, The Life and Death of Colonel Blimp, A Matter of Life and Death, Black Narcissus* and *The Red Shoes*, was to direct. When he met Dirk he knew he was in trouble. 'He was a charmer,' wrote Powell in his memoirs, 'and I fell for it. I have said that I had seen him on stage and screen, and knew what a good actor he was, but I didn't know that he was as subtle as a serpent, and with a will of steel.'[25]

> He knew all about me and actors, and he had absolutely no intention of acting in my film. He would smile (he had a charming smile), he would dress up

(fancy-dress costume), he had a good figure (light and boyish), and he would speak the lines – or, rather, he would throw them away – with such careful art that camera and microphone would have to track in close to see and hear what he was saying and doing.

Powell wanted 'a flamboyant young murderer, lover, bandit – a tough, Greek-speaking leader of men, and instead I got a picture-postcard hero in fancy-dress. He would listen with attention to me while I told him what I wanted, and then he would give me about a quarter of it.' In the end it was, he decided, a mess.

Nevertheless, Dirk, Tony and everyone else had a good time in the Alpes Maritimes. Tony wrote to Laurence Harbottle that Dirk was 'enjoying the film immensely', despite the long days from 3.30 in the morning until 9 at night. 'Michael Powell has chosen wonderful locations, usually having something to swim in when the heat becomes unbearable.'[26] More enduringly, they befriended Xan Fielding, who was working as technical adviser on the film, and his wife Daphne, formerly the Marchioness of Bath. Fielding and Leigh Fermor had been what the latter described as 'cave dwellers in Crete for a couple of years'. Leigh Fermor wrote at the time how 'terrifically exciting' he found the filming: 'Dirk Bogarde, who is doing me, is charming, a brilliant actor, and the whole thing is bewilderingly strange.'[27] He said much later how Dirk 'was fascinated by Greek guerrilla life' and how, although they looked nothing alike, he and Leigh Fermor decided jokingly that they should model themselves on each other while there was time. They and the Fieldings 'formed one of those close cliques which seem endemic on film sets'. There was, Leigh Fermor recalled, 'a great deal of fun and eating and drinking and jokes accumulating. We also drove about a lot, when there was time, with Tony at the wheel, and he and Dirk did a lot of singing as we went, in the most complicated and unfaltering descants, mostly tunes from – *My Fair Lady*, was it? "You don't need analysing, it is not so surprising" [from *Call Me Madam*] etc. They did it beautifully.'[28]

Three months after shooting finished, Dirk saw a rough cut of the film and wrote to Powell, with a number of suggestions about the film in general and about his own contribution. He evidently felt he was not sufficiently prominent, because Powell had to reassure him that John Davis and Earl St John considered him outstanding and they 'wouldn't have thought so if they couldn't see you':

It is quite true that you have always been a close-up actor ... but, my dear Dirk, that was more self-preservation. I know perfectly well why you have cultivated the close-up and 'thrown away' medium shots, and put your heart and soul and excellent voice and technique into post-synching. You can't fool me, even if you want to: and to your surprise you are going to get quite exceptional praise for your performance in this picture – because you steal it in the most unselfish manner: by being better than the other people with you in the scene.[29]

Both said that they hoped another project would soon materialise for them. Dirk would claim later that he refused to play in Powell's controversial *Peeping Tom* – 'which irritated him a little, so that we lost touch for a time'.[30] Powell, however, wrote: 'I liked Dirk, and he liked me, but we never wanted to work with each other again after the fiasco of *Ill Met by Moonlight*.'[31] Patrick Leigh Fermor felt the film 'slipped away into cliché' and should have 'stuck rigidly to the actual concatenation of events'. Dirk, resplendent for a while in the outfit of a Cretan chieftain, cut a dash; but it was a photograph of himself in beret, battle-dress top and jodhpurs tucked into knee-length boots which he kept as a memento of his career as action hero – his 'favourite still'.

This is not the place to discuss the financial woes of the post-war British film industry and the particular problems of Rank, with its network of cinemas gobbling up the ever-more expensive product. Rank's films were doing well abroad, but, crucially, not in the United States, which remained impervious to their charms and eccentricities. John Davis's attempt to break into the American industry directly, by establishing a distribution operation there, was an igno-minious failure. As Michael Powell put it, Davis 'almost started World War III'. 'The Yanks murdered him', said Powell, and when the dust had settled British film production was back where it was before the days of Alexander Korda.[32] Although more than a thousand million cinema tickets were sold in Britain every year from 1940 to 1956, there had been a steady decline from a peak in 1946. *Doctor in the House*, *Genevieve* and Norman Wisdom's alleged comedy *Trouble in Store* had done wonders for Rank itself, but television, with the arrival of an independent channel, was now serious competition and, as the company began to diversify into the wider 'leisure market' and into photocopiers, so film pro-duction and distribution became increasingly a poorer relation. Earl St John, no imaginative genius at the best of times and by now in his mid-sixties, found it increasingly hard to raise funds from the much younger Davis for any subject which was not formulaic 'family' fare. Dirk was undeniably busy, but doing what? For a start, re-inhabiting his housecoat as the newly qualified Simon Sparrow, this time fending off the attentions of a predatory nurse – interestingly named Nan – who, according to the script, 'can make the patient without disturbing the bed'.[33] The screenplay of *Doctor at Large* owed a fair amount to Dirk. Just as he rewrote some of the dialogue for his final scene with Bardot in *Doctor at Sea*, so he contributed again here. Musing on why people become doctors, Sparrow says there are easier ways of earning a living, and it is not for the glamour, the uniform or, emphatically, the money: 'I think it's because they feel that the most precious thing we have in the world is life – and that there's nothing more important than helping to give everyone their full share of it.' *Doctor at Large* was indeed more thoughtful than its predecessors, thanks in part to the shafts of political attitude – 'The NHS is all very well, but some people still prefer manners with their medicine'; in part, to the maturing Dirk. As one critic noticed, his 'unforced charm, his quiet and grave approach to hilarity, have more appeal than all the gags strung together'.[34] Mind you, there was one gag which had an impact of 'bleeding time' proportions on audiences. 'Big breaths, Eva,' commanded Sparrow, stethoscope in hand. 'Yeth,' came the reply, 'and I'm only thickthteen.'

Dirk's involvement with screenplays was based more on necessity than on desire, as he disclosed in an article for *Films and Filming* at this period:

> The good novelist and the good playwright is not necessarily a good film writer. In all my career I can honestly claim that there have been only a handful of scripts which I have not been forced to 'muck about' a bit. I cannot use the phrase 'rewrite' because that is far too pompous and indeed, is not what I do; but I do spend many hours rewriting dialogue to make it possible for me to say.[35]

The thrust of the piece was to try to stop people calling him a 'film star', because 'there are only about forty *genuine* film stars in the whole world, most of whom are in America or on the Continent'. Seeking a definition, he added that 'stars are the people with the extrovert personalities and the sparkling quality that puts the glamour, the glitter and the "stardust" into a very tough work-a-day job. All of these people are highly talented and highly accomplished performers. They are the ones, if you like, who put the show into business. They are also larger than life in every possible way.'

> The rest of us – and I include myself – are what I would choose to call star film actors, a very different thing. We are the people who without being great extrovert personalities or looking particularly glamorous, still manage to hold a strong position on box-office takings; but who, at all times, have been trained in the craft of acting. People who have studied their jobs for many years and who, after ten or twelve films, can probably claim, justifiably, to be sound knowledgeable technicians.

Dirk wondered aloud whether he might be living on borrowed time. He had reached a position where he was 'able to pursue exactly the kind of acting pattern I want', playing a form of high comedy in one film and 'whimpering, neurotic young men' in offbeat drama the next, thus avoiding being strapped into an artistic strait-jacket. Sometimes, however, 'one gets the impression that the British film industry in some respects is in its own strait-jacket'. With no little presumption he recommended that the studio bosses send their directors and writers to Rome, Hollywood or Paris for a while, 'studying their methods and generally snooping around'. He might even have to go to Hollywood himself.

In fact, just after he had written the article Dirk and Tony did set off for America – but not to make a film. They sailed on the *Mauretania* to spend Christmas with Rex Harrison and Kay Kendall on Long Island. Harrison was appearing on Broadway in *My Fair Lady*, a legendary marriage between actor and role, in which Dirk and Tony always claimed to have had a hand, by arranging clandestinely for him to meet the lyricist, Alan Jay Lerner, one Sunday at Beel. It is, alas, nonsense. Lerner knew Harrison already and had no need to resort to subterfuge. None the less, it is perfectly true that at the time he was completing the score with Fritz Loewe, he, Nancy Olson – the third of his eight wives – Harrison, Kay Kendall, Lewis (*They Who Dare*) Milestone and a few others did spend a Sunday at Beel, where most of the party were told for the first time about the work, provisionally 'Lady Liza': 'After tea, in the fading March light, we all gathered round the spinet in the Long Study, which was the only form of piano I possessed, and even though it was a full octave short Alan played the entire score, and sang, in a rather wavering voice, all the songs of his show, for the first time to a full audience.'[36] Asked about this occasion, Nancy Olson, who was known to Dirk and Tony as 'Miss Personality', said: 'Alan couldn't play the piano! He could sing, charmingly, and he might have played the opening chord for the song, but even with an audience of friends he wouldn't have dared sing "Why can't a woman ..." ["A Hymn to Him"] without a piano.'[37] In the history of the musical theatre, the event was a minuscule, blurred footnote. To those who were there, even if they heard merely a few bars hummed, it was momentous enough. Nancy Olson says: ' "My Fair Lady" is the one case I know where a writer set out to create a masterpiece.'

He might have been less of a godparent to the show than he made out, but Dirk was certainly committed to passing the word on its brilliance. When it opened at Drury Lane on 30 April 1958, it was he who provided a pre-recorded interview and a commentary on the music, for a celebratory midnight broadcast. By then, his one chance to work with Lerner had been dashed. Five months after *My Fair Lady* went to Broadway, the lyricist flew to Hollywood to discuss the possibility of a musical based on Colette's novella *Gigi*, about the gentle art of seducing a rich young man. Maurice Chevalier had agreed to play the uncle; Audrey Hepburn was to be considered first for the title role, but wondered whether age was against her. Even as he wrote it, Lerner had Dirk at the back of his mind for the part of Gaston, the bored moneybags, who on screen must not be boring. He knew Dirk had a 'very serviceable singing voice', as Patrick Leigh Fermor has confirmed. The script duly followed, but Rank had put too much on Dirk's plate, and the dates could not be made to work, with the result that Louis Jourdan played opposite Leslie Caron. In April 1959 Dirk presented one of the film's ten Oscars; his feelings would have been even more mixed had Jourdan beaten Danny Kaye to Best Actor in a Comedy or a Musical.

Kay Kendall was determined that the Christmas and New Year which Dirk and Tony were sharing with her and Rex Harrison should be one to remember;

and in Dirk's account it was, with an immense tree 'decked in silver and sprayed-on frost'; the drawing-room so full of parcels that it resembled 'the Fairies' Grotto in Selfridges' – parcels containing gifts of crazy extravagance; 'food and drink in such quantities as would have delighted Pickwick or Jorrocks and must have frightened the wits out of Rex at the cost'; and a procession of visitors including Cathleen Nesbitt – who was playing Harrison's mother in *My Fair Lady* – Margaret Leighton, Glynis and Gareth; and incessant music from the gramophone – above all, Judy Holliday and Sydney Chaplin singing 'Just in Time' from the newly opened musical *Bells Are Ringing*. There was, however, serious concern about Kay's health. She had taken blood tests, but Harrison, suspecting bad news, refused to hear the results until after the holiday and until she had left for Los Angeles, to start work on *Les Girls*, an MGM musical directed by George Cukor.

To see in 1957, they all went to a party in the sumptuous apartment of the producer Gilbert Miller, where Dirk caught a fleeting glimpse of a departing Greta Garbo and was introduced to Judy Garland. In the excitement, apparently, the tip of his cigarette burned a hole through the bodice of her dress: 'She gave a little scream, and then we laughed, and she pulled me down beside her and made me sit there on the floor and I stayed there, on and off, for almost ten years. Almost.'[38] It is not recorded whether he told her at that first meeting that she had inadvertently broken his heart. As a teenager, he had seen one of her films and written her a letter of undying love. Back came a signed photograph, which he placed in polythene and kept between his pillowcase and his pillow as he slept. He showed it proudly to a friend, who looked at the autograph and said: 'It's just a stamp.' All was now forgiven: she suggested they might film a Cole Porter musical together. The following evening, after Harrison's show and her own at the Palace Theatre, Garland, her husband Sid Luft, Terence Rattigan, Margaret Leighton, Kay, Dirk and Tony dined at the Plaza. On 2 January 1957, Dirk and Tony saw Kay off from Idlewild Airport. She was miserable at the prospect of the West Coast, and sat slumped in a corner of the car, snuffling and hiccuping, while her sole companion for the stay in Hollywood, Gladys Cooper's corgi, June, whined crossly in its travelling cage. Dirk and Tony sent them on their way: 'She was still sniffing and teary, and looked pale and wan, dishevelled and weary, as if she had spent a week at sea in an open boat.'[39] That afternoon, between the matinée and evening performance of *My Fair Lady*, Harrison visited the doctor, who told him – with some reluctance, not only because of what he had to say but also because Harrison was still married to Lilli Palmer – that Kay had myeloid leukaemia and a life expectancy of two years. Harrison agreed with the doctor that no one – Kay above all – was to know. Somehow he did his evening show, then sat up for much of the night with Dirk and Tony. He mentioned nothing about the prognosis to them, then or later. Meanwhile, as Tony noted, Kay called 'about every hour' to say how she hated Hollywood.

The night before they left New York, Dirk and Tony went to see Judy Garland's show at the Palace. With them was Rex Harrison's sister Sylvia, whose husband David Maxwell Fyfe – the former Home Secretary who had commissioned the Wolfenden Report – had recently been elevated to the peerage and, as Viscount Kilmuir, was now Lord Chancellor. Which is why one of a pair of pug dogs given to Kay by Dirk and Tony was named Woolsack; the other, less complicatedly, Higgins. As the *Queen Mary* sailed out of New York, with Michael Redgrave among their fellow passengers, Dirk and Tony could reflect on an eventful three weeks and on the ill-fated, adoring couple who had been so generous to them. Apart from anything else, there had been an opportunity for Dirk to observe Rex Harrison at close quarters, and it is not hard to see why he found much to admire in this difficult man, thirteen years his senior, who, like Tony, was the son of a feckless father from a family that had made its fortune in Liverpool. Alan Lerner memorably described Harrison as 'a human thermostat who changes the temperature of every room he enters, turning summer to winter or ice to steam in a matter of seconds'. He was 'a man of charm and the unexpected'.[40] He was also famously rude, but his patrician air enabled him to pass with ease in the highest circles. Dirk referred to him over the years with a respect that disguised a moderate envy. In *A Particular Friendship* he wrote of the elegant figure in black who, like everyone else at the memorial service to Anthony Asquith, sat spellbound as Yehudi Menuhin played his violin in salute, then touched Dirk on the arm and whispered: 'Never could abide a fiddler!' Harrison's remark 'broke the grief, beautifully'.[41]

One of Dirk's first actions on returning to Pinewood was to give an interview which highlighted how his hard-to-get attitude towards Hollywood had done nothing to dampen the ardour with which he was being pursued. At a more basic level it was the same in England, where, as the *Evening Standard* observed, 'to a large proportion of the female population of this country Bogarde is bliss'. The increasing rarity of his public appearances was simply fuelling curiosity; but, Dirk said, familiarity breeds contempt: 'If you give the public too much of yourself, they get sick of you.' He and the writer, Thomas Wiseman, discussed his somewhat unlikely allure:

> I often wonder myself. I must appeal to the maternal instinct in women because I'm no great hulk of physique. Little girls always like to play with dolls. I suppose they prefer to put me to bed than to take me to bed. As long as you can appeal to the maternal instinct you're all right: it's stronger than the other instincts – and it lasts longer. Anyway, most English women hate sex. American women, on the other hand, think about nothing else, 'think' being the operative word.[42]

A few days after the article appeared, John Davis went on his own to have dinner at Beel. Tony noted that he offered Dirk 'any leading lady of his choice from Hollywood', but quite how Davis thought he was going to achieve this is unclear. In any case, when Dirk proposed Judy Garland, Davis flatly refused. It was back to work with Betty Box and Ralph Thomas, for three films on the trot. Dirk's feelings, generated at a lunch with the 'Chief Accountant' two years earlier, that Davis intended to manufacture him 'like a stick of seaside rock' – and 'as sweet and sickly and forgettable as that product' – had not been dispelled.[43] And when Earl St John came to dinner just two days after Davis, and became so drunk that he 'tried to piss in the fireplace in the green study', the portents were not good. At least Dirk could do some of his brooding far from Pinewood, for he and Tony were about to spend much of the next twelve months on location abroad.

With *Gigi* turned down, and just one bright spot in the distance – the possibility of playing T. E. Lawrence – they took their recently acquired Rolls-Royce onto the Silver City air ferry at Lydd Airport in Kent and once more motored leisurely through France. They had two nights at the Negresco in Nice, from where they made an expedition to St Paul de Vence, lunched at the Colombe d'Or and, as Tony remarked, drove up the valley 'house-hunting'. What they had seen while working on *Ill Met by Moonlight* had started Dirk thinking seriously, not merely of buying a property in the south of France, but of moving there. When they reached Cortina d'Ampezzo for the shooting of *Campbell's Kingdom*, Tony wrote to Laurence Harbottle: 'He feels that as from "Lawrence of Arabia" he must only make two pictures a year, and that if he lives in England he will not be able to bear this, whereas if he lives in a warm climate he will be able to find things to do to occupy him.' There was, said Tony, no question of trying to avoid taxation in England 'because he wants to do his 2 films a year for Rank, but one feels that later on he might want to settle there [in France] permanently & remove all assets from England'. For the moment, Dirk was considering selling Beel and buying a house in France but keeping a foothold in England where he would work and keep the Inland Revenue satisfied. If this happened, Tony added, 'it will need to be carefully handled press-wise as there is always prejudice against anyone who prefers to live outside our rain-sodden isle!'[44] Cortina and its surrounding Dolomites were standing in for the Canadian Rockies, the siting of Hammond Innes's adventure story about a young man come to claim his inheritance – a valley in danger of being flooded by a ruthless contractor determined to build a dam. Dirk was nearly granted his wish to play a pine tree, because Ray Milland had pitched heavily for the leading role; but in the end it was a whey-faced Dirk who tottered into frame, looking as if his number was up: Bruce Campbell had been given six months to live. However, the character had more to do than remain rooted to the spot, and by the end of the picture was glowing with vitality – and passion, of course.

Barbara Murray had come under contract with Rank at the same time as Dirk and had been in two of his films, *Boys in Brown* and *Doctor at Large*, but saw little of him on or off the set. It was entirely different in Cortina, where they had not only a good deal of screen time but also many evenings together – once Dirk had forgiven her for bringing her three young children and nanny to the location. 'I was in a very difficult position because my then husband thought that if you were a mother your children were supposed to be with you wherever you went. I was very dutiful and obedient. Dirk didn't like domesticity, home lives and so on. He thought that everybody should be wedded to their art.'[45] Rock Hudson, too, was in Cortina, making *A Farewell to Arms* for David O. Selznick and not getting on at all well with his leading lady, Jennifer Jones, alias Mrs Selznick. Dirk and Tony had met him in England and enjoyed his company. Barbara Murray frequently made up the table. 'The phone would go,' she recalls, 'and Dirk would say, "Rock's here". I would have the most enchanting evenings with them. Rock was totally divine – he would flirt all night. He bucked Dirk and Tony up no end.' It is a fetching image: Dirk and Hudson laughing together, each with his ultra-masculine one-syllable Christian name, each a matinée idol – sometimes they were featured in adjacent fan magazine spreads; in August they would be first and second respectively in a *Daily Mirror* poll to find 'the No. 1 Dreamboat' – and each living his lie in his own very different way. Sometimes Dirk would see Barbara Murray courteously to her room: 'One night outside the door he put his hands on my shoulders and said, "You know, I've got to fall half in love each time." Then he kissed me on the cheek and pissed off.'

The 'slightly ambiguous, close chumminess' between Dirk and his younger, married, leading lady gives a telling insight into his attitude towards women. 'Strange things went on,' Barbara Murray recalls. 'He said he was going to buy me a present. It was a blouse. He took it frightfully seriously, so I felt I should wear it all the time.' Whenever they were filming together he would say to her, 'Come back with us in the Rolls.' It became such a habit that one day she moved towards the car without thinking, 'and he cut me off at the knees'. One weekend, he said he would like her to come with him and Tony on a drive: ' "Of course you can't bring the children with you." So I had to make arrangements with the nanny, which didn't go down well. Then he went on about the money: "I hope you don't expect me to pay for you everywhere." We arrived somewhere for lunch and of course I reached into my bag for my purse, and he said, "Put that bloody thing away." You never knew where you were with him.' On a day when bad weather set in, they shot a love scene, which went fine. As usual the stills photographer moved in afterwards to do his work, first in colour, then in black and white:

> Dirk was lying on top of me, chatting, 'I wonder when the weather will break', that sort of thing. I caught the photographer's eye, and it was clear that he thought all feeling had gone out of the scene. So I looked up at Dirk in a sexy way. He said, 'Oh yes – and what about that husband and child of yours?' Smacking me down. He used to terrify the life out of me, because you'd never know where he would turn. He had the ability to be the most charming person on earth, and then . . .

The hold he kept on his tongue in front of women journalists was not necessarily so firm in the company of a female co-star: 'To me his language was offensive. Not just the swearing, the effing and blinding – it was the way he would talk about women's anatomy. He had a fascination with how women had the curse and how it impeded their work. I realised the focus was on me and that he was quite interested to know when it was happening to me, but I never let him know. It was an undue fixation. He would talk about the sexual act between a woman and a man with real distaste.' Curiously enough, Barbara Murray was by no means the only woman to raise the most delicate of subjects during the preparation of this biography. Nor indeed was she alone in saying that she had seen the darker side of his relationship with Tony: 'He could be evil towards him, belittling him in public. "Call yourself a manager?" he'd say.'

For well over a month Barbara Murray observed Dirk at unusually close quarters. 'He was somebody who took the work enormously seriously. He was a most amazing technician. He would have been a wonderful director. In a way he was too intelligent to be an actor, because intelligence is not necessarily the most important thing.' She thought that having conquered his fear of comedy he had 'struck exactly the right note on the "Doctor" films – it is not an easy one to strike and to hold on to – and he was getting his just rewards. But he rather thought that it made him more common currency than bullion. He was struggling to get out of the commonplace and find more intellectually challenging work.' He taught her a valuable lesson: 'Not to trust people who go overboard to begin with. On every movie he did – at least, every movie which wasn't too cynical a choice – he would need to fall in love with everybody around him, and the script, and get passionate about it. Two-thirds of the way through he would become bored and waspish, and couldn't get away fast enough.' This one was no exception. Even the Diary records that 'it had not been a happy location'. It seems that Michael Craig and Stanley Baker – both Rank contract artists – 'and above all their wives' were jealous of the preferential treatment which they felt Dirk was given. His leading lady agreed: 'It was a fairly split company and fraught.'

One lasting benefit emerged from the shoot. A young Canadian called Arnold Schulkes turned up in Cortina one day with his far-from-well wife on a far-from-reliable Vespa scooter. They were, as he put it, 'going putt-putt-putt' through Europe, with the aim of seeing his relatives in Holland. As they stopped to watch the filming, one of the crew said, 'Do you want to work? Would you like to be a stand-in?' 'What's a stand-in?' came the reply. Before he knew whether it was Cortina or Christmas he was at the top of a dam, dressed as Stanley Baker, and trying not to betray any hint of vertigo. People began to notice that there was a likeness to Dirk. Schulkes was an inch taller, 'an inch all round bigger', although slightly narrower in the shoulder. From the back the two men were almost indistinguishable. Dirk already had a regular stand-in, John Adderley, who had worked with him for some years; but Adderley wanted to join his family in

America. Thanks to him, Schulkes managed to obtain a union ticket reasonably quickly and by the spring of 1959 he had the job. From that unpromising beginning Dirk and he developed a partnership which lasted for ten years and – by his reckoning – twenty-three films.

Dirk arrived back at Beel and was promptly given the sack. Not from Rank, with whom he had now been for ten years – 'It's like being married. Perhaps that's why I'm not.' – rather, from the presidency of the Amersham Film Society. At the annual meeting of that august body, the auditor, Mr E. Bramley, was reported as saying: 'Why on earth we should have as president a person who takes no interest in the Amersham Film Society, I don't know. We don't even use his name on advertisements. No Dirk Bogardes for me.' Mr Bramley proposed that Lieutenant-Colonel Alan Hanbury-Sparrow should take over. A brief correspondence ensued, in which it was made clear that Dirk had accepted the presidency four years earlier on the understanding that his life was 'full from dawn to dusk' and that he would seldom, if ever, be able to attend a meeting. The Colonel, who had been abroad when the decision was taken and had no idea he was to be proposed, let alone elected, explained that the society's finances were so parlous that a president was needed who could devote time and energy to its affairs. Dirk was said to have taken the fuss 'in good heart' and calm returned to Buckinghamshire.[46] For a while.

Once again the Rolls-Royce was stowed in the hold of the Bristol air freighter at Lydd, and Dirk and Tony took off for France, accompanied by Margaret and Ulric, who had just retired from *The Times*. In four days they were back at the Colombe d'Or, where they spent more than a week and where, as Tony pointed out, Dirk had to relax because the overpowering heat made it exhausting to do anything else. His parents flew home and Tony set a course north-west to Bourges, the location for *A Tale of Two Cities*, in which, as Ronald Colman did so effectively in a 1935 production for MGM, Dirk was to play the dissolute, work-shy Sydney Carton who goes to the guillotine to save another man's life. Before leaving England he wrote to Betty Box and Ralph Thomas: 'This is probably the most important thing I have done during my film career.' He had, he said, never felt so excited and frightened by a part; it was 'a long way to go from "Doctor In The House" to "A Tale Of Two Cities" … and any confidence, or stature I might have gained is entirely due to you both'.[47] Betty Box's witty title for the chapter in her memoirs devoted to the film was 'We Kept our Heads'. They needed to, for they had overlooked the fact that it was harvest time in central France, and when they arrived at Bourges, plumb in the middle of France, there was a drought of potential extras. Betty Box reckoned she was several hundred revolutionaries short. Luckily, there was a large American Army base nearby, so Uncle Sam's finest were crammed into their *citoyen* costumes to hurl insults and rotten fruit at the condemned souls travelling by tumbril to their rendezvous with the executioner. When Ralph Thomas cried 'Action!', Dirk trundled magnificently towards martyrdom amid a hail of overripe plums and rotten apples, launched with shouts of 'Hang the bum!' Worse was to come. A startled horse decided to head for home and dragged its by now empty tumbril into the side of the Rolls-Royce, which was parked reasonably discreetly out of shot.[48] It was exchanged on its return to England for an S-Type Bentley. Two weeks later this, too, was damaged in a collision with a lorry and swapped for an identical model.

The critics rightly pointed out that Dirk's performance as Carton lacked drunken dissipation but compensated with sincerity and chivalry. *The Times* considered that the final oration – 'It is a far, far better thing I do than I have ever done. It is a far, far better rest I go to than I have ever known' – and the act of sacrifice 'lose none of their emotion'.[49] For audiences, well, it was a kind of mass slaughter as the nation's womenfolk, and not a few of its men, were reduced to snivelling into their hankies. If there were moments in the first half of the career when Dirk crossed decisively from the 'put to bed' into the 'take to bed' category, this was one of them. The designer Beatrice 'Bumble' Dawson, who with the art director Carmen Dillon had become regular guests at Dirk's house, repaid his hospitality by kitting him out in a wardrobe to die for: frock coat, patterned weskit, ruched cape, silk scarf, knee-length boots, tights ... the sort of thing that Cornel Lucas or George Courtney Ward might have caught him wearing as the Squire of Beel. The image of Dirk in this costume became so familiar that when Ulric did a pencil portrait he wisely produced a head-and-shoulders which to their common delight was chosen for the Royal Academy Summer Exhibition. Dirk described it as 'too flattering'; his mother said: 'The jaw's too strong.' He was wrong; she was right.

It gives some indication of the importance Dirk attached to the film that he agreed to extend from twenty-six weeks to thirty-two the contractual period under which he worked that year for Rank. He did not want the production to be hurried for financial reasons if its artistic merit would be compromised. The protracted stay at Pinewood spanned both a celebration lunch given by John Davis to mark Dirk's tenth anniversary with the company and a twenty-first birthday party for the Studio itself. As *A Tale of Two Cities* finished, so the Box–Thomas team was already preparing its next project with Dirk, *The Wind Cannot Read*, part of which was to be shot in India. It has to be said, however, that at this point Dirk's eyes were elsewhere. He writes in *Snakes and Ladders* that he tried to interest the Studio in buying the rights both to John Osborne's play *Look Back in Anger*, which had shaken not just the Royal Court but the whole of the London theatre to its foundations; and to Alan Sillitoe's novel, *Saturday Night and Sunday Morning*, of which Earl St John asked him 'how I imagined that anyone could consider making a film which began with a forty-year-old woman inducing an abortion in a hot bath?'[50] Certainly, John Gielgud came to Beel to talk to Dirk about a possible film of *Richard of Bordeaux*, which had dominated the former's acting life for well over a year in the early thirties. It was written by Gordon Daviot, a pen-name for Elizabeth Mackintosh, who was best known for writing novels under another pseudonym, Josephine Tey; and, as Gielgud's biographer Sheridan Morley noted, it was an 'urbane, romantic, and often witty retread of Shakespeare' which in its use of light-hearted modern language to convey medieval history had no equivalent for three decades – until James Goldman's treatment of Henry II in *The Lion in Winter*.[51] It gave Gielgud the biggest personal success of his career, with fans besieging the stage door, visiting the play thirty or forty times, following him home, and even telephoning him in those days before going ex-directory was either fashionable or necessary. It is easy to see why Dirk was tempted by the role of the King who, in Shakespeare's version, says: 'Thus play I in one person many people,/And none contented'. Gielgud told him that there was 'a wonderful opportunity for you to get gradually older, beginning as the flighty hysterical youth, then the embittered tyrant, and, in the final scenes the saintly gentle victim'. As a postscript, Gielgud added: 'Somebody once told me you disliked wearing tights, but I can't think that would be an insoluble obstacle. Or would it?'[52] Alas, the tights never became an issue. The rights belonged in some way to Jack Buchanan – the nearest Britain had produced to Fred Astaire – and many of the documents in his estate had been destroyed in an air-raid during the war.

It had been a tantalising prospect, and Dirk was badly in need of those. The annual *Motion Picture Herald* survey of the British box-office found he was the world's biggest draw, ahead of Brando, Monroe, Sinatra, Peck, Audrey Hepburn, Presley and all. It prompted Milton Shulman of the *Sunday Express* to comment: 'If this poll really reflects the thinking of either cinema managers or the British public then few will mourn that cinemas have been closing at the rate of some 200 a year both in 1956 and 1957.'[53]

Eleven

'To have news value is to have a tin can tied to one's tail'

To some on the set at Pinewood, *The Wind Cannot Read* was known as 'The Illiterate Fart'. It would be fair to say that the atmosphere was indeed far from fragrant as production started on Richard Mason's adaptation of his own novel about a doomed wartime love affair between a grounded RAF officer and a Japanese language teacher. When John Davis called for Betty Box and Ralph Thomas to shoot a second, more upbeat, ending, Dirk made his feelings known in no uncertain terms. Word reached Davis, who wrote a strong letter expressing his hurt at Dirk's apparent lack of confidence in him, and his distress that Dirk should feel he was not keeping his word. It gives some idea of the state of the film business at this time that the managing director should have to justify his request on the grounds that an alternative ending could be inserted into this 'intelligent piece of picture making' if market conditions, or people's tastes, were to change.[1] Davis told Dirk that, like everyone else in the industry, Rank was fighting for its life, but, unlike everyone else, it was continuing to make films. This one, he said, fitted into the plan for the development of Dirk's career – the 'recipe for seaside rock' – that Davis had promised when they lunched together some years earlier. In a separate letter at the same period Davis also warned Dirk off going to Hollywood, believing that to work there would not help his international career. It was a depressing place, full of fears and lacking in direction, but if Dirk wished to pursue the idea, Davis would not stand in his way.[2] A little shadow on a happy relationship was how the 'Chief Accountant' described their disagreement over *The Wind Cannot Read*; but there were other signs that all was not well.

Bob Thomson* had been camera operator on six of Dirk's films, starting with *The Woman in Question* when he formed the impression of 'a rather uncertain character – anything but confident, never forthcoming'. To him Dirk off-camera was 'a negative personality, insofar as he didn't have an impact. All of the big stars I've worked with have been open personalities. He was closed. One or two

---

* Bob Thomson – H. A. R. Thomson, Bob Thompson, Harold Thompson, Russell Thomson; according to the British Film Institute database, he is 'The Man with a Million Names'.

of them were aloof, but Dirk wasn't. It was different somehow with him: he was there, and you accepted him, but you didn't like or dislike him. There always seemed to be something in his mind which wasn't with you at that moment; he was in his own world.'³ Dirk wrote in *Snakes and Ladders* that one day on *Doctor at Sea* – the fourth time they worked together – Thomson stared gloomily at him and said: 'You don't know a bloody thing about the camera, do you?' Thomson had a reputation for plain-speaking, but he would never have addressed Dirk, or anyone in his position, like that. He was, however, happy to advise when asked. For the rest of the film, remembered Dirk, he 'taught me the basics of cinema technique. Everything from lenses, to lights, to sound. I was a greedy pupil, he was a thorough tutor.'⁴ In later interviews Dirk would tell how Thomson, like a language tutor, steered him through the territory of the '2K', 'the Four' and the 'inky dinky', explaining every trick to take advantage of the camera's all-seeing eye – the lens which, as Dirk never tired of saying, 'photographs thought'.

Thomson recalls that Dirk's interest in the craft grew out of a lack of direction. Just as Ian Dalrymple had more or less left him to find his own way on *Esther Waters*, so too Ralph Thomas was felt to be more a *maker* of films, shooting as rapidly as possible what was on the page and not engaging fully with the actors. On one of the *Doctor* pictures, Dirk asked Thomson, 'What size am I in this shot?' This led to an explanation of the various lenses and what they did, then in due course to lighting techniques, how to avoid the hated right profile – 'odd, because there was nothing particularly wrong with it' – and how to mask the crease in Dirk's forehead which became more accentuated as the years passed and, in Thomson's words, 'perhaps made him look crueller'. 'He would ask me about his mannerisms – raising his eyebrows, flicking his ear, touching his nose. These were instinctive, and he would tell me to point it out if I saw him doing them. Which I did.' Towards the end of *A Tale of Two Cities* Thomson said to Ralph Thomas that he thought Dirk was doing a particularly good job on the film. 'Why the hell didn't you tell him so?' replied Thomas. But it was not so easy: 'I was never that close to Dirk.' Even though Thomson, too, had been involved in camouflage work during the war, they never talked about it, or about anything except the immediate job in hand and the possibilities of the equipment at their disposal; 'In fact, Dirk very seldom had a long conversation with anybody.' Thomson, too, was on *Campbell's Kingdom* and has a vivid recall of the location, when 'we were stuck out on the side of a mountain'. Dirk, he said, would occasionally 'try to be one of the boys, to be more "normal", especially with strong language, which I thought he used unnecessarily. He also had this slightly whiny Cockney accent which kept popping up. I never understood where he got it from.'

Again, this detail is important because of what happened subsequently. In his last long interview for television, Dirk told the story of his 'tutor' and said: 'Of course, he's dead now.'⁵ Which was as much of a surprise to Bob Thomson as imminent adoption was, in the same programme, to Jon Whiteley. More immediately, with *A Tale of Two Cities* behind them, Thomson and the director of photography Ernest Steward began the military operation of shipping their several hundredweight of gear to India for *The Wind Cannot Read*. 'I went into the machine shop, and one of the engineers said, "It's time somebody told you – you're not going." I went to the studio manager, and he wouldn't tell me why. So I went to see Betty Box, and she said, "Dirk would rather you weren't on the picture." It was horrible for a short period, but I knew I had a very good reputation as an operator and it wouldn't affect any other work I was going to do. So I wasn't terribly put out about it, but I was very surprised.' In retrospect, Thomson believes that Dirk was looking for a way to break up the partnership with Box, Thomas, Steward and Thomson, 'and to break away from the routine of having the same crew and the same type of picture'. In fact Bob Thomson did go to India, on second-unit duties, and at one point was in charge of a sequence in which Dirk stumbles through a kind of no man's land: 'He behaved absolutely normally towards me, as if nothing had gone between us. At times I felt a sympathy towards him.' However, the small cloud over Dirk's relationship with John Davis had grown big enough to cast a shadow over the studio floor.

The company's month in India was not without incident. To help Dirk sleep in the intense heat, Ralph Thomas emulated Hugh Jolly by giving him a pill to keep beside his bed. Reaching for it in the night, he swallowed instead the tiny white jacket which during filming he would slip onto a recessed tooth because in close-up it appeared darker than the rest. Betty Box recalled that Dirk bravely ordered an extra large dose of castor oil in order to effect its disagreeable recovery.[6] Halfway through the shoot, in Jaipur, he sprained his right ankle jumping from a four-foot wall. The following night he hosted a party, and attracted no little kudos by having as his guests of honour the Maharajah and Maharani of Jaipur, whom he had met in England some years before through Tony's friends the Hall Caines. Champagne was shipped in from Delhi and a splendid time was had by massed maharajahs, other dignitaries and the unit; but not by Dirk, who fainted with the pain from his injury and had to miss the return fixture arranged by the Jaipurs the following night. The Red Fort was visited, the Taj Mahal was swooned over, polo was watched, Indira Gandhi was met and a perfectly serviceable film made, its faintly risible action outweighed by the Flight-Lieutenant's tender romance with Suzuki San – played by Yoko Tani, who had posed enthusiastically with Dirk for pre-production photographs in Paris and on the terrace at Beel. For collectors of those few moments when Dirk and Tony share a screen, however, *The Wind Cannot Read* yields the prize: an exchange of dialogue, with the latter as a senior officer, interrogation on his mind, telling Dirk as they enter a compound full of Japanese prisoners: 'Shan't keep you a minute. I'd like to take another crack at Corporal Tanaka.'

A hobbling Dirk flew home to finish the interiors at Pinewood and, once they were out of the way, to have his leg set in plaster. At last a project was nearing fruition that genuinely excited him. He had worked once before with Anthony Asquith, on *The Woman in Question*, for which the director had wanted an American actor. Dirk told Asquith's biographer, R. J. Minney:

> I was utterly terrified of him, for no reason of his, simply because of my own realisation that I was not what he wanted. I did my very best – was attentive, willing, desperately anxious to win his approbation as a screen actor. About five weeks into shooting he came up to me after the lunch break, cigarette dangling from his lips, hair streaked with nicotine, the old faded boiler-suit and the scratched leather belt, the worn red and white spotted scarf round his neck. He said: 'I really think it's all coming along terribly well . . . and you are really very good . . . I like the accent enormously.' I said something like 'Thank, you, Mr Asquith', and he smiled, removed his cigarette, and said, 'My name is Puffin, you know. Because of my nose.'

He would make Dirk play a scene 'three, five, or eight different ways, always with a gentle ironic smile':

> He told me that it amused him to see how rapidly I could 'shift gears', as he called it, and give a completely dissimilar performance. It was hard to do but stood me in marvellous stead in the time to come. That was the first lesson Puff taught me. Total concentration at all times, and an elasticity of ideas. 'I always think that one should have lots of different hats in the bag,' he used to say . . . 'You can't do much with just one.'[7]

Eight years on, the headgear Asquith hoped Dirk would wear for him was that of Thomas Edward Lawrence, alias John Hume Ross, later Thomas Edward Shaw. From the late summer of 1957 everyone at Rank from John Davis down was convinced that the film with which Dirk would follow *The Wind Cannot Read* was to be *Lawrence of Arabia*, from a script by Terence Rattigan, whose several successful collaborations with Asquith and the producer Anatole de Grunwald had included *French Without Tears*, *The Way to the Stars* and *The Winslow Boy*. From infancy Rattigan had lived with the Lawrence legend because his father, a diplomat, had been a close friend in Cairo of Lawrence's principal proponent, Sir Ronald Storrs; and when *The Mint*, Lawrence's long-suppressed account of his experiences in the ranks of the RAF as Aircraftman Ross, was published to a general audience in 1955, Rattigan started work on a screenplay. This was to be a film on an epic scale and yet intimate enough to examine why a man who had achieved astonishing celebrity during the Arab Revolt should seek not merely privacy but total anonymity. Since the mid-thirties, when Lawrence himself told Alexander Korda that he was flatly opposed to the idea of being 'celluloided', all attempts to make a film based on his adventures had come to nothing. When Rattigan completed his first draft at the beginning of 1956, he deemed it 'Slightly longer than Seven Pillars. But much more moving.'[8] At that point he, Asquith and de Grunwald had as their first choice for the title role Alec Guinness, who seventeen years earlier at the Old Vic had played Michael Ransom, a character based on Lawrence, in *The Ascent of F6*, and, like Rattigan, had become fascinated with the man, his book and his legend. But his success in *The Bridge on the River Kwai* had convinced its director David Lean that he could play Gandhi in a projected film about the Mahatma, and, while waiting for that, Guinness agreed to star as Wormold, the vacuum-cleaner salesman and spy, in an adaptation of Graham Greene's *Our Man in Havana*.[9] To make matters even more complicated, Lean had for five years been in and out of the frame as the possible director of a film about Lawrence for Sam Spiegel and Columbia, the latest inheritors of the original thirties project started by Korda.

Eventually Dirk was cast by Asquith and de Grunwald – against the wishes of the author. 'Rattigan was not all that pleased. I was at the time more popular than Rock Hudson and Doris Day in England ... but hardly the person, one would have thought, to play Lawrence!'[10] For over a year, Dirk recalled, 'I steeped myself in the man.' Geoffrey Woolley, son of the archaeologist Leonard Woolley, and a colleague of Ulric at *The Times*, sent Dirk books on Lawrence, letters to his father and a mound of tattered cuttings. Friends of Lawrence wrote with vignettes: 'I read and read and read.' Asquith tactfully kept up the pressure. 'It was rather like being "crammed", with a very silvery-tongued professor asking you what you had studied!' On 4 January 1958 Asquith, de Grunwald and his co-producer Teddy Baird went to Beel for an intensive script conference. Ten days later Dirk was fitted for a blond wig. It 'cost a fortune' and had 'an odd "essence" of Lawrence; and although I was the wrong complexion, and height, something began to build'. No photographs were taken of Dirk in his 'rug'. 'I was very nervous about the wig,' he told the film historian Adrian Turner, 'and it was to be photographed only when absolutely complete and when I had the robes on. The "Ross" outfit was easy but the main effect had to be the Arab sequence.'[11] Many evenings were spent in the Pinewood make-up rooms, 'fining things down', until Dirk had to leave for India, but even during the shooting of *The Wind Cannot Read* he was discussing Lawrentian detail with personnel common to both films. The day after he returned to England he went to talk to de Grunwald at Pinewood about the logistics and facilities in Iraq, where the producer and Asquith had been scouting for locations and where British Petroleum was putting one of its well-equipped desert bases at their disposal. It was very much 'green for go': already John Davis had been writing to him about projects to *follow* 'Lawrence'. And then, at 6.30 on the evening of Friday 14 February, Dirk received the least welcome of Valentines when Olive Dodds telephoned. The film was off. At Pinewood on the Monday morning, he was given no proper explanation by Earl St John or Olive Dodds – just the offer in compensation of *The Captain's Table* – 'a jolly comedy set on board a Cruise Liner'.[12]

This episode was, noted Tony some years later, 'the beginning of the end of Dirk's love affair with Ranks'. The official reasons for what Rank called a postponement were uncertainty about the British film market and the burden of Entertainments Tax, which seized more than thirty per cent of box-office receipts. In that climate, a production costing £700,000 was too much of a risk. Dirk had his doubts: was it a sudden tremor about 'the exposing of a very private man'? Was it politics, and a fear of upsetting the Turks? Was it, as would be rumoured later, something more sinister, with links to the assassination in July of King Feisal? Or was it simply that the Sam Spiegel/David Lean project, with a script by Robert Bolt, was taking wind, and Rank did not wish to upset its powerful producer, who a few days later would be laden with Oscars for *The Bridge on the River Kwai*? No one who knew was saying. Nevertheless the official line was enough to see Dirk a fortnight later tottering on his crutches into the House of Commons at the head of a posse of actors and producers to lobby MPs against an iniquitous levy.

Rattigan was able to salvage something from the wreckage by reworking his material into a play, *Ross*, which had a long run with Alec Guinness in the title role. However the cancellation, for that is what it was, came as 'heartbreak' to Asquith and a crushing blow to Dirk – 'my bitterest disappointment'. It was, he reflected fifteen years later, 'the greatest part I had ever been asked to do'. Asquith had told him at the outset: 'No one can look like Lawrence, but you can probably make us feel how he felt. Much more important.'[13] The director was surely right. 'Romance and enigma seem to have become an inseparable part of T. E. Lawrence's reputation' is how Jeremy Wilson introduced his 1989 Life – ingredients which in the late fifties were already firmly part of Dirk's public profile.[14] As they worked on 'fining down' the character, Dirk had asked Asquith: 'Puff, tell me really and truly, now we have it all before us, was Lawrence homosexual?' Asquith's face, according to Dirk, 'was a study in white horror. The cigarette dropped its ash; with an unsteady hand he removed it, then stubbing it out, he replied. "Not practising." I know that I should not have asked it.'[15] Again, given Asquith's own ambivalent sexuality, that story is either disingenuous or ludicrous; but it is Dirk's way of illustrating how important that element was to their, and Rattigan's, approach. For Rattigan, to understand Lawrence's character one had to appreciate 'the predicament of his masochism', his dormant homosexuality, his self-discovery – under brutal humiliation by the Turks at Deraa – 'and consequent degradation and despair'.[16] There was a passage in the draft of *Seven Pillars of Wisdom* where Lawrence wrote: 'I liked the things beneath me and took my pleasures, and my adventures, downward. There seemed a level of certainty in degradation, a final safety.' Jeremy Wilson cited this as evidence of Lawrence's wish to submerge his real identity – part of the 'inclination towards ground-level' which he mentioned at the time he was enlisted as Ross into the R.A.F.[17] Dirk had no need to tax his imagination unduly in order to relate to much of what Lawrence revealed about himself. Permanent anonymity was not an option for an actor, let alone a film star – reluctant or otherwise; but Dirk might use his art and his very prominence to help shed light on a figure with whom he could empathise.

Lawrence wrote: 'To have news value is to have a tin can tied to one's tail.'[18] For Dirk the tin can of celebrity was becoming decidedly uncomfortable – so much so that he felt the need to strengthen his defences. The day before Olive Dodds's fateful call, work had started at Beel on a twenty-foot high, fifteen-foot wide and two-hundred-yard long mound which was to be grassed and planted with trees, in the hope of shielding the house from a view of the projected girls' grammar school and, more important, from its 540 denizens. A reporter arrived to find a small fleet of lorries dumping tons of earth along the perimeter of the garden, and a morose Dirk gazing over his blighted landscape, saying: 'If this doesn't work, I shall emigrate to the south of France. I mean it – it's not a gag. I just can't face the prospect of 600 squealing schoolgirls practically camped in my back yard.' He told his inquisitor: 'I've got to do it – it's the only way to keep the blighters out. If I didn't do something like this they'd be running amok all over the grounds. Why, it would be like St Trinian's around here, old boy.'[19] The mound promptly achieved its own national celebrity as 'Bogarde's Bastion'. Then a representative from the local newspaper pottered along to check on progress, and was told by 'Mr Bogarde's manager, Mr Forwood' that reporters were 'not too popular at the moment' as Dirk had been misquoted. Nevertheless a meeting was arranged on the terrace, where the bold scribe 'relaxed into a Bogarde deckchair and drew on a Bogarde cigarette' while the position was clarified. At the suggestion that when the school was built he would probably be asked to open it, Dirk replied: 'They will have to tunnel through my bank to get me.'[20]

Shortly afterwards a public inquiry was held, as a result of objections to the planned school from seven local residents, of whom Dirk was the most vehement. Adopting a more guarded approach, he said he had bought Beel only because an application to build houses in the Park had been turned down, and the new scheme would not only defeat his purpose in acquiring a secluded house – on the restoration of which he had spent 'considerable sums' – but also 'disastrously lower its value'. Surely, he wrote, 'the government has some responsibility for the preservation of the English countryside'. The solicitor for Buckinghamshire County Council tried to derail Dirk's case by saying that he seemed not to have obtained planning permission for his 'bastion', but Laurence Harbottle replied that his client had 'taken a pessimistic view', believing the school would be built whatever anyone said; if it was not, the earthworks would be removed.[21] Two months later, Dirk and Tony returned in the Bentley from another holiday in the south of France to learn that the Minister of Housing had approved the plan for the school. Laurence Harbottle remembers that the inquiry was chaired by Professor Colin Buchanan, arguably the most distinguished of all post-war planning experts, and 'a very amusing man'.

When he went to inspect the site, he said: 'Mr Harbottle, if I decide in favour of your client, how's he going to *move* that ruddy great pile of earth?' And I'm sure it was my answer that lost the case. I should have said, 'The lorries are waiting outside.' I think I did say, rather feebly, 'Oh well, we got it there, we'll get it away.' I had been absolutely alarmed when I arrived, because I hadn't known what Dirk had done. It was a vast bloody great erection. Utterly hideous.[22]

Dirk presided dutifully over the Little Chalfont Horse Show. But one might say that the Minister's decision was the beginning of the end of Dirk's love affair with Amersham.

While battle was fought over 'Bogarde's Bastion', Asquith and de Grunwald moved rapidly to compensate themselves and Dirk. Within a few weeks Shaw's *The Doctor's Dilemma* was under way, with Dirk playing the nervy, tubercular artist Louis Dubedat, whose plans for the Season are very simple: 'I'm going to die.' The role was, as Tony noted, a respectable substitute for Lawrence, and the production an enjoyable one, with Robert Morley, Alastair Sim and Felix Aylmer among the physicians windbagging on about 'stimulating the phagocytes' and removing the nuciform sac. Dirk recalled Asquith setting up a scene which involved the entire cast sitting at a large round table. He asked for some ad-libbed conversation, before the Shaw dialogue began, which should be in period because the sound would be running. 'I thought about Bonnard and light,' recalled Dirk. 'My doctor on my right was Robert Morley. On the word "Action" I turned to Robert to say my invented line about Bonnard and light only to hear him say to me: "Dubedat! What did Oscar Wilde do?" The take was in ruins.'[23] Dirk was especially proud of his death scene with Leslie Caron as Dubedat's devoted wife. Rightly so: Dilys Powell in *The Sunday Times* regarded it as 'the most moving and deeply felt playing the actor has given us on the screen'.[24] Everyone involved knew there was a risk that on release the film would be mistaken for the next in the *Doctor* series. Sure enough, said Dirk, 'a great many seats went clacking up'. But it had been a challenging and serious piece of work with a director of whom he was fond. In that respect Asquith was in a minority. It gives some idea of Dirk's general frustration that while he was still at work on *The Doctor's Dilemma* he gave an interview to *Photoplay* magazine in which he agreed that his career was static, if not slipping. If *The Wind Cannot Read* turned out to be a flop, he would, he said, be 'up the spout'. Neither *Campbell's Kingdom* nor *A Tale of Two Cities* had done as well as hoped at the box-office, despite the latter's impact on those who wrenched themselves away from their television sets to see it. *Doctor in the House* had been, in its own way, what he called 'a crossroads picture', and he needed another one. But what? 'What I want is a good director to tell me. I'm sick of worrying. My first experience of a British director was when I made *Esther Waters*. I asked how I should do something. "I don't know," he said, "you're the actor. I'm only the director." All my career it has been the same – with a few exceptions of course.'[25] Peter Tipthorp, his interviewer, remembered that Dirk's actual words were far more damning: 'He said,"They're fucking useless. Half the time they don't know what they are doing", but because of his position with Rank at the time, he asked me not to publish that, and I agreed.'[26] Dirk told Tipthorp that he needed to disappear from the British screen for a while; he had made fourteen films in five years and had 'over-saturated it'. He had not reached the contempt stage, but familiarity was breeding a certain apathy at home. He really did wish to do something in Hollywood, or perhaps a Broadway play?

In the event Dirk stayed away for about nine months, continuing to reject American suitors. The director Irving Rapper tried hard to tempt him with *The Miracle*, a Peninsular War story about a vow-breaking nun in love with a British soldier and an odd intervention by a statue of the Virgin Mary. The bait from Warner Brothers was $100,000 – no mean sum, even at an exchange rate of two dollars eighty cents to the pound; but only a third more than Dirk would earn on any film made for Rank in addition to his contractual commitment. It was eventually Roger Moore who took the Warner dollar and ran. At the same time David Merrick, the scruple-free New York impresario, wanted Dirk for *The World of Suzie Wong*, to be directed by Joshua Logan, but Dirk knew of Merrick's reputation and was having none of it. Instead, he concentrated energies on playing host at a redecorated and recarpeted Beel; on providing sanctuary from the press for Rex Harrison and Kay Kendall as the former prepared for the London opening of *My Fair Lady*; on more formal entertaining at his recently adopted home from home, the Connaught Hotel, where he repaid the hospitality to the Maharajah of Jaipur; on having with Ulric a joint exhibition of their paintings at the Rose and Crown pub near the latter's latest house in another Sussex village, Fletching; and on becoming more active behind the scenes. Dirk had bought Motley Films, a company that once belonged to Errol Flynn, and was using it in a similar way to Bendrose, buying options on plays and films, and investing in theatre productions, as well as retaining the services of Dirk himself and friends such as Anne Leon, who was engaged for £500 to act in two productions. Thus Dirk spread his wings in a modest way as an 'angel' – backing individual productions to the tune of, say, £100 for a thriller at the St Martin's – and a philanthropist, giving £500 to the Lyric Hammersmith. His most significant act of charity, however, was to brave the stage again, for a pittance.

He did so in part as a favour to Frank Hauser, a good friend of Laurence Harbottle and an inspirational director of the Oxford Playhouse, which had been in dire financial trouble until an Anouilh play had saved the day, and which was now hoping to consolidate the position by staging another. For £7 a week – he offered to do it for nothing, but the actors' union insisted he took the Equity minimum – Dirk agreed to appear with the redoubtable Hermione ('Totie') Baddeley, in *Jezebel*, a study of a family in turmoil, and a platform for Tony's old flame to appal as an ageing, drink-sodden nymphomaniac, happy to knock off

her sanctimonious husband with a poisoned mushroom in order to acquire the
50,000 francs needed to keep her lover from jail. Dirk was to play the son –
damaged, of course, and with worrying signs of taking after his mother; but
desperate to escape from the moral degradation both around and inside him.
Shades of *The Vortex*. Hauser knew that he could exploit the natural capacity for
self-pity that made Dirk so suited to the French dramatist's work: 'Anouilh's
"heroes" are nearly all put-upon, awful, cowardly. Self-pity was Dirk's besetting
vice, and it destroys more English actors than anything else. He would come
into rehearsal in the blackest of glooms, thinly disguised by his desire to prove it
wasn't his fault. He was very nervous, very flaky. Until about three nights before
the opening he didn't really rehearse, and then he went into overdrive, started to
act, and be *heard*.'[27] The play opened on 22 September 1958, and John Barber
reported that 'Dirk Bogarde, the slim dandy of the cinema, spent most of the
evening seizing women by the arms and shaking the living daylights out of them'.
His performance was 'vigorous yet graceful'.[28] The *Manchester Guardian* decided:
'It is Dirk Bogarde who sustains the acting, with a high romantic seriousness
that scarcely wilts even through the most daunting moments. This is a notable
performance, and an important step, one would judge, in his career.'[29]

On the second night Dirk noted in the Diary: 'Very good performance – no
one to see it!' By that he meant no critics, because the production played to
ninety-seven per cent capacity throughout, and, just in case, the Chief Constable
of Oxford had arranged for a constable to be on duty each evening at about 7,
and again at about 10.15, to control the crowds expected for Dirk's arrival and
departure. Unfortunately Kenneth Tynan had been present on the first night,
and his verdict at the weekend did Dirk's self-esteem no good at all: 'Dirk
Bogarde, who has one expression that is grave and weak, another that is grave
and wry, and a capacity for sudden shouting that serves to break the monotony,
rings what changes he can on limited acting resources.'[30] The 'deep despondency'
he had felt at some of the notices for *The Vortex* was never too far away. He
needed all the morale-boosting that his trusted theatrical confidantes and staunch
allies, the Withersby sisters, could give him when they attended both performances on the second Thursday: he had just learned that Columbia were
refusing to pass the budget for a Western on which he had set his heart, called
Kid Rodelo.

The play moved to Brighton for a final week, at the end of which Dirk was in
a bad way. He had pains in his chest and difficulty breathing. He and Tony
retreated to Beel, where on the Monday the doctor diagnosed an inflamed
duodenal tract; by Wednesday it was pleurisy, and Thursday double pneumonia.
When he began to wander about deliriously, Tony moved into his room to stop
him heading for the door. A nurse came to take charge. Agnes Zwickl remembers
how worried everyone was: 'He was very ill. And he isolated himself completely.
We all moved about as quietly as we could. It was the only time I saw him really
ill, because he was a very healthy man. He loved the fresh air.'[31] His reserves of

strength stood him in good stead, because all agreed that for a short while it had been touch and go. Even though he made a steady recovery under Nurse Keegan's watchful eye, it was a fortnight before he felt strong enough to go downstairs for a meal. The household had managed to stop news of the illness leaking to the outside world. By the time it finally reached the newspapers, Dirk was taking stock. 'It's sickening,' he wrote to the Withersbys, 'but I really have to face the fact that the theatre is not for me. This makes the third time, and was a bit too close for comfort. I really thought I was getting away with it too.'[32]

Frank Hauser remembers how during the week in Brighton, Dirk had been 'like a friendly lobster, twitchy'. He had said generously to Hauser that they should find not the best theatre but the biggest, so that they could make a huge profit very quickly: 'Let's take Wembley Stadium.' But, after the Playhouse, Brighton it had to be. By the end, said the director, Dirk's troubles – whatever it was that made him 'there to be chastised' – had grown into 'a huge nervous breakdown'. Unfortunately, too, Dirk's and Tony's living expenses made a serious hole in the profits which Dirk himself had done so much to generate; but this was forgiven because of the attention which Dirk had attracted to the Playhouse and by bringing in an audience new to the theatre. The director enjoyed working with him: 'He was very much up and down, but when he was up he was charming, funny, and just scandalous enough to have a bit of fun with. He was good for a couple of hours.' A young member of the cast, Susan Travers, was making her professional debut after leaving the Royal Academy of Dramatic Art. On her first pay day she and another actress were sitting in their dressing-room when Dirk came in, handed her his own pay packet and said: 'There you are girls. You need this more than I do.' Now married to Cornel Lucas, Susan Travers has never forgotten that kindness.[33]

It is Frank Hauser's belief that Dirk was never able to work out his own attitude to being a film star, or a star of any kind, and that adulation had prevented him from being 'really devastating' in the theatre; adulation for a matinée idol brought with it as a corollary the threat of derision. 'I remember sitting chatting with one of my nieces, who was then a schoolgirl of about fourteen or fifteen. Somebody mentioned Dirk Bogarde. She said, "Dirk Bogarde – he's queer isn't he?" Dirk was always terrified of being pronounced queer. He was so anxious to present a macho image. If he had a riding crop, he would swish it – but he was fooling nobody.' Hauser is convinced that the 'chink in the armour' – the possibility of, and consequent fear of, derision – prevented Dirk from achieving the stature of his almost exact contemporary, Gérard Philipe, who flitted between stage and screen to equal effect. Hauser agrees with Kitty Black that Dirk had some of the Frenchman's insolence – that air of 'take it or leave it' – but 'I saw Philipe doing "Lorenzaccio" and he was acres beyond Dirk or any of the other English actors'. There was another noticeable result of the path that Dirk's career had taken: 'He was not afraid of directors any more – they were afraid of him.'

The year ended with Dirk at number two in the *Motion Picture Herald* poll, having relinquished the top spot to Alec Guinness – which, Tony noted, 'he does'nt resent!' Two weeks of Swiss mountain air had revived him, as he had spent Christmas in Klosters with his parents. Indeed it had started him thinking seriously again about living abroad – in Switzerland rather than the south of France, and from as early as the spring of 1960. Tony and Laurence Harbottle had a long discussion about the implications of this for Dirk's relationship with Rank which, for all its frustrations, afforded the security and the sense of 'team', if not exactly 'family', that he in his odd way needed; and there was also his reputation to consider. Perhaps rashly, he had told an interviewer during his stint at the Playhouse that, with taxation as it was in Britain – more than eighty per cent for earners at his level – to seek refuge on the Continent was 'really the only reasonable thing to do'. Under the headline 'Another one goes ...', he was reported as being about to join the ranks of Noël Coward and the writers Alistair MacLean and Elleston Trevor as 'highly paid expatriates'.[34] It is a moot point whether that headline was written in sympathy or with cynicism. Dirk's reasons for a possible move were, as we have seen, more involved. In any case, nothing could be done about it at present, because he had gone to Switzerland in the knowledge that he was to make two films which would keep him busy for most of 1959.

Relations with the Studio had been soured by comments he had made to *Picturegoer*, some flippant, some less so, which had appeared under a headline wailing 'What a blunder this would be! – if British filmdom drove Dirk Bogarde away to Hollywood'. Without mentioning such names as Curt Jurgens, Horst Buchholz and Hardy Kruger, he said: 'These days, it appears, you have to have a German accent to impress the film studios in Britain.' More seriously, he added: 'I've turned down many films from Hollywood before because they were not right for me. But the scripts I'm being offered now are worth while. Americans see me quite differently as an actor. Over here they have set ideas about the kind of thing I can do.' Since the collapse of *Lawrence*, he said, 'I've had one offer from the Rank Organisation' and 'apparently it has nothing for me in the foreseeable future. It's a sign of the changing times. Everything's altered here.'[35] Reading this, John Davis wrote to Olive Dodds, asking whether Dirk had been misquoted, and saying that such articles did a grave disservice to the industry at a particularly difficult time. Olive Dodds agreed, saying that it sounded as if Dirk and Rank were at odds, if not loggerheads.[36] Dirk's reply is not recorded, but his actions spoke as loudly as any words. Finally Tinseltown's entreaties had come to something and for a fee of $100,000 – less Rank's slice for loaning him out – he was to have the title role in 'The Franz Liszt Story', to be directed by Charles Vidor, a specialist in musicals and romances, who had done something similar with the life of Chopin in *A Song to Remember*, starring Cornel Wilde. The part had become available because Van Cliburn, the twenty-four-year-old winner of the International Tchaikovsky Piano Competition in Moscow, had

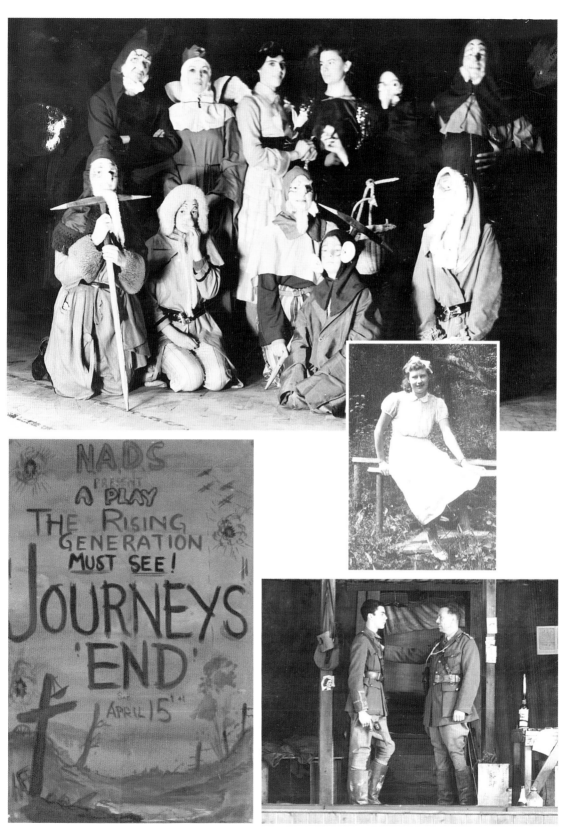

Clockwise from top Guy Fawkes Night tableau at Newick, 1938: Derek as Snow White, Christine Clegg as the Prince, Margaret as the Queen, Lu as the Witch and the Cox family as the dwarfs; Nerine Cox, photographed by Derek, 1938-9; Derek as Raleigh and Lionel Cox as Osborne in *Journey's End* at Newick, April 1939, photographed by Ulric; Derek's poster.

Clockwise from top left Margaret and Gareth; Derek (centre) in *You Never Can Tell* at Amersham Playhouse, November 1940; William Wightman; Gitta Alpar, the 'Hungarian nightingale', whom Tony tried to manage; E.L.L. (Anthony) Forwood; Derek's 'fiancée', Anne Deans, in a later wartime production at Amersham, Clemence Dane's *Granite*.

Left Derek's impression of the dressing-room he shared with Peter Ustinov at Wyndham's Theatre for *Diversion No. 2*; *Above* 'In for a Dip', with Vida Hope, Joan Sterndale Bennett and (right) Peter Ustinov.

Right The raw recruit within days of arrival at Catterick in June 1941, adopting an unorthodox approach to military formality.

Below Almost one of the family: Jack ('Tony') Jones with Margaret, Elizabeth and Derek, photographed by Ulric at Hillside Cottage, Clayton.

A portrait, one of a series by Ulric, which Derek gave to Jack in June 1944 with the inscription: 'to Tony, who shares my life'.

Clockwise from top left The gang of four, pictured by Bill Warhurst (one of Ulric's staff photographers), at Sommervieu, Normandy, in August 1944: (left to right) Kenneth Costin, Christopher Greaves, Derek, and Sydney Allen; the photographic interpreter in his mobile office; Derek and Chris with the 'family' at Eindhoven, 1945; a pen-and-ink memento of the carnage at the Falaise Gap, August 1944.

Clockwise from top left With Eve Holiday in Calcutta, November 1945; with Bert Garthoff and 'Milly' at Radio Batavia, December 1945; Major-General Douglas Hawthorn in Bandoeng, 1946; distant confidante: Dorothy Fells; with Hugh Jolly at Nee Soong transit camp, Singapore, August 1946; a snapshot for Jack: at Tandjoengpriok, July 1946.

Clockwise from top left Dirk with Maureen Pook in *Power Without Glory*, New Lindsey Theatre Club and Fortune Theatre, 1947; on location near Lullington with Kathleen Ryan for *Esther Waters*; with his brother at Pinewood on *Esther Waters* (Gareth is clutching his wages, a five-pound note); Jack and Dirk in London, 1948 - the last surviving picture of them together. *Opposite page, clockwise from top left* Tony Forwood and Glynis Johns, after their marriage at Westminster Register Office in August 1942, with Beatrice Lillie; with Glynis; Tony and his son, Gareth; Tony's cousin, later Mary Dodd; an early version of the drawing in *Snakes and Ladders* of Dirk's first house, shared with Eve and, from May 1948, with Tony.

44 CHESTER ROW. 1947.

Tony as Will Scarlet in *The Story of Robin Hood and His Merrie Men.*

As Tom Riley in *The Blue Lamp.*

As Captain Molineux (right) in *The Shaughraun* at the Bedford Theatre, with (from left) Catherine Finn, Richard Longman, Lucienne Hill and Richard Johnson.

turned it down. 'I've been waiting all this time for the right part,' said Dirk. 'This is it. I don't mind being Franz Liszt. I've read the script and am very keen.'[37] One astute commentator suggested that what really attracted him to the role was the Hungarian composer's flamboyant 'wickedness'. Dirk said he had been reading about his subject and had 'the general idea', although the foreign names were 'difficult to remember'. Liszt, he said, 'had affairs with all the most beautiful women in Europe. For the purpose of the film we shall probably have to concentrate on just three or four of them. But we shall definitely have dear old Lola Montez, and then there's the countess something or other, and then one of those princesses – I forget what she was princess of exactly.' If a composer seemed 'colourful', he rationalised, film-makers went ahead and told the story without being too 'stuffy' about historical authenticity.[38] He was due to report to Columbia early in April, but the schedule was tight. Asquith and de Grunwald had another job for him.

Libel, adapted by de Grunwald from Edward Wooll's play, was put together in a hurry because MGM were delighted at the unexpected success in America of *The Doctor's Dilemma*. It gave Dirk the chance to play three roles, as the silver-haired Sir Mark Loddon, an amnesiac baronet who might or might not have been killed in the war; as a weaselly small-time actor who might or might not be masquerading as the baronet; and, scarcely recognisably, as a cripple, his face remodelled with scar tissue, who holds the key. 'It was certainly melodrama,' Dirk reflected; 'we knew it was and we hammed it up to the elbows.' He said: 'I haven't seen it but I think it was a load of shit.'[39] In fact he had, and it was not. Melodramatic, certainly, but dignified by some fine acting from himself, Paul Massie as the alleged libeller, and Olivia de Havilland as the American Lady Loddon. The *News of the World* decided that, after years of good, bad and excessively indifferent films in which he never gave a 'duff' performance, greatness had eluded Dirk; but now, in *Libel*, 'we see a Bogarde of authority and command'.[40] Others agreed, saying it was the performance of his career and comparing him with Guinness. For reasons best known to himself, he did not keep his script for binding, which is a pity; there are some lines in the finished film which can have been written only by him: 'I remember that I had a linnet in a cage. It was given to me on my fifth birthday by the head gardener. I remember his name, too. It was Mr Searle ... The cage was too small. [The linnet] kept fluttering ...'. The free spirit was always flexing his wings, as we know, but the reference to Lally's father, which can have meant nothing to anyone outside the two families and a few of their friends, is significant. During the making of the film Dirk told *Picturegoer* that he had been keeping back the best stories of his personal life – particularly those from childhood and the war. 'I'm writing a book about my early life. Dear knows when it'll be finished, though. I might use a ghost writer, but I'd prefer to try and do it in my own style.'[41]

On 26 March, armed with a new sixteen-millimetre cine-camera, Dirk and Tony sailed on the *Queen Elizabeth* for America. Dirk's thirty-eighth birthday was spent while the liner hove to, in mighty seas and a howling gale. 'No fun,' noted Tony. As the winds and waves lessened slightly over the next two days he and Dirk were able to make their five circuits of the boatdeck, then sit out on the sundeck, 'swathed in steamer blankets, & shivering' in the afternoon. In the evenings they watched films – *The Thirty-Nine Steps, Room at the Top* and, with a pang, *Gigi*. As they arrived at Pier 90 in New York they learned that the seas had officially been declared the worst of the century, although the crossing in the other direction would have been still more hellish. There to meet them on the dockside was the composer of *Gigi* himself, Alan Lerner, with his latest wife. For two days they alternated socialising – the Lerners, Kay Young, Joanne Woodward and others – with business, including a flurry of interviews that resulted in little coverage; Dirk was, after all, just another movie actor passing through. He and Tony flew overnight to Los Angeles and were greeted by Minna Wallis, of the Famous Artists Agency, with whom Dirk had signed at the beginning of 1958. It was she, sister of the *Casablanca* producer Hal Wallis, who had been zealously searching for the bait to lure Dirk to the West Coast. At last he was safely installed at the Bel Air Hotel. Columbia gave a reception, and Minna Wallis threw a party with a daunting guestlist of Wylers, Wilders, Hathaways, even Gary Cooper and his wife; but otherwise there was to be little lotus-eating during this project. On the contrary, for the first month, without a scene being rehearsed or a foot of film shot, Dirk was to be worked harder than he had since training for battle in 1942.

His tormentor was Victor Aller, a fifty-five-year-old pianist, graduate of the Juilliard School in New York, and brilliant interpreter of Brahms. His family had moved in the thirties to Hollywood, where he established a reputation as an inspiring teacher. It was he who enabled Cornel Wilde to pass muster as Chopin in Vidor's *A Song to Remember*. Now he was engaged to turn Dirk into a credible Liszt – pianistically anyway. More than eighty minutes of music had to be learned at the dummy keyboard, then synchronised for the camera with the pre-recorded playing of Jorge Bolet and the Los Angeles Philharmonic Orchestra. They set to. For three weeks they toiled as fellow perfectionists, with Victor a hard taskmaster, given to strong language. Initially, says his daughter Judith, Dirk was scared of him, but soon realised that they were not unalike: 'Dirk found something in that sad, suffering Russian Jew'. And Victor found something *needy* in Dirk.[42] Victor's sadness and suffering stemmed largely from family jealousies in his early years, and opportunities missed; he had an invitation to Europe and would almost certainly have triumphed on the concert circuit, perhaps even as another Liszt, so powerful was his absorption in the *sound* of the piano; but his humility and insecurity made him demur. Instead, he did all he could to pass his gift to others. Dirk, says Judith Aller, became the most dedicated student Victor ever had, and the most loyal. They formed a sweet alliance, each from his own 'incredibly unsweet profession'; the music world is – and as a professional violinist she should know – 'even worse than the movies'. At the end of the film Liszt says to his mother, 'Here it is, the piano, with its memories . . . of ten hours practice a day', and adds: 'Remember, Mama, the little bleeding fingers?'[43] Dirk needed no motivation for that sequence. But nor did he hold any grudge. On the contrary, he was to remember Victor Aller as 'a most powerful influence in my life', who 'taught me, more than anyone else, what determination and dedication could do'.[44] Like the puppy Dirk adopted in Holland, Victor was christened 'Pee Wee'.

There was no need to find a nickname for Capucine. 'My friends call me Cap,' she said to her first American interviewer. 'You may call me Capucine.' It means Nasturtium, and it was the name under which this glacially beautiful creature, born Germaine Lefebvre in Toulon, had modelled for Dior and Givenchy. In the mid-fifties Capucine was travelling the world to show off their clothes, but she had never been to America. One Wednesday she felt bored, so on the Friday 'I went there'. She did some modelling, then bumped into John Wayne and the agent/producer Charles Feldman. The latter put her under contract and sent her to California both to learn English and to become more heavily involved with Mr Feldman. By the time the producer William Goetz took his 'four-and-a-half-million-dollar gamble' by casting her opposite Dirk as the Princess Carolyne Sayne-Wittgenstein, she had never made a film or appeared on a stage, but her English was pretty good and her attitude towards the industry pretty refreshing. Why do I have to be interviewed, she asked the luckless publicity man deputed to look after 'The Franz Liszt Story', by now retitled 'A Magic Flame':

'To get yourself in the public eye and to be utterly frank to get the name of the picture in print.'
   'Why should I care about getting the name of the picture in print?'
   'Because you are one of the stars in it.'
   'First I want to know where the title "A Magic Flame" comes from. Am I the magic flame or is it Liszt or Dirk Bogarde?'

A cigar was chewed thoughtfully.

'The magic flame is the inspiration. You are the inspiration for the film.'
   'Huh. Go ahead if you want to ask questions, shoot.'[45]

It is easy to see why she and Dirk had a rapport.

Tony and Dirk, his fingers battered but nimble, took a polar flight home, where they had three days before heading for the locations in Austria. They stayed at the Bristol in Vienna – the start of a second love affair with a relatively small, nineteenth-century hotel which, like the Connaught, combined comfort, elegance and an excellent restaurant with discretion and an indefinable embrace. They were to depend on it for some while. Shooting began at the Schönbrunn Palace, the Habsburg monument with its beautiful ballroom and baroque theatre built for the Empress Maria Theresa. Despite the magnificence of the surroundings, the piquant smell of disaster began to permeate the production. Dirk described it as 'a grinding and profoundly unhappy experience'.[46] Vidor, he said, was 'a foul director who screamed at everyone and shook Capucine like a dead cat, roaring at her to relax'.[47] There was an incident when an anti-Semitic member of the crew released a sandbag above the spot where Victor Aller was standing; it narrowly missed him. Days off were spent either practising with Victor or seeking solace by driving with Capucine, sometimes with Victor too, into the countryside and the mountains for picnics, their idylls captured on Tony's cine-camera. Then, late in the evening of Thursday, 4 June, Charles Vidor died of a heart attack – it was said *in flagrante delicto*, with a bit-part player from the cast. On the Monday Dirk sent a card to his parents: 'Our Director died suddenly 3 days ago (much to my relief!) – and now we wait for a replacement. But I still work at the piano like an idiot!' The film, he wrote later, 'foundered like a holed galleon'.[48] The replacement duly arrived in the comforting non-heterosexual shape of George Cukor, the witty multiple Oscar nominee, famed for encouraging actresses to give of their best. He had directed Kay Kendall in *Les Girls* two years earlier, so there was an immediate point of contact. Another good sign: he could read – and brought with him a copy of Sacheverell Sitwell's 1934 Life of Liszt. Cukor, wrote Dirk, had dealt with the greatest names in the cinema – Garbo, Colman, Gable, Holliday, Garland, Tracy and, above all, Katharine Hepburn – so 'he was not about to be dismayed by taking over a shipwreck with an almost, to him, unknown crew'.[49] His biographer, Patrick McGilligan, tells how Cukor arrived in Vienna to find 'an "idiotic" script, dull sets, costumes and furniture whose awfulness he could not believe, and an inflexible cameraman (James Wong Howe), who had to be despatched in favour of one more compatible with Cukor (Charles Lang)'. Also in Vienna, struggling with an equally unhappy project starring Sophia Loren, was the screenwriter Walter Bernstein, to whom Cukor showed the script of 'A Magic Flame'. Bernstein said: 'My best advice to you is to get rid of Dirk Bogarde and get Sid Caesar. Then, just film the script.'[50] It was that bad.

Under Cukor, however, life improved markedly. At the end of the second month, while Dirk conducted *Tannhäuser* and Somerset Maugham visited the set – 'Have *another* sip, Somerset'? – Tony wrote to Laurence Harbottle: 'All now going well on film, but D really earning his lolly!'[51] They ploughed on, travelling to Bayreuth and Munich, before Dirk and Tony were free to fly home and find Ulric and Margaret who had been minding the shop for the Zwickls. Three months had already been spent on 'the unhappy epic', but it was only the end of phase two. Within a week they were in the air again, to New York and on to Los Angeles. Shooting restarted at Columbia's studios, and for Dirk there was no let-up; on non-filming days he was closeted with Victor for yet more practice on the dummy keyboard. Nevertheless he was beginning to enthuse about Hollywood, at least as a place to work: 'I love it,' he told the *Los Angeles Times*; 'make no bones about that at all. And studios never alter; one is like another; so I can't possibly be homesick.'[52] This time a house had been found for them, at

8930 St Ives Drive, in West Hollywood, a few minutes from Cukor. At the end of August, Tony was writing to Laurence Harbottle that they had 'a delightful house with a beautiful view and a small pool, and we live a fairly Beelish existence. However it's all dreadfully expensive.' Everyone seemed 'really terribly excited with the film out here, and particularly with Dirk, and it really looks as if it may all turn out to be the right thing to have done. Everyone is confident that it will put the boy on the map of America in a very big way, and from what I have seen I am inclined to agree, except that I am always a bit cautious about getting too excited about rushes.'[53]

During this period Dirk and Tony saw more of Gladys Cooper, whose orange trees in Napoli Drive led to her being christened Dirk's 'Marmalade Aunt'. She had, he told her grandson Sheridan Morley, 'all the charm of an electric carving knife: she was precise, hard, efficient, very cool, very beautiful and I was terrified of her. She once hit me on the head for talking too much, and yet we did manage to become very great friends. Perhaps that was because we never had to work together.'[54] However, they soon had to rally together. At 7 in the morning on 6 September, Dirk was woken with the news that their mutually adored Kay Kendall had died at The London Clinic. She was thirty-two. A week later, when memorial services were held in both New York and Los Angeles, Dirk was asked by Rex Harrison – who had married her in 1957 – to give the address at All Saints, Beverly Hills; but, Dirk said, he was too overcome and Gladys Cooper read instead, 'with tears pouring down her face'.[55] Much later, in a treasured letter, Harrison wrote of his constant doubt about obeying the New York doctor's instruction so fully as not to tell Dirk and Tony of Kay's real condition. He described her last days and how she had been buried at Hampstead Parish Church in a plot he had managed to secure for her between those of Sir Herbert Beerbohm Tree and the du Maurier family, which she would certainly have considered 'not bad digs'. Harrison warned her two staunch friends to watch out, because she was 'still around, you know'.

It was an emotional low point for Dirk, and it came just as the professional future looked a good deal brighter, anyway as far as America was concerned. Tony reported that they had received and rejected 'quite a lot of approaches' because the feeling about the film was positive enough to allow for caution; it looked as if it 'might easily be the biggest thing that has ever happened to Dirk'.[56] The mood was still optimistic when Capucine threw a 'wrap' party for Dirk and Cukor at Charles Feldman's house, with a marquee in the garden, a dance band and 'A-list' company, including James Stewart, Henry and Jane Fonda, Judy Garland, Leslie Caron, the Wilders, the Wylers, Frank Sinatra and the ubiquitous Roddy McDowall, a new close friend. It was head-turning stuff. So much so that 'I had no urgent desire, now, to return to Beel, in fact I was not even sure that I wanted to see it ever again'.[57] As he left Los Angeles – 'the richer by half his fee again, because the film had overrun significantly – he gave an interview to Sheilah Graham in which he said that he would be returning in a few weeks to make a film with Susan Hayward; followed by *The Short Cut*, to be directed in North Africa by Jules Dassin.[58] Such is the volatile world of film that by the time the article appeared a few days later, he had signed for neither and was instead packing his bags for Italy, to make what was then called 'The Fair Bride' with Ava Gardner – for a fee of £70,000. Nearly forty years later he alleged that the change of plan – Italy instead of Los Angeles – had been engineered by Charles Feldman, who was jealous of the closeness between Dirk and Capucine.

There was a week at Beel, ever more unloved, and where changes were afoot. Because they believed their employers were soon to move to the Continent, the Zwickls, too, had decided to work in America, where, in addition to a more benign economy, Hans could be guaranteed first-class medical attention for an ailing shoulder. They ensured that Dirk and Tony were not left in the lurch by arranging for two Austrian friends, Willi and Greta Sendelhofer, to take over for the time being and to brave the recalcitrant Annie. The introductions were made, affectionate farewells bidden, and Dirk and Tony flew to Rome, to be met by their latest car, a Rolls-Royce – with the same number plate, BH5 – which had arrived intact at the hotel where MGM were putting them up, the Grand. Before setting out on a three-day drive and a ferry crossing to Sicily, however, they inspected the Hassler, near the Spanish Steps; it was to become favoured city hotel number three.

Dirk had left behind him in England a ticking time-bomb, in the form of another forthright interview – this time with Derek Monsey of the *Sunday Express*, whose marriage to the actress Yvonne Mitchell afforded him a privileged vantage point. Some years earlier he had asked rhetorically whether Dirk could survive on a diet of stereotyped and unsympathetic roles. He classified him as 'a Peter Pan type, reaching, with a vague wonder at his own success, into early middle age, but still looking as if he had only just said farewell to adolescence'. Now he was quoting Dirk: 'I'm absolutely potty about Hollywood. For working in, that is, not living. I can't wait to get back. There's a punch in the air. The pressure is terrific. And they're making movies. Dozens of them. And great subjects. With the best directors in the world.'[59] Every crisp sentence was an arrow into Rank's heart; and even though that organ was not quite as cold as Hollywood's, there might have been a grunt of vindication from the corridors stalked by Earl St John when the most recent *Motion Picture Herald* box-office survey placed Dirk fifth, behind Kenneth More, Alec Guinness, Norman Wisdom and Stanley Baker.[60] After two years of supremacy, the star was waning. Nor was there much comfort in the laurel for which he was listed towards the end of the decade. Each year his wartime friend in Calcutta, John Gawsworth, issued an honours list, turning high achievers and old chums into dukes and duchesses of his seagull-splattered island, Redonda; J. B. Priestley, Rebecca West, Michael Denison and his wife Dulcie Gray were all so elevated. On the same list as Diana Dors, honoured 'for services to beauty', Naomi Jacob, 'for services to Literature and Italy', and Frances Day 'for launching the State-barge "Frances" in the Grand Union Canal Paddington', was Dirk – 'for military collaboration at Bally, Bengal'. Unlike the Denisons, who received their document-of-dukedom backstage at the Cambridge Theatre, it seems Dirk's ennoblement was never ratified.

Twelve

'Il faut le voir pour le croire'

Nunnally Johnson was a small-town boy from the Deep South who exemplified the Hollywood all-rounder. By the time he met Dirk he had more than fifty films to his credit as writer, producer, director – or various combinations of the three – including *The Grapes of Wrath*, *My Cousin Rachel* and *The Three Faces of Eve*. Johnson had been released by Twentieth Century Fox to direct a picture for MGM – his own adaptation of a novel, *The Fair Bride*, which was, as Dirk summarised it later, 'about a priest and a tart in Spain during the Civil War'.[1] The casting of Ava Gardner – 'The World's Most Exciting Animal' – as the tart had been settled long before, once Johnson had beefed up the character from the original novel who, he said, would not have made a nickel during Navy Week in San Diego. The troubled, bewildered, Hamlet-like priest was more of a problem. Dean Martin, Kirk Douglas, Glenn Ford, Rock Hudson and Paul Newman were all approached; Montgomery Clift had almost signed but chose instead to do a film with Elia Kazan. At which point Dirk was proposed, and Johnson felt that, given Clift's personal habits, he had perhaps had a lucky break: 'I am quite satisfied with Bogarde, who is not only a good actor but customarily sober.'[2] The production was beset by problems with the trade unions, the weather and the politics endemic in filming a story in Italy about a fallen priest; worried letters whisked between Sicily, New York and the Roman Catholic adviser to the Motion Picture Association of America about the job description of a 'bar-girl'. Ava Gardner's liking for a sip of 'schnapps' did not help either, but, as one of those outwardly tough, been-through-the-mill, glamorous broads, she appealed greatly to Dirk. Tony described the company's base, Catania, as 'a dump, not at all pour les vacances, but this n'est pas one so it does'nt matter!'[3] Dirk noted, after another day of torrential rain and word games in Ava's room, that 'boredom prevails!' The film lurched to a conclusion, with Johnson doing his best to resist MGM's attempts at prettification into what Dirk called an ' "A Man and a Girl in Blazing Madrid" kind of thing'.[4] At 2 o'clock one morning, Johnson – in Dirk's eyes a gentle, civilised director – found himself sitting on a slippery Sicilian rock, huddled against the winter cold, ordering the camera to be placed at a certain spot. He decided that from then on someone else could do that kind of job while he stayed at home in bed. He never made another film.[5] By the time this one opened, 'to ten Eskimos in North Alaska', its title had passed from 'The Fair Bride', through 'Temptation', to *The Angel Wore Red*. It 'closed the next day and sank without trace'.[6]

Interiors and dubbing kept Dirk and Tony in Rome through Christmas Day, when an interesting group was assembled at the Hassler: Ulric and Margaret; Glynis, who turned up unexpectedly from Australia; the fourteen-year-old Gareth; Capucine and Charles Feldman. The arrival of the last was depicted in *Cleared for Take-Off* as a body-blow to Dirk's romantic hopes, with Capucine descending the steps from the aeroplane and his smile slipping 'like melting butter' when, 'elegant and lithe, Mr Feldman followed her down carrying his Louis Vuitton briefcase'.[7] In fact Feldman followed six days later, and Tony described his joining them in Rome as 'flattering'. Also in the Christmas party was Irene Howard, casting director for MGM in Britain, sister of the actor Leslie and full member of the Out-Patients Department at Beel. And elsewhere in the Hassler were Alec Guinness, Audrey Hepburn and her husband Mel Ferrer. Christmas was, said Tony, 'all very film-world and really rather fun'.[8] The Rolls-Royce, which had not escaped unscathed on Italy's roads, finally pulled out of Rome on a rainy morning in early February. In Dirk's luggage was a shooting script for a new film, which he had agreed to do for Rank. It was called *The Singer Not the Song*.

Two days later Dirk and Tony were in Cannes, from where they went house-hunting again. They saw a highly promising property between Vence and Cagnes, and another within walking distance of the Colombe d'Or. Their biggest sadness was to discover that La Caravelle, a 'completely unfashionable' beachside con-cession between Cannes and La Napoule, which they had found on their first visit and where they had spent many happy days either with Elizabeth or with Dirk's parents, had been pulled down – 'a chapter finished'. As reconnaissances went, this brief visit to the area on which Dirk had set his heart was informative but not productive. On the other hand, as a collecting mission, it was exciting. In Cannes Dirk acquired two good paintings by Monneret, including a view of the Bastille, which he would keep for the rest of his life. Into the Rolls they went, joining a Nino Caffe entitled 'Celestial Trampolines', which had been given him by Charles Feldman, and a street scene by Orry Kelly, a present from George Cukor. Already in England, but held up by customs at Dover who claimed 'thirty odd pounds duty', were a set of four sixteenth-century flower prints, an early nineteenth-century engraving of a Rubens painting, and – presents from Cap-ucine – a pair of Italian Renaissance bronze frogs which once adorned a fountain. Where all of these *objets* were to reside was a moot point, because Dirk had now resolved to sell Beel. Even Bogarde's Bastion would not be adequate protection from the four-storey monstrosity planned to house those 540 young ladies, whose behaviour might be even less predictable once they had seen pictures of Dirk in his black leather trousers.

It all started calmly enough. In 1958, Dirk had been approached by the producer John Stafford, whom Rank had entrusted with a novel by Audrey Erskine Lindop about a power struggle in a small town in the Mexican mountains, where Father Keogh arrives to take over from a priest who has cracked up under pressure from the local tyrant – Anacleto, or 'Malo, the Bad-One-of-the-Cats' – and his gang. Can Father Keogh bring Anacleto back into the Church? Can he withstand the temptation afforded by the beautiful Locha? Does he realise that Anacleto, too, has a crush on him? Ken Annakin was to direct this potentially sizzling confection, and produced a script that concentrated on a second duel, between the enlightened country priest and his heavyweight archbishop in Mexico City. Peter Finch and Marlon Brando were his ideal antagonists, but the latter was sailing the south seas looking for an island retreat, and out of contact. John Davis recommended Dirk, and he and Stafford met. A fine actor, said Annakin, but no thanks – not for this movie. John Stafford suggested they make a second film which he had up his sleeve, and hoped that in the interim Davis would see reason enough for them to try again for Brando.[9] Time passed. Roy Ward Baker, who had delighted Rank by directing two immense hits in succession – *The One That Got Away* with Hardy Kruger, and *A Night to Remember* with Kenneth More – was handed the Erskine Lindop novel. 'A great subject for Dirk,' said Earl St John. 'I read the book and rejected it out of hand,' Roy Baker recalls:

> I had no wish to make any portrayal of the ins and outs of the Catholic religion, which has nothing to do with me. It seemed to be somewhat derogatory of the religion, which didn't appeal to me at all. I managed to keep them at arm's length for about fifteen months, but then I was forced to do it. 'You are ideal,' said John Davis. 'It's the last picture under Dirk's present contract, he's a big star and we don't want to lose him. Don't worry about the cost, don't worry about anything. We are going to throw everything we possibly can at him so that we can induce him to stay. He can have the top brick off the chimney, and so can you.' So I went to see Dirk.[10]

Dirk was in Hollywood, finishing the Liszt film, when Roy Baker came to call. Baker had also to consider who should play opposite him, so he was going through a list of possibilities. At one stage Dirk had indeed been at the head of the 'wish list' for the priest, with Richard Burton as the bandit; even earlier than that, Dirk was behind Sinatra, Richard Widmark and Montgomery Clift for the bandit, with Paul Newman and Laurence Harvey in line for the priest. By the time they met, it was set in concrete that Dirk would play the villain. Baker recalled in his memoirs: 'I'd had no dealings with Dirk before this and didn't know him at all. He impressed me at once with his undoubted charm and humour and the sheer speed of his sardonic wit. He certainly had the fastest brain of anyone I've ever met.'[11] Baker tried Richard Burton, who read the book and felt the part would be 'somewhat namby-pamby'. He tried several American actors, including Widmark, to no avail: 'No Hollywood star would want to come and co-star in a British picture that had no, or almost no, possible chance of a release in the United States.'[12] Baker's next meeting with Dirk was in Rome, while the latter completed *The Angel Wore Red*; they were joined by the novelist-in-(tax)-exile Nigel Balchin, who was writing the *Singer* screenplay at his villa near Florence. It went happily enough, recorded Baker. With a start date of mid-March the second central role had to be settled quickly. Baker hankered after Paul Scofield, but Earl St John rejected the idea, saying he favoured John Mills – to which the director had no objection. But Dirk had already told Baker that he did not want to see John Mills as the priest. This was dismissed out of hand by Earl St John, which confused Baker: 'I thought they were supposed to be bending over backwards to please Dirk.'

> What Dirk had against Johnnie he never explained. As far as I know, they had never played together.* Whatever personal reasons there may have been for this attitude Johnny [*sic*] is a scrupulously professional actor of vast experience and has been a star since the early thirties. Later, when I told Dirk that Johnny had agreed to appear, Dirk declared, 'I promise you, if Johnny plays the priest I will make life unbearable for everyone concerned.'[13]

He was, reflected Baker many years afterwards, as good as his word.

The writing was on the wall as soon as Dirk declared that to play Anacleto Gonzalez Flores Comachi Alvarez he wished to wear leather. He had found a tailor in Rome 'who could make the most wonderful leather trousers'. The slight snag was that 'he only makes them in black'. Baker thought nothing of it. 'He got on the phone and the trousers duly arrived.' They surely did. George Courtney Ward's still photographs of Dirk in his black shirt, black hat, black gloves, black gunbelt and those black trousers, sometimes carrying a black whip and sometimes stroking a black cat, have achieved iconic status. In one, there is clear evidence of tumescence. In others, a flash of white supplies extreme contrast: a shirt; a second cat – a Persian; a horse, which had to be shipped especially from England under 'D'-notice conditions, for Dirk to be plonked upon. Ralph Thomas, who called in at the location, tried to reassure Baker that all would be well, 'as long as Dirk's trousers fit' – but all was not well. Baker recalls that during the shooting near Torremolinos and Granada, Dirk's behaviour was so odd that John Mills frequently asked: 'What's the matter with the fella?' 'It was', says Sir John, 'a very unfortunate experience.' For him there were two illuminating moments, the first of which he inserted into the revised edition of his memoirs,

---

* But see *The Gentle Gunman* – of which, at the time he was interviewed for this book, Sir John Mills had little recollection.

published after Dirk's death: 'We had always got on well before this, but on the set one day one of the chippies, who had not noticed Dirk standing there, remarked, "Of course it's Johnnie Mills who's going to walk off with this picture." Dirk heard him, and it caused a great rumpus. He wouldn't speak to me off the set, and he cut the family dead in New York. I was very unhappy about it.'[14] The second, he had never mentioned publicly before being interviewed for this biography:

> There was a thing with Tony's son, on location. He was staying up rather late and nicking a bit of brandy and having a cigarette. Glynis came to me and said, 'You can trust me completely, Johnnie, I'm very worried about my son. I hear he's drinking brandy and smoking . . .'. I said, 'It's not bad at all.' She said, 'But it is happening.' I said, 'Well, he's having a nip at night for fun . . .'. She said, 'That's all I wanted to know. You've put my mind at rest.' She went straight and phoned Dirk up. And that really did it. Put the cat among the pigeons. It was very bad. He went right off me. It didn't come out in the open, but I knew. For years he wouldn't speak to me.[15]

Although the detail differs, the essence of this affair is confirmed by Gareth Forwood, who remembers that John Mills returned to London from location earlier than Dirk. 'He bumped into Glynis at Les Ambassadeurs and gave her the opinion that I was being badly brought up and that Dirk had an unhealthy effect on me. Mother wrote a panic-stricken letter to my father. Panic ensued all round. There were still several weeks to do at Pinewood. And Dirk refused to speak to John ever again.' It went very deep, said Sir John: 'In New York, he was really awful to the family; he didn't behave very well at all. In my seventy-seven years of acting Dirk was the only actor who I had any trouble with. Even though we were poles apart and he could be difficult, I admired him very much, and liked him, and so was very, very sad.' At the end of Dirk's life a telephone call from Sir John produced a friendly response, which gave the latter, at least, some satisfaction. Sir John believes that at the heart of the problem was Dirk's discomfiture at having been 'pitchforked' into a role for which he knew he was unsuited: 'I think he knew he was terribly miscast, and he wasn't at all happy. He got into all the wrong gear – too tight fitting black jeans and all that stuff . . . He knew it was wrong. So he played it not very well.' There was another difficulty, which Sir John mentioned with characteristic tact and a chuckle: 'In the picture we were supposed to be *very* close!' That is so. And the fundamental problem was that Dirk refused to countenance his character falling in love convincingly with one played by John Mills. The shooting script had some dialogue between Anacleto and Locha, played by Mylène Demongeot, in which Dirk was required to say: 'It must be heart-breaking to fall in love with a man whom you can never have – *particularly such a man as that one* [Father Keogh]. I understand – *because, you see, I am fond of him myself.*' In Dirk's copy, the italicised passages are deleted.[16]

In different hands the homoerotic undercurrents might have exerted a more powerful tow. Stephen Bourne wrote of the film: 'One can only imagine the tension and excitement [. . .] if Marlon Brando and Montgomery Clift had played the bandit and priest! Bogarde and Mills are simply too polite and well-behaved, and there is an obvious lack of chemistry between the two actors.' For Bourne, Dirk was 'as camp as Christmas. But take away the outfit and we're left with an unconvincing performance.'[17] For Donald Sinden and the others at Pinewood: 'It never crossed anyone's mind that he was camping it up. We just thought he was being himself!'[18]

After the press show of the film the following year, there was a lunch, attended by sixteen critics, all but two of whom cold-shouldered Roy Baker. 'None of them would speak to me,' he recalls. The reviewers plunged their knives into a rotting turkey. *The Times* decided that 'Mr Bogarde, whenever he is allowed to act with more than his left eyebrow, enters with some enthusiasm into the slightly lunatic mood of the piece (there is, in particular, an hallucinatory moment when he appears, tightly sheathed in black leather and carrying a white Persian kitten, for all the world like a latterday Queen Kelly)';[19] the *Evening Standard*, that Dirk's 'each scene is a victory over the costume designer'.[20] The unkindest cut was delivered later, in France, where the title became *Le Cavalier noir* and *Paris-presse* announced in a headline: 'Il faut le voir pour le croire'.[21] At the first London screening the audience laughed so much that Roy Baker hid under his seat. This was derision and, perversely, Dirk had courted it. In doing so, he told an audience at the National Film Theatre a decade later, 'I had a great love affair with me.' Amid much hilarity, he added: 'Can you believe that not one single person in that bloody organisation knew what I was up to.'[22] Roy Baker, whose ideal pairing had been Burton and Scofield, suspected Earl St John of cooking up one of those Machiavellian plots, whereby a studio hopes 'rivalry will produce great chemistry'; if so, 'it didn't work at all'. He has given much thought to what had happened on his unhappy set. Just as Bob Thomson feels that his demotion on *The Wind Cannot Read* was a symptom of Dirk wishing to break with the existing structure, so too Baker believes that his deliberate act of sabotage was 'all part and parcel of a very difficult transition period for him. He didn't want to do this film. He wanted to make pictures on the Continent, and I can understand that at the time he was in a very highly strung and nervous state. I have a lot of sympathy for him.' Baker's attitude is generous, because *Singer* damaged beyond repair his career as a director of feature films.

There is a story, from an anonymous but impeccably placed source, which illustrates Dirk's state of mind while he had been in Spain. The unit was shooting in its village location, and Dirk was due on the set in the late morning. A harassed associate producer came up to Baker:

'We've got a bit of trouble.'
'What sort of trouble?'

'It's Dirk.'
'What's the matter with him?'
'You'd better come and have a look.'

So Baker did. The Rolls was parked around the corner, with Tony sitting in the front and with Dirk on the back seat, in floods of tears.

'For God's sake,' said Baker, 'what's the matter?'

There was a good-looking young man, possibly South African and with a degree of charm, who had been taken on as a member of Anacleto's gang. He had no speaking part, but he could play the guitar and sing, and Baker thought he might be able to make use of that in the film. Dirk had collapsed because he thought Baker was training up the boy to take over his part. It was that bad. The ultimate twist in this peculiar tale is that *Singer* became a hit abroad, especially in the Roman Catholic countries, and eventually went into profit. In the late sixties Dirk sent a card to Baker: 'I have *always* thought "Singer" as one of my preferred movies – It was ahead of its time, & the unforgivable casting of JM all but ruined it – but it holds up jolly well – and, as you know, is "très snob" in France & Germany! – Funny after all that time.'[23] Matthew Sweet, who acquired Roy Baker's papers while researching a history of the British studio system, wrote: 'For Baker, there was nothing very funny about it in 1961,* and nor does there seem to be now. But the archive documents Bogarde's incognizance of his own cruelty, or at least his willingness to forget it. And that's something that a more fetishistic souvenir of the production – a pair of leather trousers, perhaps – would not record.'[24]

Dirk had recently been dubbed 'probably the most skilful tightrope walker in filmdom today',[25] and now he was about to cut a large hole in his own safety net. Under his existing contract he was guaranteed £40,000 a year for two films, with payment pro rata for any extra production. This agreement was due to expire in 1962. At the end of May, after returning from the *Singer* location via Normandy and a visit to the battlefields, he wrote to John Davis, asking carefully whether the existing arrangements could be varied to take account of two concerns. First, he had for some time intended that when the contract ended he would take advantage of the 'better tax situation accorded to Swiss residents'. Beel, he said, had been sold 'sooner than I envisaged, and I shall soon find myself without a home in England', so he was thinking of 'accelerating my change of residency to begin in April of next year'. Second, he viewed 'with some apprehension the lack of suitable subjects which have been offered to me over the past two years in England, both from within the Organisation and from outside. There are

---

* The film was shot in 1960 and had its première in 1961.

indications however that a certain amount of work may be available to me in America, although perhaps only with the kind of string attached that present arrangements preclude my accepting.' He felt it would not be ethical to ask to be released from his contract, but hoped it might be possible for their respective advisers to 'work out a scheme taking both of these considerations into account which would be acceptable to both sides'. He concluded: 'I regret that I find it necessary to bother you with this, but forty is a crucial age in any actor's career, and I am very concerned that in the next five years I shall be able to build up some kind of financial security before the demand for my services wears too thin.'[26] As Tony explained in a letter to Laurence Harbottle, Dirk was hoping the contract might be tweaked so that the four remaining films could be spread over a longer period, allowing for a clear financial year away from the United Kingdom. He had in mind Richard Burton, a British citizen and Swiss resident working in America, who 'seems to have this buttoned up'.[27] Davis refused. He would not even discuss a variation. This severe blow was received initially with calm, but by the end of June Dirk had been plunged into a deep depression. So much so that he wrote to Freddy Joachim – who had not known of the approach to Davis – saying that he wished to bring an immediate end to their own association, which by this time had lasted nearly fourteen years. Freddy replied in great distress, pointing out that Dirk had made wonderful progress of late and that wider horizons were opening up before him, 'but before they are within your grasp you are pulling everything up by the roots. And now it is my turn!'[28]

Although there was a reprieve for Freddy – at least until a parting of the ways with Rank – a great deal of bitterness swirled in the air off-set as *Singer* neared completion at Pinewood. Earl St John reported to Freddy that Dirk showed no sign of being depressed; indeed, he was 'doing a splendid job on the film', but when Freddy finally saw Davis to ask whether he would be willing to make any concessions, he was told: 'Why should I?'[29] As the rumour mill churned away, Tony reassured Freddy that Dirk intended to see out his contract 'in a businesslike way avoiding both enmity and friendship as regards Davis and St John insofar as possible, but he has no sentiment in regard to the past, and at the moment no particular faith in their intentions or abilities'.[30] From now on, at any meeting of importance with the company, Dirk insisted on having reinforcements, in the shape of Freddy or Laurence Harbottle. The marriage was ending in acrimony.

Meanwhile, 'A Magic Flame' had become 'Crescendo' which had become *Song Without End* – it might just as well have been 'Titles Without End' – and a New York opening was imminent. Dirk's American courtship pursued its on-off course. The producer trying to set up a remake of *The Four Horsemen of the Apocalypse*, with Vincente Minnelli directing, encountered resistance to Dirk from Sol Siegel, head of MGM, and the role went to Glenn Ford – a lucky escape, as the picture was a catastrophe. On the other hand, Spyros Skouras and Darryl Zanuck at Twentieth Century-Fox were on Dirk's side: in May there was talk of a possible 'several picture deal', and a discussion between John Davis and the

head of the studio, Buddy Adler. Charles Feldman encouraged Dirk by saying
that he felt sure Rank would change their mind about releasing him, because
with such a short period to run on the contract, time was on his side. At various
stages Dirk was in line to play Dick Diver in an adaptation of Scott Fitzgerald's
Tender Is the Night which was eventually made with Jason Robards Jr; and, a
more remote possibility, Jesus in a biblical epic written by Zanuck, in which the
principal starring role was to be that of Judas. Alas – if only for the cognoscenti
of that genre – the project came to nothing. For the moment there was nothing
concrete, just a finished piece to promote. Dirk and Tony sailed for New York
in late July, and were greeted at Pier 88 by a deputation from Columbia and two
of the renowned Rockettes from Radio City Music Hall, where the film was to
play. Dirk was in for ten days of 'Total Exposure', which would include at
least forty separate interviews, a cocktail party for 250 journalists and a guest
appearance on *What's My Line*. Fortunately he had left town when the *New
York Herald Tribune* gave a perfectly friendly piece the daunting headline:
'Millions Riding on Dirk Bogarde – Columbia Betting American Teenagers
Will Take to Him'.[31] There was very little chance that many of their mothers
would, thanks to a comment he made while in New York about women
tourists in Europe. He described them as 'ogre-like females', adding that hotel
lobbies were 'crammed with great crushes of these blue-haired ladies, carrying
huge handbags and being followed by their depressed looking, haggard and
money-bled husbands'.[32]

Whether George Cukor refused a director's credit on *Song Without End* out
of genuine respect for the unfortunate Vidor, or because he caught a whiff of
another carcass, we do not know; but he did the right thing. 'Keyboard clunker',
decreed *Newsweek*.[33] *The New Yorker* said little apart from noting that *Song
Without End* 'sometimes threatens to be' and that Dirk was 'a master of the
slightly agape mouth and the lifted left eyebrow'.[34] All those, however, who
mentioned Dirk the pianist echoed *Variety*, which found that 'his mock keyboard
fingerwork is a positively brilliant match to the exciting pianistics of soloist Jorge
Bolet'.[35] Things did not improve greatly on this side of the Atlantic. Dirk
summarised the position by saying that the film played successfully in New York
for a short time, did exactly the same in London, then died the death everywhere
else; 'it floated down the river of no return'.[36] After the British opening at the
Columbia Cinema, Tony noted that he and Dirk were 'very disappointed' by the
final cut, which suggests that they did not see a screening during the 'Total
Exposure' in New York. However, the première attracted the customary wave of
excitement, with the added ingredient of feverish speculation about the romantic
prospects of the two principals. 'Press lurking around house all day,' Tony
noted in the Diary. 'Dirk doesn't pop the question'; a 'too-theatrical-to-be-true
friendship', 'one of the most eligible (and most entrenched) bachelors' – an
innuendo here, a sly dig there – the gossip columns kept up the pressure. Dirk
found himself labelled naïve because he used the phrase 'just good friends', a

'comment he isn't often called upon to make'. Capucine, too, was a target. A diarist ruminated knowingly about how fond Dirk was of Judy Garland, Ava Gardner and Jean Simmons, all of whom were or had been married, whereas Capucine was not: 'It is something I find quite inexplicable.'[37]

She and Judy Garland were among the last visitors to stay at the Out-Patients Department. Judy Garland was preparing for one of her spasmodic comebacks, this time at the London Palladium, where her performances were to become a sort of homosexual Haj. One of her biographers, Brad Steiger, wrote:

> For those who live vicariously, a Garland concert had the exciting lure of a hurricane in Florida, a train wreck in Kansas, or an earthquake in California. It was like waiting for the unpredictable future on the edge of the world. Her professional and private life vacillated from the sensational to the disgraceful. She could be cheered by crowds in London and, a few months later, be heckled following her late arrival at a Melbourne concert with cries of 'Have another brandy, soak!'[38]

The novelist Paul Bailey remembers how whenever she was in town he and his fellow homosexuals were 'lured from the dark recesses of the twilight world' to pay homage: 'The atmosphere inside the Palladium was electric on Garland nights. The term "drama queen" might have been invented for her alone.'[39] There are various eyewitness accounts of one or more occasions when Dirk was singled out by Garland for special treatment. On 28 August 1960, as Dirk sat rigid with embarrassment on the stage in front of her, Garland crooned 'It Never Was You' at him. Paul Bailey recalls how 'she serenaded Dirk with "You Made Me Love You". He kept his smile in place as she warbled "I didn't wanna do it, I didn't wanna do it", and the audience applauded him for being such a good sport.'[40] Brian Baxter and the late Søren Fischer – who later organised an important talk by Dirk at the National Film Theatre – remembered how in 1963 he sat at her feet for the ordeal: 'At the end he got up, and as he walked off the stage, she shouted "Give my love to Tony!"'[41] The friendship somehow survived even that awkward moment. So reliant was Garland on the strength of the bond between herself and Dirk that during one of the many meltdown periods in her marriage to Sid Luft she apparently directed that her daughters, Liza and Lorna, 'are to be given to Dirk Bogarde or Capucine'.[42] It is perhaps worth noting the use of the word 'or', not 'and'.

At the time of Garland's two 1960 concerts, Dirk was, as he put it himself, in limbo. There was nothing to do for Rank and nothing definite from America. The plan to move abroad was very much on hold: he had not, as one newspaper blithely asserted, bought a chalet in Liechtenstein. However, he had disposed of Beel – with its proud cedars and the trees on Bogarde's Bastion coming along nicely – in a swift and private sale to Basil Dearden and his actress wife Melissa

Stribling.* A new house was needed, urgently. Guided by Bernard Walsh, an estate agent with a reputation for the utmost discretion, Dirk and Tony looked at Tickerage Mill, a Queen Anne property with five bedrooms beside a lake three miles from Uckfield. They were charmed, and tempted, but decided it was too small and too far from both London and the studios. They recommended it to Vivien Leigh, and it became her final home; when she died seven years later, her ashes were scattered on its lake. They looked at a Lutyens house near Silchester: 'foul,' noted Tony. And they looked at Birchens Spring, near Beaconsfield. As he handed over a cheque for £12,000, any doubts as to whether or not Dirk had inherited *folie de grandeur* from grandfather Aimé were about to be well and truly dispelled. Dirk was to christen his new residence 'The Palace'.

Birchens Spring was built in the thirties for a South African diamond merchant called Rissik. It was designed by John Campbell, who at the beginning of the century worked successfully in Germany, and had what Nikolaus Pevsner described in *The Buildings of England* as 'a strange, informal, rural monumentality'.[43] Set in about twelve acres on a rise alongside the road to Amersham, it was approached through a coppice of oaks. Two storeys tall, with three in the principal block, it was built of whitewashed brick and grey slates. There were seven bedrooms, three reception rooms and a staff bungalow. The dining-room, the pivot of activity in the household, was at the angle of the house's L-shape, at the base of a round tower with a conical roof. From the outside, it looked as if a monastery had made a merry match with a fragment of Loire château. On the inside it was, like the gardens, a bit of a mess – hence the knockdown price. For some years the house had been in the hands of the Invalid Children's Aid Association, but was empty and neglected when Dirk and Tony went to see it on 24 August; oddly enough, a Rank film crew had been using the exterior as a backdrop during the summer. Squads of landscape gardeners and interior decorators set to work, and on 24 October, after three days of packing with Ulric and Margaret at Beel, Dirk, Tony, the Sendelhofers, their belongings and their assorted creatures were conveyed in a fleet of vans and cars the few miles to Beaconsfield. Dirk's parents stayed for three weeks, Ulric's diary recording a heavy involvement in painting, distempering and woodwork. Elizabeth's husband, George, came with a team to returf the lawns and to work on a pond for the goldfish. About halfway through, there was a fireworks display in the courtyard. And at the end of the third week their first guest arrived – Elspeth March, bearing a leather-bound visitors' book engraved in gold lettering with the words Drummers Yard.

There had been much toying with names for the new house. At the back of Dirk's and Tony's sparsely kept Diary for that year is a list of sixteen, many of

---

* Basil Dearden and Melissa Stribling were killed in a car crash in 1971. Beel House was bought in the mid-eighties by the rock star Ozzy Osbourne; then by the songwriter Matt Aitken; and is now the home of the television presenter and politician Robert Kilroy-Silk.

them Germanic – Bitterfeld, Landshut, Ravensburg, Homburg – conceivably to reflect the architect's German influences, but more likely as a tip of the hat to Wolvenhof in Izegem, because penultimate on the list is Wolfsburg. Dirk seemed to have settled, for whatever reason, on Raiding Hall, because a full address is laid out, as if on a visiting card, above one of Tony's sketches of a sleek automobile. However, the list was disregarded and the final, punctuation-free, decision was Drummers Yard – after the tall figure in lead of a drummer boy which stood outside.

John Troke – purchaser of *Doctor in the House* from the railway bookstall in 1953 – had been involved in the summer filming and was struck by the monastic feel of the house. 'I have never seen anywhere so secluded,' he said, just after Dirk had bought it.[44] The need for invisibility was heightened by an event which took place at the end of October: the release of a long-playing record so execrable that when Elvis Costello came to choose 'the 500 albums essential to a happy life' he introduced his selection by writing: 'Ever needed to get rid of unwanted guests in the early hours? Just reach for Dirk Bogarde's *Lyrics for Lovers*, on which the actor inhales audibly on his cigarette before reciting Ira Gershwin's "A Foggy Day" amid a swathe of violins. Then there are the good records.'[45] All 499 of them. The origins of this felony against musical taste lay in an approach by Marcel Stellman, who was in charge of the international division at Decca. 'I used to go to the cinema and watch his terrible Rank movies,' he recalls. 'I thought, "This is a man that the women like – and the fellows don't object." '[46] Stellman wanted to find some way of using Dirk's voice, which he thought was 'of more than usual warmth' and not best served by the 'somewhat "boxy" acoustics of cinema soundtracks'.[47] After two years of trying to 'capture' Dirk, Stellman finally arranged through Laurence Harbottle to go to Beel, where Dirk and he discussed the idea in principle, rejecting a collection of Romantic poetry as no novelty, and deciding instead on one of pop song lyrics. After all, they agreed, 'there must be some out of all the thousands that have been written which can stand on their own two feet and be spoken like any other poetry'. Stellman returned, laden with the sheet music for about forty songs, saying: 'These are what I consider beautiful words.'[48] Dirk picked 'a baker's dozen' and a recording date was arranged. Stellman asked if he wanted any special facilities, and Dirk replied: 'It would be nice if you darkened the room.' At the beginning of June, Dirk went into the Decca studio. 'Twenty minutes of this,' he said to Stellman, 'and you will have had enough.'[49]

For about three hours, with just a piano accompaniment and never a need for more than two takes, Dirk breathed away at his chosen material, including 'I Get Along Without You Very Well', 'As Time Goes By', 'Just One of Those Things', 'Our Love Affair' and, with a maximum exhalation, 'Smoke Gets in Your Eyes'. 'He was very professional,' Stellman recalls, 'patient, easy to be with – no prima donna or anything like that.'[50] At the end the initially reluctant recording artist pronounced himself satisfied. The next stage was for the Eric

Rogers Orchestra to ladle some syrup onto the backing track, for a title to be chosen and a cover photograph taken. The second of these tasks was contractually the responsibility of the record company, so that, as Tony explained in a letter to Freddy Joachim, Dirk would be in the clear 'should Ranks be annoyed at the outcome. We have in fact agreed on "Lyrics for Lovers" and I presume it will be used. However I wonder if we ought to protect ourselves in the event that they might at a later stage decide on a title which might offend the dignity of Dirk's position as an actor – we wouldn't want anything like "Lover Boy"!'[51] That would have been to gild the lily; for the photograph on the sleeve, taken in full glorious colour by George Courtney Ward, showed Dirk in super-sultry mode, his back to a sculptured pillar and jacketed against the cold. The whites of his eyes appeared to have been touched-up, so Omo-brightly did they gleam. Seven months after the recording session, they shone out at the record-buying public like those of a big cat in the jungle night; in this case, the kill lay inside the sleeve. 'As a stunt,' said the *Daily Herald,* 'the record scores 100 marks out of 100. Thousands of women will sigh over it. And any two tracks, if issued as a single play, will rocket Dirk Bogarde into the Top Ten – on gimmick value alone. But even with the first-class lyrics of Cole Porter, one cannot class any of these vintage songs as poetry.'[52] It was even rumoured that Dirk had tried to suppress the record – a sure-fire way of enhancing sales. By the end of 1960 it had amassed royalties due to Dirk of £232 16s 9d.[53]

He would always disparage *Lyrics for Lovers,* telling Clifford Castle at Rediffusion Television in 1967 that it 'ought never to have been made!' He said it made him sound 'a twit'.[54] Yet something remarkable happened at the beginning of the eighties. Exactly twenty-one years after the original release, Decca put the record out again, on a budget label. It attracted more correspondence and enquiries than any other record that had ever been played on *The David Jacobs Show* and led to a press officer at the company saying that Dirk, who had acquired cult status, 'has been quoted as a source of inspiration by many of today's leading figures in the pop world'[55] – but not, please God, because of *Lyrics for Lovers.*

The first name in the Drummers Yard visitors' book was that of Capucine. In fact she wrote 'Capucine Froguy' – a little joke on her origins in Toulon. She came to stay for Christmas, thus exciting further speculation about Dirk's intentions. 'Our friendship is a very dear and wonderful thing,' she said when she was back in London, trapped in a corner by the man from the *Daily Herald,* which kept a closer watch than most on Dirk's activities. A 'cosy family party' completed by Dirk's parents, was how the newspaper described the holiday; it would have been too complicated to explain that Gareth Forwood, too, was there, as was Irene Howard. She remained the most prominent of that tight circle of regular guests, dominated by Dirk's and Tony's women friends: 'Bumble' Dawson, Olive Dodds, Elspeth March, Daphne Fielding, Ann Firbank, Julie Harris, Alexis Smith – when in England – and Philippa, Lady Astor, who was seen from time to time on Dirk's arm at a première. Among the newer recruits were Rex Harrison's son Noel and his wife Sara, plus their brood who seem to have been tolerated. All these were augmented by the 'irregulars' – usually people in or connected with the business, and sometimes with the projects in which Dirk's two companies were making their modest investments. In each of the houses during the late fifties and early sixties the big fixture was Sunday lunch, and here again we are indebted to Barbara Murray for a description of Dirk's preparatory week:

> From Monday to Wednesday afternoon, he would grumble incessantly about the ghastly people he had had down to his house for the weekend, how they had drunk all his booze and bored the pants off him. On Wednesday evening there would be the slight beginnings of panic, about who he was going to ask for the next weekend. On Thursday and Friday there would be frantic attempts to get somebody to come down – that famous charm would ooze from every pore. The poor bastards on the other end didn't realise how they would be maligned the following week. Dear old Dirk.[56]

Many are the accounts of the entertaining, especially in that round dining-room with its green-and-white-striped canopy, and with the simplest of food: Irish stew a speciality. None is more bizarre than that of Willis Hall who, with Keith Waterhouse, had been engaged to adapt John Osborne's play *Epitaph for George Dillon*, which Dirk intended to produce under the Bendrose umbrella and in which he might be persuaded to star. Waterhouse and Hall, who had just had a big success with *Billy Liar* on both stage and screen, were invited to lunch at Drummers on their own, but with the strong possibility that Capucine might be in residence. They were agog, because the word fizzing round the entertainment world at the time was that Mademoiselle Lefebvre was in fact a fellow:

> I don't drive, Keith does so rarely, and as a 'social invitation' hinted that there could be a drink or three involved, we hired a chauffeur-driven vehicle from a well-known showbusiness car-hire firm of that time titled Miles and Miles. As we passed through the impressive gates, the first thing that caught the eye was Tony Forwood, in an apron, adroitly manoeuvring a Hoover on a long flex – vacuuming the lawn.
>
> Dirk appeared and welcomed us warmly. Tony, having discarded both vacuum-cleaner and apron, poured champagne. As the four of us chatted, I took the opportunity to sneak a glance at Dirk's collection of pictures. I noticed that he had a couple of 'Leaping Nuns' by Jonathan Routh – a friend of mine at that time who, not long before, had given up *Candid Camera* to become an artist. The house was enormous, luxurious and immaculate, but there was no sign of any servants – nor, disappointingly, of Capucine.
>
> One bottle of champagne led to a second, with Tony topping up glasses.

After some minutes, Dirk excused himself and disappeared in the direction of the kitchen. Muted raised voices drifted back. Dirk returned and instantly became the perfect host again – and as charmingly and as courteously as one would expect Dirk Bogarde to play such a part on the screen. Time passed pleasantly enough – occasionally though, he would disappear and the voices from the kitchen grew a little louder . . .

Eventually we went into the dining-room. It was a circular room, with a conservatory-style glass ceiling. The table was impeccably laid: gleaming cutlery, crystal glasses, neatly folded napkins. Champagne gave way to Chablis . . . Two p.m. was fast approaching but still no sign of lunch. Dirk excused himself yet again. The voices from the kitchen sounded a little louder and a little more strained. I had assumed by now, and I guessed Keith was of the same opinion, that the other voice in the kitchen was Capucine's and that for whatever reason – servants' day off? – she had been deputed to prepare the meal. Dirk came back, wearing an apologetic Bogarde half-smile. We moved on to a second bottle of Chablis and the elegant French clock on the dining-room's elegant marble mantlepiece ticked on towards 2.30 . . .

We were, I think, all of us a little tipsy when Capucine swept in, bearing a large silver salver. She slammed it onto the table. 'There you are, cunt,' she said conversationally, and swept out. We all looked curiously at the covered dish. Dirk raised an eyebrow, that half-smile again, then leaned forward and lifted the cover. Lunch was revealed: Heinz Spaghetti in Tomato Sauce. And in some quantity.

Dirk was in no way fazed. He picked up the server and ladled tinned spaghetti onto all our plates. We took up our cutlery and ate. The spaghetti was unheated. Capucine's culinary skills had been stretched so far as to open three or four tins of Heinz Spaghetti and empty them into the salver. We all carried on as though nothing at all had happened out of the ordinary – indeed, as though cold tinned spaghetti was our all-time favourite dish. Perhaps the waiting time, coupled with champagne and Chablis, had added an edge to our appetite? I seem to remember that we were offered, and accepted, 'seconds'.

Afterwards, we thanked our host profusely, made our farewells, and moved back towards the waiting car with its attendant uniformed chauffeur. No mention had been made of the lunch itself.

Neither of the guests has any idea what was really going on that day. 'I don't believe that the row had anything to do with the lunch,' says Hall. 'I think it was something that had been simmering all morning, or possibly even longer. Whichever way – it was an extraordinary luncheon.'[57] Needless to say they never found out whether Capucine was indeed 'a chap in a dress'. Sadder to relate, their 'George Dillon' screenplay remained unfilmed, as did another treatment for Bendrose, 'Covenant with Death', from a novel by John Harris about the

Battle of the Somme. But the two writers had enjoyed the company, and the unorthodox hospitality, of Dirk and Tony.

Basil Dearden and his wife Melissa, Beel's new owners, were among the occasional visitors to Drummers Yard. On 29 December 1960 Dearden came alone to see Dirk and to talk about a script which was to have an impact far beyond its authors' expectations. Janet Green and John McCormick were a husband-and-wife writing team whose skill was to present strong social argument inside a more palatable – and commercial – veneer. In collaboration with Michael Relph, as producer, and Dearden as director, they were responsible for *Sapphire*, a straightforward police thriller attacking the racial prejudice which had led to recent riots in London and the Midlands. In May 1960, sight unseen, Rank paid 'Janet and John' – as they were usually addressed – £10,000 plus the promise of a five per cent slice off any producer profits, for the rights to a screenplay entitled 'Boy Barrett', which would be filmed by Relph and Dearden. Its subject, again thinly cloaked inside a thriller format, was the blackmailing of homosexuals – specifically, a barrister, Melville Farr, at the height of his career.

Some idea of the difficulties entailed in approaching the issue of homosexuality under the law can be gathered from correspondence shared between the British Board of Film Censors with both producer and writers. At the synopsis stage the Board's Secretary, John Trevelyan, was warning that most intelligent people came to the matter 'with sympathy and compassion, but to the great majority of cinema-goers homosexuality is outside their direct experience and is something which is shocking, distasteful and disgusting'. He stressed that the subject had never actually been banned from the screen in Britain, but because the American Motion Picture Production Code would not allow it to be dealt with at all, there had until recently been little censorship trouble. In fact the only problem the Censors had had so far was with rival and practically simultaneous films about the trials of Oscar Wilde; but historical fact and the suppression of detail about homosexuality itself eased the path to a certificate. Trevelyan felt that public education might be desirable, but would need to be undertaken with caution by any film-maker. In the very week that Trevelyan gave the writers his thoughts about their first full script the Wolfenden Report was debated in the House of Commons and, he said, indicated that a majority was still opposed to the compassionate treatment of homosexuals. He was especially concerned that the script of 'Boy Barrett' gave the impression, unwittingly, that 'the world is largely peopled with queers'. He took issue with thirteen specific scenes, but more generally was reassured that the writers were concentrating on the essential courage and morality of the central character.[58]

Relph and Dearden laid out their stall in a letter to the writers, in which Relph said that 'Boy Barrett' was likely to be the first wholly adult and serious approach to homosexuality that the British cinema had made: 'What I think we want to say is that the homosexual, although subject to a psychological or glandular variation from sexual normality, is a human being subject to all the emotions of other human beings, and as deserving of our understanding. Unless he sets out to corrupt others, it is wrong for the law to pillory him because of his inversion.' It was, added Relph, 'a story not of glands but of love'.[59]

As the months went by, and traffic with the Censor decreased while that between the producers and the writers grew in quantity as well as heat, casting became a worry. Relph and Dearden were part of Allied Film Makers, which they had founded with Richard Attenborough, Bryan Forbes, Jack Hawkins and the director Guy Green, to work independently but with a financial attachment to Rank. Their original thought for the role of Mel was Hawkins himself. However, by November and with a projected start date in mid-January, there were doubts about whether he would be available because he was needed for the part of General Allenby in the David Lean *Lawrence of Arabia*. That, at least, was the official version; in fact *Lawrence* could never have been under way in the time available. Even so, Hawkins did not entirely rule himself out. With that problem unresolved, Rank began to worry about both the content and the title. John Davis took a copy of the script with him on a business trip to America. Earl St John felt there were still too many queers in the picture – alas, we do not know his precise phrasing. Dearden's suggestion of calling the film 'The Blackmailers' found no favour whatever with Janet Green, but Relph's 'Boy on the Scaffold' might do, provided there was no risk of people thinking a hangman was involved. The writers pleaded that a line about homosexuality being almost as grave a so-called crime as robbery with violence should be reinstated because it had been fundamental to the Wolfenden Report. All in all, the business of setting up a movie was just as fraught as ever.

By Christmas it was still 'Boy Barrett' and still on – by the skin of its teeth. And then, on 2 January, Relph wrote to Janet and John with an exciting development. Hawkins still did not like the script – 'for *me*' – and finally said no; it is now received wisdom that he was concerned the role of Mel might compromise his image as a British star as masculine as they come – might even, as Dirk put it, 'prejudice his chances of a Knighthood'.[60] James Mason turned it down because for tax reasons he could not make another film in England. Stewart Granger was not free, and in any case John Davis would have vetoed him. Relph and Dearden thought again. It was a story of a man whose marriage and career are threatened by the consequences of homosexual impulses: 'Provided he is old enough to have a brilliant career in the Law, isn't it more moving and more urgent for predominantly youthful audiences if it is a younger man and a younger marriage?' Suppose they made him a young barrister about to take silk, rather than a judge who had been married for thirty years and for whom 'the sexual side of life would not be of vital importance'? At which point – whether by divine inspiration or misplaced malice is unclear – Earl St John suggested Dirk. With him in mind, Relph and Dearden studied the screenplay microscopically, and decided that 'astonishingly little adjustment was needed to make it fit him wonderfully well'. They sent it to him and, 'in spite of obvious dangers for him, he jumped at it'. There is no doubt, Relph told the writers, that 'this is the most commercial casting one could have hoped for, and that he will give a wonderfully sensitive performance'.[61] Shooting was to start on the 30th.

Thirteen

'It is comforting to think that perhaps a million men
are no longer living in fear'

irk's final shooting script for the film which brought him back to Pinewood has on its first page: 'BOY BARRETT (Working Title)'. This he has scored out and replaced with 'VICTIM'. Bound inside, under his specific instructions, is a fascinating chart, plotting Melville Farr's emotional course through the story, with circled scene numbers interrupting the snaking black line; and above the thirteenth of these roundels, highlighted with a star, Dirk has written 'Final break down'. Scene 112 of *Victim* was, and remains, the most important of his acting life. Much of it he himself wrote, or rewrote. Confronted by his beautiful wife, Laura, the barrister is asked to explain who this Boy Barrett was, how they knew each other, and why Mel stopped seeing him. Eventually Mel says:

> Alright – alright, you want to know, I'll tell you – you wont be content until I tell you will you – until you've *ripped* it out of me – I stopped seeing him because *I wanted* him. Can you understand – because I *wanted* him. Now what good has that done you?*

Originally the speech read: 'You won't be content till I tell you. I put the boy outside the car because I wanted him. Now what good has that done you?' The force with which Dirk delivered his extra dialogue to Sylvia Syms made it unforgettable. It was the moment when the matinée idol donned a new cloak of seriousness; when 'Peter Pan' grew up; when 'Dorian Gray' allowed us with him to take a peep into the attic.

Dirk had a writer's hand in many of his scenes in *Victim*: there is a fine Bogardian simile when he describes one of his former fellow undergraduates at Cambridge as 'possessive as a vine'. But he did not need to alter – only highlight on the page – a Green/McCormick sentence which had Mel say: 'Of course the

---

* Author's italics.

young must be protected, but I've come to believe that adult men, who by nature are different, have as much right to find a partner in kind as the normal man or woman.'[1] On the final page, where Mel prepares to place on the fire a photograph of him with a weeping Boy Barrett and tells Laura how desperately he will need her when 'the shouting has stopped', there is also, uniquely, an amendment in Tony's writing: 'You must have time to decide.' This was a role about which they had no qualms. While *Victim* was still in production, an article appeared in *Films and Filming* which stated that Rank were to make 'a film about homosexuality starring Dirk Bogarde'. Dirk wrote sharply back saying that Rank were *not* making the film – Allied were; nor did Rank have any controls. He had accepted the script 'as it stood with no changes or alterations whatsoever, neither has the Rank Organisation requested any on my behalf', and its subject 'is not an "examination" of homosexuality but deals simply with the break-up of a man's marriage and life owing to the fact that he is flawed by homosexual tendencies'. He added: 'It is distressing, in a paper of your kind, to read such inaccurate reporting especially for once when one is trying to get out of the Simon Sparrow category (however excellent and delightful he was to play) and join forces with a team who are honestly trying to develop with a new and exciting trend in the Cinema today.'[2]

In later life Dirk would pooh-pooh the commonly held and almost invariably spoken belief that he had been 'brave' to play Melville Farr. He once said that no homosexual actor would appear in the film, 'so we had a lot of very straight heterosexuals camping themselves silly in it'.[3] Which, of course, was nonsense: Dennis Price, for one, was at the time well-known to be living with another man. Over the years Dirk talked and wrote of Relph and Dearden holding a meeting on the first morning and announcing that there was to be no reference on the set to homos, poofs, queens, queers, fags or faggots. 'So what the hell *do* we call them?' enquired Dirk. Basil said: 'We use the word on this set "inverts".' Another favourite story involved the reverential air during shooting – 'like making the Life of Christ backwards' – and how it was broken only when on the second Monday a chippie bent down and a voice cried from the gantry: 'Watch yer arse, Alfie!'[4] Or, sometimes, Charlie. Sylvia Syms was five months pregnant when, after several other actresses had turned the part down, she agreed to play Laura. 'We had to do it all in ten days,' she recalls. She agrees that the film itself was a brave undertaking – even 'revolutionary' – but she does not sign up completely to the general view that it was an act of courage for Dirk to play Mel: 'They say he was so brave to play this man with those feelings. But look at the lines he himself wrote. He was frightened of those emotions, and didn't want to admit them, but, when he had to, he wanted to play them with great truth.'[5] After watching the 'I wanted him' scene again recently, Sylvia Syms said that Dirk 'obviously felt about it very passionately. It was deeply moving.' She remembers that at one point she had to be stopped from crying, because tears were unnecessary – 'you just needed to see the pain really'. And in Dirk she recognised 'the pain behind the eyes'. She considers that in their big scene he revealed 'quite a lot about himself – which I don't think was just about whether he was in love with somebody or not – of either sex'. She believes he had the characteristics of the celibate, of one who, like the late Kenneth Williams, 'loves to watch, to tell dirty stories, but who does not like the messiness, the untidiness of sex'. Certainly the monastic simplicity with which Dirk always furnished his bedrooms would tend to bear out that theory, at least in part. At the same time, Sylvia Syms feels sure, he was 'capable of great love'; and he certainly loved great beauty, at a cerebral but uncomplicated level. When she and her husband Alan Edney – who had nothing to do with the film business – visited Drummers Yard, the latter would spend much of the time with Dirk in the garden discussing and admiring the plants and flowers. And when Sylvia Syms lost the baby she was carrying at the time she made *Victim*, and was extremely unwell, her hospital room was a riot of exquisite blooms carefully chosen by Dirk. The pain behind his own eyes made him the more sympathetic to that in others.

Bob Thomson operated the camera on *Victim* and remembers that although there was not a feeling on the studio floor of a 'ground-breaker', the crew did recognise that something out of the ordinary was going on. 'This was mainly because Dirk was giving such a sincere performance. It gave an atmosphere, and made us think we were making a film that was different from the normal run. Perhaps he was at ease.'[6] Not everyone was. At lunch after the press show of *No Love for Johnnie*, its director, Ralph Thomas, told the film critic of the *Evening Standard*, Alexander Walker, how concerned he was about Dirk taking the leading role in 'the homosexual picture now on the set at Pinewood'. Thomas thought it would ruin Dirk's career. A few days later Walker noted in his diary that a mutual friend had told him of Dirk's 'attitude of bewildering exploration with which he has approached new film on homosexuals. Apparently those who urged him not to make it – i.e. Ralph Thomas – are in bad odour.'[7]

The problem with the cinema is also its advantage. Unlike the theatre, where the verdict is delivered on the night and every night, a film is not judged until long after it has been shot, cut, tinkered with and sometimes made unrecognisable. The arrangement usually suited Dirk down to the ground: he worked under protected conditions, without the terror of facing an audience as he did so, and by the time his efforts came under public scrutiny he had long gone on to the next project. A flop could be dismissed with a shrug; there was something better coming along behind. The difficulty now, as Dirk turned forty, was that he would not know for at least five months whether the risk he had taken in seizing with both hands the role of Mel had paid off. Once again, there was nothing in the pipeline for him to do. In May, Tony had lunch with Earl St John to discuss ending the Rank contract, and went away reasonably confident that John Davis would finally agree. At this point Alexander Walker was pleasantly surprised to be invited to spend a Sunday at Drummers Yard, on the understanding that he would not breathe a word to anyone that Judy Garland was staying; '[Dirk] said that a Mr

Needle of the *Mirror* had already been needling him'.[8] Dirk's relationship with the press was very much at arm's length, with a few exceptions – notably Derek Monsey, Tom Wiseman and Margaret Hinxman, the last of whom had been a faithful and friendly monitor of his progress since the earliest days. Walker travelled to Beaconsfield, to be met by Dirk and Tony and driven to their 'huge white L-shaped house with notices saying Mastiff At Large' – there was, too, in the shape of a nineteen-month-old bitch originally called Mandy but now Candy.

It was, recorded Walker, a 'wonderful, wonderful day', during which Judy Garland, on her best form, regaled the small company with stories about John Kennedy and the White House – he arrived to find its parquet floors pocked by the spiked shoes of his predecessor, 'Ike', a famously avid golfer – and enthralled them by playing on the gramophone a first pressing, which had just been flown from New York, of the recording from her triumphant Carnegie Hall concert three days earlier. Dirk confided in Walker that his plans were not going well; he felt he had 'missed the tide' with *Epitaph for George Dillon*, and no American company was interested in financing 'Covenant with Death' because it was about the First World War: 'He seemed regretful at having played to his fans so long.' Walker was invited back two months later, and although he found Dirk excellent company, felt he was 'a bit lonely and rather out of things' – something of a recluse in his huge house where, to Walker, he seemed at that time to be living alone, so discreet was Tony's presence. Many years later, Walker said: 'I think Dirk could hardly get work. He was begging his agent to get him a part in *HMS Defiant* as a sea captain! In Nelson's day! No one was offering him parts now, because they associated him with being queer. To that extent the apprehension of directors like Ralph Thomas was borne out.'[9] Sylvia Syms put it another way: 'After making *Victim*, Dirk couldn't get *arrested*!'[10]

It was not an easy time for the agent, Dennis van Thal. In a warm, even 'hearty', letter Dirk had said goodbye to Freddy and was now signed to London Management, which van Thal, a former musical arranger, casting director and producer, had established two years earlier with another, younger, casting director, Jean Diamond. There was no problem about possible insularity here: because of his background in theatre and film van Thal, born in London of Dutch parents, was impressively connected, and his roster of clients would soon be second to none. On his hands now, though, was someone who had deliberately cast himself adrift – in June Rank announced that at Dirk's own request his contract was at an end – and who was now professionally dislocated, dependent for his future career on the reception for a highly controversial and possibly doomed little thriller. Yes, Dirk had the trappings: the newest BH5, the resident staff – Hans and Agnes were back from America, but not for long – and his stylishly decorated and furnished mansion. Already, though, its attractions were wearing thin: Tony noted on the Whit Monday bank holiday that Dirk was unable to work in the vegetable garden because of sightseers, which slightly begs the question of how secluded Drummers Yard really was. Alexander Walker's diary mentions Dirk telling him of 'the fan letters and the fan *attacks* he has made on him by letter and assault as well as people who spy on the house'.[11] When Betty Box and her husband Peter Rogers came to Drummers Yard for drinks, they offered to buy it; Tony logged the proposal with an exclamation mark, but logged it just the same.

Inside the entertaining continued at an impressive level. Overnight guests would be shown the best available films on Dirk's and Tony's sixteen-millimetre projector, and played the latest Broadway recordings on the gramophone. On a larger scale, Noël Coward noted in his diary that he had attended 'a charming party given by Dirk Bogarde for Judy Garland at Beaconsfield. Joyce [Carey] and I drove down and enjoyed ourselves enormously.'[12] This was the 'shimmering evening' when, 'in the fading light of the summer sun, everyone sat round the grand piano' while Garland and Coward 'sang for their suppers' and their duet on 'If Love Were All' 'brought the packed room roaring to its feet'.[13] Sylvia Syms recalls that Garland was on her best behaviour: 'She talked to me very sweetly, and I couldn't see that there was anything wrong with her. Noël sat at the piano and started to play the entire score of "Sail Away", and Judy fell asleep on the sofa.'[14]

Dirk had to work, and not simply to finance the keeping-up of appearances; two years earlier his accountant had reported to Laurence Harbottle that although Dirk was earning a very large income, he was also spending 'a very great deal' – that year alone, about £16,000 from his own account, excluding taxes.[15] He used to say that he was lazy, but he could never be accused of idleness. For someone so powered by nervous energy, and leading an existence with elements of the preposterous about it, activity was essential; otherwise the demons might hold sway. With nothing to do, Dirk became depressed – seriously, if not clinically so. 'Like gardening – where he planned things meticulously – maybe Dirk found the work was his therapy,' reflects Sylvia Syms. 'It is for many of us.'

It might be worth pausing here to look from a different perspective at Dirk as he began his fifth decade; he himself had carried out a form of stock-taking by signing up with *Woman* magazine for an interview which was published under his signature for five successive weeks shortly before the fortieth birthday – the closest he had come so far to telling his life story at any length. For the present book Renata Propper, a graphologist who lives and works in America, was sent half a dozen samples of his handwriting for analysis. To her, knowing the name of the subject makes no difference, and in this case she knew nothing about Dirk, had no idea that he had written any books, and had seen only two of the later films. The samples, she says, have to be seen as 'snapshots' because at least a decade separates them; however, like the scenic chart in his *Victim* script, they make a coherent progression. The seventeen-year-old Dirk, who had left Allan Glen's, was a gifted, highly intelligent young man, with a pleasant, sympathetic personality. Not the typical boarding school boy, but a sensitive and artistic youngster, who tries to reach out, seeking understanding. While he is still dependent on the family structure, he must have received sufficient nurturing that made a basic self-acceptance possible. He seems an assertive young boy, who already had developed a certain ego that demanded acknowledgment and recognition. He had little doubt that there was a place for him, once he decided on the direction to take. The handwriting is controlled, hemmed in by the conventional limitations of the background he depended on, without much rebellious spirit.

He might have been unhappy, added the graphologist in conversation, 'but it didn't get him down. He had enough sense of self. And he had enough basic nurture from home to be able to handle it. A resilience. He wants to impress.' She detected 'a great attachment – a bit of a Momma's boy. And the handwriting could be as much a girl's as it is a boy's. There is a definite feminine touch.' By contrast, when Dirk was twenty-four and with the Army in Europe, his writing 'suggests strong mobility and drive, having acquired a more active, aggressive character. While spontaneous and outgoing, it also reflects the inner "fermentation" of conflicting currents and under-currents that must have influenced his state of mind and mode. Also, his ego and need for recognition are growing. While he is a talented young man on the make, he stays susceptible and reactive to the vibes of his environment.'

At forty, she found that Dirk's 'always-sensitive personality seems particularly vulnerable'. He had from the start 'a good vitality to back his efforts, but in 1961 they seem at a low ebb. There could have been some emotional or physical setbacks, making him feel more susceptible than usual and low in spirit.' Again, in conversation, Renata Propper added: 'There is a deficit of energy and strength. You see the struggle, the conflicting currents. He looks a bit defeated, a bit weak. There is anxiety. He wasn't that sure what he was doing.' More generally, she said that Dirk was 'so multi-lateral, he had so many facets'.

> While in his life they were very heavy to bear it was possible to find an outlet in his work. Without that he would have been very miserable, and in a constant depression. He has his basic vitality to thank, which must have come from a strong and happy family childhood. Although he might have been miserable [in Glasgow], he had had the right nurturing. He was happy in his nuclear family – it was 'money in the bank'. That was the cement on which he could build. Without that he would have fluctuated more.[16]

The references to the 'cement' provided by the Van den Bogaerde family are especially interesting, because Dirk continually drew on its strength and protection. As we have seen, on foreign holidays and on location, either his parents or sister frequently joined him and Tony. There was a hint of the chaperone about these arrangements. Elizabeth recalls how the telephone would ring, and it would be Dirk, saying he and Tony were off to the Continent within forty-eight hours and would she like to come? Of course she would – which made life a little difficult at home for her husband George with two young children to handle; but a great deal of understanding was shown. Dirk was constantly in touch with Ulric and Margaret, who frequently 'house-sat' for him if the staff were away. But with brother Gareth? Not if he could help it.

Gareth was now twenty-eight and his existence on earth had not been forgiven. It never truly would. Hopelessly dyslexic – without him or anyone else being aware, as was common in those days – he had grown up with a deep inferiority complex. He describes his treatment at his public school, Hurstpierpoint, as 'inhuman' because, like so many with his affliction, he was regarded as simple. Immediately after the brief art school period, when he stayed with Dirk, Tony and Eve at Chester Row, he somewhat rashly tried to be an actor. Nothing would be more likely to stir Dirk's green-eyed monster than his own flesh and blood working in the same milieu. Playing Will Latch's son, at fourteen, in *Esther Waters* was one thing; acting as a decoy, so that Dirk could escape from fans outside the Theatre Royal in Brighton, was positively welcomed. But to go into the profession? And to use the name Bogarde? That was in the high-risk category. With an introduction from their father, Gareth presented himself at the Q Theatre, where Beatie de Leon said he could paint scenery – oddly enough, with Tony's cousin Mary Forwood – and could sit in on readings, for a pound a week: 'You pay us. At the end of six weeks, if you are satisfactory, we will pay *you* two pounds a week and you can also do some walk-on parts.' So there, among the Q programmes from the early fifties, is Gareth Bogarde in the cast of Rattigan's *Who Is Sylvia?* and appearing alongside Barbara Murray in a farce called *To Dorothy, a Son.* National Service in the RAF might have steered him on a different course, but after three months be was invalided out because of an ear infection, and sought work first at the Arts Theatre Club, where he helped with the stage lighting, then at the Theatre Royal Windsor, where he appeared in *A Midsummer Night's Dream*: 'It didn't last – I used to be sick every night before going on.' Fortunately the newsreel division of Gaumont British had a vacancy in its foreign news department, and Gareth went to Denham Studios to learn how to cut and to 'feel' film, under the guidance of 'a wild homosexual who used to throw his typewriter out of the window and go cottaging at Marylebone railway sidings. When I asked him why, he said, "My dear – the *fear!*" '

At nineteen Gareth was foreign editor of Gaumont British News, where, after helping to complete an acclaimed documentary on an Italian underwater expedition to the Red Sea, he knew that his future lay in editing film. There was a brief but eventful interlude when Orson Welles appeared in the West End as Captain Ahab in *Moby Dick*. Kenneth Williams was in the cast and recalled seeing at the theatre one day a young man with an uncanny resemblance to a famous film star:

> I asked him if he was Dirk Bogarde and he replied, 'No, I'm his brother Gareth.' He went on to explain that he'd been appointed personal assistant to Orson. 'Then don't stay here,' I warned him, 'the last one left after only a week, and the one before that wasn't much longer.' Gareth was assuring me he knew how to handle temperament when Orson appeared expostulating, 'Why haven't you found me somewhere to live?' and dismissed him before he had time to reply. Gareth went the way of all the others.[17]

By the mid-fifties Gareth was installed on the first floor of the cutting-room block at Pinewood, the very studio where Dirk was now in his pomp. Bogarde major came to work by Rolls-Royce; Bogarde minor, by bus. They hardly ever met or spoke, and when they did, it was very much as superior and underling: 'He was offhand and terribly self-important. He didn't like me associating with stars.' Unlike his brother, Gareth did not avoid the bar at the end of the day, and spent many happy hours there with Kenneth More and Peter Finch. He struck up his own friendship with Kay Kendall, who, he says, 'could sense that Dirk and Tony had some weird thing going'. The stars were invariably affable towards him: 'Everybody was normal, nice, and would pass the time of day. I used to go to the make-up room, and onto the sound stages, and loved it. I never dared to go on to one of Dirk's sets.' A low point in their relationship came when a writer from the *Daily Sketch* came to Pinewood, met Gareth, and produced an article printed under the headline 'ALL HE WANTS IS TO BE AN ACTOR – Brother keeps him from fame', in which Gareth was quoted as saying that the similarity with his brother caused producers to 'take one look at me and decide I'm too much like Dirk'. He was made to sound almost as aggrieved as one of the homosexuals in *Victim* who says: 'Nature played me a dirty trick.' The piece finished with Gareth declaring: 'My greatest dread is that if I stay here long enough I will have to edit a film with my own brother in it. That would be too much.'[18] In fact, Gareth was having the time of his life, doing what he really wanted to do and, for the most part, doing so in congenial company. By 1961 he was producing commercials and had his own company, Quebec Films, for which he was writing screenplays; one of them, a comedy intended for television under the title 'Coaches Welcome', was bought by Dirk's and Tony's Motley Films for the princely sum of £120. He was married, to a soldier's daughter, and had three sons. He was no longer any threat to Dirk, but even so would never be approached as his equal. 'My inferiority complex was hatched at school,' Gareth reflects unemotionally, 'and incubated over many years by my brother.' Theirs was, he says, 'a love-hate relationship. I loved. He hated.'

As for Dirk's own complexes at this delicate moment, the thinly kept Diary inevitably discloses nothing. There is uncorroborated information – at second

hand, but from a disinterested source – that at the end of the fifties and the
beginning of the sixties Dirk would be admitted, once a year and under conditions
of great secrecy, to University College Hospital, where he would receive treatment
in a ward devoted to homosexual aversion therapy. It should be borne in mind
that at this time homosexuality was still listed officially as a mental disorder, and
remained so until 1973. Dirk, if the account is correct, would spend a week on
the ward, where he would be shown erotic pictures of men while being administered drugs to make him vomit. His only visitor was a doctor. All the staff were
sworn to confidentiality, and were instructed never to refer to him by name, but
always as 'Sir'. There is another story, again unauthenticated, that Dirk was for
a short time – perhaps just once – a patient of the late Masud Khan, a charismatic,
controversial and now discredited psychoanalyst who had been a protégé of
Freud's daughter, Anna. Khan was married to the Royal Ballet prima ballerina
Svetlana Beriosova and, largely thanks to her, had gained access to the highest
reaches of London society and the new artistic aristocracy, through which he
prowled like some tall, sleek, feral cat, name-dropping, gossiping, drinking too
much, even having affairs with a woman patient and with the wife of another.
His behaviour – and, as it became clear, his analytical methods – were utterly at
odds with his professional discipline, but somehow Khan flourished. According
to a harrowing memoir by Wynne Godley, the former government economist
whose seven years in Khan's clutches were a systematic psychological torture,
'culminating in a spiral of degradation', Khan would slink about at parties, giving
the rich and famous instant analyses, and telling disagreeable stories about their
contemporaries.[19] This was the Anglo-Pakistani charlatan whom Dirk is alleged
to have seen at the height of speculation about his relationship with Capucine.
The technique was to 'look for the weakness' and, as Godley confirmed in his
memoir, Khan was terrifyingly adept at doing so. 'I don't think you are looking
for Capucine,' he is alleged to have said to Dirk. 'You are looking for Mr
Forwood.' Which will not have been of very much help. A leading London
doctor who knew Khan and came into contact with Dirk, not professionally but
through connections with the film industry, says it is extremely unlikely that any
consultation took place, 'because Khan was so indiscreet that he would have
boasted about it to me'. In any case, if Dirk was seriously attempting to do
something about his sexuality, 'they made a bloody bad job of it!'

Victim opened while Dirk was on the high seas off Spain, shooting sequences for
HMS Defiant, in which he was able to release any latent sadism as Lieutenant
Scott-Padget, a ruthless first officer ambitious for the job of the decent skipper,
played by Alec Guinness. So low was Dirk's status with the American studios
that the director, Lewis Gilbert, had to fight for him to be cast. Guinness, too,
took his side, saying at one point in the negotiations: 'No Dirk, no Alec.' It was
the first and only time that they acted opposite each other, and provided uneven
contests both for the memory and for the affections of the audience. Dirk's

character was a chilling combination of charm and irredeemable nastiness, while Guinness 'slapped his thigh from time to time in a grey wig which looked remarkably like a tea-cosy'.[20] Guinness, who had commanded ships in the war, noted in a letter to his wife Merula that Dirk was 'quite sweet but he bears no resemblance to any naval officer and is totally un-period in manner and looks. He's gay and amusing but pretty silly.'[21] Lewis Gilbert, who had made *Cast a Dark Shadow* and *The Sea Shall Not Have Them* with Dirk, said that he cast him for the former and for *Defiant* because of a sinister quality – in his acting, but not in his personality, which Gilbert found kindly and charming. In the director's opinion Dirk seemed to enjoy himself far more with the cracking whip and the quiet exercise of domination than he ever did in the films where he had to attempt a love scene, no matter how delightful the object of his attention. Gilbert saw Dirk as 'kind of feminine in a way, because he couldn't do much that was masculine. By that I mean he didn't do much running, or fighting, or jumping around; he couldn't even drive a car, which was pretty annoying in a film, really, when you had to let him jump into a car, and then substitute him with a double, and so on.' On *Defiant*, it was swordplay, rather than driving or helmsmanship, that was required, and Dirk made a hash of it, drawing blood from the stunt-double playing his adversary and putting himself in 'a terrible state'. He was not good at action, said Gilbert; 'he wouldn't have made James Bond'.[22]

The unit was based at Denia, near Alicante, where the English newspapers arrived several days after publication. *The Sunday Times* of 6 August reached Dirk on the 9th, carrying a review of *Victim* in which Dilys Powell welcomed not only a film which 'takes a stand, has a point of view, says something' but also 'a thriller (and a good one) with characters which could not have been shown and on a subject which would have excited horror or ribaldry up to a few years ago. To treat the theme as a thriller may not be particularly bold, but to treat it at all was brave.' She left her comments about Dirk to the final paragraph, saying he 'gives the commanding performance one has long expected from him. With a fine control of gesture and tone he conveys both the suffering of the man condemned by nature and the resolve of the man bent on sacrifice.'[23] He immediately wrote her a note by hand, 'to thank you, from the bottom of my heart, for your kindness & for the word "command" – with regard to "Victim" – You cannot alas, ever know how much happiness you gave me today'.[24] Dilys Powell's was not a lone voice. 'AT LAST BOGARDE BECOMES A HEAVYWEIGHT'[25] and 'BOGARDE PULLS OFF HIS BIGGEST GAMBLE' proclaimed the *Evening News* and the *Evening Standard* respectively. In the latter, Alexander Walker wrote: 'At last, after years playing paper-thin parts in paperweight films, Dirk Bogarde has a role that not only shows what a brilliant actor he is – but what a courageous one he is, too.' He said that Dirk ran the risk of 'curdling the adulation of his fans', but predicted that his 'brave, sensitive picture of an unhappy, terribly bewildered man will win him and this film a far wider audience'.[26] Walker expressed his reservations about the film itself; he noted in his diary that at the press lunch Basil Dearden had 'actually *boasted*' to him of 'its tact'.[27] Yet tact was necessary. At Walker's own newspaper, the proprietor, Lord Beaverbrook, almost forbade any mention of homosexuality, particularly in a sympathetic context. The deputy editor had warned the critic: 'I'd ignore it if I were you.' Walker pleaded that the film would make headlines, and was told to be careful. After the notice appeared, and was echoed in the *Standard*'s counterparts, Walker heard that Beaverbrook said to the editor, Charles Wintour: 'Ah, Mr Wintour, I thought I gave instructions that your newspaper was not to advertise these perversions?'

One of the supporting players, the late Alan MacNaughton, recalled that when the rushes of the 'Because I wanted him' scene were screened, Dirk said: 'Well, they'll send me up for that in Scunthorpe.'[28] They didn't in Liverpool, where in the queue outside the Odeon for one of the early showings was a young clerk in a shipping office, named Terence Davies. Now a much honoured writer-director, with a series of idiosyncratic, autobiographical films to his credit, he was then, in the autumn of 1961, fifteen, confused and somewhat frightened. Four years earlier he had looked out of an upstairs window and realised that he admired the bodies of the builders working in the yard next door for a firm called, appropriately enough, Smittens. Like Dirk with 'Mr Dodd', at that moment he *knew*. *Victim* helped Terence Davies to realise that he was not a freak.

> It was an incredibly traumatic thing for me – being gay, and it being very much against the law. That moment when Dirk is in the police station and the policeman says, 'You of course knew that Barrett was a homosexual?' And the camera tracks in on Dirk and he says, 'Yes, I had gathered that.' 'Homosexual' was a word that *no one* ever said. The word in those days was 'queer', which was derogatory and very unpleasant. And I don't know why the gay community have taken it up now because to me it is *so* derogatory; because it used to be said with such hatred. And I just thought, 'And yes, and so am I.'[29]

Davies, a devout Roman Catholic who had had a miserable childhood under a tyrannical father, sought refuge constantly in the cinema; but Dirk was an actor he had scarcely noticed. The *Doctor* films had not been as popular with the working class as they were with the middle and upper classes, and even in *A Tale of Two Cities*, where Dirk was at his most romantic and handsome, for Davies the memorable performance was Rosalie Crutchley's as Madame Defarge, knitting manically beside the guillotine. And as for *The Singer Not the Song*, 'even at fifteen I was embarrassed'. As a rule the young man preferred to watch the American stars – 'passionate, sexy and very powerful' – whereas 'English actors seemed, by comparison, anaemic and vapid'. Understatement and suppressed passion were supposed to be English acting at its best:

I must confess I found our film-acting style so understated as to be virtually non-existent. But in *Victim* Dirk Bogarde changed all that for me. Here was an actor whose range of expression and subtlety of gesture electrified me. He was powerful, he was sexy and, what's more, he was *British*! In *Victim* the sheer sensitivity of his performance was a revelation. In the last scene with Sylvia Syms he is exceptionally moving, his final speech to her being full of shame, embarrassment and anguish, all expressed by that wonderful cough by the fireplace. After that film he could no longer be the pretty face in light comedies.[30]

That night at the Odeon, says Davies, 'you could have heard a feather drop'.

For Stephen Bourne, the release of *Victim* 'had an enormous impact on the lives of gay men who, for the first time, saw credible representations of themselves and their situations in a commercial British film'.[31] Andy Medhurst, in his perceptive 1986 essay about Dirk, wrote: '*Victim*'s intentions were to support the recommendations of the Wolfenden Report, which advocated the partial decriminalisation of male homosexual acts, but the emotional excess of Bogarde's performance [. . .] pushes the text beyond its liberal boundaries until it becomes a passionate validation of the homosexual option. Simply watch the "confession" scene for proof of this.'[32] Not everyone, however, was so convinced. Kenneth Williams wrote in his diary for 2 September:

> To see Dirk Bogarde play the homosexual barrister fighting a blackmail ring in the film *Victim* – it was all v. slick, same team as *Sapphire* (Relphs) and like that, superficial and never knocking the real issues. Never touching on what Kenneth Walker [author of *Sex and a Changing Civilisation*] once described as 'playing out the tragedy of the heart, alone, with no one knowing of their troubles . . .'[33]

The film's international career started well, with high praise at the Venice Film Festival; but the Motion Picture Association of America refused a seal of approval under its Production Code because of the 'candid and clinical discussion of homosexuality' and the 'overtly expressed plea for social acceptance of the homo-sexual, to the extent that he be made socially tolerable'. The news was reported in *Variety* under the heading: 'Code Denies Seal To Homo-Hailing British "Victim"'.[34] The distributors went ahead anyway, and the reception was in the main enthusiastic, although *Time* accused the screenwriters of accepting the 'Nature played me a dirty trick' idea for a medical fact when of course it was nothing but a 'sick-silly self-delusion'. Pauline Kael, broadcasting on Radio KFPA, took *Time* to task, saying 'the hero of the film is a man who has never given way to his homosexual impulses; he has fought them – that's part of his heroism. Maybe that's why he seems such a stuffy stock figure of a hero. Oedipus didn't merely want to sleep with Jocasta; he slept with her.' She concluded: 'The dreadful irony involved is that Dirk Bogarde looks so pained, so anguished from the self-sacrifice of repressing his homosexuality, that the film seems to give rather a black eye to the heterosexual life.'[35] Nevertheless the film did well enough on each coast, pushing it into profit. The Roman Catholic National League of Decency recognised its purpose, and the Jesuits in Panama gave it an award. Earl St John pronounced himself 'very happy'.

The ultimate accolade for what Dirk called this 'modest, tight, neat little thriller' would come to him in the summer of 1968, a year after the Sexual Offences Act passed through Parliament and into law. On 5 June Lord ('Boofy') Arran, who in 1965 had introduced the legislation in the House of Lords, wrote to Dirk that he had just seen *Victim* for the first time – on television – 'and I just want to say how much I admire your courage in undertaking this difficult and potentially damaging part'. He said he understood that it was in large part responsible for a swing in popular opinion, as shown by the polls, from forty-eight per cent to sixty-three per cent in favour of reform. Lord Arran concluded: 'It is comforting to think that perhaps a million men are no longer living in fear.'[36]

To promote *Victim* in Britain, Dirk gave a splendidly brittle filmed interview in the drawing-room at Drummers Yard, in which he said he had made thirty-five films and enjoyed six while under contract to Rank; that he was now 'free of them ... [pause] ... Er, they very kindly let me go'; and that his admirers were split into three: the Followers, a hard core, who stay loyal, come what may; the Fans, who 'vary'; and the Fanatics, who are 'like barnacles, with you for a while'.[37] On the film's release, he would say later and with no regret, the Fans disappeared in their droves, 'like a knife dropping'.[38] He hoped he might make work which would appeal to a young, intelligent audience – 'The average teenager is much more inquiring than I ever was' – but realised the risk he was taking: 'A draught up your kilt at any time is uncomfortable.'[39]

He returned from being beastly off the Spanish coast with nothing definite in prospect and his producer's hat looking decidedly wobbly, to find a letter from Laurence Olivier, who was forming a company to open a theatre in parkland on the edge of a cathedral town in West Sussex. The Chichester Festival Theatre was an ambitious, even hare-brained, project – the dream of a local optician who had been inspired by Tyrone Guthrie's theatre in Stratford, Ontario. Olivier explained that the new building had a thrust stage, not the usual proscenium arch, and that although the money would not be 'unprecedentedly seductive' a 'state of indigence is not proposed and decent comfort and excitement in the work is most definitely proffered'. There would be three plays in repertory for ten weeks, and a maximum of another ten weeks' rehearsal. Dirk was sorely tempted. 'What a wonderful and exciting idea it is,' he replied. 'There is nothing I think that I should like to do more, or indeed that I need more than this'. He asked for a week or two to reach a decision. A month later he was still as enthusiastic, repeating that the time was right for him. Olivier replied by hand

and at length that he knew what Dirk meant by 'a certain need for this sort of expression' and, at the risk of sounding pompous, 'when one has played Macbeth, for instance (and *only* for *instance!*) one is somehow a slightly larger person than one was before, whatever anyone may say about it. You've scaled something, you've so to speak gone up one, and ones view of life is at a slightly more advantageous angle, and ones view of oneself too. Any peak you particularly have a fancy to climb?' Ten weeks, he added, was 'a nice little pocket of time in which to indulge in a bash' – unlike ten months at the Old Vic or Stratford. 'Now, would you like to do Hamlet? or some such thing? Have you seen yourself as something? Have you a wish for some out and out character studies, or would you rather exercise less ambitiously, just normal practice in some not particularly spectacular way of casting just to sort of feel yourself in again? You could probably have a bit of all three if you wanted'. Dirk said Olivier's offer had given him 'great heart and encouragement and has tempted me almost beyond endurance!' *But* there were 'two idiotic Americans' with film projects for the following year and he needed to come to terms with them before making a final decision. At which moment the surviving correspondence stops abruptly.[40] 'I funked the honour,' wrote Dirk in *Snakes and Ladders*, 'and probably the greatest chance I had ever been offered really to learn my craft.' He admitted – but not to Olivier – that his 'fear of ridicule' was too great: 'Hoist by my own petard.'[41]

If nothing else, the invitation itself had been a welcome boost to Dirk's self-esteem, at least with regard to his professional reputation. He was beginning to think he should go rustic, perhaps even buy a farm and, with the help of Elizabeth and her husband George, whose expertise as tree surgeon and landscape gardener had been well proven at Beel and Drummers Yard, to live off the land. On a whim he bought Hale Court, at Withyham, about fifteen miles from Uckfield. 'It was being auctioned in Sussex,' Bernard Walsh recalls. 'Dirk went to look at it one weekend and said, "I must have it". And when Dirk made up his mind, you couldn't make him change it. It was a strange house, a complete wreck, with a couple of outbuildings. So I went to the auction and bought it for him and quite upset a man who was trying to buy it as well. Dirk was very excited about it.'[42] However, the existing owner was still in residence, and only when he had moved out in January 1962 did Dirk and Tony make a thorough inspection and realise how much of a proposition it was – both in time and money – to put the place in order. 'Tony rang me late one night,' recalls Walsh, 'and said "We've decided to sell Hale Court. We'll never move into it. It'll be a year before it's ready." So I sold it, with the auctioneer, to the man who was second bidder. Dirk and Tony had owned it for about two months.' The problem was that Dirk had already agreed to take up the offer from Peter Rogers and Betty Box, and Drummers Yard was sold to them for £35,000. They, their dogs, horses, pit pony and donkey were ready to move in – certainly no later than April.

The sense of panic was heightened because Dirk now had a film to make for MGM: *The Password Is Courage*, based on the adventures of Charles Coward, who as a prisoner of war had sorely tested the patience of his German captors. Shooting was to start on 12 February, but at least the initial work was in the Home Counties, so, after dropping Dirk at the location, Tony could go house-hunting. It was a hectic few weeks. Dirk won the Variety Club Actor of the Year award for *Victim*. Hans and Agnes left finally, and amid many tears, for America, to be replaced by an Italian couple, Luigi and Aigle Serafini. Script negotiations were going on for a possible film with Judy Garland called 'The Lonely Stage'. Another company sprang into life, called, logically, Bowood Productions. And Dirk turned down $5,000 for one day's filming on Darryl Zanuck's Second World War epic, *The Longest Day*. Then, after seeing and rejecting several potential properties, and while Dirk made a mockery of the Hun at a 'Sussex-type farmhouse supposed to be [in the] Pas de Calais' but actually in Surrey, the quest ended. Bernard Walsh had told them about a possibility on a hill near Godalming, Tony drove BH5 the few miles from Ewhurst and discovered 'a delightful house called Nore'. He took Dirk to see it in the latter's lunch break, and they made an offer that afternoon of £30,000. It was Valentine's Day.

Of all Dirk's houses in the fifties and sixties, Nore was the finest. Reached by a long private drive through woodland, and much more secluded than Drummers Yard had been, it was officially described as 'a large, three-bay continuous jetty house of two storeys and attics' – a yeoman's house, dating in large part from the late sixteenth century. It stood in about ten acres, with breathtaking views across the Surrey countryside towards the South Downs. It had ten bedrooms, eight bathrooms and six reception rooms, two cottages, a separate studio, a tennis court, a garage block and four pools, 'two for water-lilies, one for ducks and one for humans'.[43] There was also a contractual right to a free daily supply of 500 gallons of water. Above all, there were extensive gardens. In the twenties and early thirties Nore had been home to the parents of Brian Howard, the American-born, Eton-educated poet, wit, aesthete, homosexual, 'charismatic failure' and 'the oddest aircraftman since T. E. Shaw'. He was dark and handsome, had a Machiavellian streak and was 'quasi-sadistic mentally, quasi-masochistic phys-ically'; he also had 'pity and compassion for all human suffering, he loved the beauties of nature, literature and the arts', and according to Evelyn Waugh was 'mad, bad and dangerous to know'. A great platonic love of his was Daphne Fielding, and although she never saw him at Nore, when she went to stay with Dirk and Tony, she 'was conscious of Brian all the time, and his own very particular atmosphere seemed to dominate even Dirk's'.[44] Which was indeed saying something. Howard's parents had rented Nore from Robert Godwin-Austen, a descendant of the topographer who 'discovered' the Himalayan peak now known as K2, and whose travels yielded a miniature temple, with a 'lion-dog' at each of the four corners, which Dirk found, buried in brambles, and with 'a rather curious, and very detailed, phallic symbol standing erect in the very center! So I am not absolutely certain that it was only spirits who went there to worship.'[45]

With Dirk tied up all day and almost every day with *Password*, Tony had never had to work so hard in his life. 'The Lonely Stage' was on the point of being confirmed. Michael Relph and Basil Dearden had approached them with a firm offer: *The Mind Benders*, a study of brainwashing by James Kennaway, who was 'hot' after writing *Tunes of Glory*, which starred John Mills and Alec Guinness. The timing might not have been ideal, but, as Tony noted, it was big in the 'uplift dept!' So, on 3 April, while Dirk filmed in – of all places – Amersham, Tony was again marshalling a convoy, which this time included his son Gareth, Elizabeth and all available hands, bound from Drummers Yard to the Surrey hills, where they were joined by the ever-faithful Ulric and Margaret. The following evening, when Dirk returned from work, he was 'suitably impressed'. Tony made no bones about it: their new home was 'really looking divine'. They had nearly walked away from it, however, when the previous occupants raised the price to £40,000 after recognising Dirk and realising that he, not Tony, was the buyer. Dirk agreed to pay, but said he never wanted to see them again. He never did; and when their smooth son drove up to the house to impress his girlfriend by introducing her to Dirk, he was told to 'Bugger off'.

Daphne Fielding's sense of a presence at Nore was swiftly established: she and her husband Xan were the first overnight guests. Dirk and Tony were not going to argue. They, too, came to believe the house was well and truly haunted – at first, they thought, by Godwin-Austen, then, more likely, by Howard:

> [...] he used to bash about up and down the big staircase, lock us into rooms, scatter records all over the drawing room ... OUT of their sleeves, and cut the heads off any large flower he fancied and stick them in the ashtrays ... The dogs loved him! They leapt and danced after him ... unnerving to many guests I may add, but we all got perfectly used to him in time. He was more of a benign poltageist (cant spell it!) than a ghost ... although some people swore that there was an icy draft during his appearances.[46]

Nonetheless Dirk told the present owner that Nore was a 'house I loved with a deep and lasting passion'.

Another early visitor was Ronald Neame, the fifty-one-year-old director who had started his film career as a sixteen-year-old gofer at Elstree, was an assistant cameraman on Hitchcock's *Blackmail*, had shot *In Which We Serve* for Noël Coward and David Lean, and had just made *The Horse's Mouth* and *Tunes of Glory* with Alec Guinness. Despite Judy Garland's reputation for driving directors to the brink of despair, if not the asylum, he had leapt at the chance of working with her on 'The Lonely Stage', a custom-made vehicle about an emotionally fragile singing star who abandoned her son for her career and after fourteen years wishes the boy's father, an eminent surgeon, to reunite them – this against the background of an imminent series of concerts at the London Palladium. Would Jenny Bowman cope? Would Judy Garland cope? The life-imitates-art aspect was all the more authentic because at the time she came to England to make the film she was going through a ferocious battle with her estranged husband, Sid Luft, for custody of their three children. Neame reckoned he could handle it all, as 'an arrogant Englishman, convinced my manners and tact could overcome any difficulty that might arise'.[47] The shrewd producers, Larry Turman and Stuart Millar, had approached Dirk early on to play opposite Garland, knowing that if the seas became rough, he would be on hand as counsellor. His doctoring extended into a third area – the script, which needed a good deal of work before he agreed to take the role, and even more after he had done so. One Saturday less than a month before shooting started, Neame asked him more or less to rewrite the whole thing by Monday. Which he did. Dirk 'could write dialogue that was absolutely right and suitable for her', recalls Neame, 'and I made full use of it'.[48] But he refused to take a screen credit.

All went comparatively smoothly during the pre-production stage, and on Garland's first day of shooting, at the Palladium. She sang 'Hello, Bluebird, Hello', and to mark the occasion Dirk presented her with a bluebird brooch from Cartier. On the second day, Dirk was again not required; indeed he went out to Elstree to make a guest appearance – as a favour to Kenneth More and the producer Danny Angel – in *We Joined the Navy*, an especially dim farce, on the credits of which he was billed as playing 'Dr Simon Sparrow'. In the evening Neame called to say there were 'Judy dramas'. It was the start of a roller-coaster ride for cast and crew alike, but above all for Neame whom Garland tried at least twice to remove from the film. 'Talk about a love-hate relationship!' he recalled:

> [...] when she liked me, which was half the time, she used to call me Pussycat. She would come up to me and give me a hug, and I would hug her, and she'd say, 'We're all right, Pussycat, aren't we?' And I'd say, 'Judy, darling, we're all right.' And we'd have three days of greatness. Then she'd come on the set in a filthy mood, having been missing for three days, and then I became 'Get that goddamn British Henry Hathaway* off the set!'[49]

Everything came to a head in the usually tranquil setting of Canterbury Cathedral. First, Neame had a fifteen-minute stand-up row with the Dean, Dr Hewlett Johnson, because a dozen young extras were wearing uniforms resembling that of the illustrious King's School nearby. Johnson, who was known as 'the Red Dean' because of his left-wing leanings, said they looked 'very scruffy

---

* Henry Hathaway (1898–1985), American director and on-set bully.

and untidy' and would bring discredit on the school. Order was restored, but the altercation was as nothing compared with the one that took place after lunch in Garland's trailer, where not only abuse but also a plateful of food hurtled through the air. Dirk devotes a page and a half of *Snakes and Ladders* to the Garland tantrum. In the Diary, Tony summed it up succinctly: 'not loved enough'. Garland's younger daughter Lorna Luft has spoken about how being with her mother could be 'like having a tornado in the living-room'.[50] In a trailer it must have been something else again. The following day, at Shepperton, the storm had not abated, with Garland, in a blazing row with the producers in front of Dirk, demanding that they fire Neame, and, as Tony noted, 'all the shit hitting the fan!' About eight weeks into the filming, on a Black Friday the 13th, Judy walked out. All involved were at the end of their tether. Ultimatums were issued, and somehow she was persuaded to return for the last two weeks.

For Ronald Neame, Dirk's account of this fraught enterprise did not do justice to the positive side of the 'love-hate relationship' between the director and Garland: 'As is always the case, history gets slightly changed. He made out that Judy hated me from the start. In fact we were much warmer and closer than he suggested.'[51] Dirk, he said, 'didn't see us on the occasions when we talked quietly together and when she was obviously, in her way, quite fond of me'.[52] Neame pays tribute to Dirk, saying: 'I'm deeply grateful to him' – for his self-effacing acting, 'which I very much admired'; for his help in keeping Garland on the rails as far as was possible; and for his contribution to the screenplay. One scene above all stands out in his memory, and in those of everyone else who was on the set that day. Jenny Bowman sprains her ankle shortly before going on stage, and from the hospital's casualty department calls for David, her former lover, who then has to persuade her to let him take her to the Palladium rather than home; but she has had enough of being 'rolled out like pastry so everyone can have a nice big bite of me!' and refuses point-blank: 'It's not worth all the deaths that I have to die.'[53] Normally, a sequence of its length – four to five minutes – would have taken Neame a day to shoot, with several cuts. They rehearsed a few times, then he called for the first take. As the scene developed, he realised something unplanned was going on, and that he would never be able to capture it again: 'The room was filled with such emotional intensity that the unit became caught up in the moment. It was magic!' It seemed to Neame as if 'Judy's emotions had taken over, and we were no longer shooting a scene, we were filming *her*, her life. Suddenly it was as though there wasn't a camera there.' The director forgot about his careful strategy for the camera and signalled for it to close in on Judy and Dirk, favouring the former. Dirk, he said, 'must have had tremendous peripheral vision' because he realised what was happening and adapted not only his physical closeness to her but also his dialogue, in response to her own words, which were taking on a life well beyond what was on the page. It was completely remarkable, said Neame, even a little frightening, to see Garland becoming Garland, no longer Jenny Bowman; and Dirk, the 'consummate actor', adjusted accordingly.

Dirk would contend that as they were all professionals, they could have done the scene again, just as effectively. Neame disagrees. Dirk might have been able to, because 'his was the easy bit. He was feeding her the lines.' But not Garland, whose emotional well-tapping was unrepeatable.[54]

Before Dirk completed his part for Neame he had the welcome distraction of a second film, and was leading something of a schizophrenic life, dovetailing work at Shepperton with *The Mind Benders* at Pinewood. Garland, inevitably, felt abandoned: ' "You are walking away from me," she cried in anguish, "you are walking away, like they all do . . . walking away backwards, smiling." '[55] When her part was finished, it was Garland's turn to smile. Looking at the unit, she said: 'You'll miss me when I'm gone!' It was true. Neame has never been able to explain why, but, despite all they had been put through, when she left the set for the last time 'many of us were in tears'.[56] Their film was later retitled *I Could Go On Singing*, after the Harburg and Arlen composition on the soundtrack and, like *The Singer Not the Song*, has earned cult status – but for a simpler reason: it was Garland's last film. And if she really did say to Dirk that he was backing away from her, smiling, she was correct. Judy Garland needed to be loved, and, as her daughter Lorna put it, 'there was a bottomless pit there that could never be filled'.[57] Dirk, as we know, needed to be needed. But there were limits.

Fourteen

'I'm a gentleman's gentleman. And you're no bloody gentleman!'

It has to be said that on the domestic front this was not a golden era. Dirk and Tony were having problems either choosing staff well, or keeping them. Luigi and Aigle were given notice before the move from Drummers Yard, because they threw one of the cats out of a window. A Spanish couple, Vicente and Manolita Mirales, arrived at Nore just two days after being interviewed and were sent packing within two months. Then came a Mr and Mrs Hillier, who survived for five months before retreating down the hill, she with a gunshot wound to the leg sustained on Christmas Day. Another couple was dismissed when Dirk and Tony returned home from abroad to find evidence in polaroid photographs of serious party-giving in their absence. A gardener was fired for being 'troublesome and rude'. Frankly, things were a bit rocky from the animals' point of view, too. A month after they had settled in at Nore, Sinuhe – 'He who is alone' – was put to sleep, followed the next day by one of the cats, Missie. The dog's grave remains to this day, under a carved stone reading: 'Sinuhe – Welsh Corgi – 1953–1962.' In time, Dirk wrote, the old chap would be joined by 'countless cats, two fat pekenese (which belonged to my cook) and a small flock of birds of one sort or another. These had wooden place names which have long since rotted away ... but were smothered in bluebells and daffodils. ... and set about with primroses. We always called it the Chestnut Walk and Cemetary Lane'.[1] Meanwhile the canine, Candy the alarming mastiff, was not only to be found every now and then with tufts of her fellow family members' fur emerging from her mouth; she also made it impossible for Dirk and Tony to hire at least one potential couple because at the interview she made it perfectly clear that she wished to eat their poodle bitch. Annie, the green Amazon, continued to terrorise any human who came within range of her active beak – even, on occasion, her adoring owner. Elizabeth's son, Mark Goodings, recalls Annie with wry amusement: 'That bird is one of the very few living creatures that actually got the better of Dirk.'[2]

The animal population might temporarily have shrunk, but Dirk's and Tony's personal and business circles had widened a little. On a visit to the south of France with Tony's son Gareth, who was to enrol at Aix University, they met

John Standing and his wife Jill Melford – who had had 'a cough and a spit' in *Doctor at Sea* – by the harbour at St Tropez. A drink and 'a good laugh' turned into a dinner lasting until 3 o'clock in the morning and a friendship enduring the best part of forty years. Within a week of returning to England, the Standings were in a Sunday lunch party at Nore, and Jill Melford, who hated her given name and preferred either 'Melford' or 'Melf', was duly christened Maude, which she did not much like, either, but it stuck; one day she would be known as 'Swiss Army Knife'. And now that Dirk was a director of three companies, it is worth taking note of his employees – in effect, two decidedly colourful women, whose job it was to read scripts for possible production or investment. First was Joyce Dyson Taylor, formerly a spectacular model whose first name was anathema to her ex-husband, the writer Peter Quennell; he insisted on referring to her by her Swiss stepfather's surname, so Glur she was to all. Two years younger than Tony, she had lived with her daughter by Quennell and with her third husband on the opposite side of Chester Row from number 44, so the relationship with Dirk and Tony went back to at least 1948. A depressive, afflicted further by telephonitis, she was enjoyed by Dirk and Tony in small doses, but over many years. The other script-reader was the Ukrainian-born Baroness Moura Budberg, once the mistress of Maxim Gorky and now his literary executor. She had come to Britain in the thirties and established a *salon*, among whose adherents were H. G. Wells – whose lover she became – Bernard Shaw, and Alexander Korda, through whom she made connections in the film world. It was disclosed recently that as early as August 1950 she tried to warn the British secret services that Anthony Blunt, the then Keeper of the Pictures of King George VI and later unmasked as the 'Fourth Man' in the Burgess/Maclean/Philby spy ring, was a member of the Communist Party, but the spooks were too busy investigating her own background to take her seriously. As Miranda Carter noted in her biography of Blunt: 'She was charming and unscrupulous, and was rumoured to have spied for everyone, including the NKVD.' She was also 'rather large'.[3] In 1951, after she had spent twenty-five years under suspicion, the bulging files were closed on her, the final document recording that she was 'an unusually intelligent and amusing woman – a quite outstanding personality'.[4] Now, here she was in the sixties, working as a translator, administering Gorky's literary estate, editing Russian fairy tales and lending a hand to film and theatre producers. Dirk was paying Moura Budberg £520 a year to read scripts for possible use by Bendrose. She was performing the same service for Joe Losey.

In the nine years following their collaboration on *The Sleeping Tiger* Losey and Dirk had seen each other only spasmodically: in June 1961 the former wrote to Dirk in some disbelief, saying that they had not sat down to a meal and spent an evening together since 1958. Yet they had most certainly not forgotten about each other. Losey had made seven full-length films since 1954, including *Blind Date, The Criminal, The Damned* and *Eve*, but among the many abortive projects were several which he considered possibilities for Dirk. He offered a short story by John Collier called *Witch's Money*, about rum goings-on in a village in the east Pyrenees; Dirk had doubts as to whether he would be suitable casting, but kept the door open. In 1959, while Dirk was making *Song Without End* in Austria, Losey tried urgently to pin him down en route to Hollywood for a talk about a script entitled 'The Great Indoors'. *Hotel de Dream*, a story by Stephen Crane who wrote *The Red Badge of Courage*, was waved in front of him, and Sydney Box promised Losey his backing, sight unseen, if Dirk agreed to star. David Storey's novel, *Flight into Camden*, was another keen thought of Losey's. In early 1960 he tried so often to call Dirk at Beel, without success, that he wondered whether the number had been changed, 'or are you now a Girls' School?'[5] At about the same time, Losey wrote to Harold Pinter, telling him how impressed and moved he had been by the latter's television play, *A Night Out*, which had been transmitted a few days before and which Losey found 'both horrifying and purgative'. Pinter wrote back, saying he had heard from his agent, Emmanuel (Jimmy) Wax, that Losey had mentioned a possible film script; he would be interested to know what the director had in mind. According to Losey's biographer David Caute, there was nothing 'in mind' at that point.[6] However, there soon would be.

As early as 1955, Losey had taken an active interest in *The Servant*, a 1948 novella by Robin Maugham, the nephew of 'Have another sip' Somerset. The story was inspired by an incident soon after the war, when he rented a friend's small house in Fulham, which came equipped with a manservant. He was, wrote Maugham, 'an excellent servant. Softly moving and soft-voiced, he would glide silently around the house. But there was something about him which made me shudder each time he'd come into a room.' He was, for the purposes of Maugham's writing, called Barrett.[7] One evening, Maugham went to the cinema with Mary Soames, Sir Winston Churchill's daughter, and brought her back for a drink before driving her home. She said she would love a cold lager. Maugham remembered that he had some in the fridge, downstairs in the kitchen. There was no one in the kitchen, but the door to the servant's room, which led off it, was open and the lights were on. 'Lying spreadeagled and naked on the double bed was a boy of about fourteen [. . .] While I stared at this vision in astonishment, a soft voice spoke from behind me. "I can see you are admiring my young nephew, sahr," Barrett said. "Would you like me to send him up to you to say goodnight, sahr?"' At that moment, Maugham could see himself 'caught in the mesh of a smooth-voiced blackmailer'. He took the lagers from the fridge, pretended not to have heard a word, said 'Good night, Barrett' and went upstairs. Mary Soames stared at him and said: 'You look as if you've seen a ghost.' 'I have,' he replied. The 'beauty and slenderness' of the boy had reminded him of a lover he had had at Eton as a fourteen-year-old schoolboy. This disturbing event, and a brief fling with 'Vera', a beautiful teenaged girl who had been seduced by her riding-master, formed the genesis of Maugham's book, which was underscored by his own inner turbulence. He would write in his 1972 memoirs that he was perhaps fortunate not to have suffered from the delusion of his uncle, who 'told me in his old age that his greatest mistake had been to persuade himself that he was three-quarters normal and only a quarter queer – "whereas really it was the other way round". But though I came to accept my own similar nature – that I was mainly, but not wholly, homosexual – the torment and the guilt remained.'

The author adapted his novella as a play, which in 1955 Losey put forward to 'Binkie' Beaumont, but without success. The following year another producer, Stephen Mitchell, rejected Maugham's script because 'the people he writes about and the things they say are too trivial'.[8] In 1961 Losey seemed to have been trumped when Michael Anderson, director of *The Dam Busters* and *Around the World in Eighty Days*, commissioned a screenplay from Pinter, but was unable to raise the backing. In the mid-fifties Losey had shown the novella to Dirk, with the intention this time that Dirk would play the master: after all, he had just subverted a household in *The Sleeping Tiger*. Now, it was Dirk who heard about the Pinter script and tipped off Losey, who immediately contacted the playwright. What Losey read was 'very uneven but absolutely brilliant'.[9] The rights changed hands for £12,000, and the usual coming-and-going ensued. 'It was on and off with the frequency of a conjuror's hat,' wrote Dirk.[10] There was an extremely tense evening meeting at which Pinter, unhappy with the way he was being expected to work on rewrites, virtually told Losey to take a running jump; but after everyone – apart from the director – had had a great deal to drink, Losey asked Pinter to hand back the notes he had been given and tore them up. They started again, and never had another serious dispute. Tony, meanwhile, was worried that it was going to be 'a completely homosexual picture' and, so soon after *Victim*, might harm Dirk. In the event, no one could possibly describe it as 'completely' anything; as Pinter's biographer Michael Billington observes, whereas Maugham made his novella melodramatically explicit, 'Pinter works in more delicate shades and half-tones'.[11] Between the lines, in the spaces, is an exhilarating playground for the imagination. To Dirk, Pinter's writing was like 'a beautifully laid-out scenic model railway. A start and an end. Tunnels and level-crossings, gradients, cuttings, little stations and smaller halts, signals all the way. The whole track laid and set out with the precision of a master jeweller. Pinter doesn't give you instructions like a packet of instant minestrone. The instructions are implicit in the words he offers so sparingly for his characters to speak.' Dirk disagreed with the common theory that Pinter 'writes pauses'; rather, 'he is one of the few writers who are brilliant in the text they *don't* write. His pauses are merely the time-phases which he gives you so that you may develop the thought behind the line he has written, and to alert your mind itself to the dangerous simplicities of the lines to come'.[12]

By 20 December 1962, the principal obstacles had been overcome and *The Servant* was on, with shooting to begin at the end of January. Leslie Grade, who worked in partnership with Losey's agent Robin Fox and had made a fortune from two films with Cliff Richard and the Shadows, came to the rescue by putting up the bulk of the £140,000 budget. Losey, Dirk, Pinter and the co-producer Norman 'Spike' Priggen all agreed to deferred payments – in Dirk's case, a guaranteed £7,500, with a further £2,500 payable if and when the film came into profit. The casting of his co-stars had about it an element of serendipity. At a party Dirk met Sarah Miles, who had recently made an impact as a nymphomaniac pupil causing misery to Laurence Olivier's schoolmaster in *Term of Trial*. Dirk told her he was involved in setting up *The Servant* and made a flattering remark to her about being prepared to appear in it only if she did too. She read the script, was not too excited, and forgot about it. At roughly the same time Dirk found himself watching a television play called *The Door*, with Ann Todd and a good-looking, unknown twenty-three-year-old, working under the name of Oliver Fox. He could act, for sure. 'And there was something more. Under the grace and breeding, the golden-boy innocence, I sensed, and I don't for the life of me know why, a muted quality of corruptibility. This young man could spoil like peaches: he could be led to the abyss.'[13] Dirk alerted Losey. It transpired that the actor's real Christian name was William and he was the second son of Losey's agent, Robin Fox. Moreover, Willie Fox and Sarah Miles were what is nowadays called 'an item'. On 15 December Dirk and Tony went to the première of Bryan Forbes's film, *The L-Shaped Room*, and acknowledged the prepossessing young couple sitting in front of them. At the dinner afterwards, Fox and Sarah Miles found themselves at the same table as Tony, who asked what the actress thought of *The Servant*. 'Why?' 'Because Dirk wants to do it and he wants you for "Vera".' A squeak of mock modesty from Sarah Miles. Yes he does, confirmed Tony, 'and wouldn't your friend be good as "Tony"?'[14]

The following morning they went to the Connaught to meet Losey, whom Fox found to resemble 'an asthmatic intellectual Red Indian Chief without the feathers', and who 'rumbled on about things that had gone wrong that day, and other bad news'.[15] A week later, on primitive equipment in a flat in Kensington, Fox was tested by the director.[16] It is an indication of the slightly ramshackle nature of the whole enterprise, not only that Losey paid for the test himself, but also that Dirk missed it because he and Tony were given the wrong address. Nevertheless the director had seen 'what he wanted' and, if the money came through, the part was Fox's. It was to make him, as James Fox, a star overnight.

'Saddening' was the strange word Dirk used for the chance that brought 'Sarah Miles and the golden-haired Fox boy' – emphatically 'together' – to the seats in front of him and Tony at *The L-Shaped Room*.[17] But there were other curious coincidences in the background to *The Servant*. When he returned from National Service in Kenya as an officer in the Coldstream Guards, Fox found temporary work on the biscuit counter at Fortnum & Mason in Piccadilly, where among his superiors was a Mr Barratt. The story of *Victim* had as its catalyst, if not its leading character, the Boy Barrett. Pinter, in his late twenties and at the end of his career as a repertory actor, played the James Robertson Justice role in a touring adaptation of *Doctor in the House*. And then there is the more sensitive question of 'Tony' in *The Servant* itself. In the course of research for this biography, several witnesses pondered aloud over parallels that might be drawn between the Barrett/ Tony and Dirk/Tony relationships – the one, malign; the other, of course, entirely benign. 'The beauty of *The Servant*,' says James Fox, 'was that the domineering one, Barrett, was not the one with the most class.'

> And Tony Forwood had more class than Dirk. On the one hand you felt that Tony was not in any way somebody who would be kicked about. He would send Dirk up. But Dirk would be quite bossy with him, and Tony did not seem to mind when he was being rude, abusive, domineering. He probably enjoyed being a little subservient. Obviously there must have been some sort of psycho-sexual thing going on, but who knows? Tony was the practical one, the one who drove the Rolls. I think Tony probably saw himself as the one who *should* be driving a Rolls. Later, Tony did the cooking, but I couldn't see him wanting to do the washing-up. Dirk did that. Nor can I imagine Tony making the sauce for the spaghetti, whereas I can see Dirk with his apron on, preparing his sauce – fussing, pottering, complaining, whistling.[18]

Within both the Van den Bogaerde and the Forwood families it is widely accepted that Dirk – the breadwinner, if not the employer – needed Tony more than the other way round. In the film, the servant manipulates his so-called master into a position of total dependence. Barrett is the man of the world, the busybody, the know-it-all, while the lassitudinous Tony simply dreams of fortune-making in South Africa. For James Fox, Dirk 'in a rather royal way, was slightly cut off from real life, and Tony was the one who had his ear much closer to the ground. I wouldn't say Tony was a great businessman, a great planner, or pusher, or creator of deal-opportunities; he wasn't a *manager* in that sense; but he knew what was going on. He had a good nose.'

Certainly *The Servant* has no resonance whatever with life at Nore in its depiction of a descent into moral and domestic chaos, fuelled by Barrett's jealousy of Tony's breeding and social superiority. Pinter described the film as 'stinking of moral corruption'; for Fox it is anarchic: 'It's about disorder and destruction and overthrow. That's all right for a drama and fantasy, but Dirk didn't want that in his life. He wanted "normality" and order.'[19] Fox remembers an occasion later in the sixties when he himself had moved away from the conventional acting world and had become involved with the rock music crowd. He made contact with Dirk, who invited him to the Connaught for a reception he was giving after the première of *Accident*. Fox said he had some friends with him: could they come too? 'Oh God,' said Dirk, suddenly alarmed. So there amid the elegance and the formality were Fox and his girlfriend in fairly advanced hippie mode, with velvet trousers, cascading hair and wreathed in scarves, accompanied by Mick Jagger and Marianne Faithfull, slouching on the radiators and popping amyl-nitrate capsules. Dirk, immaculate in his suit and cut-away collar, went over to them and said if they wanted to do that kind of thing they should do it in the lavatories. As they left, he said to Fox: 'Do get washed, have a hair-cut and choose new friends.' There was much giggling, from Jagger especially. Looking back, Fox recognises his own arrogance at the period, but also believes that Dirk was unable to cope with even that modest irruption into his ordered existence, especially as it took place in front of his professional colleagues: 'He couldn't relate to anyone who was not going to play the game by his own fastidious rules. In his private life there wasn't the anarchic streak that he could exhibit so well professionally.' He was, says Fox, 'something of a counsellor – he had a Princess Diana complex in that way – but he was not an identifier. He was also quite snobby, and didn't see the ironies of social advancement. Tony did.'

To an extent Dirk wanted to control others, but much more important was the absolute necessity to be in control of himself; for the loss of that capacity was a terror even greater than that of letting an audience down and of inviting derision. Once again, we come back to the importance of release through the work; and the relish with which Dirk seized an opportunity. It is doubtful that he ever enjoyed inhabiting any character more than he did that of Barrett. In *Snakes and Ladders* there is a fascinating description of how he created this malevolent beast, working as he always did 'from the outside in' and starting with the shoes – black, squeaking a little – which dictated the walk; which in turn led to the stance and the posture. Onto the frame went the clothes, inside which 'one's body starts to form another's; another person walks and breathes in the shabby, serge suit'. The Brylcreemed hair came from Billington/Quigley, the houseman jailed for stealing from Dirk at Bendrose; the walk, 'from an ingrati-ating Welsh waiter who attended me in an hotel in Liverpool'; the 'glazed and pouched eyes were those of a car-salesman lounging against a Buick in the Euston Road, aggrieved, antagonistic, resentful, sharp; filing his nails'; and there was 'no make-up, ever'. The clothes – 'pork-pie hat with a jay's feather, a Fair Isle sweater, shrunken, darned at the elbows, a nylon scarf with horses' heads and stirrups' – were 'a mean, shabby outfit for a mean and shabby man'. With all of this, and a good deal more from the data bank accumulated by constant observation, there was 'almost nothing left to do but wind him up and set him off to work'.[20] The one essential ingredient which he did not have to acquire, because Pinter handed it to him, was a superb screenplay, presenting a character in two dimensions. As Dirk told Losey, without that, the actor's job was 'rather like hanging up a suit of clothes on a nail . . . not on a coat hanger'.[21] He expanded the simile in an interview for a special edition of the Oxford University magazine *Isis*, where he said: 'I nearly always do wear the characters a bit, but I wore Barrett really with a zip fastener down the back, it was extraordinary.'[22] No less interestingly, in the same issue James Fox described his own part as one-dimensional; Pinter's Tony was more stupid than Maugham's with the result that 'some of the depth was missed'.

Not so much at the time, but later, Dirk would make great play of the fact

that he had taken over the direction of *The Servant* a fortnight after shooting
began, when Losey succumbed first to gastroenteritis, then to pneumonia. Losey
feared that the producers would abandon the film and claim the insurance, so
he asked both Dirk and the production designer Richard MacDonald, who had
worked on the director's two previous films, to take over. Losey was away for ten
days, three of which were lost because of a dispute involving the art department,
and the pair muddled along in conditions of mutual respect rather than bon-
homie. When Losey returned, in a bad state, he ditched all their work, bar about
three scenes, and shot it again.[23] Dirk was glad to see him back. He had in the
past year toyed with the idea of directing; suddenly it did not seem such an
attractive proposition after all.

They finished shooting on 29 March, the day after Dirk's forty-second birthday
and, remarkably, they had come in under budget. The 'wrap' party in the
restaurant at Shepperton was full of the warmth that emanates from a co-
operative, with tributes paid both to Losey and to Dirk; yet there was the
underlying concern that the film was so far out of the mainstream, it could
founder on bewilderment and antipathy. The team had to hope that everyone
would see *The Servant* in the same way as Fred Harris, the head of Humphries
Film Laboratories, where the raw footage was processed. He wrote: 'I believe that
the day of the audience that go to the cinema to giggle and suck ice cream is
over, and that a type of audience is coming in that does not believe the price of
admission guarantees no mental effort required, or that one cannot be made to
think and be entertained at the same time.'[24] What a sight for Losey's and Dirk's
tired eyes. Losey wrote to the production's financial white knight, Leslie Grade,
saying that the finished film belonged to a category mostly unknown in England,
the *comédie noire* – which is not quite the same as a 'black comedy'. He thought
it might 'outrage many people, perplex others, fascinate, move and impress
others, baffle and annoy others, but I should be much surprised if it bored
anybody'. He continued:

> Dirk Bogarde is one of the top, if not *the* top popular star in England, and has
> of recent years become a name of international importance. Whatever else may
> be said of the film, his performance is certainly a startling innovation for him,
> and I think will be recognised as by far his most important performance up to
> now. As a Frenchman recently said on viewing some of the rushes: 'We knew
> about Bogarde in France as a star, but we didn't know he was a great actor.'
> Dirk tends to bridge the generations.[25]

The story of how *The Servant* limped, via Paris and Venice, towards a public
screening in Britain is comprehensively told in the Life of Losey by David Caute.
Eventually, it was the head of Warners in Europe, Arthur Abeles, needing at
short notice to fill a gap-week at his large West End cinema, who rescued the
film from a pile gathering dust as 'unreleasable'. The haunting poster, featuring

one of Losey's trademark convex mirrors, went up outside the Warner in Leicester Square, and the press were invited on Monday, 11 November. The following morning at least one newspaper hurried into print with the word 'masterpiece'; by the Sunday the acclaim was unanimous – and even those critics who felt the film was marred by its thoroughly *anti*-climactic orgy were in ecstasies about Dirk's performance. Thomas Wiseman in the *Sunday Express* spoke for most when he wrote:

> Mr Bogarde seizes this part like a hungry man confronted by his first square meal in years. Dispensing with the easy cuteness that has earned him his popularity, [he] gives us a heart-cooling portrait of the underdog having his day.
>
> With its cleverly placed homosexual inferences, this is a performance in which every move is worked out as in a game of chess. Only in retrospect can one appreciate the cleverness of the overall strategy [. . .] With this performance, the best he has given so far, Mr Bogarde places himself in quite a new category as an actor, and makes himself eligible for a whole new range of parts previously regarded as beyond his range.[26]

Dilys Powell hailed a 'flawless performance in a masterly film, which [. . .] brings to the English screen the sense of experiment. Exploring the relations between characters in differing social strata, it does not attempt the arabesques of the Continental directors – but it doesn't need to.' Losey's style, for her, was as audacious as anything to be found across the Channel.[27] Patrick Gibbs in *The Daily Telegraph* found Dirk's portrayal to be 'a remarkably effective study in the sinister'.[28] The *Sunday Citizen* beckoned its readers, and saw the point, with the headline: 'May I have your soul, please?'[29]

James Fox, too, received a chorus of praise, and would never forget the debt he owed to Dirk for choosing and encouraging him. Many talk of the generosity which Dirk showed to younger actors. In Fox's case it was not in any overt way, such as by tutoring him in the practicalities of acting when surrounded by, and having to be conscious of, a crew and its equipment. Rather, Dirk's gift was a partly selfish one: he made Fox raise his game to such an extent that the latter felt they were working as equals; and Dirk functioned best when challenged. Sarah Miles who, coincidentally, was now living in Hasker Street with her Pyrenean mountain dog Addo, stated mischievously in her memoirs that she 'lost' Fox 'both to his role in *The Servant* and to Dirk Bogarde' and that the 'delving inward' for their performances as Barrett and Tony needed 'hard work and risky soul-searching', but had to go 'even deeper'. Barrett tries to control Tony by drawing him into lechery and decadence, she wrote; rehearsal was essential and, since she was secretly seeing another man, 'on what grounds could I grumble?' In fact Fox spent a month preparing for the role under the formal tuition of the actor, director and teacher Vivian Matalon. Sarah Miles, whose reviews were 'raves' as well, remembered that Dirk, 'an absolute professional, was good fun to be with and I learned a lot from him. His knife-sharp observation made him quick to grasp that I had a problem with gravity and he christened me "Dainty" almost from day one.'[30] Wendy Craig was the only member of the principal quartet whom Losey regarded as a weak link. Dirk had recommended her for the part of Master Tony's luckless girlfriend after working with her on *The Mind Benders*, which had come out to caustic notices in mid-production of *The Servant*. Losey, doubtless prejudiced by his American background, thought she was not 'upper-class' enough; the critics found no fault at all. It was, in sum, a triumph, and no less so in Europe. The large-circulation Paris-based magazine *Cinémonde*, which had as usual on its cover a photograph of Brigitte Bardot, devoted three pages to *Le Serviteur*, describing it as a film for adults, of rare violence, continuous intensity and true audacity – a magical film.[31]

No one knew it then, but a little more language of that kind would be enough to persuade Dirk where his future, both professional and domestic, lay. Without question, the former would in some way involve Losey, to whom he had given as an end-of-filming present a small Japanese ivory frog. What was the director like to work with, the *Isis* interviewer asked Dirk: 'Well it's very difficult to answer that really, because we work together without any words ever being spoken. I never ask him anything, he never tells me anything. It's completely a mutual marriage of minds. We are completely dissimilar people, and you know that that is usually the best sort of marriage.'[32] Another, unpredictable, question was: 'Apart from Liszt's Hungarian Rhapsody No. 6 in D-flat at two places in the film, what are the pieces that you whistle?'

> I whistled that little bit because it seemed to fit there and because I'd played it until I was green in the face in a film about Liszt [. . .] and the rest I just made up. It's difficult, because every time you do those spontaneous things, if it's within 50 years, you've got to be charged copyright. Being Barrett was very simple because it was such a beautifully constructed and beautifully written part, and I was being Barrett practically all day long, which was frightfully worrying to most of my friends. So it was very simple to take something like the things he whistled automatically from him.[33]

As his family attest, Dirk was a great whistler at home – especially when the pressure was on. And in the eight months between the completion of *The Servant* and its première there had been plenty to keep that kettle boiling at Nore. The customary staff trouble was one thing; an estimated tax bill for £41,000, to be paid by 1 January, was quite another. 'Something's got to give!' noted Tony. The £500 apiece which they had won by placing £100 on Relko in the Derby was not going to be of much help. They seriously considered moving into the converted cottage, which was now called the Pheasantry. Renewed thoughts of going abroad had been dismissed by Dirk because he felt he would not find enough work. To make matters worse, and adding to rumours that Shepperton Studios were on the brink of closure, John Davis had hinted that Pinewood itself might have to shut down temporarily because the industry was in such dire straits. Dirk had made two more films since *The Servant*, both for Betty Box and Ralph Thomas, and both with an air of desperation about them – especially the first, in which, for £20,000, he had agreed to resuscitate Simon Sparrow. *Doctor in Distress* was as much James Robertson Justice's vehicle as it was Dirk's and, disregarding prolonged shots of Mylène Demongeot in the hottest of pants, proved notable only for a sneak aural preview of Dirk's Barrett accent, deployed during a telephone call. Shooting had started before *The Servant* finished, but *Doctor in Distress* opened four months sooner. It was now clear to Box and Thomas that Dirk was accepting parts purely for the money. He was decidedly reluctant to take on the spoof thriller *Hot Enough for June*, and matters were made worse when a first treatment – by the Canadian novelist Mordecai Richler – proved unacceptable to Rank. Then, as Dirk demurred, Tom Courtenay agreed to take the leading role; at which point Tony said to Dirk in front of the producer and director: 'I'm not sure, Dirk, that you can afford to turn this down.'[34] Everyone knew that 'afford' was meant in the literal sense. Once again a new BH5, this one in two shades of grey, rolled through France with Ulric and Margaret completing the party; once again Tony's sixteen-millimetre camera recorded their progress to Florence, to Padua – the principal location – and to Venice, half an hour's drive away. Dirk's attempt to play a spy had even the friendliest of reviewers struggling to find a kind word: 'He is the sort of secret agent who looks as menacing as a pop gun and probably isn't even licensed to kill grouse,' wrote Thomas Wiseman.[35] There is a moment when Nicolas Whistler – an appropriate name for Dirk – has to pretend to be a Czechoslovakian milkman, and his cry of 'Mee-lkoo' sums up the pottiness of the entire enterprise. Tony, incidentally, was recruited to walk purposefully into an immense official building, a sequence intended for the beginning of the film, while the credits rolled. On the production call-sheet he was named Antonio Avanti.

At least these films were realised. The traffic in possible projects for Dirk, either as actor or as producer/investor, was extensive, but as usual most of them came to nothing. For much of 1963 he was kept in suspense about whether or not a thriller called 'The Achilles Affair' was to be made, with Stuart Whitman as his co-star. At one point it came so close to fruition that he and Tony boarded the Rolls with John Standing and Maude, and set off for Yugoslavia. They reached Venice, where they were joined by Gareth Forwood, and stayed in limbo for ten days, waiting to hear whether the production's financial problems had been sorted out. With nothing resolved and the bills mounting at the Gritti Palace – favoured city hotel number four – they flew home, leaving the car in Venice in case the film went ahead. It did not, and the Rolls was shipped home at a cost of £91. Dirk missed a fee of £40,000, and as a result turned down a series of requests for investment in stage productions. Even though *Hot Enough for June* came partially to the rescue, the position had become so tight, the tax commitments so crippling, that he felt obliged to end the arrangement with Moura Budberg. Bernard Walsh was asked tentatively to find a buyer for Nore. 'The Rolls is going and so is the house,' Dirk said while on location in Venice. 'It is quite ridiculous that I have allowed that house, for example, to become master of my life.'³⁶ Maude recalls how Tony told Dirk that they were spending an untenable sum each month on magazines. After a little thought Dirk agreed that the order should be cancelled – 'But not *Country Life.*' Some sacrifices were beyond the pale.³⁷

Dirk's popularity at the box-office was ebbing away. Cliff Richard had headed the *Motion Picture Herald* poll for two years, and Dirk was ninth, behind Peter Sellers, Elvis Presley, Sean Connery, Hayley Mills, Elizabeth Taylor, Marlon Brando and Albert Finney.³⁸ 'A great actor who has never appeared in a great film' was the description of Dirk above a thoughtful appraisal of his work by Richard Whitehall which appeared in *Films and Filming* just before the opening of *The Servant.*³⁹ After its reception the general view was that he had now appeared in a great film, but the uncertainties in his life were as profound as ever. Preliminary soundings were made about his interest in both *Alfie* and *King Rat,* and he might have found himself revisiting *Journey's End* for MGM, until he heard rumours that it was felt he was too old for the part. At least he had now corrected his entry in the reference books, where for many years he had given his birthdate as 1920 – a peculiarly modest conceit when, just as some actresses have always cheerfully shaved a few years off their age, so he could probably have got away with adding two or three. Then again, when early in 1960 an interviewer had done her sums from existing cuttings and made him forty-four instead of thirty-eight, he was very cross indeed. There was still confusion when, at forty-two, he arrived in New York to do a play for television, *Little Moon of Alban.*

The on-off affair with America had reached a delicate stage. Hollywood, its difficulties in proportion to those in the British film industry, had gone decidedly cold and was unlikely to be stirred by the intellectually testing, claustrophobic *Servant.* Alan Lerner, who regretted the lack of recognition for Dirk in the United States, summed up the problem: 'Unfortunately, he bears the cross of good looks and all too often American critics find themselves incapable of believing depth and artistry can thrive behind a handsome face. A tortured life properly publicised will sometimes remove the stigma. A severe accident or prolonged illness will also help. Suffering somehow assures them that the actor is not a photograph.' Moreover, Dirk was further handicapped by not having an accent 'laced with Cockney' and by seeming to be educated, which was regarded as 'a perversion of the truth'.⁴⁰ Nancy Olson and Lauren Bacall, among others, said during the preparation of this book that Dirk was 'too intelligent' for Hollywood.⁴¹ Never-theless the East Coast wanted him, at least for television, which, he said, he refused to do in Britain because audiences would not come to see him in the cinema if he was 'all over' the BBC.⁴² *Little Moon of Alban* was a drama of the

Irish Troubles in the twenties, in which Dirk appeared as a wounded officer tended by a novitiate, played by Julie Harris, who had created the part of the nursing sister opposite Christopher Plummer, and performed it subsequently with George Peppard and Robert Redford. The play was written with Dirk in mind by James Costigan, after they had met on one of Dirk's and Tony's transatlantic voyages; Costigan incorporated into the text some of the 'dirty stories' that Dirk had told him during the crossing. However, Dirk's British film commitments prevented him from taking part in the original Hallmark Hall of Fame production. Rehearsals and recording at the NBC studios in Brooklyn took nearly three weeks, during which Tony kept busy working on a script from a novel called *Barbouze* by Emlyn Williams's thriller-writing son Alan. Dirk had bought an option, and for a while it looked as if he might star in the film with Orson Welles, under the direction of Bryan Forbes, but the project was another that fell away. After *Little Moon* was finished Dirk and Tony stayed on in New York for another two weeks, principally to help with the promotion for *The Servant* which opened while they were there, but also to enjoy the social life afforded by old friends such as Kay Young, Lerner, Lauren Bacall and Roddy McDowall, and newer ones such as Richard Burton's ex-wife Sybil and an agent from the Deep South, Alice Lee 'Boaty' Boatwright, sister-in-law of the English actor George Baker who had been in the cast of *Doctor at Sea*. Dirk and Tony were bowled over by Carol Channing in *Hello Dolly*, but 'haunted' by the Mills family at the theatre and at the party afterwards – doubtless the occasion when, as John Mills recalled, they were snubbed. As part of the promotional round, Dirk was a guest on Johnny Carson's *Tonight* show, accompanied by Eva Gabor and a chimpanzee. Just before leaving for home he learned he had won the Variety Club Award for his performance as Barrett. With all that, and excellent reviews in the New York newspapers not just for *The Servant* but also for 'the telly', it had been an uplifting visit. Tony wrote to Laurence Harbottle that 'Dirk is rather taken with America this time, so if he sells the house we might move here!'[43] They left the Plaza 'not without regret'.

They returned to news of another award – the British Film Academy's, for best actor – and of a possible third film with Joe Losey. *King and Country* was based on a stage and television play by John Wilson, which had in turn been expanded from an incident in a novel by James Lansdale Hodson about a First World War deserter, and the relationship formed with the captain who is given the task of defending him at a court martial. Losey described the film as 'a class conversation in which the officer is educated by the boy's simplicity'. When Captain Hargreaves ends Private Hamp's life with his revolver after a bungled execution by firing squad, the former is, in a sense, 'ending his own life as well as the boy's'.[44] On a wider and more explicit level, *King and Country* is also a devastating indictment of war. Evan Jones's script describes Hargreaves as slim, erect, dark-haired, much decorated and, although he is still in his twenties, 'the war has aged him so that he looks almost forty'. His façade of complete control hides 'a ruthless man with a taste for violence' who despises Hamp as the strong despise the weak, but is responsible for him 'as the gentleman is always responsible for his retainers'. The story – to emphasise Losey's point – is that of Hargreaves being 'moved by Hamp's faith in him to a new awareness of that responsibility'.[45] The film was shot in eighteen days at Shepperton, on a budget of £86,000. Losey said the film was realised only because of the risks and sacrifices made by people with whom he had worked before; this gave them a freedom to shape the material according to their own ideas – none more than Dirk. He told David Caute that Losey had shown him the 1959 television playscript, then called 'Hamp', while they were in New York at the time of the *Servant* première; Dirk in turn gave Losey a copy of 'Covenant with Death', which Bendrose had failed to produce, and suggested Losey visit the Imperial War Museum. Evan Jones's effort, initially entitled 'Glory Hole', did not impress Dirk, who came to the subject with both specialist knowledge, from his time as an Army officer, and, just as important, the commitment of the amateur, who had grown up obsessed with the imagery of the First World War. Losey would acknowledge Dirk's 'immensely helpful' contribution. To give just one example, there is a scene in which Hargreaves questions Hamp about his motives for running – or rather, wandering – away, and the Private replies that he had been blown into a deep shell hole where he thought he would drown until he was rescued by two of his comrades who pulled him out with their rifles. In Dirk's copy of the script is a passage in his own hand: 'I saw it happen to a bloke before once – He just slipped off the duckboard – wasn't pushed, just fell – into the hole, he went bobbing up and down in the mud like an egg boiling in water – with his pack and everything you know'.[46] The egg and the water: just as Lally described Ulric's recurrent waking nightmare.

Rats, sludge, rain, the rotting carcass of a horse, sometimes all four at once – no wonder the cast and crew were glad to be out of Shepperton. They had worked at such a pitch that on one day they shot an astonishing twelve minutes of screen time. Dirk was exhausted, but knew that he had done some of his best work. Just as with *The Servant*, there would be cold feet among the distributors before *King and Country* found an outlet in Britain. There were accusations that it was not only downbeat – which suggests that the point had been missed somehow – but also anti-establishment. Fortunately a pillar of that same establishment was John (Lord) Brabourne, Earl Mountbatten's son-in-law and himself a prominent producer; he had been involved in the financing of the film and stood by it. *King and Country* went to the Venice Festival, where Tom Courtenay won the Volpi Cup for his portrayal of Hamp. Losey said that both he *and* Dirk 'should have got it because Tom, who is an extremely good actor, would be the first to acknowledge that he could never have given that performance if Dirk hadn't been so generous'.[47] Indeed Courtenay remembered how kind to him both Losey and Dirk had been during the making of *King and Country.* He and Dirk never worked together again, but more than twenty years later they met at a dinner party in London. In his text for a volume of letters written to him by his mother, whose husband had worked for the fishing industry in Hull, Courtenay recalled that Dirk greeted him with the words: 'How's the fishwife's son?' It was said with affection.[48]

For the rest of Dirk's life *King and Country* remained a source of pride. None of his films had been made so cheaply and so quickly, and none, arguably, to greater effect, although one or two of the critics felt its dice were too heavily loaded. In 1967 Dirk lectured at the Philharmonic Hall in Liverpool, to two full houses of fifth- and sixth-form pupils from local colleges and grammar schools. He chose *King and Country* as his subject because he found it the most satisfying of his forty-odd films to date, and also because it had been shown to so few people; it had been a commercial disaster. Seeing there was a clear majority of girls among his listeners, he added his hope that the screening which was to follow his talk would not be so horrific as to result in aisles full of the fainted.[49] There were no reports of casualties, just of a shocked and much moved young audience. Eleven years later the film was 'apparently still in the red'.[50]

Two days after leaving the noisome set at Shepperton, Dirk and Tony were heading for the sun. Betty Box and Ralph Thomas had persuaded Dirk to do a ninth film for them, *The High Bright Sun*, a thriller set against the background of the Eoka terrorist campaign on Cyprus in the fifties. For obvious reasons, the island itself was not an option, so the location headquarters were established first at Bari, then at Foggia, in the heel of Italy. Betty Box recalled that for the only time in their ten-year association Dirk was 'a less than happy member of the unit'. He immediately christened Foggia 'Hot Watford' and on arrival at its 'rather iron curtainy hotel' set about rearranging the suite he and Tony had been given, by commandeering furniture from other rooms. Something close to a tornado struck the town on their first night, knocking out the electricity – not for the last time. Halfway through the shooting, Dirk and Ralph Thomas had an unprecedented row. Betty Box remembered that she came back to the hotel after viewing some rushes at the local cinema, and said to Dirk how good they were. 'I don't care a fuck about the rushes,' he said in a voice loud enough for all to hear. 'Finish the fucking film and get me home.' A shocked Betty Box walked away, to be pursued by an anxious Tony, saying: 'Don't worry, Betty. He doesn't mean it.'[51] This was the occasion which, above all, prompted Betty Box's husband, Peter Rogers, to say: 'Dirk could be a petulant beast.'[52] Within forty-eight hours the air was cleared and an apologetic Dirk was carrying on with the job as if nothing had happened. In fact he was not at all well. A doctor found that he had an inflamed liver and a touch of heatstroke, but he continued to work. On one of his free days, he and Tony took Dirk's co-star George Chakiris and Arnold Schulkes to see the memorial to Rudolf Valentino at his birthplace in Castellaneta; they found what Tony described, and as his cine-film bore out, as 'the most hideous purple ceramic statue'. There was a fair amount of beach activity with male companions from the unit, including frolics on swings and slides which Tony's camera duly, and somewhat embarrassingly, captured for posterity.

Another day was spent on Capri, where he and Dirk sought out Gracie Fields's restaurant: 'All very flash & crowded with what one would expect.' Dirk 'rather bravely' introduced himself to the Lancastrian singer-in-exile, who was at first 'coolish', then asked him to repeat his name as she was deaf. She warmed up and proved 'friendly in a North Country way', looked 'marvellous', and admitted she spoke no Italian. Her restaurant served the best food Dirk and Tony had ever had in Italy.

They were away for a month, and returned to find Nore at its most ravishing, but with more staff difficulties. One member of the team was finding it hard to get on with the cook/housekeeper, Mrs Knight, who had arrived in the spring after working for several 'good houses', including seven years with Queen Mary at Marlborough House. Alas, Mrs K herself would last only six months. The search for a buyer had taken on a new momentum. Bernard Walsh brought the twenty-seven-year-old singer and actor Tommy Steele, and his wife Ann, to look at Nore. The following day they offered £59,000, and Dirk and Tony agreed 'with great reluctance' to accept £60,000; but there were doubts about whether or not the sale would result in a significant tax burden for Dirk, and about the Steeles' commitment. The deal fell through, but with no animosity: Tommy and Ann Steele would soon be welcome dinner guests at the house they nearly bought. In any case, Dirk was far from set on selling. Despite the financial pressures, he was still living pretty high on the hog. Another BH5, blue and black, would soon be installed in the garage, alongside a new BH7 – a white Alfa Romeo Spider. A handsome rectangular gold Longines watch adorned his wrist. He was again backing theatrical ventures, in a small way, through Bendrose – losing £125 on *The Striplings*, which at least had given a showcase to a young man called Michael Crawford; and putting another £100 into a Kitty Black production, *Maxibules*. There was enough spare cash – and goodwill – to spend, through Bendrose, £100 in support of the satirical magazine *Private Eye*, which had been founded in 1961 and was undergoing one of its periodic crises. He and eight others, including Jane Asher, Bernard Braden, Peter Sellers and the publisher Anthony Blond, made contributions to the magazine, knowing full well that there would probably never be a return on their 'investment'; Laurence Harbottle suggested to Dirk's accountant that the most sensible way of explaining this arrangement was to call it 'a loan which disappears'.[53] After a while a certificate arrived, showing that Dirk owned 103 shares, but even when the company became highly profitable he neither sought nor reaped any financial benefit for himself; instead his stake brought him a case of wine each Christmas for the rest of his life.

The entertaining achieved a peak when Dirk threw a party for about a hundred at the Ad Lib Club to mark the departure to New York of Sybil Burton. The *Sun*, in those days a broadsheet newspaper, dedicated its entire page three to a report and photographs of this star-spangled affair, at which on the stroke of midnight Dirk, Tony and Alma Cogan sang their own version of 'Hello Dolly':

'Ta ra, Sybil/Well ta ra, Sybil/It's been good to have you back where you belong./You're going away, Sybil,/To USA, Sybil/You can stay there, you can play there/But for not too long!' – and so on. The following day a judge told the club that neighbours had complained about the noise from its 'beat music' and ordered that it had to stop, even if it meant £10,000 would have to be spent on sound-proofing.[54]

No listener would have guessed, but it was on the morning after the Ad Lib party and with just three and a half hours' sleep that Dirk went to the BBC to record *Desert Island Discs*. The programme's creator, Roy Plomley, asked him whether he could endure the isolation of the castaway and Dirk replied: 'I think I'd go absolutely stark, staring bonkers.' Out came many of the stories, about his family being Dutch, about being bashed on the head by Max Adrian, about being billed as 'Bert Gocart' outside the Brighton cinema screening *Esther Waters*. He chose two of Liszt's compositions played by Jorge Bolet, Elisabeth Schwarzkopf singing 'Vilja' from *The Merry Widow,* Beethoven's Fifth Symphony and songs by Yvonne Printemps, Judy Garland and Carol 'Hello Dolly' Channing. There seems to have been great confusion about the eighth and final disc: Rex Harrison singing 'I've Grown Accustomed to Her Face', from *My Fair Lady.* For some reason it was not played, but Dirk said he wanted to take it with him because of its 'most marvellous backhanded love lyric' and because Harrison had 'influenced my acting life in the theatre and on the screen more than any other actor or living person'. The song would remind him of 'that beautiful purity of diction and the splendour and power of the English tongue'. Asked how he would manage on his island, Dirk replied that he would be able to live off the land – 'I'm very good at gardening'; that he was excellent at catching fish if he had to, but did not like killing them; and that he would hammer some sort of craft into shape. Reminded that nails would not be available, he said: 'Well, then, I'd lash things together.' Would he try to escape? 'Yes, every four minutes.' The invidious choice of a single record came down to Beethoven because after five years he might be bored by 'Hello Dolly'. His book would be *The Swiss Family Robinson* by Johann David Wyss, which Dirk 'bought for twopence in Lewes High Street when I was about fifteen' and which 'tells you exactly and precisely how to live on a desert island'. And his luxury item was John Singer Sargent's portrait of the Sitwells, 'Conversation Piece', which was not only the most haunting picture of its kind that he had ever seen, but also 'very large', so he could make it into a tent or a raft.[55] It had been a congenial encounter – for a fee of 40 guineas to boot.

Four days later Dirk was back in Broadcasting House, for a long discussion with Philip Oakes of *The Sunday Telegraph* and Mary Holland of *The Observer.* Here was an opportunity to try out for a radio audience some of the anecdotes and one-liners that would be the staple for countless broadcast interviews in the years to come. Talking about the way in which the Studio would accommodate his wish not to be photographed from the right profile, he said: 'I was rather like sort of Loretta Young, you know', which would be sharpened to: 'I was the Loretta Young of my day.' He said he had spent seventeen years as a 'sort of pop Cliff Richards'. Hollywood was 'most appalling' and 'a wonderful place', a 'mixture of New Delhi and Golders Green', described by Dorothy Parker as 'seven suburbs in search of a city'. The Bob Thomson saga – 'I'm just wondering how the hell you've ever stuck' – was given an airing, but at least Thomson was not killed off. And, in a nice Bogardian simile to capture the unpleasantness of promoting a film at a festival, 'you really do walk around like a bandaged thumb'. Philip Oakes wondered if Dirk felt any professional rivalry, to which he replied that he had envied some rather bad actors their good fortune, some their 'Hollywood chances', but he preferred to stay 'professionally dull': 'Tyrone Power once said that he was a very good journeyman actor, and I think that's what I would like most to be.' Dirk wanted to be not too high, not too low, but 'on an even keel, hurting no one too much, and loving no one too much', just enjoying the cinema's equivalent of a 'comfortable, solid, middle-class existence'.

Asked about the sacrifices that had been demanded of him, Dirk said that he had 'tried the marriage caper, shall we put it that way, without ever getting married, three times', but he had never yet found a relationship with a woman in which he was not 'the possessed' rather than 'the possessor': 'I don't mind possessing and showing off my possession but I hate being possessed.' He made the comparison between his own situation as a free spirit who could, like Gauguin, just pack up and leave, as opposed to other members of his profession who were making a lot of money, had put the son down for Eton and the daughter for Heathfield, built a swimming-pool, laid the tennis court, bought a donkey and given the wife a mink, but were now 'trapped in a sort of vortex of necessity'. Better to be, like Dirk, 'a draft of one'. Most intimately, he said that he had been a very fortunate child who 'never had any unhappiness or lack of love or money or anything' and whose parents were 'very intelligent and sensible'; the highest compliment he could offer them now was to succeed in the job he chose to do. And he could repay them in some measure by taking them away on holidays. It was a lively discussion, but the chief producer of arts talks was unhappy, suggesting that the allotted time of forty minutes should be cut to thirty, mainly because of Dirk's rapid speech which did not make for easy listening. Three months later, the assistant head of talks decided that too much of the programme was 'gabbled' and recommended it should go out in a twenty-minute spot or even a seventeen-minute 'concert space'. Eventually it was transmitted, much depleted and under the title 'It Takes All Sorts', five months after the recording was made. What a waste.[56]

During the discussion, Dirk mentioned that in four days' time he was starting a new film which contained the best part for a British actress in ten years. It was about 'a little predatory beast who claws her way through four men and ruins them, finally ending up as [an] Italian contessa and is ruined in turn'. That, in Dirk's nutshell, was the story of *Darling*, which was to star Julie Christie – one of his guests on the noisy night at the Ad Lib – as Diana Scott, the beautiful, amoral, blithe spirit haunting fashionable London. Dirk, as so often, was not the first choice to play her lover Robert Gold, a journalist and television personality; although, bizarrely, his name is mentioned in Frederic Raphael's first treatment of the story: 'She sees DIRK BOGARDE (or a comparable star) in a smart furniture shop and promptly goes in.'[57] The most likely candidate for the role was Maximilian Schell, until possible legal action was threatened by a woman who believed the story was based on her, and last-minute changes in nationality were required. Letters whisked across the Atlantic to George Maharis and John Cassavetes, but no American company would provide financial backing, so the director, John Schlesinger, and his producer Joseph Janni eventually decided to go for 'marquee names' in England in order to secure British funding. Dirk was engaged as Robert, and Laurence Harvey as the sleek and unscrupulous tycoon Miles Brand. If ever a film captured the *Zeitgeist* of the mid-sixties, it was *Darling*, with its cold eye trained on what one writer described as 'a phenomenon of detribalisation' in a world of promiscuity both sexual and social.[58] Nearly three years before he started shooting, Schlesinger said it would be about the rich and the *nouveaux riches*, but would not be made as a satire; there would, however, be irony – 'There is an element always of something that is ironic in everything I do.'[59] Which, of course, suited Dirk just fine.

Frederic Raphael quotes Dirk as saying of Julie Christie that she was 'the most exciting English talent I've worked with for years' and of Laurence Harvey: 'His taste is between his toes.' As for Dirk himself, Raphael found him, at forty-three, 'still pretty, like some neat zoologist's exhibit. Full face, he has a dreadful knowingness; in profile he retains the spent innocence of a second-hand mid-shipman.'[60] The film took three months to shoot, at locations which included Bristol, where Dirk went into the streets as a 'vox pop' interviewer, and Lord's cricket ground, where on a spectacular summer's day hoses supplied rain, with disastrous consequences for the continuity sheets maintained by Ann Skinner; photographs survive showing Dirk and Arnold Schulkes on their haunches with her in the middle of the hallowed turf, pegging pages of the script out to dry. One scene, featuring Julie Christie, Dirk and the Oxford don Hugo Dyson, was filmed in the office at Nore, on the day after Mrs Knight's departure; Maude and Tony kept the unit victualled with bacon sandwiches and coffee.

Throughout it all, Schlesinger quite naturally never betrayed his feeling that the film had a fundamental flaw; afterwards he wrote to the camera operator, John Harris, that all the performances were very good but that Dirk had been miscast in the most difficult and unrewarding role. Frederic Raphael dismisses this: 'Schlesinger, and directors in general, are a race who are preternaturally disposed to giving the impression that it is they from whom all blessings flow. Clearly, if Dirk gives a good performance when he is "miscast", it must be to do with how brilliantly he has been directed. It's very unwise to assume that because John said something he meant it. He meant it to *do* something.' And perhaps the same applies to actors: four days after finishing work at Shepperton Dirk wrote to 'My very dear Schlesch' that he had found Robert 'a sod to play ... because he did'nt always seem to be within my grasp ... but with your help and mending I hope it wont be too disgraceful as a perf.' He thanked the director for his kindness when 'I got gritty from time to time out of funk' and guaranteed that 'it is going to be a tremendous film', 'eight billion times better than it's script ... and that was pretty good for a start'. Dirk concluded with a plea to be allowed to work with Schlesinger again: 'actors need direction and only directors proper can do that ... and genius directors are a bonus ... but DOLLY GENIUS DIRECTORS are super bonus'. He said he would be 'delighted and happy to play a fir-tree or an egg-whisk or a try of Escargots anytime you asked me!'[61] Thirteen years later he told Ann Skinner: 'I still think "Darling ..." was his [Schlesinger's] best, in spite of everything that followed. And Julie has never been as good again.'[62]

Frederic Raphael confirms that Dirk had been accepted for the part with some reluctance by Schlesinger, but that in the final result 'he served us extremely well':

> He was also very good with Julie – which is not a constant characteristic of slightly older star actors with new talent. He deserves a lot of credit for Julie's performance. I don't in any way wish to suggest that I thought he was a selfish actor; I saw no evidence that he was ever a selfish actor. It is a virtue; it is not simply the absence of a vice. One can contrast it with a certain gracelessness off-screen which certainly did not extend to being *on*-screen. In other words, he probably chose the right métier! He did have that quality – he did manage to do extraordinarily little in such a way that it looked like a lot. Which may be why he wasn't quite a star. He was a model, and that is what screen actors have to be. The ability simply by *being there* to seem to be expressing something. The old montage trick is that if I sit here looking soulful and you cut to a woman it's because I'm dreaming about her; if you cut to a ham sandwich I'm dreaming about it; and if you cut to a plunge in the Caribbean I'm dreaming about that – each time you're thinking 'I don't know how he conveyed his longing for the woman, the sandwich and the Caribbean'. The answer is, he didn't; the scissors did that. But he *allowed* the scissors to do it. And it's not nothing.[63]

A few unsuccessful scenes with Julie Christie were cut, because, says Raphael, 'they were flirty. He wasn't awfully good at the flirty, any more than Alan Bates was. At pain, at need, at all sorts of things like that, Dirk was immensely good.' The writer also remembers Dirk saying to him on one occasion: 'I find Robert very weak in this scene, dear.' 'To which I replied: "Why the fuck do you think we asked *you* to do it?" I was more outspoken in those days! After that, he referred to me always as The Author – "What does The Author think?"' In similar vein,

Raphael tells a story about Dirk which travelled from *The Servant* to other productions, including *Darling*. Puzzling over whether Barrett was lapsed or fake, he asked Pinter: 'Well, dear, is he a gentleman or not?' To which Pinter is said to have replied: 'Don't give a fuck, dear.'

Fifteen

'I have never felt quite so abandoned and destroyed as I do today'

Early in 1965 Dirk was interested to learn that he had been picked up by police on a drunk-driving charge in New York, and that he had 'complicated the situation by throwing a punch at one of the officers who hauled him into the station house'. This information arrived in the form of a cutting from the *National Enquirer*, a 'Scandal Sheet' of which neither he nor Tony knew anything, and had been posted to him by 'a completely psychotic fan in America'. The sole accurate fact was that Dirk had been in New York. He and Tony spent ten days there at Christmas, basing themselves as usual at the Plaza, and being much fêted. The visit coincided with the presentation of the New York Film Critics Awards, at which Dirk missed by the narrowest margin being honoured as best actor for *The Servant*. The judging panel had six ballots, at the end of which they voted seven–six in favour of Rex Harrison for *My Fair Lady*. Pinter won the award for best screenplay. Dirk was far from downcast: theirs had been a cheap British picture which had opened nearly a year before, while the Lerner/Loewe musical had been recently released with all the oompah of a Hollywood blockbuster. In any case, who better for him to lose to than Harrison? The critical response to *The Servant* was such that Dirk went on the offensive. With the Oscars three months away, he wrote a long letter to Hedda Hopper in Hollywood, suggesting that after the success of the film in New York perhaps it was not such a long shot to think of 'recognition from the Academy'. He said that it was clearly not the kind of film which benefited from a big exploitation programme: 'So I suppose it's up to me as much as anybody to try and make people at least aware of our existence!' He conceded that he was 'nothing like as well-known in America as I am at home', but that as Hedda Hopper had been kind enough in the past to mention films in which he had been involved, perhaps she would forgive him for 'bringing us to your attention at this very important time'. He mentioned that *King and Country* was proving another outstanding success for the 'same team', but that naturally 'we do long for approval from Hollywood, which is after all the Movie Centre of the World!'[1] The Christmas visit to New York had also brought Dirk a team of 'personal managers' in the shape of Robert Chartoff and Irwin Winkler, to complement the work of his agent Robert Lantz. They advised him that it would be worth spending something in the region of $3,000 on a campaign to bring his name to the Academy's attention. The attempt failed: nominated for best actor were Rex Harrison, Richard Burton, Peter O'Toole, Anthony Quinn and Peter Sellers; and the winner was ... Harrison. Nevertheless the initiatives indicated how Dirk and Tony were following their resolution to make it 'push Bogarde year – in the right direction one hopes!'

There was no shortage of ideas. Peter Shaffer's *Black Comedy*; Iris Murdoch's *A Severed Head*; L. P. Hartley's *The Go-Between* with Anthony Asquith; a version of the life of Mary, Queen of Scots; a suggestion from Tony that Losey and Dirk do Henry James's *The Wings of the Dove* with Lee Remick – all were floated in the first few days of the year. Otto Preminger appeared to be keen for Dirk to play in *Bunny Lake is Missing* – nothing to do with the former headmaster of University College School – but gave the part at a late stage to Laurence Olivier, which, given Preminger's reputation, was probably no bad thing. There had been a difficult series of negotiations with the Boulting Brothers regarding a crime caper called *Rotten to the Core*, from which Dirk finally withdrew because he felt unhappy with the probable casting of Alfred Marks. And, a full twenty-five years before his dream became a reality, Richard Attenborough wondered whether Dirk would consider playing the title role in *Gandhi*. Amid the hail of scripts, and telephone calls about possible scripts, there was a health scare: tests showed that Dirk's liver was malfunctioning, so a course of injections was prescribed, with good results. However, the overall picture was full of gloom. By April, three years after they had moved to Nore, Dirk was being assailed by his black dog. The only 'work' he had done, apart from one or two extra shots for *Darling*, was a television appeal for thalidomide children, and the only firm commitment was another charitable gesture – the commentary for *Exile*, a film about Tibetan refugees directed by John Irvin. One night, Dirk dreamed that he was 'Hitler's favourite soldier', and in the morning a script arrived for a play about the Battle of Stalingrad, as seen from the German Army's point of view. He wisely turned it down.

Things were dark enough for Tony to note at one point that although Dirk's mood had lifted slightly from the previous day, when they had shared a 'rather monosyllabic drive' through the Hampshire and Sussex countryside, there were still undercurrents – 'running at least partially in my direction – something I have said [...] but I don't know what except I think to do with acting'. They toyed briefly with the idea of operating the garden as a nursery, but in reality they knew that the house must finally be sold. Bernard Walsh was instructed, and on to the market it went, with offers sought at around £60,000. An alarm bell rang somewhere among Dirk's advisers that the Inland Revenue might begin to take an interest in the fairly rapid turnover of houses – three sales within five years – but his accountant, John Don Fox, reassured him that in each case there seemed to be a perfectly sound and valid reason. The property columnist of one newspaper reported that Dirk was not planning to look for a new home until the middle of the following year because he was 'committed to making four films abroad until then'.[2] Chance would be a fine thing. In fact the only firm prospect was a second narration – for a BBC documentary, 'The Epic That Never Was', about Alexander Korda's doomed attempt to film Robert Graves's *I, Claudius*. And there might just be another Losey film, *Modesty Blaise*, which would occupy about ten weeks in the late summer, with locations in Sicily.

Among those who expressed an early interest in Nore were Vivien Leigh's daughter, members of a family which had once owned the house, and Ringo Starr. Eventually Bernard Walsh brought another Liverpudlian, a racing driver, Max Wilson, and his wife to see it and they offered the asking price, behaving impeccably as the deal went through. By the time it did, *Modesty Blaise* was confirmed and contracts were exchanged two days before Dirk left for Italy. He agreed to hand over the keys in the middle of October. Once again it looked as if he and Tony would be homeless.

Their last spring and summer in Surrey had been notable for inactivity and for an illustrious long-stay guest. Ingrid Bergman had been engaged to appear in *A Month in the Country*, the opening production of the Yvonne Arnaud Theatre in Guildford, six miles away. Michael Redgrave was to direct the play and a member of his family asked Dirk if he would be prepared to provide digs. She proved a delightful companion, 'an honest no nonsense woman', noted Tony; 'quite lovely to look at & seems very sweet'. In her own memoirs she said that Redgrave had introduced them, and that Dirk 'thought it was terrible for me to live in a Guildford hotel because then I should meet my audience every time I went in or out'.[3] Which sounds very like Dirk, but was not quite the sequence of events. Her stay lasted a month, with no shortage of emotional ups and downs thanks to problems in rehearsals, incompatibility with Redgrave and poor reviews. Certainly there was no criticism of Dirk, who had been recruited to speak a prologue written by Christopher Fry, and so uttered the first words from the new theatre's stage as well as his own first from any stage since 1958. There came a moment after the notices were printed when a decision had to be made about whether or not to take the play to London. In a long, late-night discussion at Nore, Dirk and Tony advised against. It was good enough for Guildford but not for the capital. The actress duly spoke to Redgrave, who thought it should transfer. Her desire to appear in her first West End play overcame her better judgment. Returning from the theatre late one evening, she found Dirk had gone to bed, so left him a note saying she had gone against his and Tony's advice. The play went to the Cambridge Theatre and was a commercial triumph. Whenever they met subsequently, Dirk and Tony reminded her not to heed any advice of theirs: 'We told you not to go to London, and you could have run forever.' As she left Nore she gave Dirk a Dior dressing-gown, and Tony an outsized bottle of Scotch and a 'decision coin' for the office, to be tossed as often as necessary.

There was not much indecision – on Dirk's part anyway – about *Modesty Blaise*. Here was a chance, for £22,500, to camp it up wildly, and with licence, for his beloved Losey, whose working methods were now so familiar that Dirk had recently described him as 'the only woman in the world that ever had a baby'.[4] With a $3 million budget, it was an attempt to create 'pop art' on screen. There were the usual preliminary dramas over the script. Indeed the writer, Evan Jones, wrote to Losey of some 'wild thrashing about' by Dirk in the early stages because he was unsure how to play the role of Gabriel, who was intended to be 'slick, satiric, kinky, the international gangster weeping crocodile tears, the nouveau riche master criminal'.[5] Dirk needed a gimmick, and after an intensive talk with Jones, had found one: he wanted to be the black-sheep son of a dowager Scots countess who wrote detective stories, hunted stags and gave her boy psychoses about violence and power. And he had found a white wig.[6] Shooting had already begun in Amsterdam, where he was not required, when Dirk cabled joshingly to Losey that he was 'DEEPLY DESIROUS FOR CALM PEACE AFFEC-TION TRANQUILLITY AND MAJOR STAR TREATMENT FOR MY ARRIVAL', and wondering whether Terence Stamp had yet killed the unit hairdresser.[7] This time Dirk and Tony left the Rolls behind, flying to Rome and then, in decidedly un-star-like conditions, taking the 'peasants' express' to Calabria and across the water to Messina and Taormina. There they were billeted at the San Domenica Palace, a thirteenth-century convent which had been Field Marshal Kesselring's wartime headquarters. At first all went comparatively well; the lighting cameraman and one of the principal actresses were fired during the first week in Sicily, there were the customary organisational problems, some difficult weather and Terence Stamp was in a sulk. Dirk and Monica Vitti – the star of Antonioni's *L'Avventura* and *The Red Desert* – seemed to be getting along fine. Losey's wife Patricia recalls that

at the beginning Dirk adored her. We used to go to the beach every lunchtime and she would swim out miles. She swam beautifully. But Dirk said that on land he found her coarse and ungainly: 'She looks like the cook.' He was ambiguous about women – I remember he once said, 'It's a pity she's a woman. It's been proved that they have smaller brains than we have.' He was full of admiration and condescension.[8]

Clearly the latter prevailed, because an unspecified remark was taken the wrong way by Monica Vitti and a *froideur* descended which not even Tony could dispel. According to Frederic Raphael, Dirk began to intone: 'Miss Veetee is a peetee.'[9] After a week he sent her some roses and a note, and relations improved, but only marginally. For Losey, Monica Vitti was spoiled and impossible. Some months later he wrote to Darryl Zanuck at Twentieth Century-Fox: 'God help the next director!'[10] She, too, wrote to Zanuck, saying how she had loved the character of

Modesty before beginning the film but knew now that she had suffered 'four months of bitterness and humiliation for nothing'.[11]

Ann Skinner, who said that without Dirk's and Tony's kindness she would not have been able to get through *Darling*, her first film as continuity girl, found *Modesty Blaise*, her third, an uneasy production, on which Losey 'made big mistakes'. Dirk, she said, enjoyed 'doing something different'. He and Tony found her in the hotel, too distressed to go out alone because it meant running the gauntlet of the young Sicilian men:

> I was about thirty and you couldn't go anywhere without being touched. I couldn't bear it. When I explained this to Dirk and Tony they didn't believe me. They said, 'Right, we're going to take you to dinner. You go on ahead and we'll walk about a hundred yards behind you and see what happens.' They did, and when they saw what went on, Dirk said, 'From now on you eat with us every night.' It was a shock for him. He lived in this ivory-tower world where unpleasant things did not happen. But he took care of me.[12]

Just before they left England, Dirk had given an interview to, and been irritated by, Clive Hirschhorn of the *Sunday Express*. The piece appeared, under the heading 'I LOVE BRITAIN – BUT NOT THE PEOPLE says Mr Bogarde', while the unit was in Taormina. The tone of the encounter was plain to all, from Hirschhorn's account of arriving at the Connaught in 'light trousers', prompting Dirk to go in front of him into the dining-room 'so they won't notice'; on through an excoriation of the English as 'a nation of conforming sheep'; to a final paragraph about whether or not Dirk intended ever to marry: 'He sighed heavily. "That question," he said, "is like a stray puppy dog that has been following me remorselessly and relentlessly around for at least eighteen years. No matter what answer I give, people will automatically think I mean the opposite – so let's just leave it an open question, shall we?" '[13] Tony described the article as 'Filthy'. Dirk immediately sent a cable to the Editor:

INCLUDED IN SOME RATHER ODD DIALOGUE WRITTEN BY MR CLIVE HIRSCHORN AND ATTRIBUTED TO ME [...] IS THE SMUG SOUNDING LITTLE SENTENCE QUOTE I THINK I CAN DO WITHOUT THE PRESS UNQUOTE THIS COULD ONLY BE TAKEN AS UNGRATEFUL AND RUDE TO THE MANY FRIENDS I HAVE MADE IN THE PRESS OVER A LONG PERIOD STOP FEEL I MUST EMPHASISE IN THE INTERESTS OF ACCURACY THAT I VERY CLEARLY STATED I COULD DO WITHOUT A CERTAIN KIND OF JOURNALISM WHICH FOR ITS OWN ENDS DISTORTS BOTH STATEMENTS AND CIRCUMSTANCES STOP OUR BUSINESS NEEDS THE SUPPORT AND INTEREST [OF] THE NEWSPAPERS BUT MOST OF US RESENT MISREP-RESENTATION AND [PERHAPS] MR HIRSCHORN WILL COME TO ASSOCIATE [*sic*] THIS STOP INCIDENTALLY I REALLY DONT GIVE A DAMN ABOUT MY

AGE BUT AS MR HIRSCHORN APPEARS PREOCCUPIED WITH IT A VISIT
TO SOMERSET HOUSE IN WHATEVER COLOURED TROUSERS HE FINDS
APPROPRIATE WOULD PROBABLY SET HIM RIGHT STOP ASSUMING OF
COURSE HE LISTENS CAREFULLY TO WHAT THE MAN SAYS.[14]

Unfortunately for the newspaper's readers, who now believed that Dirk hated
them all and that he was born in 1919, the Editor chose not to print his cable.
The contretemps caused much embarrassment to Theo 'Thumper' Cowan, who
had fallen foul of 'the Rankery' after a blunder by one of his staff at the première
of *No Love for Johnnie*, and who, to Dirk's delight, was now looking after his
press relations on a personal basis.

Dirk and Tony were in Italy for five weeks. They returned with a pair of life-
sized faience leopards, but not many good memories of the shooting. Losey
wrote that he was sure his job as director 'would have been a quite impossible
one without your support and without the pleasure of your scenes on a picture
which was otherwise almost entirely without joy'.[15] It was good to be home, but
they realised that they had begun to turn their backs on Nore in the knowledge
that it had been sold. Yet again, as Dirk finished his work on *Modesty Blaise*
at Shepperton, Tony resumed the hunt. This time, even furnished flats were
considered: they looked at one owned by Nunnally Johnson in Grosvenor Square,
but it was too dark. Eventually Bernard Walsh took them to see number 56
Ladbroke Grove, a decent-sized house, which they agreed to take, furnished, for
six months at fifty-two guineas a week. It was such a temporary measure that
even on the way back to Surrey, they stopped to investigate two more houses,
but decided that the better of them was, at £26,500, expensive at the price. Their
last Sunday of entertaining at Nore was Tony's fiftieth birthday, spent happily
with Irene Howard, Ingrid Bergman, her eldest daughter Pia, and the photographer Eve Arnold. However the final few days were full of melancholy – not
helped by the collapse of Gareth Van den Bogaerde's marriage and uncertainty
about the fate of his three sons. Fortunately Elizabeth and her husband George
were on hand to help with the upheaval, as were the latest resident staff, Hilda
and the bachelor houseman, Fred. Once again a convoy assembled, and Dirk
and Tony drove down the hill, sad but satisfied that they had left Nore in
impeccable condition, with enough fixtures and fittings to fill nine A4 pages,
and a number of extras – including 5,000 bricks, two sofas, a pair of fire-dogs,
two motor mowers and two hammocks – which the Wilsons bought for a further
£800. But Dirk was not well. He had his first liverish attack for several months
and then, shortly after arriving at the new house, began coughing blood. For
about a fortnight, while specialists examined him and tests showed nothing amiss
apart from old scars left by his pneumonia in the fifties, the worries continued:
had the three packs a day of Kent cigarettes done irreparable, indeed dangerous,
damage? He and Tony indulged in some retail therapy by buying a Joan Eardley
painting apiece – Dirk, 'The Field in Summer', a companion to a winter

landscape, 'A Cliff-Top Field', which he already owned; and Tony, similarly, a companion to an earlier, smaller work. They noticed that the artist's prices had more than doubled. The following day arrangements were made for Dirk to be admitted to hospital for a bronchoscopy.

Nothing from this period throws a clearer light on their seventeen-year relationship than the entries in the Diary. Dirk had been 'hating it all but behaving very well of course'. On the night he went into the Brompton, Tony had supper with his son Gareth, who was appearing at the Hampstead Theatre Club in a Strindberg play, then went back to Ladbroke Grove, where it felt 'strange & horrid without D here'. Tony passed the next morning at the hospital, until Dirk was sedated, then spent 'from one to three p.m. in various forms of agony' until their doctor telephoned him to say 'no cancer' – 'the relief even now is almost numbing. D has been so controlled about it all, but terribly frightened as indeed I have.' It turned out that Dirk had been conscious throughout much of the examination as the Pentathol had not worked properly, but by 3.30, when Tony went to see him, was fully awake and 'naturally very happy'. Alternating with visits to the hospital, Tony had tea and supper with Maude before returning home at 11.45 – 'very tired & strange feeling, but more grateful than I ever remember feeling'. Tony fetched him the next morning, and by the afternoon they were on the road again, inspecting Woodside Dower House, a 'miniature Regency-Gothic manor' at Old Windsor, with a coach-house, lodge and extensive gardens, for which the owner, Sir George Bellew, wanted £50,000. Woodside was very much what they had in mind, although the coach-house was unnecessary. They offered first £40,000, then £42,000, but negotiations stalled. It was back to Ladbroke Grove and to square one. But at least Dirk's scare was over. He arranged to take his parents on another holiday, this time in St Moritz, and bought himself another picture: Christopher Wood's 'From the Studio Window, Paris', painted in oils three years before the artist's suicide in 1930 at the age of twenty-nine. Dirk paid £1,500 for the canvas, which he and Tony saw in an exhibition of Wood's work at the Redfern Gallery. He would never part with it.

Fortified by gulps of alpine air, they began the search again. An extra spring in Dirk's step had now been afforded by stunning reviews both in Britain and America for his performance in *Darling*. Even Kenneth Tynan, who was not keen on the film, said Dirk was 'imaginatively cast' and the scenes between him and Julie Christie were 'written and shot with fierce, unflinching honesty: we believe in her happy dependence on her lover, and his acid disdain ("I don't take whores in taxis") when she deceives him. Even his TV work is credible'.[16] The *New York Post* believed that he had given a performance 'surely equal to his best, if not superior';[17] the *New York Herald Tribune*, that 'he couldn't be better'.[18] It was doing well, too, at the box-office, which meant that Dirk's deferred fee was secure and that his share of the net profits – just over eight and a half per cent – would lead to a steady trickle of income. Maybe. Frederic Raphael wrote many years later: 'When the movie was a huge hit with all the people it was meant to scandalise, only a minute proportion of the receipts came back to the UK.'[19]

Bernard Walsh led Dirk and Tony even further into the southern English countryside, this time to the border between Kent and Sussex, where on the edge of Ashdown Forest they found a 'perfectly lovely house a bit like Nore'. Adam's Farm comprised a fifteenth-century main building, a Tudor barn, a seventeenth-century oast, a staff bungalow, a number of outbuildings, a landscaped garden planted with 'choicest shrubs and trees' and, bounded by a stream, four acres of pasture grazed by a neighbouring farmer's sheep and Jersey cows. There were in all about nine acres. Its views, while not as magnificent as those at Nore, were nonetheless very fine. The principal buildings had been cleverly transformed in the mid-fifties by a bachelor of unprepossessing aspect but immaculate taste called Charles Kearley, who lived there alone, entertaining a succession of lady friends. A builder himself, he amassed a considerable collection of modern paintings which on his death became a cornerstone of the Pallant House Gallery in Chichester, some sixty-five miles to the west. His conversion of the barn into a forty-foot drawing-room and gallery, on the walls of which many of his pictures hung, enhanced its attraction to Dirk. The only problem was the location, a far longer drive to any of the studios than had been the case at Nore; but perhaps that was beginning to matter less. So in went an offer for £27,000, which was accepted the following day – a few hours before Dirk was to meet Fred Zinnemann and discuss playing Thomas Cromwell in his film of *A Man for All Seasons*. Another painting seemed like a good idea, too: at an exhibition of work by the actress Lilli Palmer, Rex Harrison's second wife, Dirk bought a still-life, 'The Red Cabbage', for £185. The walls vacated by Mr Kearley would not be bare for long: Dirk and Tony had about £10,000 worth of pictures, posters – including a particular favourite, of Mistinguett – and tapestries.

They moved in on 28 January 1966, with spirits higher than for some time. A final examination of Dirk's lungs had revealed nothing untoward. A script had arrived from Harold Pinter, entitled *Accident*. Another, for a big-budget production called *The Night of the Generals* – in which a high-ranking Nazi turned out to be a Jack the Ripper – might compensate for rejecting *Tobruk* opposite Rock Hudson and George Peppard at a fee of $150,000. Dirk had a new, keen New York agent, Sue Mengers, and in London had decided, with some pricking of his conscience, to move away from Dennis van Thal to Robin Fox. Dirk was invited to give the address to the Queen at the Royal Command Film Performance, to which he was accompanied by Julie Christie. A few days later both won British Film Academy awards for *Darling*, and Julie Christie was on her way to Hollywood to receive an Oscar. At Adam's Farm the Drummer was placed under an old apple tree, looking towards the Downs; at Nore he had faced away from them. A statue of Oscar Wilde, which had been presented by Xan and Daphne Fielding, stood in a wilder patch of garden, with, as Tony noted, 'a Yucca up his arse'. There were two sadnesses. The first, for Tony especially, was that after fourteen years they had finally decided the Rolls was an unwarrantable luxury, so it was traded in against a white Mercedes 250SE, which was bedecked with the BH5 plates and which even he had to admit was not exactly 'slumming'. The second was the departure to auction of a Sutherland dining-table at which had sat at one time or another in the last three houses an extraordinary roll-call of famous names: Coward, Garland, Bardot, Cukor, Gielgud, Milestone, Simmons, Elizabeth Taylor, Gene Kelly, Cary Grant, Anouk Aimée, Moss Hart, Ava Gardner, Trevor Howard, Margaret Leighton, John Osborne, Capucine ...

In the wider world, the House of Commons approved Lord Wolfenden's recommendations, thus easing the path to reform of the law on homosexuality – 'a tremendous achievement for Lord Arran who got it going in the Lords,' noted Tony. Politics was not an overriding preoccupation with either him or Dirk, who once wrote: 'I'm as political as a garden gnome.'[20] When Harold Macmillan had resigned in 1963 after being misdiagnosed with prostate cancer, the bitter struggle in the Tory Party to choose a successor exercised Tony enough for him to record in the Diary that the appointment of Lord Home 'amongst a good deal of derision' had been one that they both favoured, 'so time will tell – anyway not Ld Hailsham which is something'. Now, in March 1966, they watched until midnight on television as Harold Wilson was returned to power in a Labour Party landslide; neither of them had voted because they were not yet on the electoral roll at Adam's Farm, but Tony observed that he would not have been able gladly to vote for either side.

Suddenly, as *Accident* edged towards a start date, the offers of work began to trickle in. *The Night of the Generals* was off, because its producer, Sam Spiegel, now preferred Omar Sharif; but Sue Mengers said that Arthur Hiller wanted Dirk almost immediately to star opposite Natalie Wood in an MGM comedy, *Penelope*, for $150,000. The problem was that it would overlap with *Accident*, and to the Americans' astonishment Dirk's loyalty to Losey won the day. Joseph Janni wanted him for John Schlesinger's next film, Thomas Hardy's *Far from the Madding Crowd* with Julie Christie; but, again, the Losey commitment might rule him out. He turned down a cosmopolitan operation entitled *Cervantes* which would have seen him star with Alain Delon and Gina Lollobrigida. And, to his considerable pride, Alain Resnais flew to London specifically to talk to him about *The Adventures of Harry Dickson*, a Sherlock Holmes pastiche hugely popular in France and Belgium during the twenties and thirties, for which the director also had Vanessa Redgrave in mind. This, however, would not be until the following year, at the earliest. Once more, it looked as if 'the marriage' to Losey would provide the lifesaver.

Harold Pinter describes how Sam Spiegel financed the adaptation of Nicholas Mosley's elliptical novel, *Accident*. When the producer had finished reading the script, he summoned Pinter and Losey to his office, where he stared at them and said: 'You call this a screenplay? I don't know who these people are, I don't know what their background is, I don't know what they're doing, I don't know who's doing what and why, I don't know what they want, I have absolutely no idea what is going on, how can you call this a screenplay?' Pinter and Losey sat in silence. Finally the latter said: 'I know what's going on.' 'So do I,' said Pinter. 'You two might know what's going on,' Spiegel said, 'but what about all the millions of peasants in China?'[21] Sam Spiegel made plain what he felt about the casting. 'What do you want Bogarde for? Who's ever heard of him?'[22] He said he could get Richard Burton, and duly did so – except that they would have to wait a year because Burton was so busy. Losey and Pinter were not prepared to wait. Anyway, they had always had Dirk in mind for Stephen, the Oxford philosophy don confronted by a moral dilemma and no little sexual electricity. So they bought the rights off Spiegel for $30,000 and a percentage of the profits, and started looking for the money elsewhere. Dirk's nearly contemporaneous version of the story came in a letter to Dilys Powell:

'Accident' was never actually meant to be my part ... it was intended for another actor, and an American company was going to do it for Joe and Harold. I was given the script to read from kindness ... and almost wept when they told me the actors name. I begged them to try to get Scofield ... but he was 'unknown' to the American producer. No longer! However when the Producer read the script he pronounced it to be 'thick'. Which none of us fully understood quite, and then he finally handed it back to Losey and wiped a gentle oriental hand ... and we were alone the three of us, and they offered it to me.[23]

By the time Dirk and Losey went to Cannes for a screening of *Modesty Blaise* – at which Princess Margaret and Lord Snowdon were booed for arriving late – the financing for *Accident* was in place. Losey wanted to meet Michael York, with a view to him playing the undergraduate whose equally aristocratic fellow student Anna is the catalyst for much of what happens, and does not happen, in the story. York was in Rome, making *The Taming of the Shrew* with the Burtons and Franco Zeffirelli, so flew to Nice one Sunday morning and arrived at the Colombe d'Or laden with the English newspapers, upon which Losey and Dirk fell 'with masochistic avidity' to see sentence passed on their months of painstaking work with 'Miss Veetee' and the others. The verdicts were mixed. An hour or two later York went down into Cannes with the two men and watched them fielding the questions, 'both hostile and flattering', at the *Modesty Blaise* press conference. Losey handled them with 'native bluntness'; Dirk, with 'characteristic debonair charm'. Losey and York then went for a walk along the Croisette and talked about *Accident*. After lunch York flew back to Rome. An odd audition, he thought, but illuminating. The part was his. 'Dirk told me afterwards that he managed with some difficulty to persuade Joe that a British aristocrat can have a broken nose!'[24]

Michael York is unique among Dirk's fellow players in writing at any length about him. As an undergraduate at University College, he had seen *Victim* at an Oxford cinema and thought: 'That takes guts.' His first brush with film-making came when he appeared as a student for a scene in *The Mind Benders* and now, four years later, he was returning as 'a young, eligible juve' to his alma mater, location for the first ten days on *Accident*. For a tutorial scene with Dirk the don, he wore his old college tie and gown; he was impressed to find that Dirk himself was sporting 'a fine old tweed jacket that had already done duty in many films'. York says he was never fully aware of how the Dirk–Losey relationship worked, but seemed to be based on 'the attraction of two opposites'. Losey, he recalls, 'was nice to me, but I was never invited into his inner sanctum'; nevertheless York came to respect him profoundly as a man of cast-iron integrity, with a 'taciturn shyness'. Stanley Baker, playing Charley, the zoologist, novelist and inciter of jealousy in Stephen, kept to himself; York was aware of 'a certain tension' between him and Dirk. In all of this the twenty-four-year-old found himself 'firmly in Dirk's camp': 'He and Tony welcomed me into their trailer and we got on immediately. There was the ritual of the mid-morning Guinness, which Tony poured. I was in seventh heaven – doing a film of that kind with a distinguished cast.' Dirk became York's tutor off-screen as well as on:

> He taught me about film acting both by instruction and example. His own method was a fine blend of intense concentration and instinct. Cinema, it has always seemed to me, is essentially filmed thought, and you could almost hear Dirk thinking. Concentration was essential as the slightest peripheral disturbance – a technician yawning or some unnecessary movement – could demolish it, making it vital to clear the actor's eyeline. Indeed, the eyes were the essential doors to the soul of the film. Playing a scene together, Dirk instructed me how to look at the eye of his nearest camera so that both of mine could be captured on film.[25]

York learned from him about camera lenses and about 'the supremacy of the script', which had to be used constantly as a reference, not only in preparation for the next day's dialogue, but also on the set.[26] A fellow Aries – he was born on 27 March – York found they had in common an impatience, especially in feeling about the theatre that 'rehearsals are wonderful, the first couple of months are fine, but then boredom sets in and it's torture'. Film, by comparison, was 'a salvation'. The relationship was such that when Michael York wrote his memoirs twenty-five years later and mentioned how on an Italian epic younger actors were in need of encouragement and advice, he offered it willingly, remembering 'how Dirk Bogarde had oiled and seasoned my own salad days'.[27]

   Nicholas Mosley, who says that at the heart of his story are 'the interweavings of responsibilities', fused aspects of himself and of his friend Raymond Carr – Fellow and future Warden of St Antony's College – into the characters of Stephen and Charley.[28] He remembers visiting Dirk in his 'rather grand caravan': 'He was enormously charming to someone like me – funny, nice and patient. I was awe-struck.'[29] Losey asked the author whether he would like to play a don in a High Table scene with Dirk, Stanley Baker and Alexander Knox. This was the sort of chance, replied Mosley, 'for which people wait all their lives, hanging about on street corners!' 'The only tip I can give you', said the director, 'is: you can't *under*act. Underact as much as you can.' 'I sat there and watched the camera on Dirk and Stanley Baker. They so did not *act* or ham it up; they seemed to be doing nothing. When I saw the rushes it didn't seem like that at all: they were being very effective while I was the only one overacting.' Mosley spent a day or two with the unit. 'There was a tennis scene. None of them – Dirk, Stanley Baker, even Michael York – had the slightest idea about how to play tennis. Dirk couldn't even hit the ball. Poor Joe: I don't think he was able to use any of it.' Losey concurred with the author's summary of Dirk *le sportif*: '[He] is a completely non-physical man. He can't ride a horse, he can't swim, he can barely walk. The only thing he can do is garden.'[30] Mosley was apprehensive about how Dirk, whom he had presumed to be homosexual even before *Victim*, would carry off the scenes with Jacqueline Sassard, as Anna the glacial foreign undergraduate:

> I thought that Dirk can act this, he can act that, but I didn't really see how he could smoulder with lust for this young girl – or indeed for the older woman played by Delphine Seyrig, in the middle of the film. But he did the scene with her very well; I don't know that he really put over Stephen's intense frustration, his longing for the girl and his frustration with his pregnant wife; but I don't think anybody could have done it better. I didn't think it mattered that he was not able to give that *air* of smouldering with lust. There is a scene where he takes the girl for a little walk in the country and they pause by a stile: he handled that very well.

The biggest bone of contention between author, screenwriter and director was over the climactic scene when Stephen takes the badly injured girl into his house and takes advantage of her while she is near-catatonic. Mosley ended his novel on a note of optimism, with Stephen deliberately refraining while his wife – played in the film by Vivien Merchant, who was then married to Pinter – expected their baby in hospital. Pinter wrote a long letter to Mosley, to be opened only after the latter had read the script, explaining that a dramatic structure makes its own unique demands and that in the light of their 'final complicity' it was inevitable that Anna and Stephen should sleep together. Mosley was not convinced, particularly when the suggestion of consent on Anna's part was nullified by her state of shock. Dirk told David Caute that he had objected – in his word, 'resisted' – as far as he could, 'but Joe wanted it desperately badly ... It was bestial and I think Joe wanted that crudity'.[31] One suspects that Dirk's resistance was some way short of 'over my dead body'. David Caute quotes the critic Raymond Durgnat as describing Stephen as 'a "can't quite" man' – someone who thinks himself very civilised, but he 'can't quite declare himself to Anna, he can't quite get Charley's TV job, he can't quite be honest, and in a fury of despair he concludes with a near-rape'.[32]

The sequence was shot towards the end of the filming, on a twelve-hour day, after which Tony noted that it had been too difficult for Jacqueline Sassard, 'so D must do it for them both'. Dirk was already tired after being on set practically every day for two months, but now there followed four night-shoots in succession. Losey had indicated that the last of them would be short, but it was not. At 7.15 in the morning, Dirk walked off the set. Losey, it seemed, had knocked back 'one or two too many vodkas' and had blasted off at him about nothing. It was only the second time in Dirk's career that he had downed tools – the first having, presumably, been in 'Hot Watford' two years earlier on *The High Bright Sun* – and he did so in exhaustion and rage. It took two days for him and Losey to make up, but they did, and the film was finished at the end of the same week. As the Rolls – yes, the withdrawal symptoms had been too much, and the Mercedes had given way to a 1961 blue-and-black Silver Cloud – purred back to Adam's Farm, Dirk was unprecedentedly emotional. He cabled Losey the next day:

THANK YOU FROM MY HEART FOR THE LAST THREE MONTHS STOP STEPHEN HAS COMPLETELY GONE AWAY AND IT SEEMS HAS TAKEN PART OF MYSELF WITH HIM STOP I HAVE NEVER FELT QUITE SO ABANDONED AND DESTROYED AS I DO TODAY BUT IN THE VACUUM THAT REMAINS THERE IS GREAT HAPPINESS THAT YOU TRUSTED ME TO PLAY HIM EVEN IF HERE AND THERE I MIGHT HAVE FAILED YOU THOUGH I TRIED CON-STANTLY SOMETIMES DESPERATELY NOT TO STOP I MISS YOU GREATLY AND LOVE YOU MORE THAN YOU COULD EVER GUESS.[33]

Tony, too, wrote to Losey, thanking him for the handsome gift of a book on Bonnard, which was

proving a great consolation in what cannot be described as a particularly jolly few days. Dirk is feeling more than usually bereft, and I find that I am not immune myself. I think that the making of 'Accident' has been a unique experience for a lot of people. Instinct tells me that *one* has been allowed to take part in the making of a film which will make history – whether time will prove this right or wrong, I am more than grateful for the experience.[34]

To Dilys Powell some time later, Dirk wrote:

When I had finished with 'Stephen', one sunlit day at Oxford, I was almost a dead person. I drove from there to here in a sort of haze. I confess that I wept for a day (exhaustion I suppose as much as anything . . .) and then took all the clothes which 'he' wore and put them away. And for three weeks after I waited for 'him' to, sort of, die. It was a very odd feeling . . . and I thought to myself, 'Well.' I thought . . . 'You've gone a bit potty, no one will see the effort or find the man. It is too buried. You should laugh more, and sing perhaps or go back to [Betty] Box.' But I think I was wrong . . . something does happen if you have the inspiration [. . .][35]

A little later still, he wrote of *Accident*:

It is a masterpiece of its kind, and it's not 'easy'. You have to work at it, and it can be painful too . . . the yearning and the search for lost youth . . . the squalor of Male Menopause . . . the loneliness among a group of No Longer Young academics in Oxford. Certainly go and see it. It won't be ninety minutes of Doris Day![36]

For Delphine Seyrig the experience was altogether positive. She wrote to thank Losey and asked him to give her love to everyone – 'especially that English Bogey – ah, what a wonderful actor – and partner – he is'.[37] And another to receive compliments was Arnold Schulkes, to whom Losey sent a tea-set, in appreciation of his being for many years 'consistently thoughtful, helpful, kind and considerate, bridging many difficulties and often functioning as a most capable assistant'.[38] Dirk's stand-in had, in his quiet and loyal way, just done his boss an extra favour. During the interior work on *Accident* at Twickenham Studios he heard from a colleague that Jack Clayton, director of *Room at the Top*, *The Innocents* and *The Pumpkin Eater*, was preparing a film called *Our Mother's House*, from a macabre novel by Julian Gloag about a family of seven children who bury their mother in the garden and give a hard time to her estranged, spivvy husband, who returns in search of his inheritance. Dirk said: 'That's the last thing I should do – to be the father to a lot of kids.' But Schulkes said it would be right up his street. Tony agreed. It was going into production very soon, but might be manageable once they were back from another trip to New York, where Dirk had been invited to play in a further Hallmark Hall of Fame production for NBC, as Charles Condomine in Coward's *Blithe Spirit*. He was not in the best of heart, feeling the play was an obligation rather than a desirable prospect, and suffering both from bad toothache and from a recurrence of internal bleeding. Just before they set off, he was prescribed codeine for his tooth and given a hefty shot of vitamins, which perked him up so much that late one night he began wrestling with a trap-door, and so enraged Tony that the latter reported in the Diary: 'I berate him that he never does what he's advised to do & always does what he's told not to do – & so ends my fifty-first birthday!'

With Ulric and Margaret, Dirk and Tony sailed on the *Queen Elizabeth* to New York. Apart from the comfort and the avoidance of jet lag, one significant advantage of travelling the slow way was that lines could be learned; so although he was feeling far from his best Dirk arrived, as usual, word-perfect at the NBC studios to rehearse with Rachel Roberts, Rosemary Harris and Ruth Gordon. The social highlight of their three-week stay was a party given for him by Sybil Burton and her husband Jordan Christopher at the 'in' nightclub, Arthur. Among the guests were Ethel Merman, Bette Davis, Sidney Poitier, Michael Caine, Stephen Sondheim and Barbra Streisand, who had spent a May day at Adam's Farm while making her London debut in *Funny Girl*. She and Dirk had got on well; Tony noted that she was 'basically straight like most true artists & preserving an identity despite all the blue-alpaca shit around her'. Her visit was marred only by the loss of an earring in the paddock – an incident replicated a few months later when Natalie Wood, 'a pretty, rather kitteny little creature with a headache', did exactly the same thing; only hers was real gold, 'and the fuss made v. considerably less'. Most welcome of all the partygoers at Arthur, which became a regular haunt during the three weeks, was a new friend, Jean Kennedy Smith, sister of Bobby Kennedy and the late President, to whom Dirk and Tony had been introduced by Alan Lerner. On one of the days when Dirk was rehearsing, Tony took her to lunch and had a long and deep discussion about, among other things, God, biography and the loss of privacy for the families of the famous; Tony found himself defending 'the right of qualified men to write on great men', such as Lord Moran on Winston Churchill. When he mentioned the name of President Kennedy's successor, Lyndon Johnson, the subject was swiftly closed. Jean Smith was good company, and would remain a chum.

However, the play aside, this trip was not all wining, dining and discos. One of Dirk's and Tony's concerns was that they had not seen the £10,000 representing the deferred part of Dirk's fee for *Darling*, let alone any of the net profit of which he was entitled to a share of a little more than eight and a half per cent. In the summer Tony had written to Laurence Harbottle, saying that the film had won three Oscars, which he understood could make a difference of several million dollars in the box-office receipts. Dirk and Tony had been told that Joe Levine, whose company, Embassy, distributed *Darling*, did 'not take to parting easily with his money' and that its producer, Jo Janni, 'does not hurry to someone else's bank bearing bags of gold', but 'I don't propose that we should all go and have a nap while they wish us nothing but sweet dreams'.[39] John Schlesinger, the director, was in the same position. By the time of the New York visit, they had still seen nothing, although the film was a success: Dirk had received a letter from the secretary of his fan club in Rosario, Argentina – seemingly, and curiously, the only one to which he gave any semi-official approval – saying that in a week at fifteen Buenos Aires cinemas the film took more than £24,000, which indicated that it was doing well enough in South America. A high-powered firm of New York lawyers was engaged to find out what was happening. They discovered that the gross receipts were just under $3.5 million, but they were unsure whether this figure was worldwide or just for the Americas. Nevertheless the inquiry seemed to have some effect. An interior decorator, Susan Wilding, whom Dirk and Tony had met on two of their transatlantic crossings, including the most recent, bumped into a close associate of Levine's, who told her that Dirk was owed the equivalent of £12,000 but she would be given a £1,000 commission if she could persuade Dirk to accept £6,000. This did not go down well. Next, Tony bumped into Janni, who said that the profits were in the region of $130,000 (about £55,000) which would entitle Dirk to about £10,000 – less than the lower figure mentioned to Susan Wilding, and a drop in the ocean compared with that secured by Dirk's co-star Laurence Harvey, whose deal had made him richer by some $400,000. A little later a cheque arrived, for £12,700, which Tony inter-preted as the deferred £10,000, plus a profit share roughly on the lines of that offered through Susan Wilding. By the early nineties, that share had yielded Dirk just over £16,600.

They flew home with some honour satisfied, with a decent 'telly' in the can – 'Dirk Bogarde was a solid thespic rock as the pivot of all the action', declared *Variety*[40] – and with New York a little deeper under the skin. At least they returned to a relatively stable staff situation. In the spring they had lost Fred Strayton, the bachelor houseman, who had been with them for two and a half years but found the work at Adam's Farm too demanding and, as a non-driver, the isolation too much. He eventually worked for Joyce Grenfell's friend and correspondent, Virginia Graham, who said he was 'tiny, sixty-one, & very clean & neat & makes the beds & dusts with the best of them'.[41] Fred had been replaced by a Mr Foster, who came, festooned with references, from Bangor; a fortnight later, he took two days off to 'get married'; and then, while Dirk and Tony were in Cannes for *Modesty Blaise*, installed his recent bride and stepdaughter in the house, where they occupied both his employers' bedrooms. He was fired within the hour, not so much for the act, but for not owning up. Now, the staff was all-female: Hilda, who had been at Nore with Fred, and a friend of hers, Helen Vaughan. Calm prevailed.

Four days after landing from America, Dirk had turned himself into Charlie Hook, 'a balding, green-toothed horrid little man with seven children' for Jack Clayton.[42] There was nothing exceptional about the fee – $35,000 – but the two months of working with Clayton and the young cast were 'a magical experience', unblemished by visits from the film's Hollywood backers, because 'Jack wont have them near'.[43] It was one of the happiest films Dirk had made: 'The children were fantastic, good actors, kind, funny, devoted and professional. Clayton was a demanding, challenging, exciting director.' And, despite its selection as the official British entry to the Venice Festival, the film would be judged a 'dis-tinguished failure'.[44] As would Dirk's next – but without any such adjective. 'Mr Sebastian', as it was then called, was another spoof spy story, played far straighter than *Modesty Blaise*, in which Dirk appeared as a 'brilliant, complex math-ematician who heads the decoding division of British Intelligence'. He explained to an American woman journalist why his character would have a hundred girls working for him:

Well, first of all, women have a much higher degree of that niggling, nit-picking sort of concentration one needs for breaking codes. During the war, I worked with a number of girls – not in code-breaking, in another sort of espionage work – who looked like those vulgar, idiotic British layabouts, with long blonde hair and long red fingernails. But the more stupid and idiotic they seemed to be, the more useful they were when it came to the real work. In a minute, they could rip off the fingernails and get to it.[45]

Not long before, Tony had tried to suppress an interview Dirk gave to a British newspaper because it had been 'all a bit too personal': 'he really never learns to guard his tongue with reporters & it always upsets him in the end'. At least on this occasion, a compliment seemed to emerge from the insults. And at least Eve Holiday was no longer alive to read them; she had died in New York in 1962.

Apart from his fee of £32,500, there was little of merit for Dirk in *Sebastian*, as it finally became known, apart from the chance to work for the first time, over just three days, with John Gielgud. Arnold Schulkes, whose last film it was as Dirk's formal stand-in, recalls a bizarre moment in a bedroom scene with Susannah York, when Dirk casually reached for a book from a bedside shelf, opened it and found inside his own 'annotations'. It was a children's story called *A Peep Behind the Scene*, about an orphaned girl, and when Lally read it to him and Lu forty years earlier at Cross Deep Gardens in Twickenham the tears had been duly jerked. The young Derek had inscribed the volume with his own name and marked it in places with crayon – additions which had survived when it was acquired by the nearby studios as part of a job-lot to decorate sets.[46] The coincidence was all the stranger because shooting on the film had begun in the same month as two significant events which in their separate ways would lead towards Dirk seeing his own, revised, name adorning a book in gold lettering – but this time on the spine.

Sixteen

'FORCE memory!'

Just before Christmas 1963 Dirk had received a letter from Edward Thompson, a director of Heinemann Educational Books and an avid theatregoer, who had paid one of his less frequent visits to the cinema and seen *The Servant*. The performance as Barrett prompted him to write saying that someone should persuade Dirk to write a book, 'and if that someone could be me, then I would be very happy indeed'. Yes, he added, 'I know that an actor should not be expected to turn author, but, nonetheless, when an actor can be persuaded to commit his ideas on his art to the permanence of a book, then the result is often very happy, especially for that author's readers.' Had Dirk perhaps considered the possibility of writing? If not, would he like to consider it?[1] Dirk replied that he was flattered:

> Heaven knows I talk enough, but whether this would be of any use in writing a book I don't know. I have often written bits and pieces and embarked on numerous 'books' about my life and childhood none of which have borne fruit owing to the fact that I am lazy and the cinema occupies a lot of my time.
>
> I have very few views on my 'art' that would be of any interest to any other actor or actress I feel. I am not a tremendously dedicated player and writing on that subject would be difficult for me because I know so little about it and boring for the readers for the same reason!

He was grateful for the suggestion, which 'certainly gave me three or four days pleasant thinking'.[2] No self-respecting publisher would give up at that point, and sure enough Thompson wrote back, saying he was happy to have given Dirk a few days' pleasant thinking but would be so much happier 'if I could provide you with many more days of such thinking, which, at the end, demanded action. I'm sure it's really only a matter of application. I've heard you talk on the radio and it seemed to me you were not only articulate but excitingly so. This, to me, suggests that you could write in the same way – even if a tape recorder did part of the work.'[3]

He proposed dinner after a charity concert at the Festival Hall, where Dirk was to read *Harmony in an Uproar*, an eighteenth-century satire aimed at Handel; and where Antony Hopkins, both a friend and an author of Thompson's, was to conduct the Pro Arte Orchestra in aid of the Citizens Advice Bureaux. Dirk said he would not be able to meet then, because of another commitment and because 'all I want to do at the Festival Hall is to read my piece and get to Hell out of it'.[4] But he kept the door ajar. Time passed, with its many distractions and the three further Losey pictures. Now, early in 1967, he had begun to think seriously about writing at length, and started at the typewriter on some memories of childhood under the provisional title of 'The Canary Cage'. At this stage, Edward Thompson was not in the picture. Who prompted whom is unclear, but a meeting was arranged with James Price, from Secker & Warburg, who came to see Dirk at the Connaught and tried to persuade him that the book should be extended to cover a longer period, but Dirk resolved that it should be restricted to those early years. And there the matter rested.

On 27 February, the day Dirk started his role as Sebastian, Dorothy Webster Gordon sat down at home in New Haven, Connecticut, and wrote a long letter. A friend in England had sent her a magazine article about an English actor, the text of which was, on the face of it, uninteresting. What seized her was a photograph showing him at home in the country. Thirty years earlier, the house had been hers. Now, according to the magazine, it belonged to Dirk Bogarde.

Dorothy Webster was born in Berlin, to American and non-German-speaking parents, in 1902; her father was assistant to the Kaiser's dentist. Her childhood was a lonely one: as 'the American girl' she was an outsider, and she had few friends of her own age. However, her father, a voracious reader, taught her to love and to respect books. She accidentally tore a page in a copy of *Little Women* which had been lent to her, and when she asked her father if he would repair it, he said no – she must save her pocket-money until she could buy a new copy for the owner. When she was twelve the family moved to America, where she was taunted by her fellow pupils at school for being the 'German' girl. It left deep scars. In the early twenties she was back in Europe, with Edward Blair Gordon, whom she had met when he was studying economics at Harvard and who was now working for J. Walter Thompson in Paris. They married there; and while he was at his office she haunted the bookstalls beside the Seine. By 1924 the couple were in London – in Dorothy's eyes a still greater paradise for the book-lover – where, despite her inveterate shyness, she established a modest literary *salon*. Among the couple's firmest friends was the artist and writer Mervyn Peake, whom they met when his wife, Maeve Gilmore, took a job as a copywriter at 'JWT'. Peake's biographer Malcolm Yorke tells how Dorothy reminisced in a letter to Maeve about his 'obscene drawings on tablecloths and menus at the Café Royal' and how 'he taught me all I knew about painting – long afternoons at the Tate'.[5] Peake painted her portrait in oils, a study which suggested a likeness rather than providing one. In the spring of 1933 Edward bought as a country retreat a house in east Sussex, part of which dated from the fifteenth century. It was called Adam's Farm. They became so fond of it that they moved permanently out of London. For Dorothy the only significant drawback seemed at first to be its isolation from the society and the shops which helped to sate her appetite for literature. However, she was fortunate, because in the nearest town was the Crowborough Book Club, run by two formidably well-read women, one of whom, Elise Santoro, has been a friend in Rome of D. H. Lawrence and of his wife Frieda before the novelist had made his reputation. Salvation was at hand.

As war loomed, the Gordons helped many Jewish friends – especially from Vienna – to flee Hitler, and brought them to Adam's Farm. However, in 1938, leaving the refugees to stay on at the house, they themselves took ship for the United States, where Edward Gordon continued to work for the agency in New York. They settled in New Haven, a short train ride away. A college friend who had encouraged in her an enduring love of verse supplied a list of American poets whose work he felt she should know, but to her chagrin she discovered that even in the town which harboured the great Ivy League university of Yale she was unable to find much of their work. However, a contact in the hotel business introduced her to a former publisher called Mitchell Kennerley, who had been born in England and who was now dealing in rare and antiquarian books. In 1940 he opened a shop on Lexington Avenue in New York, from where he was able to supply Dorothy with the titles she sought, and for the next ten years they engaged in a substantial correspondence. In 1948 one of her poems, 'To M.K.', was published in the *Saturday Review of Literature*. It contained the lines, 'Lonely in wisdom, he has long since learned/Collection's folly, since the worm is king'; and concluded: '[. . .] Love makes deep music here,/And immortality surrounds my friend.'[6] Because of geography they seldom met, but their minds did, constantly, until Kennerley's suicide in 1950.

Dorothy had a daughter, Carol, who described her as 'a most peculiar mother and a most fascinating friend'; an 'amazing woman – delightful and eccentric as they come', who 'carried on an old-fashioned tradition into the modern world she hated so much'.[7] Despite the small group of friends who constituted her new *salon*, Dorothy remained essentially lonely – an outsider. She was never happy in America, remembering how as a teenager she had been taunted as the 'German' girl. Her husband left her in 1947, but she was able for a while to continue her comfortable life, every now and then selling off a piece of jewellery or a painting. Eventually she needed to find employment, and took several jobs before joining the staff at Yale in 1956, as an administrative assistant in the Department of Physics. In 1961 she went to work in its library, where she could transmit her passion for books of all kinds to at least two younger generations. A new head of the Kline Science Library, John Harrison, understood and appreciated her as somebody with a quiet zeal to encourage learning; somebody who had herself amassed a huge number of books but had not set out to collect; as Dorothy used to say, *they* had collected around *her*. So while not a bibliophile in the strictest sense, she was, like her father, a literary omnivore. Despite her economies, she had retained in the brown-shingled house on Bishop Street a few mementoes of her former life: a Picasso from his Blue period; an Archipenko sculpture; a Modigliani drawing which hung over the fireplace in the living-room. An upright Bechstein piano that had travelled from Adam's Farm stood in her study upstairs. However, it was at one end of the large mahogany dining-table that her typewriter came to rest, and it was here that she produced her stories and her many poems. Here, too, shortly after Carol had joined the Madonna House Lay Apostolate in Canada, Dorothy tapped out a letter to the Englishman in the magazine and enclosed some snapshots of the property they now had in common, in case he might be interested in its history. Neither of them could possibly have imagined the consequences.

   Usually, mail from strangers was dealt with by Dirk's and Tony's secretary, Peggy Croft, who had succeeded the long-serving Val Geeves on their move to Sussex. Only very occasionally did Dirk himself reply, and, if so, he did not write a second time. However, in this instance 'it seemed that we were not total strangers, for we both shared the common love for one particular house, and we both knew it intimately'.[8] He wrote back at length, enclosing a photograph of the exterior. Dorothy was impressed by his 'amazing empathy and sensitivity', struck by his descriptive flair – in high winds, he had written, one of the rooms 'creaks like a galleon' – and touched that he was as 'foolishly fond' of Adam's Farm as she and her husband had been. Avid for information about what he had done to the house and its grounds, she wrote again, inquiring, among much else: 'Do you ever listen to the silence?' Back came another long letter. And for three years scarcely a day went by without one of them sending to the other a letter or a card. The correspondence began formally, but, as was happening on a less prolific scale with Dilys Powell, rapidly became a conversation in which streams of consciousness were exchanged at essay length. When Dirk's filming commitments made this hard to sustain, he sent postcards which would sometimes – especially during industrial action – accumulate in the post and arrive as one in Bishop Street, where, Dorothy told him, they seemed to 'fly about my head like huge flocks of birds'. She called them 'starlings'.[9] His letters, in their elongated envelopes, were 'blue jays' or 'familiars'. Dirk swiftly recognised that Dorothy was lonely and that she needed above all else the stimulus of a sharp intelligence. He, in turn, thrived on tapping into a developed intellect, formed by years of immersion in books. Shortly after their correspondence began, Dorothy discovered that she required surgery. His need to be needed was to work to their mutual benefit: '[. . .] I knew, in some strange way, that I *had* to write, that I wanted to do so above all else, and the most important thing was that I had a recipient'.[10]

   The timing of Dorothy Gordon's approach was perfect. Dirk had started 'The Canary Cage' and was writing by instinct, as he always had, governed either by his own spontaneity and impatience or – as had been the case at *The Fighting*

Cock – by the joint imperative of space to fill and a deadline. This was different. A book, even in embryo, was going to require an element of discipline. To someone with such a respect for the elegance of prose and the refinement of verse, Dirk's chaotic letters must have seemed like the steps of a witty dance partner with two left feet. 'I am very well aware that my syntax is "all to hell",' he wrote, '... so is my spelling and punctuation ... relics of a mis-spent youth ...'.[11] By Dirk's own account he was at first amused, saying it was reasonable for him to spell 'cough' as 'koff' if he so wished, but that it was ugly. 'I carried on, explaining that she was bloody lucky to get letters from an overworked, illiterate movie star in the first place and she correctly countered that it just seemed a waste not to do it "properly" '. 'Sometimes she would carefully correct an entire page of one of my letters, have it photocopied, and send it back for my thoughtful examination. And sometimes I tried, but the efforts made her laugh so much that she decided that the best way to try and penetrate my thick head was by reading. Books were sent. We spent a fortune on books which flew to and fro across the Atlantic.'[12] Dorothy recognised that the strength of Dirk's writing was in its directness – the feeling of sharing a confidence, given straight from the shoulder, with no rules, no pedantry, no *Fowler's Modern English Usage* to weaken the impact. She conceded that he should do it his way: 'I'm used to it now and would HATE the letters to be any other way, they are vivid, funny, alive. I see all you see, all you share with me, and that is more than enough for a grumpy University critter like me ... it's no good stuffing you in a strait-jacket of correct literature-behaviour! I'd far rather you were free to wave your arms about, and shout freely. And that you certainly do!' As for 'The Canary Cage', of which she eventually saw the first pages in draft, she advised him that in order to recapture Time Lost he should concentrate on the voice of the child. 'FORCE memory!' she wrote. And he did. In Dorothy Gordon – 'Mrs X' – he had discovered his first 'needlewoman'.

It took two months for Dirk to be persuaded that it was worth his while to accept $165,000 from MGM for a starring role in *The Fixer*, an adaptation of Bernard Malamud's novel about a Russian Jew falsely accused of murder who becomes a quasi-Christ-like figure. John Frankenheimer wanted him to play Bibikov, a Spinoza-reading examining magistrate, opposite Alan Bates, and negotiations reached a stage of near farce when the two principals were squabbling through their agents for the right *not* to top the bill. Eventually all was agreed and, with Elizabeth, Dirk and Tony once again took the Rolls across the Channel: destination Budapest. They were not altogether sorry to be leaving England for a while. Autumn, with its melancholy, was upon them. *Our Mother's House* had taken a beating from the critics; the much applauded *Accident* had done appallingly outside London. They had been shaken by the death of Vivien Leigh, with its ripples of sadness affecting many mutual friends; Dirk wrote to Losey that her memorial service at St Martin-in-the-Fields was 'quite remarkable ... and very moving ... pouring rain and huge still and silent crowds and a thousand of us crammed into the church and Larry hunched up like a dead man behind a pillar ... and Gielgud's address was most moving and beautiful. But I can do without these things ... they are unutterably sad, because they make the fact of death so horribly final ... and who wants a tribute like that really I wonder'.[13] At home, the staff problems had not eased, with the cook resigning and Hilda the housekeeper being given notice, then two married couples – one of them called the Leavers – arriving and departing within six months. So fraught was it all that the question of foreign residency was back on the table, reinforced by the ever-worsening taxation position under Harold Wilson's Labour government. For the first time, Tony had sought advice about Dirk's forthcoming fee being paid into a tax-free sterling area – specifically, in Nassau – and they were now even wondering whether to base themselves in the Caribbean for a year or longer. One idea was to lease Adam's Farm to a member of Dirk's own family, but after an acrimonious falling-out with Gareth Van den Bogaerde in the summer and a pessimistic forecast from the accountants, that was never a serious option. They decided to stay. After all, they could not fault the sudden realisation by the designer 'Bumble' Dawson that the whole point of the house was 'its outward-looking purpose, and the stillness and tranquillity'. And they believed that, wherever they went, they would miss the 'softness' of England. They would stay put, for the moment, and do what they could to avoid the punitive attentions of the decidedly un-soft Treasury. So, on their way to Hungary, they stopped for one night at the Lancaster in Paris, and the following morning signed the papers establishing Connaught Productions Limited, a partnership arrangement under the Trust Corporation of Bahamas Limited, which would also do business under the name of Connaught Enterprises, and which would provide a home for the *Fixer* fee, as well as other sums earned outside the United Kingdom. A visit to the Trust Corporation headquarters itself would be beneficial – and, in the Caribbean, far from disagreeable – but that could wait until the film was finished. At least the money would be free of the Inland Revenue's clutches.

Dirk's expectations for his time on the film were not high: 'It all seems very grotty indeed,' he wrote to Losey, even though he was to have a 'nice little salary' for 'ten pages of script and about two and a half weeks ... I'd really rather not go ... my costumes are smashing! A pony skin coat to the floor with otter collar and cufs and a great hat ... and pince-nez and a beard ... and a lousy part. Aw fuck. This is a dreary letter ... I'd better get the hell out into the garden and do a little tulip planting ...'.[14] Losey was in Sardinia, making *Boom!*, an adaptation of Tennessee Williams's *The Milk Train Doesn't Stop Here Anymore*, with Elizabeth Taylor and Richard Burton; and with Noël Coward as the Witch of Capri, a part that Losey apparently had in mind at one stage for Dirk. He did not get Dirk, but he did receive from him a small eighteenth-century Chinese jade toad, a companion to the Japanese frog in ivory, a 'clenched fist' and some 'fornicating toads' that had brought them luck on earlier films. Dirk apologised as he sent the latest talisman, for breaking 'his fingers on the right hand … foot'. He said it was to be grasped firmly, to warm, like a worry egg, and the sharpness would soon be smoothed away. A grateful Losey replied that the broken edge was keeping his 'blood running' while he grappled with the fresh hell of his latest production. Soon afterwards he wrote to Dirk in contrition. On the day before he shot Coward's first scene he offered him the toad to touch for luck. 'Thank you, dear boy,' said the Master, and took it. And that was that. From then on Coward constantly referred to the toad, calling it 'Losey-Linger-Longer'. Losey did not have the heart to reclaim it from that 'extraordinarily sweet' and 'devastatingly sad' man. A few weeks later, when Losey was back in London, Dirk brought round to him a stone Roman foot, said to date from the second century. It weighed about forty pounds, recalled Losey, and was a little unsuitable as a pocketable charm; but, as Dirk told him, at least he would not lose it. The foot resides to this day with Losey's widow, Patricia.[15]

Dirk took to Budapest Losey's present to *him* – a gold watch. It did not bring him luck. He was scheduled to work on thirteen days between 16 October and 22 December in a city where he expected 'no toilet paper, Alka Seltzer, Dom Perignon, Kent Cigarettes, good Petrol, London papers, and only three exit visas and entry visas'; 'What *am* I to do with all the days in between!'[16] Many of them were spent across the border in Vienna, where he and Tony retreated as often as they could to the Bristol. Elizabeth found her few days in Hungary depressing and flew home in relief. The filming itself started promisingly, and the rugged John Frankenheimer was surprisingly affable; but after a break halfway through, during which Dirk and Tony had time to return to Adam's Farm for some domestic crisis management, it all went sour. They were appalled at the way in which the Hungarians were treated by the American members of the unit – 'Quite the worst Ambassadors in so sensitive and wounded a place.'[17] By the middle of December Tony felt moved to record – uniquely – that Dirk and he were 'not popular on this film, & a good deal sent-up by the younger players I suspect – jealous perhaps of the Rolls & the suite and the isolation'. Personalities clashed. Dirk had a showdown with Frankenheimer, who was – rumour had it – taking drugs, facing an imminent divorce and livid that his new Ferrari had been immobile for three days because he had allowed the battery to run flat. The director, in his turn, told one of the cast that he came in every day wearing boxing-gloves ready to face Dirk. Frankenheimer recalled some years later that Hungary was a terrible place to be in the late sixties, and he hated it as he had never hated anywhere else. 'Alan Bates was divine, but Dirk Bogarde was mean; he makes life difficult for all the other actors. We did not end up friends.'[18] Dirk told his 1970 audience at the National Film Theatre: 'I did practically everything I could, short of shooting Mr Frankenheimer.'[19]

David Warner, at twenty-six already a renowned Shakespearean player and the star of *Morgan – a Suitable Case for Treatment*, had coveted the part of Bibikov, but his disappointment was tempered when he knew it had gone to Dirk. Instead he was to play a Tsarist count as foppish as they come. The two had not met before, but Warner was an admirer of Dirk, especially of his refusal to be typecast and of the way in which he had developed from *Hunted*, through *A Tale of Two Cities*, into 'this really fine screen actor'. When Warner arrived in Budapest, 'I had flu or something, and we had to delay my scenes. I went straight to bed for a few days. When I shook his hand in his suite, I was feeling really ill, and I was sick on his shoe. Not a good start. I wrote him a little note, apologising, which began, "Dear Puked-on . . .". And he wrote a nice letter back, signed "Puked-upon". He was very gentle about it.' In the film they had one scene together, at the end of which, as was usual on a big production such as *The Fixer*, the stills photographers came on to the set. Inevitably, because they already had many pictures of Dirk, the focus of attention was the younger man, who, after his Edward II, his Hamlet and his Morgan, was 'hot'. To start with they stood behind Dirk and took their photographs of Warner.

Which was fine. The only trouble was, that they didn't then go round and take stills of Dirk. His reaction wasn't one of anger. Tears welled up in his eyes. I can't remember exactly what he said, but it was something like, 'Nobody's interested in taking a photograph of a faded old man.' And he just ran off the set. What surprised me was that here was a man who was successful, and wonderful, and he should feel so hurt. I know why the photographers did that: he was in so many scenes, they had hundreds of pictures of him. They were behind schedule: 'Let's move on now.' But Dirk obviously took it personally. Or he was aware of something deep within himself and it hurt. He felt a rejection of some kind, even though he had this wonderful part and he had hundreds of stills taken of him. Perhaps he felt that I was young and he was getting into a middle-aged thing; young people were coming up. Maybe he thought, 'My time is over . . .'.[20]

It was *The Singer Not the Song* revisited.

Ian Holm, who was juggling his work on *The Fixer* with performances as Romeo at Stratford, had not met Dirk before, either; but his experience was different from that of Warner, who was on the film for only a week or so. Holm and his 'other half', Bridget ('Bee') Gilbert, arrived in Budapest just as Dirk and Tony had been forced to change hotels and were suffering at 'a ghastly place with dim lighting and a dreadful orchestra which came round the tables'. All four were, says Bee Gilbert, 'thrown together in our misery', and they spent a good deal of time together on the off-days, or travelling between Budapest and Vienna.[21] While the avuncular Tony took Bee Gilbert under his wing, Dirk treated Holm, who was just breaking into film, as 'a sort of protégé'. How, Holm asked, did Dirk manage to make his cheek twitch for the camera? 'Grind your back teeth together,' came the reply. It was technique, not tricks. 'It's all the eyes,' said Dirk. 'They will know what you are thinking through your eyes.' Later, as

Holm became successful in the cinema, Dirk's attitude towards him cooled – they became more 'gladiatorial' – but in Budapest and back at home immediately afterwards there was a firm bond. In Bee Gilbert's case it never loosened with either Dirk or Tony, who christened her 'Snowflake'. She describes Tony as 'a powerful moon around Dirk's creative planet' and their relationship as one based on 'the most incredible affection and symbiotic need – more than in any I have ever seen. There was never a hint of anything sexual between them. Occasionally Dirk would tap Tony on the knee and say "Thank you, Wifey", but there was nothing untoward about it. Theirs *was* a marriage – of two minds.'

In all, the Rolls covered about six thousand miles and crossed the border between East and West ten times. Dirk and Tony arrived home to a parrot-free zone: after buying a companion for Annie, they had realised the folly of their ways and passed both birds to the owner of a large and opulent house a dozen miles away who promised them a life of tranquillity. Dirk had many a pang about his beloved Annie; Tony, none whatsoever: he was delighted to be shot of the 'beastly, savage' things. Another Christopher Wood painting, 'French Cyclists', was just the tonic for commiseration and celebration respectively. A Spanish couple, Eduardo and Antonia Boluda, had started and were full of promise. They would have to become used to an otherwise empty house, because there was a business trip in the offing and, if any projected film materialised, it would be shot abroad. A treatment of Morris West's novel, *The Shoes of the Fisherman*, for a time a probability, had fallen away; but there was still the possibility of 'Harry Dickson' for Resnais; and now a script had arrived from Jean Renoir, 'very simple, Belle Epoque, tender and full of enchantment, especially if directed by him'. *The Servant* and *Accident*, even his performance in *Our Mother's House* – they had been shown in some of the right places and the right people were taking notice. First, however, it was more 'Total Exposure'. This time New York meant four days of television appearances, starting at 8 in the morning with *Today* and finishing with Johnny Carson at night; audiences with a procession of journalists boasting bylines as big as their egos; and a full-scale press conference for the opening of *Sebastian*, which was the principal reason for the summons to America. At least he had one pleasant duty: to give Edith Evans an award for her performance in Bryan Forbes's *The Whisperers*.

From New York Dirk and Tony flew to Nassau, where they found on the board outside a splendid colonial house, headquarters of the Trust Corporation of Bahamas Limited, the freshly added name of Connaught Enterprises. Dirk was now in partnership, to all intents and purposes, with himself – as owner of ninety-nine per cent of the capital assets, and with Connaught receiving five per cent of any profits. A cheque for nearly £60,000 was on its way from *The Fixer*, as were the fees from the various television programmes of the previous week. A board meeting followed by lunch a short ride from their beachside hotel was a pleasant way to do business, but Dirk and Tony did not tarry on Nassau. That night they flew to Kingston, Jamaica, and twenty-four hours later, after being driven by a 'most pleasant negro' in a large Mercury to Frenchman's Cove, Tony was moved to prose:

> The hotel is lovely – cottages situated well apart and well screened one from another, round or near a magical cove with a small sandy beach with palms & banyan trees beside a saphire coloured river which runs into a tiny bay where Atlantic rollers foam – even on this dull & rainy afternoon it is magical & D finds a colony of tiny blue fish who feed tamely on the crushed shellfish he gives them from the rocks. The cottages are staffed by maid [Norah] & waiter [Tom] who also waits on one in the restaurant – the food is excellent & all, including D's Dom Perignan & caviare for dinner, is included. Paradise?

It was to be better yet. A few days later – after they had been joined and rapidly left by Sybil Burton and her husband Jordan Christopher, who could not take the lack of pace – Dirk and Tony were directed to a 'collection of shacks' on the south of the island, beyond which was 'the tropical beach of one's dreams, palm fringed, golden smooth sand for miles & not a soul but an old man with a dog & an athletic built young one with harpooned fish. D's X-ray eye immediately picks on a bleached toy plastic sheep in the sand so I decide that the house we must build here has to be called Sheep Cottage'. In a letter to Dorothy Gordon Dirk described a second day at Pera as one 'of unbelievable beauty and solitude. I have never felt so happy and relaxed and lost to the world.'[22] A decade later, he wrote a travel article, 'The bay of the little lost sheep', in which he disguised the location; it concluded: 'I have never gone back there. I probably never will again. But I have never forgotten it nor ever shall. It has "marked" me. I loitered there with Time. I am very contented.'[23]

They returned home via New York, and one night at the Plaza, from where they called a few friends. But there was little time to socialise, and, even if there had been, the short hop to New Haven was not an option. He had now been corresponding with Dorothy Gordon for a year. At the outset he had issued an open invitation for her to come to Adam's Farm, but she replied that life had taught her 'there is no going back'. Dirk knew exactly what she meant. As they wrote, and wrote, and wrote, so it became understood that they would never meet, because there was real danger of jeopardising what she described as 'the fragile egg-shell delicacy of the strange bond we share'. Dirk explained:

> Affairs like this are for the secret places of one's hearts and minds, to be held securely in the private-times. To expose them to the harsh, probing light of normal, ordinary living would be disastrous. They would not survive the brutality of reality. You see: I don't *mind* if you look like the back of a bus, if you have green teeth, three legs, or wear cotton stockings and eat unskinned oranges . . . I just don't want to KNOW these things. Equally I do not want

you to see that I am going thin, just a bit, on top; that I am not ten feet high, with hips as slim as this, a chest as broad as that, arms as strong as a Viking. I don't want you to SEE that I am just ordinary. Nothing matters more to me than preserving the illusion we have created of an almost perfect relationship and a quite beautiful world which only we know about, and which only we can share. It is ours and ours alone.[24]

The understanding extended, tacitly at least, to the telephone. In years to come, Dirk would say that he once dialled the number, heard a voice and replaced the receiver immediately. In fact he *did* speak to 'Mrs X' from his room at the Plaza. And, just as the post-war rendezvous with Mrs Fells – strangely enough, another Dorothy – had been a disappointment, so too was his call to Connecticut. There was awkwardness, embarrassment and a blurted remark by Dorothy that she knew immediately had overstepped the bounds of their 'particular friendship'. She wrote afterwards that they should 'keep their little tangential, momentary world of pen and ink in good faith'. Nevertheless, she had revelled in hearing his voice: 'It was delightfully as I thought it would be. Your endearing little laugh I hadn't expected. It sounded almost nervous. Were you? Or just tired, and wishing the blasted woman would hang up?' Given Dirk's ambivalence, she was probably correct on all counts; but no lasting damage had been done. He and Dorothy would not speak again, but the bluejays and the starlings resumed their busy passage across the Atlantic.

Almost the first news to greet Dirk and Tony when they returned to Adam's Farm was that Luchino Visconti had made an enquiry about Dirk's availability. The great Italian director had much admired Dirk's performance in *Our Mother's House*; and, although the character he had in mind was in sharp contrast socially and economically to Charlie Hook, they had in common that they were both outsiders. For Dirk this was heady indeed: no fewer than *three* masters of the European cinema were interested in directing him. A month or so later a script arrived via Robin Fox – 'a sort of *Macbeth* loosely based on a family like the Krupps … Germany in 1932'. It was called *La caduta degli dei*, otherwise *Götterdämmerung* and – because to The Money 'The Twilight of the Gods' did not have a sexy enough ring – for its eventual release in English it would be renamed *The Damned*. Dirk asked his agent to tell Visconti, in the most tactful way, that the part of Friedrich Bruckmann, lover of the widowed Baroness Sophie von Essenbeck, was 'just too wet'. Back fairly promptly came an amended version, which was an improvement; at least there was somebody he could begin to grasp now – somebody who, as a non-relative, might believably have climbed to the upper reaches of a once mighty family firm. Yet there was still some way to go, both with the character and with the fee. Meanwhile, Dirk had been offered $25,000 to make a television commercial for Foster Grant sunglasses. Like Olivier, he had always refused – although, as a joke, he did John Schlesinger a favour by sliding into the background of an advertisement which the latter shot with

Julie Christie for Vosene shampoo. Now, just as Olivier succumbed to the blandishments of Polaroid, Dirk agreed to make the commercial, provided it was not shown on British television. It would require a day's filming in Rome. Oddly enough, fashion was on his mind. He had been approached, Tony told their accountant, by

> three very young but very talented designers who wish to open their own fashion house to cater for both men's and women's clothes. Their idea is that Dirk, who they consider to be an arbiter of elegance and distinction (which is flattering of course) should be their sole sponsor, lending both his name and money to the project, which is planned to service a modern-minded clientele who wish for clothes better designed and made than the run-of-the-mill boutique, and therefore more expensive while being less so than the big Paris houses.

Dirk met the designers, looked at their ideas, and was full of enthusiasm – until he heard how much money they needed: £9,500. Tony had to explain 'to disbelieving young ears that film-stars are not necessarily millionaires' and a 'graceful and unhurtful disentanglement' ensued.[25]

Dirk had to earn his dollars, donning the sunglasses countless times in sweltering heat and shimmying down the Spanish Steps, without uttering a word. Crowds milled, not all of them friendly because of the disruption, and the work spilled over into a second day. Never again, he reassured Dorothy Gordon, when he confessed that he had debased himself for dollars: 'My shame is complete.'[26] However, the trip was doubly profitable because Visconti, who had sent a further version of the *Damned* script to the Hassler, now came to see him there. Tony noted that he was a fine-looking man, bigger than expected, and 'very definite as a personality'. The Count and Dirk responded to each other, and it looked as if they would work together in June. But timing was delicate because Twentieth Century-Fox had offered Dirk the part of Pursewarden in *Justine*, from Lawrence Durrell's *The Alexandria Quartet*, and this was to start in September, with locations in north Africa and interiors, not as he had hoped in Paris, but in Hollywood. Once again, famine had turned, if not exactly to feast, at least to a square meal. And once again thoughts turned to where they should base themselves.

While Dirk spent his second day on the Spanish Steps, Tony wrote to their accountant about the immediate plans and said that they both felt the moment had come 'to take the oft-discussed action and move Dirk abroad'. He asked John Don Fox to see if a scheme could be devised whereby Dirk would leave Britain as from the beginning of shooting on the Visconti film, which was only a month away. They suggested putting the house in Ulric's name and at the same time placing it on the market; if Dirk returned after completing the period out of the country, he would in any case want to live in a smaller house. Once the two films were finished, he and Tony thought they would probably settle in Rome; it was important that Dirk should be 'close to a centre of film-making activity'.[27] And, leaving that thought with the accountant, they drove to the Colombe d'Or – it has to be said, nowhere near Rome – where for a few days they house-hunted unsuccessfully under the guidance of Simone Signoret. They left France just in time, as the country was about to be paralysed by the student rioting and trade union action which were to become known as *Les événements de mai*.

The big *événement* in Dirk's social calendar on returning to England was a summons to Buckingham Palace. The Queen at that time was felt to be somewhat remote, and through her equerry, Patrick Plunket, asked a few people prominent in various walks of life to join her for lunch. Dirk, whose shyness caused him to quake at formality on anything like that scale, had politely declined the first invitation, but Plunket, a former major in the Irish Guards whom he had known in the war, made it fairly clear that a second refusal might be frowned upon. So, on 6 June, in the Rolls but with a professional chauffeur at the wheel, he glided through the gates to his dread appointment. In the event, he had a delightful time. His seven fellow guests, all male, included Sir Max Aitken, son of Lord Beaverbrook; the guitarist Julian Bream; and the painter, collector and con- noisseur of the Surrealist movement, Sir Roland Penrose. Princess Alexandra arrived late and in a flurry, straight off a flight from Germany, and immediately enchanted everyone. But, as Tony noted, Dirk 'has fallen in love with HM'. Dirk found the Queen 'completely relaxed, very jolly indeed and surprisingly frank on all sorts of topics'. On the subject of the rioting French students, she said: 'I *am* so relieved we haven't got any cobblestones over here!' The only cloud over the proceedings was the announcement earlier in the day that Robert Kennedy had died overnight after being shot in Los Angeles. 'I've sent off the official letter,' the Queen told Dirk, 'but what on earth am I going to say to Rose?'* He himself had cabled Jean Kennedy Smith on hearing news of the assassination: 'There are no words.' In the Diary, Tony wrote: 'God, what a loathsome country America is today.' Within the month Jean Smith was at Adam's Farm, finding some solace with Dirk, Tony and Gareth – a visit recorded in *A Particular Friendship*: 'She is very strong and calm. Seeing her sitting here in the sun, relaxed, laughing ... it was difficult to relate her to the wild and dishevelled creature in all the news photographs leaning over her dying brother in the Ambassador kitchens only three weeks or so ago ... My God! I SO admire that kind of courage and faith. I wish I had it.'[28]

Eduardo and Antonia went home to Valencia, to marshal their forces for what might be a long period alone at Adam's Farm. In their place came a six-foot-plus Antiguan called Kenneth Dalton Kennedy Richard who, Dirk wrote,

---

* Rose Kennedy, mother of John, Robert and Edward Kennedy.

was, I think, once a Body-builder. At any rate he does exercises all the time he isn't cooking or polishing, and has a great box of iron bars and wheels and things in the Staff Sitting-room. His main extravagance, as far as I can see, is one dozen raw eggs consumed every morning with a quart of milk. To keep his waist at thirty and his chest at, one imagines, three hundred. He is a very impressive sight doing his press-ups on the lawn in nothing but a silver chain and a jock-strap. The baker got quite a shock.[29]

They wondered if he had been brought to England when very young, and probably very handsome, by a white man who subsequently ditched him. He worked hard and willingly for Dirk and Tony, and seemed sad to leave. While he was there, the house went discreetly on the market. Bernard Walsh was called in, and a guide price of £36,000 agreed. That weekend he escorted to the house a 'shabby and quite toothless man' called Lambert Burton, who told them of his antiques business and his property in the Seychelles, said he very much liked Adam's Farm, and within a couple of hours had made an offer of £50,000. Dirk and Tony were taken by surprise, but agreed in principle. On the Monday Bernard Walsh called to make sure that Dirk still wished to sell and arranged to take an inventory. By the evening the crestfallen agent had learned that Mr Burton, a 'confirmed bachelor' who had said a few days earlier that he would be buying a second house in Belgravia for £150,000, was a fake, with a long track record of confidence trickery. It looked as though Adam's Farm was to be Dirk's for a while yet. Nevertheless he asked the Crane Kalman Gallery to keep safe his latest painting – a 1932 Ben Nicholson, 'Still Life, Bocquet', in oil on wood, which he bought on the same day that he met Charlotte Rampling, one of his projected co-stars in *The Damned*. 'Very pretty girl,' noted Tony.

The unresolved mess surrounding 'The Achilles Affair' and the coming and goings on *The Fixer* were as nothing compared with what faced Dirk and Tony on the Italian film. It began with days of uncertainty at the Hassler, while guarantees were sought that Dirk's salary of $100,000 would be paid, and while they waited for news of when exactly Dirk would be required. There followed a breakneck dash in the Rolls to Salzburg where at first there was no sign of Visconti. A day or so later, they spotted him in a group on the terrace of their hotel, but Dirk, 'terribly shy of them and in a state of nerves because no approach has been made to him', could not bring himself to go over to Visconti. Only when Tony persuaded him to go to talk to a macaw in a cage in the garden was Dirk noticed by one of the great man's aides, at which point everyone finally united for a perfectly relaxed drink. Dirk sent a card to Dilys Powell that day: 'The Italian Cinema is very odd indeed. I rather think I'm a bit too old for this kind of lark! – I was better off with Rank – at least I could speak to them!'[30] Within three days of Dirk's first shot on location at Unterach, the authorities more or less impounded the wardrobe vehicles because of disputes about unpaid bills; a week later the unit was threatening strike action because no one had been paid; then the producer shut down a location, telling Dirk and Tony that they were free to return to Rome, with the hint that Dirk and everyone else might be out of work. They were packed and ready to go when the producer said it was all on track again and shooting would resume the next day. On it went, with fewer days of shooting than not, until a Terrible Tuesday, when Dirk's salary failed to arrive; he blew his top, and said he refused to work until he was paid and until his final shooting date was agreed; the production office accused him of being uncooperative, but Visconti took his side, saying that he, too, would not go on set the following day unless Dirk's problems had been sorted out. It was, noted Tony, 'all mad'. And to make matters more complicated, on that very day Bernard Walsh called to say a buyer had been found for Adam's Farm – at the asking price. Yet somehow all their problems paled into insignificance beside the news that Russia had invaded Czechoslovakia. 'I feel almost close to tears,' wrote Tony in a long Diary entry virtually reproduced by Dirk in *A Particular Friendship*. 'This must alter the whole world for many years.'

Tony wrote to Laurence Harbottle, summing up their position:

I have never known a film sailing so close to the wind in my life, and the latest news is that they can't afford to get the sequence shot in Germany out of customs in order to show it to a potential American company who could get us out of what is politely known as trouble. Through a series of well-engineered circumstances Dirk has so far been paid up to date, partly because Kaufman* managed to obtain some sort of guarantee directly from the distributors and partly because the Rolls is always at the door with its nose pointed in the direction of France if not England, but one begins to feel slightly guilty that almost nobody else gets paid including the crew, particularly as they are so extremely nice. It all seems to have a political background, the film having been backed by the previous government and evidently not so liked by the new administration. Visconti, as one of those aristocratic millionaire communists that abound in Italy and France, is also considerably less favoured by this administration, and emphasis to the whole thing seems to be given by the fact that most of the cheques come, when they do, bearing Vatican signature. I didn't know priests were allowed to have cheque-books although the best restaurants are certainly full of them looking worried about their shares in Pill manufacturers.

The next crisis is due on Monday when D has to be paid again, and we can't afford any further delays because he has only four weeks left and some of the others far less with almost all their parts to play. The pity of it is that what has been shot seems to be really good, and the old man is certainly a genius of some sort. I don't see how it can possibly be finished unless everyone comes

---

* Hank Kaufman, Dirk's agent for a while in Rome.

back next year, but this is Italy and they have their own approach to things. Certainly Visconti refuses to be panicked or unduly hurried, and is outwardly calm and very good to his actors.

It has taught us something about the prospect of living in Italy, but has not completely cured us of the intention to do so. The light compensates for much inconvenience and hence you may be in for a lot of trouble making it possible![31]

With his living allowance safely arrived – and with his parents in Rome, too – Dirk was back in the studio with Visconti. Tony observed how the latter worked:

He is unique in that his interest in detail is minute. Every part of every costume is scrutinised and all afternoon was spent sitting hunched in a chair on the set watching the set-dressing changed (including all the carpet) towards something he would approve of. I suppose he is an anachronism, and his kind of film can only be made for large expenditure over as long as he needs to get it right & may then not appeal to popular-taste audiences, but one can only respect it & regret its probable impractibility in face of the mighty dollar. All the unit love him, but it is the love of respect, and D says he's never heard a set so quiet. Although one knows his rage would be fearful his gentleness to everyone is what one remarks upon.

In a lunch break at a favoured trattoria across the road from Cinecittà, Visconti told them that he understood much about how to handle actors from having trained horses for ten years before going into the theatre: 'he says the sen-sitivities & need of attention & petting are very similar, and the smell & challenge of a racecourse are to a horse like the smell & challenge of a good scene to an actor'. He admitted that the film might never be finished and 'would end up as a collection of snippets as "What would have been Visconti's greatest film"'. But for Tony and Dirk it was an eye-opener to spend some time at close quarters with this 'fascinating & unusual man'.

For Charlotte Rampling, too, it was an extraordinary experience. She arrived, she says,

at twenty-one, completely untrained as an actress, having just done a couple of Boulting Brothers comedies. Here I was, playing a *grande dame* with children, and I had no idea what I was supposed to do. Visconti took me under his wing like a little bird. He loved the way I looked, my youth, my wildness, my fragility, and he said, 'You *have* to do this film for me.' He wasn't paternal, exactly; he was all-encompassing. He powerfully imbued me with a great sense of myself for the role – which was rather magnificent.

Off-set, however, it was Dirk and Tony who were her mentors:

I had come in, in a Swinging Sixties sort of way, and was completely uncultured in terms of the cinema. I didn't have much idea about Dirk. I'd seen one or two Rank films, and I suppose I thought of him as a romantic lead. I hadn't seen *The Servant* or *Accident*. There were long, long periods on *The Damned* when we were doing nothing. We started talking. I began to ask him and Tony about the cinema and its history, and they taught me. Everything. Tony knew about all the mechanics, how it worked with the dealing and the wheeling. Dirk told me about its poetic side, about what it meant to a feeling person. I was discovering this extraordinary world.[32]

Dirk helped to instil in her a particular kind of endurance –

how to bear the waiting and the tension for those very few moments when you have to be supremely on form. You never know when those moments are going to come in your day or in your night, and you can't not be feeling absolutely ready for them. It's about forms of self-discipline that are really essential. It's self-control – *maîtrise de soi*. You also have to know how to let go of that self-control for those moments. But if you don't have it in preparation, you arrive at them exhausted, irritated, not collected together – a fragmented, chaotic thing. Dirk taught me about that.

They quickly discovered that there was a more complex connection between them, based on a restlessness, a sense of dislocation, inherent in their upbringing. They recognised that they were part of the same rootless, nomadic tribe, searching for the place where they truly belonged; the skin in which they might feel most comfortable. And they both had their demons, their torments. 'You link up with people whose form of suffering has the same way of translating itself,' says Charlotte Rampling. 'And Dirk had a way of covering up his own form of personal nightmares which was exquisite. I felt close to him because I'd never met anyone who could do it like that.'

Towards the end of September, with Dirk due in Tunisia for *Justine* on 7 October, there was still much to do, and disillusionment had set in. Visconti was favouring his new protégé, Helmut Berger, cuts were being made in Dirk's part for the wrong reasons, and again the production seemed to be in jeopardy. Dirk and Tony began to feel that Visconti was a bully who needed bullying, 'but it would take a big bully to do that!' It became clear that the film would have to shut down temporarily, but, God willing, the unit would reassemble and Dirk would join it in the New Year. On his final day, he gave a party at the studios for the cast and crew, but arrived to find the tables turned by Visconti, who took over a sound stage, dressed it lavishly and organised the presentation to Dirk of an inscribed gold and silver cigarette case from the entire unit. Tony was assailed with comments about Dirk being a joy to work with, how he was 'the perfect

English gentleman', and how everyone was 'in love' with him. It was, in that respect, quite a contrast to *The Fixer*.

Joseph Strick, the director of *Justine*, held a meeting with the cast at the house where he was staying on the beach at Gammarath, their base in Tunisia. Dirk had arrived that morning from Rome, and he emerged from the reading with 'misgivings'. A few days later, he and Tony recorded, fifty journalists were flown in by the unit publicists 'to witness the massacre of a superb book'. That, coupled with the heat, the 'runs' and much incompatibility, made for a depressing stay in north Africa, brightened only by the presence of Arnold Schulkes; reunions with Anouk Aimée and the Magnum photographer Eve Arnold; and by an introduction to the photographer-peer Patrick Lichfield and the writer Kathleen Tynan, who were on assignment for *Vogue*. 'Well,' Dirk wrote to Dilys Powell, 'it seems that I will never learn – here I am with Anouk Aimée and Durrell and a simply ghastly "Carpetbaggers" sort of picture. To break your heart! – How I miss, and long for, Visconti. Tunisia is *lovely* – but the rest is silence.'[33] Somehow he kept his counsel for three weeks, then, after yet another sequence involving 'people standing in a row like the Village Players', Dirk had a row with Strick. The location work finished in an unseemly rush, and the unit packed for Hollywood. There was just time to spend a couple of nights at Adam's Farm.

The first prospective buyers had pulled out because of problems over planning permission, but another couple, the Fishers, had agreed at the full price and would be moving in when Dirk and Tony returned from America. Despite the volatile position, Eduardo and Antonia were proving amenable throughout. Then news came that Strick had been fired. Dirk and Tony flew to Los Angeles, not knowing who was to take over the film. They settled into the Beverly Hills Hotel and hoped for the best. Their prayers were answered. In a bizarre case of *déjà vu*, the white knight was George Cukor, with whom, since *Song Without End*, they had established a firm friendship: to him, Tony was known as 'Fortune'. Cukor duly ditched a good deal of what had been shot in Tunisia and started again, but not even he could clear the air around this doom-laden affair. There were hideous problems with Anouk Aimée, whose love affair with Albert Finney not only was the talk of, but also kept her away from, the set. Michael York found himself on the receiving end of disapproval, probably based on nothing more than the fact that he was a young inheritance, new to Cukor. 'I was in limbo,' York says of this miserable period. 'I had gone from being the golden boy who could do no wrong, to the whipping-boy who could do no right.' Whereas on *Accident* he had been so warmly treated and encouraged by Dirk, he was now 'shoved out into the cold'. York believes that Dirk 'slightly resented the fact that I was becoming successful, that I was a competing talent; but I couldn't reconcile this at all – I hadn't changed.'[34]

Patricia York – they had married earlier in the year – remembers that her husband was interviewed by *Women's Wear Daily*, which had mentioned the salary he was receiving for *Justine*. 'It seemed to infuriate Dirk. He made a lot of sarcastic remarks about it. The same thing happened when we told him once that we were staying at a grand house on the water in France – it drove him nuts. He was, as Thoreau put it, "guilty of condescending envy".' Shortly after their marriage Michael York had taken Pat down to Adam's Farm to meet Dirk and Tony. She found the day deeply uncomfortable:

Dirk didn't say a nice word about anybody. I found myself laughing once or twice at other people's expense, and I hated doing that. He was very vindictive about England. He loathed America. There was vituperation on his face. The second time I met him he started talking about Tampax and cunts and so on. It was bizarre. For a man, whom I hardly knew, to be using language like that, or even to bring the subject up, was distasteful. I really thought he was a horrible creature. But then I thought about it and realised that he probably hated himself. He wanted to be another person. *Il n'était pas bien dans sa peau*. And self-hatred and self-pity combined is a horrible thing to have to witness. It is really so sad for someone not to recognise who they are.[35]

Dirk's Pursewarden was never going to be the physical reincarnation of the character in Durrell, who was 'little, fattish and blond', but he could certainly convey the seedy novelist, the author of 'poetry and prose of real grace', who 'gave the impression of a young man lying becalmed in his mother'. After he did so each day, to great effect, at the Fox Studios, he returned to bungalow number 3 at the Beverly Hills, which he and Tony came to regard with some affection, largely because of the steady traffic through its door of their friends – either in transit or Hollywood-based – and, in the case of Yves Montand, Simone Signoret and, for a time, Ingrid Bergman, their immediate neighbours in the hotel. Establishing their own social circle meant that Dirk and Tony could 'steer almost clear of the horrors of local society'.[36] Tony kept especially busy trying to organise, at a distance of 6,000 miles, their future, which involved the completion of Dirk's work on *The Damned*; ensuring financial security and access to funds; their final departure from Adam's Farm; and finding somewhere to live. Thanks to a problem with exporting fees from *The Damned*, it now looked as if the last of the problems would resolve itself, anyway in the short term, by making Rome their base. They flew there at the end of January 1969, apprehensive that Dirk would be 'ragged-out' by the polar flight and the nine-hour time difference, with just one day to prepare for 'a key scene, and a most important one for him personally', almost a monologue of five pages, 'with the problem of getting back into a character he's by now far away from'.[37] Inevitably, the one day became several, and there was time to look at houses; but nothing was suitable. Dirk's final scene was shot at a steelworks at Spoleto, in the foundry, which was 'like a great beast that must be fed, day & night, with white hot slabs of iron to be crushed in its jaws' – a portentous conclusion to an assignment which, for all its traumas, left him in awe of Visconti, whom he considered an Emperor, a true intellectual, a giant – whereas none of those titles applied, quite, to Losey.

Back at Adam's Farm, they found all their possessions labelled, and their home disappearing around them. At least they had been through this before, and were not – as others were having to do – giving up a family seat dating back for generations purely because the taxman made life impossible. However, they wondered when and where they might see their ornaments again. Elizabeth and her family volunteered to take Dirk's remaining pair of birds, as well as Candy and the aged cat Mister, who was on the point of being put down. Eduardo and Antonia went home, for the time being, to Spain. And Dirk and Tony handed over the keys to Mr Fisher and his wife, who were to be somewhat cruelly described in *Snakes and Ladders*. 'They were delightful people,' recalls Bernard Walsh. 'They'd met Dirk two or three times. They weren't intrusive, didn't bother him at all. They didn't arrive with their aunt and their grandmother to see "Mr Bogarde", or anything like that. When the book came out I felt rather traitorous.'[38] Dirk and Tony retired to the Connaught for a couple of weeks, during which there was a round of valedictory entertaining, and a private screening of Richard Attenborough's *Oh! What a Lovely War*, shot mainly on Brighton's West Pier, where Dirk had worked for one day in a scene with Susannah York. They found the film, Attenborough's first as a director, 'outstanding' and spent hours afterwards talking about it in their suite with him and his wife Sheila. On the last day of February they distributed their luggage between BH5 and their latest second car, a Simca, and loaded on to the latter spare tyres for the Rolls. This time the convoy was to be just two-strong, with Arnold Schulkes at the wheel of the Simca. After downing a dozen oysters apiece, they left the Connaught, ensuring that it was only *au revoir*. For the rest of his life Dirk would keep a modest 'moneybox', or 'oilwell' to keep him in credit at the hotel; the manager would let him know whenever it needed topping up. After all, this was Dirk's and Tony's home from home. The question now was: where is home?

Seventeen

'I did a great look'

Dirk told Tony that as they drove on to the ferry at Dover it was like a portcullis coming down; 'it's time for roving spirits to leave England while they have a chance'. None the less, they did so with some trepidation. The cars were subjected to an inch-by-inch search by customs, suspicious about possible breaches of the currency restrictions; at that time no United Kingdom citizen could leave the country carrying more than £25 in sterling and £300 in foreign currency or travellers' cheques. But since they had only about £350 between themselves and Arnold, there was little to worry about. When they first stopped in France, Arnold handed them $500 from his pocket, which he had, if necessary, been prepared to justify as he was the holder of a Canadian passport. 'Dirk was furious,' he recalls. 'He was always scrupulously honest about things like that. The press and everyone knew he was leaving the country. The idea of his ex-stand-in and double taking money out for him was too much.'[1] Leaving them, somewhat wanly, at the Hassler in Rome, the ever-loyal Arnold flew back to Britain.

After three days Dirk and Tony were taken by an estate agent to a house off the Via Flaminia, in Labaro, an ugly village a few kilometres outside the city. The Villa Berti was, in Tony's words, 'a modest house, although big enough for our needs & with plenty of bedrooms & bathrooms and a large, green & pretty garden with an adequate swimming pool'. Crucially, it was on a hill, well above the impoverished blocks of flats and the garbage-tips, and with superb views towards the mountains and towards Rome itself. There was even a small vineyard. They decided to take it for a year, at five and a half million lire a month, from its owner Signora Berti, whose husband had been killed in a light-aeroplane crash while he was on safari in Africa. Dirk and Tony moved in, augmented the meagre furnishings and equipped themselves with essentials such as sheets, towels, lamps, kettles, and a phrase-book. By the second evening, a small dog with uncertain parentage and a broken leg, which had been haunting them from the moment they arrived, had moved in, was dining off a plate of spaghetti and had been christened Labaro. A pretty, but kleptomaniac tomcat was just as persuasive. Eduardo and Antonia arrived from Barcelona and took an instant

liking to the house, and within a week there had been visits from Julie Christie
and Capucine. After ten days or so Dirk wrote to Losey:

> We have just about settled down ... the *dust* is settled anyway ... and the villa,
> which is not a St Simieon ... or whatever the place is called that Hearst had in
> Calif. is really a bit pretty ... it is well built ... on a hill among olives and
> pines and mimosa ... overlooking all the slums of Rome and the rubbish tips
> of Labaro and Porta Prima ... but somehow actually living IN the place is
> better than those awful no-living places on the Appia Antica ... we are actually
> residents of the Commune da Roma, and we are finding it rather nice, thank
> you very much.[2]

None of the household could manage more than 'Good morning', 'Thank
you', or, if put to it, 'How much does this bolt of muslin cost?', but the natives
were, if nothing else, patient – 'as long as one is not a Yankee ... whome for
some reason they don't seem to care for ... I suppose they have had a belt of
Frankenheimer once.' The gardener, Antonino, 'as bent and sturdy as an Olive
tree, as enduring and as incomprehensible', was planting 'beans and garlic and
lettuce and peas and radish and chick peas and Dhalias', and most days they
went to the stalls in Porta Prima 'and stagger back with wonderous bunches of
artichokes, of parsley, of Broccoli ... and the first of the broad beans ... small as
the nail of your little finger and as tender as a virgin nipple!' Dirk and Tony were
beginning to feel at home – the more so, as the friends and relatives from Britain
came to stay. Elizabeth was the first – she christened the cat Prune – and before
long, 'we really do seem to be running a rest home for our English Chums, which
is fun, expensive, exhausting, & quite *lovely* when they go!'[3] Labo went to the
vet, to be wormed, splinted, injected against rabies and generally repaired. It
turned out that he and Prune had simply been abandoned by the former
occupants of the house when they left: 'Americans, I fear,' noted Tony. The
restoration took three weeks, but was well worth it: Dirk had become devoted
to the dog.

The one item missing from the agenda at this time was work. The odd script
came Dirk's way: 're-makes of "Accident" or of Knife In The Water or very often,
a terribly "Nazi-Hates-Yanks??-Hates-The-World" kind of crap'; a film about
Ovid, to be made in Rumania, singularly lacked allure. However, he and Tony
were none too exercised. They were enjoying a life of relative ease and, just as
important, relative lack of luxury. 'I garden a lot,' he wrote to Losey; 'not your
idea of joy, I know, but useful therapy ... and I read a great deal ... and get
pissed again in the velvet evenings and shop and market and wander about
feeling happy and smug and on holiday'.[4] Visconti invited them to a screening
of *The Damned* in a rough cut, which both impressed and disappointed – not
least because an important scene, from Dirk's point of view, had gone. The film
was, he wrote, 'staggering ... it is far too long ... by about almost half an hour

... but where to cut!' He thought it was 'tilted towards the boy [Berger]', yet that was understandable because Visconti had done the same with Alain Delon in *Rocco and His Brothers*; 'but the sheer spectacle ... the detail ... the splendour of the high opera acting ... is unforgettable. It is not something that an American Audience in the Bahamas will readily cope with.' It was obscene, 'if cruelty is obscene'; perverted, 'if fucking your mother is perversion'; and unrelenting in its castigation of 'the People in Berlin', the Krupps and the Thyssens, 'and it wont make a sodding penny. Unless Warners cut it, and play it all for the Queer element, the incest and the tarts ... Not to mention the hero dressed as Marlene singing "Ein richtiger Manne". Thats not me dear.'[5] He and Visconti had a long talk, at the end of which Tony recorded that Dirk 'feels a certainty now that his talents as an actor, in which he is sure, as most informed people are, will be doomed by the crude demands of commercialism, and that he must state his own terms for retirement'. Tony felt Dirk was justified in his attitude, 'but this is a strange world & a strange business in which logic does not always work. So long as his qualities as a man are not upset it does'nt really matter.'

Dirk was buoyed to hear from George Cukor in Hollywood that his performance in *Justine* had power, originality and edge, and was moving and funny – all of which was correct, but counted for little, coming in a letter from his friend the director, and when laid against the scorn poured on the film more generally and publicly. In huge type the *Los Angeles Herald-Examiner* began a long article about the 'ten years of muddled thinking' behind *Justine* with the words: 'Occasionally – and still all too often – a motion picture can make a critic cringe and groan from first frame to last.'[6] *The New York Times* was kinder, but Dirk's concerns from that first read-through at Joseph Strick's beach house in Tunisia had been borne out. 'I really think,' he told Losey, 'that the most successful thing I have done in ten years or more is a one-minute bit in "Oh! What a Lovely War" ... which gets applauded every time. *Now why?* What was wrong with three hours in "Accident" or two in "The Servant" ... are'nt people funny.'[7]

As the guests – Irene Howard, Moura Budberg, Laurence Harbottle, Maude, Gareth Forwood and others – continued to ascend the hill in rapid succession, and Visconti came to lunch on veal and ham pie and trifle, there was a cold reminder of how some doors had shut. Dirk and Tony learned of Judy Garland's death, not by cable or telephone, but by reading it in the newspapers. Clearly 'what was always going to happen one day finally has done,' recorded Tony; 'it seems, almost, that more years of misery could have been spared if she had really done it many years ago. D is very upset, I think, & feels guilty that he has deserted her in recent years – but in this he is only one of many who could not stand the pace. I feel that what one loved, in public & briefly in private, vanished a few years ago.' Dirk told a BBC Television team some time later that in the end, after all the telephone calls at 3 in the morning, 4 in the morning, 5 in the morning, and the letters, the cables, the 'I, I, I', he and a lot of her friends 'couldn't take the stress of it'. As he, somewhat confusedly, remembered her telling him: 'One day you'll walk away from me, and you'll have your back to me. You won't walk away facing me.' Yes, said Dirk, 'we did turn our backs and we did – yes, we did walk away'. He recalled a link-line from one of her records, 'He was from Hell alright', and, Dirk added, 'that's where she came from'. She had spread her dislike, her distrust, her terrors, to everyone – and, during *I Could Go On Singing*, particularly to him. 'But everybody got a wallop of it, we all got it.' She was one of the most profound actresses that we had, and she was schizophrenic; she had magic, and she was a mess. For Dirk, finally, that was Judy Garland.[8]

Eleven months passed without Dirk facing a film camera. When he finally did so, it was for an NBC documentary, 'Upon This Rock', about St Peter's in the Vatican. His task was to read from the letters of Bonnie Prince Charlie, while those of James I were 'delivered' by Ralph Richardson, who twenty years earlier had accused Tony of 'carrying-on' with his wife Meriel Forbes when they appeared together in *The Philadelphia Story*, but who now, to Tony's relief, seemed to have acknowledged an error. Others involved in the project were Edith Evans and Orson Welles. The bonus for all concerned was that the filming took place, under a special papal licence, at night inside the Basilica, where they were able to wander at will, alone apart from a twenty-strong crew and a few guards. It was, said Tony, 'a pretty rare experience', and one of which Dirk made melo-dramatic capital in *A Particular Friendship*.[9] A more measured account in the Diary relates how, with his own contribution already 'in the can', he and Tony went back to St Peter's to see Dame Edith do her piece, but found she had finished, and was dining at a nearby trattoria, where they were expected. During the meal she said she would like to return one day to see the tomb of Pope John XXIII, 'Little Jesus', deep in the catacomb. Dirk brought his powers of persuasion to bear on the authorities, and late in the evening the three of them, escorted by two Vatican chiefs of police and a guard, were taken down:

> [...] she stood there in her long black dress & mink coat, 81 years old saying 'You see I did love him so'. Then the guard broke a carnation from a vase, laid it on the tomb for a moment & handed it to her. And then she walked forward to the tomb & bent to kiss it. It was a rare & deeply moving moment; the greatest actress alive, in her old age with such humility & wonderment – the flower may well go to the grave with her, although no Catholic she. But like all of us she holds Pope John above any creed. It was certainly an experience one will not forget.

One Sunday in the summer of 1969, Visconti had telephoned, first to express his dismay about reports that Warner Brothers were planning to cut *The Damned* by even more than he had agreed; Dirk, by this time, was both unsurprised and sanguine. What really took his attention was the second reason for Visconti's call: would Dirk play von Aschenbach for him? Dirk was confused: there was a character in *The Damned* called Aschenbach and surely there was nothing more to be done with him? Once a tetchy Visconti had made it clear that he was talking about Thomas Mann's protagonist in *Death in Venice*, the answer was, as Tony noted, 'yes with no consideration'. The novella, initially published as a two-part serial in a periodical and then, in 1913, in book form, has been described by the novelist and critic Gilbert Adair as the story of 'an ageing writer in febrile thrall to the ultimately fatal charm of a Polish adolescent' and 'the catastrophic loss of dignity suffered by a great and mature artist infatuated by a very much younger object of his lust'. It was based on a series of incidents from Mann's bleak, supposedly recuperative holiday with his wife and brother in May 1911, during which, at the Grand Hôtel des Bains on the Lido, his eye had been drawn to a Polish family, and, in particular, to the youngest child, a boy of 'near supernatural physical beauty and grace'. The Manns' stay in the city known as *La Serenissima* was abruptly cut short by a cholera alert, and on his return to Bavaria the writer began work immediately on a story of just seventy pages which was to become not only one of the undisputed classics of contemporary European literature but also 'the paradigmatic master-text of homosexual eroticism'.[10] There has been conjecture over the inspiration for Mann's protagonist, but he was most probably a mélange of Goethe, who in his sixties fell in love with a seventeen-year-old girl; of August von Platen, a homosexual German poet and aesthete who died at the age of thirty-nine, leaving verse that spoke of 'beauty's arrow' – 'Whoever has beheld beauty with his eyes/Is already delivered into the hands of death'; and, above all, of Gustav Mahler, who had died in the month that the Manns took their Venetian holiday: 'His princely progress towards death in Paris and Vienna, which was reported, step by step, in the papers, made me decide to give the hero of my story the passionately strong features of this artist whom I knew.'[11] At least the origin of von Aschenbach's given name was indisputable.

The photographer Horst – for whom Dirk sat at Nore in 1965 – told Laurence Schifano, Visconti's biographer, that when they met and became lovers in the thirties Visconti would carry around with him three books: a volume of Proust's *A la recherche du temps perdu*, André Gide's *The Counterfeiters* and Mann's *Death in Venice*. They represented, respectively: roots and love of family; alienation, and hatred of family; and homosexual temptation. In those days, according to Horst, Visconti still fought against his own homosexuality.[12] When he became a film and opera director, he would one day try to pay homage to both Proust and Mann; and by the late sixties it was inevitable that he would find a way of using the music of Mahler. He had tried to do so with *The Damned* but The Money insisted on 'the ponderous thumpings of Maurice Jarre'. He hoped to fare better with *Death in Venice*. But how were those backers going to take to a story which, at another level and like *The Damned*, was about a conflict and a crisis where 'disease, irrationality and self-destructiveness overwhelm the peaceful, reassuring but false order of middle-class life'?[13]

Two days after calling Dirk, Visconti went to dinner at Villa Berti, and further outlined his intentions. He explained that in the film Gustav von Aschenbach would be a composer rather than, as Mann had made him, a poet. The author, said Visconti, had based his character on Mahler, whom he 'once met on a train from Venice to Munich, wearing heavy make-up', and the film would have the composer's music on the soundtrack. The biggest stumbling-block to his plan was that Helmut Berger was keen for his master's next film to be 'about young people, starring himself, of course'. Time would tell. For the moment it was a tantalising prospect, with a touch of fate about it. Some twelve years earlier Glur Dyson Taylor had come to lunch at Beel with a young, clinically insane writer, Richard Rumbold, who not long afterwards committed suicide. He had brought with him as a present a copy of *Death in Venice*, hoping that Dirk would be able to set a film in motion: 'I was far too young to play the role, I thought ... but he was convinced.'[14] Now Dirk could no longer trace his copy and wondered with some regret whether he had mislaid a first edition.

Throughout the autumn Dirk was kept fairly reliably informed of progress. At Visconti's urging, he and Tony had bought a lot of records, expanding the Villa Berti repertoire from its Broadway base and leading Tony one evening to confide, wistfully, to the Diary: 'Tonight I sit up & listen to Mahler's 3rd Symphony. Some of the loveliest & most gentle music I've heard; one misses so much in the world – why only now does one hear Mahler, just because Luchino relates him to a possible film character for Dirk. I suppose he, D, will never listen to it – he cannot permit music to wash over & through him as I can; I suppose I'm so placid.'

By the time they attended the Brussels première of *The Damned* – where Dirk received compliments at first hand from, among others, Fellini – many of the usual obstacles seemed to have been overcome. Then, to everyone's chagrin, they learned that the film rights to the novella were already in other hands. The actor José Ferrer – Cyrano de Bergerac and Toulouse-Lautrec himself – and a producer, Joseph Besch, had acquired them for $18,000 from the Mann estate in 1963, and commissioned a script from the British writer H. A. L. Craig which was faithful to the novella in having von Aschenbach as a writer not a composer. Ferrer intended to direct, rather than star, but eventually backed away in favour of Franco Zeffirelli. At the end of 1965 the leading role had been turned down by, among others, John Gielgud, Burt Lancaster and Alec Guinness – his 'greatest missed opportunity', according to Piers Paul Read, who cites Kenneth Tynan as saying that Guinness was 'one of the few people alive who could play a genius convincingly. How seldom one sees an actor playing an author, whom it is possible to imagine constructing a coherent sentence, let alone a masterpiece.'[15] The Ferrer version was shelved, but before he and Besch would re-sell the rights to Visconti, who Ferrer knew was deeply committed in pre-production, some serious brinkmanship took place, during which it became clear that the actor-director wanted to play the part of von Aschenbach himself. Eventually the contract was signed in March 1970, with $72,000 changing hands, but the lawyers were still haggling six days before shooting was due to begin.

Dirk's own contract was for $120,000. He signed it as a non-resident of the United Kingdom – and that was now official. In September Tony had written from Villa Berti to Laurence Harbottle that Dirk 'did not feel any call to home', although he 'gets a little rattled by the graft here'. He was, however, rather 'leaning in the direction of France':

> The French are less likeable, but a little more grown-up! At the moment the 'game' season has opened and one can really hardly leave the house without being potted at by some idiot dressed for Safari who is wandering around in a hopeless search for something that he did'nt kill last year. The only thing left, apart from an abundancy of Rats in Prima Porta and a few sparrows in the stubble, is a small Screech Owl of whom we are rather fond. I fear they've got our pair of Hoopoes already. We have to keep the gates closed so that our wretched little dog does'nt put himself in the firing line.[16]

The 'wretched little dog' might be hard to train, but he was emphatically part of the family. Tony wrote to their solicitor, saying that because he and Dirk were about to do a good deal of travelling and because 'the roads here are a daily invitation to disaster', provision should be made for the Boludas to have £1,000. If they were unable to look after Labo, and if Elizabeth could not take him, he must be put down properly by the vet; 'on no account must he be abandoned'.[17]

Dirk was not merely 'leaning towards France'; he had become determined to move there. In November he and Tony were back at the Colombe d'Or for a concerted hunt. Yvonne Mitchell, who lived near Mougins, introduced them to Clair Loschetter, an agent based in Cabris, who took them to a farmhouse called La Treille a few miles east of Grasse, below the village of Châteauneuf de Grasse. It needed work, but was in a glorious position facing south, with – when visible – the mountains of l'Estérel making a distant arc towards the west and the sea 'shining some way off like a sheet of silver paper'.[18] They pronounced themselves 'very keen' but, at about £70,000, the house, with its workshop, garage, ten acres of land and 400 olive trees, might be beyond their budget. There was an outbuilding, or *dépendance*, a hundred yards or so away. The following afternoon, after two fruitless visits to properties in the area, they returned, in mist and rain, with Mme Loschetter, to meet the owner, Jean-Pierre Boursier-Mougenot, a good-looking, rich and eccentric artist in stained glass, whose Maoist wife lectured at the university in Nice. Despite the fog and the lack of any view, Dirk and Tony still found La Treille 'an enchanted mess' and coveted it badly. The owner was prepared to split the property on condition that Dirk and Tony found someone to buy *la dépendance*, which he used as his glass-making studio, within a year. A further afternoon tramping the boundaries, again in poor weather, did nothing to dissuade them. They returned to Rome, and made an offer of 740,000 francs – roughly £56,000 – which the admirable Monsieur Boursier-Mougenot, surprisingly sympathetic to the hideous problems for United Kingdom citizens in extracting sterling, accepted in principle. They did not know it at the time, but he was anxious for a quick sale because he was disposing of the house clandestinely; he wanted to expand his work activities by moving to a more elaborate studio elsewhere, but did not wish his relatives – even his wife – to know that he was severing ties with a property that had been in the family since the seventeenth century. Now Dirk and Tony were at the mercy of the fluctuating 'property dollar premium', which had a tendency to put houses out of reach overnight. Dirk wrote hurriedly to Lloyds Bank, saying that after searching extensively and finding nothing in the price range 'with a quarter of the amount of land or in such a splendid position', he was anxious not to miss 'a remarkable opportunity': 'I am advised by an eminent local architect that La Treille is probably the last unadulterated 17th century farmhouse in the residential part of the coast, and although my primary interest in it is as a home there is little doubt that, with some minor improvement to the living accommodation, it has a great investment potential, especially with its approximate 10 acres.'

The eminent local architect was Clair Loschetter's husband, Léon, who had established himself in his native Luxembourg, helping with the country's recon- struction after the war, and who now had a thriving practice in Cabris. He joined Dirk and Tony on a site visit, for which he had low hopes, knowing that Dirk was 'in the movies' and therefore expecting to be asked 'to gut the house, build a sauna and a swimming-pool, and string Venetian lanterns from every ceiling'.[19] After a slightly edgy introduction he rapidly discovered that Dirk – 'unlike most actors, who are silly' – was a man of rare cultivation with a keen interest in, and understanding of, the architect's world. The house, which dated from 1641, was on three floors, with no proper foundations. The ground floor was in three main sections on different levels, formerly stabling for donkeys, sheep and chickens; one of these 'rooms' had been roughly transformed into a kitchen, a second into a small studio. Upstairs were the Boursier-Mougenots' living-quarters: a sitting- room, three small bedrooms and a bathroom. There was further accommodation on the top floor, once a hayloft. This was no palace, just a simple, straightforward *mas*, largely unaffected by the passage of time. Léon Loschetter recalls that apart from its outlook there were three main reasons why Dirk chose the house: 'It was difficult to find, hard to get at. It was ancient. And it was big enough for him to make out of it some kind of reflection of himself.'[20] When they met, Dirk had no fixed ideas about what he wanted, apart from a substantial terrace and a means of translating the ground floor into one large living-room. 'In a way the terrace was the more important to him because from 15 June until 15 September the Provençal people eat, drink and spend most of their day outside.' As they talked, the architect realised that Dirk's ideas were different from those of most English people. For him history did not stop in Great Britain. For him the light was more important than the heat. He wanted an alternative to the conventional, perhaps with an element of the mysterious about it. He wanted the tiles on the ground floor to be irregular. He wanted to keep the old chicken-stains. His choices were a reflection of 'a British Continentalist', says Léon Loschetter. 'He had one foot on the Continent, and his heart was here.'

Dirk became a householder in France on 24 January 1970, with due ritual at the office of the *notaire* in Cabris. The property, of which he would be able to take possession in about six weeks, reverted to its ancient – and grander – name, Le Haut Clermont; La Treille remained part of the address. He, Tony, Clair Loschetter and M. Boursier-Mougenot repaired for a celebratory beer. And Léon Loschetter was entrusted with the task of transforming the back-of-a-table-napkin plans into a reality. He would have about six months, but he would be left alone. In his experience that, too, was unusual. Back in Rome Dirk wrote to Losey about the house, saying that he was 'ravished by it', but that there was a good deal to do – throwing three rooms into one, building another bathroom and another kitchen, and making an apartment for the Boludas. In the meantime he had to concentrate on *Death in Venice*.

> I have 18 changes . . . and we shoot also in the Tyrol and in Munich . . . because the TRUE story of DIV was that Mann, an old friend of Viscontis, was travelling on a train from Venice to Munich in 1910 . . . and in the compartment was a strange being in full slap . . . desperately unhappy, his dyed hair streaky . . . his false eyelashes coming off in his tears. They spoke . . . It was Gustave Mahler . . . and he had just fallen in hopeless love with a child of thirteen in Venice . . . and so from there it went. So, although *we are not telling anyone*, I am in fact playing Mahler . . . and look rather like him with the putty-nose job and the rimless Lennon-glasses . . . long hair . . . oh! dear I am a sight at the moment . . . So I rather fear that what my father calls a 'slender little tale' will end up with fifteen weeks shooting and then some, and so the house must wait . . . because this comes very much first . . . although how I am going to manage on the piddling little salary I dont know . . . we are back to OUR days of the Servant again . . . no lolly and everything needed.[21]

As part of a substantial amount of commuting, Dirk and Tony sought and gained the approval of Eduardo, Antonia and Labo for Le Haut Clermont. They also took Dirk's agent Robin Fox and his wife Angela to see it, and negotiations began for them to take on the *dépendance*; but these never progressed far. Next, the Boludas and Labo went to inspect lodgings in Venice. Dirk and Tony had found a house on the Giudecca, called Ca' Leone, which was owned and evidently not often occupied by the Volpi family – 'an acre of garden, and a simple house with silence all around'.[22] The central heating had collapsed, the electrical wiring was suspect, the legs of all the furniture on the ground floor were stained by the annual flooding, but it faced due south across the Lagoon towards the Lido and had that Venetian rarity: a large garden at both the front and the back. It was 'super, if sodden'.[23] Yet, with ominous echoes of *The Damned*, the production was by no means guaranteed. Dirk and Tony went to have dinner with Visconti, and found him none too well – nauseous and off his food, as he had been for more than two months. Tony suspected pleurisy, not helped by Visconti's gruelling mission to Austria, Hungary, Finland and Scandinavia to find the film's 'angel of death', Tadzio; it had ended successfully in Stockholm when he auditioned the fifteen-year-old Björn Andresen. During dinner, Visconti kept growling: 'Death in Venice – Dead in Rome.'

There was growling from another quarter, too, as Losey took exception to an interview published at length in *The Sunday Telegraph*, in the course of which Dirk mentioned the incident during *Accident* when he walked off the set before the end of a night's shooting. He had moved a prop, a child's tricycle, he said, and Losey shouted: 'Can't you ever learn to be disciplined?' It was, Dirk told Margaret Hinxman, 'the one thing he knew would hurt me because I've prided myself on being professional above everything. Of course, he didn't mean it. It was [. . .] the terrible strain of that film.'[24] Dirk did not keep Losey's letter, but his own response, headed 'Dearest Josieposie' and with a warning in red ink that what followed was supposed to be 'a funny letter', was blunt in the extreme. Of the article – which proclaimed Dirk as 'the most accomplished film actor in the world. After the death of Spencer Tracy, there is Bogarde. It is that simple.' – he wrote:

> I *knew*, the very second I read it . . . 'Watch it! Loseys going to be pissed off about this one.' Well; I *loved* it . . . and *approved* it, and was terribly pleased to get the coverage . . . things on which you did not comment . . . like us both trying to work for English Films and make them go . . . seem to have passed over your huge head . . . the fact that I did NOT say you were pissed out of your mind, and disgusting, the night I walked off the set . . . and took ALL the blame; you choose to ignore . . . correctly, I suppose . . . if one thinks one is God one must behave as God . . . but I just honestly and calmly, do think that we have done all that we can together. I dont, honestly, see how we could work together again . . . we have said all there is to say as actor-director . . . and you decided, a while ago, to take another path my dear . . . the one with the lolly and the lushness . . . I have kept to my rather wobbley one; it has been a bit of a wrench . . . but, after all, I had the lush one before Our Time, with Rank, I suppose . . . so now it is refreshing to be free . . . and to choose. It is frightning like shit . . . but it *is* honour regained.[25]

The reference to 'the lolly and the lushness' applied above all to Losey's espousal of the Burtons, unquestionably the Royalty of the film world at that period, and one or both of whom he had directed in his last two films to be released: *Boom!* and *Secret Ceremony*. Dirk expostulated at Losey's claim that he was going to California 'to "help Burton" get his Oscar' for *Anne of the Thousand Days* – 'as if it were some noble deed . . . something in which you felt you should share . . . so "that my usefulness is not entirely gone." Jeasus! What are you doing for the

Welsh bastard? How can you help him get an Oscar for an indifferent performance that has already, sickeningly, been purchased by Hal Wallis?* Why lend yourself to that stuff?' There was more. Dirk reminded Losey about *Death in Venice*:

> I know that you have long wanted to make it. You told me until I was blue in the face ... but you never asked *me* to do it ... or offered me the chance, or remotely thought that I even could! Visconti, in May last year, did ... I was amazed and thrilled to my marrow ... he gave no excuses or reasons, except to say, in a rather grudgning way, that I was 'like a dead pheasant ... hanging by the neck, and almost ready to drop' the reference being, I hope, that I was RIPE. And also, that I do look like Mahler, and that I was 'one of the most perfect actors in the world today on the screen'.
>
> You have never even said that I was more than passably good. To me anyway ... And from your interviews and books and all those itsy-bitsyes you hand out to 'Isis' and papers of that ilk ... I was lucky to have you. Instead of the other way round, sweetie!!
>
> You ARE a naughty fellow ... you know, full well that you are deeply loved by me ... and that you always will be. No matter what. But you are a solitary ... there is no helping you ... you eat love like candy and vomit it straight up again: like a dog.

It was strong meat and, with the wisdom of hindsight, it is easy to say that the 'warning' was not sincere. Another letter, now lost, winged back to Dirk, eliciting an apology for having caused 'such anger' with his previous missive, which Losey had described as 'paranoid'. 'It WAS supposed to be funny,' insisted Dirk.[26] Nevertheless it is hard to believe that the first letter did not signal, even mark, the end of their working relationship. David Caute notes in his Life of Losey how their extensive correspondence reflects the contrasting temperaments of the feline Dirk and the canine Losey: 'Bogarde cheerfully outrageous, Losey gloomily responsible. Both were vulnerable but Bogarde wears his scars on his sleeve in a bright patchwork quilt; Losey's wounds bleed through layers of armour.'[27] There would in the coming years be overtures on both sides, but it seemed pretty clear that, for Dirk, Losey's reign as the King of Film was dead. In any case, he now had to go to work again for the Emperor.

In 1953, back in the days when the stars made their varying entrances to the restaurant at Pinewood, Dirk found himself within earshot of Alan Ladd, who was making *The Black Knight* and who tended to be the butt of much mockery wherever he went. The diminutive figure clanked to his table and sat down with some colleagues who, intent on mischief, asked him: 'Wal,

---

* Hal Wallis (1898–1986), producer of *Anne of the Thousand Days;* brother of Minna.

Alan – waddayadoterday?' Ladd thought long and hard, then said: 'I did a great *look*.'[28] His companions were too stupid to take the point, but Dirk did. He never forgot it – even though he varied the location from Pinewood to Hollywood, and abandoned the armour, according to whether his audience was British or American. The great look had served Dirk well; well enough for him to tell Ann Guerin, as he waited for Visconti, that one of the highest compliments he had ever been paid by a critic was to be bracketed with Spencer Tracy, 'the absolute film actor. I think there are only about six in the world and I'm one of them.' He hoped to reinforce his claim with *Death in Venice*. 'I've always been good in bad pictures,' he said. 'I would like just once to be great in a great picture.'[29]

Seldom since the silent days had an actor been afforded the chance, or the burden, of carrying a film almost entirely on one 'great look' after another. In *Death in Venice* von Aschenbach speaks fewer than thirty times and utters about eight hundred words in all. The enormity of it dawned on Dirk after a lunch alone with Visconti, from which, Tony wrote, he returned 'devastated by the responsibility of the part, which will certainly be the hardest of his whole career'. The English script arrived four days before the film began, and he declared himself 'scared'.

The Hôtel des Bains had reverted to its Edwardian glory with the help of six pantechnicons full of art nouveau when Dirk arrived for his first scene. He had spent three hours with a quaking male make-up artist, sometimes under the supervision of Visconti himself, and at the end looked more like Thomas Mann than Mahler, and reminded Tony strongly of Rudyard Kipling. Dirk thought he resembled Lloyd George. For the next three months he would be lucky to have more than half a day off, 'but of course,' said Tony, 'he is happy about that really'.[30] After a fortnight, most of it on night-shooting, Dirk wrote to Dilys Powell: 'DIV goes well. A *very* odd experience for me. No words, just, as someone said from Warners, a "lot of looks". I pray to God they are the right ones! The Boy uncanny & quite magical – the Budget smaller than a telly commercial, but V is making it look like "The Leopard".'[31] The same day he wrote again:

Visconti is doing something magical . . . we have absolutely NO money at all . . . Warners are 'behind' us, but would have preferred 'a little girl', instead of a little boy . . . this was their own suggestion. They thought it would be more 'youth oriented' . . . (For God's sake dont tell anyone) . . . but there it is in a nutshell. Now they are bemused, and wonder how to sell a movie about 'This old fag who digs kiddies.'

One has, always, to catch ones breath and clench ones fists, and be nice to them . . . the Yanks I mean . . . but in ALL degrees they are dreadful. And I use the English word . . . one is full of DREAD for them . . . & they are full of dread too – from Cambodia to Kent . . . to the idiotic values, or non values, which they attach to Mann and 'DIV'.

He waxed nostalgic and lyrical about the atmosphere during the night work at the hotel:

> Shivers up ones spine when one sinks into a stuffed leather armchair and reads the 'Times' of June 11th, 1911 ... to see pictures of the review at Spithead ... (what a huge Navy we had) ... and on the opposite page a sad picture of the Prince of Wales with his Welsh Gear. What an odd, odd feeling it is ... almost ... no, not almost, clearly a case of Priestly ... I have been here before ... and in this room ... this odd mahogany room with mirrors and art nouveau lamps.

Night added a timelessness to it all:

> ... and the women look so beautiful. So elegant ... mincing along on their heels ... fans clacking ... skirts a shimmer ... hats brimming ... what we have *lost*! Oh! Dearie me ... not comfortable, I agree, but that has never been a reason for correct behaviour, for elegance ... for beauty even ... but how much nicer it was then ... just before the sky went dark, and 'the lamps went out'.

With that he said he had to close because he needed to snatch an hour or two's sleep 'before I have to trail across to the Lido to be turned into (I hope) a fiftytwo year old Jewish genius with a "hang up" (as Warners call it) on kids. Male.'[32]

By the middle of June Dirk and Tony were so settled at Ca' Leone that they were almost tempted to ask the Volpis if it was for sale. As usual, they tended to keep to themselves and saw little of the unit when off the set. 'Venice seems to be full of people one knows,' wrote Tony; 'lovely in some ways but D finds it not possible to cope very much with people at the moment because the part is really tiring enough in itself.'[33] Among their welcome visitors were Alain Resnais, who brought a script – a near-monologue about the imprisoned Marquis de Sade, which Dirk agreed immediately to do; Kathleen Tynan and Patrick Lichfield, on another assignment for *Vogue*; Rex Harrison and his latest wife-to-be, Elizabeth Harris, who invited Dirk and Tony on board their sumptuous motor-yacht, tied up to 'the queasiest mooring in Europe' and Peter Adam, a German-born film-maker working for the BBC, who was at work on a documentary about Visconti. 'Bogarde was the only person who refused to be part of the Visconti court,' wrote Adam in his memoirs:

> The relationship between the two men was distant but full of respect and affection. Visconti had a great admiration for Bogarde the actor, but Bogarde the man he found too serious, too English, not outgoing enough, more an actor than a film star. Visconti was used to the glamour of Alain Delon, Romy Schneider or Maria Callas. Dirk Bogarde is a generous man without pretensions

or false vanity. He would never indulge in the little games actors often play. He was totally genuine and slightly melancholic and laughed at what he called the 'Italian theatre' that most people on the film affected, 'the constant flatteries and the insincerity which seem to be their daily bread.' He preferred to be alone to read a good book.[34]

Adam observed that Dirk would take on to the set Mann's novella, rather than the script, and that he was a man of words, whereas for Visconti the words were always secondary to the images. Later, Dirk wrote to Adam that he had always hated the 'stuff' that Visconti had written and that was not in the book. Indeed, some of the sparse dialogue was impenetrable, even risible. Yet Visconti would justify himself by saying: 'This is a film, not a novel. I am trying to tell the human drama of an artist, his solitude and his desperation.' Age, decay and mortality were themes that had begun increasingly to preoccupy the ailing Visconti, who reputedly told Dirk before the death scene on the beach that his face should express 'pity, pain, love, fear, indignation and ten other things – you must know what they are'.[35] It took three days to shoot von Aschenbach's demise in his deckchair on the Lido – a sequence vividly described over three pages in *Snakes and Ladders*. Dirk made much of the process by which the make-up man achieved the effect of the barber in Mann's novel, who applied cream and carmine to the face of the *signore* and deluded him into thinking he was 'a young man in earliest bloom', able to 'fall in love as soon as he pleases', with his pallid lips 'now burgeoning cherry-red'. After four hours at the hands of Mauro – soon to be sacked, because Dirk considered his mind was more on a career in front of the camera – Visconti was satisfied. Dirk then had to wait beneath his 'scalding mask' until the light was deemed satisfactory, at which point, Tony told Kathleen Tynan, his 'will to die had ebbed a bit'. He 'passed on over and out about ten times, and Visconti told everyone how good it was. It was the first and only time that Dirk heard him cry "Bellissimo".'[36] Another hour was passed in discarding the 'dead' face, which, Tony noted, had been created with 'stain-removing paste which may or may not be good for the skin!' But there were no awful consequences, and the following day it was business as usual. Dirk and Tony were, in fact, rather more concerned about the health of Robin Fox, who was to have an operation on his lungs for possible TB, or worse.

Shooting in Venice lasted nine weeks. As it finished, Visconti took the unit to dinner on the island of Torcello, where he proposed a toast to Dirk, which resulted in a full minute of applause. Visconti had felt, while working on *The Damned*, that Dirk *was* Mann's von Aschenbach: 'I knew I could make a film based on his eyes. When he sees Tadzio kissed by another boy on the beach, he must smile from the interior a special amused smile, in no sense broad. And Dirk found that smile at once.' Dirk wrote and said often that Visconti only once gave him formal direction, when he shouted through a megaphone from a boat on the Grand Canal that Dirk must stand as his own boat emerged from the shadows under one of the bridges into the light – a moment which Visconti had choreographed in his head to a Mahler crescendo. More discreetly, he also told Dirk to be 'a little self-ironic' as von Aschenbach, 'since true tragedy makes you laugh'; and to approach his strawberries 'with more relish': 'Remember you have travelled south to eat fruit like this.'[37] Of Björn Andresen, von Aschenbach's 'Aphrodite', we learn little from the Diary. He and Dirk met seldom off the set, and when interviewed by the BBC in 2001 after nearly three decades in retreat from celebrity, bore out the general impression of Dirk's isolation in Venice; Andresen had hardly any memory of Tony, believing they met only once and that he was Dirk's agent. The young Swede respected Dirk, and not just as a player. It should perhaps be noted here that in 2003 a tabloid newspaper ran an interview with Andresen dominated by a large still photograph from the film, with him in the foreground as Tadzio and Dirk lurking at a distance behind him; the heading was: 'How beauty (and Dirk Bogarde) ruined the life of the world's prettiest boy'. Nothing in the accompanying text backed up that scurrilous assertion. On the contrary, the writer found that Andresen remembered Dirk fondly, and quoted him as saying: 'He was always very courteous to me. He was very kind and very British. He was the first foreigner to be specific about learning how to pronounce my name and he actually succeeded. I found that charming. He certainly never behaved improperly towards me.'[38] Dirk was equally respectful towards Andresen. He told Kathleen Tynan that 'Once you hold his eyes, he holds yours, fixes you like a python. It's not like playing with a child actor, he's a *proper* actor.'[39] To Patricia Losey, Dirk wrote that the sole problems with the boy were his 'shooting up feet in days ... and staying up until seven every morning doing the "Frug" or something frightful with the kids on the Lido and arriving for shooting with hoops of black under each eye ... our pure unblemished "Canava [*sic*] Marble" falling in dust before our eyes; stuffed with Pot and pea nuts and chewing gum'. He was, said Dirk, 'sensational', 'absolutely extra-ordinary': 'We worked together as if he had been in the business as long as I ... which is 36 years this June ... and he was [...] utterly professional'.[40]

Björn Andresen had completed his part when the unit moved to Rome for the final stages of production. There, Mark Burns was recruited at the eleventh hour to play Alfried, a character added by Visconti to represent von Aschenbach's conscience and saddled with mouthing a fair amount of pretentious bilge. No matter: it was a big opportunity. Dirk had remembered him from a series of Saki stories on television many years earlier, been reminded of him in films such as *The Charge of the Light Brigade* and *The Virgin and the Gypsy,* and had now recommended him to Visconti, whose sole instruction to the young actor was to play Alfried 'like a devil'. Burns recalls how Dirk was both paternal and helpful towards him:

> I have never worked with an actor who was so concerned for my well-being and my ability to do the work. He could have just left me to my own devices,

but he didn't. I've never understood actors who don't want to work with the other actors. It's a cliché, but if you're playing tennis with a really good player you're a much better tennis player yourself. So obviously it was to his advantage that I knew what I was doing. I would go to his dressing-room or he would come to mine and we'd work the lines, or we'd ring in the evening. There was a line in the script, a very flowery Italian translation: 'Tell me, do you know what lies at the bottom of the mainstream? Mediocrity!' I didn't understand it then, and still don't to this day. I called Dirk and asked 'What does "bottom of the mainstream" mean?' He said, 'Don't ask me, love, I haven't a fucking clue! You're the one who's saying it!'[41]

Burns remembers Dirk taking him to one side at the end of a scene, and watching secretly as Visconti set up the next with his lighting cameraman and his first assistant on an otherwise deserted stage. Visconti had worked out every movement that Dirk and Burns would make, and methodically went through them. The two actors crept away. Hours later, the actors were summoned to rehearse the scene. Each time he asked Dirk and Burns what they felt they should do, they copied what they had seen Visconti do, to cries of 'Bravo!' and 'Perfetto!' 'He knew we knew, and we knew he knew we knew. He probably knew Dirk was behind the scenery. But it was quite sweet, really.' What struck Burns more than anything was the silence whenever Visconti walked on to his set: 'It was like a cathedral. But not the silence of terror, as it was with Otto Preminger. The silence for Visconti was one of absolute adoration and admiration. He was the Maestro, and the Maestro was in their presence. And they were so *privileged* to be working for him. They hung on his every word, his every move. He was a huge personality.' Burns thinks it was inevitable that Dirk and Visconti would work together: 'They were both discreetly gay and they had a huge admiration for each other, a very bonded mutual feeling – but absolutely not in a homosexual way. I thought that the way Dirk called him "Papa" said a lot about their relationship. Perhaps Dirk did see him as a father figure. On the other hand, Dirk would argue with Visconti if he didn't feel comfortable with something: he was no pussycat.'

Burns recalls also how Le Haut Clermont dominated the conversation during their evenings in Rome. 'They talked about little else when we were on our own. Tony would report to Dirk how it was getting on, and Dirk was permanently on the phone, saying, "Put in this, put in that", and "God, I bet he's done it wrong".' They took the chance to see for themselves, when Visconti had to leave for a confrontation with The Money. In a new white Maserati – the fourteen-year run of Rolls and Bentleys was at an end – Dirk and Tony made yet another border crossing, and on a spectacularly fine day met Léon Loschetter at the house. They were thrilled by what they found. The architect's plans had been beautifully translated, and Le Haut Clermont was 'really everything we felt it could become'. They scurried back to Trieste and then to Bolzano, for Dirk's last, and perhaps most moving, scene in the entire film, with Marisa Berenson as von Aschenbach's wife. And then they were free. They moved into their new home on 5 August 1970.

Eighteen

'There is a movement afoot to take Dirk Bogarde seriously!'

So began the happiest period of Dirk's life. It was achieved against a background of responsibility, whereas the Lullington days had been, in the true sense, carefree. At the same time, most of the surface gloss applied through stardom had now – like von Aschenbach's make-up, but less painfully – been peeled away; and many of the days to come would be enjoyed in the spirit of uncluttered, unpretending simplicity which had characterised his and Elizabeth's enchanted childhood. No door in his corridor had been open as wide as the one which beckoned on that dull afternoon when he caught his first sight of Le Haut Clermont, or, as he knew it, Clermont. Now, confronted by the reality, he was still convinced; but he knew full well that in his metaphorical room there would be furniture for unsuspecting shins to be barked upon, low beams for heads held complacently high, and large insects to cause discomfort. Furniture – ah yes, that was all too soon a very sore point. In *An Orderly Man*, where Dirk most fully records the early days at Clermont, he describes the day the yellow removal vans came up the path, like 'elephants ambling slowly towards a water-hole', and disgorged the wreckage of his belongings.[1] Most of his Meissen was 'smashed to bits', he told Ann Skinner; '... lamps were broken ... books lost ... tables and veneers of various pieces ripped apart'.[2] Paintings were pock-marked, the film-projector had disappeared and even the Drummer was broken in two. Almost the only objects to have escaped intact were the two leopards, which were safely in an auction house back at home; they failed to reach their reserve and would eventually end up gracing the lobby of Denville Hall, the home for retired actors and actresses. Suffice to say here that the wrangling over compensation from the firm of shippers lasted more than a year and was settled at a measly £1,300.

One of the first long despatches from Clermont went to Patricia Losey, informing her that 'here we are in a beautiful place, where I have always wanted to be, and that should jolly well be enough. And, in truth, it is.' They had done 'a hell of a lot' to the place – 'opened up walls and floors and closed doors and windows and generally transformed a stable, workroom and kitchen into a fifty foot room with a great terrace and windows out over the whole of the Provence countryside to the sea at La Napoule'. The biggest problem was that Antonia had discovered a lump and, after three years of loyal service on a par with that of the Zwickls, she and Eduardo might have to return to Spain; they were there now, for a check-up, and, wrote Dirk, 'we sit in our bergerie on the hill "doing" for ourselves. I loath it [. . .] Floors to scrub, beds to make, food to prepare, eat and wash up ... windows and shutters to lock up and open, and the fucking incinerator to relight every morning!' Otherwise, 'we sit and write and read and garden and play music and shop and eat and wander about hanging pictures and dusting books ... and generally settling in for a stay':

> We really do rather adore it, and keep hoping that God, or the fates, will allow us a little time to stay here ... apart from the always present hazard of age and health there should be no real reason why not ... I dont have to work again for twenty years, which will take care of me anyway! And I am not all that eager to do so ... Joe and Visconti are terrible spoilers for one ... no one else quite hits the same mark.[3]

His financial position had improved in a relatively short time. He was right when he told Joe Losey during their 'paranoid' exchange that: 'My "exile", as you quaintly call it, was not emotional, but very good business.'[4] The balance at Connaught in Nassau was certainly healthy and there was a chance of some profits from *The Damned*. He would see his full fee of $120,000 for *Death in Venice* only if it moved into profit; otherwise his participation was almost philanthropic, at $50,000. There *was* a possible film: the Resnais, 'a Marienbad about de Sade. Original. Confusing. Brilliant and un commercial' – so that was far from being a *fait accompli*. In fact it would be two years before Dirk worked again on a film set. But now that there was so much to do in his life as an *agriculteur*, the depressions and liverish attacks which had so often coincided with boredom seemed a remoter possibility. When he moved to Nore, he added 'Farm' to its postal address, which caused bewilderment in Bernard Walsh and others; but there was no intention to adopt for his letter-heading 'La Ferme du Haut Clermont' – the property's historical name was quite grand enough.

The first lunch guests were Richard and Sheila Attenborough, to whom Dirk mentioned that the *dépendance* might soon be available – to everyone's benefit. The first long-stay visitors were Dirk's parents, now both in their seventies. Their relationship, and that with their son, is the secondary theme of *An Orderly Man*; and a poignant one it is too. Never before had Ulric confided so deeply in Dirk, who reported his father saying of Margaret, 'I really shouldn't have married her,' and 'If I had had the money then that *you* had at that age, we would have been divorced in four months.' For fifty years, they had 'muddled through'.[5] (These remarks are disbelieved by the family, who describe them as utterly out of character.) After their first stay at Clermont – there would not be many – Dirk told Patricia Losey that Ulric was as 'devine as ever pottering about painting and smelling the air, and trying to "capture" Cezanne's light on paper. But she sat in a heap, with tired legs rather hating the whole thing and most of all me. As usual! I feel it so wretched that she is utterly incapable of enjoying a thing. Except the bar of the Colombe and a good flask of wine. And we all know what that leads to.'[6] Harrowingly, after he and Tony had seen them off from Rome the previous year, Dirk confided that he no longer *liked* his mother, and felt disconsolate about it; but she assumed a false personality when she was with him and he could not stand it. He had come to respect his father more and more; but he took no pleasure in the fact that the particular mother–son bond which had underpinned his early life and quickened his desire to act was now irreparably frayed. The sadness was all the greater because Margaret had taken much vicarious pleasure from Dirk's success; now, with his professional stature at a new level, she was in a sense no longer there to enjoy it with him.

Even before the opening of *Death in Venice*, a debate about Dirk's qualities as an actor had begun. Geoffrey Moorhouse, writing in *The Guardian*, compared him unfavourably with Alec Guinness, saying the latter was the 'outstanding actor as distinct from performer', who 'can act and assume someone else's personality, appearance, caste marks and all'. By contrast, to find an example of failure to get into a subject's character 'you need look no further than the average performance by Dirk Bogarde':

> As performances, I can enjoy and applaud them as much as most, but I wouldn't call them acting. There was scarcely any difference at all between the human being who appeared as a Great War subaltern in 'For King and Country' [*sic*] and the one who appeared as a 1935 German industrialist in 'The Damned'. There came moments when both raised their right eyebrow, just so, and dilated their nostrils, like that, and looked very levelly at someone they despised because that was another Bogarde stock response. I saw nothing which suggested that whereas one was the product of middle class Home Counties the other was most distinctly a scion of the Ruhr's elite. And this gap between them should have been something infinitely complex and subtle.[7]

At the National Film Theatre, however, they felt differently. In recent months Alfred Hitchcock, Graham Greene and Noël Coward had all given talks as part of a John Player Lecture series, and to this illustrious roster they now added Dirk. To the organisers, Søren Fischer and Brian Baxter, he was, with Trevor Howard and James Mason, 'one of the three great film actors whom Britain has produced'; and they acknowledged the foundation for Margaret Hinxman's claim that he could be bracketed with Spencer Tracy. The recent pictures – including even the unlamented *Justine* – had seen him break through 'not just in terms of performance but films of major interest' and his absence from British cinema was symptomatic both of the current malaise in the industry and of the internationalism of film.[8] Shortly before his recent death, Søren Fischer recalled how there was a technical rehearsal for the talk, because it was to be illustrated with clips from several of Dirk's films. When the scene Dirk had contributed to *I Could Go On Singing* was screened, the theatre technicians and the BBC production team who were filming the event applauded him to the echo. Tony told Dirk: 'If you're not careful, you'll have written the whole film next.' The talk itself was, as we have already seen, a splendidly irreverent affair – at Dirk's insistence. Only Billy Wilder had made a John Player Lecture audience laugh so much, recalled Fischer and Baxter, 'but he was more acerbic. Nobody else had Dirk's slightly self-deprecating, camp, frame of reference.'[9] It was Dirk at his best: relaxed, engaging, forthcoming, sharp, occasionally slanderous but not malicious, and very, very funny. He enjoyed himself immensely, and decided that the NFT's governing body, the British Film Institute, should have his collection of leather-bound scripts, some thirty in all, sprinkled liberally with his annotations, amendments, additions, doodles and sketches.

Death in Venice was given a royal première before the Queen and Princess Anne. The former was in a 'distant' mood, noted Tony, and the audience was 'sticky', applauding only tepidly, perhaps because the royals trooped out promptly, the Princess looking distinctly glum. Björn Andresen was coached by Dirk in how to bow to Her Majesty. 'What do you find most entertaining in London?' she asked him. 'Madame Tussaud's Horror Cabinet,' he replied.[10] It was probably her best moment of the evening. The critics accorded Visconti's work the respect it deserved. Patrick Gibbs thought the 'dropping of Mahler and his music into a work that has generally been regarded as fiction' fatally flawed 'what might otherwise have been a masterpiece';[11] for Dilys Powell, the film made 'grave demands' on the audience, but none in the previous twenty-five years had been 'more truly a work of art'.[12] In America, Judith Crist decided that it was 'essentially a triumph of ambiance, a Dirk Bogarde performance and the viewer's willingness to settle for face value, an exquisite one';[13] *The New Yorker*, that it was 'a peculiar mixture of unearthly beauty and almighty carry-on'.[14] For that Dirk Bogarde performance, Gibbs had 'nothing but admiration' and George Melly declared: 'If he doesn't win an Oscar, there's no justice.'[15] *Variety* did not go quite that far, but conceded that Dirk, 'vastly improved now that he is getting into roles that match his own intelligence, is both pathetic and compelling'.[16] The harshest verdict was probably that of John Simon, who wrote:

Though meant to be only fifty, Bogarde tends to effect an eightyish dodder. Meant to look cold and intellectual, Bogarde's face is pouty, pettish, and rather vapid. After pretending to be infuriated by a hotel error obliging him to stay on in Venice – which he wanted to do all along – he gives a prolonged little smile of secret self-satisfaction that must be the coyest, smuggest, most obvious bit of facial play this worthy actor has ever permitted himself. Shambling along the hotel beach, officiously ordering about the beach attendant (one of numerous twentyish, corrupt-looking youths with whom Visconti populates his movie), eating a strawberry with exaggeratedly fussy gusto, or merely ogling Tadzio with a sheepishness that keeps spilling over into bovineness, Bogarde, in his white togs and funny hat, looks less like *Death in Venice* than like *Monsieur Hulot's Holiday.*[17]

Dirk and Tony philosophised that as usual the male critics had been made uneasy at the film's 'sexual connotations', which 'Americans are a bit unsophisticated about or scared of'. The women writers seemed to love it. Except the critic of *Nice-Matin*, who, according to Dirk, 'said it was the most boring thing she's seen since measles'.[18]

More privately, Kenneth Tynan would later annoy his wife Kathleen by describing Dirk's 'highly artificial' performance in *Death in Venice* as 'A middle-aged man pretending to be a young man made up as an old man.'[19] Tom Courtenay told Piers Paul Read that if Alec Guinness had, as proposed, portrayed von Aschenbach as the writer, 'it would have been a greater film. You would have felt that he *was* a great writer. With Dirk you didn't.'[20] And Keith Baxter – opposite whom Dirk would have played had he agreed to create the role of Andrew Wyke in the stage production of Anthony Shaffer's *Sleuth* the previous year – voices a widely held view when he says that the tension of the novella is lost from the beginning by Dirk's performance in the film: 'There is no *coup de foudre*. The twitching, the loathing of the painted face – all that repression is established too soon.'[21]

When *Death in Venice* went to Cannes, it fell foul of the politics which have always bedevilled that festival. Although shot in English, it was shown to the jury dubbed into Italian, thereby putting paid to Dirk's chance of winning the prize for best performance by an actor. The screening of the original version was a triumph, Tony noting the applause of the packed house when von Aschenbach decides – or Fate impels him – to return to the Lido. By one of those ironic twists, the Palme d'Or was awarded, not without controversy, to Losey for *The Go-Between* – a subject much discussed between him and Dirk. Visconti had to be satisfied with a special Festival silver jubilee award, which was greeted with undiluted approval by the audience.

Disappointments over the film added to a general malaise at Clermont during what should have been a contented, if not exhilarating first spring and summer. Dirk was having a dreadful time with his back teeth, which at one point fell out when a bridge collapsed and had to be replaced at huge expense. More worrying was a suspected nodule in his throat, which cause him to cut down overnight from sixty cigarettes to none. Tony, who followed him in support, noted that it was 'probably only a polyp on the vocal chords, but we're all so desperately over-aware these days, & D is a highly sensitive creature who has to suffer for his talent'. After weeks of concern Dirk finally summoned up the courage to see a specialist, who said it was all in the mind. Disconcerting also was a peremptory summons to the British Consulate, for a meeting with a Foreign Office representative who flew out specifically to see him. It was a mysterious encounter, never fully explained, but at its heart was 'a vague warning about possible Russian trickery'. Whether this had something to do with the potential for blackmail, which in all the circumstances was non-existent; or with publicity surrounding Losey's next film, *The Assassination of Trotsky* – in which Dirk had at that stage turned down the title role – is, one imagines, known only to a retired spook and, perhaps, a dusty file. About none of this was he made to feel better by the fact that he was now fifty – the event marked by lunch at the Colombe d'Or with Patrick Campbell and his wife, James Baldwin and Simone Signoret; and by Tony remarking that 'it does'nt seem so long ago we celebrated his mother's ditto & thought poor old bag!'

Trotsky was not the only historical figure to be smartly shown the door. De Sade was still a hope, but diminishing, and according to Tony within the space of a few weeks Lord Randolph Churchill – offered by Richard Attenborough – Somerset Maugham and Chaucer had all been rejected: 'Torquemada is currently in the post and will most likely be dealt with in similar fashion, but we must earnestly hope that someone will soon turn up who will strike a chord of response and bear a purseful of dollars at the same time, and we ought to be ready for him even if it's Stanley Baldwin!'[22] Then came an offer which had some appeal. Edward Thompson, who had last written in 1964 about the possibility of a book for Heinemann on Dirk's craft, was prompted by *Death in Venice* – 'quite the greatest thing to hit us for years' – to make another approach. Dirk replied: 'Now about writing . . . well. I can not even spell . . . and as for knowing ANYTHING about acting I could'nt begin. It sort of happens. And one only hopes it works. As Edith Evans said once recently . . . "I just dress them up and play them, dear." And thats about it for me too . . . I'm not bright I'm afraid.'[23]

Four months later, taking a leaf out of Ulric's manual for 'constant dripping', Thompson had prevailed. He visited Dirk at Clermont, and gave him books by Gielgud and Redgrave. The former went down well, but 'I dont awfully care for Redders. He reminds me, always, of a bossy old School Teacher . . . which indeed he was and still, to my mind, is. With pretty legs long ago.' Dirk agreed to attempt 'a sort of Auto Bio' through which some of his thoughts about what he did as an actor might be conveyed. Each actor has his own Method, he said, whether it be Stanislavsky's, 'in various disguises, or just plain super Rex-Harrison. I have one myself . . . but I would no more be able to explain it to you, or to a reader, than I can explain the Telephone or the Auto Loader on a Bofors Gun.'[24] He said he would write it *for* Thompson – it was important to have a reader in mind – and explained that for several years he had been corresponding three times a week with a woman in America. He then set out his synopsis:

> The beginning is not unusual . . . the struggle and push . . . Peter Ustinov and
> Paul Scofield my contemporaries . . . the West End the War and all that crap

... the coming back and starting again after seven years away ... the Casting Couch and odd gentlemen promising one fantastic jobs to dress up as an Hussar in breeches and boots and then to cook them supper! And then the horrors of Rank and all the sixty films that followed and the people who came along and passed out of ones ken ... or on to higher things ... fat Welsh Pit Ponies who became Richard Burton and people of that ilk ... but all of it funny. With serious undertones!

He even had a choice of possible titles:

I might call it [...] 'Dangerous To Lean Out ...' or else 'A Movement Afoot ...' which is part of a phrase used by an Actor once at Farnham Rep where he was heard to say, in deeply shocked tones ... 'There is a movement afoot to take Dirk Bogarde SERIOUSLY!' which I have always found delicious! And my first chapter heading is 'Who The Fuck Is Clair Bloom?' ... in quotes, like that, and said aloud at one of the first Theatre Parties I ever had to go to when I had just Become A Star in the Theatre after the war. I suppose that would'nt be allowed though, would it? I would'nt actually be being RUDE to CB although I could (and shall in tiny print!)

The following day he began to plan his book, with the working title of 'A Movement Afoot'. Tony approved. As he remembered it, the original remark had been made to his son Gareth. The source was believed to be James Cairncross, who is troubled by the reference to Farnham because he never acted there; but he and Gareth *did* appear together at the Oxford Playhouse, 'and I am afraid it is the sort of thing I might have said in those days!'[25] Gareth Forwood confirms that Cairncross is off the hook: 'It was Alfred Burke who said it at LAMDA when I was a student ASM and in the chorus of *The Bacchae* in the early sixties. I told Dirk and he thought it was the funniest thing he'd ever heard.'

Alas, Dirk was soon writing again to Thompson, saying that however hard he tried, he simply could not 'get the thing off the ground'. There was a book about, he thought, 'and a very funny, sad, at times ugly one at that, but it aint no Educational Book Department deal'. Nevertheless he would 'muck about' with 'Your Book' during the long dark winter evenings, and promised him 'the first "look" at it'.[26] Two months later, Dirk admitted defeat, having not put a word to paper – but he had dug out the three chapters of 'The Canary Cage' from five years earlier, and sent them to Thompson, who read the first pages to his secretary and assistant, and found himself brushing away a 'cursory tear at the sweet pathos of the kid'. At the end 'the only thing I wondered about is why the hell you have been saying you can't write'.[27] The encouragement worked for another brief while, until Dirk reported that he had exhaustedly set the book aside:

The whole thing really becomes so 'cute' and 'sicky' … and I fear that too much will be like eating plates and plates of Ice Cream and hot chocolate! […] What more is there to say about hills and fields and Lally and rivers and skies … there has to be some sort of *core* and I cannot really find one. There is no 'adventure' as it were, and really, as Mrs Ritz said after the Occupation years in Paris from '40 to '45, 'nothing very much happened'.[28]

So, while there was work in abundance outdoors at Clermont, there was another halt in the studio, and nothing to take him back in front of a camera. Losey and Dirk had fallen out badly over *The Assassination of Trotsky* and an unrealised version of Malcolm Lowry's *Under the Volcano*, for which the director again chose to go with Richard Burton. News of this reached Dirk on a 'Bloody Monday', when he also heard that he was unlikely ever to see an estimated $80,000 which he thought he was owed for *The Damned*, and one of his agents told him that although he was recognised as one of the greatest actors, he was 'difficult to sell'. He missed Robin Fox, who had died, and in whose memory Dirk wrote a poem, 'At Santa Monica'. The care he took to polish this verse is evident from the several drafts that survive among Dirk's papers; the 'definitive' text, published in a memoir by Angela Fox in 1986, supplied the lines that are carved on Fox's headstone in the churchyard opposite their house in Cuckfield, Sussex:

> Gone now:
> Your raven's eye,
> the dancing grin,
> head held high
> and soldier's
> unastonished stride.[29]

With the loss of a man who had been a friend and guide as much as an active agent, the question of Dirk's representation had become uneasy; dismissals were frequent, because he felt he was not being sent the kind of material which might enhance his reputation – or, as in one case on 'Bloody Monday', was not being kept informed: the agent who had been sworn to secrecy about Burton and *Under the Volcano* was fired by telephone.

'Since "Death in Venice",' Dirk told Penelope Mortimer, 'I am only asked ever to do senile old sex-perverts or schoolteachers in love with their nymphetts … or whatever they are called … so I have called a halt for the time … almost two years now … and prefer to sit up here on my hill and regret nothing … rather than make all that awful crap and regret it all.'[30] Penelope Mortimer had written to Dirk, introducing herself as the author of *The Pumpkin Eater*, which had been filmed by Jack Clayton from a Pinter script. Feeling strongly that Bette Davis was misused in sub-*What Ever Happened to Baby Jane?* material, she had approached the formidable actress, offering to write something for her. Back came an ecstatic letter, saying: 'If you could think of an idea for Dirk Bogarde and me – well – I would be so truly thrilled. It is my ambition to work with him at this point.'[31] Oddly enough, Dirk had received a script a few weeks earlier which Davis had agreed to do, and which would have required him to be 'a suave man of the world with a Franco-Greek accent and a way with women', who, like the Davis character, would spend a great deal of time 'nipping about the railway lines' in Geneva, when he was not 'Feaverishly Unbuttoning Aunt Cecilias Neices Knickers'.[32] He had declined. The idea of collaborating with Davis and Mortimer was, if nothing else, novel.

An actor who had worked with Davis long ago, wrote Dirk, 'said it was like coming through Hell and he needed Intensive Care until a year ago ... he almost fell into his Moules at lunch when I mentioned her name ... and his wife is quite ill still'.[33] It goes without saying that the idea never advanced far. However, from that initial enquiry by Penelope Mortimer came another 'particular friendship', another relationship at a distance, with a fiercely intelligent, uncompromising, amusing and *safe* woman correspondent. Her timing was almost supernaturally good.

Dorothy Gordon lost her battle with illness in April 1972. She had undergone an operation which left her with – as she and Dirk put it – a 'banjo belly', but somehow kept writing to him with vigour right up to the end, which came unexpectedly. A letter typed on the eve of her death acknowledged receipt of his latest 'starling', which had brought her 'a measure of relief'. It was overtaken in the post by a telegram from America, which carried the sad news to Dirk. She had died suddenly, at home, of a heart attack. Dirk was particularly touched by a note thanking him for the happiness his letters had given during her employer's last years, and saying that Dorothy had often said they should be 'put in a book'. It was signed: 'Paula J. Gary – her friend & maid'. 'I felt rather empty and wretched,' he told Penelope Mortimer. 'A habit of love suddenly whipped away like a dusty rug from under ones feet. Three letters a week for seven years. And suddenly nothing to write to ... or no one. And collecting dotty things to tell her ... like buying presents for a cancelled Christmas.'[34] The question was, what to do with the immense transatlantic correspondence that had accumulated since 1967? It was, after all, the transcript of 'a love affair without carnality' – as Dirk would always refer to it – with a heated intensity of its own and a purity unblemished by any meeting. The eventual fate of his letters to her had troubled Dorothy for some time; but Dirk had not given it quite the same priority. At one stage he had suggested that Dorothy publish them; she felt not. She suggested giving them to a university archive, but Dirk resisted, saying it would leave them open to inspection by 'hippies'. She reassured him that they would be subject to restricted access, would be seen by properly qualified scholars alone, and could, if he so wished, be locked away for a hundred years. He then said they should be destroyed, which made Dorothy ask whether he would destroy a Bonnard or a Schiele just because the artists had painted to divert themselves or a friend. She

Earl St John.

Olive Dodds.

John Davis.

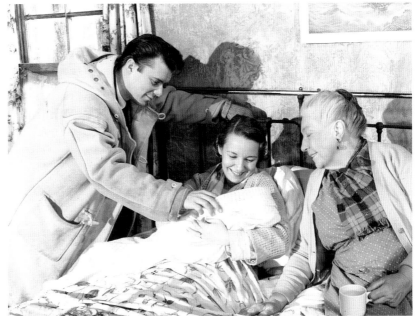

Bedside manners: in *Doctor in the House*.

With Ralph Thomas . . .

. . . and Betty Box.

Theo 'Thumper' Cowan on Festival duty at Cannes.

Jean Simmons with Chug.

With Agnes and Hans Zwickl on the set
of *Ill Met by Moonlight*.

With Irene Howard.

With Noël Coward.

Above As Patrick Leigh Fermor – Dirk's
favourite still.

Left Christmas in America, 1956, with
(from left) Kay Kendall, Rex Harrison
and Margaret Leighton.

Right Arnold Schulkes.

Idol of the Odeons – especially Leicester Square.

The price of fame?

An early brush with royalty.

Right How the fan magazines saw things in the late Fifties.

Inset With Rock Hudson on location in Cortina d'Ampezzo, 1957.

DIRK BOGARDE

and now let's meet

Rock Hudson

another star who has found heartbreak and love are seldom far apart.

"I LIKE my steaks rare," said Rock Hudson.
"And I like mine well-done," replied the pretty girl sitting opposite him, whose name was Phyllis Gates.
Rock, up till then Hollywood's number one bachelor, gave a long, happy sigh.
"I'm just crazy about you," he said, smiling into Phyllis's eyes. "I guess you know that. But I like my steaks rare, and you like yours well-done. We're so different, you and I."
"That's what makes it such fun, Rock," said Phyllis, "that's why we'll never bore each other."
Rock laughed and leaned across the table towards her. "If I believed that, I might—" he said softly, "I might—just possibly— ask you to marry me."

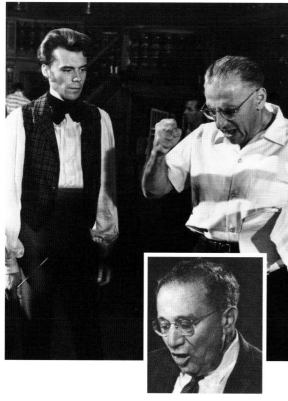

Left Under tuition from George Cukor; *Inset* Victor Aller on *Song Without End*, 'a holed galleon'.

Above A statement: on location for *The Singer Not the Song*

Left The turning point: as Melville Farr in *Victim*; *Inset* Basil Dearden.

Above With Tom Courtenay (left) and Joseph Losey (right) on *King and Country*, the third of Dirk's five collaborations with 'The King'.

Above As Barrett, 'a mean and shabby man', in *The Servant*.

Capturing the *Zeitgeist*: in *Darling*, with Julie Christie.

On location with
John Schlesinger.

Left At Bendrose with Jon Whiteley, his co-star in *Hunted* and *The Spanish Gardener*.

Below On the terrace at Beel House, with Elizabeth and her son, Mark.

At 'The Palace', Drummers Yard; *Inset* Capucine and Judy Garland, Christmas 1960.

Clockwise from top The finest of the houses, Nore, and Candy the mastiff; with Annie (left), believed to be the only creature who ever had the better of Dirk; with Labo, the waif of indeterminate age; the ugliest of the houses, Villa Berti, outside Rome; Gareth Forwood and Kay Young at Adam's Farm.

Staked-out as Gabriel in *Modesty Blaise*.

With Jacqueline Sassard and Michael York in *Accident*.

Consultation with Jack Clayton on *Our Mother's House*.

With Ingrid Thulin in *The Damned*.

said that many of the letters were 'things of great beauty, too lovely to perish', and she felt that *he* should edit and publish them ... '*Letters to an Unknown Woman!*' In *A Particular Friendship* Dirk writes of Dorothy recommending that for publication 'My death would be the appropriate moment'. However, she added, 'I never know when you are being tongue-in-cheek.'[35] Dirk claimed that, in what turned out to be his last 'starling' to her, he said she could do what she liked with 'my ruddy letters. Yale, Harvard or the British Museum, or try St Pancras, why not? Do as you like, if it makes you feel better, I really do not care.'[36] Dirk's version of events is suspect, but he confessed to being cruel and thoughtless at a time when Dorothy was gravely ill. There is no question that he was needlessly belligerent in his attitude towards what had become for her an upsetting dilemma. In her last letter she regretted ever raising the question with him, and accused Dirk of emotional blackmail – 'And blackmail is not the art of a gentle man. And gentle, you are.'

After her death, a friend reported to Dirk that Dorothy had considered all the possibilities that lay in the range between a bonfire and editing for publication, but felt ill-equipped to take on the latter task herself; so she had resolved to return his letters to him. And that is what the executors did on her behalf. Dirk went to the post office in Grasse to pick up the box – 'all intact and fewer than I had thought,' he noted in the Diary. He had expected a tea-chest full. In the meantime he had written yet again to Edward Thompson regretting that he was too busy with guests to be able to work on a book. 'What would you say to 2,000 letters written by me over 7 years to a woman in America whome I never spoke to, or met? She died & has left the collection to Yale – unless I want them back – & I do! – (her copies too) – quite a Saga – "Love Story" unseen!'[37] Thompson thought 'Love Story Unseen' a 'splendid' title, and volunteered to do the editing; but he was still dedicated to 'The Canary Cage'. Then the letters arrived and, Dirk told Penelope Mortimer, they were 'FRIGHTFUL ... and off they go to the fire. After the shock of reading a random few [...] I decided I was not much cop at the writing ... and the person who emerged from the typed pages was a mixture of Shirley Temple, Doopey, and Oswald Mosley ... so off with their heads.'[38] Another year went by, with no word of a bonfire, but with Dirk still thoroughly off the idea of publication because the letters were 'terribly personal and "near" to me'; and then, to his pleasant surprise, Thompson received a card from Dirk – addressed to 'Dear Persistant' – saying he had started again on the memoir, and was calling it 'The Eggshell Summer'.[39]

Some time in 1972 the writer Beverley Cross spotted a familiar face in a supermarket some miles west of Grasse. It was Dirk, and he was looking closely at the prices. 'Lobster at fifty francs a kilo!' he protested. 'Good heavens, I'll have to make another film!'[40] And he did. The director Henri Verneuil had an 'interesting idea', *The Serpent*, in which Dirk would play 'a sort of Kim Philby'. At $75,000 it was, recorded Dirk in the Diary, 'Too much, for 15 days work, to turn down'. And he liked Verneuil, journalist-turned-director, immediately. For the Paris segment of the shooting, Dirk and Tony travelled overnight on the Blue Train from Nice, and arrived at the Lancaster at about 9.15 on a Sunday morning. Fifteen minutes later the telephone rang, and it was Gareth Van den Bogaerde, to say that Ulric had died at Cherry Tree Cottage. This was a profound shock to Dirk, who had spoken to his father a few days before, when he sounded as right as rain. Ulric and Margaret had returned to Châteauneuf in the spring, when she was the one to be afflicted by problems. The day they arrived – Dirk's fifty-first birthday – she fell and severely fractured her shoulder. While she recuperated, in full 'tragedy queen' mode, Ulric spent much of the time trying, as ever, to capture with his paints the light as Bonnard had done. He and his elder son were closer than they had ever been. Now, at eighty, he had suddenly gone. Trapped in Paris by his obligations to the film, Dirk had a business lunch with a potential new agent at Brasserie Lipp, where he 'drank a lot and was amusing and "on"' – then walked with Tony back to the hotel through the silent Sunday streets; 'the tears came finally, in the loo where it was sort of private . . . and I sat on the bidet and blubbed like a five year old instead of a fiftyone year old'.[41]

The funeral was delayed until the following Saturday, so that Dirk could be there – which he was, just. On the Friday evening he was shooting until 8.30, then began a fiendish journey by train, boat and car to Fletching. Tony stayed behind at Cherry Tree Cottage with Margaret and Gareth Van den Bogaerde's wife, Lucilla, while, as Dirk put it, 'we sang those dotty hyms and watched them bung [Pa] into a hole. Then back to the house for a vast reception for all the super people who had come to be there.'[42] At 9 o'clock the next morning Dirk was on set at the Travellers' Club in the Champs-Elysées. The film finished a few days later, and Dirk returned to Sussex to deal with, and burn, his father's papers, while Elizabeth disposed of the clothes and 'personal gear, his shaving brush and tooth brush . . . silly things. Mother sat in black; mute, brave, and sipping white wine while her family ransacked her house. Ghastly. But inevitable.'[43] He 'loved his father,' noted Tony, 'as did I'. The black dog curled beneath Dirk's heart had stirred itself again.

The Serpent, in which Dirk's co-stars were Henry Fonda and Yul Brynner, had required Dirk 'to do very little except stand about in a black raincoat looking enigmatic'. His was, in the main, 'apart from the raincoat, what I call a "cardigan and knitted-tie" part'.[44] A very different wardrobe would be needed for his next film, which was to follow hard behind: a peaked cap, a riding-whip, jackboots and an SS armband.

Liliana Cavani arrived at Clermont with the Rome-based producer Robert Gordon Edwards to discuss *The Night Porter* and found Tony with his right hand swathed in bandages after he had nearly lopped off two fingers while mowing the meadow. Dirk had not only to do Diary duty, but also to switch into Barrett mode for a few weeks. It was a state of affairs unusual enough for him to record that after attempting to discuss the contract and the film 'in three broken languages', and having dined well, 'I tidy up the table & stack the stuff in the washing machine'. There was nothing so mundane about the content of the script they were considering. Dirk first read Cavani's screenplay during the making of *Death in Venice*, on which Edwards was the associate executive producer. It was hard going, heavily politicised and, for Dirk, unfilmable in that state. It meant him playing yet 'another degenerate'.[45] However, at its core, 'buried like a nut in chocolate', was – he insisted – a love story set in the kind of hell which he had glimpsed in the area around Hanover when he was twenty-four; a love story based on a vignette from Cavani's own experience, when, while she was making a television documentary about the concentration camps, a smartly dressed woman came to place roses on the site of the hut where she had once been held and where she had begun an affair with one of her Nazi captors. Cavani, said Dirk, wondered what would have happened if the SS man had not been executed by the Americans, but had gone to ground and, years later, they met again unexpectedly – perhaps in a hotel where she was a guest and he the night porter, with his politics unchanged and his predilection for domination and humiliation as intense as ever. In Cavani's own, slightly more prosaic account, she had interviewed for her documentary two Italian women – both partisans, neither Jewish – who had survived the camps. One of them had been in Dachau between the ages of eighteen and twenty-one, and, since the war, had returned there every year *on her holidays*, for reasons she would not – perhaps could not – explain. The other, a *bourgeoise* from Milan, had found on being freed from Auschwitz that she could not go back to her husband and children because she was treated like a wretch, and made to feel she was an embarrassment, a reminder of something too disturbing. She had experienced cruelty, horror, ordeals – but what she could not forgive was being made by the Nazis to perceive the depths of human nature. She told Cavani: 'Don't think that all victims are innocent.' So the director, troubled by what she had heard, set out to tell a story that took human nature 'to the limits of credibility', through a sado-masochistic relationship made possible by the extreme situation in which the principals find themselves.[46] In the same interview, Cavani did not use the word 'love'. She stated openly that because of the way human nature worked, for her, the basic text in life was de Sade; it should be taught in schools. However, in Dirk's much publicised view they were to tell a 'love story' – 'rather like a tiny flower thrusting through the brutality and degradation of a battlefield'.[47] At a different level, the role of Max the porter was one that afforded an extraordinary opportunity to exorcise – a cynic might say exercise – demons, at very high risk.

It took about three months for the script to be fashioned into an acceptable state: at one point not only Dirk, but Tony too, was involved in its doctoring. And once more uncertainty hung over the entire project until the last moment, with repeated hiccups over money. At least the casting was settled at a fairly early stage. Cavani had wanted Dirk from the start because of what she called his *façon pâle* – a quality that enabled him so effectively to convey hidden depths of

extreme anxiety. Dirk, in his turn, had never worked with a woman director –
apart from his walk-on for Wendy Toye in *We Joined the Navy* – but was
encouraged to do so with the thirty-five-year-old Cavani because he had seen on
television a film she had made about Galileo, starring Cyril Cusack. Although
made in Italian, dubbed into French and therefore aurally incomprehensible for
most of the time, it was visually brilliant. For Lucia, Max's 'victim', Cavani
thought longer and harder. At first she had imagined Mia Farrow in the role;
then Romy Schneider – who turned it down – and Dominique Sanda. Eventually,
with both Dirk and the producer already convinced by their experience on *The
Damned*, Cavani came to see that Charlotte Rampling would be perfect casting:
she had the same *inquiétude* that so struck the Italian about Dirk. With the
principals agreed, if not actually signed, the production teetered for weeks on
the edge of collapse, and Dirk was reduced once again to gloom: 'I have suddenly
found that I simply LOATH the acting bit [...] its such balls ... and I want
out. I think after the Cavani that'll be it as far as I am concerned.'[48] Tony was
more positive: 'We feel in a state of semi-retirement up on our hill & are far
from discontented with our lot.' But finally, the film came together and in a
cold, wet and miserable Rome, Dirk began his porter's duties. On the fourth day
he was on location at a former tuberculosis sanatorium, strutting about in full
SS uniform and inspecting fifty stark naked extras of all ages, with, in their
midst, the brutally cropped Charlotte Rampling. For her in the coming weeks,
there would be no shortage of indignity – moments when perhaps it might have
been better if Romy Schneider *had* accepted the role. Yet the understanding she
had formed with Dirk on *The Damned*, the feeling of 'a kind of brotherhood in
terms of where his demons lay', enabled her to face the ordeal – for that is what
it was – with some confidence. It was, she recalls 'the ultimate catharsis; you
couldn't do more on that theme'.[49]

When she was given the script, Dirk told her she *had* to be aware that it was
not an analysis of why the Nazis did what they did and how they atone for it.
'It's not about Nazi guilt,' he said. 'We must never forget that, because otherwise
Liliana is going to pull the film into another, colder, more analytical area. It has
to have the essence of a real love story, not just a sado-masochistic essay.' Taking
advantage of Cavani's improvisational shooting method, they would play scenes
her way, then theirs; proving a point while never quite sending her up, or
belittling her. Dirk would push her harder and harder to 'bring out the essence
of the love story', and, says Charlotte Rampling, 'in the end ours were so much
more searingly real than her rather stagy versions'. And, therefore, all the more
shocking, because 'it showed how unbelievably powerful the forbidden fantasy
inside us is. When we have power, it is *very* exciting. And that is a subject which
is as ugly as it is fascinating.' They filmed a scene which exemplified, probably
better than any of those which became the subject of controversy, the tightrope
they walked in portraying domination as an aphrodisiac: 'It was a flashback,
from the concentration camp period. I was dressed up as a little girl and taken

by Max, in full uniform, to a restaurant, where he feeds me. There was a perverted joy in it.' In the end, even Cavani decided it was too much, and cut the sequence, but Charlotte Rampling remembers it as having an exceptionally potent charge and illustrating just what dangerous territory they were visiting.

For her the entire shoot was

> unbelievably traumatic, and Dirk and I steered each other through a precarious journey. Two things stopped me from completely cracking up. I had my two-month-old son with me, so his nanny would try to keep him awake until I came back from the set. That way, I *had* to switch off at the end of the day. Also, my own youth helped. When you are young the impact of reality has not actually sat on you yet. I felt I could stand it better because I hadn't been through anything like that: I could only *imagine*. For Dirk it was harder: he had been in the war. I remember we did all the flashbacks, the concentration camp scenes, first. On the second day I had to do my song in front of the Nazis [at the end of which her character, like Salome, is presented with a decapitated head]. After shooting that day, Dirk was completely wrecked.

They never talked about what he had done or seen in the Army; she just knew that parts of his experience at that time had added to his torment. She saw parallels with her soldier father, a medal-winner in the Berlin Olympic Games in front of Hitler, and 'rather a Dirk sort of man'; but Dirk was more fortunate in having an outlet, however temporary, for his demons: 'Dirk was able to release himself through his work and his creativity.' Never more so than on the Cavani film, during which, Charlotte Rampling noticed, he was drinking quite heavily. It left her feeling that had he not been able to find that release through his work, either for the screen or in his writing, Dirk might have been 'very scary' indeed.

According to Charlotte Rampling the account in *An Orderly Man* of the making – and the hazard-strewn selling – of *The Night Porter* is accurate; in particular, the incidents while they were on location in Vienna which showed how terrifyingly little was needed to awake the barely dormant beast of Nazism.[50] A more contemporaneous, but brisk, summary of Dirk's experience on the film came in a letter to Ann Skinner where he said that once Charlotte Rampling had been cast,

> all was magic. However there DID come a point, after my fifth simulated orgasm … lying on my back, flies open, being straddled by Charlotte like Harvey Smith and wallowing about like a stranded whale … with a vast pizza stuffed crew watching with bored eyes … there was a point when I though 'What the hell am I doing here like this, at fifty three, Flies open and Bald spot gleaming.' In 17 years Rank had *never* prepared me for THIS kind of a lark. However I did it. And I got on with it like a good boy. And I never care if I

work in the Movies again . . . after sixty of the buggers I really do need tempting terrifically.[51]

When Dirk saw a cut of *The Night Porter* he found it 'rather extraordinary. Marvellous. Erotic . . . (They are shit scared to show it in America and refuse to show it in Italy [. . .]) You'll probably never see it at the Essoldo or the Odeon . . . five simulated orgasms . . . and all very well done indeed . . . with beloved, brilliant, scorching Charlotte Rampling [. . .] we have out tangoed "Tango" . . . which is about time I think.'[52] As for his 'alive', 'pretty', 'tough' young director, he had, he said, offered to marry her on the spot, but she had replied: 'No. We get married AFTER we do "Faust".' With Dirk playing all *three* parts.

Mentions of a partial abandonment of his career were becoming consistent enough to have a hint of truth about them. 'I am too old, too rich and far, far too distinguished to be trailing about the Sound Stages any longer,' he wrote in reply to the latest fly cast by Edward Thompson:

> So I have decided to semi-retire now . . . and go and do a little 'bit' (for excellent money) when I need something new for the house . . . a kitchen, a tree, rewiring the electricity, planting a hedge of Oleanders . . . that sort of thing, otherwise the whole sheebang has quite lost it's charm . . . and after 'Death' I really felt that I had done all I wanted to for the Cinema . . . better stop before one ends up flopping about in middle-aged Dad parts on Telly. Or advertising Wincarnis or something frightful.[53]

So it was no to being photographed by Patrick Lichfield for Winston cigarettes, which would have brought in £12,000 and easily covered the cost of a badly needed new kitchen. Dirk and Tony were now fending more for themselves, having found that they were not really getting their money's worth out of the most recent couple, Henri and Marie Danjoux. Daily help was at hand thanks to Madame Martinez – christened 'Lady' – and shirts were laundered to perfection by Bruna, the wife of their skilful stonemason Marc Isoardi, who lived a mile or two away; once a fortnight Tony would drive down to exchange the laundry.

Their increasing independence, if not exactly self-sufficiency, at Clermont was both desirable and to some extent necessary; Dirk was teasing when he described himself to Edward Thompson as 'too rich'. Compared with the rewards being reaped by his contemporaries in Hollywood, or even just working regularly in Britain, Dirk's earnings were meagre, almost derisory. Certainly he and Tony had more than enough to manage comfortably, but their concern was to put enough aside not only for a rainy day but also for the anticyclone of old age. Already Tony had had a scare, which turned out to be a benign cyst; and Dirk, with his history of liverishness and other symptoms brought on by nervous tension, was vulnerable at any time. So too, therefore, was their earned income. Sound financial advice had become a high priority. Fortunately they had been put in touch with a highly astute wealth-management expert in Geneva, Jean-Pierre Aubert, and his colleague Anton (Tony) Troxler, a lawyer who Dirk said looked like 'Jesus Christ Superstar'. In Britain, both Bendrose and Bowood were wound up, and their modest assets transferred to Motley Films. The Connaught arrangement in Nassau was ended, too – a wise move, as the Inland Revenue had begun to launch attacks on offshore partnerships. It all took time – some years, in fact – and, of course, money, both in fees to advisers and to satisfy the Revenue; but the result was a streamlined and more efficient financial set-up, with a Swiss-based company, charmingly named Labofilms, of which Dirk was the sole employee, and which received any monies earned outside France, where he was officially resident. 'He certainly regards here as Home,' wrote Tony to Laurence Harbottle.[54] And he always would.

On 25 October 1974 Dirk was the sole guest on London Weekend Television's *The Russell Harty Show*, as part of a campaign to beat the drum for *The Night Porter*, which had finally moved into a single West End cinema. Since being completed a year and a half earlier it had had a stormy passage. As far back as January, when the prospects of finding a British distributor were almost nil, Dirk had suggested a private screening for a few selected critics – Margaret Hinxman, Dilys Powell, Felix Barker of the *Evening News* and Alexander Walker – expecting that they would go into print only if they felt positively about what they had seen. The initiative backfired when the *Evening Standard* immediately published Walker's prominent and damning verdict: 'Degradation without illumination doesn't invite interest after the curiosity has been satisfied,' he wrote. For him, the other story of 'chamber-sadism', *Last Tango in Paris*, had brought a dawning understanding of why people play dangerous games of pain and humiliation; not so *The Night Porter*, which 'just breeds disgust'.[55] The Powell, Hinxman and Barker reviews were unanimous in their praise, and anxious to reassure. Margaret Hinxman – whose book about Dirk's films was shortly to be published – declared the picture 'shocking because the subject is shocking', and one of the most powerful she had seen in years. Practically every other film she reviewed was 'more explicit in its viciousness and perversity than this', she wrote; and it contained 'the best performance Dirk Bogarde has ever given and one from Charlotte Rampling that establishes her as a great, glowing star in the Garbo category'.[56] Dilys Powell said she refused to believe 'that today's cinema audiences, so quick in response, are inferior in comprehension to the audience for written fiction'. She hoped she would not have to waste time by travelling to Paris for a second viewing.[57] Sure enough, the French were queuing round several blocks to see it. In Italy there was a summary ban, thereby attracting immeasurable free publicity for the moment when the authorities relented. In America, the knives were out even before a critic had clapped eyes on it. In a letter to Dilys Powell explaining why he had set up the sneak preview, Dirk said the word in Hollywood was that *The Night Porter* was 'incomprehensible ... lewd ... badly acted and

pornographic on a par with "Deep Throat" and "The Devil And Miss Jones"'.
This was not the intention. 'Somehow, deep in my heart, I *cannot* believe that
Cavani and Charlotte and I were trying to make a porno-Movie [...] We
never even saw "Tango" for that reason [...]. However. Never Explain. Never
Complain.'[58] In due course, the producer Joe Levine took the film for distribution
in the United States and launched it with a party in New York that makes
Charlotte Rampling shudder to this day: 'It was the kinkiest thing you've ever
seen, and I caught the first plane home.' Pauline Kael condemned Cavani's film
as 'a porno gothic' which might as well have been called 'Tales from the Nazi
Crypt', and said of Dirk: 'After such pictures as *Victim, The Servant, Darling,
Modesty Blaise, Accident, The Damned, Justine,* and *Death in Venice,* he isn't just
overqualified for Max – he's also overexposed. We know his neurasthenic tricks –
the semaphore eyebrow, the twitching mouth, the sneaky vindictive gleam, the
pinch of suffering. His warmed-over performance here has all the surprise of the
César Franck Symphony in D Minor.'[59] A correspondent to *The New York Times*
echoed a widespread view of the film: 'By treating victims of concentration camps
as freaks in a sexual parade, she has taken away their humanity. And this is the
worst kind of pornography.'[60] In similar vein was the condemnation from an
untraced source, that the film was 'bumming a free ride on the gas chambers' –
a comment, incidentally, that Peter Hall remembered the following year when
he saw the Trevor Griffiths play *Comedians,* in which the central character, 'an
old wise comedian who knows about truth and falsehood', has become the
cautious, sage-like figure he is because he visited Buchenwald after the war.[61]

Now it was London's turn to see for itself, and Dirk gave Russell Harty the
principal reason why he felt people should watch this story of 'burning, passionate
love'. It was, he contended, 'a kind of a warning film', and backed this up by
speaking of his wartime experiences. Why was the United States so hostile
towards the film? The reaction there was entirely predictable, he said, because
'America is full of guilt'. He cited the recent Watergate scandal, the massacre at
My Lai and the throwing of Vietcong prisoners out of helicopters as three good
reasons for the nation's shame, and added: 'A country doesn't want to be reminded
of its guilt.'

Given all that has been mentioned above, it is easy to see that the motives
behind the making of *The Night Porter* were imbued with a certain amount of
confusion. Nevertheless, Dirk gave a good account of himself on the programme.
He hoped his job as an actor was that of an educator as much as that of an
entertainer. The *Doctor* films had in a small way helped to change the image of
the general hospital – especially in making them seem less frightening to children.
Victim had helped to modify, if not remove, another fear. He hoped he could,
every now and then, address big themes. 'I want to be a teacher,' he said. Russell
Harty had been a schoolteacher, and he and Dirk seemed to hit it off. Dirk won
a loud and slightly shocked laugh from the studio audience by announcing to
his host at the outset: 'They say you're a bit shitty.' In fact, the first five minutes

of the show were more of a flirtation than an interview, but once he had settled down, Dirk spent forty minutes exhibiting his flair as a storyteller, with an eye and an ear for detail. It made a favourable impression in an entirely unexpected quarter.

Nineteen

'You felt you were in the same room with him'

Norah Smallwood was not a great watcher of the television; indeed she did not even own one, preferring to be enlightened and entertained by the 'steam radio'. Nevertheless she found herself in front of a set on that Friday night when Dirk was doing his 'turn' for Russell Harty. Legend has it that on the Monday she went into her office and at the first meeting with senior staff asked: 'Did anyone see that chap Dick Buggered, or whatever he's called, the other night?' The story is almost certainly apocryphal, because Norah Smallwood was far too culturally aware not to know of Dirk. What is beyond doubt, however, is that as her colleagues mumbled their regrets at having missed something of significance, she then said: 'Well, if he writes as well as he talks, he might have a book in him.' She telephoned Harty's assistant, Patricia Heald, to ask how best to make contact with Dirk, and on 1 December one of her editors and co-directors, John Charlton, wrote to ask whether he had ever considered writing about his life. If so, on the strength of what they had heard the other evening, their firm would be delighted to publish him. 'This is not something that we are saying lightly,' he added; 'it is based on the belief that you have an unusually interesting story to tell, and that you would write it in a way that a great many people would value and enjoy.'[1]

The firm was Chatto & Windus, whose list included Aldous Huxley, Mervyn Peake, Compton Mackenzie, V. S. Pritchett, Laurens van der Post, Laurie Lee, James Lees-Milne and Iris Murdoch. And Norah Smallwood was its driving force. A slim, stylish woman in her mid-sixties, with a fondness for black felt hats, a short fuse to her temper and a tongue as sharp as a scalpel, she had a fearsome reputation in the world of publishing, where she was known as 'a tough egg'. To her authors, she had the heart of a lion and would defend their interests to the last; Iris Murdoch said 'she was a combination of comrade, leader, mother, business partner and muse', and 'an unenvious cherisher of the talents of others'.[2] She had joined Chatto in her late teens as a secretary, or, as her father put it, 'a type-writer'. When war came and her boss, Ian Parsons, went into the RAF, she took on responsibility for design and production, and her role in helping to keep the imprint alive during the difficult days of bombing, shortage of manpower and lack of paper was acknowledged in 1945 when she was made a partner in the firm. Both her husband and a greatly loved elder brother had been killed in the war, and she never married again. One of Chatto's authors and editors, John Goldsmith, wrote: 'If there was, as one sometimes sensed, an eye of loneliness in the magnificent storm of Norah's professional and social life, it was because of that double loss; certainly, thereafter, she threw herself completely into her career.'[3] By the time she asked John Charlton to make his unconditional approach to Dirk she was regarded as the most formidable woman publisher of her generation.

Dirk knew none of this when the letter eventually emerged from a postal backlog caused by a strike and arrived at Clermont. He wrote back to 'Mr Charlton' saying that the week of promotion which had included the Russell Harty programme had left him feeling 'as overexposed as a blank negative' and that some of the stories he had told were included in a series of essays he had been writing on 'the odder highlights during my career':

> ... there are VAST problems about libel, of course, it is quite useless to try and fake this stuff ... it does'nt work. So I get a bit hung up from time to time with worry! Ken Tynan said 'write it and let the Publishers worry ...' well ... I dont know. Anyway I am going on with it slowly, and without much incentive. I *do* feel that books by Film Stars are beastly boring ... and the few recent ones which have thudded onto the market prove my point. I am not a David Niven* ... so that is out ... and I truthfully feel that what I have to say has all been said before and usually better. However if you want to discuss it I'd be delighted but I dont think anything I have to say is really much cop.[4]

Charlton replied immediately, saying how encouraged Chatto were that Dirk was 'doing very much what we had hoped – that is to say writing from within yourself about the things that have mattered to you'. He offered to look at some of the existing material, and to consider the likely 'central issue' of libel: 'We would also have a much better notion of the terms that we could offer you if you would like us to draw up a contract. These won't, I should say at the outset, be equivalent to a film contract, but then I don't imagine this is what you are expecting. David Niven, for example, started off with a £500 advance, I am told.'[5]

Dirk was now being actively courted by two suitors, neither of whom knew of the other's involvement. It was to stay that way for some time, but a letter to Penelope Mortimer, which must have crossed with John Charlton's second to him, makes clear Dirk's confusion. 'Are Chatto and Windus any good?' he asked. 'I don't know. Heinemans I sort of think are better ...'. Both want books, he

---

* David Niven's autobiography, *The Moon's a Balloon* (Hamish Hamilton, 1971), had been a huge bestseller.

explained. 'So easy to say. Harder to manage. Chatto is sounding warm and more interesting. Not the Usual-Film?-Star-Bio. Better than that. Apparently I was good on the telly. Rude too and vastly irreverent and libellous almost, I fear, and they want THAT. But I have a feeling that they are a bit tatty . . .'. By the end of the letter he was saying that because he had had no 'practice' for nearly two months, 'I'd better get on with a chapter of Chatto's and get eased up.'[6] It sounded as if the stop-start relationship with Edward Thompson was cooling, although one would never guess from their correspondence that it had reached the chilly state depicted in *An Orderly Man*, where the Heinemann director is multiplied into a series of 'educational Toms and Dicks and Harrys', who had sent as incentive 'slim books written by distinguished players' which had 'as much life as a smoked haddock and as much inspiration going for them as the Albert Memorial', and which 'crushed for ever any remote curiosity I might have had about acting as a craft. Or writing about it.'[7]

For a few months Dirk successfully avoided having to take any difficult decision about his writing, because he had agreed to return again to Vienna for a reunion with Ava 'Snowdrop' Gardner on 'Kickback' – later *Permission to Kill* – a 'nice simple CIA-Chase-Round-The-Airport sort of movie' which would yield $125,000 and 'take care of a new terrace at the back of the house . . . more covers for the chairs and settees' and – alas – 'my mothers wine bill at the Hotel'.[8] Margaret was now in a decidedly up-market nursing home, having nearly broken her neck in a fall at Cherry Tree Cottage, and, as Dirk would record in *An Orderly Man*, was refusing to read, write, knit or undertake the necessary physiotherapy: 'I honestly think that she has given up for good. She's started to die.'[9] Privately, he confessed that he had

> absolutely no guilt whatsoever; no reason to have. I have been an excellent child . . . thats it. I have FAR more guilt about the big toad I hacked to pieces with the grass cutter last summer. He simply would'nt die . . . and stared at me with those golden pheasant eyes . . . I had to finish him off with a spade; and then was sick behind the log-shed door. Guilt because I could have cleared the land before . . . oh shit. There is guilt and guilt. I have none about Humans. At all.[10]

He did, however, have a twinge of conscience that Elizabeth, now living at Cherry Tree Cottage with her husband, must carry most of the family's burden in visiting and trying to boost the spirits of their mother, who, more resentful than ever, was still able to call on reserves of feistiness – a lethal combination for those closest to her. Elizabeth was, Dirk acknowledged, 'her only contact with any form of life at all'. Brother and sister had never been distant: witness the wartime letters and the journeys to the Continent during the Rank era when, to her embarrassment today, she would drop everything at minimum notice and leave George holding the fort at home, while she joined Dirk and Tony to their mutual enjoyment and, it must be said, benefit – for appearances' sake. Now, with geography keeping them eight hundred-odd miles apart and with responsibility for their mother unequally shared, they spoke constantly and wrote copiously. For Dirk the letters to his sister were part of an extraordinary outpouring from his studio in the former olive store, which he reached by a separate, outdoor staircase at one end of the house. Gossipy, newsy essays, often about very little, rattled off his Adler typewriter until its ribbon was so worn by the italicised keys that pages would be almost illegible. He needed to write, but he also needed the identifiable audience, which is perhaps why he was finding it hard to persist with the book. Dorothy Gordon was no longer there as his chief correspondent, but Elizabeth, Penelope Mortimer, Ann Skinner, Glur Dyson Taylor, Olga Horstig-Primuz, Irene Howard, Maude – all regularly received letters of uncommon length and density; and usually they felt better for doing so.

It was from one of these epistles that Elizabeth became the first member of the family to know that Dirk had a book under way. The news came at the end of a summer when Dirk and Tony agreed that after five years their home had finally 'come together' as they had wished. There was a moment earlier, one August morning after a Mistral had cleared rain clouds from the sky, when Dirk recorded in the Diary 'a light to break ones heart – of *such* beauty. This is why we came to Clermont.' At that point there was still much to do; there always would be. But at least they had their house in order. They had their new kitchen. They had their two terraces, ablaze with plants and flowers. They had their *bassin*, with its limited occupancy. And during the summer months they had their procession of guests, most of them as anxious as their hosts that their welcome should not be outstayed. Tony was developing into no mean chef; Dirk, an incomparable *plongeur*, whistling as he stood at the sink. There is scant evidence of him doing anything creative in the kitchen, apart from making twelve pounds of piccalilli in 1974 and, the following year, some pickled cabbage. He would sum up his lifestyle dismissively by saying he worked 'bloody hard, grubbing round olive trees, feeding dogs [Labo had been joined by a boxer, Daisy] and cleaning out the lavs'. He might have added: running up curtains, making hutches out of packing-cases for abandoned rabbits, mowing the terraces and planting, planting, planting...

What he and Tony had achieved in the relatively short time that they had been on their hill was a source of genuine pride. *House and Garden* magazine devoted six pages to Clermont – with an unsigned text written largely by Tony, but with no trace of his presence – showing what an exquisite home Dirk had made for himself; its *pièce de résistance* was necessarily the three-level drawing-room, but there was a harmonious feel throughout.[11] Even the dramatic, stark black-and-white chequerboard flooring which Dirk preferred for his bedroom, and which was repeated in the dining-room, seemed somehow in keeping. The countless visits to second-hand shops inside a radius of twenty miles or more had resulted in a hotch-potch of carefully chosen furnishings which

complemented the pieces that had come out from England. At last everything
was in its place: the Staffordshire china tucked into niches; recently acquired
pictures by Ben Nicholson and Egon Schiele, which had been consigned to a bank
vault, now hanging with those by Christopher Wood and Leonard Rosoman. As
in all Dirk's houses, there was only one place at Clermont where any clue could
be found of its owner's profession: a wall of his office was hidden by a montage
of photographs from his career; another was decorated with postcards – 'starlings' – from his friends. It was, as all who went there agree, a house of immaculate
taste which never overpowered and always exuded a warmth, even a modesty.

A few journalists visited Clermont during this period, usually after 'vetting'
by Theo Cowan. Alasdair Riley of the *Evening Standard* hit the nail on the head
when, moonlighting for a magazine under the pseudonym Mark Carter, he wrote
of Dirk:

> Today, at fifty-three, he is still very much the gentleman, and lives in the
> country, but the idea of the country gentleman that this conjures up is decep-
> tive. Elegant as ever, well-spoken in a clipped English voice, he is nonetheless
> a new man. A toiler of the soil, a drawer of water and hewer of wood, a painter,
> carpenter, bricklayer, farmer and gardener rolled into one. He seems happier,
> too. More content and peaceful. He plays his new role eagerly and with
> conviction, as if it is the one he wanted all along.[12]

Ever since childhood on the Sussex Downs, in fact.

After shooting *Permission to Kill* – in which Tony had a line or two as an
MI5 chief – Dirk had kept his counsel from the publishers. 'The Canary
Cage'/'Eggshell Summer' had been in a drawer; the Dorothy Gordon letters
tucked away; but a book was still an attractive prospect: at one stage he and Tony
considered a joint effort based on the Diary and recollections of their time away
from England. The turning-point had come when, after months of restraint and
polite silence, John Charlton wrote to say that he and his family would be
spending a late-summer holiday near Grasse, and might it perhaps be worth
coming to see Dirk to talk about the whole idea? Dirk replied that he was running
a cross between the YMCA, the NAAFI and a cheap doss-house, but that
Charlton would be more than welcome to call. He did:

> John Charlton didn't look remotely like a director of an extremely august
> publishing house. A tall, lean, angular man with a strong nose and an absurdly
> boyish cockscomb of hair which sprang in a high curve from the back of his
> neat head, he seemed, in his flannels and plain tweed jacket, far more suited
> to a sports field blowing a whistle, perhaps, on the sideline, or shouting LBW!
> triumphantly to some unfortunate youth in cricket pads and gloves.
>   An illusion which he quickly dispelled.[13]

On a thundery evening they talked about a 'formula' which Dirk had contrived the previous day, and Charlton went away with a 'sample chapter'. And with five words making a peculiar music in his head: *A Postillion Struck by Lightning*. There are several versions of how Dirk happened on this quaint but arresting title. In some form it had appeared in an ancient *Baedeker* English–French phrase-book, but no one can be quite sure whether he discovered it at Allan Glen's or at Chelsea School of Art (as Bill Lockie and Jean Thomson respectively believe); or whether his sister-in-law Lucilla Van den Bogaerde mentioned it to him on a postcard from a sodden camping holiday with her children in northern France (as he remembered it in *An Orderly Man*). Then again, he told Elizabeth that the book belonged to Ulric, and contained other indispensable phrases such as 'This muslin is too thin have you some thicker'. The least likely story is the one which has Lally on a beach at Wimereux, reading out extracts of a book owned by the Hatfields as its pages flapped in the wind: ' "Travelling! 'The Postillion Has Been Struck By Lightning' – well!" she cried laughing "That wouldn't get us far today, would it?" '[14] Least likely, because although that sounds like the authentic Lally, she never went with the family to France. Again, it is of small consequence; what is important is that John Charlton liked the title, as he told Dirk, 'from the moment you came out with it'. While the publisher finished his holiday, Dirk retired to the olive store, enthused. 'Praise, when it comes, often embarrasses me, and I don't handle compliments as well as I should [. . .] But encouragement is something absolutely different. Encourage me and I will part the seas; if you want me to.'[15] A few days later, he despatched four more chapters and part of a piece about Hollywood, saying that six further 'stories' were either complete or in the pipeline. 'You remember I told you I was writing a "book" about us and Lally at Alfriston?' he told Elizabeth in an end-of-summer letter. 'Well . . . I have been bashing away at it for years now and am well into chapter 7!' Chatto & Windus, he added, 'are dotty about what I have done so far and are considering publishing it! What about that?'

To describe Chatto as being 'dotty' about what they had seen so far was a trifle premature. An internal memo from Charlton to Norah Smallwood shows how the former was concerned that the stories from childhood alone might not make a publishable book, and that Dirk needed to bring in some from his adult life, 'if only to present a more varied picture of himself'. Most people, he added, would want to read about the professional life. So Charlton envisaged a 'selective autobiography', a mixture of the childhood and adult experiences that had impressed themselves on Dirk's mind and which, Charlton was convinced, he was capable of telling. The childhood stories had 'a very attractive quality about them', and Dirk, who had 'a marvellous ear for dialogue', managed to convey atmosphere and mood without apparent difficulty.[16] Before he could write back to Dirk with his opinion, Charlton was felled by pneumonia. Nearly six weeks went by. Dirk wrote, saying he assumed *Postillion* was not acceptable, and asking for 'the stuff' to be returned, or left for him to collect at the Connaught, where he would be staying again soon. In fact, an apologetic Charlton had already dictated a letter, explaining how others at the firm had read his chapters and were unanimous in liking them very much. The question was, how to proceed. Everyone felt that the book should not be limited to childhood scenes, but should go on to reflect Dirk's adult and professional life. Back came the reply:

> Thanks for your observations on 'Postillion' . . . I have been working away at it for some time now and have reached the end of the First Part . . . the Second part will go up to my start on the Stage and the start of the War. After that I really AM not interested in writing. I am not a David Niven . . . alas . . . and I think I'll just stay with this 'story' rather than go into the Career bit. All far, far too boring for me, even if not for 'Anxious Reader'. But thanks all the same.[17]

And yet . . . and yet. Not only did he return to the Adler with renewed vigour; he also made contact with Dennis van Thal's brother Herbert, for two reasons: to equip himself with a literary agent and to find someone to convert his chaotic typescripts into a form which might be presentable to a distinguished publishing house such as Chatto & Windus. Bertie van Thal willingly took on the first role and arranged the second. At 4 o'clock one Friday, in the middle of a spate of interviews which Dirk was doing for *Permission to Kill*, a young mother from Hertfordshire who worked for a secretarial agency called Freelance Services presented herself at suite 152–4 in the Connaught. Her name was Sally Betts, and, having worked at the BBC, she was neither starstruck nor overawed; her first job at the agency had been for the playwright David Storey. On that November afternoon Dirk handed her his latest drafts of the first three chapters and said: 'Let me know if you think it's "icky".' She didn't find it 'icky'. On the contrary. Sally Betts was struck immediately by the essence of Dirk's style: 'You felt you were in the same room with him,' she says today.[18] They were to work together, and scarcely ever see each other, for twenty years.

Dirk wrote to Lally, to let her know what he was doing. He explained to Penelope Mortimer:

> When [. . .] I said that she was to be the star of the story and that I was going to change all the names except her 'pet' name, she wrote back from her Caravan at Steeple, and said that she was very happy to hear the news, that it was about time I got away from That Acting Business, and what else could I possibly call her except her real name? 'I'm who I am, dear, whatever you do to change me, I'm sure I'll come through all your fiction no matter what. So you MUST use my name because I should'nt like to be fictionalised at all after all those happy years: and after all *I* shall know.' So she's herself.[19]

'I have changed ALL the names except Lally,' he told Elizabeth; '. . . I cant find a better name for her ... she simply IS Lally, and she emerges as the Star. Quite rightly, too ... for she was ...'. Both Lally and Elizabeth provided notes to help prod Dirk's memory, the former with a delightful stream of anecdotes about pets being banned upstairs after Ulric and Margaret found meal-worms in their bed; about mice and the tortoise being smuggled on board the OM; about Dirk dressing up as an old lady for a 'Christmas entertainment'; about putting on another show for an unwell Granny Niven; and about Lu's screams from the garden shed causing a neighbour to believe a murder was taking place rather than one of Dirk's plays ... 'there were lots of screams but by then I was used to it,' Lally added, deadpan.

By 5 January 1976, the first half of the book, 'Summer', was complete. A month later, Chatto made an offer of £1,500, because they had 'a kind of blind faith' in Dirk's ability to 'pull off Part 2 as well'; their confidence was reinforced almost immediately when the first three finished chapters of 'Winter' arrived. The style had not changed in any fundamental way, but the atmosphere had, dramatically. Dirk was entering the 'Anthracite Years', and what John Charlton described as 'the change of gear' had worked perfectly for him and his fellow directors at William IV Street. However, at William Heinemann, the mood was far from bright. Dirk had heard from Edward Thompson and told him that the 'Telly' had 'caused a flutter, it would seem, in various Publishing Houses' who had been 'paying court ever since ... even sending earnest chaps over to "persuade" me and making pleasing offers of something called "Advances". I have not been beguiled.' He had taken on an agent 'to preserve my sanity'. There were, he concluded, 'more fishermen on the river bank than there are fish in my river alas!'[20] Alarm bells jangled, but Thompson kept calm. In his next letter, more or less passing the buck to Herbert van Thal, Dirk explained that he had written about 70,000 words and had another five chapters to go: 'It gets depressing at times ... and I find that I can only manage about three to four thou. words a day ... not finally good enough.'[21] Only three to four thousand! – most of Norah Smallwood's authors would have had a coronary at the mere thought of progress at that rate. Thompson made contact with van Thal, established the position and wrote again to Dirk, prompting a reply which began 'Oh dear! Of *course* you are miffed', but offered him little hope.[22] The publisher's last resort was to plead 'benign moral consideration', and he sent to van Thal a detailed diary of his thirteen-year pursuit. To no avail. The agent wrote curtly to Thompson, and John Charlton told Norah Smallwood that Dirk did not feel morally obligated to Heinemann. 'Hooray!' she declared, '& good for Bertie!' The contract was signed, 'Winter' was delivered, and Dirk wrote a final letter to Thompson, saying that 'the moral obligation (if it exists at all) relates more to the publisher who not only made a businesslike offer on very slender material, but was also able to suggest a shape and form which finally made it possible for me to finish the book'.[23] The first suitor took his jilting with good grace. Some years later he received another letter from Dirk which he found so upsetting that he tore it to pieces on the spot. It may have had something to do with 'educational Toms and Dicks and Harrys'.

Dirk had written the second half of the book not only at great speed but also with some trepidation. Yes, he felt that 'the "Yukkie" stuff' could not be continued any longer; but now he was concerned about libel. 'Many of the people in the book are still very much alive, and I am reluctant to cause distress or embarrassment to them,' he told John Charlton. 'I think that it might be wiser to have one member, my sister perhaps, read the MS to be sure that I have not caused offense. I am not so worried about Lally for example, but AM worried about the reaction of my Aunt Sadie who is very beady-eyed and flourishing.' He concluded that it was wise to be cautious: 'The Second Half, after all, is not Fiction!'[24] Charlton reassured him that he had little to worry about: the one possible cause of upset was 'the bathroom scene with your uncle', but neither he nor Norah Smallwood foresaw any potential libel problems. Attached, as was becoming the habit, was a list of comments and suggestions about the latest chapter to have arrived at the office; receiving the book piecemeal was on the one hand exciting, with an element of the serial about it; on the other, he said, it was frustrating because he and his colleagues were impatient to know what happened next. Their principal concern, stylistically, was over Dirk's use of Capital Letters and of '...' as punctuation: 'Capitals in "Sunday Best" all right [...] But why capitals for canary, camel, village, stalls, roundabout, dodgem cars, etc?' As for dots in punctuation, surely a comma, a semi-colon, a dash or a full stop would be preferable, especially in continuous prose, as opposed to dialogue? Would he allow them to use their discretion?[25] Even at this early, sensitive stage, here were tutors more rigorous even than Dorothy Gordon. Irritating, but constructive. Dirk could handle that: he respected perfectionists. And he was enjoying himself in this new, ultimately private endeavour. So much so, that the ink was hardly dry on the contract when he began talking of a second book which he hoped to start in the autumn. He already had a title: 'Enter Daemons'.

Chatto's encouragement and his own enthusiasm were not the only reasons for Dirk's sustained burst of creativity during the winter of 1975–6. Scripts continued to arrive, most of them offering 'queer' or, as Tony sometimes called them, 'ambivalent' roles. Liliana Cavani wanted him to play Nietzsche, and much as he liked the idea of working again with her, he declined firmly. Cavani was bitterly disappointed. 'Italy is rent from the toe to the Alps with [...] Screams,' Dirk reported to Penelope Mortimer; but, as he and Tony agreed, it was not the time for him to be making films about the sexual hang-ups of long-dead philosophers: 'All fumbles, and women peeing in pots and elderly men fucking youths in old railway station loos ... I don't know if that has anything to do with the great philosopher ... but it has nothing, whatever, to do with me.'[26] L'Histoire d'O came with the promise of an enormous cheque, but 'after "Porter" enough is enough ... and I wont wag my private parts on anyones screen. Why should

I?'[27] Joseph Losey, who wrote a generous foreword to the Hinxman–d'Arcy book about Dirk's films, admitted confidentially to Margaret Hinxman that the relationship had been strained in recent years; however, he had not entirely abandoned the idea of their working together again. He was to send a script by Thomas Wiseman, *The Romantic Englishwoman*, but for Dirk it was already condemned by its title: 'A bit twee . . . Englishwomen are singularly un-romantic, I always feel . . . in most cases. They have yellow teeth like dogs, bark like them, and generally behave like them.'[28] When he read it, he felt he had been there before: 'that Author with the Hampstead-Life . . . the elevator in a grand hotel . . . the wandering enigma of a Poet . . . shades here of better things . . . Darling . . . Pumpkineater . . . Accident . . . none if it is very new, really . . . and someone seems to have shares in Kentucky Chicken'.[29] Losey tried again, with Pinter's screenplay from *A la recherche du temps perdu* – the history of which is in itself a saga – but no part was specified, and Dirk was not interested. So much for the King. And the Emperor was no more.

While making *Ludwig* in 1972, Visconti had a stroke, and on their way back from the *Serpent* location in Munich Dirk and Tony went to see him at his house on Lake Como. They found him wrapped in a tartan rug, frail, almost shrivelled, 'the lion reduced to the size of a crippled whippet', but with his mind still alert and eager to show them the photographs of his new film, the latest and most lavish 'present' to Helmut Berger.[30] They doubted he would ever work again. Dirk as Puccini, which had been a vague idea at the time of *Death in Venice*; Dirk in Mann's *The Magic Mountain*; Dirk in Proust, on which Visconti, long before Losey, had set his heart – all would remain pipe-dreams. Astonishingly, however, Visconti *did* continue to work, in film, theatre and opera, while smoking at an industrial – some believed suicidal – level. On 17 March 1976, with his film *L'Innocente* in post-production, he died at his apartment in Rome. Dirk heard the news from Simone Signoret. 'We were very lucky to have been drawn into his orbit for those few years,' wrote Tony. And it was Tony who drafted a letter for Dirk, taking issue with the English newspaper that had said *Victim* prompted Visconti's choice of Dirk to play von Aschenbach; in fact it had been *Our Mother's House*, scorned by the critics but much admired by Visconti, who saw it three times and 'discerned a certain quality in my work which he found suitable to "The Damned" '.

At the first rough cut screening of the latter film, Visconti 'apologised in advance for having edited my performance to "one of the longest back-to-camera roles in cinema history" in order to alter the emphasis of the story; but promised me, however, a "present" in recompense'. The present was von Aschenbach. Dirk took the opportunity to add a few words in tribute to Visconti: 'Like most of us who had the rare good fortune to work for him, I found myself enriched not only as an actor, but more importantly, as a person.'[31] Tony noted in the Diary that Visconti would always be 'a major figure' in Dirk's life. The reverse did not apply – how could it when, apart from anything else, they knew each other for such a short time? – but the principal studies of Visconti's life and work accord Dirk little more than a passing mention.

The lion had roared his last, but a tall, pale, grey-haired man, whom Dirk first saw 'bundled up in a shabby raincoat' – not for the last time – was about to reward Dirk for his patience. With the failure of both 'The Adventures of Harry Dickson' and the de Sade film to reach the floor, it had begun to look as if Alain Resnais and Dirk would never collaborate. Now, however, there was a script entitled *Providence*, by the playwright David Mercer, about a dying novelist 'with a vicious tongue and a love of the bottle' who struggles during the night, fuelled with pain-killing drink and pills, to create a new work, using his family as his characters; and then confronts them the next morning, his seventy-eighth birthday.[32] It was a black comedy – allusive, weird and dense, with five succulent roles. When Dirk received his copy of the screenplay he was uncertain whether it was a work of genius or pretentious rubbish; he had a sneaking suspicion that it was the latter. However, two things he was sure about: first, that playing the barrister son was something he truly wanted to do; second, that John Gielgud, who was to be the patriarch, would, like Raffles, sneak off with the picture. Ironically, Resnais recalled that when they were trying to set up 'Harry Dickson', he had been too afraid to approach Gielgud. Dirk said: 'Don't hesitate. He would love to do more cinema.'[33]

The summer of 1976 was one of the hottest on record, but not all the time. Shooting took place under conditions of acute discomfort in Paris and not, as originally planned, in New Hampshire and Montreal, but in Belgium and Limoges. On their first free day in Brussels, Dirk and Tony made the pilgrimage to Izegem and trailed about the churches looking in vain for Van den Bogaerde tombs before going to Wolvenhof, where a farmer said that the Belgian equivalent of 'the Guv'nor' was at home; but Dirk's shyness overcame him and they drove away. After two weeks in Brussels, Antwerp and Louvain, the unit moved to France and to its principal location at Ambazac, nine miles from Limoges. Here, at the Château de Mont-Méry, which had been built in the late nineteenth century for the American porcelain maker Theodore Haviland, Dirk worked for most of May as part of what Resnais described as his chamber quintet, with Ellen Burstyn as the violinist, Elaine Stritch the double-bassist, David Warner as the viola player, Gielgud the cellist, and Dirk at the piano.[34] In a despatch to Penelope Mortimer Dirk reported that Resnais was 'brave and clever and patient. And as long as he knows what it's all about I don't give a damn. I feel wonderfully safe . . . and I think, only think mind you, that I have found a way of dealing with Mercers brilliant nonsense.' He summed up the script as 'a disillusioned Marxists hymn of misery' and predicted that the film 'will either be a load of pretentious crap or else Resnais masterpiece'. All in all, it was 'a fascinating experience which will make Mrs Kael Wail'.[35] To Elizabeth, he described it as 'a hell of a film. Much harder for me than "Death in Venice" was . . . and that WAS hard' – not 'horrid or anything, just deadly boring and "actorish" and I never did like actors much'. Quite by chance, he found an effective way for young members of the company, and even the occasional exponent of the Method, to be brought down to earth. One weekend, after lunching with Gielgud, Dirk and Tony drove into the countryside north-west of Limoges and happened upon a sign to Oradour-sur-Glane. They had not heard of the village, but in France it had earned its place in infamy.

On Saturday, 10 June 1944 the Waffen SS moved into Oradour and killed almost its entire population. In all, 642 men, women and children perished, some of them visitors from nearby villages and farms; some from Limoges, come to shop for food or to fish in the River Glane. The reason for the massacre had always been slightly imprecise, but the theory with the greatest currency was that the Nazis were acting in reprisal for an attack by the *Maquis* near Oradour-sur-Vayres, fifteen miles away, and had sent an execution squad to the wrong Oradour. The terrible events of that summer afternoon were marked in an extraordinary and profoundly moving way: once the bodies had been given a dignified burial, the heart of the village, including the church where some two hundred women and children were herded to their death, was to remain untouched. 'The smell of ashes and burnt brick still hangs in the air,' wrote Dirk to Elizabeth,

> . . . the bullet holes are still in the doors which were not burned . . . the skeletons of Singer Sewing machines, and clocks on the walls still . . . the cooking pots in the fireplaces, the scorched refrigerators and twisted iron bedsteads . . . everything that would not burn, still remains inside the shells of the houses . . . and the gardens have been carefully preserved [. . .] And totally deserted, silent except for the birds and the distant bleat of the sheep in the lush green fields which surround this hateful, sad, ruined little town.

At each of the three gates to the ruins was a notice: 'SOUVIENS TOI – REMEMBER.' Like many before them and since, Dirk and Tony were affected by what they saw. They returned there twice, the first time with some young members of the unit; the second, with Ellen Burstyn and her assistant, Blossom Plumb. Dirk felt that in an environment on-set where they were hearing 'of "progressiveness and the moral language of Man" and all that crap', it would 'do them good to see just what man can do to man . . . and only thirty years ago'.

For David Warner *Providence* was 'quite a neurotic ship. Not a desperately unhappy production or anything. It was just slightly mad.'[36] He remembers meeting Dirk for the first time since *The Fixer* in the bar of their hotel in Belgium. 'He looked quite reluctant to be there. I don't suppose he and Tony hung out in bars very much. He said, "We'll all have a round of drinks. But we mustn't make it a habit! It's very expensive." Tony reached into his pocket.' The strongest impression that Warner retains from the filming is of Dirk and Tony at the Château de Mont-Méry,

sitting on two chairs, slightly away from the rest of us, and Dirk with his back
to everybody; even if we were outside. That kind of isolation seemed to me to
be the image of how he was. There was an ice-thin veneer of unhappiness, which
some people could see and some people thought was arrogance, aloofness –
somebody who was not quite still and serene. Not that many of us are. I never
really felt comfortable going and chatting, having small-talk with him, but not
everyone can go out and socialise. I preferred Dirk to somebody who sits on
the set telling jokes all day.

Dirk and Resnais had an excellent relationship – 'a sort of marriage between
us ... no words are wasted, all sign language ... exhilarating, lifting';[37] the
occasional disagreement resulted usually from nuances in their respective languages. Dirk's waspishness could surface without too much provocation. Warner
recalls: 'Alain asked Dirk to do something, and Dirk replied, "Oh, don't ask me
to do that. I had enough of that with *Visconti*." He was only half-joking. There
was a deep, deep insecurity there.' A humility too. When Dirk took some
suggested rewrites to Resnais at his office in the château he approached as
nervously as a schoolboy submitting his work to the headmaster; he and Tony
were too nervous even to smoke. Yet Resnais was no humourless tyrant. Warner
recalls a montage sequence, during which he and Dirk examined a hedgehog.
'We turned to Resnais and said, "Alain, does this hedgehog *mean* something?"
"No," he said, "it is just to give the intellectuals of *Cahiers du Cinéma* something
to discuss." ' Gielgud found the whole exercise strange, fascinating and, on some
days at the château, bitterly cold as he and the others sat outside trying to look
as if they were basking in warmth while the crew huddled in windcheaters. He
wrote to Dirk later, saying 'what fun it was – even with the vileness of the
weather, hot and cold in all the wrong taps, but I shall always feel proud to have
worked with you so happily and to have got away with a character which I
frankly feared was too butch for me to make convincing. I know I could never
have done it on the stage, but somehow the location and strange speeches gave
me a sort of courage to let myself go in a new way – for me – in trying to act for
the screen.'[38] To another of his correspondents, Gielgud said that Elaine Stritch,
her husband John Bay 'and Dirk Bogarde and his friend Tony Forwood were
OK but not wildly exciting'.[39] For their part, Dirk and Tony revelled in Gielgud's
company. After another lunch with him near Limoges, they recorded a classic
Gielgudism: 'I've always been lucky in having very un-sycophantic friends who
said "Oh put a crown on her and shove her on!" '
    Elaine Stritch played Dirk's dead mother and – in Mercer's topsyturvy world –
his mistress. She marvelled at his acting: 'He was the most comfortable person
to work with. Demanding, but, with me, gentle and sweet. I don't play the love
interest in movies. I play women who are funny, amusing and dangerous. He
dug me right away.' They met over tea. 'He said, "I am a very disciplined worker.
I do not stay up late. I do not have affairs. I am a nine-to-fiver. I don't want any

knocking on my door at three a.m." I let him go on. Eventually I said, "Dirk, I'm married." He laughed. With relief!'[40] Elaine Stritch is another of the professionals who believes Dirk was too intelligent, too sensitive and, perhaps, too effete for Hollywood.

The quintet broke up finally in July. It had been a taxing three months, and not free of friction. But Dirk told the columnist Rex Reed it had been 'the most thrilling thing I've ever done in my life. I never thought I'd say that again after "Death in Venice". It's like having a great love affair when you think it will never happen again. But it does'.[41] Like Visconti and Losey, Resnais was preoccupied with solitude, memory, anxiety and time; and, like those other great directors, he did not tell actors what to do, only what *not* to do. The big difference was that he had asked his cast to play each scene three separate ways, virtually assuming three different identities. 'After weeks, I asked him which one of the three characters I was,' said Dirk. 'He asked me to give him one more week, but he still hasn't said who I am.' The 'Style demanded is immense,' Dirk told Penelope Mortimer, 'partly Wilde ... partly Congrieve ... partly Sheridan and *lots* of Resnais! [...] and the film, amazingly for Resnais, is very, very funny ... black funny and not always comfortable funny, but funny!'[42] There is a moment when Gielgud's Clive Langham asks his son to list the values by which he lives. Dirk's Claud replies: 'Honesty, scrupulousness, discrimination, protectiveness, tenderness, aversion to violence, and the conscious practice of terror.' We do not know whether the list, or any part of it, was the result of a Dirk rewrite. At least it did not include 'equenamity', a mangling in another sequence, which a fully anglophone director would surely have prevented Dirk, as a fastidious barrister, from uttering on the finished soundtrack. It was of no lasting consequence – unlike a few of the words he would be given to speak in his next film. David Warner remembers that as he and Dirk parted in France they compared notes about their future commitments. Warner was to co-star in *Cross of Iron* for Sam Peckinpah, director of *The Wild Bunch* – and, surprisingly, the single American film-maker with whom Dirk by this time had a hankering to work. As for Dirk, he was going to Holland almost immediately to appear in *A Bridge Too Far*. 'I'm only doing it,' he said, 'because it's going to pay for a new fence. And because I have The Line.' He was to wish he hadn't.

Richard Attenborough, their occasional next-door neighbour at Clermont and a knight in the 1976 New Year Honours List, had sent a courier from England with William Goldman's script of *A Bridge Too Far*. Dirk did not think much of it, but agreed, provided some dovetailing could be done with the schedule for *Providence*. 'I have said yes to Dickie's picture,' he told Elizabeth, 'it is not a great part. Boy Browning, who was Daphne du Mauriers husband and one of the planners of Arnhem. Rather a prick, I think ... however it's loot and it's going to be a massive picture on the lines of "The Longest Day" and all that sort of thing. Nothing to do with me ... but if they want me to play and pay I'll do so

happily! Cant afford to be proud now dear!' Even so, when the producer Joseph
Levine – who had kinked-up, if not sexed-up, *The Night Porter* in America –
offered $80,000, Dirk refused. 'It's a lousy part anyway,' noted Tony. A renewed
offer of $100,000 – for approximately twelve days' work spread over three weeks
and an extra two days subsequently – did the trick, and exactly a fortnight after
finishing Resnais' chamber piece in Paris, Dirk joined the mighty symphony
orchestra which Attenborough had assembled at Deventer, east of Amsterdam
and some twenty-five miles from Arnhem itself. The unit was 250 strong, the
biggest Dirk had ever seen, and the organisation was itself on a military scale.
Dirk had often used the term 'epic' to describe his films and for once it was
justified. The budget was $23,500,000 and the cast stellar: Caan, Caine, Connery,
Edward Fox, Gould, Hackman, Hopkins, Kruger, Olivier, O'Neal, Redford,
Schell, Ullmann. He would always say that he was used as a sprat to catch
Hollywood's mackerel, but the other British names were also engaged early.
Certainly the pay was sprat-like by comparison: none of the Americans was to
receive less than $100,000 a week; Robert Redford's fee was $2,000,000 for three
weeks. At least everyone had equal billing and as they were listed alphabetically
on all promotion material for the film, it was, as Tony observed, 'useful to have
a surname beginning with "B"'.

General Sir Frederick 'Boy' Browning was an Old Etonian, a former Olympic
athlete, and an exceptional soldier who by the age of twenty had won the DSO
and the Croix de Guerre for his deeds with the Grenadier Guards in France
during the First World War. In the Second, he created and commanded the
British airborne forces. In September 1944, he was summonsed to Brussels where
Montgomery outlined his strategy for 'Operation Market-Garden', which had
been prompted by recent V2 rocket attacks on London, launched from sites in
Holland. 'Market' was the drop and 'Garden' the armoured advance across the
'airborne carpet' laid by the paratroops. When Montgomery issued his orders
Browning expressed reservations. How long, he asked, would the 1st Airborne
Division be required to hold the bridge at Arnhem? 'Two days,' replied Monty.
'They'll be up with you by then.' 'We can hold it for four,' said Browning. 'But
I think we might be going a bridge too far.'[43] Hence 'The Line' that gave
Cornelius Ryan the title for his scrupulous account of the operation,[44] on which
the Levine/Attenborough film was based. Dirk's salary might have been a pittance
but at least he had 'The Line'. Or something like it.

The problem began with the decision of the film's high command to strip
away the top layer of the military hierarchy. Eisenhower and Montgomery would
not be depicted, therefore there would be no meeting between 'Monty' and
Browning at which the latter could voice his doubts. The crude ethos of the
Hollywood School of War has usually dictated, first, that there must be a fall guy
for a failure and, if joint operations are involved, he should be British; second,
that characterisation must be black and white, with no shades of grey. Here,
history made life easier. A twenty-five-year-old intelligence officer, Major Brian

Urquhart, deeply troubled by confirmation from the Dutch Resistance that SS Panzers were being refitted in the Arnhem area, took his worries to Browning and another senior officer, who told him that the information was probably incorrect, and that in any case the German troops were refitting, so would not be up to scratch. 'This reaction,' wrote Urquhart, 'confirmed my worst suspicions about the attitude of Browning and his staff, and I concluded that Browning's ambition to command in battle was a major factor both in the conception of "Market-Garden" and in his refusal to take the latest news on German opposition seriously.' Five days before the operation was due to begin, Urquhart, who at one of the planning conferences had asked with bitter irony whether the so-called 'airborne carpet' was to comprise live or dead Allied troops, requested the RAF to carry out low-level reconnaissance around Arnhem. Armed with five photographs which showed beyond doubt the presence of SS Panzers, 'I rushed to General Browning with this new evidence, only to be treated once again as a nervous child suffering from a nightmare. Even in my overwrought state I got the message very clearly. I was a pain in the neck, and only our long association and his natural kindness prevented the general from saying so.' Later that day, the chief medical officer visited Urquhart and ordered him to go on sick leave.[45] The encounter with Browning gave the film-makers a key scene, in which Urquhart was disguised as 'Major Fuller'; and established Browning as the villain of the piece. Browning's 'natural kindness' need not concern them. Nor, of course, did they have any idea that Urquhart realised when Ryan's book was published how badly he had misjudged Browning's initial attitude. 'Market-Garden' had been born of Monty's desperation for a British success to end the war; Browning had tried to apply the brakes, with 'The Line'. But such a little detail need not stand in the way of characterisation. And there was the added advantage that, unlike some of the other principals in the story, Browning was no longer alive to throw a legal spanner in the works.

Lady Browning had approved of the treatment afforded by Cornelius Ryan to her late husband, whom she called 'Moper'. According to her biographer, Margaret Forster, she liked the description of him as 'lithe, immaculately turned out ... [with] the appearance of a restless hawk'. However, her own experiences with the movie world had taught her enough to be suspicious when she learned, quite late in the day, that Ryan's book was to be the basis of a film. She wrote to Richard Attenborough, asking to see the script. He assured her that proper respect would be paid to Browning, as to the other main figures, and of course she would see William Goldman's screenplay. At this point she heard that Dirk was to portray her husband, and expressed her concern that the latter would emerge as 'effete and mincing'. Attenborough said that Dirk had been an intelligence officer with the forces involved at the time and that his personal knowledge of the operation would help the authenticity of his portrayal. The shooting-script which reached Daphne du Maurier in mid-March enraged her. Browning had been cast as a minor character and 'came out of it with no credit at all';

worse, he had been made 'the fall-guy of the whole Arnhem disaster'. Where was his crucial warning? What was the evidence for the scene with the aerial reconnaissance photographs? And why did the script constantly harp on his appearance, making him sound 'like a dandy who shrank from dirty work'?[46] To Oriel Malet, her friend and correspondent of more than twenty years, she wrote: 'I didn't like the scenes with Moper in them (to be acted by Dirk Bogarde), because they made him out to be a typical Guards officer, who only thought about polished boots, sort of thing. I made a fuss, rang up Attenborough, and he was polite and said they would make changes. But I bet they won't! Bogarde may be a good actor. I saw him in *The Servant*, and he was a homo in that. Whatever Moper was, he certainly *wasn't* a homo!'[47] The curious aspect of Lady Browning's reaction is that 'The Line' was missing altogether from the version of the script which she read. It had, presumably, been there in some form when Dirk first accepted the role – hence his remark to David Warner. However, Attenborough told Lady Browning that he would 'try to fit it in at the end'. He also said that he had spoken to Dirk, who 'agreed that Boy's concern for his men must be shown and due attention paid to all her other points'.[48] According to a newspaper report from the period, Richard Attenborough received a letter from Lady Browning full of gratitude for the trouble he was taking to allay her fears.[49] There is no evidence to back up Dirk's claim in at least one interview that he wrote personally to her – no such letter exists in the family archive; nor does her son or either of her two daughters remember any direct contact between him and their mother. Margaret Forster said that Attenborough's attempt to mollify Lady Browning failed; but, realising that it was useless to resist the advancing might of a Hollywood-financed blockbuster, she simply awaited the worst.

There is nothing in the Diary to indicate a sense of foreboding about Dirk's portrayal. On the contrary, he thoroughly enjoyed working with the 'thoroughbreds' and 'any race is the more exciting if you know you've got the best horses'.[50] One day the call-sheet read 'Dirk Bogarde, Sean Connery, Gene Hackman, Ryan O'Neal', prompting him to say 'I'm Still Here!' He sang the praises of all three: Connery – 'liked him a great deal'; Hackman – 'very Methody but nice and respectful'; O'Neal – 'very nice, clever, bright and not at all Peyton Place'.[51] Only when he had to return to the film after an interval of seven weeks to play the reconnaissance photograph scene with Frank Grimes, and found William Goldman on the set, did he express any discomfiture: Tony noted that Dirk felt inhibited by the writer, because 'he [Dirk] wants to change all the dialogue'. In retrospect, he told Penelope Mortimer, 'the more I played [Browning] the more a prick he emerged. Casting historical accuracy to the wind I managed to cut the crap and hope that I have made him Brave, Courageous, Wise and a Gentleman. At least the yanks will understand him now. Whereas in Goldmans Script they would have been forgiven for thinking him to be a cross between Terry Thomas and Ralph Reeder.'[52] As for 'The Line', it is odd to rediscover that the production notes distributed during the making of the picture carried on the title page Browning's original words: 'I think we might be going a bridge too far.' In their reworked form they occur in scene 860 of the script, where, in its penultimate version, Browning says to Major-General Roy Urquhart, Commander of the 1st Airborne Division and no relation to the troubled Brian: 'We just tried to go a bridge too far.' In the last version, it has changed to: 'As you know, I always felt we tried to go a bridge too far.' And on the soundtrack, Dirk says: 'Well, as you know, I've always thought that we tried to go a bridge too far.' At least Daphne du Maurier had set them thinking, but, as events would prove, not enough.

It is odd, too, that Dirk should have used the phrase 'Nothing to do with me' in his letter to Elizabeth, because, quite to the contrary, his role in *A Bridge Too Far* had more direct resonances than any other of his career. He had served as an officer in the very theatre of 'Operation Market-Garden'. In the months afterwards he had crossed repeatedly one of the bridges which, as he said at the time on his postcard to Elizabeth, would take their place in history. His work was the study of aerial reconnaissance photographs. And he alleged that he met Browning in the course of his duties, which is possible; but one might have expected the 1976 Diary to mention the fact. His two stints on the picture done, he retired to Clermont and thought about it only when his next-door neighbour reported from time to time on progress through the various stages of post-production. The first sign of trouble came on 24 June 1977 when Patrick Gibbs of *The Daily Telegraph* wrote that were Browning alive 'what is shown of him appears to be actionable'. 'As portrayed by Dirk Bogarde and, of course, by the script-writer, who is William Goldman, this general is not one I would have trusted to run a cocktail party.'[53] The following day a long letter appeared in *The Times* from General Sir John Hackett, damning Dirk's portrayal of Browning as both untruthful and unkind: 'It is untruthful because it shows a superficial, heartless, shallow person who is uncaring – even almost flippant – about the fate of brave men committed to his charge and displays, instead of strength of character, a petulant obstinacy born of weakness. He was not like that at all and could not have commanded such widespread loyalty if he had been.' It was unkind, he added, because it would 'affront very many men who knew Browning well' and would deeply and unnecessarily wound 'those still living who were closer to him still'. Hackett pointed the finger at Goldman, supposing that the scriptwriter 'needed a character like that for structural purposes' and that 'a director should probably not stray too far from what he is given. The pity is that a tragic conflict in a high-minded man, of a kind that carries an echo of Racine, might have provided for an actor as good as Bogarde, under the sensitive direction he could expect from Attenborough, a memorable and moving role.' A great opportunity had been missed.

For the next two weeks, the correspondence column rang to the clarion call of Dirk's supporters and the film's detractors. The writer Cyril Ray, who had flown in with the 'Market' troops, said he did not recognise the man he knew: 'Boy Browning was debonair in manner, dapper in appearance. So was Field

Marshal Alexander and so is Lord Mountbatten. So was Nelson. I do not know that anyone has ever been the worse a general or an admiral for keeping his voice low and his boots clean. All those I have mentioned were compassionate towards the men they led. But the dapper and debonair is one all the easier to caricature by anyone wishing to please a box office, and easier still if he is dead'. Colonel Frederick Gough, who was one of Browning's unit commanders in the early days of the Airborne Division and, as a major, took over from the wounded Lieutenant-Colonel John Frost at Arnhem Bridge, did not know whether the director had 'assumed a right to trample on people's feelings and to play ducks and drakes with historical facts in order to dish up an extravaganza fit for the American massed cinema market. But the fact is that great offence has already been caused'.[54]

Daphne du Maurier refused to see 'that bloody film', but, on the strength of what she heard from people she trusted, became obsessed with having it condemned. There were potential allies in very high places indeed, because almost immediately after the war Browning had been appointed to the Royal Household as Comptroller and Treasurer to the then Princess Elizabeth, and, on her accession, he became Treasurer to the Duke of Edinburgh. Lady Browning asked Lord Mountbatten to boycott the première, but he refused because it was for a charity he supported. After seeing the film he wrote that, even though Dirk was not 'ideal' casting, he could find 'nothing really detrimental to Boy'; 'nobody could think Boy's magnificent reputation tarnished'. After all, 'Market-Garden' had been a disaster and Browning was one of those responsible. Hardly surprisingly, she considered this bizarre response a betrayal. James Orr, Extra Equerry to Prince Philip, was another she approached in aid. He was more robust, saying that 'Boy would have laughed it off as tripe'[55] and that she need not worry about the reaction among the Royals, who knew and loved Boy. The press and the film world, Orr felt, seemed to think they had a licence to lie.

When Browning's son Christian first saw the film, he said that if he had not known the history of 'Market-Garden' he would have thought that the general being portrayed in the film 'was working for the other side – it was so peculiar'. Nevertheless he understands how it happened: 'It was American money and they wanted a fall guy. They knew there would be too much flak if they put Monty in a bad light, so they went for Dad. It is very difficult to know who might have played him more convincingly. John Mills was by then too old for the part. David Niven? Peter Bowles would have been a little too young, but he could have done the suave without being camp. Dad was a very strict disciplinarian and a lot of people were frightened of him, but he loved his men – his "boys".' Christian Browning confirms his father's elegance: 'In the 1950s he was the best-dressed man in London; his shoes were immaculate. But he was not all that serious a man: he said during the campaign, "I'm the first person to piss on German soil". That was much more him than poncing around with white gloves. Those gloves! Dirk played Anacleto in "The Singer Not the Song" more or less the way he played Dad.'[56] James Fox, himself a former Guards officer and a friend of the Browning family, almost hoots at the memory of seeing the film: 'The first thing we all said was, "What the hell are they doing casting Dirk as Freddie Browning?" We went into the cinema and were appalled. It was the most peculiar performance ever. He was impersonating Freddie Browning completely wrongly. It was as if he set out to play him as a poofy waiter, or a poofy bank manager – not that I've ever met a poofy bank manager. Dirk just *wasn't* a general.' For Fox, Ryan's book had been 'a powerful account of a failed campaign' and 'they could have made a heartbreaking film, but they lost their marbles'. It was, he adds, 'the end of British cinema being taken seriously about putting our boys into battle dress. Hollywood finally decided they had to take over: "These Brits have lost the plot!" '[57]

At Clermont the reception in the newspapers had a profound effect. This was public derision – Dirk's dread. What is more, much of it was being levelled in the pages of *The Times*, of all places. What *would* Ulric have said? Dirk used to tell how, when his name first appeared outside a cinema in Brighton, implausibly billed as Berk Gocart, his father had called to protest that he had brought shame on the family. That was a joke. This was a different matter. As the attacks continued, Tony recorded that Dirk was in some distress. They tried to work out what had gone wrong. Had a scene been cut? Was there some 'editorial cause'? Or was it, most disturbingly, 'a performance failure'? Whatever the reason, to be the target of hostility was a novel and highly undesirable experience. After about a week, distress turned to anger, because Dirk began to feel he had been set up. He considered donating his salary to a charity of Lady Browning's choice. But Dilys Powell, who went back to see the film for a second time, said: 'Apologise to no one.' She found the performance straightforward, military and cold – which, she supposed, was what generals were meant to be. Dirk sent a card to apologise for a 'fearful imposition' and to thank her: 'It all seems like a storm in a tea-cup – But to dis-honour a man's memory for gain seemed to one frightful.' He said he would now quieten down 'and get on with my many chores on the land'. It is hard to know whether Dirk was being disingenuous or deluding himself. He was certainly in need of his own fall guy. 'I have learned a bitter lesson!' he wrote on the same card. 'One *never* does "business" with a friend!'[58] How much worse when the friend is also living, anyway for part of the year, next door.

Dirk telephoned Sheila Attenborough and told her that the family was no longer welcome at Clermont for a pre-arranged dinner and, by implication, on any other occasion. He also wrote in venomous terms to her husband. 'It was the most awful letter, which I think I destroyed on the spot,' recalls Lord Attenborough, for whom the episode is painful to this day.[59] Never in his life had this legendarily affable, benevolent and emotional man received anything like that letter; nor had any of his personal or professional relationships, let alone one of thirty years, come to such a brutal end. To make it worse, 'Dirk was someone for whom I had an amazing deal of affection and a massive amount of respect. I found it really distressing.' The letter accused him of both a personal betrayal and of 'treachery' by presenting the character based on Boy Browning in an untrue light, knowing full well that it was untrue. 'On the contrary,' insists Lord Attenborough. 'I believed it to be true.' Dirk, he says, played the part as it was conceived and written: 'He knew what he was doing – he had a considerable brain – and he knew perfectly well what was on the page. But it was not until the picture came out that he uttered a word.' Much of the background detail is now lost or forgotten, but at the time when Attenborough was seeking to reassure Lady Browning, he wrote to Dirk, saying that the General, for all his 'urbane sophistication', nonetheless cared greatly for the men under his command; if Dirk could add that aspect of the character to the scenes as scripted 'it will result in a man, not only of considerable stature, but, indeed, of real flesh and blood'. Tellingly, this was the only piece of correspondence from his director that Dirk kept. As for his own 1977 letter, it contained another assertion which Lord Attenborough will not forget: that by giving him the part, 'You have absolutely ruined any possible recognition that I might receive nationally. And I shall never forgive you for that.' He was, of course, thinking about Browning's stock within the Royal Family. Little did he know that in the light of Noël Coward's knight-hood, awarded despite his exile in Switzerland, the influential Attenborough had for some time been pressing for Dirk to be given such 'national recognition'. And would go on doing so.

Two weeks later, the freezing divide between the two houses at Châteauneuf had thawed enough for the Attenboroughs – shocked not only by the personal crisis but also by the opprobrium heaped on the film – to cross the Clermont threshold with their other friends of long standing, Bryan and Nanette Forbes. Inevitably, Tony had been the mediator. Later still, when *The Sunday Times* ran a long article on the controversy surrounding the film under the heading 'The Second Battle of Arnhem', Attenborough wrote to correct any misunderstanding about the interpretation of the part. He said that although Dirk bore no physical resemblance to Browning, 'he most certainly had the qualities, experience and skill to be able to depict a character as complex as the one required. The characterisation eventually arrived at was as a result of discussions between us but, finally, of course, what appears on the screen is the responsibility of the director.' Dirk, he added, 'is, without question, one of the supreme actors in world cinema and we were fortunate indeed to be able to acquire his services [. . .] In my opinion he gives a quite superb performance and if the end result, in terms of interpretation, is, to some, unsatisfactory, then the blame accrues to me and not to Mr Bogarde.'[60] It was a loyal gesture and it appeared on a day when Sheila Attenborough, staying alone at their house, came to supper with Dirk and Tony. For her 'the whole episode was very sad and upsetting. I don't think Dirk ever really got over it. He believed that Dick hadn't behaved honestly.' Lady Attenborough, who was on the Dutch location, remembers there being no clash during the shooting – 'It was a happy time' – nor in the period leading up to the film's release. 'The only explanation can be that Dirk never understood the impact the role would make, and he may have been angry that he had allowed himself to fall into what he saw as a trap. When he was criticised, he became irrationally upset. He was like that. He had this insecurity and he couldn't control his emotions. He would get on the wrong side of people and that was it.' They 'patched things up and it was possible to go on living side by side, but that was very much due to Tony'.[61] Relations continued much as before with Sheila Attenborough, whom Dirk had christened 'Garnet' after a spectacular set of jewellery she had worn with a ball-gown to a première in the early days of their friendship: 'He was very observant – frighteningly so.' But those between Dirk and her husband would never fully be restored. As he had proved with John Mills, Dirk could be remorselessly unforgiving.

Twenty

'The world is full of dotty people'

I t is just possible that Dirk's eye was not properly on the ball when he accepted and participated in *A Bridge Too Far*. After all, he had a lot both on his mind and his hands. '[...] we live a very do-it-yourself life here,' wrote Tony to Laurence Harbottle, 'and I am gardener-cook-chauffeur-housepainter-secretary (unpaid, of course) and Dirk is wood-chopper, housemaid, kitchen-maid, bar-maid, handy-man (unpaid) and WRITER ... (paid). Neither of us sit down very often, but it might be quite good for our figures.'[1] True enough: Dirk was indeed now a WRITER, even an AUTHOR. The final portion of *Postillion* had gone to Chatto at the end of February 1976, and the usual processes of revision, indexing, proof-reading and selection of illustrations began. Two months later he wrote to John Charlton from Brussels, where *Providence* was under way: 'It would appear that I am thinking more about poor old "Postillion" than the work in hand!'[2] He enclosed a drawing which he had just done at his hotel of the kitchen at Lullington, because it had dawned on him that the kitchen was where much – or, as he put it, 'most' – of the story in the first half of the book took place. From Holland he sent a postcard of Van Gogh's 'Field and Skylark', thinking it might be good for the jacket, then had a change of heart: 'I cannot think what possessed me [...] I was either deeply depressed by Holland (which I was) or else overcome by the sheer beauty of the exhibition at the Rijksmuseum ... which I also was! But it was a very vulgar and common idea and I beg you to forget it right away. I really feel quite ashamed at the idea of trying to pinch a Master Work for my slender copy. The shame prompted me to try my own ...'.[3] He enclosed a painting – an idealised view of the cottage and Great Meadow, with a storm-cloud looming – and, apologising that 'my presumption is great', made suggestions about the typeface and position of the lettering. This was swiftly followed by a sketch for the title page, showing a carriage on a rainswept country road; it was seen from the rear, so that Dirk did not have to draw the horse, one of his few blind spots as an artist. Norah Smallwood and John Charlton were delighted: it really was turning out to be a case of All My Own Work – with a famous name attached. There was a slight hiccup when both the new illustrations came back to him for adjustment:

Infuriated about the Title-sketch. I took a good deal of trouble with the damned thing because I was, am, positive that you wanted it to be Vertical! [...] The Jacket is becoming a bit of a bore. The sketch which I sent you is clearly useless if it is to be smothered in text [...] Why not simply junk it, it is far too busy, and use a perfectly plain colour ... white or blue or something simple ... with lettering to delight your Home and Export Sales Directors. Why not, even, use the title sketch for the cover, set in an oval, and bursting with advertising all round?

He begged them not to use a photograph of himself on the front, adding 'I really would prefer the whole thing to be cancelled (an impossibility I know alas!) than to face my first book as if it was a Film Stars Paper-Back.'⁴ All was quietly resolved, and then the proof copy arrived. 'It is a rather daunting thing to hold ones very first book in ones hand ... not altogether a comfortable experience. I'm not dotty about it, I fear. Some is good, some awful.' He gave it little chance. 'I think, paradoxically, that Summer is a good deal better than Winter ... which is sad. And I cant think it will have the LEAST interest to an American reader. However time will tell ...'.⁵ He sent Norah Smallwood as a present a spontaneous drawing of Virginia Woolf, co-founder of Chatto's subsidiary, the Hogarth Press, who strolls, unnamed, into *Postillion* while Derek, Reg Fluke and another chum, Percy, are fishing for a pike: 'She was tall and thin, with a long woolly, and fairish hair which looked rather wispy as if she had just washed it. She was carrying a walking stick and a bunch of wild flowers.' She is lost, and Reg gruffly gives her directions. 'They say she's a bit do-lally-tap ... she writes books,' says Percy. Derek 'just lay back quietly in the grasses, and watched the sky and wondered why there were so many witches in Sussex'.⁶ And to his publisher's further pleasure, even as he worked on the corrections, the second book was beginning to take shape in the studio – the working title now changed from 'Enter Daemons' to 'The Honey Waggon', 'a Military term for a mobile latrine ... it seems to cover most of the contents ...'.⁷

The title had changed again – to 'Starting with Exits' – and the three opening chapters were already in John Charlton's hands when on 1 February 1977 Dirk stepped into the Chatto office in William IV Street. 'I was strangely instantly secure in the familiar feeling of the place.' With its discrete scent compounded of paper, cardboard, print and dust, and its atmosphere of serious work, it reminded him of *The Times*.* John Charlton welcomed and introduced him to Rosalind Bell, who was responsible for the firm's publicity and who was to become another of the principal players in Dirk's life. Then he and Tony took the lethal lift, 'a shuddering coffin', to the second floor. Here, in the doorway of

---

* Dirk's description in *An Orderly Man* of the office and its denizens is engagingly complemented in *Kindred Spirits* (HarperCollins, 1995), the autobiography of a former Chatto & Windus editor, Jeremy Lewis.

a room identified by a small wooden plaque as the lair of Norah Smallwood, Dirk met Dorothy Gordon's successor as his 'needlewoman':

> She was tall, very slender, elegant in a white silk blouse and a coral-red wool skirt. In her hands she held two books, one bound in blue, one in yellow; she thrust them towards me.
>
> 'Which colour d'you like?' She left the books in my hands and turned back into her room. 'I'll get my jacket.'
>
> I stood there in the corridor holding two copies of *A Postillion Struck by Lightning* and knew that nothing as wonderful could ever happen to me again.[8]

It was, as they say, a well-made book, with its artistically licensed Lullington landscape bleeding from the front of the jacket on to the spine, its quiet lettering, and on the back a portrait by Jurgen Vollmer of a smiling, sweatered Dirk. The endpapers were a photograph of Great Meadow, the two cottages and the church – an aerial view dated 1931, which Ulric had organised as part of his experimental work at *The Times*. Scattered through the pages were seventeen of Dirk's pen-and-ink drawings and twenty further photographs, mainly of the family, but with four from his early days in the theatre. Apart, of course, from Lally, only two 'outsiders' were given prominence: Bill Wightman and, above a caption reading 'Lieutenant Anthony Forwood RA, Summer 1940', Tony, standing nonchalantly against a pillar, hands in the pockets of his uniform. One picture above all, which enchanted everyone who had seen it, was dated July 1927 and showed Derek and Lu sitting together on the bottom step of a steep, narrow staircase, he in shorts with a model car balanced on his knees; she looking waif-like beneath a straggle of hair. The author explained in his preface that he had drawn in the main on material he had found when sorting the papers in Ulric's studio in 1972, which included a packet and a cigar box labelled simply 'For Dirk'. They contained diaries, letters, school reports, photographs, glass negatives, cuttings and 'written notes in his own hand on dates and times', which Ulric had begun to assemble for him when Dirk left England in 1968, with an eye to a possible book of the latter's childhood memories. For the rest, 'I have had to depend on my own memories and those of my English family and my friends.' The dedication was to 'My Father and Mother, Elizabeth, Gareth, Tony and Lally. With my love'; and there were acknowledgements to Elizabeth, Lally, Tony, Bill Wightman and Gareth – and to Glur Dyson Taylor who was 'godmother' to the book. She had read the embryonic chapters on a visit to Clermont and had urged him to press on.

John Charlton and Norah Smallwood took Dirk and Tony to the Garrick Club for lunch, with representatives from the paperback house, Triad, and the American publisher, Holt, Rinehart. The former had paid £14,000 for the book; the latter, $10,000. The former was, understandably, more optimistic about its chances; one of the Triad directors, Jim Reynolds, considered *Postillion* worthy of comparison with Laurie Lee's *Cider with Rosie* and was mystified that Dirk had hidden an extraordinary literary talent from the world for so long. The Americans might not have had *Postillion* at all. 'I really *dont* want the thing published in the States,' Dirk wrote to John Charlton, before relenting slightly: 'Holt seems to be promising, from the booklet you sent me, but one is slightly bemused to see that they have cornered the market for "Peanuts" and Cook Books!'⁹ At the lunch he told his hosts that he was going to send one of his copies of the book to Elizabeth, and if she hated it, or was upset by it, 'or thought it was beastly or vulgar to anyone', he would insist they cancel publication. 'That caused a bit of a stir, I can tell you! But they were very sweet and put it down to sort of First Night Nerves!' In the evening, Chatto gave a party for Dirk to meet booksellers. Rosalind Bell recalls that 'it was held in the packing room at the office. The cleaners were in the corridor, soap-suds everywhere. As Dirk and Tony picked their way past, one of the cleaners said: "Ere, do you know who that was? Humphrey Bogarde."' At the end, Dirk told his hosts: 'When the book comes out I'm going to have a proper party – at the Connaught!'¹⁰ After a spate of interviews, including a third and more serious fixture with his sparring partner Russell Harty, he and Tony returned to Clermont, leaving the publishers in no doubt that, despite an initial reluctance, he was 'doing his bit' for them. Now, all he could do was to await the verdict. 'I dont think, to be fair, that I have ever been so scared before,' he wrote to Norah Smallwood,

> never with a film ... sometimes with a Play ... but this time the fear rises in my throat and threatens to strangle me. It is all perfectly idiotic I know; I am a grown up person and face the full responsibility ... but I am *not* Laurie Lee ... however nice it might feel to be him ... in a few days, almost, it will be all over and the stress will pass. I hope. And I shall go contentedly, banished no doubt from Chatto, back to my REAL work.¹¹

So on edge was he that he became convinced he had invented Henry Moore's presence on the staff at Chelsea School of Art; after a sleepless night he rang Graham Sutherland's wife Kathleen, who assured him that they had all taught at Manresa Road in Dirk's time. An early copy of *Postillion* went to Moore, who said he 'dimly' recalled the young Derek, and offered his congratulations on the book. They were as nothing to the hymn of praise which came, to Dirk's intense relief, from Elizabeth. She described her brother's book as 'heaven' and said he was a 'gentle writer', who made no *demand* on his audience but, rather, asked whether they would *like* to read about him. For having transported her back so effortlessly to the happy times they had shared as children, she said he was a magician. There was no need to stop the presses. Publication day was 24 March, just before Dirk's fifty-sixth birthday. By then 13,000 copies had been sold into the trade – a substantial figure. On the day itself, with Tony and Elizabeth he arrived at Hatchards in Piccadilly to find the royal booksellers under siege. An hour and a quarter later, 670 copies had been sold and signed. Clearly, the public was in a mood to be beguiled by the first-time author. What about the reviewers? That morning, the literary editor of *The Daily Telegraph*, David Holloway, bracketed *Postillion* with a so-called 'autobiography' – in fact a series of short essays – by J. B. Priestley. This was not only a nice coincidence, given that Dirk's first West End engagement was in one of Priestley's plays; it was also an indication that he was to be treated on the same terms as a literary giant, albeit one who, at eighty-two, was running out of puff. Within the covers of *Postillion*, said Holloway, were 'two quite different books'. The first half 'might almost be a novel, an idyllic summer remembered, spent partly under the shadow of the South Downs and partly in Normandy'; it was 'really remarkable, a childhood brilliantly recalled'. The reporting was exceptionally vivid, the conversations were real; Dirk had unselfishly assumed the role of observer and 'feed', giving the best lines to Lu and to Lally. In the second half, the sketches of 'his two "wicked" grandfathers' found favour. The 'show biz' part of Dirk's life was 'conventional enough, better written than most of its kind, but when you have read of one attack of first-night nerves, and of one helpful older actor giving good advice, you have read them all'. Interestingly, Holloway was struck by the unclear picture that Dirk had drawn of Ulric and Margaret: 'Mr Bogarde's exile to Scotland seems to have been particularly heartless, as he tells it, but clearly despite this he was very fond of both his parents and they of him.' Like Priestley's book, *Postillion* was 'decidedly odd', but Holloway had enjoyed them both.[12]

The point about Dirk's parents had surfaced elsewhere, notably in a thoughtful appraisal of the book at an early stage by John Knowler, the London representative for Holt, Rinehart. He said he recognised that much of the point was their almost Victorian remoteness and their substitution by Lally, but there evidently was great mutual affection and the children saw more of them than the reader might think; he had in mind particularly the 'Remember Game' – the Pelmanism – which helped to forge Dirk's remarkable memory for detail.[13*] Dirk wrote in reply to Elizabeth's congratulations shortly before publication: 'The thing which interests people so much, so far, is the way that Parents are shadowy at that age to children ... always there and loved, but distant ... and then they start coming into ones life as one gets older.' He would compensate in years to come – especially with *An Orderly Man* – but for the purposes of *Postillion*, he was content to let the shadows flicker. Mind you he had tried. He told Elizabeth that he had sent to Margaret and to all the Scottish relatives a questionnaire on the Nivens, and had 'absolutely no answer from anyone. Sadie said she could'nt

---

* John Knowler identified another missing element: sex. The author, he wrote, 'seems to have ended up engaged without ever encountering the phenomenon. I (the common reader) get the feeling it is deliberately avoided. Perhaps it was a perfectly natural part of the children's lives; perhaps it was a taboo – the subject is so absent, I have no idea which.'

comment, and would pass her letter on to Roey! It was the same letter to them both . . . and very polite and asking for careful help. Not a word. So screw them. There is an AWFUL lot I HAVE'NT said about my little Scottish Trip, I can tell you . . .'.

What he *had* said was already quite sufficient to cause the most almighty stink when copies of the book began to circulate in and around Glasgow. We have seen in an earlier chapter how miserable the teenaged Derek was in Bishopbriggs and, to a much lesser extent, with Aunt Hester in King's Park. In *Postillion* it was as if most of the unpleasantnesses visited on him by anyone at any time from 1934 until, well, Earl St John, should be laid at the door of number 42 Springfield Square. It is hard to reconcile this with the letter which Dirk wrote on Hester's death in 1954 to 'Dearest Aunt Sadie', saying that her closeness to her younger sister, and the fact that she been with her through the last unhappy weeks, 'must have given her great heart & peace – I know that she will have had every possible kindness & help & love from you – & must have been content'. He added: 'How very important you are to "our" family – & may God bless you for the way you have helped us all.' He signed the letter, 'Your loving nephew/Dirk xxx'. In that context, her failure to answer his 'questionnaire' twenty years or so later seems insufficient grounds for Dirk to take his 'screw you' attitude to the extreme that he did. Forrest McClellan, Dirk's cousin, describes the impact of the book in the Murray household at Bishopbriggs as 'a body blow'. Hilda Niven, wife of Sadie's brother Munro ('Roey'), told Dirk with admirable understatement that she was 'disappointed' by his writing of the 'Glasgow episodes' in such a way while Sadie was still alive. Some fifteen years after *Postillion* was published, and in a long letter of thanks to Forrest McClellan for sending a copy of *Some of My Aunts and Uncles*, Dirk explained that life with the Murrays was 'far FAR worse than anything I wrote in my book':

The scars that the time there, three years, burned into me never healed. But, and this I have said before, and repeat, without those awful years of bigotry and loneliness I would never have got through life. Those years made me strong, determined to save myself, and to get away from all that was 'dainty' 'false' and 'genteel' and, no need to put a fine point on it, cruel. Uncle Murray was deadly cruel. He falsified my school reports, censored my letters home every week, watched me with curious intensity when I took my weekly bath, and although my parents were paying them pretty well a weekly wage for my board and lodging, he made certain that I accounted for every penny I was allowed by my parents for my 'Saturday Pennies'. I spent most of my time quite alone in their 'front room' because the boys I knew at school were either, in his opinion, 'rough and common' or 'dirtying your aunts carpets'.

He denied that his account in *Postillion* was 'vengeful': 'I did my best to explain that it was mostly MY fault. The absolute impossibility of the two very different temperments joining or even understanding each other.' Once, when Uncle Murray went briefly to Ireland, 'Sadie was a quite different person. Almost jolly, always smart and trim, and ready to do something exciting! Like going to the cinema or to hear the Orpheus Choir, or some thing . . .'. In which case, why, when she was still alive, did Dirk go so savagely on the attack, and return to it time and again in subsequent volumes? None of the family knows, let alone fully understands.

It has to be said that some of the most laudatory notices for *Postillion* came from well-disposed writers whose usual beat was the cinema. Dirk enjoyed their praise but wanted his book to be treated on its literary merit, not as some kind of a spin-off or by-product from his usual milieu. When proof copies had been sent to national newspapers for possible serialisation, the reaction was far from wildly enthusiastic. One features editor said it was written in a lively and agreeable way but was not substantial enough to make good extracts; Mark Boxer at *The Sunday Times* took the same view. It finally went to *The Times*, where perhaps, if only for sentimental reasons, it properly belonged. Now *Postillion* was out in the world, the judgment of the colder-eyed and the disinterested was bound on occasion to cause Dirk to wince. In recent months he had been reading the books pages of the English newspapers with heightened interest, and had come to the conclusion that the winds of criticism blew even more harshly in the literary world than they did in the cinema. He would not be spared. Peter Forster in the *Evening Standard* said that there was no point in 'smiting a perfectly pleasant little book with a steam-hammer, but the fact remains that whatever the postillion was struck by, Mr Bogarde was struck by a talent for acting rather than a genius for writing'. Noting a remark by Visconti that in Dirk was a mixture of jelly and steel, Forster concluded that 'subsequent volumes need more of the latter'.[14] There would be – plenty of it. Indeed, some was already in Chatto's hands. But Dirk had to pause in the pursuit of the new career, to return to what he told Norah Smallwood was his REAL work – in Munich.

The call from Tom Stoppard had come out of the blue at the end of October 1976. He and Dirk had never met, or had any dealings before.

'I gather that you aren't making any more films; am I right?' enquired the thirty-nine-year-old playwright.

'No. Wrong. I'm not making any more crap.'

'I don't write crap.'[15]

Stoppard, who had recently 'doctored' Thomas Wiseman's script of *The Romantic Englishwoman* for Losey, said he was adapting Vladimir Nabokov's 1936 novel *Despair* for Rainer Werner Fassbinder, a wild man of the German cinema, who at thirty-one had directed some twenty-five full-length films. The first-person narrator in Nabokov's story is a Russian émigré who owns a chocolate factory in Berlin during the last days of the Weimar Republic. The business is in trouble, his marriage is on its uppers, and he decides to commit the perfect crime by taking out insurance on his life and murdering his so-called double, and then do a bunk with the money. In the Fassbinder/Stoppard version, as Wallace Watson remarked in *Sight and Sound*, the protagonist would be less cold-blooded and infinitely more sympathetic, 'a sort of existential hero whose madness seems the only respectable way out of the vulgarity and absurdity of the modern world'.[16] However, in both novel and film, Hermann is 'a witty, ironic aesthete and philosopher of sorts' – a combination perfect for Dirk – and he was immediately interested. Stoppard sent a draft screenplay, noting regretfully that the boss of the Munich studio where the film would be based was one Doktor Krapp.

Dirk thought the script 'extraordinary'. The wordplay was dazzling; the chance to work with another exciting young talent, irresistible; the fee of $225,000, more than useful; and the part, huge. 'If, as I felt certain in the deepest recesses of my heart, my days as a working actor of the kind I had been for twelve years were beginning to fade out, I was determined that they would not fade out on a cameo role. At least I would go out above the title; a position to which I had grown accustomed ever since my first film in 1947.'[17] There were three problems, the first of which would swiftly be resolved. Dirk had been wooed to the point of acceptance in principle by the producers of *Under the Volcano*, to be shot in Mexico; but this collapsed amid uncertainty about that country's economy. Second, if *Despair* did turn out to be his swan-song, the title was not the happiest way to bid farewell. And third, the script called for Hermann Hermann – as the protagonist was now called, with a nod towards Nabokov's Humbert Humbert in *Lolita* – both to drive and to appear in the nude. 'I have no intention, at my time of life, of wagging my genitals about on a screen!' he reported to Stoppard; 'and I cant bloody drive. Apart from that I THINK I can play your chap.'[18] The driving was easily dealt with; the nudity became briefly something of an issue. A body double was suggested. 'Might be the best solution,' he wrote to Stoppard. 'If you insist on nakedness at all in a middle aged man. I think it is a total bore, nakedness, anyway … and not the least bit erotic.' He felt, however, that if Fassbinder did use a double, 'I really ought to have approval; dont you?'

I mean, after all, I have been 'teasing' the buggers for over thirty years as to what I actually have between my legs, and although it is'nt that great it is'nt too bad. So, supposing it was suddenly discovered that I was endowed with a sort of chippolata instead of a really sound Cervella or even a good Bratwurst?

I'd be terribly saddened. So would all those now elderly people who dreamed otherwise [...] I do think it is something we shall have to have a serious talk about one fine day … you see in a cod-piece, breeches, or even ordinary old slacks, you can cheat delightfully. Kleenex, a banana … that sort of thing. I know one Famous Film Star, now aged and retired to Marbella, who actually had a little bomb from a Soda Syphon thing slung round his waist. It dangled provocatively in his tightish pants and had them in fits from East Croydon to Matlock Spa.[19]

Into the contract it went: 'The producer agrees that the employee shall not be requested to undress during photography, that he shall, however, in the corresponding shots, perform waist-high dressed according to the instructions of the producer.'

Dirk and Fassbinder met for dinner at the Colombe d'Or. 'I didn't know what to expect because I'd never seen him. He arrived in a white tuxedo with his hair combed back, soaking wet, and a huge tie with a naked lady on it and black evening dress trousers, motor cycle boots and granny glasses and a big moustache because he hadn't shaved.'[20] Maybe not; but Fassbinder's immersion in a bath had caused a commotion: his companions told Dirk it was the first he had taken in four years. In fact one of the director's closest friends wrote that Fassbinder had more baths than the average German and that his image of dishevelment and disreputability was carefully cultivated as a reaction against a genteel upbring-ing as a lonely child; it was a classic case of an artist wishing to *épater les bourgeois*, and, at times, succeeding. To Tony, he resembled 'a small round Joseph von Sternberg' and 'not too geary as we had been led to believe'. The image he had put about of a 'homosexual sado-masochist' and a 'dirty old man' was, Dirk reflected some time later, 'completely untrue'. 'He was the gentlest, quite the sweetest man, loathing the new Germany, hating what had happened in the past and refusing to bear any responsibility for what the Germans had done.'[21] And he, too, was shy; his bursts of violently aggressive or exhibitionistic behaviour were compensation. As one of his biographers, Ronald Hayman, noted, Fassbinder's hysteria was 'often genuine, but he could also fake it in order to get his own way by frightening people, and to a large extent his life consisted of putting on a performance, living up to the public image that was partly his own creation and partly that of the press. But he never overcame his shyness.'[22] There was common ground between him and Dirk.

Postillion was happily ensconced for the fourth week in the top ten bestsellers, and *Providence* was belatedly running to capacity houses after a bout of promotion in Paris, by the time Dirk and Tony arrived at Interlaken for the start of *Despair*. During the two-month progress to Berlin, Hamburg and Brunswick misunderstandings with Fassbinder, mainly linguistic, gave way to mutual respect, then, towards the end in Lübeck, an almost complete breakdown in relations because the organisation was – uncharacteristically for the Germans – a shambles. Dirk issued an ultimatum: he would leave on the agreed finishing date whether or not his work was complete. Which concentrated the minds of all, including Fassbinder who, the Diary records, was 'brilliant, but capricious & spoiled'. On the last day of shooting, the director did not attend the 'wrap' party in the unit hotel, choosing instead to stay in his room, where he wrote to Dirk, saying that he was unable at the moment to 'speak about the things, which happen in my head'. He thanked Dirk for Hermann – 'I hope, it will be *our* Hermann like his madness is a little bit our madness' – and for giving Fassbinder his 'authority without making fear, because fear makes sick, and normally authority goes together with fear'; Dirk, he said, showed him 'how to combine authority with freedom, which I knew so far only theoretically and what is one of the most important ideas for work and life'. More than likely, he added, 'there is more despair than anything else. But – and that is what I think – life is timeless and end is endless. And this means, it is not so sad like it seems.'[23] Dirk, and Tony too, found the letter 'very touching & extraordinary'. Back at Clermont, Dirk wrote to Fassbinder:

> I suppose I've never worked with anyone before who had a 'Death Wish,' and being a very adventurous, curious believing kind-of-person myself, I find it very difficult to understand. Although, God knows, I do understand the atmosphere in Germany after only three months stay . . . it cannot be easy for a person of your age and generation to bear easily. But you must fight that terribly dangerous atmosphere . . . and push it aside . . . You say in your letter to me that 'more likely there is more despair than anything else['] . . . I assume you mean Life? That is fundamentally NOT TRUE! Life is full of hope and promise.

He warned Fassbinder off the 'Clubs and Discos and Pills . . . and Pot', saying he should use them from time to time for the relaxation he needed 'but not as often as you do. Dont live by them or by the mindless people who exist in that world. They will only swamp you and kill you off far, far quicker than your own feelings of disilusion or so-called Despair.' Although he thanked Fassbinder for the kindness and 'security' shown him in the past weeks of 'a very difficult and bewildering (at times!) assignment', he said he had not actually *learned* anything from him; nevertheless he hoped that he, Dirk, had been able to bring to the younger man some of the learning acquired from 'people like Cukor, Milestone, Clayton, Losey, Visconti and Resnais and the rest of them [. . .] I was simply handing on the "baton" in this extraordinary business of the Creative Cinema. And to see you take that "baton" is HOPE, Rainer . . . NOT ever despair!'[24] Dirk had seen self-destructiveness in his professional world often enough to discern when it was the real thing.

After an interval, for recovery and reflection, Dirk wrote to Stoppard, saying that Fassbinder had been

> all I could have possibly wanted as a Director, and brilliant to boot. And nice. Really nice. Under all the chains, leather, thigh boots and grannie-glasses a soft-center lies snuggled. And I found it and liked it enormously. Sadly the people who surround him are the most awful lot of scrubby, pot smoking,

squealing little Leather Boys ... pretty tiresome; and dangerous too for I do think that they have a tremendous effect on Reiner who desperately needs love, as he calls it, and insists on rejecting it at the same time.

Dirk mentioned Fassbinder's thanks for teaching him 'authority without making fear'; 'I'm happy if I was able to show him that. For it is exactly the one thing which he lacks himself! He has Authority WITH fear. They were all shit scared of him from the head Dr Krapp to the smallest fag in the make-up rooms ... and no one, but no one, would say no to him. Except me. And he liked me for that.' And the film itself? Dirk believed it was 'a very important one indeed' but they all had now to sit 'nibbling finger-nails' while its running-time was considerably reduced – by an hour or more.[25]

The next time that actor and director met was two months later, at a dubbing theatre in Paris, where Dirk was to add his dialogue to the soundtrack. With him and Tony was Dirk's eighteen-year-old nephew, Brock Van den Bogaerde, who had been staying at Clermont and who remembers that Dirk had spent a long time training with a dialogue coach to pin down the precise Prussian accent that a White Russian exiled in Berlin would have acquired.

It was very important to him that he got it absolutely right. So for the two weeks before we went to Paris, he spoke with a German accent the whole time. He really was this man Hermann. We arrived at the dubbing theatre, and I was introduced to the production people. There was no sign of Fassbinder, but the decision was made to go on without him, even though there was a risk that everything might have to be done all over again. It was my first experience of post-synching. Dirk had to do a sequence of about a minute and a half where he has gone mad and is at the top of a spiral staircase, and then you see him rolling down it, crying and laughing at the same time. He did it in one or two takes. After a while Fassbinder appeared. He was wearing motorcycle gear, leather jacket, a leather hat, chains, a pair of jeans and boots. He smelt to high heaven. He'd just smashed up his hotel room, and had been arrested on the way to the dubbing theatre in a pink Cadillac. He and Dirk embraced each other affectionately, then did two days' worth of dubbing in four hours. It was extraordinary.

With the French actress Andréa Ferréol, of whom Dirk and Tony became extremely fond during the filming, they saw a rough cut of *Despair* and felt confident. Nothing in the Diary indicates alarm. Indeed, a few days later Dirk was writing to Fassbinder: 'I love the film. I am proud, immensley, of it, of you and of Andrea, Klaus [Löwitsch] and even of my own work [...] I am, like you, never really satisfied; but this time I think that I can honestly say that you have enabled me to do my best work for the Cinema. It is not perfect. But it is the best I have done. Thank you.' He went out of his way to praise the director for doing a 'fantastic job' with the editing, adding: 'Stoppard called yesterday and I was happy to be able to make him so happy ... he is now convinced that we have done a marvellous film, and is very excited.'[26] That excitement lasted no time at all once the playwright sat down to watch the film 'in the company of friends and loved ones, all predisposed to loving it'. The very first words, he told Dirk, were 'a lighthearted compendium of Russian clichés (wolves, samovars etc.)', and were spoken without the intended irony. He had begged Fassbinder to 'keep the playing light, dry and quick', and found it weighty and introspective. All the voices came over 'as if talkies were invented last week'. The crux of the matter, wrote Stoppard, was that 'I wanted to write the script because it was Nabokov's book, and Fassbinder wanted to film the story *despite* its being Nabokov's book'. It was, he decided, 'a turkey, which I believe is American for lemon'.[27]

Despair was shown as the German entry at Cannes on 20 May 1978. At the morning screening Dirk and Tony found the film 'rather slow and at times a bit confusing'. In the evening, after frenetic attention for Dirk and Andréa Ferréol from both the press and the crowds outside the Palais des Festivals, they saw it again with a more responsive audience. There was no sense of a disaster. Yet, time and again in the years to come, Dirk would tell how, as he arrived for the morning showing, he was collared by the tearful lighting cameraman, Michael Ballhaus, and warned to stay away. In the eight months since Dirk had seen the black-and-white rough cut in Paris, Fassbinder had taken his scissors and cut the film to shreds. The warning was correct, Dirk wrote to Wallace Watson: 'The film was a mess. Scenes were transposed, cut, eliminated, and all, or nearly all, of Andrea's performance was ruined. The comedy, and there had been valuable comedy, had gone. So, too, had many other splendid "set pieces". I was pretty shattered. There was still a sort of movie ... but not the movie I had seen last in Paris in black and white.'[28] Professor Watson established from the editor of *Despair* that the version Dirk saw in Paris was the final cut, lacking only some effects, the music and, of course, its colour.[29] It is as if Dirk developed an increasingly active bee in his bonnet about the film, about being associated with what he perceived as a failure; for in *An Orderly Man* Dirk described it, with far greater restraint, as 'A sort of Jacob's coat of a film: a curate's egg somehow. Whatever went wrong, and something did somewhere along the line, it was, however, an incredible, detailed, study of madness by a brilliant director. And that, of course, might have been one of the faults. Madness embarrasses people to watch; it makes them uneasy and uncomfortable.'[30] His own performance was universally applauded. At Cannes, right up until the final afternoon of the festival, it seemed highly likely that he would win the prize for best actor; a flurry of press activity, including a long interview for French television, suggested that it might be in the bag. But, after a three-way tussle with Marcello Mastroianni and Jon Voight, it went in the end to the American. 'I was immensley relieved,' he wrote to Ann Skinner. 'I would have detested a prize in that foul collection of people. And anyway I had'nt got a clean shirt and it's a haul down the hill to Cannes and no one to keep an eye on the house etc.'[31]

Dirk was disappointed, but not surprised. He believed that in *Despair* he had achieved distinction, and as the film made its way without much fanfare into cinemas throughout the world, he found that opinion shared – above all, in America, where Jack Kroll told the readers of *Newsweek*: 'Bogarde is superb; you seldom see such a sustained, moment-by-moment characterization on screen: he finds a feverish wit in Hermann's self-destructing looniness. It's a performance by one of the best movie actors ever, at the peak of his talent.'[32] In the light of opinion such as that, a flop at the box-office did not seem so distressing. A few years before, when the French film magazine *Ecran* ran a long, respectful piece on Dirk, Tony noted in the Diary: 'Lots of recognition but no offers! I'm sure most people think he's besieged with scripts. Still, glory is a compensation & a bit of a drug I suppose.' At about the same time, a twenty-five-year-old pho-tographer from *Vogue* came to Clermont and tried to impress on Dirk how much of a 'legend' he was among the young in Britain, partly because of his 'remoteness' – and not simply in the literal sense. This was gratification indeed. Now, with the exhausting, exciting Fassbinder behind him, no shortage of critical 'glory', and the writing life ever more dominant, would it matter if he never made a film again? On returning from Germany he had written to Dilys Powell – whom he forgave, but never forgot, for saying of his performance in *The Serpent* that, given too little to do, he did far too much – 'I have decided now to give the Movies a rest [. . .] it is not something that I like any more. I *detest* the work, I detest the job, and most of the time I detest the people. I started over thirty years ago . . . and it is not one whit better. The fact that I have been chosen by Resnais, or Visconti, or Fassbinder, helps tremendously . . . of course . . . but, really, when all is said and done, it is what my Father always said. "No job for a man." . . . it isn't.'[33] The door remained ajar, however. After 'all that heavy German Klong Klonk', he had a hankering to do a comedy: 'I'd do a re-make of "Quiet Wedding" even . . . anything that was funny . . . or even quite funny [. . .] But, of course, I'm too old now . . . but you can be funny *and* old surely?'[34] What he categorically did not wish to do was a script he had been sent by Michael Winner: 'Honestly. It'll make a fortune,' Dirk told Ann Skinner. 'They fuck on the first two pages and rape each other on the fifth and sixth and two boys masturbate happily in a hedge on the tenth and eleventh . . . awash with sperm I swam towards the end to find out what I could possibly be playing. He was very nice about it . . . and just said, "Well . . . perhaps next time?" ' A year later Dirk was still waiting and hoping: 'I'm in the market for a comedy and Woodey Allan is my last ambition.'[35]

The *Vogue* photographer had inadvertently paid Dirk the greatest compliment by remarking on his connection with the intelligent young. Not only in Paris, but in London too they had gone in number to see *Death in Venice*, *The Night*

Porter, Providence and now *Despair*. As he approached sixty, he became ever more appreciative of the respect and the company of the two generations junior to himself. His nephew Brock had arrived at Clermont one day in 1975 as an unsettled, unkempt sixteen-year-old, and, after some initial fencing – 'You can put your tent there.' 'Haven't you got a spare room?' – became such a welcome visitor that in the winter of 1977 Dirk paid for him to spend three months learning French at the Berlitz School in Cannes. 'When I turned up the first time, we knew we were family,' Brock remembers. 'It wasn't going to be a short hello. It was going to be a very long goodbye.' His presence in the house was, as the Diary repeatedly recorded, a breath of fresh air; his keenness and aptitude for working on the land was a bonus. 'Brock arrived in full power,' Dirk wrote to Laurence Harbottle as the Berlitz course began, 'and the house is no longer, shall we say?, peaceful – but at least as he pointed out – he has "got us out of our elderly rut!" – Goodness me!'[36] It is clear now that Dirk and Tony were sensitive to the delicate situation caused by having a teenaged boy living with them; so it is the more surprising that Dirk, somewhat clumsily, suggested he assume the role of guardian to Brock. The motives were altruistic – there had recently been a particularly nasty custody battle between Brock's father and mother – but the offer was crisply and wisely rejected by Gareth Van den Bogaerde. Wisely, for everyone's sake. Nevertheless during this period a bond was forged between uncle and nephew which, despite extensive intervals when there was little or no contact, would before all that long prove beyond price to Dirk. Brock, too, benefited from experiencing a way of life which within a few hours could waft him from olive-picking and terrace-mowing to dining at one of the best tables in France and dancing arm-in-arm up the Champs-Elysées with Dirk, Tony and Capucine, 'the most beautiful woman in Paris'.

As the cinema receded and the writing began to occupy more and more of the working time, so Dirk and Tony became inevitably more insular, and so the stimulus of youth became more necessary – in smallish doses. Mark Goodings, who was staying in Cannes with his parents and a friend, recalls being invited with the friend to Clermont to meet Elton John, who had just returned from a ground-breaking tour as the first Western rock star to perform in Russia. The singer had been asked for pre-lunch drinks at 11.30:

This open-top Bentley turns up and there's Elton in a track suit and his terribly nice man-servant, chauffeur, whatever. We're all sitting around, and my friend and I are fascinated by their talk about the Russian trip. So is Tony. After exactly an hour and twenty minutes Dirk gets up and starts whistling. You know that Elton's time is up. Dirk and Tony had gone down to Monoprix and bought the cheapest bottle of champagne they could find – not that they didn't have any in the house, but they weren't going to open a bottle of decent brew. The rest of us have been drinking beers. Elton and his chap have got through half of the champagne when Dirk, whistling away, starts clearing the table.

He goes into the house, empties all the ashtrays, comes back out and says, 'Well, I dare say you'll be rushing off, keen to get back to have your lunch. I know we are. And it's been lovely seeing you.' Poor Elton. He got halfway down the terrace and Dirk said, 'Hang on, you're forgetting something. I bought this specially for you.' And he made them take the other half of the bottle. Off they went with the cheap champagne nestling between Elton's knees as the Bentley disappeared down the drive. And that was the last we saw of him.

'We had a Real Pop Singer,' Dirk reported to Ann Skinner, 'in Elton John who was lovely and funny and very bright indeed, and fascinating about the Moscow Tour ... thats a story.'[37] They also had a real Royal, the forty-two-year-old Princess Alexandra, whom Dirk had met at the Palace in 1968. A great friend of Kenneth More's ex-wife, Billie or 'Bill', the Princess was staying on Cap Ferrat, had read *Postillion* and, according to Dirk, 'longed to talk about it. That was rather pleasing.' So Bill brought her to tea. 'She was in a bit of a fuss and wanted to change from a tee shirt into a long frock for the event, was politely told not to, came and ate a vast amount of squashy shop-cake, many jam tarts, and was utterly adorable, funny and pretty as could be.' She told Dirk and Tony that the house was 'my sort of place', which was no less pleasing. 'What I particularly loved,' Dirk wrote to Norah Smallwood, 'was her sincere concern for Lally! If poor old Lally ever knew that she had been the subject of a very long conversation with a Royal she'd have had a "proper turn" I can tell you ... not to mention Elizabeth who arrives tomorrow and has threatened to curtsey when we meet.'[38]

There were also uninvited and unwelcome visitors – some *ad hoc*, as it were; some, habitual. In the first category were the ultimate dread: the fanatics, one or two of whom tracked down the house. On a Saturday in August a girl from Paris arrived at the bottom of the drive, and delivered a note saying she would stay there until Dirk gave her a smile. She was there for four days. Eventually, while cutting the lawn, he shouted at her and she fled. On their arrival back from shopping in Grasse, there she was again, in the drive. This time Tony did the yelling – 'very politely' – and she left for good. A far more insidious intrusion was that by an obsessive in Bromley, who bombarded Dirk with letters at the rate of about ten a month in the belief that he was communicating with her via coded messages in the newspaper. Laurence Harbottle was called in, and advised that any response of any kind would probably encourage the madness, so, unless she was dangerous – and there were stories in the past of fans threatening acid attacks on the basis of 'If I can't have you, no one else will' – it would be wiser to mark the letters 'return to sender' or throw them away. However, when 'Barmy Bromley' appeared to be on the point of descending on Nice, and therefore ascending to Châteauneuf, action was needed. A lawyer's letter zoomed to Kent, and back came a grateful reply, with an assurance that the only communication in future would be constant thoughts for Dirk's well-being. 'I'm afraid that the moon guides her fairly closely,' reported Laurence Harbottle, slightly apprehensive from her tone that affections might be on the point of transfer to him. Effusive thanks came from Dirk:

> You are a good fellow. Thank you so much for dealing with Balmy Bromley ... there is another one in Herefordshire ... older, and prone to Moon Troubles too; however, she has just written to say that she has left me 15,000 (pounds) in her recent will. And I have'nt written to her either! The world is full of dotty people. Last week, from Bromley, a huge parcle of dead leaves, hazle nuts, holly berries, and moss ... to remind me of the sweet scents of an English Autumn.
>
> Those, apart from Mrs Castle and Mr Wilson,* are precisely the reason I left England![39]

For about two months the guns were silent, then a four-page letter and an essay entitled 'Autumn Thoughts' landed in the box at the bottom of the drive. 'She's at it again!' wrote Dirk. 'Help!'[40] The postal stalking went on for well over a year, and culminated in word of another intended visit; a telegram to 'Barmy Bromley' saying the French police had been alerted to a possible imminent trespass; and an 'astonished' reply. 'I am glad she is astonished,' wrote Laurence Harbottle, 'although unfortunately she needs a doctor rather than threats.'[41] As for Unhinged of Herefordshire: she was last heard of when Cartier told Dirk that 'a client' wished him to choose a watch up to the value of £1,000. Tony wrote to Cartier saying Dirk never accepted anonymous gifts. A few days later she confessed. 'Silly bitch,' noted Tony. She had been an elderly, ailing 'pen-pal' of Dirk's until, as Dorothy Gordon nearly did, she overstepped the boundaries of their friendship. At least, however, she did not turn up. The second category of unwelcome visitor did so, without fail, each January. In their hundreds.

If Dirk's proudest achievement inside Clermont was the three-level drawing-room, outside, it was The Pond. It has to be said that Léon Loschetter, the distinguished architect, had nothing to do with this creation. And it showed. Dirk 'designed' it, and built it himself out of assorted stones, with help from Marc Isoardi and Ahmet, the Tunisian labourer. The result was what Monsieur Loschetter, somewhat disparagingly, calls 'a swimming-pool for ducks, arranged rather badly and a bit sillily'. Dirk could be forgiven a little silliness. After all, the stocking of the pond was an adventure; he bought a plastic bag of goldfish at one franc apiece from Monoprix; Elizabeth brought waterlilies from England; Ulric, roots of 'real English mint' in his sponge-bag. The resulting comings and goings both in and around the water gave hours of untold pleasure:

---

* Baroness Barbara Castle (1910–2002), Labour MP for Blackburn 1945–79; Minister of Transport 1965–8. Baron Wilson (1916–95), Prime Minister 1964–70 (and 1974–6).

Then came the 'people' . . . voles and shrews plopped along the sedge, dragon-flies of every size and colour darted across my pond, water wagtails came, the yellow and the grey, swallows and swifts and once, to my astonishment, a bewildered heron lost on his way to the Camargue. Waterboatmen, water beetles, dragonfly lava, water spiders and mosquito lava multiplied. I bought half a kilo of eels and three carp from the fishmonger. Small green frogs with gold eyes and yellow bellies sang in the mint and sprang from rush to rush with the dexterity of trapeze artists.[42]

He sat entranced before his pond, little realising that the local ecology was being thrown ever so slightly off kilter. The Diary records that on 23 January 1977 no fewer than thirty mating toads were collected from the pond, scooped into a plastic dustbin and carted a mile and a half down the road to a stream. The next day, the same procedure, with about forty; and more were converging. On the very morning that they left for Paris and London to do the promotion for *Providence* and advance publicity for *Postillion*, Dirk and Tony despatched another thirty. It was a Forth Bridge operation. When they returned from their travels, they bought two carp in the hope of keeping down the tadpoles which would teem in their millions during the summer, so that 'we slid and skidded on the squashed bodies of tiny toads who seethed like boiling black rice beneath our feet'. The sex-starved adult toads immediately took a fancy to the carp, but slithered and somersaulted into the water, their passion unrequited. Reluctantly, Dirk decided that the only answer was to fence off his pride and joy. 'So far this season only two pairs have managed to get over the wire,' he wrote in 1979. 'I knew there would be a great many strange changes in my life when I came here to live ten years ago, but lugging dustbins filled with furious mating toads was not one of my expectations.' Nor, to be honest, was being on the hardback and paperback bestseller lists simultaneously.

Snakes and Ladders – formerly 'Enter Daemons', 'Starting with Exits', 'The Honey Waggon', and even at one point 'An Ass in the Mirror'* – was published in October 1978. Its progress had been like that of a racing-car: periods of fast and furious activity alternating with stasis. After sending Sally Betts the final chapter, he wrote to Norah Smallwood: 'A sudden fear hits me. I wonder if, perhaps, the book is too "personal"? Kate, Judy, St John, Nan . . . is it too much of an ego trip? Is it anybodies business but mine? . . . I who have spent the years keeping out of things? I shall need honest, considered, advice. But it nags and nags now that it is all finished.'[43] He sketched two charming endpaper illustrations, one of 44 Chester Row and Cliff the cat, the other of Clermont. The dedication was

---

* Dirk had found a quotation from Georg Lichtenberg (1742–99): 'Books are mirrors and if an ass peers in, you can't expect an apostle to look out.' The title was rejected because it was felt to be either too self-deprecating or disingenuous.

to Elizabeth and her husband George, who had contributed vastly to Dirk's and Tony's peace of mind by looking after Clermont and the dogs – and, in George's case, the trees – sometimes for months at a stretch, when a film or promotion called. The 'continuation of my ego trip' was, Dirk, explained, 'an endeavour to portray just a few of the people who have helped me to become whatever sort of an actor I may be. Living their own lives, they are also my life.'[44] It was also, as he stated in an early letter to Norah Smallwood, an attempt to 'try and Investigate my theory of Acting . . . to show, if I can, what the loss of privacy and annonimity meant to me and how much pain it caused. To re-call my Father and Elizabeth and Forwood as often as I can . . . because they were always, and thank goodness in two instances still are, the keel to my boat.'[45] Tony was in charge of the index and occupied by some margin its longest entry, over that of Visconti. And yet his presence in the book is ambivalent – the more so because of the use of his surname only. He seems to hover eternally in the doorway, seldom stepping into the light and never the limelight. It was with the publication of this second volume that reviewers and readers alike began to speculate on the precise role of E. L. L. Forwood, who is thanked for his 'care and patience' with the indexing, and credited with the colour portrait on the back of the jacket. The single image of him is minute, in a group with Dirk, Rex Harrison, Kay Kendall and Gladys Cooper's dog June, during the Long Island Christmas in 1956. Why is he treated almost like a hanger-on? Even a handyman, a jobbing gardener? As the notices began to appear, the most frequently used adjective in describing Dirk the author was 'reticent'.

Revelling in the success of *Postillion*, Chatto had ordered an initial print-run of 15,000 copies for the new book, and Rosalind Bell arranged a strenuous programme for its launching. Signing-sessions in Bristol, Birmingham, Oxford, Cambridge; radio, television and newspaper interviews from breakfast to cocktails – it was the literary equivalent of 'Total Exposure'. In Birmingham, after inscribing *Snakes* for a large and friendly throng, he signed another hundred while at the same time giving four interviews. The crowd that greeted him at Heffers in Cambridge was thought to be 'a bit pompous' and relatively thin; nevertheless 400 copies were taken away bearing Dirk's confident signature. There was one tricky moment, at Harrods: 'Stuck half way between Soft Furnishings and the Record Department I did, at times, feel that I should have had a lable in my lapel.' It was there that a woman made a remark he never forgot: 'My God! How disgusting. Selling himself in public.' 'Well I was, after all . . . and jolly glad! No one would have bought her. At auction even. Or anything, I venture to guess, which she had to offer.'[46] In two months that single store would sell nearly a thousand copies. Norah Smallwood – now known to him as 'Madame Petitbois' – threw a publication-day party at the Chatto office, where the guestlist was so full of important people whom he and Tony had never met before that they began to feel he really *was* beginning to be taken seriously as a writer; and when John Carey, the Oxford don and principal book reviewer on *The Sunday Times*, gave

Snakes and Ladders his exclusive attention, Dirk was at once humbled and thrilled: 'His prospects as a writer look rosy,' said Professor Carey. 'His first volume of autobiography ... was a triumph: so is this. Quite apart from his startling visual gifts, he has gained, from years of acting and scriptwriting, an infallible ear. Every dialogue, every voice, rings true. The book fairly yammers with life; and when you look up from the pages you're surprised to find how quiet it has gone.'[47]

The most penetrating notices came from Alexander Walker, both on radio and in print. 'A sad book,' he told Sheridan Morley on Radio Four's *Kaleidoscope*, 'and also a reticent book. I think he stands somewhat back from the edge of truth ... because I really don't think that Dirk Bogarde is at all happy with having been an actor [...] the book shows a certain sense of a current self-disgust at the worthless roles'. Walker was most interested in the way that the second volume picked up the image of the tortoise, George, who is lost at the beginning of *Postillion* and later found in a hole, eaten out of its shell by ants. Dirk, said the critic, was continuously trying to go to ground, but having to come out into the open air and exercise his profession as an actor, thus risking being devoured by insects in human form, such as producers and the press. Walker detected an element of snobbery and a 'fatal attachment' to the good things of life, as well as a sense of displacement, through not being truly an Englishman. Finally, he regretted that in the extensive accounts of working with Visconti, Dirk did not even mention Helmut Berger by name. Noël Coward's commandments not to go into the cinema or to compromise had been broken, and Walker felt sure that Coward would have advised Dirk to be generous in writing about a younger talent: 'But he might not have been heeded this time, either.'[48]

Much to Dirk's annoyance, Kenneth More's autobiography, *More or Less*, was published at the same time. Inevitably, a number of reviewers placed them together. For B. A. Young in *The Financial Times*, More wrote 'as if he were chatting to you at the north end of the bar at the Garrick Club' – which he often did; Dirk, on the other hand, 'an intensely private man', had produced 'a work of conscious art', containing 'so much pseudo-verbatim dialogue that it often takes on an appearance of fiction in which the characters have real names'.[49] Hilary Spurling, in *The Observer*, felt that More was wise to settle for more amusement and 'a less ambitious prose style'.[50] Within a fortnight Dirk was having the last laugh: not only was *Snakes and Ladders* at third place in the bestsellers and *More or Less* at eleventh; in addition, *Postillion* was simultaneously in the top ten paperbacks, in the company of Richard Adams's first two books, *Watership Down* and *The Plague Dogs*, and of *Jaws 2* and *Grease*.

Postillion's history had been eventful. About 27,000 copies were sold in its first three impressions, and orders for the Triad paperback had reached 60,000 before publication. In France, it was translated under the attractive title of *Une enfance rêvée*, and praised by, among others, *Le Monde*, which decreed it 'une belle "composition" de Bogarde', offered with that chill modesty – *pudeur glacée* – to

which we have become accustomed from his other roles.[51] Alas, the public was
not convinced. To the chagrin of his publishers, Alta, Dirk declined to go to Paris
to appear on the influential and intellectual television programme *Apostrophe*, in
which the discussion was invariably conducted in 'out-of-my-depth French'; the
result was a 'three-page telegram of fury and rage from Madame Messager saying
that I have ruined her "house" and that she intends to send the remaining unsold
copies of the book (4,000) to my "villa" next week. And revoke all my rights in
the Contract.' It was all 'hateful ... and hysterical ... and not a bit good for
Womens Liberation which I warmly supported up until lunch time yesterday!'[52]
The United States also, and more predictably, had been indifferent to *Postillion*.
The astute John Knowler explained to Dirk that Americans liked stories by film
stars to be full either of funny anecdote, as in David Niven; or of trauma and
scandal, viz. Brooke Hayward, Liv Ullmann, Vivien Leigh. Holt, Rinehart had
published Dirk's book precisely because it was not like that. To make a lot of
money, he said, you have to go on the road and dish the dirt, invented if necessary.
Dirk, who was frank but private and wrote like a gentleman about the stars he
had known, would have to be content with a respected and limited reputation
as a writer.[53] Holt were happy to take *Snakes and Ladders* on the same modest
terms as its predecessor.

In Britain, by the end of publication month, 25,000 copies of *Snakes* were
sold. Dirk was justifying the confidence of his London publishers, who had given
him an advance of £7,500 – five times larger than that for *Postillion* – against a
royalty of ten per cent for the first 3,000 copies, twelve and a half per cent on
the next 17,000, and fifteen per cent on further sales. The hardback sales of about
27,000 for *Postillion* were rapidly supplemented by 65,000 copies in paperback –
one of which brought an unexpected and disconcerting reaction. Since initial
publication there had been silence from those quarters where one might have
expected trouble, especially Glasgow. The only minor agitation came when a
London doctor and bibliophile wrote to Chatto, suggesting a change of title
because he had in his collection a volume of verse by Patricia Beer called *The
Postillion Was Struck by Lightning*; a second correspondent, who went further by
accusing Dirk of plagiarism – and thereby displayed his or her ignorance, because
there is no copyright in a title – was slapped down by John Charlton, who
explained that the inspiration had been an early *Baedeker*. Now, more than a year
and a half later, a letter from a firm of solicitors in Oxfordshire arrived at
Clermont, seeking satisfaction on behalf of one Mary Elizabeth Rolls. Who? It
transpired that this was the married name of 'Nurse Hennessy', who had delivered
Gareth at Highfield Avenue in July 1933, and who 'crackled like a twig fire and
was less friendly'.[54] The solicitors accused Dirk of painting her as a hard-drinking,
hard-swearing Irishwoman who treated the birth with callous indifference and
was prepared not merely to engage in, but also to encourage, unhygienic activities
at, or shortly after, the birth. They allowed for the fact that the three contentious
pages purported to be a recollection of a time when the author was twelve, and,

therefore, a little licence might be appropriate; but what Dirk had written was a gross distortion and entirely without foundation. Miss Hennessey – the correct spelling of her maiden name – was now seventy-seven and her long, distinguished career stretched back to well before Gareth's birth. Furthermore they were given to understand that, actually, Dirk had been very fond of her. In their dreams. Nevertheless, although he suspected the whole thing was a belated 'try-on', Dirk realised he had been a clot to use, albeit imprecisely, the nurse's real name; so a damage-limitation exercise swung into action. He wrote to Mrs Rolls, assuring her that he had had no intention of 'reflecting on' her professional skill and expressing his deep concern that she had been caused distress: 'I had hoped that, within the context of an unhappy boy's point of view, it was clear that he was seeing all grown-ups at that time through his own focus of distress.' He was careful to explain but not to apologise. For six months letters drifted between Oxfordshire, Laurence Harbottle's office and Clermont until, finally, the aggrieved ex-nurse accepted £1,000 and £200 costs. No amendment was made to the text in subsequent editions of the book. Lally told Elizabeth that, if anything, the portrait Dirk had painted was too kind. It was a warning, however; as Dirk observed to Norah Smallwood, 'I must be more careful in future.'[55] Even in a novel.

In the interval from completion to publication of *Snakes and Ladders*, Dirk, with the bit between his teeth, had worked on two more ideas for books. The first was an edited version of his correspondence with Dorothy Gordon, which, along with the Diary, had been a valuable source for the second volume of memoirs; he acknowledged as much – without naming the recipient and with an inaccurate date – at the front of *Snakes*. He estimated that there were about 650 letters, plus 200 postcards. He would edit them '*vastly*'; cut all 'the mushier bits',

> and there were quite a lot, to my astonishment, and sometimes embarrassment [...] I'd use her as a sort of 'hook' for a set of essays and so on ... events and thoughts ... points of views ... morals and manners [...] We wrote about books, music, food (a lot about food since she could almost no longer eat anything at all ...) love, death and each other. So much about each other. God! But I also told her every detail of the things I was doing, people I was meeting, places I went to, music I heard, and things like Viv Leighs funeral and so on ... many of which I have, until recently, quite forgotten.[56]

Norah Smallwood was excited at the prospect: what a searchlight it would bring to bear on Dirk, she said – perhaps rashly. For a while the idea 'seethed about' in his head 'like a simmering casserole'. He had a provisional title, 'Postscript'.[57] But there was another ingredient in the pot. A novel, based on his time in Java, with the working title 'Never Look Down'. It is hard to see how, during those hot summer months, Dirk had the time to look up. He lurched between the two, deciding one day that he was over-writing the fiction; the next, that the letters were too full of whimsy and boring. Yet, shortly before publication of *Snakes*, he sent Sally Betts the letters and the first three chapters of the fiction, some 37,000 words.

Dirk abandoned the idea of publishing the letters about a year after he had told Norah Smallwood, 'that tiresome fellow L-M with his diaries has made it impossible for anyone following him to do as well' – a remark which amused James Lees-Milne enough for him to include it in his journal and in his collected diaries for 1975–8, adding: 'Flattering from him; but nonsense of course, for there is no artistry in my diaries. They were just a day-to-day jumble of thoughts and recorded events.'[58] Dirk had seen *A Particular Friendship* – the latest title, after that phrase's occasional appearance in the letters – as one to be read at odd moments, 'a bed-book', one that was not over-long. However, by the spring of 1979 it was out of contention as his next publication. So too, for a while, was the novel, which, as the chapters arrived at Chatto, was not being received as positively as his previous two books. 'Sadly it took me longer to realise than it took clever you, that it was'nt really very good,' he told Norah Smallwood.[59] So he put aside his story about a young Army captain, serial number 269237, who has spent much of the war interpreting reconnaissance photographs on attachment to the Air Force, and who is despatched as a Draft of One to a dangerously unsettled island in the Java Sea, where he becomes ADC to a general with a peculiar retinue, and falls in love with a Eurasian ... There was also a character who had latched on to the general, with more than a passing likeness to 'the Petit woman' of the Doulton diaries. 'I have shoved Miss Foto into a drawer with her crowd,' Dirk told Norah Smallwood. 'They can stay there for a while.' He believed he had become 'most dreadfully carried away in creative euphoria or whatever it is. Parts of it are frightfully good I think. Parts. [...] Marvellous experience for me ... after all I am still trying to teach myself how to write. Nothing has been lost except perhaps a possible book for you.'[60] To the Diary Tony confided: 'I don't really think Norah understands about men & war, & the effect of war on men, & even on women. And John [Charlton] might be too young to understand for that matter.' With little further reference to the letters, except as source material, Dirk decided he should 'stick to the Autobio Bit ... a little longer. Then cut my teeth on something less grand than a twelve-hander Novel. I am in a difficult position really because of the modest success of the other two. *First* two. A first Novel is a brute. And they will all wait for me to fail at my first attempt. Rather as if I HAD gone and done my ruddy "Hamlet" for Larry O at Chichester. So I must take extra care and not just "rush at things".' Volume three was already 'coiling about in my head', and would bring his life up to the shooting in Berlin of *Despair*: 'that ought to be quite amusing. Me and the youthful Marxist-Red Brigade Set all getting on splendidly together!'[61] In the meantime he might turn the fiction into a film script: it was, after all, alive with dialogue.

As the ideas swirled in his head, he could be excused a certain amount of distraction. Daisy the Boxer, part of the household since before their first Christmas at Clermont, had contracted cancer and become, very suddenly, very ill. She was put to sleep by the vet while Tony held her in his arms. 'We spent a pretty glum day I fear,' Dirk told his Needlewoman. 'T tremendously brave and v. quiet. I sort of in an ache [. . .] Part of the fabric of ones life here. Idiotic to mourn a dog. However one mourns for oneself really.'[62] In truth, both he and Tony were close to tears all day. Labo, still going reasonably strong and ever-independent despite the rickety leg, was without company for just two months. Sixteen hundred francs worth of Phoebus, a six-week-old Boxer puppy, arrived one Sunday afternoon and was renamed Bendrose – Bendo for short. 'I expect I'll have to train it & make it "my" dog,' Tony ruminated. 'But D will feed it.' The next few weeks were the mayhem familiar to all sensitive puppy-owners. No outside kennel for Bendo; he slept beside his joint-master's bed in a cardboard box, itself inside a protective cage, and insulated with two old cashmere cardigans. 'My bedroom floorboards don't look too good,' Tony noted after three vigorously disturbed nights. 'The house is rent with shrieks and wails and deep howls,' reported Dirk; 'both ends of the beast function splendidly all over everything. "A change of diet" we say cheerfully, hearts sinking with each lugged bucket of bleach and hot water and rags . . . "New surroundings of course" we say brightly . . . "It'll soon settle down." When? Hardly any sleep at nights . . . I should have bought a bloody Lion.'[63] It was enough to drive a man back to his office and fish a typescript out of a drawer – perhaps the one about Miss Dora Foto and 'her crowd'?

Twenty-one

'Would you call camouflage deceit, lying,
or merely a means of survival?'

The adventures of Captain Benjamin Andrew Rooke, APIS, on an unnamed island 400 miles south-east of Singapore and 150 miles north of Java were, Dirk said, based on one real fact: the attempt by the British and Indian armies to 'hold the ring' in the crumbling Dutch Empire of South-East Asia, and their suffering heavy casualties while doing so. The island, the inhabitants, the Division – '95 Ind. Div.' – and its personnel were 'all entirely imaginary and exist, or existed, only in my mind'.¹ Once again, the title underwent serial change. 'Never Look Down' became 'Come of Age'. Consideration was given to 'A Bamboo Cage' and to 'A Touch of the Sun', 'The Freedom Sign' and 'The Scoundrel Dawn' – all taken from the text. A John Charlton suggestion, 'Jungle Green', which Dirk agreed was 'snappy and commercial', received short shrift precisely for that reason; 'it does sound to me rather like an Army Manual ... and is a sight too "war-like" I think. After all, the book, if book it is, is not about a war. It's about the people who are in a war. A comedy of manners rather than a "saga of people in a war-torn Island, awash with blood, sweat and tears ... and sex!" Oh dear. I can see the blurb now.'² 'Jungle Green' reminded him of films he had managed to evade in the fifties, such as 'The Red Berets' and 'Operation Bamboo'. 'Whatever Title we finally use I do want it to reflect on the very modest start I have made with the other titles, and styles. I dont want, above all things, a terrible "Dirk Bogarde's FIRST BREATHTAKING novel!" '³

For a while the strongest contender was 'Batik', which emerged from a discussion between Dirk and Tony on the day the typescript was completed. The reference to a process of printing on cloth, where wax is used for masking off the area to be left untouched, was apt and subtle enough to qualify for a volume of Dirk's non-fiction. Eventually it was his own proposal, *A Gentle Occupation*, that won the day. 'I always hoped that my particular war would be a gentle occupation,' says Major Geoffrey Nettles, Rooke's smug, predatory, fellow officer. 'Vain hope. It never is.'⁴ Dirk contended, rightly, that the title 'has a bit of style to it, is wonderfully ambiguous, and has a bitter connotation':

It can, on the one hand, apply to the Japanese Occupation, which was, to start with, gentle … it can apply to Miss Foto's whoring … her intriguing and general use of her wiles and sex … another Gentle Occupation … or Nettles and Rooke searching her out, so to speak, a sort of 'spy catch spy' business done in quiet serenity … another Gentle Occupation … it can equally apply to the supposed Gentle Occupation of the British Forces who thought that their war had ended four weeks before, and that they were off to a Treasure Island where all they had to do was herd the wretched Internees home and sit in the sun with a glass of gin and tonic. I think it can apply to all kinds of things in the 'book' …[5]

By the time the contract was signed – for £15,000 – the book was already at proof stage. One afternoon, while Tony was out in search of the London newspapers and Dirk was on the terrace pulling up the last of the summer bedding plants, a voice boomed almost in his ear: 'Hunted you down!' There stood a large, white-haired man in glasses, with his daughter and with a fair number of close relatives lurking in their car at the bottom of the drive. Didn't Dirk remember him? 'I'm Kit Rook.' In letters written on the same day Dirk told Norah Smallwood that he had no idea who the chap was, but apparently they had been at Catterick together in 1942; and John Charlton, that he and Rook had last met in 1946. Not impossible, of course, but odd just the same. 'I was extremely impolite, I confess,' he told Charlton, '… and sent them away coldly.' Dirk was left, 'rocked with shock'. Whether this was because part of a buried past had stirred, or because of any implications for his novel, we shall never know. In any case, the intrusion was enough to rattle Dirk. He seized his proofs and immediately changed the first name of his protagonist from Christian and 'Kit' to Benjamin and 'Ben', telling Charlton: 'I dare'nt have another Nurse Hennessy on our hands.'[6] At least it was a Rook who had so suddenly materialised and not a Nettles – an altogether more unpalatable piece of work.

That said, it is Nettles who is given many of the best and most pertinent lines in the novel. Consolidating one's position is crucial, the Major tells Rooke.

After that we come to camouflage. A *sort* of lie I suppose, don't you? Would you call camouflage deceit, lying, or merely a means of survival? You will realize, I know, that we are still in a war, and sometimes you have to fight dirty, as they say, like our friends across the perimeter hacking us all to bits in the name of Freedom. If the word lie really distresses you, Rooke, and your angelic conscience, why not soothe yourself with the word improvise?[7]

It is worth bearing in mind, when reading the above passage, that Dirk told Norah Smallwood: 'I […] work out *my* philosophy of life through *other* peoples voices.'[8]

Improvisation was much needed for the next bout of 'Total Exposure', for which the itinerary alone was 'mind-boggling'. 'Now and again, on the crammed schedule, I would notice a small bracketed "SC" which, I was informed, stood for "Shirt Change"; and that was the only break one got [...] Publishing and the cinema were not so very far apart, after all. In both, one had to sell the product hard.'[9] Dirk was honoured at the 477th Luncheon given by the redoubtable Christina Foyle, whose first guest speakers in the thirties had included Haile Selassie, Bernard Shaw and Oswald Mosley. Introduced wittily by the composer and lyricist Vivian Ellis, Dirk explained in five off-the-cuff minutes how his life had been 'a series of flukes' and how his own gentle occupations were writing – 'I always wrote my own plays and my own parts because I did not think anyone else could do it as well' – and gardening, which at 500 metres, on terraced land and in boulder-strewn limestone soil, was 'rather hazardous'. Apart from the blazing heat of summer and the bitter cold of winter, 'tractors and things fall on me' and he was reminded of some doggerel by Nancy Mitford:

> The kiss of the wind for lumbago,
> The thrust of a thorn for mirth,
> You are nearer to death in a garden
> Than anywhere else on earth.

He told the story, after a fashion, of 'Mrs X' in Connecticut and of the chain of circumstances which had led to Norah Smallwood advising him most recently to take a break from autobiography. 'I said "I do not know how to write a novel." She said "All you need for a novel, dear, is a beginning a middle and an end. Try." '[10] Which was why the dedication of *A Gentle Occupation* read: 'This book is for Norah Smallwood, who said, "Try ..."'. The visit to London, which included another siege at Hatchards and another 600 copies signed and sold, was besmirched when the diarist of the *Daily Express,* 'William Hickey', reported the lunch under the heading, 'Dirk launches his latest book, and Tony comes down from the hills for the occasion'. Tony, described as a 'ram-rod backed ex-Royal Artillery officer', had sensibly told Mr Hickey's lackey that he was not going to talk about his private life, prompting the latter to muse about Dirk's lot: 'What with an acre of Paradise, Tony dancing attendance, and his books a success every time, is it not Somerset Maugham revisited?'[11] In their own Diary the next day Tony recorded how the piece virtually stated that he and Dirk were lovers, and that it was 'quite foul and slimey, but just within the bounds of being actionable I think'. They were both upset, he added, 'but one must not give in to that sort of hurt'. Fortunately they had little time to brood before Dirk was on his feet at a second literary lunch, organised by Blackwells in Oxford, where he gave a slightly modified version of the successful Foyle's talk. It was almost a case of 'If it's Tuesday, it must be ...', because on the Saturday Dirk and Tony flew to Amsterdam, where the novel was published simultaneously. Here, the reception was of a different order. First, he did his bookshop duty, and was approached by several people he had known in Java but had now forgotten: 'All I could do,' he wrote a few days later, 'was ask gently, "Who were you?" and "Where?" ... some were grannies ... and some grandpappas ... it made one feel pretty ancient.' More sticky were the newspaper and television interviews: 'The book there is considered very hot. Politically that is. I was a bit thrown by that. Had to deal with all aspects of the Dutch Press from the very far Right to the Communists ... vocal and beligerant indeed. Salutary.' He was challenged about his use of the word 'terrorist' when, some felt, 'freedom fighter' was the correct term for those who bombed and who mutilated, as well as simply splattering 'Merdeka!' in red paint on every available prominent surface.

Well before publication, orders for *A Gentle Occupation* stood at about eleven thousand, far above the norm for a first novel. More important to Dirk as he returned, exhausted, to Clermont were the notices. 'So he can write novels, too,' began Victoria Glendinning in *The Sunday Times*, identifying the real subject of Dirk's 'gently malicious' book as survival – the price of which, 'though it may have something to do with avarice or snobbery, is principally a matter of sex. "We all suffer from it in one way or another; whatever our gender," says elegant Major Nettles, a charming, cynical-sentimental creation who talks like Noël Coward.' Mrs Glendinning said the book's only real weakness was 'an enthusiastic repetitiveness. This may be all too true to life, but it slows up art. It is as if Mr Bogarde, who has experience of practically every branch of film-making, had missed out on the cutting-room. Nevertheless, don't wait until "A Gentle Occupation" is the book of the film before reading it.'[12] Tim Heald, in the weekly magazine *Now!*, said that Dirk's ironic title belied gruesome killings, 'rape and seduction, intrigue, duplicity, love, loyalty, blood. Indeed all human life is here. It is not only a skilful, sensitive picture of men and women somehow making do under almost intolerable circumstances. It is also an adventure story full of excitement and suspense. It succeeds, in other words, on two levels – as a "literary novel" and as a thriller.'[13] Stephen Glover, in *The Daily Telegraph*, while finding fault with the 'sudden jumps of sequence' and the 'multiplicity of adjectives which tend to cancel each other out', was in awe of the 'remarkable' dialogue and concluded that Dirk had 'triumphed in the primary task of a novelist – to create another, credible world.'[14]

There was also a private appreciation which Dirk took just as seriously. Jack Jones had renewed a spasmodic correspondence: the letter from Dirk quoted above, about his experiences in Amsterdam, was sent to Suffolk. Jack's memory of the 1945–6 letters from Europe and Java was that Dirk's writing was truly *him*, 'unbeholden to any *one* influence'; after reading *A Gentle Occupation* for the second time in a fortnight, the only influence which Jack had detected – if it could be called an influence – was that Dirk had 'lived the same sort of life, and come to the same sort of post-War outlook as Simon Raven in his ten *Alms for Oblivion* books'. Jack was able to pick out a good few of Dirk's principal characters, 'amalgamated as some of them are, and all mixed in the DvdB medium of an uncomfortably discerning eye for character and manners'. It was, said the sixty-four-year-old Jack, 'a bloody good book' by 'a bloody good writer' – and he hoped that it was from him that Dirk had picked up the absurd Victorian expression, 'an elegant sufficiency'. Back came a card from Clermont, thanking Jack for his 'very generous' letter: 'I have never read Raven! So you'll have to think again about that'. Much had changed in thirty-five years, but not Dirk's sensitivity.

Dirk's fifty-ninth birthday fell on a Friday. The next evening his mother died of heart failure at her 'hotel' in Sussex. It was a release. The vibrant, zestful, laughing, life-enhancing Little Madge had long since taken her last applause, and her latent resentment at once being denied the chance to shine had multiplied a hundredfold as she dwindled in widowhood and dependency. Dirk would write, later and bluntly, about the wonderful wife and mother who ended her days 'as pissed as a fiddler's bitch'.[15] More immediately he told Norah Smallwood:

> I was glad, indeed, of the London Trip, for the main reason that I got down to see her that Sunday before I started 'work'.
>
> As I told you, I think, she looked so astonishingly beautiful and vivid that I knew, in a strange inner way, that she was actually dying.
>
> I knew that she had made a supreme effort for me ... and was exhausted when I left. I knew, driving away from the pleasant house, that I would never see her again ... and I am certain that she knew it also. However her happiness was that I was happy launching my book ... that I was busy and working ... she knew, more or less, about the reviews, and had, she said, started to read the thing herself ... but when I left, on the Sunday ... she was so proud that I had been on the Television and that the Telegraph had given me a cover.
>
> Very important factors to an actress-mother!
>
> So the week had it's double burden in a way ... I did my job and she got on with hers, and did it very neatly after supper, alone.[16]

He also wrote in deeply moving terms to Elizabeth, saying that without her constant care and love he could not imagine what their mother's life would have been. He urged her not to feel any guilt: 'You did everything, and more, that was possible, not just in these last wretched days, but in all the weary years of trailing about getting her the little things which made her happy, taking her out, having her to the house ... a million things which I did not do.' To him, and to Gareth, it had often seemed that she and her husband George were left to 'carry the can'. Margaret, he hoped, was now with Ulric: 'It is, I know, something she longed for ... this she said often enough. She missed him dreadfully.' In *An Orderly Man* Dirk would write: 'When the two great tent-poles fall, which have, for so long, supported the fabric above the circus of one's life, the guy-ropes fly away, the canvas billows down, and there is nothing left to do but crawl out from

under, and go on one's way alone. "A Show For All The Family!" is over.'[17] The
funeral was to be the following Thursday, Easter week. This was one occasion
when Elizabeth and George would not be able to look after the house and dogs,
so he and Tony tried to book the quickest possible return flight. There was
nothing, even via Paris, Brussels, Geneva or Zurich. They gave up, Dirk at once
relieved and guilty. Elizabeth reported on the evening after the funeral that much
had gone wrong: the traffic was so appalling that Gareth only just made it in
time; Lally could not find the way; and the parson lost his voice. Maybe, they
thought, 'Little Madge' was 'busy stirring it up'. And why not? There had been
little gaiety in her life for many years. Loneliness can be the cruellest state,
particularly for someone who has known what it is like to be 'always applauded'.

For her elder son, the applause was a quieter but more constant affair than it
had been during the fifties and sixties. He had tapped into a young audience
with 'difficult' cinema. Why, asked Léon Loschetter, had he made *The Night
Porter*? 'The job of an actor is to make people uneasy,' Dirk replied. 'Then they
start to think.'[18] The trouble was that the chances to do so at a level which could
satisfy Dirk himself were almost non-existent; and, anyway, he was fed up with
the strains and stresses, the early calls and – as he told a visiting television team
from New York – a culture where 'the prime consideration is the budget, the
running time, the cost, the cutting time [and] whether they will understand it
in Milwaukee. The hell with whether you acted or whether the movie tore your
guts out. That is what I think is so appalling, and I don't want to be in it – and
I am not in it any more.'[19] He had not been forgotten, however. After a long
silence, Losey called: about a script by Dennis Potter, which he thought might
interest Dirk, Alec Guinness and Tom Conti. It was on its way. Then Guinness
called, worried because although it was brilliant he did not altogether understand
it. Dirk replied that he had *never* understood any script sent him by either Losey
or Resnais but that it all came clear in the end. The script arrived. Dirk did not
like it. Guinness was relieved. Joe was 'disappointed', but said he might try for a
Graham Greene story which they could all do. At which point a multi-millionaire
called Jeffrey Pike offered to finance a film of Dirk's choice to the tune of $5
million. Dirk put him in touch with Losey. Graham Greene's new novel, *Dr
Fischer of Geneva*, might be just the thing to perk everyone up. Talks went on for
more than a year, but it never happened – at least, not on the big screen and not
with those originally interested. Dirk could have done with the money, but he and
Tony were managing, thanks to Aubert's and Troxler's husbandry of Labofilms in
Switzerland. He turned down a huge fee for a commercial, as much because it
would have involved a flight to Australia as for reasons of integrity. In fact the
only formal involvement with the film world for two years was his presentation
of the 1980 Palme d'Or at Cannes to Akira Kurosawa, who shared the prize with
an absent Bob Fosse. And the books, while never earning a fortune, kept both
the wolf from the door and the toads – some of them – from the pond. There
was something else. 'It is an astonishing thing to me,' he told Norah Smallwood,

'to find that I am really not a bit happy unless I am writing.'[20]

At the moment he typed those words *A Gentle Occupation* was with his publishers and he had two more books on the go – neither of them the Dorothy Gordon letters. A third volume of autobiography, provisionally entitled *An Orderly Man*, had been jockeying for Dirk's attention with a second novel, 'Thunder at a Picnic', and the fiction was winning. He had promised 'a smallish book ... set today. No film, no theater. People behaving. My heroin, or is that the spelling for a drug? is to be called Cuckoo. Since she is seventy it will be less objectionable ... and she is'nt a cuckoo. Really. Skin under skin. Like an onion and a catalyst to peel them away after so many years ...'.[21] There was much stumbling on the way. At Christmas, 'My Muse is pissed of: and sulks in the shadows. No sign of her coming out to play again until she is certain that I am there to stay.'[22] She did come out to play, and a year to the day after Dirk typed 'Chapter One', the last chapters of 'Thunder at a Picnic' arrived at Chatto. Dirk had harboured fewer doubts than usual over the title, which he took from W. H. Auden – 'Death is the sound of distant thunder at a picnic' – and gave to a character, not unlike Tony, to speak in a scene at the end of the book. But when, at the first stage of editing, the scene was cut, the thinking caps went on at Clermont and at William IV Street. 'A Walk in the Garden' was considered; so, too, was 'Candle in the Wind' – possibly as a result of a second visit to Clermont by Elton John, who had brought with him a personal stereo and a number of tapes, and, just to be on the safe side, a bottle of Crystal champagne. 'Lifelines', a John Charlton suggestion, was 'loathed' by his colleagues – 'I sort of do see why now,' wrote Dirk, 'all those Phone In Shows.'[23] Finally it became a toss-up between 'The Big Time' and a title that had come to Dirk after Rosalind Bowlby* had mentioned a line from Robert Browning's 'A Serenade at the Villa': 'When the garden-voices fail'. *Voices in the Garden* it was. Chatto offered the same advance – £15,000 – as they had for *A Gentle Occupation*; Dirk accepted, but it was a mark of his growing confidence as an author that he took issue with the contract and refused to sign an option clause relating to a two-book deal. Some 35,000 copies of '*AGO*' had been sold in Britain, and it was being warmly received in the United States, where – after some ill-feeling and lack of communication with Holt, Rinehart – he was now in the prestigious hands of Alfred Knopf; the arrival at Labofilms of a £13,000 royalty cheque was a pleasant surprise. His success was undoubted and yet, as he became wiser to the ways of publishing in an ever more competitive climate, an air of impermanence began to hang over the arrangement with Chatto, which was now based fundamentally on loyalty to Norah Smallwood, his 'discoverer'. A strong enough foundation, one would think, in an environment where the author–publisher relationship

---

* Rosalind Bell was married in 1979 to Nicholas Bowlby, who became known to Dirk and Tony first as 'Lungs' because of an operation two years earlier on a collapsed lung, then as 'Norman'; she would soon be 'Brenda'.

was far more about trust and satisfaction than about money. But there were signs in private correspondence that Dirk was quite prepared to jump ship if Chatto were unhappy about his new novel, and that he was irritated at some of the minutiae of the editing process. 'No! Over my dead body!' he wrote against a suggested deletion among five pages of editorial queries from John Charlton. And for the first time, there was open speculation about what would happen at Chatto when Norah Smallwood retired; she was, after all, seventy and increasingly arthritic. One intimate told Dirk and Tony that on her departure the firm would 'collapse like a house of cards'.

For the moment Dirk still had his Needlewoman Number Two, who had once told him to 'write from your heart and hurt the reader in his'.[24] She declared *Voices in the Garden* 'a triumph'. More important to him, however, was the opinion of Nicholas and Rosalind Bowlby, to whom he and Tony had become strongly attached. Unbeknown to her employer, who was already a little jealous of the growing friendship, Rosalind Bowlby had secretly received a copy of the typescript. Her enthusiasm, and that of her husband, bucked Dirk greatly, Tony recorded, 'as they are young and it means they approve of his young characters'. Those young characters were a golden youth, Marcus, and his girlfriend Leni, who enter the lives of a seventy-year-old military historian, Sir Charles (Archie) Peverill, and his wife Cuckoo, a 'Raffish old girl who once knew the Murphys, the Fitzgeralds and danced a tango in a restaurant with Isadora Duncan . . . faded glamour'.[25] This relic of the Riviera's glory days – the epoch which Tony had known at first hand – was modelled by Dirk on Daphne Fielding and Lady Diana Cooper. It was a novel about illusion, self-delusion and deception, written with a serious intent. Under the surface of Dirk's romance was 'a cry of despair for the things we are losing', a lament for past values, decency, *manners*. It was also about class, lost love and – necessarily – sex. While staying at Clermont, 'Madame Petitbois' had wondered aloud whether Dirk's treatment of this last, awkward, subject might perhaps be 'a "little more overt" . . . not for Chatto, God forbid! but for the booksellers'. Dirk saw her point: the sex, especially the homosexual variety, in *A Gentle Occupation* had been ever present between the lines, but pretty much absent on the page. So he 'made a stab at it. Anyway . . . it amused me . . . one hopes it will amuse a reader. Or a Bookseller!'[26] And so, breasts which 'could have suckled Romulus and Remus' were blessed with nipples that pointed 'hard at the sky like tiny Howitzers':

> With a sudden move which took him completely by surprise she knelt across his body and straddled him, trapping his thighs between her massive ones, crushing them together tightly.
>   'Oh Christ!' he gasped and tried to sit up again, but was pressed firmly backwards by the superior weight of her body which she folded over him, her lips close to his, her hair falling about his head like a heavy, fragrant curtain. 'Oh no . . .' he moaned. 'Oh no, don't. I . . .'

[...] Her hands glided firmly across the taut blue cotton of his straining
slip, caressing, stroking, nipping. He rolled wildly beneath her, trapped
at the knees, beating his hands at his sides, crying out in little strangled
gasps.

'No! No! No! For Christ's sake, Sylva ... let me free.'

'I let this one free firstly,' she cried, and with a swift tug unclipped the
buckle at his hip and stripped him.

He gave a helpless sob, reared upwards. 'Oh! Stupendo!' she cried happily.
'Si robusto! Si robusto!' and quickly untying the cord at her own hip, she
removed with one swift, and practised, move the last shred of modesty she
possessed. And raped him.[27]

John Charlton thought that Marcus's helplessness was somewhat over-stressed.
Dirk replied that Sylva was 'a very hefty lady. Ever tried one in this position?'[28]

The cast of characters was sprinkled with familiar names: Bruna, Minna, Bea,
Tonnino ... even Dr Poteau, a homage to Dirk's and Tony's own physician, who
was now retired but still looked after them privately. A monstrous Italian film
producer, Umberto Grottorosso – who comes to consult Sir Charles about the
historical accuracy of a script dealing with the life of Napoleon's son – was, Dirk
insisted, *not* based on Visconti. Their principal scene together, discussing the
film's approach, contains references which resonate in the present context: '[...]
I can not, and will not, accept the odious suggestions which you make that
l'Aiglon, of the Duke of Reichstadt, was an invert!' says the historian. 'It is
companionship, not carnality!' contends the producer.[29] It was, Dirk told Nicholas
Bowlby, a book he wanted badly to write, without really knowing why. 'It does'nt
really say a thing. Its not very original. All the people are very cliché ... I suppose.
But somehow I do KNOW them.'[30] Whether others would find them persuasive
remained to be seen. The initial response from Bob Gottlieb, the charismatic
head of Knopf in New York who had done Dirk proud with the production and
marketing of *A Gentle Occupation*, was cool. He thought the ending of *Voices*
was too 'cute and pat', and the book as a whole not astringent enough; it was
too sentimental – an adjective that stung Dirk: 'it IS sentimental I suppose.
Although I much prefer the word romantic.' He had spent the weekend 'feeling
strangely like Mrs Cartland', and it was not a pleasant sensation. 'I detest
sentimentality in any form. Have I really erred? Or is it that tough Jewish-
American-New York attitude which is revolted by any form of understatement.'[31]
Gottlieb took the book, but without great expectations.

The melancholy in Dirk's second novel was reflected to a degree at Clermont.
For much of 1980 Dirk was unwell, having been beset by an intestinal parasite
that the good Doctor Poteau thought had probably lain dormant for many
years – most likely, since the sojourn in Rome; at one point Dirk's weight was
down to an alarming nine stone. Tony had been in increasing discomfort from
a calcified foot, for which there was no hopeful prognosis. More upsetting to

him, however, was his sixty-fifth birthday. He neither felt nor looked his age, but overnight was classified officially as old and qualified for a pension, if he could be bothered to claim it. What with this 'dawn of old age' and Dirk constantly on edge about his health, Tony confided for the first time that they both were beginning to believe their days together were numbered. Another shadow fell over their lives when Labo became infirm and, three days before Christmas, had to be put down. They believed he was about thirteen. It was, wrote Tony, 'the end of a long chapter' which had begun when they took in the 'crippled waif' at Villa Berti. 'He cost us dear in many ways, but none of it grudged as he gave full value in loyalty & affection.' Dirk told Norah Smallwood:

> My little beast could'nt make it in the end. We sat and watched him battle away and loose [. . .] A gentleman, and he was that, of such impeccable manners . . . I carried him about, he could no longer even stand, and finally we reached the Decision and it was done; well stage-managed I admit, in my arms in the patch of sunlight he used always to seek just beside my chair. He had no fear nor awareness. Only the very splendid Vet knew the grief; and simply left immediately after without even a farewell . . . which was tactful and kind. And so Tote and I put him in his hole quite near the greenhouse, under a flourishing bay, and shovelled in, together, not just the last of a dog but fourteen* years of our own lives.[32]

There was a further and more general reason for their malaise. As we know, Dirk was 'as political as a garden gnome'.[33] Considering the length and the frequency of those that have survived, his letters are remarkably free of partisanship, let alone engagement. In his demonology there seems to have been little to choose between Harold Wilson and Edward Heath: both had made the country of his birth a less agreeable place in which to live, although the latter's positive attitude towards Europe had been encouraging. Margaret Thatcher's stridency did not appeal. What really disturbed him, however, was the global picture. Czechoslovakia had just been invaded when he and Tony went to live in Rome, a couple of autoroutes away from the Eastern bloc. They had seen enough from working behind the Iron Curtain – albeit in comparatively pampered conditions – to know at first hand of the debasement of communism within its barbed-wire and watch-towered boundaries. After working on *The Night Porter* in Vienna, a few miles from the Czech border, Dirk appeared for the second time on Russell Harty's television show and 'scared the hell' out of his host by explaining why we should all be fearful of the naval build-up in the Red Sea and the massing of 'metal and steel and huge, huge armies'. It was, he said, just like the thirties. 'Think how quickly Portugal happened,' he added.

---

* As Tony once observed on a birthday, Dirk had 'his own form of inevitable mathematics'.

'Think how very quickly Cyprus happened – on a summer's day there wasn't a Cyprus any more.'[34] At the beginning of 1977 he and Tony talked seriously about moving to Switzerland or the United States. During the 'Total Exposure' for *Snakes and Ladders*, Ian Jack, who wrote the 'Atticus' column in *The Sunday Times*, joined Dirk on a train from Bristol to London and, after being entertained with reminiscences about the Bogarde career, asked whether he would ever think of leaving Provence and settling in Britain again. 'Never,' came the reply, 'or at least not until the Russians come.' Ian Jack thought he had misheard, and that Dirk might have been using the film-world term 'rushes' to mean something portentous like death, or just itchy feet. 'And of course the Russians *will* come, sooner or later. I may be lucky. I should be in my early sixties by then and, if I stay, my age may save me from the internment camps. Either that or I shoot the dogs and quit.' It had recently taken him just twelve hours to drive from Vienna to Clermont. Marvellous, he said, 'we've done it easily in a day. And then I thought my God, what am I saying? If it takes *us* a day's driving it will only take *them* a day too.' It was twelve hours not only to the Hotel Bristol but also to the Hungarian frontier. He hated to sound like a Jeremiah, but it was his honest belief, held since the end of the last war: they *would* come.[35] In 1980, with the Russians having trooped into Afghanistan, Tito at death's door in Yugoslavia and Soviet eyes on Rumania, there was little reason for cheer, but, so far, no threat of imminent invasion. The best thing to do was to mow a terrace, plant a petunia, or hunker down in the former olive store. And then came the call. Would Dirk replace Alan Bates on a film to be shot partly in Hollywood – in three weeks' time – and partly in England, with Glenda Jackson as co-star and Anthony Harvey directing? It was a 'cardigan-and-knitted tie' role, but one with a difference.

The man he was being asked to play was no fictional creation. Like Patrick Leigh Fermor, but unlike 'Boy' Browning, Roald Dahl was very much alive. Dirk and Tony knew him and his wife, the Academy Award-winning actress Patricia Neal, from the Amersham days, when they would occasionally go to each other's houses for dinner; they had all last met earlier in the year at the Foyle's Luncheon. The projected film was based on a book by Barry Farrell, *Pat and Roald*, which charted Dahl's battle to rehabilitate his wife after a series of strokes she suffered in 1965, a battle so successful that she was able to resume her acting career and a fully active life.[36] It was the true story of a kind of domestic heroism, one of great intimacy, and in the wrong hands it would be ripe for mawkish treatment. Although Harvey and Dirk had never made a film together, the signing of the director, who had won an Oscar in 1969 for *The Lion in Winter*, seemed a promising start. The script was by the playwright Robert Anderson, who had among his credits *The Nun's Story*. Above all, there was Glenda Jackson, about whom Dirk had for a time been uncomplimentary in private, mainly because of the excesses in Ken Russell's *The Music Lovers* and her not-infrequent chest-baring; however, her later work had impressed him. They had never met. When

Dirk visited the set of *The Romantic Englishwoman* and Losey asked her whether she would like to be introduced to his friend and collaborator, she declined, saying she was working and therefore concentrating. She laughs at the memory: 'Nothing must deflect from the process!'[37] 'I am told that she is very dedicated to her work, and she doesn't suffer fools gladly,' Dirk writes at the conclusion of *An Orderly Man.* She was most definitely someone after his own heart – and even, he said, his Lorelei: 'No one else on earth but she could have got me back to Los Angeles.'[38]

Before he agreed to take the role, and the $300,000 that came with it, Dirk's first priority was to ensure that the Dahls approved of what was being done with their lives. The entire family was against the film, which had a working title of 'Gipsy House', after their home in Great Missenden. When it was announced that Alan Bates had been cast as Roald – who was born in Wales to Norwegian parents – his daughter Tessa snapped at a reporter that 'they've got an over-sensitive Englishman playing my father and a Northern shopgirl playing my mother'.[39] Dirk made contact with Dahl, who said he had tried a hundred times to have the film stopped and never wanted to have anything to do with Hollywood again after what had been done to his book, *Charlie and the Chocolate Factory.* The producer, Larry Schiller, assured by his lawyers that there was nothing the family could do about it, had gone ahead anyway, and made a somewhat unusual deal with CBS Television and Proctor and Gamble, which would result in the film being shown on television in America and in cinemas elsewhere. Faced with the inevitable, Dahl – unlike Daphne du Maurier – decided that it was 'better to help them to get it right than to leave them to get it wrong'; so he contributed to the script, which he admitted was a good one. And when Dirk made contact to seek his endorsement, Dahl said he was 'ecstatic' that the former was prepared to break *his* promise never to go back to Los Angeles, a.k.a. Gomorrah, in order to take the role. Dahl gave him certain dire and unrepeatable warnings about the producer, then offered a few pointers to his own character and behaviour. He never displayed his emotions; he was unsentimental and both cool and competent in a crisis. He was, 'like all writers (you included) a good organiser, tidy, neat, orderly, except in my dress which is purely for comfort': open shirt and cashmere cardigans the year round. Every day while his wife was in hospital he arrived on the dot of six in the morning – an indication of the intense and sustained drive to make her recover, which came, he said, from the tenacity and endurance common to all good writers: they do not give up. 'The act of rehabilitating Pat was like writing a long and difficult novel. That is why you are so perfect for the job. You *know.* Acting alone is not enough. The secret is knowing.'[40]

Dirk went shopping in Cannes and found a pair of black, lace-up semi-brogues – the kind which his mother used to call 'good women' shoes. Rummaging in cupboards produced a pile of old 'cardies', gone at the elbow, and Viyella shirts with discreet checks in beige and brown. Out came the Huntsman hacking-jacket which had been made for *Esther Waters*, and old sweaters gone at the elbow. And a few neglected knitted ties. It was a ritual: start with the feet, then the wardrobe, then the 'look' . . . His bags packed, he and Tony flew from Paris to New York on Concorde, no less. It was, he reported to the Bowlbys, 'absolutely amazing' – even to someone with a hatred of flying, its claustrophobia, the sensation of being shut in a lozenge-shaped drawer with a bunch of deeply suspect strangers. No, this experience inside the graceful supersonic bird, was 'exactly like travelling in the Old Days before the Proles went to Benidorm or Florida'. On board all was elegance, 'no fur-fabric, *all* sable'; take-off was 'staggering and magical'; the wine 'perfection' and caviar in half-pounds. 'Hostesses in "frocks" wearing their own jewerlery and looking so chic you could faint . . . it was All Too Much.' Outside the tiny windows 'the world was a strange aching blue . . . infinity . . . real infinity . . . shading to black'. Even a visit to the lavatory had curiosity value: 'I mean having a pee at twice the speed of sound *is* a bit interesting.'[41] The onward flight the next morning to Los Angeles was altogether more mundane, but, to judge from the Diary, not quite the purgatory that Dirk would take no fewer than eight pages to describe in *Backcloth*, with 'Margie', 'Barbie', 'Tracey' and 'Cindy' dispensing warm, sweet Californian 'champagne', three-day-old menus and chicken that tasted, if anything, of fish in formaldehyde. 'Imagine two hundred people with diarrhoea,' mused Tony, leaving Dirk no alternative but to place his knife and fork back on the tray.[42]

Conditions were a great deal better at the Beverly Wilshire, where Dirk and Tony were given a corner suite. After three days, Dirk sent Norah Smallwood a postcard view from the hotel: 'This is the view from my window – only I'm 7 floors up and wondering how I can afford it all.'[43] His living allowance was $2,000 a week, but this establishment catered for the likes of Warren Beatty, whose pay-packets were of a bulk unknown to Dirk. Because the film was being shot on location in Pasadena, he and Tony moved out to a hotel nearby, where the rooms were somewhat dingy but half the price; ten nights at the Beverly Wilshire had cost them $4,300. What with the expense and the arduous hours – 7.30 in the morning was considered an exceptionally late call – they were tempted to stay in the camper van which had been laid on for Dirk while shooting. More than forty feet long, 'with loo and shower, beds, cooker, fully stocked fridge (from Dom P. to Carnation Milk) cocktail cabinet which lit up, red, fully stocked also, big deep arm chairs, thick pile carpet which you could get lost in, orange, and a TV and radio. Colour TV of course. What more does a boy want? Even a great bowl of fresh flowers daily on the make-up table!'[44] Trundling between locations like a Pullman train, it added to the enjoyment he felt at facing a camera again after so long. The contract stipulated that Dirk's Winnebago 'shall be substantially equal to the one provided for Glenda Jackson's use'; but it was part of Dirk's greatest pleasure in making this film that his co-star could not give a damn about that sort of nonsense. Glenda Jackson, whose arrival had been delayed by a bereavement, was proving not only the ultimate professional and a joy to work with, but also a companion off-set who had endeared herself to Dirk by her complete lack of side: 'The night she arrived from a fifteen-hour flight via Birmingham, she was in my room in her dressing gown, arguing that Brecht was a load of cobblers'. He had welcomed her with a cuddly toy. It was, she recalls, a kind of love at first sight.

Glenda Jackson said Hollywood was 'like a set waiting to be struck. It doesn't exist.' Dirk called Los Angeles 'the town of deceptions'. *Backcloth* tells how they became united in 'a battle for banality against quality' and how it 'raged unabated' as thirty minutes of script was removed to meet the demands of the network and the sponsors; as the financing began to look dicey; and, above all, as the producer fell out with his director.[45] It was 'a destructive shambles', within which the leading players managed some of the best work of their careers. 'We were a great team,' said Dirk. If feelings were running high at executive level, there was nothing but respect and co-operation on the floor. Glenda Jackson recalls how quickly Dirk broke any ice that might have existed with the crew: 'He regarded himself as one of them – and after all they are always the ones you are working with most closely. There is something about the sheer professionalism of making a film in America. There is an expectation that what is required will always be there. I remember we were shooting somewhere miles from any human habitation, with no proper road. One of the guys got out of his truck, lifted up a piece of grass and plugged in the generator. You just thought, "Bugger me!" ' They worked flat out for fifteen days over three weeks, gobbling up at a remarkable rate the surviving pages of the script. One evening Dirk took a call from the film's most vociferous opponent, Tessa Dahl, who was in LA and had seen the footage shot so far. Dirk wondered what was coming next. She had gone to the screening ready, at best, to giggle. In fact she was reduced to tears for all the right reasons: Glenda Jackson was 'wonderful' and astonishingly like Patricia Neal; Dirk was 'towering'. Dirk said Roald Dahl was hard to play, because he was a genius. Tessa Dahl replied: 'So are you.' So on the players went, buoyed by the unexpected praise. At the end, the rugged fellows from the Teamsters Union presented Dirk, his co-star and Tony with cigarette lighters shaped as pearl-handled revolvers – a further mark of respect for these unusually committed and un-snooty limeys. 'I had been used to working with the English actors of Dirk's generation,' says Glenda Jackson. 'The prevailing attitude seemed to be that acting was not really terribly important. It was something you did in between doing the *Times* crossword. That was never a problem with Dirk. He was someone with no hang-ups about the fact that it was the most important thing in his life.' Dirk would repay the compliment. She was, he wrote, 'as strong as teak, as pliable as plasticine, as professional and dedicated as any actress I had ever worked with.'[46]

Because Glenda Jackson had an engagement on Broadway to fulfil, there was a four-month gap before the second part of the filming could go ahead, in England. For what would be the last time, Dirk and Tony flew from Los Angeles with no regrets at leaving that 'sad town' itself, but with a reminder of how

stimulating its *raison d'être* could be. Soon after returning to Clermont he wrote
to Norah Smallwood that he had enjoyed finding that

> my work was as good as ever, and, frankly, better for the four year pause. One
> can become very mannered without being really aware. I caught myself just in
> time I think ... the odd thing about walking onto the 'Set' that very first
> morning in California after so long away was that I was not even remotely
> concerned. The only thing which caused me grave anxiety was the fact that I
> had asked someone to get me an egg and bacon sandwich ... and it had'nt
> arrived. It did later. And I suddenly realised that I had 'gone back to work'
> quite unaware and unworried. A moral there somewhere I suppose?[47]

The Diary bears him out. In the past Dirk had invariably been in a state of nerves
before the first day on a film. This time, all was unnaturally calm. Reflecting on
the experience, he said it was 'rather like a captive duck being hurled into a pond
after years of the security of a hen-run in a farm yard ... I merely swam.'[48] And
now, he told the Bowlbys, 'in a DREADFUL way I do rather miss the panic
and hurry and the work there. I equally miss the spoiling I got. That was
terrifically nice, thanks.' It had, he added, been 'a wild trip', which had yielded
'lots of material for a book'. He intended to call it 'Have a Nice Day'.[49]

It drizzled on Dirk's birthday, which was unfortunate for Marie-Christine Isoardi,
the daughter of his stonemason and his laundress. That afternoon she was
married in the neighbouring village of Magagnosc, and Dirk and Tony dutifully
turned up. The bride looked like 'a Telephone Doll in yards and yards of white
tulle stuffed with pink rose buds'. To Tony she resembled 'a big creamy cake'.
For some reason, Dirk reported,

> we got into a pew which filled to the brim with rotten little bridesmaids [...]
> picking their noses, and swiping each other with their Dorothy Bags. I thought
> my chum would go under. But he stayed gamely on to the end, complaining
> that he could'nt hear the Priest, and asking, in that boring British Voice, what
> they were 'up to' with all the wafer chewing and swigging out of chalices. He
> got a bit unnerved by the Acolyte who kept swinging a rattle on a chain to
> mark the end of each part of the Ceremony. And the incence made his throat
> hurt. Oh dear.[50]

Tony had a quiet chuckle in the Diary: 'D thought the choir was lovely, up in
the gallery – it did'nt seem to occur to him that it was all on tape. But as today
is his 60th birthday he was allowed a little vagueness.' The Bowlbys sent Dirk a
telegram which, he said, arrived on a 'delicious card covered in doves and crippled
children'. In the message he was addressed as a 'sexygenarian', which went down
extremely well.

Here he was, at sixty, and understandably confused. We have seen how he had declared himself truly happy only when he was writing. But now, pausing in his portrayal of a man who – as Robert Altman described it to Glenda Jackson – 'reached into his wife's grave and pulled her out', Dirk realised just how powerful a draw his 'real job' continued to exert on him: 'The thing I simply adore is "being" another person. Trying to use his mannerisms, finding what he'd do in a given crisis, how he'd move, walk, use his hands ... if he would perhaps have a particular "tick" in distress ... tiny things which when added together give the audience the illusion that I am someone else. I dont always get this together fully. Sometimes I do.' They had been shooting at a hospital in Pasadena when the surgeon who had performed the operation on Patricia Neal, and who was technical advisor on the film, approached Dirk. He had spent much time with Dahl during those emotion-charged weeks. Dirk did not look like Dahl, but he *was* him. He was behaving exactly as Dahl did: the same calmness, the same 'angularity' in his walk. Dahl, said the doctor, 'only ever showed his distress in his hands. As you do. Behind his back.' Dirk was delighted and called Dahl, thinking the latter might be relieved to know that the surgeon he had admired for looking after his wife was impressed by the way the portrayal was going. 'Of course you'd behave like me,' said Dahl. 'We are both English [*sic*] and we are both Gentlemen. Something the Yanks dont understand yet.'[51]

The English portion of the film was shot in the Home Counties in June, by which time it had a new title: 'Miracle of Love', which to Dirk's and Tony's ears sounded like a documentary on birth control. Schiller had sacked Anthony Harvey and replaced him with Anthony Page, the original choice of director, who had turned it down 'because I had done so many "Disease of the Week" TV movies'. He, Glenda Jackson and Dirk worked on the script in Dirk's and Tony's suite at the Connaught; 'I remember Roald Dahl ringing Dirk constantly and saying that unless the producer and I accepted all his rewrites he would "walk out". He felt he was not being treated sympathetically enough. Dirk was very sensible about it all. Very thoughtful.' The shoot itself went as smoothly as could be hoped. 'There were no problems: Dirk liked the fact that the thing was very economical. He was extremely focused and professional and always ready to deliver. He was so at home in front of the camera.'[52] 'Always ready to deliver' is a pertinent phrase, and not as trite as it sounds. It is at the heart of what Charlotte Rampling said Dirk taught her when they met on *The Damned*. And it is the essence of what Dirk himself has described as 'Actor's energy'. Both mental and physical, it is the life force behind a performance, and it depends upon intense concentration.[53] Glenda Jackson says: 'It is what one is there for. Without it, there are no perks, no money in the world, that make the job worth doing. Most films are shot in very, very short pieces, and you might have to wait hours before the moment comes. When it does, you have to be ready for it. You can't waste energy, or fritter away time while waiting, because it is the only reason for being there. Dirk believed it very strongly and in that I think he was in a way unusual.' Never, for either of them, was it a way of filling in time between solving crossword clues.

The subsequent history of the film to which they had jointly given so much 'Actor's energy' is too convoluted for this narrative. All those who saw it at an early stage were convinced of its outstanding merit, to the extent that Larry Schiller decided to open the cinema version in Los Angeles before it had been screened on television, in order to qualify for the Oscars. Rave reviews were forthcoming. So, too, the coast-to-coast broadcast early in December was a success, but only on those two coasts. In Dirk's account, after fifteen minutes the Midwest, 'that giant's tablecloth', switched over *en bloc* to watch an episode of *Hart to Hart*, starring Robert Wagner and Natalie Wood. Ironically, the Hollywood 'golden couple' had become close to Dirk and Tony on visits to Provence. But any twinge of regret about a lost ratings tussle paled into insignificance beside the genuine tragedy which had just befallen the Wagner family: Natalie Wood had drowned just nine days before. 'She was a dear, bright & funny girl,' recorded Tony, '& a good friend to us.' Rabid press speculation about her fate had, it was said, caused the greater part of the United States to tune in to watch one of the last small-screen performances she had given: the competition on other channels had no chance. Nor were there any glittering prizes for 'Miracle of Love', or 'An Act of Love', or *The Patricia Neal Story*, as it became en route to England. Roald Dahl wrote saying he did not like the film – 'a bit of a botch-up' – but that Dirk should not be downcast: he and Glenda Jackson had done 'a fine job'.[54] More important, where it was shown, audiences saw how by determination, tenacity and sheer bloody-mindedness a massively damaged stroke victim had made an extraordinary recovery. 'I want my wife back,' Dahl declares in the film, and what he did to achieve his aim offered a message of hope. For that alone it had been worth Dirk's and Glenda Jackson's while. As for the fee: some years after the film was first screened, Dirk and his lawyers in America were still trying to extract nearly half the money due to him. Not that it was unusual. Ever since he had broken free of Rank and begun to make contracts where he would be paid a relatively modest salary plus a deferment and perhaps a percentage of any eventual profit, he had risked never seeing a cent beyond the initial payment. Once *The Servant* moved into profit, a trickle came his way each year for the rest of his life. On the other hand, twelve years after the release of *Death in Venice* he asked Laurence Harbottle to make sense of the latest distribution statement, in case it indicated that he might one day see some of the $40,000 that he had been promised as a deferred payment. The upshot was that gross receipts appeared to be $5,300,000 but that after all the deductions, including a staggering interest figure of nearly $2,500,000, the *deficit* was $3,300,000. None of the deferments had been paid and, Laurence Harbottle added sorrowfully, they probably never would be. 'Oh dear!' replied Dirk. 'That's exactly what I felt certain you would have to say! And everyone thinks I'm a millionaire. Never mind. It was fun to make it – & I'm glad I did!'[55]

At least Dirk's publishers paid up without having to be asked. The advances were paltry by comparison with the cinema, but there was satisfaction for Dirk in seeing them earned out and then receiving royalties. On the same day that Tony had his first pension – £545 for six months – a cheque reached Dirk for £13,000, his share of the proceeds from the three books to date. By the middle of 1981, nearly two hundred thousand paperback copies of *Postillion* had been printed, and another one hundred and fifty thousand of *Snakes and Ladders*. These excellent statistics did not prevent Dirk complaining to his hardback publisher that when he passed through London Airport in the spring he found not a sign of either title, but 'yards' of Peter Ustinov and of 'Jolly, Breezy' Kenneth More. *A Gentle Occupation* had done well, with about thirty-two thousand copies sold, and had been translated into French and Dutch. For *Voices in the Garden*, Dirk was offered the same terms as for the first novel: with royalties rising from ten per cent on the first 5,000 copies to fifteen per cent on any over 20,000. This time, however, he declined to submit to 'Total Exposure' and stayed at home: there was, after all, a danger that 'Total' might become 'Over'. He would do a very few interviews the next time he was in London and concentrate instead on launching *Une aimable occupation* in Paris, while doing as much as he could to help the new novel's American fortunes without leaving Provence.

On publication day for *Voices in the Garden*, 3 September 1981, Clermont was struck by lightning. William Boyd's notice in *The Sunday Times* three days later did not knock out the electricity and the telephone, but it winded Dirk enough for him to doubt in a letter to Norah Smallwood whether 'we' – he and Chatto – had this time 'pulled it off'.[56] Boyd reviewed *Voices* with *July's People* by Nadine Gordimer, who had won the 1974 Booker Prize, and the comparison did Dirk's book no favours. It failed, said Boyd, 'to arouse even a suspicion of curiosity about the destinies of the empty characters that populate its pages'; characters who 'swim, drink, eat, make love and indulge in very long dialogues about their various pretty inconsequential problems' and who 'appear to be assembled there not to satisfy any demands of plot but rather to provide excuses for elegant descriptive set-pieces'. These, he added, Dirk did 'very well, albeit with a heavy emphasis on up-market consumerism', making the life of sybaritic languor almost palpably appealing: 'We have a close and precise acquaintanceship with the objects and accoutrements of this world – the drinks, the decor, and the clothes – but Bogarde's descriptive abilities fail to enlighten us about the individuals who inhabit it.'[57] To see in *The Times* a few days later that it was a 'delicious' novel must have caused confusion in those who read both newspapers. 'Mr Bogarde's virtues as a writer,' concluded John Nicholson, 'are precisely those which made him the most compelling screen-actor of his generation: a flawless but unobtrusive technique, miserly economy of effort, and characterization which starts at the roots. Praise enough to say that admirers who were once horrified to hear he had no further film plans must now be praying that no-one sends him a script good enough to lure him away from his new career.'[58]

Dirk, predictably, took the *Sunday Times* notice to heart. 'I do confess to being a little dumped,' he wrote. The printed word stays, 'even wrapped round the fish'. He found it curious that some of the reviewers believed people like the Peverills no longer existed, a nineteen-year-old must *de facto* be 'a Punk or a Rocker' and Grottorosso-plus-entourage must be creatures only of the imagination, so farcical were they in the story. 'But they are absolutely real ... I know the sources, and I have seen wilder displays, I assure you, than I ever dared put to paper! But dealing with Critics who don't know that world is a problem [...] Better, I suppose, be that ghastly chap who writes The Hobbits! [...] Because HIS world is clear and bright and easily imagined because it is *not* real. And is therefore not beyond the comprehension of the reader.'[59] Rachel Billington, for *The New York Times*, found much to praise in *Voices*, which she judged 'an honourable defeat': 'The descriptions are always excellent. The colour, the touch, the smell of the South of France is vivid around us [...] The cadences of speech move with their own entirely successful swing and balance. It is clear that Mr Bogarde must be judged as a writer rather than as an actor writing.'[60] By the time he read that, he had set fiction aside and consigned to the 'back burner' some rich ingredients from his brief stay in Hollywood. It was on with 'Bio. 3' and, simultaneously, an idea which might just produce a further *bonne bouche* from the Lullington/Alfriston days, for which he had in mind the title 'Lally'.

Twenty-two

'You are very good indeed at saying an interesting bookful without
in fact saying anything *really* personal at all'

Never go back. Like Dorothy Gordon, Dirk believed it was the wisest course. But, as we all know, the past can travel too, and sometimes arrives entirely unexpectedly. When the silver-tongued broadcaster David Jacobs played one of the songs from *Lyrics for Lovers* on his long-running and highly popular radio programme, the BBC received more written and telephoned enquiries about the record than about any other in the show's history. For several weeks Jacobs gallantly placed it on his turntable and endured the horrors of an LP which the writer Mark Steyn more recently accorded special treatment when considering the regrettable tendency of non-singing actors to indulge themselves in a recording studio. Dirk, remarked Steyn, 'recites the words in dramatic fashion' – i.e. they bear no relation to the music: ' "You must remember" Long pause. "this a kiss is stillakissasigh" Longer pause. "IS! JUST! A sigh??" '[1] Decca, caught pleasantly by surprise, hastened to ask Dirk if he would mind them re-releasing the album. He suspected that it had been played on the radio 'as a bit of a send-up', but did not *mind*. 'What the hell,' he philosophised. 'I'm an Entertainer first and last I hope ... and although I am some little way towards shame about the way I did the thing, under rehearsed etc., I know that it is yukky and sentimental, but equally know that there HAS to be a revival of sentiment soon, so why not give the patient the medicin it requires?'[2] And dispensed it was, at a budget price, but with the same photograph of the gleaming, white-eyed Dirk on its sleeve. One of the company's press officers who took *Lyrics for Lovers* to various publications directed at the young, reported on an 'amazing' reaction both to the record and to Dirk himself, who, she said, now enjoyed cult status as one of those in the fifties and sixties whose style represented the current 'high fashion'. Furthermore he had been cited as 'a source of inspiration by many of todays leading figures in the pop world'.

Dirk did not take all this seriously enough to submit to a round of questioning by *New Musical Express* or *Rave*, nevertheless the response was a gratifying complement to the enthusiasm of those who had queued for his recent films. At the same time, thanks to the books, he was either clinging on to, or recapturing, some of his more senior admirers. If they had known how he referred to them in private, they might have scurried back in perpetuity to Messrs Niven and More: 'Timid letters on pale blue Basildon Bond, and worse, are beginning to flop into the mail box saying that they think "Voices", in their phrase, "just lovely". So thats one achievement! My Old Fans are not yet dead it seems ... and if they think that the thing is "lovely" who am I to say "What a lot of fat fools ..." I only wish they'd stop putting their names on the library lists! One blasted woman has been waiting eighteen months for "Snakes and Ladders".'[3] That was in a letter to Norah Smallwood, whose position at the head of Chatto had begun to come under harsh – or, as Lu would have said, 'vile' – scrutiny. Towards the end of 1981 *Private Eye* printed an article, seemingly prompted by the fact that *Voices in the Garden* had been entered for the United Kingdom's foremost literary award: 'for the publishers of Proust, Daisy Ashford and a hundred other great literary names to submit the outpourings of the novelist Dirk Bogarde for this year's Booker Prize [...] is indication that all is hardly rational at 40–42 William IV Street'. It described Norah Smallwood as 'an aggressive old battleaxe, more noted for reducing her secretaries and staff to tears than caring for her authors'; and suggested that Carmen Callil, the Australian founder of the feminist house Virago and 'at least as outspoken as Smallwood', was waiting in the wings at the behest of Chatto's recently appointed managing director, Hugo Brunner.[4] Dirk was livid. 'What a perfectly filthy world we seem to inhabit now, when all grace, all decency, all honour is sacrificed for a tuppeny, two penny?, bit of paper. What amazes me, and always will, is that there are people who actually read the damned thing.'[5] He was wise not to take up the cudgels publicly on her behalf: the *Eye* tended to have the last word, and, even as a shareholder, he might not have been spared. At least he was now 'the novelist Dirk Bogarde' – satirically or not, it sounded good.

The autobiographer Dirk Bogarde submitted the final chapter of *An Orderly Man* to Chatto in the summer of 1982. He had started it in 1979, intending a 'VERY mordantly funny book', which would contain set-pieces about Cavani, Fassbinder and others, but which was really the story of settling at Clermont and 'finding out about how to cope with a "simple" life from bed-making to washing-up and sadly murmuring to myself at the sink ... "God! To think that once you were Britains No. 1 ..." But there are also the losses [...] My fathers sudden, shattering death, Visconti going too ... and suddenly realising, shaving one morning, that I had aged and not liking the way my face had set-in for the winter of my life.'[6] He had completed about two-thirds when he realised that what was emerging was a 'sad' book, mainly because his parents had become such key figures in the story, and by the end, both would be dead. His account of Margaret's wretched widowhood would affect the stoniest-hearted reader. As he finished, he decided that it was 'a book as much about a house as about myself', and yet in a paradoxical way it was more intimate than anything he had published so far, more spare, and less self-conscious, while at the same time containing a deeper self-analysis than before in the explanations of why he, a man governed by the need for 'precision, order, plan', was so 'pinched by doubt'. It also dealt with his birth as an author, paying generous tribute to Dorothy Gordon, 'Mrs X', whose existence had become momentarily the subject of intense interest in the English press when Dirk told John Higgins of *The Times* about his 'friendship through the mail' with an American woman, now dead, who had become his literary mentor. The very act of focusing on her – while continuing to conceal her identity – undoubtedly made him apply further rigour to the prose in this new book. In addition, answering John Charlton's minute and pertinent queries on the first four titles; being formally *edited* both by him and, sometimes on the terrace, by Norah Smallwood; noting, to an extent, the nuances in how the books had fared abroad – all this had made Dirk a great deal more aware of his own writing, and of the process of writing, which he now felt qualified to describe. For him it was not the lonely, solitary, reclusive job that he had been warned about. Yes, he was ostensibly alone in the olive store, but his Muse sat sulking in the shadows, needing to be wrestled and beaten about like a drunk until some bagatelle – 'a match-box' rather than a cornucopia of riches – could be prised from her grasp. The room would resound to voices remembered and imagined; often to his own voice as he experimented with the dialogue that so many of his critics acknowledged as being unusually authentic.

> It is an extraordinary sensation, spending hours with my people. Exceptionally pleasant most of the time, irritating often; especially if a character takes off on his or her own path against my better judgment and I lose control of them. Then I rip them from the typewriter, screw them into a ball and chuck them away, insert a new sheet into the machine, and start again. 'Now, this time get it *right*!' I say. Of course I suppose it is all a form of lunacy (so is acting come to that) but certainly it is not lonely.[7]

It was an indication of just how 'personal' it had turned out to be that *An Orderly Man* was dedicated to Tony. Dirk gave him the choice of how he should be addressed – Anthony Forwood, E. L. L. Forwood, E.L. L. F., Tony – and decided that, in all the circumstances, the most appropriate formula was initials and surname. Throughout the book he was, as usual, Forwood. He had been doing some writing himself. When they were living at Villa Berti and Maude had come to stay, she was enraptured by his stories of childhood and encouraged him to put them down on paper. For a while he set to work, with a clever title, 'The Five to Four', a reference to a train which passed near where he lived as a boy and which was the signal for tea; he was also to be fifty-four that year. Now he was sixty-six, and although he had occasionally taken the typescript from its drawer, it remained a work in progress. He had, however, written for the Bowlbys' private pleasure his short, barely fictionalised 'The Last Summer', prompted by his taking them with Dirk to the Hôtel du Cap in Antibes and by the memories which that visit revived in him of the weeks before war was declared. Unlike Dirk, Tony lacked confidence in writing for a wider audience, but his letters and his entries in the Diary display the good sense, the ease and the humour which all agree he possessed in spades. He was also the first reader, and critic, of all Dirk's output; he had been 'a bit damping' about the five initial chapters of *An Orderly Man* – to such an extent that Dirk was on the point of giving up. So exercised was he that he sent what he had written so far to Rosalind Bowlby, in the strictest confidence, because he had come to value her opinion more than that of John Charlton and even of Norah Smallwood. He explained that although he had 'always, all my life, worked my road but taken advice *if* it suited me', Tony's presence at every event, and his knowledge of all that truly happened, meant that 'my somewhat "arranged" version will irritate or bring to mind memories which he himself carries'. He acknowledged that they were both 'a bit too close to the wood to see the trees' and that if the book was not working he would 'shove it out of the way and concentrate on something else'.[8] To his relief Rosalind Bowlby reported that it was his best achievement to date. Dirk was on his ninth chapter, Tony observed, while he, working at his own story in a desultory fashion, was still on his first.

Just as the black cloud threatens the bright blue summer's day on the cover of *Postillion*, so the interval between the completion of the new book and its publication in March 1983 was marked by a build-up of unwanted forces beyond their control. The elegant jacket photograph by Sheila Attenborough which showed a laden Orderly Man moving away from the camera at a snow-covered Clermont, had about it a valedictory feeling. Jean-Pierre Aubert, who with his wife Brigitte had become close friends, was so pessimistic about the political and financial future that the prospect of a move to Switzerland was ever more real. To make matters even less palatable, Dirk and Tony had begun to realise that the house, and all that went with it in constituting their corner of paradise, was too much for them. Worse still, Tony was not well. The funeral of his eighty-eight-year-old father at Amersham in February 1982 had been an ordeal, not because of the family reunion which gave him more pleasure than he had expected, but because he had been feeling – in a favourite word of his – 'mouldy'. As the months went by, he logged a combination of high blood pressure, a slight tremor, a touch of rheumatism in one shoulder and the already problematic foot. As if that was not enough, visits to Dr Poteau alternated with those to the dentist. Pills seemed not to work, and Tony became uncharacteristically listless and depressed. There was unquestionably something amiss, and lacking the French to talk confidently about his symptoms – 'Be ill in your own language'[9] – he bowed to Dirk's insistence that they should go to London for a thorough check-up. Norah Smallwood, herself suffering badly from sciatica, recommended her doctor, Michael Linnett, who carried out comprehensive tests and X-rays before referring Tony to a Harley Street neurologist. 'Waiting room full of Arabs,' Tony noted. At the end of it all he was found to have a 'slight liver weakness' and a localised, early form of Parkinson's disease. The doctor said the latter should respond to pills which replaced missing natural chemicals. While not exactly offering a rosy prognosis, the visit to London had at least pinned down the main problems and had removed some, but by no means all, of the apprehension. On the new pills he felt better.

Dirk had been anxious, for both their sakes, to make the stay at the Connaught as much as possible like business as usual. He took the opportunity to do some editing of *An Orderly Man* with Norah Smallwood, who had left William IV Street but continued to work with her authors from her home in Vincent Square. As he and Tony arrived, they bumped into James Lees-Milne, who that night confided to his diary a first impression of Dirk as a 'short, well-preserved, still youthful man with dark hair': 'I said, "I saw you three evenings ago in the best film in the world." He asked what film that was, and whether I had not mistaken him for Humphrey Bogart. "*Death in Venice*," I said. "I've never seen it," he said. "You're like me, then, I never read my own books." "I read mine all the time," he said. There is something rather camp about him.'[10] On the one hand it gave Dirk pleasure to see his devoted publisher free of the cares of office in an ever more febrile book trade; the 'kissing cherubs' who formed the Chatto imprint were, he thought, quite likely to give way to hissing vipers. On the other, Norah Smallwood was increasingly disabled and frail, and, if truth be told, redundant to his future as an author. Nothing would fray the ties between them – above all, loyalty; but also a mutual understanding, a certain shared snobbery, a common code of behaviour, of *manners*. However, they both knew that the working partnership was more or less at an end. If the new brooms at Chatto finally decided they did not like *An Orderly Man* he would take it elsewhere and give them 'Lally', which they would find considerably harder to handle. And that would be it. In fact he had decided to leave anyway after doing what he could to promote the third volume of memoirs. From all he had heard, he and Carmen Callil were not made for each other. Dealing with John Charlton had become edgier. Rosalind Bowlby was pregnant and felt her days, too, were numbered. Like the other small groups with whom he had always flourished – in the war; at Rank, albeit highly selectively; and in the Losey era – his Team at Chatto was breaking up. There would be no crisis of conscience about finding a new home for the books, which kept on demanding space inside his head, urging him to grapple with that recalcitrant Muse; in fact another one was already there, nudging 'Lally' out of the way. What he needed was a strong, effective, literary equivalent of Clair Loschetter to guide him and a new novel towards a different house.

Another useful distraction from worries about health during the London visit was a possible film. The only prospect that had held much promise in the past year or so was brought to him by David Puttnam and Hugh Hudson, producer and director respectively of *Chariots of Fire*. Dirk and Tony had pushed the boat out during the 1981 Cannes Festival and hosted a *fête-champêtre* among their olive trees for those connected with the all-conquering picture which seemed for a while to herald a renaissance in British cinema. Puttnam and Hudson had tried to set up a Cold War drama 'The October Circle', from a Robert Littell novel about a Bulgarian champion cyclist planning to escape to the West. Hollywood was not impressed. So they made *Chariots* instead, and now The Money would probably fund their interpretation of the Sofia street directory if they so wished. Puttnam and Hudson recruited Robert Bolt to write a new screenplay and approached Dirk, who was interested: to shine a light on the ogre of communism in such good company might be tempting indeed. Even the great Bolt – *Lawrence of Arabia, Doctor Zhivago, A Man for All Seasons* – failed to make the role intended for Dirk appealing enough, and he turned it down. The film never happened.

Within a week or so, there was an equally promising approach: Granada Television wanted to adapt a 1908 novella, *Buried Alive*, by a writer whose productivity put even Dirk's in the shade: Arnold Bennett. It was the story of a suburban widow whose second husband might or might not be a bigamist. He is a shy artist, who enjoys having his every whim indulged, but whenever his wife talks about paintings he 'feels that she sticks a knife into his soul, for her remarks are of "exceeding puerility" '.[11] The producer, David Payne, wished to reunite Dirk with Glenda Jackson, who was first to accept in principle. The attractions for Dirk were considerable. Negotiations went on for a year and a half, with meetings at Clermont and at the Connaught, during the visit for Tony's tests:

> [Payne] brought clutches of new Young British Directors to see me each evening, just as if I was choosing material to cover a chair [...] what amused me, after initially shocking me, was that on the third day David [...] said that all the Directors we had met, and who had swallowed all my Scotch and Vodka, were 'too scared to work with you'! It seems that I have become a 'legend' to most of them. And they dont want to work with Legends [...] Forwood had to admit, after a pause for shock, that Glenda and I might sound a 'bit overpowering' to some of them who considered, for example, Jeremy Irons as a Superstar! [...] A legend! Fuck that![12]

Eventually Mike Hodges, who made the underworld thriller *Get Carter* and was a mere eleven years younger than Dirk, accepted without demur. A final script arrived, which Dirk said could be made to work if he and Glenda Jackson were allowed to have fun injecting the necessary vitality and energy into their roles. With Hodges, that seemed likely. Dirk and Tony flew to London. Dirk's wardrobe was chosen and fitted, the studio at Wembley was made ready, and all looked set when Hodges was whisked into hospital. For a long while there had been doubts about whether or not the money was in place; these continued after Hodges returned, ready to work, and, with no guarantee of a definite starting date, Dirk pulled out. Glenda Jackson remembers little about the disappointing affair, which had seemed a perfect vehicle for renewing her partnership with Dirk: 'I had some lovely costumes fitted. And then the film just stopped. A pity.' But through no fault of Dirk. He and Tony returned to France, their feelings a combination of regret at the collapse of a film in which they had invested so much time and hope; and of relief – because, like Mike Hodges, Tony too had been under the surgeon's knife.

Thanks to the pills prescribed in England, the incipient Parkinson's was under control, but Tony was worried about other new symptoms, including weight-loss of twenty-four pounds in nine months. He went to see a young doctor called Gilles Cabrol who had moved into a house down the lane from Clermont and whose aspirations to make a career as a singer and songwriter were as pronounced as those for his future in the medical profession – prompting Tony to ask rhetorically, 'what it is that makes an Elton John or a Rolling Stone?'* Cabrol sent him for more tests, which Tony summarised as 'Pee-Pee, Bindies, Blood, Happy Snaps up the bum and down the throat taken while I was in the most improbable positions, some of them highly embarrassing'.[13] They allayed his greatest fear by disclosing no trace of cancer; and the weight-loss was easily explained by Tony's having cut down on drinking. But a colonic polyp would need to be removed before too long and his prostate was enlarged. So he and Dirk resolved that when they went to London in the spring for *Buried Alive* – and also to promote *An Orderly Man* – the position would be monitored. It was then that an endoscopy showed Tony's polyp to be 'something other' and must be removed forthwith; so arrangements were made with the King Edward VII Hospital.

Backcloth contains a version, based on Dirk's entries in the Diary, of what happened during the four weeks from the middle of February 1983. It is cool, almost detached, but at the same time self-regarding, as if the events are being watched in a mirror. There is, for example, a peculiar description of walking past Miss Selfridge, where 'a whole window, it appeared, of young women started screaming and waving and jumping up and down. Maybe they thought I was someone else? Will buy tweed cap at Purdey's tomorrow for safety.'[14] None of that is in the Diary entry; instead, a far more plausible line in which he says of the 'wonderfully kind' hospital staff: 'Grateful I did the "Dr" films.' There is a narcissism about the published account which is all but lacking in the original. After about ten days, when he has returned to the Connaught from lunch with Charlotte Rampling, he writes: 'Amused, in retrospect, that the only person who has not recognised me was the concierge at Claridges.' It appears, slightly amended, in *Backcloth*, and comes over as arch. In the Diary it seems to matter

---

* Dirk and Tony had met both species: Elton John had visited them at Clermont, Mick Jagger had come to the *Accident* party at the Connaught. And they coincided twice with Keith Richards: first, at the 1967 Venice Regatta, and later at Nice Airport where he declared himself to Dirk as 'a fan'.

less to him. What shines from the busy handwritten pages is evidence of the devotion and the interdependence of two men for whom age was beginning to be a trial. It should be said that a few days before he took Tony to the King Edward VII, Dirk, who, as we have seen, was no stranger to health scares on his own account, was passed A1 by the doctor who carried out the obligatory insurance check for the film. Now he could only stand by while Tony's major surgery took its course. The patient, who approached the ordeal with resignation and with fewer nerves than he had expected, felt quite genuinely and typically that the whole thing was worse for Dirk. At least there were supportive friends close at hand, and distracting engagements for him, too, thanks to the impending publication of *An Orderly Man.*

No one in the audience at the National Film Theatre on St Valentine's Day, twenty-four hours after Tony's admission to hospital, would have guessed for a moment that Dirk was beside himself with worry. His contribution to *The Guardian* Film Lecture series did not, perhaps, have the sparkle that made the similar event in 1970 so memorable, but the conversation with Tony Bilbow was lively enough, with a string of anecdotes and character sketches, many of them familiar to readers of the autobiographies and watchers of the Harty interviews, supplemented with newer thoughts teased out by his informed and affable questioner. What was your relationship with Losey? 'Grumpy.' They said you retired for a while after *Death in Venice?* 'I've never retired! I retreated.' What sort of scripts were you sent at that time? 'Oh, kinky schoolteachers, neurotic priests walking through corridors towards confession, one or two mad bishops, a couple of bent coppers ... You name it, I got it!'[15] The only sticky moment came when the audience was invited to join the discussion. First to his feet was a man who introduced himself as Peter Ewing and announced that he had been at Catterick with Dirk during the war. 'Can I go back to 1941, or will it stir up too many memories?' he asked. 'Too many memories, Peter,' replied Dirk flatly and, he hoped, finally. Not a bit of it. Ewing began to recount how they had been born on the same day in the same part of London and been called up on the same day into the same unit. 'This is *my* interview, darling,' interrupted Dirk icily. But on Ewing went. To avoid peeling potatoes and cleaning the latrines he and Dirk had 'joined everything in sight', including not only the dramatic society and the choir, but also – to everyone's astonishment – the rugby club. 'Could we have the question, Peter?' asked the host politely. There was no question ... 'Wrap it up, Peter,' said Dirk. 'Wrap it up.' Eventually, amid mounting murmurs of embarrassment and irritation in the audience, he did – until the end of the talk, when Dirk told Tony Bilbow that he regretted not taking two roles: Christopher Isherwood in a mooted production of *I Am a Camera*, with Glynis as Sally Bowles; and 'the Louis Jourdan part in "Gigi"'. 'Did you not do "Gigi" because you thought you could not sing?' came the insistent voice from the back of the auditorium. 'You could sing beautifully at Catterick!'

The curious aspect of this dialogue is not that Ewing, a former teacher at the

Italia Conti drama school, had indeed been a colleague in the Royal Corps of Signals – they appeared together in *Judgment Day* – nor that they *were* born on the same day in north London. Rather, for reasons that are hard to understand, Dirk kept two letters from him, both sent after the NFT talk. In a postscript to the first, Ewing asked whether Dirk had heard about a new biography which alleged that Olivier had two homosexual affairs with actors before being taken to one side by Sybil Thorndike and her husband Lewis Casson, and told that if he wanted to get anywhere he had to change his ways. On which subject, wondered Ewing, should he burn Dirk's wartime letters, or return them to him 'for a laugh'? In the second, thanking Dirk for a 'long and most personal' reply, he wrote that Godfrey – clearly Ewing's lover – destroyed all Dirk's oldest letters and photographs in a misplaced fit of jealousy when Ewing went to America at the time Dirk was filming *Song Without End.* Whether Dirk wrote again is not known. Ewing was suffering from leukaemia and within eighteen months was dead, drowned in a north London park. It is odd that his two letters should have been allowed to survive, given the care with which Dirk removed from his 'archive' all trace of Jack Jones.

His talk was received with acclaim. 'Good audience, clever, alert,' records *Backcloth.*[16] 'All goes v. well – warm house (packed),' Dirk told the Diary. He tried to call Tony, but the coin-box at the NFT was jammed: 'Typical.' And perhaps, too, it was typical of him to attempt to use a public telephone; not, as most in his position would have done, request access to the manager's office. With a small group of supportive friends from both careers, he managed to see out one of the most testing evenings of his life, and to have acquitted himself so well he must have had to draw copiously on reserves of 'actor's energy'. He had already used up a fair amount two days before Tony's admission to hospital, when the BBC spent six hours with him for an *Omnibus* documentary to be broadcast on the eve of his birthday. He would need a good deal more in the days to come, even when not under public scrutiny.

Ian Todd carried out the operation for bowel cancer on the afternoon of 16 March. Dirk, who had been 'numb' with apprehension, was there when the patient was brought down from the recovery unit; and although Tony was asleep, he seemed to hear when Dirk spoke to him. 'I touch his hand so that he might remember I was there,' Dirk wrote in the Diary. 'It's going to be a long haul.' It was. After twelve days Tony was judged well enough to leave hospital, but it was another two weeks before they could travel home, with Elizabeth and George, who would, as so often before, come to the rescue. The idea of Dirk coping with Clermont and a debilitated Tony was beyond anyone's imagining. In the meantime there had been an important development professionally. Even as *Buried Alive* was proving true to its name, and even as finished copies of *An Orderly Man* were arriving at Chatto, Dirk's next novel was sold, on the strength of a few chapters, for £44,000. The news came on the morning of the operation, and it surprised Tony as much as it had Dirk, who suddenly had a new publishing house – Allen Lane, the hardback arm of Penguin Books – thanks entirely to a new agent for his writing; his literary Clair Loschetter. Ties were severed with London Management, whose involvement had in any case always been so notional as hardly to justify a percentage, and with ever-chillier winds wafting up kilts in the book world, he needed strong representation. Both Kathleen Tynan and Rosalind Bowlby recommended Patricia Kavanagh of A. D. Peters, which had a formidable stable of authors living and dead. She came to dinner with Dirk and Tony at the Connaught. 'Pretty and intelligent & rather nice,' decided Tony; 'tough, v. bright, a lady and nice too,' concurred Dirk in a letter to Norah Smallwood.[17] For him, Pat Kavanagh's effectiveness was already in no doubt. For *Voices in the Garden* and *An Orderly Man*, both of which he had delivered before being paid, Dirk's advance was £15,000 apiece. *Voices* had topped the bestseller lists for a month and, although it had not been as successful as *A Gentle Occupation*, just under thirty thousand copies were sold. His advance for the new novel, admittedly covering both hardback and paperback publication under one roof, was almost three times as high. Now, he confided to the Diary, 'All I have to do is finish the damned thing.'

As we know, when he first returned from Los Angeles and the American shooting of *The Patricia Neal Story*, Dirk felt he had enough ingredients from his 'wild trip' to form the basis of a novel which might even be called 'Have a Nice Day'. By the summer of 1981, when the 'coiling' began in his head, he was thinking of 'A Helluva Time in La Jolla', inspired by a drunken passenger on the flight home who had enjoyed himself in what Dirk called that 'rather ghastly' hangout of actors, writers and intellectuals on the coast. As yet nothing was written, but he was wondering what might have happened to the principal characters of *A Gentle Occupation*. Supposing Nettles and Rooke were now in a Californian writers' colony? Maybe not: they were probably 'divorced' by now. However he did not want to lose 'the material I grabbed during the Hollywood Experience. It's not startling. But it *is* odd.'[18] That material, one might think, would be pretty thin. Dirk was in California for less than a month; the working schedule was tough, with crack-of-dawn starts, late finishes and few days off. To judge by the Diary, there was no hectic round of social engagements; just enough to keep him and Tony amused, but, it transpired, more than sufficient for Dirk's antennae to pick up the signals which would lead to another comedy of manners. Kathleen Tynan was their principal hostess, and dinner at her rented house in Brentwood not only provoked a good deal of talk about writing but also gave Dirk the basis for at least one of his characters in the extravagant personality of Shirley MacLaine. The Sunday brunch Roddy McDowall gave in his honour, with a guestlist including Christopher Isherwood, Don Bachardy, Rock Hudson, Coral Browne and John Schlesinger, was even more productive; and that same evening Larry Schiller threw a sponsors party which swarmed with slightly awful people. All grist to the mill. Dirk's now somewhat distant association with Moura

Budberg was a foundation for Irina Miratova, a Russian émigrée in her eighties, marooned in a wooden gothic pile on the cliffs at Santa Monica, slowed by arthritis and her 'general heaviness', and joylessly downing her vodkas, alone. Kathleen Tynan herself, widowed and planning a biography of her husband Kenneth, supplied an outline for the protagonist. Dirk told Norah Smallwood that 'this thing, if I ever finish it, wont be just about films or film people. I have made sure of that, but it is about the type of person I seem to know best.'[19] For the title he toyed further with 'The Corner of Sunset' and 'Third on Sunset', before settling for *West of Sunset* because, he observed: 'Nothing lies west of Sunset Boulevard except the Pacific Ocean, and nothing lies west of the sunset itself but eternity . . .'.[20] It was Olivia de Havilland who, just before he left to make *Song Without End*, advised Dirk to remember at all times that Los Angeles was an 'Oriental city', quite alien to the European mentality; with that in mind, it could be survived. Dirk had managed to do so, and had even come to regard the place with 'wry affection'. He had spent little time in its sprawl, but had seen enough to people his olive store with a disparate bunch in self-imposed exile, 'like driftwood cast high on a beach'. Some people, says one of his characters, 'do not transplant easily'.[21] And nor do some novels: within days of Pat Kavanagh securing the handsome advance for *West of Sunset* in the United Kingdom, Bob Gottlieb, Dirk's New York publisher who had been given the same six chapters, turned it down flat. Viking Penguin took the book instead, for $30,000. There, and in Britain, its reception in the outside world would not be decided for a full year.

The response to *An Orderly Man*, meanwhile, was healthy enough for Dirk to feel that his swan-song with Chatto was no flop. In the first six months 23,500 copies were sold, more than earning out his advance. A letter from Emlyn Williams, whom he did not know but whose play *Night Must Fall* had inspired him in the Newick days, wrote to say that it was his best to date: 'Your wonderful portrait of your mother could not be bettered – lethal dialogue and yet (though it's completely unflinching) there is the ache of pity there'.[22] Another private and acute notice came from Jack, who said he liked the new book, but preferred *Voices in the Garden*. 'You are very good indeed', he added, 'at saying an interesting bookful without in fact saying anything *really* personal at all.' Sales had been given a flying start by the promotion Dirk undertook during that fraught week of Tony's operation. The *Omnibus* programme, all sixty-five minutes of it, was regarded particularly as a boost because of its serious approach; the interviewer, Saxon Logan, remained unseen as he asked about both the work and the man. Dirk said that he was a shy, timid person and that, as such, 'you're inclined to put an awful lot of camouflage on to hide yourself, so that people think "Ah, I know him", and they don't, actually, because you've covered yourself with so much gunge and rubbish'. Pressed about the image he had helped to contrive for himself, he replied: 'I'm not a liar. I've never cheated an audience in my life. I hope I've never cheated a reader of any book I've ever written. I've never cheated –

you're always found out if you cheat. I had to do those things; you had to go along with it. It's all part of the pattern of selling the product, and the product was me. And as far as I'm concerned, I'm the only thing that I care about.'[23] Of course we know differently about that final, utterly selfish-sounding remark; but for the purposes of the interview Dirk was hardly going to say he was worried sick that the person he cared most deeply about was facing a dangerous operation. A few days afterwards – on the morning of the NFT talk, and with Tony by now in hospital – he did a single national newspaper interview. He was more cautious than ever about the press: the coverage at the time of the 1980 Foyle's Luncheon and subsequent sniping convinced him that the *Daily Express*, for one, had it in for him. He was 'filled with doubt' about the English newspapers, he told Norah Smallwood. 'The sheer vulgarity of most of it. Even, to my shocked surprise, The Guardian and The Times stoop to snidery and sneers. I am so impressed by Alec Guinness ... who NEVER sees the Press and gets away with it all comfortably.'[24] Out of duty to Chatto, he duly agreed to see Nicholas Wapshott of *The Times*, and was much relieved: 'V. attractive. Gentleman. Informed and, I gather, on my side – anyway liked all 3 books.' Not only did Wapshott stay for lunch – '6 oysters. Cheddar cheese. Guinness' – but also Dirk allowed him and his wife, Louise Nicholson, to return the compliment the following week. 'Pretty pair,' Dirk decided. The article duly appeared just before the book was published, when he and Tony were back at Clermont. To read it now, no one would bat an eyelid: it seems both factual and positive. But Dirk found it harmful and deceitful; so much so that, when the Wapshotts telephoned from Eze three months later to suggest they get together again, Tony told them that he and Dirk were 'away'. Presumably the reasons for upset were, first, that in explaining why Dirk had been holed up at the Connaught for six weeks Wapshott mentioned not only the uncertainty over *Buried Alive* but also that 'he has been waiting for his friend, Tony Forwood, to come out of hospital'; and, second, that with *Victim* he 'radically rejected his type-casting and came clean about himself'.[25] Presumably, too, these statements counted for more because they were printed in Ulric's old paper. Worse was to come.

'Friends have been amazing & kind in these last weeks,' wrote Dirk, as he and the convalescent Tony made arrangements for their return to France. That afternoon Richard Rayner had come to the Connaught to do an interview for the weekly 'listings' and arts magazine, *Time Out*. 'Boring and, at first, sticky,' recorded Dirk. 'Finally all OK. Until they print the thing.' How right he was. Rayner's article, headed 'Rank Outsider', was published two months later, and announced at the start that Dirk was 'not ageing with grace. "I hope I never grow up," he announces petulantly. "Who the fuck wants to? Not me, I'll tell you that." [...] As far as age is concerned, he's not raging against the dying of the light. He's spitting at it.' Rayner observed that Dirk was 'still youthful, a Peter Pan figure with a full head of (too?) black hair', with a lined and pale face but sharp eyes; 'still unmistakably a fine looking man'; alert and arrogant in conversation, and in manner 'scrupulously polite and yet bitchy'. He asked about an episode in *An Orderly Man* when the woman owner of an antique shop, who had allegedly tried to swindle Dirk in selling him a table, was found murdered. Was it not a touch malicious to describe the singularly gruesome circumstances in such detail? 'It was her come-uppance for being such a shit to me,' Dirk replied. 'And to everyone else she'd cheated [...] She was an absolute old fuckpig [...] And it served her fucking well right. No one was happier than me.' Bogarde, wrote Rayner, 'doesn't care to hide his cruel streak. In part this side of his character is instinctive, in part it's a reaction born of the battles he's had to fight, for acceptance as an actor, for acceptance as a homosexual, for acceptance as a writer.' Dirk's comments about England, the British economy, London's cinemas, the country's newspapers and its youth – all were delivered 'with tetchy and eloquent intolerance'. And for reasons best known to himself, he had unburdened himself of the observation that 'You simply dare not risk the lavatories, my dear.'[26]

Before a copy reached Clermont, the *Daily Mirror* had picked up the story and applied its own 'spin', accusing Dirk – in Tony's words – 'of using foul language & hinting that he frequents public lavatories'. They decided it was a scurrilous, wicked, unfair and mean-minded piece, but knew it would be futile to sue because the newspaper had been careful to use inference. However, when the *Time Out* article arrived two days later, they were devastated. Rayner's perceptive thoughts about Dirk's acting and compliments about his on-screen passivity – 'a quality unusual among film stars' – counted for nothing when buried in what they saw as an 'abominably cruel and distorted' piece, one which was 'altogether not to be believed'. What to do? In some ways it would be better to let sleeping dogs lie and hope the article would be forgotten. But what if other papers took advantage? Then again, should not someone try to make the press think twice about printing such misrepresentations and cruelties in future? They sought advice from Laurence Harbottle, who said it would be unwise to sue, because it would drag on for two years, cost a fortune and attract wide publicity. He felt the magazine was ephemeral and had a small circulation. John Charlton agreed, saying nobody would take the piece seriously. With some reluctance, Dirk decided to take no action; but, as Tony noted, 'to attack D, of all people, of hanging round public conveniences etc is so dreadfully unfair – he's lived the most discrete existence to the point of dullness!'

Dirk resolved never again to speak to the British press. He also harboured second thoughts about moving back to England, an option which had become more likely than Switzerland or Paris because of the problems with Tony's health. At the beginning of 1983 they contacted a local estate agent, Stuart Baldock, and decided to put Clermont 'very quietly' on the market in the late spring. They would ask three million francs and hope to realise at least two and a half. In June, with the French property market in a slump and still with no sensible plan of where they would live, they went ahead. Half-hearted would be an inadequate description of their attitude as vendors; every time they looked out beyond their olive trees towards the Mediterranean, or across to the mountains of l'Estérel, or even the length of their split-level living-room, they knew with a pang how much they would miss Clermont:

> I [...] sit here mooning through my small windows down across the tiled roof of the woodshed, vividly green with the unfurling vine, out across the valley towards the hills ... soft plum in the morning sun. The clouds are spilling over the rim of the hill and trailing down like liquid to douse the sun [...] the ox-eye daisies are tall in the waving strands, the buttercups spread golden light everywhere, and sorrel floursihes in scarlet spears [...] the nightingale is back, a reluctant cuckoo does, from time to time, 'cuck' ... and we have, for the first time, a pair of ring doves who sooth the ear cooing in the cherries. And eating them all.[27]

When the first prospective buyers came to see it, Dirk took to the woods.

Only two couples were brought up the hill by Stuart Baldock and his staff. The first – a husband with an unpronounceable name and a possibly English wife, plus their son – liked what they saw, but wanted to take possession sooner than would suit Dirk and Tony, who had the end of the year in mind. Next, Dirk wrote, came a 'perfectly enchanting young couple, Belgian, two small children, saw the house, loved it instantly, asked no single question, accepted to the last sou the asking price and went away showering me with gratitude'. They confirmed the following day that they would pay the full asking price. 'There is much to discuss,' recorded Tony,

> but I suppose we have got to face up to it and agree to sell, but it's going to be such a wrench. To sit on the terrace on a perfect evening and contemplate such a different life is'nt joyful making. But we're too isolated. D can't drive a car & perhaps I wont be able to if my Parkinson gets a hold on me; and we've had one bad scare this year. Perhaps London will have alternative pleasures to offer, & possibly more work for D. One must trust one's judgement, but I wish my instinct was more clear. And quarantine for poor Bendo.

For days they agonised, miserably, over whether or not to go ahead with the sale. The local removal firm who brought their belongings in 1970 came to discuss storage and shipping. By now their thoughts were veering towards Paris rather than London as their destination, but the prospect was too depressing. One week after the Belgian couple had agreed to buy Clermont for three million francs, Dirk rang Stuart Baldock and cancelled the sale. He told Norah Smallwood that 'it just could'nt be done. I dont know why ... T was clearly deeply sad and I feared that he might become ill again. Is'nt it strange to love a place so deeply, solidly?' When the Bowlbys came to stay a few days later, champagne awaited them. As they all sat on the terrace in the cool of the evening, the nightingale went through its repertoire, the fireflies darted, and Clermont was at its most un-leavable. It was, wrote Dirk, 'a sort of breath released. Of pleasure.'[28] As long as Tony's next check-up in the autumn proved satisfactory, they would hang on for another twelve months or so.

Although he and Tony never integrated socially, preferring to keep themselves to themselves, France – specifically Provençal France – was where Dirk belonged. He had known that to be so ever since his first visits in the fifties. Now, in the eighties, he would talk of going 'back' to England, but never 'home'. That was here, in the Alpes-Maritimes, and spiritually it always would be, wherever he was. The French, in their delightfully haughty way, had not acknowledged his presence among them, had made no concessions. Nor did he desire or expect any. Away from his professional work he had wanted only a simple life on the land, and his wish had been realised. Now, by one of those gentle ironies, just as he was having to contemplate leaving them, his hosts began to show him overt respect. One day, a certificate arrived in the post, accompanied by a letter from President Mitterrand's Minister of Culture, Jack Lang, announcing that Dirk was *un Chevalier dans l'Ordre des Arts et des Lettres.* Despite the informality of its bestowal, it was a proud moment. In fact, Lang's office had approached him four years earlier, during the Presidency of Valéry Giscard d'Estaing, with a short questionnaire and a request for some documentation as proof of Dirk's existence, but he heard no more and had forgotten completely about it until the 'natty little scroll' arrived. He was entitled to wear the discreet insignia of the Order in his buttonhole, and received the permission of the Queen to do so without restriction when in Britain. Next, at the gala opening of the 1983 Cannes Festival, Dirk was fêted with a special award for his service to the cinema alongside Sophia Loren, Vittorio Gassman, Liza Minnelli, Fernando Rey, Robert de Niro and Ingrid Thulin. Introduced by Michèle Morgan, he was greeted with gratifying warmth.

Then came the publication by Acropole – his third French house – of *Des voix dans le jardin*, and in the Parisian equivalent of Total Exposure the press swarmed to meet him. The press – but not the populace. Both he and Tony had warned the publicity people at Acropole that a signing-session might not be a good idea. They were right. When he arrived at the Printemps store, no queue snaked from the books department into radio and television as it had done at Harrods, or out into the street as it did at Hatchards and Blackwells. He sat there for an hour or more, with five pens and with 200 copies to sign. Ten were sold. The weather; the wrong day; not long to Christmas were among the excuses offered. It was, he told the Bowlbys, 'very salutary' to sit at a table for an hour and a half 'like one of those wretched people demonstrating potato peelers or Home Knitting Machines which no one, but NO ONE, wanted'. Three copies were bought by English people who said they 'just happened to be there' and probably could not read French anyway; perhaps it was a sympathy purchase.[29] Tony was furious that his and Dirk's advice had not been followed, but Dirk kept his sense of humour, telling the gentleman from *Libération* who came to interview him afterwards: 'I've just received a custard pie full in the face!'[30]

The novel was dedicated to Charlotte Rampling and her husband, the musician Jean-Michel Jarre. To work with her for a third time was a further reason for the two-week stay in Paris. They had agreed to contribute to a documentary for French and Japanese television on the Louvre, and, in addition to a 225,000-franc fee there was the privilege – similar to the one he had had at St Peter's – of working for six nights in imposing and almost deserted surroundings which by day thronged with thousands. The series, *Le plus grand musée*, was to be on the lines of Kenneth Clark's fabled *Civilisation* and Dirk's responsibility was to talk with as much authority as possible about Greek sculpture in the Mediterranean basin – 'A lot of pots and dusty bits of terracotta' – and 'The Golden Age of Flemish Art'.[31] 'I knew as much about both as I know about taxidermy,' he wrote later. 'Less, frankly. But we mugged it all up from guide books and the rather dire script provided. I never saw a foot of the two-week epic – I rather think that the Japanese had the same good fortune – but I was paid a whacking great fee which covered the fares on Air France and the bills at the Connaught when the London visits arrived.'[32] The world of documentaries was proving to be more rewarding and, in truth, satisfying than it once had; he used to say that one of the reasons he left England in the late sixties was because the only work on offer was from the Forestry Commission. Worthy as that might have been, at least he was now being approached for subjects which interested him. Just before going to Paris he had spent a morning at the studios of Radio Monte Carlo, narrating a Thames Television film about Oskar Schindler, the factory owner and 'minor god of rescue' who had saved some twelve hundred Polish Jews from the exter-mination camps, and whose story was the basis of Thomas Keneally's *Schindler's Ark*, winner of the 1982 Booker Prize. Dirk was approached because of 'the Concentration Camp passages' in *An Orderly Man*. Again, he found the script lacking, but this time the main incentive was not the fee of £7,000 for a morning's work at a microphone: 'It's worth doing because I feel it important that the Young should realise just what happened to the Jews in the war.' The programme was to be shown shortly before Christmas: 'An odd time, I'd say, to put on such a depressing subject. What the Americans would call "the Big Turn Off" programme!'[33] In the event it attracted widespread praise.

So, too, did a further sign of how Dirk's adopted country was steadily taking him to its heart, when at the beginning of the year Robert Favre Le Bret, founding father of the Cannes Film Festival, telephoned with an invitation to be president of the 1984 jury. Caught somewhat off-guard, Dirk asked for time to consider. He rang Olga Horstig-Primuz, who said of course he must agree; it was a terrific honour. He would be succeeding to a chair occupied in the past by Cocteau, Simenon, Pagnol, Fritz Lang, Visconti and Losey; no Briton had ever been president. But it would mean a fortnight of unusual intensity, with the risk of controversy that always attended the most prominent and, arguably, still the most prestigious event of its kind. Politics, whether local, national or international, had been known to irrupt into the auditorium of the Palais des Festivals; the venality of the film industry was ever present. Of greater concern to Dirk, however, was Tony's condition. It had stabilised, but a check-up in London was due. How would he be in four months' time?

> Thinking ahead was a pretty silly thing to do now; there was the constant pricking of fright, like a buried thorn in the thumb, about the result of every three-monthly trip to Harley Street, the concealed look when a glass was lifted, a plate set down, a saucepan filled, a page turned, and handwriting grew smaller. Trivial things became, very slightly, hazardous. But I tried to batter along and find things to do which would be convincing proof that everything was, in fact, perfectly normal.[34]

Every absence from Clermont brought with it the worry of who would hold the fort and look after Bendo. Marie Danjoux, who with her husband Henri had more or less alternated house-sitting duties with Elizabeth and George, was now an elderly widow, and could not be expected to take such responsibility; apart from anything else, burglars were rife, habitually helping themselves to the Attenboroughs' belongings next door. Fortunately the Isoardi's daughter Marie-Christine and her husband Thierry were prepared to take over, often at short notice. For the fortnight of the Festival, Elizabeth and George would be happy to house-sit; it would give Tony a break from the oven and the mower to be pampered for two weeks at a good hotel, even if the town pullulated with riff-raff. He and Dirk went to meet the dapper Monsieur Favre Le Bret, who agreed that everything would be done to make them comfortable and free from worry. Dirk took the job.

First, though, he had to see *West of Sunset* on its way, with a more moderate bout of Exposure, not because demand had slackened. Far from it. He told Rosalind Bowlby – who had left Chatto and was looking after his publicity on a freelance basis for Allen Lane/Penguin – that he would not be interviewed by any national newspaper. Nor would he appear on David Frost's television programme, let alone on Terry Wogan's, which had wanted to set up a joint chat with Cliff Richard; 'one sees what they would make out of it,' noted Tony, 'so D says no thankyou'. He would, however, see the provincial press, do radio interviews and a *Pebble Mill at One* with Anna Ford. Of course he would sign at a couple of bookshops; and speak again at a literary lunch in Oxford. As for a return engagement at one of Christina Foyle's Luncheons – he was honoured to be asked back so soon. Among all these events was the far more important matter of Tony's check-up with the surgeon. Before they left for London, Tony had been deeply apprehensive, but Dirk gave him 'a good talking-to'. He 'really holds one together', Tony recorded. Another heartfelt compliment went privately in the same direction on the day of the appointment with Ian Todd, when Tony wrote that he wished Dirk's shoulders 'did not have to be so broad, which they certainly are'. Three days later, they were both 'somewhat numb with relief' when the surgeon reported that all was well and that Tony need not see him for a year. If the eight hundred or more copies of *West of Sunset* which Dirk signed that day at Hatchards and Waterstones were inscribed with an extra flourish, there was good reason.

There can be no quieter condemnation of the conduct of the British press than Tony's decision to stay away from the Foyle's Luncheon because of what the *Daily Express* had written four years earlier and because of the more recent 'sniping' exemplified by the *Daily Mirror* during the *Time Out* affair. Instead, Maude kept him company at the Connaught. The sadness was all the greater, first, because it was Dirk's sixty-third birthday; second, because when he returned from the Dorchester he said it had been perhaps the most moving morning of his life. The cause of his delight at being humbled was the chairman's speech by Peter Hall, his director on *Summertime*, who at Christmas in 1978 had read *Postillion* and *Snakes and Ladders* 'back to back', praised them in his own diary as 'magnificent stuff'[35] and written Dirk a fan letter. Now, on his feet in front of some four hundred guests, he explained why he held the guest of honour in such high regard, and why he admired him for the same wholesale dedication and 'honesty of expression' with which a member of the Peking Opera had once made Hall cry, and with which the ice-skaters Torvill and Dean had held the nation rapt in preceding days:

> He is a dangerous man because he is a man of so many parts that, in this pigeon-holing world, he has frequently taken the risk of having himself written off. He does so many things, and so many things superlatively well. He was, and is, a great movie star. When a great movie star, he was patronised for not being a great actor. But he went on until the world recognised that he was a great actor – a great, great cinema actor; someone whose craft is so seamless that the seam is invisible; someone who is so honest with himself and what he is doing that he does achieve that quality of absolute honest communication [...]
>
> He then went on to be a great writer – and I am using the word 'great' very carefully, not loosely. I believe that the memory of one's childhood and what childhood brings one is something that we all live on for the rest of our lives. It is given to very few people to have the technique and the grace to express the memory of their childhood with the richness and complexity that Dirk has expressed. There is the same naivety, the same honesty, the same simplicity and artlessness in that writing which there has been in his great performances.[36]

In an exemplary and brief reply, Dirk quoted Voltaire, 'just to prove that I am a little bit educated and that I do live in France. Voltaire said that the art of boredom was telling someone everything. I am not going to tell you everything.

And I have not done so in anything I have written.' What he did say, however, was that Hall's tribute had seemed to be 'to someone I do not know anything about'. Only those already 'in the sod' received such 'extraordinary homage'. He wrote to Hall later, saying the speech had 'got to him'; it had – to use another of his preferred expressions – 'unmanned' him. Hall was unrepentant and is so to this day. When his words were quoted back to him recently, he said: 'I'll stand by that.'[37]

Twenty-three

'But I'm still in the shell, and you haven't cracked it yet, honey'

Comforted by the surgeon's report, and with the Parkinsonism under control, Dirk and Tony put the question of selling the house to one side. There were reinforcements of local labour to help with the land and life could go on as normal, even if it required extra afternoon naps and a slight reduction in invitations to stay. Every now and then they would be reminded of how fragile was their hold on privacy; Clermont was no fortress, surrounded by high walls and electric gates; Bendo, no baying Baskervillian. One day, while Tony was out shopping and Monsieur Martinez – husband to 'Lady' the maid – was trimming the cypresses, a fan arrived. She flung her arms round Dirk's neck, said her name was Thelma and insisted that they had known each other in 1943. She had written letters, assuring him that she was 'in touch with Judy, on the other side'. Dirk, at his iciest, gave her short shrift and she went on her way, accompanied by an embarrassed younger man. A padlock was placed on the gate. A month or two later, another of the loonier tendency turned up in the middle of lunch. This time Tony was on hand to repel boarders. 'How one dislikes having to be dislikeable!' he recorded. Shortly before they left for Festival duty, they returned from a visit to the doctor and found a woman in a white cloak and white boots pacing their lawn, 'like some dotty E. F. Benson poetess'. She too was sent packing. With so much publicity surrounding Dirk's presidency of the jury, they would just have to keep their fingers crossed that it did not act as a magnet to the barking; quite enough madness attended the Festival in any case.

'I cant imagine WHY I agreed to be President,' Dirk wrote to Dilys Powell:

Maybe because it IS an honour and because I live in France, and what the hell ... why not? I seldom see a Movie. I do hate dubbed versions of things. So now I shall watch two a day in shaking despair. Oh! The miseries of the Czheck, the Russian and the Bolivian entries ... and those interminable Chinese bits! However my Jury is distinguished and sounds as if it will really be serious ... and we have no idiot American writer to hinder us this year! They get so dreadfully drunk, cast the wrong vote, and insist that as America is spending

so much money in the Town they HAVE to win the Palme d'Or. But this year
things will, I hope, be different. We'll see!'

Losey, who held the presidency in 1972, issued dire warnings about its hazards.
A potential killer, he called it. In the twelve years since he had done the job, the
Festival had changed. For Dirk it was 'a rather tacky affair, a film market attracting
a host of unattractive customers, porno films, bums and tits, dope and drugs'.
The glamour had begun to fade and the big stars stayed away. More to the point,
'the film-makers kept their best films out of the Festival – its increasing (perhaps
apocryphal) reputation for splitting the vote, juggling of the Jury votes, and
general under-the-bar-counter chicanery to suit individual interests had frightened off many serious studios and directors'. Word had spread that a decent film
stood no chance unless 'a wallet was placed on the table'. At least he had a good
idea of what to expect as he met his nine fellow jurors on the eve of the opening
gala. 'I felt rather like a member of the Salvation Army: I was in for a battle to
save lost souls indeed. How to restore dignity to a crumbling Festival?'² The first
promising sign came in the delightful shape of Isabelle Huppert, 'the most
adorable, sensible, grown-up, VERY brilliant actress I have met in years. I
immediatly made her Vice President of the Jury.'³ Among their companions were
the director Stanley Donen, the composer Ennio Morricone and the novelist and
scriptwriter Jorge Semprun. They were, as Tony observed, a 'distinguished and
valid' lot. Dirk escorted Isabelle Huppert to the gala opening, where the crowds
greeted them with unbridled enthusiasm. It was like old times – only a lot more
gratifying.

For two weeks, in the worst May weather since 1926, Dirk commuted along
the Croisette between his hotel – the Majestic, not the oick-infested Carlton –
and the auditorium. Most of the screenings he attended were at 8.30 in the
morning; during more conventional film-going hours he was constantly in
demand from press and television interviewers, to whom he was introduced by
a 'terrifically efficient ADC' called Frédéric de Goldschmidt – although Dirk
insisted on referring to him as de Rothschild. Sometimes Tony went with Dirk
to watch the 'very mixed bag of fillums from pretty good down to plain bloody
awful' and, on one occasion 'slept through a good half of what I was supposed
to be looking at'.⁴ On the penultimate day the jury met to decide the two leading
players, emerging after two and a half hours with a split decision in the male
category because they could not separate Alfredo Landa and Francisco Rabal,
the stars of the Spanish film *Los santos inocentes* (*The Holy Innocents*); and with
Helen Mirren as best actress for *Cal*. When Dirk disclosed the choices to the
Festival authorities, there were blank looks. Who *are* these people, they asked.
What films are they in? 'Helen Mirren? – she's a *nobody.*' The powers that be
wanted 'big names' to add lustre to their Festival in the eyes of the world. Sorely
tempted to remind them that it was they who had selected the damned movies
in the first place and that therefore the actors and actresses might have rung a

bell or two, Dirk ignored the splutters of indignation. Worse was bound to follow in choosing the winners of the other prizes and especially the Palme d'Or for best film. On the final afternoon the jury was incarcerated at a villa high above the town. Their deliberations were sometimes 'stormy'. 'I behaved exactly like a British Officer in Aden!' he wrote to Norah Smallwood on 29 May. 'I dealt, in my jury, with Italian, Hungarian, Russian, USA and French ... No cheating, absolutely none. I forced them to vote according to MY ethics and standards, a pretty hard task ... but we WON hands down.'

Backcloth contains a confusing account of the proceedings and their immediate aftermath, when 'Authority' came to hear the result before Dirk made the official announcement in front of the Festival audience and millions watching on television. The winning film was *Paris, Texas* by the German director Wim Wenders; the jury's special Grand Prix would go to *Naplo* (*Diary for My Children*) by the Hungarian Márta Mészáros; the best director was Bertrand Tavernier for *Un dimanche à la campagne* (*A Sunday in the Country*); and the cinematographer Peter Biziou had made the best artistic contribution with his work on *Another Country* – a film which, incidentally, Dirk had turned down, because it would have meant 'another queer part'. At these names, the face of 'Authority' fell. Where were the Americans? *Paris, Texas* was set, rhapsodically, in the United States, but directed by a foreigner. What about something for John Huston, director – finally – of *Under the Volcano*? He was here, in Cannes, having flown thousands of miles. At which point in the discussion, according to Dirk, a male juror said: 'Listen: you do *not* win the fucking Palme d'Or for *travelling*!'⁵ The story is a good one, but the remark, if true – and it has a definite Bogardian flavour – must have come earlier in the proceedings; the jury had already decided unanimously to pay homage to Huston for his *oeuvre* and for his 'extraordinary contribution to the cinema'. In *Backcloth*, but nowhere in the official record, the *hommage* is given *in absentia* to Satyajit Ray, who also had a film in contention but who had been too unwell to do any travelling at all. Huston and the other winners enjoyed their night of triumph; so did Dirk, knowing the significance of every word he uttered on the stage of the Palais.

One or two of the newspapers carped at his jury's choice for the Palm, but he himself attracted a good deal of favourable publicity, as he had throughout the two weeks. Aristocratic; gentleman to his fingertips; *grand seigneur* – they like paying that kind of compliment in France when they feel it has been earned; and even though the decisions from the jury room exasperated 'Authority', the general view was that Dirk had been an excellent president. He really did work hard, reported Tony, 'both in doing an ambassadorial job for his own country [...] and also in controlling a quite distinguished but sometimes not very tractable jury who all wanted a piece of the cake for their own countries, quite under-standably [...] even the mayor of Cannes (who is a forceful lady) told him that he had brought the festival back to what it had once been.' Not the least cause for pride was the way in which Dirk had somehow managed to achieve confidentiality in a set-up which usually leaked like a sieve. It helped that he insisted on a late and secret ballot. Tony recorded: 'Forty-five minutes before the ceremony he and the jury were rushed back to the Palais de Festival in convoy with a police escort with sirens, flags flying on all the cars, and all other traffic stopped as they tore through all the traffic lights whether red or green. Rather like the procession of a South American dictator and his minions. I think he rather enjoyed that bit.'[6] Thirty-six hours later, tired but satisfied at a job well done, he was dodging the showers to plant his petunias and geraniums. Losey's warnings had been useful in preparing Dirk for the worst; 'it' had not, after all, killed him.

There had, as we have seen, been little contact between the two men. At the end of 1982 a letter arrived from the University of Wisconsin, in Losey's native state, asking Dirk to support its award of an honorary doctorate of humane letters. Dirk wrote back, expressing some surprise that it had been felt necessary to write to *him*:

> We in Europe have known, for many years now, that he is one of the greatest living cinema Directors. His presence among us brings us honour. There are very few indeed who have reached his position in the Cinema, and fewer who have had such a profound influence upon it: he is, in a humble Englishman's opinion, very well worthy of a 'seat' in such a respected institution as yours and those of us who love and respect his works pray that he is spared to us for a good time to come.[7]

Losey duly received his cap and gown, but Dirk's prayer was not answered. The last time they met he was perturbed by how ill his friend looked. Then, in June 1984, Patricia Losey telephoned from her house in Royal Avenue, Chelsea, to say Joe was dying. The next day Dirk rang, and before they could speak she was called upstairs. Losey was dead. That afternoon, Dirk wrote: 'I did'nt expect Joe to die, for some silly reason. I suppose I thought that because he had been so very much a part of my life he would stay on, the grumpy, cantankerous, loving genius that he was.' Losey had given Dirk 'the courage to extend myself in my work: he never told me what to do, but watched closely what I did and asked for more ... extending, demanding, fullfilling me as an actor, helping me to expand and to experiment. And the pleasure was intense: and rewarding; as were the letters which he wrote after each film ... noticing things which I had thought that perhaps he had not seen: but old Joe had seen all, nothing escaped him.' The reflections were, inevitably, bitter-sweet:

> I remember, with constant joy, the day he showed me his Cartier watch from Liz Taylor and his enraged reaction when I said that I liked him better in the days when he wore a 'tin one'. He knew just what I meant by the remark, and finally, ruefully, he removed the watch and put it into the pocket of that huge

house-coat thing he used to wear. I know the watch went back on the moment I left the room! But the one thing I will always, always remember him for was his blinding courage, his passion for the Cinema and good players and good Crew, and his burning determination to make magic on the screen. That he did. He has at *least* four Great Movies to his credit [...] [which] may seem a small sum for such a rich life: but they were Movies which altered the way all Movies were to be made in the future. I think thats a pretty wonderful record: and maybe four is too modest an assumption on my part ... but it's enough to be going on with. Clever sod! Shitty bugger! Goodness HOW I shall miss him.[8]

Dirk paid tribute in public, too, giving an interview a few days later to the BBC *Arena* programme and hurrying to Losey's defence when *The Guardian* printed a grudging obituary. He was, said Dirk, 'the most European of American directors, and he knew a great deal about the British and our often complex behaviour and emotions and placed these blindingly on the screen'.[9] And perhaps in that sentence is the essence of the understanding between these two very different men. For Dirk, surely, could claim to be the most European of English actors.

A 'Final Wrap Party' in honour of Losey was given at Twickenham Studios by his widow. Organised by Theo Cowan's team, with long-distance input from Clermont, it was timed to coincide with the next visit by Dirk and Tony to London for the latter's medical checks. 'It was a happy event, rather than a miserable one,' Dirk wrote afterwards to Patricia Losey. '[...] We were all there because we had loved him, admired him, been nourished (theatrically speaking) by him. And everyone spoke of him with such terrifically warm pleasure that he HAD to be a decent bloke underneath all the humph and huff and blowing.' Informality had been essential: 'No weary Knight bleating from a pulpit: no quotes from John Donne, no singing of 'The Lord Is My Shepherd' ... none of the crap. Just an end-of-picture party for a most particular man.'[10] It was, Dirk concluded, 'a chapter closed'. Unfortunately it was not the only one. Indeed, Losey's death was symptomatic of what seemed to Dirk and Tony to be heightened activity by the Reaper. The 'gathering', they called it. Tony's father, Lusia Parry and Irene Howard had all died recently – the last, touchingly, leaving £1,000 apiece to her staunch friends. Cukor and Fassbinder, too, had gone. So had Ingrid Bergman, at a mere sixty-seven. Now, there were serious concerns about Norah Smallwood who, apart from her other afflictions, had collapsed with abdominal trouble and been admitted to the Westminster Hospital for an emergency operation. Twice during their stay Dirk and Tony visited her there, and she seemed to be making good progress. On the day after the Twickenham party, Dirk went alone and was shocked by her deterioration. 'She lay back on the pillows as transparent as egg-white on a windscreen,' he would write in a poignant passage at the end of *Backcloth*.[11] They returned to Clermont, at once encouraged by Tony's progress and deeply worried about her. Daily checks with either the hospital or Rosalind Bowlby indicated a roller-coaster alternating between resilience and resignation, until finally on 11 October 1984 she died. 'She will make a big empty hole in a lot of people's lives,' recorded Tony, 'and D & I were very lucky to enjoy her intimacy & confidence.' Behind that somewhat flat Diary entry lay immense sorrow at the loss of someone with whom Dirk had conducted another 'love affair without carnality'.

It had been less than eight years since his first tentative contact by letter with Needlewoman Number Two, his 'patcher'. During that time, he variously referred to her as 'the Reverend Mother', 'Head', 'Madame Petitbois' and, by extension, 'Chips'. Once, in honour of her fondness for dashing headgear, he addressed her as 'My dear Hat'. Inevitably, their correspondence was less voluminous than that with Dorothy Gordon because they talked often by telephone and because they saw each other at least two or three times a year either in London or at Clermont, where she would stay in the spare room known as the 'Tart's Parlour'. Nevertheless, it was carried on at a level of genuine openness and – yes – an 'intimacy & confidence' from which Dirk held back in his transatlantic letters: astonishing as it might seem, Dorothy Gordon never knew of Tony's existence. Both women had played an essential role in Dirk's life as a 'sounding-board'; both in their loneliness satisfied to different degrees his 'need to be needed' and they themselves benefited greatly from doing so; but to Norah Smallwood Dirk opened his heart without reserve. When she told him privately in 1982 that she would be retiring from Chatto the following spring, her decision 'weighed as heavily with me as bricks in the pockets of a drowning man'.[12] That was true, but only from the professional point of view. After she had left the firm, he was angered to learn that people said to her, 'I expect you don't hear from Dirk Bogarde now.' He was reminded of a note that Visconti had sent after Dirk and Tony called to see him at Lake Como on their way back from filming in Munich; it thanked Dirk for 'coming so far out of your way to see me: now that I am no longer of any use to you'.[13]

I think that that remark, although I understood why he had written it in my heart, hurt me more than any other he had ever made, or anyone had ever made! Did he, I wondered, really think that my admiration, my awe, my respect, for him was simply founded on his 'use' to me? It was an alien feeling for him: one that he found hard to understand in the sometimes ugly world in which he lived when people DID only love him for his 'usefulness' or 'influence'. But it was not, and never could have been, that with me.

The same applied to Norah Smallwood: 'As you know, I trust by now ... (for it has been written down by me to you often enough) ... I simply love you. I love you, respect, admire extravagantly, and depend, still, on you. Even though Chatto (with its purple painted doors) is light miles from us both now.'[14] Later, when Chatto's parent company formally marked her retirement with a dinner that Dirk was unable – and, in truth, unwilling through shyness – to attend, he wrote: 'How little I thought, that evening when I "did" the dreaded Russell Harty Show, that my whole life was about to be altered by a stranger from quite another world. And that through that stranger I would be permitted to set foot, all be it modestly, into that world. And that the stranger would shortly become so very dear to me."¹⁵ How thrilled she was to see her protégé-author earn the description by one of the leading French newspapers as 'Bogarde le proustien' – especially as she had recently overseen a new translation of *A la recherche du temps perdu*. How proud she would have been that, one month after her death, Dirk was invited to accept an honorary doctorate of letters from St Andrews University. And, despite her possessiveness, how gratified she was to have been a conduit for Dirk to acquire a sounding-board from another generation in Rosalind Bowlby and her husband. What Norah Smallwood can never have imagined is that less than a fortnight after her death someone who commanded as much respect in a different but related milieu, and who, just as she had been in the mid-seventies, was a complete stranger, should write to Dirk with a request that was a good deal more unexpected than an offer of potential publication; let alone that it would lead to another particular, and mainly epistolary, friendship. This time the woman who unwittingly chose the perfect moment was French. Her name was Hélène Bordes, although she would become known before too long as 'La Planche' – 'The Plank'.

West of Sunset, which Dirk dedicated to the Bowlbys, had not done as well as hoped. It flickered among the bestsellers, but in hardback never came near the figures achieved by the first two novels or the non-fiction. No blame attached to anyone, and certainly not to his new 'team' at Allen Lane/Penguin. He had first met them a week after the novel's 'auction', while Tony was still in hospital. Dirk's editor, Fanny Blake, and Peter Mayer, the assertive American who had run Penguin since 1978, took him to lunch with Pat Kavanagh and lifted his spirits by being 'V. civilised and, above all, young and pushy'. Momentary consternation was caused when as Dirk left the table he ruffled Mayer's luxuriant head of hair. Also there was Tony Lacey, a straight-talking, affable northerner who had recently set up a new Viking hardback imprint, more mainstream than Allen Lane, with authors such as Ruth Rendell and John Mortimer, into which Dirk's writing would make a comfortable fit, perhaps with the next book. There were no complaints that his first for the Penguin group had done less well than hoped; it simply failed to catch the public's imagination as its predecessors for Chatto had. There was always the paperback – kept in the same house, of course – and there would be another new title from their 'star signing' before too long. Indeed, they knew that a fourth volume of autobiography was under way. More episodic than *An Orderly Man*, it would find him looking back at the fifty-odd years he had spent scuttling about as a hermit-crab and at some of the people who had caused him in differing degrees to pop his head out of the shell. 'Kith and Kin' had been his first thought for a title, after the unofficial relatives with whom he and Lu surrounded themselves in childhood; then 'Something I Forgot ...' and most recently 'Time and Again'. However, it had not progressed well. So 'blocked' had he become by the time *West of Sunset* was launched that he had changed tack and started another novel, provisionally called 'Closing Ranks'. But the worries about Tony and about the future had made it all the harder for Dirk to drag his Muse from her corner, and at the moment of Norah Smallwood's death he had practically given up hope for either book. The position would not have been quite so grim, so enervating, if there had been a film to make.

As well as a new publisher and a new literary agent Dirk also had a new agent for his acting. While Dennis van Thal was on holiday, his assistant at London Management, Jonathan Altaras, telephoned to introduce himself, allowing Dirk the opportunity to unload some of his worries. The next day Altaras rang to say that Christopher Morahan, director of *Jewel in the Crown*, the triumphant adaptation of Paul Scott's *The Raj Quartet*, 'flipped' at the mention of Dirk's name, believing he had retired from acting. A script for the small screen would be with him in a trice. At a first reading, Dirk found the thriller 'In the Secret State' well-written but confusing. Normally that would have been the end of it; but no, he read it again, spoke to Morahan and agreed in principle to take the role. It would mean seven weeks of locations in Britain. The following morning Tony had reason to worry about his insides, and told Dirk that he might not be able to join him on the film. Dirk gave it careful thought, and pulled out. Tony was mortified that his frailties should be having such a negative impact on Dirk's career, but some good had come of the episode because Altaras, who had impressed from the word go, now took over Dirk's representation full-time with the blessing of Dennis van Thal. Then again, if the young hotshot continued to find good potential marriages between subject and client, it would be frustrating, even soul-destroying, if domestic circumstances made it impossible for Dirk to fulfil them. The next serious proposition came via Charlotte Rampling, wondering if Dirk would be prepared to do *The Quiet American* in place of Richard Burton, who had died recently in Switzerland. Where would it be shot? No one seemed to know. The script was unexciting, although it afforded a huge central role. In any case it was a re-make. Then came an offer of the husband in *Anna Karenina*, for television, opposite Jacqueline Bissett. Location: Hungary. Time: September – the month for Tony's check-ups. The answer, again, was no.

Dirk's most persistent pursuers at this stage were David Puttnam and the director Roland Joffé, who had just completed *The Killing Fields*. Puttnam, who had led his *Chariots of Fire* troupe up to Clermont for the *fête-champêtre* in 1981, had seen Dirk and Tony since; they liked him for his enthusiasm, commitment and old-fashioned good manners. First he wondered if Dirk would like to play in a new version of the 1944 *film noir, Laura*, playing the role for which Clifton Webb was an Oscar nominee; Dirk declined because it was another re-make and a 'faggy part' to boot. Then Puttnam's co-producer, Sandy Lieberson, sent a mysterious postcard which referred to Dirk joining them in the forests of South America. A rum business indeed. More than a month went by, before Jonathan Altaras called to say that Puttnam was sending a script to his office by courier for the most urgent attention. Dirk told Altaras to play it cool, and to read the script himself before sending it on. Then Puttnam called Dirk, first to protest in jest that the agent was reading the screenplay before the actor, and second to explain a little about the project. It was a multi-million-pound movie, called *The Mission*, with an original screenplay by Robert Bolt. It would indeed be shot in South America and what is more, Robert de Niro had said he would co-star if Dirk agreed. As Tony admitted, it was 'a big deal'. The part they had in mind was that of a Jesuit priest – 'a seventy-year-old man, physically weak but with fantastic strength inside' – who forms a bond with a young slave-trader full of remorse at having slain his own brother in a duel.[16] Dirk never heard, nor read, that far. He told Altaras to turn down the offer, sight unseen, as he did not want to go to South America. The same day, in white-lie mode, he wrote to Puttnam, explaining that he had just accepted a film to be made in Paris. Furthermore:

> After you and I had spoken, I checked out the map. Brazil is a hell of a long haul by air. I can just about make Nice–London frankly ... and it is also a little too far for a little too long (you said two months) ... and I feel, in my bones, that it has to be what we used to call 'a Roughie' movie. I've made a hell of a lot of those in my thirty odd years in the Cinema but I honestly dont think that I am up to 'roughies' now.*

Not reading the script, Dirk explained, 'prevents me from being put in the situation of turning it down: except for purely physical reasons'. He felt wretched about having to say no to Puttnam and Joffé: 'But I feel that I would have been more of a liability to you than a help. F. Stage at Pinewood is one thing: Brazil, at my age, alas, is another ball game.'[17] Joffé wrote, regretfully, admitting that the movie might indeed be a *bit* of 'a Roughie', and there the matter rested. Until, three months later, the director called from New York with an appeal for Dirk to reconsider; Joffé's girlfriend, the actress Cherie Lunghi, backed him up by telegram. Dirk slept on it, but still said no. 'Joffé is now the hottest director around & I think it would be very big money, but there are many problems,' noted Tony wanly. It was Dirk's 'first offer for a major movie in many a long year and I'm hardly happy to be the cause of his rejecting it'. In its way, this was a watershed; a moment when Dirk had reluctantly to pass an open door in the narrowing corridor of his life, knowing that few would ever again offer such promise. For Tony, trying to come to terms with the implications of his ill-health

---

* The part of Father Gabriel, which had been written originally with Cyril Cusack in mind, was reworked for a younger man and accepted by Jeremy Irons – Cusack's son-in-law. The film, which cost £18 million, was shot in Colombia and Argentina, and was indeed a 'Roughie' for cast and crew.

was as bad as coping with the conditions themselves. When he knew that it would be impossible for him to accompany Dirk to the degree ceremony at St Andrews University, he felt 'a retired "minder" for the first time'. The 'Leader', as Arnold Schulkes used to call him, was being led. The mutual dependence with Dirk was increasingly one-way, and Tony hated it.

When the letter arrived from Scotland's oldest university offering him an honorary doctorate, Dirk thought it might be a hoax. He wrote back, cautiously. 'You cant tell with these Students,' he said when letting the Bowlbys into the secret. 'I quite fancy a mortar-board. Though why in God's name I should be given a D. Litt I cant imagine. In a way I accepted for Norah. I think she would have been amused but quite pleased that "her" find had been elevated, and by St Andrews too. Not your actual Sussex or Bristol or Essex.'[18] Because he had also been saddled with an after-dinner speech, it meant two nights away from base at the Connaught, and from Tony. Rosalind Bowlby agreed to stand in as 'minder' – a satisfyingly direct link to Norah Smallwood and the first days at Chatto, as well as a close confidante. At the ceremony, on 4 July 1985, he found himself in company with a leading art historian, a former diplomat and world authority on Tibet, Holland's principal expert on the Old Testament, the scientist who discovered beta-blockers, and the university's first woman Rector, Katharine Whitehorn. He felt 'a terrible impostor'. There was a certain amount of 'kneeling and bobbing', which he negotiated successfully, but he said afterwards that because he was lost in a 'haze of terror' he heard nothing of the citation.[19] This was a skilful, perceptive and witty analysis by the Dean of Arts, Donald Bullough, of how Dirk had 'attained undoubted excellence in the art of *Mimesis* in both acts and words' thanks to 'an almost obsessive concern with precision and order' and a 'controlled strength'. The Dean commented that the French, 'deplorably – as so often since Waterloo', had preceded the British in recognising artistic and literary talent: 'It is, however, not too late to introduce a new element of order into the kaleidoscope of a distinctive achievement.'

At the dinner that evening, when he had to speak on behalf of all the graduands, Dirk said he was 'a thoroughly ill-educated man' who throughout his early life 'resisted, with grim determination, any form of learning whatsoever: to the suicidal despair of my parents and the exhausted hopelessness of my teachers. I found ignorance far less tedious and much more comforting. And that ignorance has brought me here tonight. Do you wonder at my astonishment?' In his career, he said, there had been room for nothing *but* astonishment, and 'to be astonished is one of the surest ways of *not* growing old too quickly'. Every day he grew warier as he confronted his work; 'more and more uncertain as to whether I should go on with it, I find reassurance only in my fears themselves. The writer, or the actor, who loses his self-doubt, who gives way as he grows old to sudden euphoria, to prolixity, should stop playing, or writing, immediately; the time has come for him to lower the curtain or to put aside the pen.' Even the honour the university had given him would not allay his fears: 'I have not yet quite got it all together.' After the dinner, there was a ball in a 'giant, chiffon-draped marquee' on the university lawns. It reminded Dirk of a Tissot painting: 'All the girls in long frocks, the men mostly in tail-coats or the kilt. Romantic and young ... and very distant from our daily life.'[20]

The proceedings had given Dirk much food for thought. 'It was, without question, the most important day of my adult life,' he wrote, '[...] apart from war, that is, and I was very much moved by the welcome and the reception which I was accorded by the Faculty and the Students themselves; I had NOT considered myself important in any way.'[21] During the long ceremony – and one suspects that the 'haze' was caused not so much by terror as by reflection – he had been aware not only of the dignitaries, 'in ranks rising high to the ceiling of this splendid hall', but also that 'behind them, far, far away, and only in my mind's eye, is the backcloth massed with the faces and figures of the people who brought me here' – above all Ulric and Margaret, Tony, Norah Smallwood ...[22] A few days later, on the terrace at Clermont, he and Tony were mulling over what had happened. The word 'backcloth' came up, and they both knew at once that it had to be the title for 'Bio. 4', on which Dirk, once stalled, had begun again to work. In fact, he had eight chapters under his belt; the events in Scotland would provide the ideal finale. And finale it must be: he had had enough of writing about his own life.

The impetus to complete the book was in large part the result of the letter he had received a few days after Norah Smallwood's death and just before the invitation from St Andrews. Oddly, it too was on university notepaper – from Limoges, where one of the principal members of staff in the Faculty of Letters was Hélène Bordes, *maître de conférences*. She wrote, not to ask him to give a lecture, but to seek his approval for a paper she was preparing on the first three volumes of Dirk's autobiography. Of course she could go ahead, he replied: 'I can not think that this would have any interest for French students however: the works are not published in France because they are considered "too local" in appeal! They have been translated into a number of other languages but I dont think that my particular kind of "dialogue" translates well into French ... as you yourself admit.' One other thing: 'I do not wish to be involved in any way with this work, for I am swamped with my own at the moment, and I do not need to read it first to "make changes" because my French is not good enough and I am certain that you will write what you feel and what you want.' He wished her good luck and thanked her for the compliment.[23] On St Valentine's Day 1985 he wrote again, having received a draft of her essay, '"Peuple" et "Pays" dans l'*Autobiography* de Dirk Bogarde': 'I am overwhelmed by the amount of work you have had to do, and the great generosity of spirit towards my humble efforts which you show [...] I had no idea that I would end up being so beautifully dissected by such *caring* hands in the University of Lovely Limoges.' Hélène Bordes contrasted him with Nabokov, who saw autobiography as a means of getting oneself out of the way so that one could write about something else;

Dirk, on the other hand, was producing a self-portrait of greater and greater transparency in order to reach a deeper and more complex truth.[24] Dirk was delighted: 'It almost manages to explain my own book to myself.' He told his 'dissector' that Norah Smallwood had made him realise that he had, after all, led 'an extra-ordinary life, as opposed to a quite ordinary one, and that, historically, one day, my comments on the period in which I had lived might be of some value to a researching writer'. She – who had published Murdoch, van der Post, Huxley and Pritchett, and had twice seen new translations of Proust into print, 'Thank God, and Norah!' – had pushed Dirk, and it had paid off, 'even more than the inspiration and bullying offered me by Mrs X. Alas! both are now dead and I am left with an immense hole in my capabilities, afraid to try anything without their criticism'. By taking such a serious interest in, and being so generous about, his work, Madame Bordes had done 'a great deal to throw, as we say, a bridge over that hole of despair'.[25] Yes, he said when she replied, 'Despair was the word I meant':

> I write like an idiot: re-write and re-write, page after page, so that sometimes I type one page, or even one paragraph, eight, ten, twenty times. And still I am not satisfied [...] So that it is crossing a deep pit of despair, dark and hopeless [...] one KNOWS one will never get 'it right' ... and [...] the way across the pit is dangerous because if one falls, from tiredness or from a lack of criticism and council, or even comfort, one could fall for ever. One HAS to get to the other side of the pit: and your letters and your thesis have provided me with the plank and the rail to go ahead. Simple![26]

When the essay, handsomely printed in a symposium of great erudition, arrived at Clermont in May, Dirk addressed her as 'Chère Madame Planche'. The form would vary – 'Madame La Planche', 'Madame de la Planche', even 'Dear Plank' – but the Plank is what Hélène Bordes would be from now on. Her status as such would be acknowledged in the book which she had inspired him to finish. Readers were not to know, however, that in her Dirk had found another clever, formidably well-read, independent-minded, sympathetic woman of a certain age, who lived some distance away, and who was quite content with an epistolary 'love affair'. Referring in *An Orderly Man* to the 'Mrs X' correspondence, he had written that a friendship based on two people meeting through letters was not unusual; 'there have been many others like it before. But it is a once only business. It can *never* be repeated.'[27] Not on the same scale and at the same pitch, perhaps. But the void left by his Needlewomen suddenly seemed not quite so deep and dark.

In their different ways the two universities provided the brightest spots in what was to become an *annus horribilis* – a year that had begun with Clermont being snowed up for a week, and with yet another burglary at the Attenboroughs. Dirk and Tony bought a sporting gun. Nothing fancy like the chased-metal devices brandished by young Tony in the thirties. This was a 'rough & ready mass produced affair'. They tried it out in the garden: a tin on a flowerpot at about fifty yards. Dirk fired three times and scored a bullseye with each shot. Tony's one attempt was a fraction low, but the tin still went spinning. They were, they decided, 'dead-eyed dicks'. However burglars were not the main concern. Nor were 'the slowness, the shaking legs, the slight wobbles now and then [...] the good days, the bad days, the buttons which wont get buttoned, the paper he cant fold, the table napkin he cant un-fold, the spoon he cant quite get into the saucer ... it's not ALL the time ... but it's there, and it wont ever get better.' These were the small signs of the Damoclean threat hanging constantly over their happiness on the hill. What would they do if Tony had to sign a form saying 'no impeding ailment' when his driving licence expired? 'I'm far too old to try and learn driving again,' Dirk told Elizabeth; 'perhaps I shall have to buy one of those awful chugging buggies old ladies have to go shopping!' Whatever else, 'I have to try and keep this place going as long as humanly possible because I have almost seen Tote "die" when he is away from it ... when he's in London it's pretty hellish. All that matters are the Tests, the results and then he wants to come immediately Home. It's pathetically sad, and touching ... so I know my duty now ... no return to a dear little flattie in London or somewhere ... we stay here until the last moment. If we are lucky enough.' By the end of 1985 the reserves of luck were badly depleted.

Gilles Cabrol came one October day to give Tony a thorough check-over. He ordered X-rays of the liver and the prostate, and although nothing untoward was found, the latter needed further examination. Dirk and Tony decided to leave for London, where, fuelled with Carlsberg Export, Tony failed to satisfy the examiners and an operation was arranged. It was back to King Edward VII, where on the last occasion he had been judged its 'star patient' and smothered with kisses by senior members of the nursing staff as he left. Once more Dirk began to plod the familiar path from Carlos Place to Beaumont Street. The operation took place on a snowy November afternoon and a dopey Tony reported that he had been awake throughout, comparing it to 'a film like Kubrick'. No malignancy was found. 'So,' asked Dirk in the Diary, 'what else matters?' While Tony recuperated, Dirk had a few distractions; principally, revising the text of *Backcloth* and, at one point, engaging in a polite wrestling bout with the lawyers over a chapter devoted to the Cannes Festival. Most of the time when not at the hospital he spent in the suite at the Connaught, seeing a few of his and Tony's closest friends and professional advisers. One day he lunched downstairs with Glenda Jackson, buying a tie – '22 quid!' – for the occasion. He noted how 'very warm and kind' the staff were as he and his guest were led to his customary place, the one once occupied by King Farouk. 'Thirty years at this table,' recorded Dirk, '– and I'm still (by the Grace of God) still there.' Another day, he visited a doctor on his own account. He was committed to appear in the new year in an adaptation of Graham Greene's short story, 'May We Borrow Your Husband?',

and had to take the obligatory insurance medical: 'A mere formality I fear,' he noted after returning from the consultation. 'I could be raving mad or slowly dying of something. He'd never know.' The gloom was increased because his role was for the small screen and, for want of anything better to do, he had watched a fair amount of television – 'in horror': 'What have I let myself in for in Feb? It's all so dreadful. Standards have dropped far below the helm.' There were few compensations in his week alone: 'no washing up at least. And no planning meals. I really *DO* like Room Service – even if I don't eat more than oysters or s/salmon. Easy. If you have the loot.' It was costing £250 a day, for the rooms alone – and that could not go on for long.

A week after Tony was released from hospital, and with a 'mind blowing!' Connaught bill settled, they were back at Clermont. The flight to Nice had been efficient, but marred by what seemed to be 'half the staff of Sothebys', on their way to Monte Carlo and 'proving by their voices and behaviour generally, that the Middle-upper (?) Class is worse, or as bad, as the Marbella lot'. That night they watched the Louvre documentary, finally transmitted two years after Dirk had made it: '*WHY* did I bother? Boring and reverential & a big Turn-off.' He told Hélène Bordes:

> I spent months studying the subject, and we were 'free' and not like School-Teachers ... and suddenly they 'cut' all my work and replace it with some stupid voice of a woman speaking EXACTLY as I did NOT want it to be! I wanted it to be alive and amusing. How else do you make 'stone' come alive for M. Toutlemond I wonder? And then they dubbed me with a terrible voice ... not like mine at all ... and only left in a few of my words ... I was very sad.[28]

Nevertheless it was good to be home. Existence, 'of a kind', could resume.

Not without drama. Two days later Tony was back in hospital, this time at the Villa Madeleine in Grasse, which he knew well from his many tests. At 5.30 in the morning he had appeared in Dirk's room, haemorrhaging badly and in great pain. Doctor Cabrol took control and, in his own car, rushed him to Grasse for an emergency operation to relieve a blocked bladder, while Dirk and 'Lady' cleared up what looked like a murder scene in Tony's bedroom. Then the doctor, cancelling his other patients, ferried Dirk to the clinic, to find Tony reasonably comfortable in a small room, 'sharing with elderly gent & anxious wife'. That evening, Dirk, in a state of utter dejection, confided to the Diary: 'I am alone, for the first time in my life, in this house. Odd and sad. Helpless too. Call Lu/Capucine/Rozzi/Olga/ – anyone who will listen. Take bewildered Bendo to Bed in my room. A bowl of soup (tinned) and now in bed (still unpacked!) until tomorrow at 10.30 a.m. with Maurice from the Bar.* It's all a strange world.

---

* Owner of a local bar, who – far more usefully to Dirk and Tony – drove a taxi on the side.

We pay for the joyouse past. But why? At 70 and 65 – ? Beats me. And T has been the gentlest of men.' To 'La Planche' he wrote of their misfortunes, saying 'the nightmare which I always dreaded has come about'. He described Tony – most unusually – as 'my partner' and explained how, after

> the six years of war, and one disasterous marriage, he came to look after my affairs because I could not handle them! Now it looks as if I must reverse the role ... and try to understand my business problems. Not easy for a person like me who only ever worked in cotton-wool, cosseted from the problems, so that I could act or write ... it is very different now. And age does not wait! [...] It is not difficult to repay all those years of care, I must return a little which I was given. But this house is so isolated! And I am so awful at cooking (very good at tinned soup!).[29]

For the first time in his life, he believed, he cooked lunch: *boudin blanc*; broccoli, mashed potatoes – and even worked out how to prepare some pasta for Bendo. 'I *hate* cooking,' he decided. But he was touched by the many kindnesses shown by those who realised his predicament. Gareth Van den Bogaerde suggested that his son Rupert come with his wife Jacquie from their house near Perpignan and 'take over'. Rosalind Bowlby offered to step in as cook/chauffeuse. A French neighbour said she would supply vegetable soup: Marie-Christine and Thierry were 'difficult' about accepting money for the month when they had house- and dog-sat. And 'Maurice Taxi' dropped his rates. 'No Grabbers,' recorded Dirk with unforced humility. But the strain was telling. Dirk had developed a bad and mysterious backache. He was drinking too much. The whole thing was 'a nightmare' – but supposing it had happened to Tony 30,000 feet above Clermont-Ferrand?

The patient came back after a week, pale, weak and gaunt, but *home*. Life, wrote Dirk, 'somehow begins again'. He went shopping and returned, triumphant, in three-quarters of an hour, having been everywhere from the pharmacy to the butcher, ready to cook his first ever lunch for Tony: sausages, broccoli and mash. It was a 'fuck-up', because the well-intentioned Doctor Cabrol arrived in the middle to see how Tony was. But Dirk forgave him; on that fateful, bloody, morning seven days before, he had, quite possibly, saved Tony's life. In general, however, Dirk was not at his most charitable. 'The Hell with Christmas!' he decided. 'The blackmail is appalling.' As the festive cards arrived, with their 'tweety' little messages, he asked rhetorically: 'Does anyone think, when they send these things, that the recipient might be in a sorry plight? Who the hell invented Xmas? It wasn't Jeasus.' On Christmas Day itself the mood improved. Tony was back on his feet, even driving, and cooked a fine turkey. 'Today is Wednesday but feels like Sunday & not the least like Christmas,' wrote Dirk. 'But we are together and safe, & happy. That's the best of all Christmas Days I find now.' The mood was more upbeat still on New Year's Eve when the

Attenboroughs came from next door for supper. Tony opened a 1978 Dom Perignon, a 1958 Beaune and a 1963 port. Dirk admitted he was 'a bit pissed' as he compiled the Diary: 'Good night '85 – please be kinder in '86.'

The year began with two fixed points: the 'telly', to be shot in February; and *Backcloth*, to be published in September. Viking Penguin, as it now was, had paid £50,000; his editor, Fanny Blake, would be coming out from London to work with him for a couple of days; he had done more than a dozen drawings; and the jacket had been chosen: a photograph by Tony, showing Dirk, again with his back to camera, painting the 'Hippo Pool' bright blue. The cleaning and repainting in June was the only time that Dirk was to be found inside the *bassin*, for his antipathy to immersion had not diminished. In 1975 he had told Russell Harty and the watching millions that he did not believe in baths. Explaining some years later to the Bowlbys that he had just completed the chore in the pool, he said he was now 'very stinky, but have LOVELY clean feet, what with a hose running over them for two hours, so that there need be no more of that agonizing heave over the washbowl to wash the fuckers. For a while. I *know*, of course, that a bath is easier. But it is not, actually, my year for a bath yet. So the washbowl has to do. With scent for private parts and all that ... I'm really pretty foul. Goodness!'[30] Even at the Hôtel Negresco in Nice, where the bathroom facilities were renowned, he would not be tempted.

With its pink, onion-shaped cornices dominating the Promenade des Anglais, the Negresco was to be his and Tony's base for a month while Dirk made 'May We Borrow Your Husband?'. Losey had once been keen to film the 1967 story, with its echoes of *The Servant*; but precisely *because* of those echoes, Dirk was not interested. It was Arnold Schulkes, as an intermediary, who had brought it to his attention again, with no more success; but a few days later Dirk's nephew Brock, who was now working with a commercials director, Bob Mahoney, made a special plea and met with less resistance. The attractions were twofold. They wanted Dirk to write the script, as well as star; and there would be no arduous itinerary, because all his scenes would be shot within easy reach of Nice. Brock brought Mahoney to see him at Clermont, and Dirk said he would have a try at a screenplay. He had been approached once or twice in the past – not surprisingly, given his proven flair both in uncredited work on his own films and also in his first six books – but none had interested him enough. To adapt a story by Greene, that master of the sardonic and of the psychological power game, was right up his street. By the evening he had produced an opening and several early scenes. Three days later the first half was complete, and in the mail to England. The remainder followed within a week. Mahoney was astounded. Auditions for the female lead, as the unhappy newly-wed Poopy Travis, were held just before Tony went into King Edward VII, and on that same London trip Dirk found himself in the strange position of passing judgment on a screen test by their next-door neighbours' daughter for a role in which she would play the object of his desire.

Charlotte Attenborough won the part, to her delight and that of her oft-burgled parents.

It is easy to see why Dirk seized on Greene's story with such relish. It is all about ambiguity, deception and jealousy, with a pair of homosexual interior decorators 'borrowing' poor Poopy's bridegroom, and the novelist narrator, for his own motives, doing nothing to intervene. Had the young man taken on a wife 'as a blind or as a last desperate throw for normality?' 'Would everything have gone normally well, if some conjunction of the planets had not crossed their honeymoon with that hungry pair of hunters?' For Poopy it was quite straightforward, although desperately sad: 'He just doesn't like my body.'[31] In the fiction Greene leaves the 'borrowing' largely to the imagination. Dirk scripted a full-scale orgy, with shaven-headed German leather boys in goggles, punks, topless girls, an obese Arab sprawled on a white sofa, another wearing hefty gold chains, an elderly man in yachting gear sporting heavy make-up and a long black wig, and 'lounging on arm of sofa a tall black man, immense height, naked but for cod-piece of cowrie shells, cuffs, high collar of same'; a Sudanese was to tow the young bridegroom about the party on a chain attached to a collar at his neck, towards the next bowl of drink or drugs. All were listening with varying degrees of interest to a transvestite bawling 'Get Happy' in full Judy Garland slap. 'No one here you'd take back to tea with Granny,' was Dirk's summary of the assembly he imagined into life.[32] For him the scene was 'the hinge of the whole thing', but he was adamant that it should not betray the ambiguity in Greene's story; so much so that at one stage, having seen a rough assembly, he threatened to have his name removed from the writing credits. The party sequence was filmed in what Tony described as 'a perfectly beastly house' above St Paul. 'Half the transvestites from Nice were there,' recalls Brock. 'The only problem was that the boy refused to go naked, so he had to be fitted with a flesh-coloured jock-strap. Dirk was absolutely on his side. "Don't do anything you don't want to do", he said.'

The base at the Negresco proved a godsend. On the first day of shooting, Yvonne Roux, owner of the Colombe d'Or, telephoned to say that some television people had been trying to get hold of Dirk. In the course of the conversation, Tony's Parkinsonism came up. They knew from Simone Signoret, who had died very recently, that Madame Roux had the disease, but until now had not discussed it with her. She continued to run her hotel, without any apparent handicap, because, she said, there was a brilliant specialist at the Institut Pasteur in Nice called Professor Pierre Martin. She would ring him on Tony's behalf. The treatment was, warned the professor when consulted, still in the experimental stage; he could make no promises. But if Tony could come to him twice a day for the next two weeks, he would see what could be done. Geography was on their side for once, and as Dirk observed, 'it was better to be at the Pasteur with *hope* than to be isolated on the hill with only apprehension'.[33] Tony undertook a course of consultations and pills of varying strengths, and, by the time they had returned to Clermont from the filming, felt a good deal better. On Dirk's sixty-fifth birthday, for which they had the Attenboroughs round to dinner, he was positively 'on a high'. But, as Dirk would write, it was 'a false dawn'.[34] A few days later he told Hélène Bordes: 'The Invalid goes up and down: some days good some not so good . . . but after three major operations in a row the body rebels, and you cannot expect miracles . . . what saddens me most is that a man of such vitality and delight, whome I have known all my adult life should be reduced now to a shadow of himself . . . that, I suppose, is life. But it is hard and cruel.'[35]

He and Tony had talked about living at the Colombe d'Or; Anton Troxler thought that might be a good idea, because they were so fond of the place, and when it came to issuing bills Madame Roux always treated them benignly. However, in the middle of April, they knew that the need for Tony to be ill in his own language had become too pressing. Dirk had spent four days with a great deal more time than usual for contemplation; they were passed in a deep armchair while David Tindle, under commission from the National Portrait Gallery, painted his likeness. Not to be writing or planting was mighty boring, but Dirk could think ahead. It made him feel 'wretched'. Worse, he now had some kind of chest infection. Tony noted ruefully that 'we're both on the way out I suppose'. On 9 May Dirk instructed Stuart Baldock to put Clermont on the market again. 'It's just too much to handle,' wrote Tony, 'especially for D who takes all the strain. But somehow it seems like issuing a death warrant.' Before anyone had the chance to view the house, they changed their minds again. 'I cant believe we'll live somewhere else,' wrote Tony. 'If I'd been more provident when we were younger we would'nt have had to – but then we probably would'nt have come here anyway.'

On the surface it was a strangely normal Last Summer. The terraces were mown, the vegetable garden tended, the Hippo Pool painted. The occasional script arrived, and was rejected: a part opposite the latest 'hot property', Mickey Rourke; a cameo in Michael Cimino's *The Sicilian*. More tempting was a ghost from the past. *Covenant with Death*, the First World War novel to which he once owned the rights through Bendrose, had ended up in the hands of David Puttnam, who wanted a screenplay written. Dirk said he might take it on, provided it was to be made 'big'. The prospect was daunting: the novel was some four hundred pages long, 'and the final scenes are those which take place on July 1st . . . the first great battle of the Somme when we lost sixty thousand men dead between 7 in the morning and mid-day! HOW can I write a film which requires so many bodies in the green corn of the Somme valley above Serre?'[36] He rather hoped that by grappling with someone else's work on a large scale he would anger his Muse, who had disappeared to 'China or Martinique . . . or somewhere and simply refuses to come back when I call'. It turned out that the film was not to be made in the way he saw it, so that was that. However, the flirtation had made the Muse jealous. Dirk started on a new novel, about a man with a crumbling marriage and two ghastly children who receives in the mail a key to a house in Provence, sent by his younger brother, whom he has not seen for many years. The brother has disappeared, leaving behind him many problems – 'an un-married wife, a hundred canvasses (paintings) and a child who is a Mongol! After that I dont quite know what happens ... trust me! But I am playing with a title already which COULD be "The Jerico Walls" ... (they fell down, did'nt they). Well, it could be a symbolic meaning. I dont know ... I'm muddled, and silly, and worried but I MUST work.'[37]

The fact was, he could not. His main efforts, professionally, were directed at 'flogging' with minimum disturbance and to maximum effect the two pieces he had completed: *Backcloth* and 'May We Borrow Your Husband?', which were due for publication and broadcast respectively in the autumn. He gave a very few, carefully targeted interviews – one, at length, to Lucy Hughes-Hallett, who encountered an 'old pro' who was 'courteous and efficient about promoting his own work, but he doesn't disguise the fact that he finds it a bothersome chore. He answered my questions. He was never rude.' She shrewdly observed that he might as well have been talking about himself when he quoted Norah Smallwood's answer to an accusation of snobbery: 'If it means that I only tolerate the very best in things, you know, like ... well, Colette, perfectly fried eggs and bacon, an Auden poem, Siena in the autumn ... then I suppose that I am.' For someone who sounded 'brisk to the point of impatience', he was surprisingly garrulous; 'in fact he seems to relish rambling on'. Yet he was 'not immune to melancholy'.[38] That melancholy was put more openly on display a few weeks later in the most searching and testing interview of Dirk's life. He had vowed to do no more television, but Rosalind Bowlby persuaded him to see Russell Harty one last time, at Clermont. For Harty, whose shows were flagging, it would be a catch: the serious, difficult, demanding subject whom no one had ever pinned down. For Dirk, Harty could be – as the latter's companion, the novelist Jamie O'Neill, put it – his gonfalonier, the bearer of his somewhat tattered standard as he retreated towards Britain. Dirk agreed, on condition that the Bowlbys came to stay and help run the house with Tony, who was unable to cope with the invasion by a Yorkshire Television crew.

It took three days, and became a highly charged affair. Harty was nervous of Dirk, still somewhat in awe; Dirk was impatient with Harty. 'He wanted to prove that Harty was very much the junior partner,' Nicholas Bowlby recalls. 'It was adversarial.'[39] Harty went straight in with questions about the war, causing Dirk to break down when talking of Belsen; Dirk's own nerves in front of a television camera, with no script, had cost him his composure. But as the conversation moved from the war – 'the single most important thing in my life' – to the career, his impatience began to show. When they broke for lunch, Dirk asked Tony and the Bowlbys, who had all been sitting within earshot, how they thought it was going. 'This is re-tread stuff,' said Tony. So Dirk challenged Harty: 'Throw me some interesting questions. Do your job. Be provocative, and I'll answer.' So Harty probed away, hoping that he would be the first person to persuade, or provoke, Dirk into explaining the relationship with Tony.

> 'It's more than an agent and client relationship, isn't it, because you share this house with him.'
>   'Yeah, he's here.'
>   'Whose house is it?'
>   'Mine.'

The replies sounded dismissive not only of Harty but also of Tony. Harty pressed on, enquiring about whose taste was reflected so exquisitely in the house – 'it just sort of happened' – and about what they did in the evenings. Would there be a post-mortem after the crew had gone? 'Well, if you're inferring that we might sit down knitting and pulling rugs, then forget it.' No, said Harty, he was not inferring that, he was just asking . . . 'No, there are no post-mortems. I listen to BBC World News at eight, because I want to know if I have to put a sheet on the lawn saying "Help, get me out!", you know, like they did in Cyprus and all those other places. And, sometimes, it's quite funny to see what Mrs Thatcher has cocked up.' The chaff was flying through the air, and Harty, thwarted, could observe only that there was a 'rather waspish' side to Dirk. 'I can be taken so far and no further,' Dirk replied:

> I don't know if that's being waspish. I have lost my temper, I suppose, about five times in my life, and it's extremely unpleasant. Because I store up all the things I find as faults in people and let them have it full in the puss. It's not a very beguiling habit, but it's my way of reasserting because I'm very often taken for granted because I'm so cuddly and so dear. *I ain't*. I haven't survived this far by being cuddly and dear. People have to be taught a lesson sometimes. But it's very rare.[40]

Harty, who looked genuinely astonished when Dirk told him that he did not like acting, tried another tack, concentrating on the 'cleverly edited picture' Dirk had drawn of himself in his carefully structured autobiography:

> 'You will allow people to know what it is you want them to know about you. There is no totality of a picture.'
>   'There is a *complete* totality of a picture as far as I'm concerned [. . .] it's all there if you want to read it. But if you're not very bright, you won't get it.'

Harty read out a passage from *Backcloth* in which Dirk writes of the hermit-crab syndrome and his dread of possession.

'Nobody's ever possessed you?'

'No.'

'And you've never felt the need to be possessed?'

'No. Family – I mean, I would mind not being possessed by family. But [...] I have no sense of possessions at all. I don't mind, as long as there's a little bit of money in my pocket, some ciggies and my bottle of booze in the evening, that's OK.'

'And somebody to talk to?'

'Yes, I think you have to have someone to talk to. But I don't talk very much. I get loquacious on aeroplanes.'

At which he paused to give Harty a smile of withering condescension, before adding: 'But I'm still in the shell, and you haven't cracked it yet, honey.'

The confidence, the arrogance, were part of the performance, and the performance took its toll. Several years before, Dirk admitted to a surprised Harty that he was a 'very frightened person'. What of? 'Letting myself down.' In other words, of losing control. And one evening during the Clermont shooting, after Harty and the crew had left, Dirk, who was drinking too much at this period, did lose control. The emotion of the day, and the circumstances in which this ordeal was taking place, simply blew the circuits. It was, recall the Bowlbys, alarming: 'We saw a man in absolute despair.' There was no doubt in the minds of anyone at the house during those three days that hanging over it was an air of finality; of the melancholy that Lucy Hughes-Hallett had detected a month before. The film made much of the bonfire on which Dirk had destroyed a mass of his papers, journals and letters – 'my private writings, and I've put them all in the books, as much as you need to know'. Tony had told him: 'That's a part of your life in ashes.' 'I've always taken everything for the day,' Dirk told Harty, 'and I never look back. There's no point in looking back. The door has closed. I've got a door now, at sixty-five, that's on the swing. It's creaking a bit. One day – I don't know where I shall be; it would be nice to think I'll be here, I don't suppose it will be – but I'll hear the bang and that'll be the door at the very end of my tunnel of life.' As for Tony, constantly there, never seen . . . When the crew left, the cameraman went up to him, hugged him and said: 'Take great care of yourself.'

Twenty-four

'Stuff this!'

'T he decision seems to have been made, as if for us,' wrote Tony on 4 August 1986. In the preceding weeks of intense heat a succession of X-rays, scans and biopsies had disclosed further polyps and, now, spots on his liver. There was no longer any choice. Treatment was required in London, and it would coincide with the launching of *Backcloth*. For the third time Dirk activated the estate agent, and also called the Belgian couple who had been disappointed in 1983. They had bought another house in the area, but Madame Lippens's sister might be interested. Five days later, Alain and Christine de Pauw came from Brussels with one of their five children. They, too, fell in love with Clermont on the spot. The contract was signed on the 28th at the same office in Cabris where Dirk had bought the property sixteen years earlier. The price was 2,800,000 francs – £275,000. He was told before the sale went through that he could have asked double that sum; to him it mattered more that Clermont should fall into hands that were *sympathiques*. They agreed that the de Pauws would take possession in the first week of October.

The hideous business of clearing out their belongings began before the London visit and would continue afterwards. Nothing, however, was more unbearable than having to decide Bendo's fate. He was seven, and not in the best of health, having had eye and foot problems. A potentially nomadic life involving city hotels was not an option. Nor would Dirk and Tony countenance quarantine if, say, Elizabeth were to agree to take him; in any case, his feet were in such poor shape that the authorities might not let him through Customs. None of the people they knew who might have given him a home in the neighbourhood had suitable properties . . . So, one hot afternoon, shortly before they left for London, the vet came. Bendo lay on his back in his favourite spot in the 'cockpit' of the drawing-room, 'legs apart like a milking stool, stump wagging joyously, yellow ball clamped in his mouth', with Tony scratching his tummy and Dirk chattering away to him, and was put to sleep. Wrapped in his old bed blanket, he was gently lowered by Marc Isoardi into the grave the faithful stonemason had dug among the oleanders opposite Dirk's studio. With the body Dirk put Bendo's ball and his food bowl, the earth was replaced and a rock positioned on top to prevent him being disturbed by foxes and badgers. The deed was done.[1] It was, wrote Tony, a 'vile day' – not only because they had despatched a greatly loved companion 'for no reason other I am ill'; but also because Bendo's death represented 'the beginning of the break-up of Clermont'. And they both knew, too, that there would never again be a dog in their lives. When, two nights later, the forest fires began to rage on the hills opposite, Dirk and Tony felt nothing but foreboding.

For a month Dirk and Tony returned to the Connaught. 'Now the weeks of worry begin again,' wrote Dirk. 'But in English!' Another series of tests, another round of promotional interviews, more meetings with advisers. It was 'all a very strange mixture – books, publicity – and Hospitals. Oh! for peace and calm again.'[2] In two days he signed nearly two thousand copies of *Backcloth*, which went immediately to the top of the bestseller lists. It was some solace. At the same time, the scans, apparently disagreeing with the findings in France, showed no cancer in Tony: more good news; but he would have to be kept under surveillance. They flew back to Nice with Elizabeth, for the final packing-up at Clermont, where they were joined by Dirk's brother Gareth – with whom relations had much improved – and his son Rupert. For six days they sorted, burned, wrapped and packed, until the professionals took over, and once again the 'great yellow elephants' rumbled up to the house, this time to swallow rather than disgorge. They left, a 'majestic, stately, lumbering pair, moving carefully down the narrow winding lane to the main road'.[3] The house was not quite as bare as it had been on that August day sixteen years earlier, because the new owners wanted to keep much of the furniture. To see its walls stripped of the paintings, to find in the olive store no trace of what had been the 'Ego Room', above all, to have no snuffling Bendo – these might have made the parting easier. But no. On 3 October, Tony's seventy-first birthday, and at the same *notaire's* office in Cabris, Dirk handed the keys to the de Pauws. 'Leaving Clermont was, for both Tote and myself, an amputation rather than a severence,' Dirk wrote many months later to his brother Gareth; '... killing Bendo a sort of suicide ... something which we'll take a time to get over'.

Dirk and Tony left behind them not only an improved and cherished property but also, as Léon Loschetter puts it, 'un excellent souvenir'. They are remembered in the area for their unfailing courtesy and modesty. Bruna Isoardi, now a widow, talks with affection of Tony on his fortnightly laundry deliveries, and of the generosity shown to her and to her family over many years – not least in supplying all their olive-oil needs; on the last day they had waved Marc Isoardi farewell, his car crammed with belongings they had given him, as 'loot'. Marguerite Galbe, a farmer's widow who lives at the bottom of their lane, has never forgotten their kindness in allowing her a key to the gate so that she could take a short-cut through Clermont to her housekeeping duties up in the village. At the mill in Opio, Christine Michel saw Dirk seldom but recalls with a smile the five or six visits Tony would make between November and February, with two hundred kilos or more of olives for processing: 'He was charming, tall, and spoke French reasonably well.' It is one of the mysteries that after so long Dirk's French was so poor; that he who could assume another character entirely, and who said he *felt* French, never came to grips with the language. No one held it against him. Wherever you go in Châteauneuf, among the natives there is a unanimous nod of respect for him and Tony, the English pair who had lived a little way down the hill; who kept themselves to themselves, but who were 'vrais gentlemen'. At the Colombe d'Or, their haunt for more than thirty years, and where they now stayed for a few days in transit to London, the Roux family remember their 'charm, politeness, elegance and discretion'.[4] *Excellents souvenirs* indeed.

Bereft, homeless, without a car – both the Peugeot and the Renault had been sold – and with their furniture in store, it was a lost and *épuisés* Dirk and Tony who drifted back to the Connaught, for more tests and with the expectation of moving to a flat in Paris. 'I have no wish to surrender my French residency and I love France far too much to abandon her,' Dirk wrote from London.[5] There was another imperative: as a foreign resident he was allowed to spend only ninety days in Britain during a financial year, and the 1986–7 ration was being rapidly gobbled up. By November they were installed at the Lancaster, with eight suitcases, two typewriters, overcoats, anoraks, shoes, umbrellas and little else. The flat-hunting was abortive and, in truth, half-hearted. Charlotte Rampling, who saw a good deal of Dirk and Tony in Paris, found them 'in complete limbo – Dirk loved France, but not Paris-France. Tony wanted to go home.'[6] By Christmas, they felt 'stymied' and deeply depressed, despite the efforts of friends and indeed the team at the Lancaster, where, as at the Connaught and the Colombe d'Or, the goodwill built up during so many years of loyal custom was entirely reciprocal. Dirk and Tony wanted to give £100 as a Christmas box for the staff, only to be told by a somewhat embarrassed general manager that 'we don't have that sort of thing at this hotel'; instead, the staff would like to put it towards a party for Dirk and Tony. Which they did. At 11.30 on the Friday before Christmas, the eighty-strong *équipe*, chefs in their white hats and chambermaids in their smartest uniforms, assembled to toast the two guests. 'The Manager made a speech,' Tony reported to Brock, 'and then D made a formal reply (I managed to become invisible) and then there was a formal presentation of a night-porter's crossed key insignia, and D was declared to be "one of them". Lots of champagne and I kissed every single maid.' A Christmas card signed by the entire staff, from the general manager to the most junior laundress, came with especially good wishes from the Conciergerie to 'le plus illustre "Portier de Nuit" '.

There were many other kindnesses: the Jarres had them for Christmas Day at their large house on the Seine; the Attenboroughs, anxious to return several years of New Year's Eve hospitality at Clermont, took them to Taillevent, one of the best restaurants in France; the Puttnams, too, provided stimulating company for several days; and Lusia Parry's actress daughter Natasha, wife of the theatre director Peter Brook, brought back happy memories of the Bendrose years. And there was some encouragement: the latest tests in London were clear, and Tony had been told to 'go away and get on with your life, and come back when you feel like it some time in the summer'. But they were beginning to feel institutionalised, bored and, soon, bronchial. Then, once again, the big decision seemed to be made for them. The BBC had sent Dirk an interesting script by William Nicholson, whose *Shadowlands*, the story of C. S. Lewis and Joy Gresham, had been lavished with awards. The same team of David Thompson as producer, Norman Stone as director and Nicholson as writer had contrived a satire about a television presenter, with a crumbling career and a collapsing marriage, who is recruited by an extreme right-wing religious group to front a satellite channel. It would be rehearsed and shot in England and Wales over about eight weeks from the middle of March. Dirk's balance of days allowed in the United Kingdom would be put 'into the red', but he accepted the part. 'I feel we'll just slide back into England for good,' he told the Bowlbys. '[...] I think I'll find something smaller, neater, and a flat of course, in Town and we can speak the sodding language and the Doctor is'nt far ... we'll be poor, of course, and there wont be any Connaughting alas! but I have to get settled and sorted somehow and I cant see it happening here. I am NOT going to make beds and wash up and skip about with Fairy Liquid any more.'[7] On 1 March 1987 Dirk and Tony flew to London. 'I feel in my heart it's the end of our French adventure,' Tony told the Diary, which was now kept only occasionally and, when by him, in the tell-tale faltering hand of a sufferer from Parkinsonism. Tomorrow, he wrote, 'we must begin again'.

Maude – who was to earn the additional sobriquet of 'Swiss Army Knife' because 'every man should have one' – had found them an attractive 1820s house to rent at number 15 Moore Street in Chelsea. It belonged to the actor Julian Fellowes,* who lived in the basement, and it was theirs for six months at £500 a week. While Dirk was working on the film the BBC would pay the rent, on top of his £25,000 fee and 'first-class' accommodation while on location. His fellow principal players would be Lee Remick and Eileen Atkins, with Helena Bonham Carter playing his daughter – a trio who suited him well, because as Eileen Atkins puts it, 'he'd got a film star, someone who had a bit of kudos as an actress, and a beautiful young girl. And beauty was *very* important to him.'[8] Helena Bonham Carter recalls how it was seen as 'a great catch' for the BBC to have secured Dirk's services, and 'a big thing for him to be coming back to England and doing a telly'. At twenty, she found it 'quite thrilling to be able to tell my parents that I was going to work with Dirk Bogarde. I was very aware that he was a legend.'[9] His heart sank when he learned that the locations were Cardiff and Swindon. But he never complained or made a fuss about being in sub-Gritti Palace accommodation. By the end of April he was writing that the Holiday Inn at

---

* Julian Kitchener-Fellowes (1949–), actor, producer, Oscar-winning screenwriter (*Gosford Park*) and novelist (*Snobs*, Weidenfeld & Nicolson, 2004).

Cardiff was full of commercial travellers and *putains*, but comfortable. The work was arduous: 'I hate filming now. It is not the job for me ... too many early mornings, too many words to learn every day, too much make-up to hide the wear and tear of the years and too much waiting about. Ouf! Enough ...'.[10] To the cast and crew, however, he was the consummate professional. Norman Stone remembers calling at Dirk's 'tatty little caravan' – no Winnebago on a BBC budget – and finding him at work on an odd-looking chart. It was the grid of the emotional highs and lows required for his performance; plotted in exactly the same way as for *Victim*. Stone, who had never worked with Dirk before, was struck that when Dirk was in front of the camera there was never any trace of *acting*: 'He made it real. And he had an astonishing ability to compress and concentrate emotion; you could feel it from a word, thudding somewhere in the soul. More than with most actors, his eyes were the window to him. You could almost fall into them.'[11]

With his fellow players Dirk was good-humoured and generous, although he startled Eileen Atkins by informing her that he would never do a 'take' the same way twice – to avoid becoming stale. To Helena Bonham Carter he seemed proud of his technique, and offered the young actress advice, 'but he never patronised me'. He was also a sport: 'I remember having to throw tomato soup at him. He was very good about my having to drench him *twice* in Campbell's Tomato Soup.' Off-set, they became good and lasting friends. She went to the house in Moore Street and was given champagne to the strains of Gershwin. 'I remember him complaining about getting older and about how boring it was, but he was very good at keeping up with young people and making young friends.' He and Tony came to her twenty-first birthday party: 'It was very sweet of him to trog up to Golders Green. He was of a different era, a different time, and of a different stature from the rest of the people there. It was odd for them to bump into him in the lavatory!' She was, however, disconcerted by his flirtatiousness. He made remarks such as 'If only I were forty-two years younger', and wrote her a card which, she recalls, 'was like a note to a lover. It was flattering to be flirted with by Dirk Bogarde, but I was puzzled. He would always make out that he was a macho heterosexual. He talked about Capucine. He said that Ava Gardner had the most beautiful feet in the world. But why bother with *me*? He was conscious of keeping the mystery, weaving webs. But he was really a hunk of self-denial.' She also found it hard to come to terms with his unpredictability: 'He could be quite forbidding, quite sharp. When you went to meet him you asked yourself, "Now, are you going to be in a happy mood, are you going to be loving? Or are you going to be angry, dark, bitter?"' And there was another aspect of Dirk that Helena Bonham Carter actively disliked – his snobbery. As for Tony:

I fell for Tony. He was so gentle, such a benign *gentleman*. He was already quite frail, and it was touching that on the first day he came, in his capacity as manager, to the rehearsal room. They were comfy together; they were nice to each other, but they weren't openly affectionate. I think Tony liked himself much more than Dirk liked *him*self. Dirk always had demons. But Tony was always happy within his skin. I think he was just 'wholler' than Dirk and forgave him his excesses.

When, with shooting finished, Dirk agreed to see Lynn Barber for the publication in paperback of *Backcloth*, discussion of Tony was, as usual, off-limits. 'There's nothing to talk about,' he told her, 'but it's all there in the books if you read between the lines.' She found him 'nervy and naked', unsure whether to move into a flat or buy a house, unable to write because of the lack of a permanent home, and deeply depressed 'just being here. It's so utterly different from everything I've been used to for the last twenty years. But that's my fault.' During their talk he had Rosalind Bowlby in attendance, 'in case I say a dreadful oath, which we will ask you to cut out'; and when Lynn Barber enquired how he hoped posterity would remember him, he replied: 'I don't care if I'm remembered or not. It doesn't matter on your gravestone, does it? It doesn't matter a bugger – sorry, Ros – it doesn't matter a row of peas. I have said that in my will: no funeral, no memorial service, just forget me.'[12]

One final, painful trip had to be made to Provence, for Tony to see Professor Martin at the Institut Pasteur and for Dirk 'to settle my affairs'. 'I *hate* to be back,' he wrote. 'So many memories and scents!'[13] He returned to London, no longer a French resident. From now on, 'home' was the United Kingdom, but he would never accept it as such, carrying in his wallet his *carte de séjour* until long after it had lapsed. The less significant matter of '*a* home' had now to be resolved. And, because of stress, he was not in the greatest shape to cope. Having completely given up smoking, he was putting on weight and drinking far too much. Their doctor, Michael Linnett, issued severe warnings, and Dirk went smartly on the wagon. A few days later he wondered, in all seriousness, whether he was on the verge of a nervous breakdown.

Bernard Walsh, whom Dirk and Tony had not seen for twenty years, joined the hunt. At the fifth attempt, they found a possibility – an early-eighteenth-century house on five storeys in a secluded street and, from the upper floors, a view into the gardens of a Carmelite priory. Dukes Lane was not Chelsea, much to Dirk's chagrin: this was neighbouring Kensington, which for some odd reason he seemed to think was in forbidden territory 'north of the park'. But Tony adored Queen Anne House from the moment he set foot inside it. 'I can not tell you what awful places I have had to look at,' Dirk wrote to Hélène Bordes. 'Flats where one would die a day after moving in from sheer sadness . . . houses full of damp, misery, children, and the feeling of divorce! Awful.' Here at least – even with no garden, just a fourteen foot by eleven foot south-facing patio – 'the vibrations feel good'.[14] The price felt less so; but it was all relative. The house was in immaculate condition and the vendors were happy to complete quickly.

So, although he would need to raise nearly a third of the funds by taking out a loan from Labofilms, he paid the ten per cent deposit of £37,500 and prepared to move in with his furniture on 24 September 1987. He and Tony went off to the removal company's store to check that their belongings had arrived safely from Clermont; what they found resulted in Dirk writing to Pat Kavanagh:

> I am in an advanced state of hysteria and deep anxiety. I move to my new abode in two weeks time: the house is too small for the furniture which lies in a tumbled mass in various outhouses [...] mostly broken, all filthy. Dont ask me why or how it happened, no one seems to know. Natch. I have rescued my Ben Nicholson and one or two others, but the Roserman jobs are badly damaged. The largest had the leg of my bed sticking through the canvass. I wonder why?[15]

In fact the damage was restricted to about a dozen items on a nine-page inventory: an antique wing-chair was irreparable, as were some Victorian pictures on glass; sofas had been spoiled, and a crate of pictures had vanished. History had repeated itself and there would be a drawn-out dispute about where responsibility lay. Oddly, the additional stress seemed to work wonders with Dirk's Muse. Two days later he fulfilled a colour supplement commission for a travel article about the Riviera. Published several months later, 'Impressions in the Sand' would stand as perhaps the finest piece of sustained descriptive writing in his career.[16]

The first sign that his fellow professionals might feel warmer towards him now that the native had returned came when the British Film Institute, under Richard Attenborough's chairmanship, awarded Dirk a Fellowship. His next-door neighbour from Clermont said that Dirk and his fellow Fellow, the Soviet director Elem Klimov, had 'altered the culture of the cinema through their undoubted courage and commitment'. After virtually absenting himself from the British cinema Dirk had been welcomed with open arms by many of Europe's great film-makers, with the result that 'he has maintained an incredibly high standard of work, second to none of his generation'. Dirk received his accolade with a modicum of grumpiness, in part because he was upstaged by a surprise addition to the proceedings: Bette Davis. She went on to the stage to a thunderous standing ovation, poked him in the ribs and said: 'You should make more films. I miss seeing you up there on that screen.'[17] As he and Tony left with the Bowlbys, a girl broke free from the crowd of gawpers and threw something into the open window of the car. Dirk shouted, and threw his body across Rosalind Bowlby's, pushing her down on the back seat, while Bob Pearson, one of Dirk's two regular chauffeurs, drove smartly away. 'It was all very quick, strange and rather frightening,' Rosalind Bowlby recalls. When they had gathered themselves, she looked down and saw a small, white jasmine flower in her lap. 'It could have been acid, you know,' said Dirk.[18]

A few days later he and Tony moved into the 'Doll's House'. Everyone who would visit them there agreed it was unsuitable. To go from the basement kitchen and breakfast room to his bedroom on the top floor, Tony had to mount four narrow, twisting flights of stairs. Admittedly, when he had done so, he could enjoy plenty of light and attractive views facing south over a ziggurat of roofs, but the effort was considerable. For the rest, while perfectly comfortable and, of course, elegantly furnished, it could not help but feel claustrophobic, especially to the free spirit. Dirk, although he tried not to show it, hated the place. In part, of course, this was because of the lessened circumstances in which they found themselves. At the least important level, space dictated that they must discard decorative pieces which had surrounded them in England and France; several items of furniture and ten Meissen birds went immediately for auction, and would be followed in the coming months by much else. Financially, too, there were pressures to sell: the mounting medical bills were threatening Dirk's and Tony's capital. The Ben Nicholson, which had spent too much of its life in vaults or packing-crates, would go at the turn of the year for £120,000.

In late October, Tony's specialist, Peter Wrigley, confirmed cancer of the liver. Tony would not, now, countenance chemotherapy: 'I'm too vain. I'm damned if I'm going to lose what hair I have; I've lost my teeth already. Clackers. I'm not doing any more.'[19] He would, however, be willing to go on a new pill, not widely known in Europe, which had been developed in Japan. It meant being a guinea-pig again, but it was worth a try. His increasing wobbliness came into sharp focus on a rare excursion to the hurly-burly of Kensington High Street, when he became separated momentarily from Dirk and had a fall, badly gashing his head. Peter Wheeler, one of the doctors from Michael Linnett's Sloane Street practice, which Dirk and Tony had attended since 1982, put in the stitches. 'I'm rather good at sewing,' Dirk quoted him as saying. 'That's a lie!' he laughs. 'It's the one thing I *can't* do – that's why I never became a surgeon. But I pulled Tony Forwood's head together and he looked a bit better after that.'[20] Even at that time, Peter Wheeler remembers, 'Tony had a twinkle, a fun smile. For a man in his seventies and not at all well, he was pretty good. Life was fun for him. He was always laughing – a good counterbalance to Dirk, who spent most of his time being morose.'

On the evening of 16 November, Dirk felt a slight paralysis in his right leg. He tried to climb up to Tony's room, but collapsed on the stairs, in what the latter described as 'a sort of heap'. Tony managed to contact Peter Wheeler's colleague Jonathan Hunt, who came to the house and confirmed Dirk's suspicion that it was a stroke – but, fortunately, a mild one. Dirk was taken by ambulance to King Edward VII, and Tony called Dirk's brother Gareth, and Maude. 'Oh Christ,' thought Gareth when he heard the news. 'Not what I expected at all – other things it might well have been, but not this.' After all the years of being held at arm's length; and, more recently, a gradual coming together; the packing-up at Clermont; awkward visits to the Connaught; 'a glimpse of the loneliness, an affection' – at the end of it, he confided to his diary, 'the most overwhelming feeling of despair sweeps through me'. He arrived at the house and took command, staying the night, chilled by the thought of the future. Who was going to look after whom? At the hospital Dirk was finding it impossible to collect his own thoughts: 'My head felt rather like a suitcase suddenly spilled in the street, things scattered everywhere. Unconnected, unlinked. Useless as they lay. I was unafraid, uncaring.'[21] He was there for about three days. In the early hours one morning he had a panic attack, waking in the belief that he had lost everything and that he was unable to walk. The night nurse was an American, Bonnie Derrick, who brought him a sleeping pill but put it on a cupboard out of reach. She told him he had to walk or he would die. 'Somehow, with her help, I managed,' he recalled many months later. 'I do believe I would have died that night. I learned that you have got to keep going ahead – and then it's wonderful.'[22] Reading those words in a newspaper, Bonnie Derrick wrote to him: 'It seems like, as a nurse, you are always trying to do and say to patients what will be helpful to them. Sometimes you get it right, and sometimes you don't. I very much wanted to get it right for you, Mr Bogarde, and I can't tell you how delighted I am to know that apparently I did.'[23]

Dirk was released from hospital ten days after the stroke. That evening he stepped on to the stage of the National Film Theatre, where *The Vision* was being shown in preview, and by doing so delivered a loud raspberry to the part of the tabloid press which had suggested he would never walk again. At home, help was on hand. By the time Dirk returned, Gareth's son Rupert and his wife Jacquie, a fully qualified nurse, had come from their house in France to take care of both patients. He had some treatment from a physiotherapist who dabbled in faith healing: 'She asked if I minded and then put two rather hot little hands on my head. I thought, "Stuff this!" But that evening I got up, walked out and bought myself the paper.'[24] He might also have been galvanised by overhearing a family conversation about residential homes. Unquestionably it was a tonic to have Dirk's young relatives about the house for six weeks. Rupert Van den Bogaerde remembers how, as Christmas approached and new depths of 'Bah! Humbug!' were plumbed by Dirk and Tony, he and his wife insisted on buying a tree: 'I can't tell you how easy it was in the end to get that tree into the house and decorated! They wanted it all along.' Gareth Forwood came to the house on Christmas Day, and Tony, for his son's sake, attempted a festive lunch. His technique was not to roast but to broil the turkey, with all the trimmings. 'The only problem was that they'd forgotten the trimmings,' recalls Gareth:

> Dirk couldn't care less – he'd already had a bottle of champagne. I asked if he'd mind opening another one. Which he did. I went down to the kitchen, and there was Pa, on every pill under the sun, with this raw turkey in a pot. We found a slightly war-torn cabbage and bunged that in, then I said, 'Some potatoes would be nice.' There weren't any, so I went out to a nearby Paki grocery, the only place open on Christmas Day, and bought two tins of

potatoes. We wrestled with this turkey and somehow it got cooked. Then we sat down at the kitchen table, and Dirk tried to carve the bird, which had now become an entertainment in its own right. Pa gave Dirk an ironic look and started singing, 'We've been together now for forty years . . .!' We all knew it was the last time.

Rituals at Queen Anne House were observed. The reading of all the daily newspapers would take place at 11 in the morning in the drawing-room on the first floor, with the fire lit, and two cans of beer as accompaniment. Dirk and Tony were reluctant to depart from the cuisine with which they felt comfortable, but one day Jacquie, an excellent cook, rustled up alligator for them, saying it was reindeer. 'We told them afterwards,' – says Rupert. 'They were appalled.' Every now and then Dirk's frustration – at his own impaired mobility as well as everything else – boiled over. During dinner he exploded at Tony: 'Don't be such a fucking old cunt!' 'Tony didn't say a word,' recalls Rupert. 'He kept his dignity while Dirk ranted and raved. You just felt so sorry for both of them.'

When the Van den Bogaerdes left in early January, Dirk wrote an unprecedentedly warm letter to his brother and sister-in-law, thanking them for making sacrifices in their own lives 'to accommodate two elderly gents in trouble'. Their 'extraordinary family' had swamped Queen Anne House with love and security 'just when it felt arid and cast-off' and, thanks to them, 'I think we might even make it!' There was a noticeable improvement. Kathleen Tynan recommended a physiotherapist with more conventional methods, Susan Pink, whom Dirk regarded as 'v. tuff' and who apparently told him he had 'a lot of "dead brain cells"'. 'Cor!' thought Dirk.[25] Tony had relented about chemotherapy, and the treatment, in addition to the Japanese pills, seemed to be having a beneficial effect – enough for Dirk to report in mid-February that the tumour was 'considerably reduced'.[26] He established an office with 'miles of shelving' for the contents of the olive store and with two desks, one for Tony, who battled on with unfailing good humour. 'Sorry about the usual typewriter inadequacies,' Tony wrote to Laurence Harbottle at the end of March. 'I'm going to try & get a machine that does not dazzle me but just writes what I tell it to!'[27] But in truth it was courage and stoicism that was keeping him going. Even as he penned that note, he and Dirk knew the pills had failed and there was little time left. Professional nurses came. On 30 April, Dirk wrote a card to Hélène Bordes: '[. . .] alas, The Patient and I have lost the battle. Day and night nursing by two nice girls, and not very long to go. It is a strain, but at least I am able to sleep again, and apart from feeding the nurses, and him, my work is not difficult. The loneliness will be when it comes. It was a good fight, valiant, determined, but the good Lord has decided that He will be the winner. Mal chance . . .'.[28]

Towards the end there were grim and ghastly times, described by Dirk in *A Short Walk from Harrods*.[29] There were gentler moments too. Lauren Bacall came to see Tony and made him laugh; she was, said Dirk, 'the force of life for him'. Rosalind Bowlby reminisced with Tony about evenings on the terrace at Clermont when they danced to the great musicals on the stereo from the Long Room. That day at Queen Anne House he was 'valiant', she remembers; 'gentle, amusing and as courteous as ever despite the terrible ravages of the disease'. Gareth Forwood brought him a last Bloody Mary of which Tony was able to take the tiniest sip. 'Absolutely delicious!' was the almost inaudible verdict. Lucilla Van den Bogaerde, Gareth's wife, recalls how, on the last occasion she saw him, Tony was happy. 'Oh, I *am* dying,' he told her, 'but it's going to be *un autre spectacle!*' This decent, kind, dignified, gentle man – this 'great "soldier"' as Eileen Atkins had come to know him – finally ceased enhancing the lives of others at 2.15 in the morning on 18 May 1988. He died, peacefully, in his sleep, with Dirk holding his hand.

'If you watch, with a steady gaze, fifty years of your life being carefully negotiated down a too-narrow staircase in a plastic body-bag you do rather come to a full stop. It is a dulling sensation. Numbing.' Dirk left the 'final untidiness of death' in the hands of Gareth Forwood. And now, as the house emptied, he was, for the first time in his life, truly *alone*. He had been solitary often enough. 'But not absolutely isolated, lost, bewildered and, suddenly, quite hopeless. The hermit-crab shell-less. I felt exactly how it must be to appear without warning stark naked in some vast cathedral at Evensong, or High Mass.'[30] It is an interesting choice of metaphor. In the months that they had been at Queen Anne House Dirk had seen from its north-facing upstairs windows the slow-motion activity of the white-haired monk in the gardens of the Carmelite priory. Once, as they watched together from an upstairs landing, Tony confided to Brock: 'Your uncle really would have been very happy over there, you know.' He was, of course, referring to the simplicity of the contemplative life, nothing more. For, one day near the end, returning home with Gareth, Dirk went through the monastery door. Gareth thought they would simply and calmly light a candle, but Dirk suddenly began a vigorous routine of genuflexion and crossing himself. 'It was extraordinary,' remembers Gareth. 'He must have learned what to do when he was playing the priest in "The Angel Wore Red".' It was probably no bad thing that Tony never knew: he was, says his son, 'extremely anti-Catholic'. Now, on this hateful morning, one of the many telephone calls Dirk made to his advisors and friends was to Bernard Walsh, and he said words to this effect: 'I have just seen Tony being carried out in a body-bag, and it has hit me rather hard. I haven't any faith, because of what I saw in the war, but I know you get a lot of comfort from yours. Do you have any advice for me?' Walsh, a devout Roman Catholic, said Dirk could do much worse than cross the road, go into the little church, sit by the statue of the Holy Child of Prague for twenty minutes and ask for help. 'It won't come like magic out of the air,' he added, but it was certainly worth a go. So Dirk did exactly that. He telephoned Walsh later, saying nothing spectacular had happened, but he thought that perhaps he did feel a little better.

In the coming weeks, he went again, two or three times. Then, according to Dirk, on about the fourth occasion, 'a wretched cleaning woman or someone' spotted him and scurried round the church alerting others to the famous person in their midst. Their stares ensured that he would never return, on his own account, to the priory or to anywhere like it.[31] The reason for doubting Dirk's conclusion to this vignette is the ferocity with which he was soon to attack Roman Catholicism. When Ludovic Kennedy produced a pamphlet in support of euthanasia, Dirk found himself 'crushed with horror' at the words of the 1980 Vatican declaration which made it 'perfectly clear' that suicide and assisted death are 'as wrong as murder', and which continued: 'The pleas of gravely ill people who sometimes ask for death are not to be understood as implying a true desire for euthanasia; in fact it is almost always a case of an anguished plea for help and love.'[32] Dirk wondered whether the Pope would have changed his opinion, had he 'dared to make that vicious, outdated, idiotic, remark in front of [Tony's] Aunt Gwen [...] who was reduced, by reason of spinal cancer, into a howling virago, eyes ablaze, feathers all about her face from tearing pillows to pieces with her teeth to assuage the pain'. And as for suffering, especially during the last moments of life, being part of God's saving plan:

So now we know. I wonder what my manager and partner of 50 years would have thought of that? Parkinson's *and* cancer of the bowel; he died wretchedly, slowly, bitterly. His night nurse, Anna, and I took it in turns to watch this paralysed, speechless creature die before us. One night, as we turned him, he whispered 'If you did this to a dog, they'd arrest you.' I had promised to 'help him' if the cancer became intolerable and when we knew that his illness was terminal. But he slipped quietly into a coma and I had no need to assist him on his way. I would not have failed him, however. My promise had given him the only peace of mind he could possibly have had.

One suspects that Dirk did not find lasting solace in the priory and, in order not to offend, or perhaps simply to make a better story, he found an excuse in his obsession with being recognised. In the recent interview with Lynn Barber he had spoken of trying to shop incognito – 'in an anorak and granny glasses' – at Tesco and being 'grabbed by a lot of screaming ladies all wanting my autograph, with cans of pineapples cascading round us'.[33] There is no suggestion that anything quite so unseemly took place inside the haven offered by the Carmelites; but for Dirk, who professed to a phobia against being stared at, perhaps this was a case of subtly tailoring to his own ends 'When in Rome...'.

Among the condolence letters which arrived in the days after Tony's death was one from the novelist Julian Barnes, who, as Pat Kavanagh's husband, had visited Clermont and established an occasional, wry, correspondence with Dirk, highlighting their shared passion for gardening and good food. Dirk now drew great comfort from Barnes's remarks about Tony, and replied:

> [...] nothing I could say or do would ever convince him that people actually did like him MUCH better than me! He never learned, the silly fellow. I realise, from the letters which have come since he died, just how much he was liked and respected, and that the balance between Sweet and Sour, if you like, he and I that is, was rather good. Anyway we had a terrific fifty years together and nothing can take any part of that away. The last five years were hell. But then one has to pay it seems. Sod it.[34]

To Hélène Bordes, Dirk wrote: 'Now I must try to begin to live again: and alone. The house is very empty without him. And my life also.'[35] The Team, in its disparate form, was more needed than ever.

There had been a second reason for telephoning Bernard Walsh on the morning of the 18th: Dirk wanted more than anything to escape as quickly as possible from the Doll's House, with its awful resonances, and move from Kensington back to less alien Chelsea. Another recipient of an anxious call was Barbara Peerless, the probate and trust manager at Harbottle and Lewis. 'Dirk rang me at home at half past six in the morning and said "Tony's died". I felt that he just needed to *tell* somebody.' But he also wanted all Tony's papers to be sorted without delay and – unless essential for estate purposes – shredded. One day, while tackling in her purposeful fashion the unexpectedly large quantity of documents that Tony had spared from the bonfires at Clermont, she came across a bundle which she put to one side. 'What's that on the windowsill?' asked Dirk when he came in to see how she was getting on. 'I know you said "Throw everything away",' she replied, 'but this is far too good.' It was the abandoned four chapters of 'The Jericho Walls', and the typescript of his partially edited letters to Dorothy Gordon. 'I will never be able write again,' he told Barbara Peerless. 'You will, when you are feeling better,' she answered. In fact, he was already committed to do so.

When, at thirty, Nicholas Shakespeare was appointed literary editor of *The Daily Telegraph*, he set out to find an 'acceptable outsider' to 'drop firecrackers into the book world's cosy lap'.[36] Acting on a hunch, he telephoned Dirk, whose autobiographies had impressed him with their frankness and lucidity, and who in the 1986 interview with Russell Harty had come across as 'someone who tells the truth'. One Monday evening, Shakespeare called at Queen Anne House, knowing it was 'a bloody time' for Dirk, but not how bloody. Earlier in the day Dirk had learned the cancer was at Tony's lymph glands and it was just a matter of time. 'I suppose I should have called and asked you to cancel your meeting with me,' Dirk wrote later. 'But for some strange reason I did not do so.' Both men's instincts proved entirely sound. After their talk, at the end of which

Shakespeare mentioned the possibility of reviewing books, Dirk, although diffident and uncertain, felt 'a mild glow of hope'.[37] A few days later they spoke again. A book had arrived, Shakespeare said, which 'might have your name on it' – *Mr Harty's Grand Tour*, a 'tie-in' to a television series presented by Dirk's long-time, frustrated interrogator. If it is no good, Dirk warned, 'I'm not going to be unkind.' The review arrived on the agreed date, and when it did so Shakespeare was elated: 'His spelling was atrocious, but the writing utterly professional, and it had the loud smack of honesty.' The book was condemned as 'light, frothy, as digestible as the wafer on a vanilla ice-cream and about as insubstantial'; its author was 'no eagle, no hawk, swooping down on his delectable prey, tearing out the gut and the heart and making us see the cities and the places which he drifts through on this tour; rather he is a jackdaw, concerned with the glittering trivia'. An irritated Dirk concluded that Mr Harty, who 'tells us that teaching is his passion [. . .] "must try harder"'.[38]* About ten days before Tony died, Dirk was offered an informal contract, for eight reviews in the next twelve months, at £375 a time – 'puny,' Pat Kavanagh admitted, while reassuring him that the *Telegraph*'s pre-eminent regular reviewer, Anthony Powell, received only £200 for passing judgment each fortnight. It was a deal; and it was much more than that. 'Nicholas didn't know it at the time,' Dirk recorded later, 'but it was he who chucked a plank across the ravine for me.'[39] Here was work which did not require sustained effort over long periods, but which would exercise his intellectual muscles and, incidentally, give him a new and different kind of platform thanks to the newspaper's Saturday circulation of about a million and a quarter. There had been two Needlewomen in his life; now he had a pair of Planks. In their different ways they were both to prove indispensable in the first years after Tony's death.

The adjective most commonly used by his acquaintances to describe Dirk at this time is 'bitter'. He had further reason to be so when the biggest-selling Sunday newspaper stated that Tony had died in St Stephen's, which, it slaveringly pointed out, was the leading hospital in the treatment of Aids, and that Dirk had become a 'tragic recluse'. Friends did their best to cheer him up. Molly Daubeny, to whom he and Tony had become close since the death in 1975 of her husband, Sir Peter, invited Dirk to a dinner party at the end of June, attended by, among others, Paul Scofield and his wife Joy, the writers John and Hilary Spurling, and Nicholas Shakespeare. Dirk wrote an effusive note of thanks for a 'civilised & amusing' evening with 'lovely food and V. nice company'. Two months later he began an article, published in *The Independent* under the heading 'A half-life in World's End', with that same evening under the flimsiest disguise, and unrecognisable as either civilised or amusing. Two similar occasions, and his hunt for a flat, were dripped in acid, before he concluded that reclusion was so

---

* A month after the review appeared, Russell Harty died; Dirk wrote a handsome tribute in *The Sunday Times* (12/6/88).

much more preferable than having to come into contact with his fellow citizens: 'On my hill, years ago, cicadas chiselled into the olives, a goat-bell clonked distantly, water tumbled into the fountain. Years ago. When I was a recluse. And happy.'[40] Lady Daubeny remembers how Dirk was always saying how short of money he was, 'but to betray his friends for a few bob! It was extraordinary. There everyone was – *mown down*!' For £300. Nevertheless she and Dirk remained friends. 'But I didn't ask him to dinner again!'[41] John Schlesinger, too, thought twice, after inviting Dirk to his large, stylishly decorated house less than a mile away, to welcome him back to what Frederic Raphael calls London's 'haute pooverie':

> He was asked to come 'at eight for eight-thirty'. Schlesinger was in the kitchen doing his stuff, which he did very well. At eight on the dot the doorbell rang, and there was the guest of honour, who had arrived *first*. And this is an *actor* – you'd think he'd know that you don't actually need to bring the curtain up yourself. For whatever reason, there Dirk was. He came into the house. Now John had stuff, and he had taste, and he had the top decorators to do it, and it was very nice. Dirk looked round and said, 'John, this is a rich man's house. And you've had nothing but flops.' As John said, 'And then, dear, we had to sit with him for three hours.'

Dirk's *angst* was, admittedly only in part, the result of uncertainty about where to live. Bernard Walsh was under instructions to find somewhere facing south – 'Dirk hated north' – with some outside space so that he could 'have a breath of fresh air'. 'He knew as soon as he walked through the door whether or not it was for him.'[42] And nothing was, until Walsh telephoned to say he had found a possibility that was only 'a short walk from Harrods'. He took Dirk to see a penthouse flat on the fourth floor of a mansion block, which, as number 2 Cadogan Gardens, had been – briefly – the home of Lillie Langtry, mistress to King Edward VII. Dirk liked to think that the flat he now seized upon had been her laundry. Certainly it was far from palatial; just two modest bedrooms, two bathrooms, a small kitchen – 'A place to boil an egg rather than roast a sheep'[43] – a dining recess in the hall, and a medium-sized drawing-room with French windows opening on to a shallow balcony. It looked out over pleasant communal gardens and, at about 11 o'clock, towards the bulk of Peter Jones, the department store where Dirk claimed to have dressed windows in his Chelsea School of Art days. At 10 o'clock there was a school playground, but the squealing would be occasional. There were tall trees, blackbirds and squirrels; he would have space on the balcony for plants; above all, there was the Light. The resident caretaker, Phyllis Hayden, could be instructed to come up every so often to 'see if I'm lying in a pool of blood'.[44] And a bonus: because his was the sole flat on the top floor, the lift at that level was for his use alone. Dirk could have the sixty-two-year lease for £380,000, and move in at the beginning of September. After one false

Previous page On the Lido with 'The Emperor' during the shooting of *Death in Venice*.

Clockwise from right Le Haut Clermont, sketched in the early days by its new owner; on the terrace with Capucine; a corner of paradise for Dirk and Tony; erecting defences against 'Barmy of Bromley' and the like.

'Dangerous territory': *The Night Porter*; *Inset* Its director, Liliana Cavani.

Above With Charlotte Rampling on the day she took the photograph which appears on the back of this book's jacket.

Left With Glenda Jackson, his co-star from *The Patricia Neal Story*, at Cannes in 1983.

On location for the 'black funny' *Providence* with Alain Resnais.

Above With Rainer Werner Fassbinder on *Despair*, 'a curate's egg'.

Left As 'Boy' Browning, with Sean Connery as Major-General Roy Urquhart, on location for *A Bridge Too Far*.

Below With Jane Birkin in *These Foolish Things* (*Daddy Nostalgie*); *Inset* 'The Genius', Bertrand Tavernier.

Left Clermont's interior glory: the 'Long Room'.

Below Dorothy Gordon, 'Mrs X', as depicted by Mervyn Peake, c. 1930.

Below (left) With his second 'Needle-woman', Norah Smallwood, and the Drummer; *(right)* 'La Planche': Hélène Bordes.

Above The second 'Plank': Nicholas Shakespeare.

Left At work in the former olive store.

Clockwise from top left In the Pond; with Lucilla and Gareth Van den Bogaerde at Clermont, 1981; with Brock, his nephew and 'heir', at Versailles, 1977; with Sheila Attenborough, next-door neighbour in France and friend for fifty years; the Bowlbys, during the filming of the Russell Harty interview, 1986.

Above The great connector, at one of his several National Theatre 'shows' or 'concerts' in the early Nineties.

With Helena Bonham Carter (left) and Molly Daubeny (right).

With Elizabeth, after being dubbed by the Queen, 13 February 1992.

Sheila MacLean.

Tony, Dirk and Alma Cogan wish 'ta-ra' to
Sybil Burton at the Ad Lib Club, 1964.

At the flat - by Bruce Weber.

start – before he had alighted on Cadogan Gardens – Queen Anne House was sold for £421,000. Tony's belongings and his clothes had gone. 'The house is now empty of him,' Dirk wrote to La Planche, 'and, in a way, I can begin again. I have adopted his very loved grandson (aged 15) so I am suddenly a Step Grandpapa! I *like* it!'[45] Thomas Forwood, then fourteen and living with his mother in her native France, had asked Dirk if he would assume power of attorney over the legacy to which he, Thomas, would be entitled at twenty-five. The responsibility came at the right moment for Dirk: 'I had a book ready for publication* [...] and had put on a terrific amount of weight since giving up smoking. I had a face like a melon, a beer gut, from far too much beer, and tits like Dolly Parton. I was altogether disgusting.'[46] The reviewing was enjoyable too: in rapid succession he had dealt with a biography of Dorothy Parker – 'I can tell you one thing: I'd have loathed Mrs Parker and she wouldn't have gone a bundle on me either'; reluctantly, with three film-world autobiographies; with a first novel by 'the multi-talented Antony Sher' – 'I dislike reading about people who "defecate", are "constipated" or, even more, sit stuck "in their own dung"'; and with a collection of short stories by Jeffrey Archer which had 'all the bite and crispness of tinned asparagus'.[47] And there was a book of his own to work on: the 'Mrs X' letters, which would need a little expansion, a prologue and an epilogue. None of these activities placed too many demands on the Muse. Things were looking up. 'I am slowly coming back to life!'[48]

On 9 September, for the first time in more than forty years, Dirk moved into a flat. Elizabeth, whose husband had died earlier in the year, came to help, as did two recent additions to the Team: Frank Martin and George Easton, respectively the builder/decorator and the plumber who had sorted matters for him at the Doll's House. They now settled him in amidst his greatly pared-down furniture and possessions. About £50,000 worth went in the sale-rooms during 1988, including both the large Leonard Rosoman paintings which had looked so well on the walls of the Long Room at Clermont, and – symbolically – the Drummer; but a smaller figure in stone, of Bacchus, survived to stand guard on the balcony as he had once done at the front door of Clermont. A different kind of sale saw a large box full of typescripts and drafts for the first seven books, as well as a few carefully selected letters, on their way to the Mugar Memorial Library at Boston University, one of the world's great repositories of literary archives. It could not expect too much: as Pat Kavanagh told Anthony Rota, the London antiquarian bookseller who brokered the deal, Dirk was 'a great destroyer of personal material'.[49] The orderly man had now shed a great deal of the excess baggage in his life, keeping just a few favourite pictures and ornaments, plenty of books, and just one typewriter – on which he went cautiously to work, in the spare bedroom, for his masters at Viking Penguin and for 'Mr Shakespeare'.

---

* *Dirk Bogarde: The Complete Autobiography,* comprising all four volumes of memoirs and published by Methuen.

A clear indication of how vulnerable and sensitive Dirk was at this period can be seen in his reaction when Robert Tanitch sent a copy of his book, *Dirk Bogarde: The Complete Career Illustrated*, with a note saying it was not only a pictorial record of his work as an actor but also a tribute to him. In the section devoted to *Song Without End* the author had written: 'When the picture was finally released, though everybody knew, of course, that Jorge Bolet was playing the piano on screen, they naturally presumed that Bogarde's hands were pounding the keys and admired his virtuoso synchronisation – only they weren't his hands but a double's.' Dirk was furious: all those hours of toil with Victor Aller dismissed. He sent a card to Laurence Harbottle: 'Completely untrue. See "Postillion" (final chapter) & "Snakes & Ladders" – & sue!'[50] If nothing else, the passage implied that he was lying in his autobiographies, so his lawyers demanded from the publishers, Ebury Press, an immediate amendment and an assurance that in the meantime no copies would be issued for sale. Seven thousand had been printed, and were now withdrawn for the offending page to be replaced, at some cost, with new wording that stated 'he mastered it so well that when the film was finally released audiences, watching his hands pounding the keys, were full of admiration for his virtuoso synchronisation. It was a very impressive feat, and rightly highly praised.'[51] However, some copies had already gone on sale, and Harbottle and Lewis sought redress. The haggling began, and eventually Dirk felt honour was satisfied by the reprinted page and a cheque for £2,500 made out to the cancer charity BACUP. Tanitch was mortified by the whole thing; he had meant only to pay homage.

So, too, had the British Academy of Film and Television Arts, when in the summer it offered to give Dirk its first Tribute Award for an outstanding contribution to cinema. He agreed and then, a few days after the ceremony was announced publicly, wrote to Richard Attenborough, BAFTA's vice-president, pleading to be excused; it was, he said, an 'anguished cry for kindness'. He could not abide the prospect of sitting in the cinema while people spoke about him; he was not that keen on being presented with anything by the Princess Royal; and, besides, he did not own a dinner-jacket. Sir Richard – as he then was – told Dirk that he did not have to be in the cinema until the end, when he would just walk on, receive his applause and accept the silver mask from Princess Anne; even black tie was not obligatory. Dirk relented, 'grudgingly', and on 9 October an event unfolded, the memory of which to this day brings a hush to the Attenboroughs' conversation. Far from crouching in his seat at the Leicester Square Odeon, its former idol chose to share the stage with the evening's presenter, Robert Powell, to comment on the many film clips from his career, and to receive the personal tributes beside those making them. 'It was ghastly,' recalls Lord Attenborough. 'A nightmare. And distressing in terms of the image which ought to have been left by an occasion like that. Dirk simply took it over and it became an awful, embarrassing ego-trip. He was foul about Cukor and about others he had worked with. The evening still has a terrible smell in the business.'⁵² Barbara Murray was first to join Dirk on-stage. 'It was a nightmare,' she echoes:

> I said something about how clever and adept he was on a film set, how amazing his grasp was on the technique of film-making. I told how he could stand on location with the sun belting on to one side of his face, and with a reflector on the other, and he would be lit with a brute – one of those enormous lamps – and those brown eyes of his would never blink, while mine were absolutely streaming. When I finished telling this story, he said, 'Stupid woman. I just have strong eyes.' It went on like that. Poor Robert Powell didn't know what to do. There was a sort of revolt in the audience. It was just awful. Dirk took over more and more, running down Mahler's music, that kind of thing. Eventually Princess Anne rose from her seat and left – I thought, 'My God ...' – but she had only gone backstage. On she swept, serene, majestic, gave a thoughtful, authoritative speech and was absolutely wonderful. This young woman comes on and shows us all up. Dirk kissed her hand, which he shouldn't have done. She looked cross. And that was more or less that.⁵³

A generous, filmed, contribution by Peter Hall on Dirk's unfulfilled potential as a great stage actor seemed to leave Dirk genuinely moved, but not for long: 'I mean no disrespect to fans,' he said. 'I don't believe that without them I wouldn't be here. Because I'm *bloody sure* I would be. But they did destroy me for the theatre and the theatre for me.' Even in the much edited Thames Television broadcast a few nights later it was painfully obvious that he had badly misjudged the mood.⁵⁴ One wonders how differently he would have behaved had Tony still been alive, fulfilling his vital role of allowing Dirk 'to present myself as a man of infinite courtesy, always amenable, usually "charming", to one and all'.⁵⁵ On that kind of occasion especially. It says much for the professionalism of everyone present that, in contrast to the grouchy, fabrication-packed interview he gave to its reporter, the subsequent coverage in *Hello!* magazine consisted of margin-to-margin smiles – none, apparently, with teeth gritted.⁵⁶ In correspondence immediately afterwards, there is not a hint from Dirk of any embarrassment. And in one respect the evening had an entirely positive effect: being in front of a large 'live' audience again did not hold too many terrors.

In her capacity as director of a ten-week festival to mark the seventieth anniversary of the Armistice, the forgiving Molly Daubeny asked Dirk whether he would like to lead a quartet of actors in a reading of short stories by 'Saki', otherwise H. H. Munro, at the National Theatre. After much hesitation, he agreed. His companions were to be Barbara Leigh-Hunt, Tim Pigott-Smith and Zoë Wanamaker. 'I don't think he had any idea of what he was committing to,' recalls Amanda Saunders, then manager of platform performances at the NT. 'He thought it was just "a nice little idea for charity".'⁵⁷ On 14 November he took his first steps on to a theatre stage since 1965, when he had delivered Christopher

Fry's prologue at the Yvonne Arnaud in Guildford; it was thirty-three years since *Summertime* in London. For him, it was 'a very big moment', says Amanda Saunders, 'and he was just standing there in the wings looking extremely trim and dapper and making jokes'.

> His biggest terror was falling over. The Olivier stage was a sandpit for one of the plays in the late Shakespeare season and because of his leg he was as worried about going across to the lectern as he was about the rest of it. It was fascinating. He took only three or four steps before he was greeted by this roar from the audience. It was how everybody felt about him: the combination of all those films and all those books. He had been living in France for sixteen years, but he had this extraordinary, huge following. The other thing about that moment was the time in his life. Not only was he vulnerable. He felt redundant, old, that he would never do anything again, he was serving no useful purpose. He was fairly resigned to that. He genuinely thought at that point that he wouldn't do a whole lot more and that he had become an elderly man with not a lot of purpose in his life. He hadn't been on a stage for years. He was recovering from a stroke. He had a gammy leg. And there was this mighty gale of applause which he hadn't been expecting.

What impressed Amanda Saunders and the other professionals was not so much the quality of Dirk's readings, which were less assured, but 'the intelligence of the interpretation, the casual sense of humour if anything went slightly wrong, and the relationship with the other actors. He was discovering all that, for the first time in years. He had a very strong sense of the correct value of things.' The evening was a triumph. All agreed the 'Saki' programme should be repeated – as it would be – and when Dirk next had a book published, he must return to that same Olivier stage to talk about it. He would, repeatedly.

When Carol Gordon returned to Dirk the mass of letters and 'starlings' he had written to her mother, she told him of her hope that one day, in his own time and in his own way, they would be published. Now, seventeen years later, they finally were, under the title *A Particular Friendship*. It is a slender book, effectively covering just the three years from the spring of 1967, when Dorothy first made contact, until the strange night in the catacomb of the Vatican; so it stops short of the move to Clermont. It is also, autobiographically, suspect. Dirk told Russell Harty in the 1986 interview that his letters to 'Mrs X' were written 'as a spur to keep her alive'; they were 'fantasy' letters, in which 'I exaggerated everything to make it more joyful'. They also seem to draw heavily, sometimes word for word, on the Diary, which at that period was kept exclusively by Tony; it is a fact that when preparing them finally for publication Dirk had the Diary to hand because he had destroyed the original letters. None the less the immediacy, coupled with his special amalgam of vigour and flair, gives the book an even more conversational tone than usual and a place of its own in Dirk's *oeuvre*. It was a one-sided conversation that not everyone found palatable. Tony Lacey, now his publisher at Viking, recalls how he showed the typescript to his colleague Peter Carson, 'not exactly a rabid left-winger'.[58] Carson said that if anything had decided him to vote Labour for the first time in his life, it was the letters; but Dirk, amused, would always attempt to justify himself by saying to Carson that they had to be read in the context of the time, when there was swingeing taxation and so on. He was, remember, 'as political as a garden gnome'. But politics was not the issue when more serious offence was taken on the eve of publication.

With 20,000 copies printed, and those for review already distributed, Dirk's old friend Daphne Fielding, to whom he had sent the book, took exception to two lines in a paragraph about the wedding of her son Lord Christopher Thynne. She was not troubled by Dirk writing of the rumour that the cake had been spiked with LSD, thus giving rise to the possibility that the Queen, who was among the guests, might have taken her first 'trip'; no, it was his reference to her own reaction on learning that the bridegroom had been arrested at the airport en route to his honeymoon after 'some pleasant sod tipped them off that he was smuggling drugs'. Dirk wrote: ' "Oh!" wailed Daph on the phone yesterday, "he was SO good at the wedding, he didn't take a thing! Silly boy!" ' On reading this the octogenarian Daphne Fielding caused what Dirk called 'a bit of a tarrididdle', with the result that the initial printing of *A Particular Friendship* had to be withdrawn and the sentence deleted. 'My book made the whole thing look like a prank . . . and that he was innocent,' wrote Dirk to Laurence Harbottle. 'Now we all know that he was convicted and charged. A total nonsense and Fielding is in a state of woe and misery for "overreacting".' Viking Penguin had, he said, been 'very decent about the whole thing'. He, in turn, had paid the bill for a libel reading by Mishcon de Reya. 'It's been a bloody week,' he lamented; 'no wonder I'm half-witted.'[59]

Viking Penguin had paid £50,000 for *A Particular Friendship* – an investment that proved sound when Dirk's first new work for three years whizzed into the bestsellers list at number two. His celebration of what he called 'an affair of the written word' was greeted in the main with warmth, but not in the pages to which he was a regular contributor. The novelist Mary Wesley, herself a latecomer to authorship, told the readers of *The Daily Telegraph* that she did not understand why he had published his letters: 'He was kind and loving to a lonely old woman. He made Mrs X happy. I, for one, would have felt happier had he kept that particular light of his under a bushel.'[60] The parallel with Helene Hanff's *84 Charing Cross Road* – another 'affair of the written word', as Dirk called it – was drawn by the biographer Hugo Vickers. He was absorbed but was also disturbed by Dirk's disclosure that his public image was an act: 'He can "paint on the fixed smile, the 'gentle and humble one' (which seems to be the most popular with the Fans) . . .". I think I know the look he means – the confused, slightly forlorn, appealing look as when the young trainee doctor in *Doctor in the House* is confronted unexpectedly by the looming figure of Sir Lancelot Spratt. I hope it is not *wholly* an act.'[61] Jennifer Rhys, who also used the adjective 'absorbing' in *Literary Review*, took Dirk at his word that he had not revised the letters and said how wise he was: 'They bear the authentic stamp of a sensitive man in his forties coming to terms with the altered world of the sixties and seventies; seeking refuge in many havens, not least in his letters to a fastidious and elegant woman of a previous generation.'[62] While it would never achieve the heights of *Postillion*, *Snakes and Ladders* or even *Backcloth*, *A Particular Friendship* – which he dedicated to a misspelled Molly Daubeny – sold just over 19,000 copies in hardback and 53,000 in paperback. Dirk's titles were not translated widely, if at all; but for some reason this one made it into a Japanese and a Korean edition.

Dirk was true to his word that he would do no more television chat shows to promote his books, but he gave a couple of radio interviews and underwent the now traditional siege at a Hatchards signing. Amanda Saunders at the National Theatre, too, was true to hers, and invited Dirk to talk about the 'Mrs X' letters with the BBC's Sue MacGregor on the stage of the Olivier, followed by questions and answers from the audience. In its now innocuous-sounding way, this event was as significant as the letter from Edward Thompson; if not that from John Charlton. It meant, if only for a few minutes, a direct, unfiltered contact with the public; an exchange with the readers who over the years had felt taken into Dirk's confidence. It was different from the talks he had given at the National Film Theatre which, by definition, concentrated on his life in the cinema; and it was altogether more meaningful and satisfying than turning up in a sterile studio or a hotel suite and dodging the tiger-traps laid by people with a predictable agenda. Amanda Saunders remembers how that evening he was 'very open, very direct, very honest, but absolutely controlled as to what he meant to reveal'.[63] The packed house was fascinated. And Dirk enjoyed himself. First 'Saki', now this: a new door was ajar in the corridor, and it would be flung wide open in the next year or two. For the moment, though, he had an invitation to go back home.

Twenty-five

'I just love to be asked to talk about *me*'

Bertrand Tavernier was not at all the figure Dirk had imagined – someone like Truffaut, 'Neat, agile, dark, intense.' No, he was 'a glorious bear of a man. Very tall, white-haired, laughing eyes behind thickish glasses, perfect English and an hysterical laugh.'[1] They met in 1984 at Cannes, when Dirk's jury gave Tavernier the prize for best direction, but their wish to work together went back further. Dirk had seen Tavernier's exquisite, sensitive films and would 'walk barefoot across Antarctica' for the chance to play in one, even if it was 'the owners Hand Book for a Japanese washing Machine'.[2] The director, who probably knew more about the English-language cinema than any other foreigner and all but a tiny handful of Britons, had admired Dirk's acting since before the vintage years with Losey, for whom Tavernier was at one time the Paris press agent. He had seen some of Dirk's Rank fare without being bowled over, but then in 1962, when he was twenty-one, along came 'a crazy film, a piece of kitsch, which had a cult following in France' – *The Singer Not the Song*, no less – and Dirk's performance as Anacleto made an impression on him for more than its campery. Immediately afterwards, with *Victim* and then *The Servant*, Dirk was established in Tavernier's eyes no longer as 'a young, beautiful romantic lead' but as 'the British actor most associated with important projects'. He was 'somebody who was totally European long before it was fashionable – he was breaking the frontier'.[3]

More than a quarter of a century later Dirk was well aware of how unsatisfactory it was that the last of those important projects should have been called *Despair*. He was also worrying about money. 'Can I afford a new suit,' he had asked plaintively of Laurence Harbottle; 'a pair of decent shoes (I wear only sneakers at the moment) and perhaps a new jacket? I ask merely because I have no OAP, no bank balance and no accountant!'[4] He claimed to be living – or 'dangling' – on roughly £30,000 a year and feeling the pinch. Small wonder when he was about to face a bill of £7,000 for a single, admittedly extensive, piece of dentistry. So, a fee for a movie would be welcome. Yet that is where things stood in the summer of 1989 when Bee 'Snowflake' Gilbert, his friend of twenty years, called – in part, to arrange lunch. How was he, she asked, to which Dirk replied that he was in desperate need of work, otherwise he would have to sell more of his paintings. Why, then, had he turned down the Tavernier film? What Tavernier film? The one about the retired English commercial traveller who has had a heart operation and knows he has little time left; his French wife, to whom he no longer has anything to say; and his late *rapprochement* with their daughter, a writer living alone in Paris. Ah yes, he remembered; a script *had* arrived at Clermont, in the dark times when *everything* was turned down – especially a piece about a dying man. So?

When the highly autobiographical screenplay for *Daddy Nostalgie** by Tavernier's ex-wife, Colo O'Hagan, was first on offer, it was to be filmed by another director; but Tavernier helped with the casting. Gielgud had been approached, as had Dirk. Enquiries were made of Peter O'Toole, Gregory Peck and even Danny Kaye. When Tavernier took over the film himself, believing Dirk had ruled himself out indefinitely, Denholm 'How Dare They?' Elliott and Paul Scofield became the principal quarry. To play the daughter, Tavernier had already engaged the actress and *chanteuse* Jane Birkin, whose brother Andrew was living with Bee Gilbert. Perhaps Dirk could provide a telephone number for Scofield? He could not – first because each respected the other's privacy; second because Dirk was rather interested on his own account. His circumstances had changed since the initial approach several years earlier; he needed work; and now that Tavernier was directing the film … 'Don't move from the phone,' said Bee Gilbert. She rang Jane Birkin, who rang Tavernier, who rang Dirk – and two hours later Dirk rang 'Snowflake' to say the title role in *Daddy Nostalgie* was his.[5] He wrote to his new director, saying 'you may find me rusty, but I *will* do my best'.[6]

On 19 September 1989 Dirk left the flat and flew to Paris – on his own, abroad and nervous, for the first time since the war. He would be away for six weeks. He had not made a feature film for twelve years. However, the subject matter of *Daddy Nostalgie* was so intimate, the cast so small, that provided he hit it off with his companions all might be well. He had done so already and immediately with Jane Birkin, whose mother Judy Campbell, the actress and great beauty, had known Tony since he and Glynis were her neighbours during the war. And now at the Lancaster, where to Dirk's surprise he found no ghosts – 'It was exactly as if a slate had been wiped clean' – he met his other co-star, Odette Laure, former queen of the French music-halls, who was to play his wife. She too was, instantly, 'adorable'.[7] With this little Team, and the Glorious Bear at its head, Dirk felt he might be strong enough not only to do some good work but also to face returning to Provence, where the film was to be made – fortunately, on the coast and mainly at Bandol and Sanary, some seventy miles from Grasse. He prayed that none of the locations would be too close to Clermont; it would be

---

* Released in Britain as *These Foolish Things* (1991); the song partially spoken and sung in the film by Dirk and Jane Birkin was performed by Madge Elliott and Cyril Ritchard in *Spread It Abroad*, the 1936 revue which also had in the cast a twenty-one-year-old Anthony Forwood.

difficult enough when the final sequences were shot in Cannes; not because of spectres from festivals past, but because it was where he and Tony used to visit the bank and the chemist, and he would potter to the *librairie* for a book or the newspapers while Tony took his turn to have a haircut. After all, the ordinary is more piquant than the extraordinary – a truth that lies at the heart of *Daddy Nostalgie*.

Odette Laure described the film as 'exquisite chamber music made with touches of colour, little nothings which are all of life'.[8] Dirk wrote: 'Nothing very much happens in a Tavernier film. Just all of life.'[9] For a swan-song, as he felt all along it would be, he had chosen well. Never before had the Dirk on the screen more closely resembled the Dirk off the set; and not since *Victim* had he put so much of his true self into a script. He said later of the character: 'I imposed my own things on this bourgeois: I decided to make him a bit of a spoiled bastard, not very kind or nice, who suddenly, at the end of his days, finds out what a shit he's been and realizes all the things he's lost, and doesn't know how to make it better. He was a commercial traveller for Yardley's, but all those stories he tells are total fabrications and lies – and I thought, Well, I can invent wonderful things around that.'[10] As an American critic, David Denby, would observe: '*Daddy Nostalgie* is fascinating because it's all about Dirk Bogarde's personality and the way people respond to it. The play of pride and regret in his face is mesmerizing'.[11]

Tavernier wanted to exploit Dirk's experience of being lonely in a foreign country. In this, logistics and *fin de saison* melancholy were on the director's side. Dirk was billeted at the most expensive hotel in Bandol, while the rest of the cast and crew lodged elsewhere, so he rattled about in a 'vast concrete slab empty apart from me and three waiters'.[12] In his postcards to friends he invariably spoke of his loneliness, but this was not wholly accurate. He established an unbreakable bond with Jane Birkin, who, too, had left Britain in the sixties. Although much more integrated in France than Dirk had ever been – she had lived for twelve years with the late Serge Gainsbourg and was now with Jacques Doillon – she knew just as well the particular pangs of the outsider, the deracinated. His paternalism towards her came to the fore even more strongly than it had with Charlotte Rampling. Jane Birkin, too, had her problems, she was vulnerable, she was stricken with nerves. Dirk took her under his wing to such an extent that at times it was difficult to tell when the day's filming ended and normal life began. Just as Dirk's had done in the fifties, so Jane Birkin's parents came out to stay on location; here, too, there was an element of *rapprochement*. She wondered, with some trepidation, how her father would regard this near-surrogate, but she need not have feared: Dirk was 'a love' with David Birkin, going in search of the English papers so that his wife could read them to her husband on the hotel balcony; placing an arm around his shoulder as he enquired after his well-being, and, when Judy Campbell went on perhaps a little too long about the stage, saying to him with a sigh: 'Boring, isn't it, the theatre?'[13] Jane Birkin saw in Dirk that 'very English way of never complaining, but at the same time you could not help but know that he was suffering'. There was, she said, something *froissable* – brittle, easily offended – about him. On two occasions during the filming, he was 'irritable, withdrawn, almost unpleasant, without any reason. I realised only later that he was silently confronting his memories.' Odette Laure, too, saw beyond the courtesy and attentiveness of the 'true British "gentleman"' – 'he knew how to hide his sadness'.[14]

The director himself found Dirk 'funny, bitter, educated, quick'; a strange combination of the intimidating, the warm and – like Jane Birkin – the vulnerable. 'I'm frightened,' Dirk said at the start, placing one of the director's hands on his pounding chest to prove it. Once, at dinner, he talked most movingly about grief and pain – which, he said, he had observed in another, but which Tavernier guessed was Dirk's own. A month after production had finished, Tavernier watched a cut of his film and realised that it needed an extra scene showing how fully the understanding between father and daughter had grown; there was more to say before they parted for what both knew would be the last time. He contacted Dirk, who agreed, and offered to write it. Tavernier asked him to use what he had said that evening at dinner. At the end of January 1990 Dirk flew back to Paris, for Tavernier to shoot the additional night-time sequence in an old Renault at a studio on the outskirts of the city. 'Pain,' says Daddy as he sits with his daughter at a motorway service station, 'is like a bad neighbour: it's always with me. But I do try to keep him at a distance.' She asks: 'He breaks in sometimes. Doesn't he?' Yes, replies Daddy; 'but, like a bad neighbour, he goes away sometimes and you forget. Equally, you forget he's going to come pattering back up the path.' And when he does? 'Pain is not intellectual; you can't rationalise it. It makes you a stranger'. Tavernier, as the film's narrator, says of Daddy: 'He was so used to hiding the pain under an elegant, ironic façade.' He might as well have been talking of his star, whose own pain was mainly psychological rather than physical, whereas Daddy's was both; but Dirk's was no less of a lousy neighbour.

At the beginning of the extra scene Dirk had Daddy reminisce about a village in Lebanon where he had watched a girl of about nine skipping along a road with a baby goat which had a necklace of flowers around its neck; later, he had seen in *Paris-Match* photographs of the same village obliterated by bombing. 'You have to look at beauty like that as if you're looking at it for the very last time,' Daddy says. 'The sweetness of life, my darling, is terribly perishable.' That remark about beauty, decided David Denby in the review quoted earlier, 'will stand as an aesthete's brutally pragmatic advice to a sadly polluted world'.[15] All Dirk's contributions to the dialogue – thoughts on England, the sceptr'd isle with its 'gnome-ridden gardens', its rain and its hatred of 'bloody foreigners'; on God, 'From what I've heard He's not over-bright' – were accepted with alacrity by Tavernier, who now reflects: 'I think I got in the film things which were very, very much *him* – the real Dirk, the Dirk he was hiding.' There is no question about that. Dirk in turn added a third figure to his private pantheon: Visconti the Emperor; Losey the King; and now Tavernier the Genius, master of our minutiae. Dirk's career as an author had begun with an elegy. If, as seemed more than likely, *Daddy Nostalgie* was to be his last film, another elegy would mark the end of his remarkable progress as a screen actor. In which case, as he wrote to his director, 'it was a wonderful way to finish!'[16]

So wary was Dirk, so alert to any possible 'tiger-traps' and so deft at taking evasive action, that he was seldom caught by an interviewer's question. On New Year's Eve listeners to BBC Radio Four's *Desert Island Discs* had the rare experience of hearing him flounder. Twenty-five years after he had first been 'cast away' by Roy Plomley, Dirk was invited back to choose the eight records that would keep him going and to tell Sue Lawley about his life. He warned her that his taste in music was 'pretty bloody awful' – and proved it when he asked for 'New York, New York' in a version by the Boston Pops Orchestra rather than by, say, Sinatra or Liza Minnelli. He thought God had leaned out of Heaven and touched him in order to play the piano as Franz Lizst, whose first concerto was the only piece common to both programmes. He said he liked being alone, but could not get used to the English Christmas. He thought war was 'a very unnecessary and evil situation'. And he did not regret that he had never had children 'because I'm a deeply selfish person, I'm too into it now, I'm better on my own'. So, asked Sue Lawley, 'is there nothing, is there no love in you to give?' A flustered Dirk replied:

No, no, there is, I think, for my family, an enormous amount. I do love them. My brother and sister had lots of children, and I'm a great-uncle and God knows what. That does take its place. But I can't say I'm an unloving person [...] no, I'm not, but I don't really want anything further than that. I don't want anybody in my life. I never have. I couldn't have done my career if I'd been married to someone; it would have been a total disaster. I've fallen deeply in love with every leading lady I've ever worked with – except Monica Vitti . . . who was a *beast*. All the others I simply loved [...] OK, Uncle Dirk's *full* of love.

By this time he had pulled himself together, stating firmly: 'Shall we put it this way – people come to meals, they don't stay the night.' But it had been a telling exchange: 'I don't want anybody in my life. I never have.' Where, then, did that place Tony? Sue Lawley had already asked Dirk about him, describing Tony Forwood as his 'friend and companion', and about the constant speculation that theirs had been a homosexual relationship. Did he resent that? 'I resented it enormously for his family, and for his grandson who is now fifteen, and for my own family. What can you do? Especially with the press we have in this country.' He also resented very much growing old, although 'there are compensations – not many'. So did he fear death? 'Not at all. I fear the *method* of it. I don't want to be in an aeroplane slowly spiralling down. I don't really want to go through what Forwood did with Parkinson's and cancer, because there's nothing more undignified and more hideous than that. That's why I'm totally for euthanasia in those circumstances. I've taken precautions for myself. It won't happen to me.' For some listeners those ten words drowned out the second half of the programme, at the end of which Dirk chose, as the one record he could not do without on his island, the fourth movement of Mahler's Fifth Symphony; as the book he was allowed in addition to the Bible and Shakespeare, Ronald Blythe's *Akenfield* – another elegy; and for his luxury object, a distillery: a more conventional large case of whisky would not last him very long.

The interview took place shortly after Dirk's return from the *Daddy Nostalgie* filming and a month before the programme was broadcast. He asked for no cuts or retakes to be made. As he left the studio he seemed perfectly happy with the way it had gone, writing a 'charming' letter of thanks to the producer Olivia Seligman, whose recollection is of 'a hugely intelligent and original man who, at the time of the recording, was saddened and disappointed by his life'.[17] She was surprised when, a few weeks later, he wrote of being subjected to 'an interrogation rather than an interview, with shreds of music tacked on at the ends of treacherous questions'.[18] So too was Sue Lawley, who had expected him to be 'rather melancholy and unobliging' but found him 'entirely co-operative'; her abiding memory is that 'he seemed resentful – the world had done him wrong'. What struck her most forcibly, however, was his attitude when they first met: 'He made a great fuss about how he had been left loitering for longer than was desirable in the reception of Broadcasting House. I said, "I'm so sorry." He said, "It's very difficult – the fans can be so tiresome", the implication being that he expected to be mobbed. I thought, how peculiar, this man is in denial.'[19]

Dirk's remarks about euthanasia were to reach further than he could ever imagine. In the past he had made occasional broadcasts for an assortment of charities: the Animal Health Trust in 1955, the Hertford British Hospital in Paris in 1963, a group supporting unmarried mothers and illegitimate children in 1966, the Lady Hoare Thalidomide Trust in 1967 ... but there had been no sustained involvement with any specific cause, apart from the Sunny Bank Anglo-American Hospital in Cannes, which during the Clermont years received the equivalent of a good *camionette* full of his and Tony's discarded *objets* for its jumble sales. In 1986 Tony's specialist Peter Wrigley introduced Dirk to a then new cancer charity, BACUP, founded by – in Dirk's words – a tiny, sparrow-like, vibrant, eager and courageous woman doctor, Vicky Clement-Jones, to 'help sufferers and their families who found themselves exactly where she had found herself. Adrift. Unsure. Frightened. In need of advice.'[20] He called her courageous because she herself had been diagnosed as a terminal case; indeed, although he did not know it at the time, she had risen from her sick-bed to meet him. Dirk quietly went to work on BACUP's behalf; it was to them that he asked for the libel damages resulting from Robert Tanitch's book to be sent. Soon he was calling it 'my charity'. But it was not the only one.

His mention to Sue Lawley of being 'totally for euthanasia' in certain circumstances, and of having 'taken precautions for myself', had touched a chord. 'There is always mail after you open your mouth on radio,' he wrote in his review of Ludovic Kennedy's *CounterBlast*; 'but the many letters I got after this were shatteringly disturbing. They did not include a single complaint. Some reached me via the BBC, others had been put through the letterbox of the block in which I live. Letters of extreme despair, delivered by hand. All of them begged one thing. Help. Where do we go? Who can aid me? What can we do? Will you help?' Help, he thought, was an 'easy' word: 'Help me make the bed, hang the picture, stir the pudding, carry the logs [. . .] But help me to die is a very different thing. From these letters, and from my own wretched experiences, it is not so singular.'[21] He was invited to become a vice-president of the Voluntary Euthanasia Society, which he saw as an opportunity 'to lend a bit of weight to the boat'. Publicity surrounding this appointment had a dramatic effect: the society's executive director, John Hofsess, told him that within a few months the VES had gained a thousand new members. 'It is extraordinary,' said Dirk. 'Friends I have known for years now talk about how much they want to die peacefully and with dignity. They believe, as I do, that so long as we are *compos mentis*, we must be allowed the right to decide – but only as a last resort – to be assisted to die peacefully. Before I spoke out they did not like to bring up the subject because in this country, I believe, euthanasia is still as much a taboo as talking about anti-Semitism.'[22]

The charity worker, the polemicist – here were new Dirks. They were joined by another: Dirk the teacher. He and Richard Eyre, director of the National Theatre, had lunch at the Connaught, after which the latter wrote in his diary: 'He's flirtatious, charming and amusing. Quite tart and quite self-analytical. Says several times that he knows he's good at his craft.'[23] A few weeks later Dirk was passing on some of that knowledge by giving a master-class at the theatre's Studio – the first of three informal sessions arranged, with no publicity, for members of the NT company. Juliet Stevenson, who had grown up with a passion for the theatre but little exposure to the cinema, remembers her disbelief when she heard that this 'mythical figure' was to take such classes; slightly suspicious, too: 'I thought he was incredibly exotic and remote from the life of London and working practitioners in the theatre.' The thirty-three-year-old actress had admired his 'miraculous' face on the screen, but 'would not have had him on my top-twenty list of actor/mentors'. As a student she had had 'a slight bias against film and that kind of performer. I always wondered how much actors like him actually *did*.' So, largely out of curiosity, she went along to the Studio where Dirk was to conduct a 'scene study' of sequences from *The Servant* and *Accident*. She arrived a little late, and found Dirk sitting at the head of a table:

He looked up, and smiled. I was immediately struck by his humility. That quality permeated the session. He was very gentle, quietly spoken and, to start with, seemed apprehensive. He seemed to have no sense of his own status.

Here was this legendary character who was slightly in awe of the actors round the table. He seemed quite vulnerable. As the session went on he warmed to the whole thing and his confidence grew. I can't remember the detail of what we studied, but it wasn't – unlike some – a highly technical exercise, and I was hooked by his gentle explanation of the scene. I suppose I imagined him sitting back on his laurels after a golden career based on a happy chance of nature. But it was an absolute revelation to me that here was this courteous, highly intelligent, generous, witty person. I completely swung around behind him. I remember worrying about him. After the death of his lifelong partner, he could so easily have stayed, tucked himself away and stewed in the south of France, living off the income from his bank accounts. Instead he chose to return to London, which had changed and was a more complicated place. I thought, how brave.[24]

The Guildhall School of Music and Drama and the University of Surrey had the same idea, of tapping into Dirk's experience. What they were given was refreshingly candid and free of actorish pretentiousness: 'I don't go in for that Method rubbish. Go into a room and pretend to be a packet of Kellog's or a tin of condensed milk. God, what crap.'[25] His reward was simply the satisfaction of being made to feel he had something interesting and useful to offer. 'I cant believe that the young people want to talk to me or to hear me talk to them, and I am terrified,' he wrote to Hélène Bordes. 'But if one does'nt hand on the information of a life what is left? They want to know. I will try and tell them.'[26] For the next few years, in different ways, and in front of audiences varying in number from several hundred total strangers to a single nephew or niece, he did so.

In the summer of that first master-class year, 1990, Dirk began to have serious doubts about whether or not he would ever again be able to write a book; his Muse had gone fully AWOL. He had abandoned 'The Jericho Walls'. 'After 3 years work I KNEW that it was going to be a failure [...] My publishers are very sad. I am relieved. I feel empty. But ready to try again. Perhaps this time a play? Who knows?'[27] A suggestion from Tony Lacey at Viking that Dirk edit an anthology about the theatre and film, from Shakespeare to Tynan, fell on stony ground; in any case it is doubtful that Dirk's patience at working on the writings of others in anything other than a review or an introduction would have lasted beyond about twenty pages. A few weeks later he told Pat Kavanagh that he felt like a frog in a muddy pond. She wrote saying that from experience both professional and personal – her father, stepmother and husband were all writers – she had always felt that no one in his right mind should embark on a novel unless driven by a compulsion to do so; therefore Dirk would have no bullying or coaxing from her. Nevertheless she felt certain that there were more novels and further volumes of autobiography 'to be fashioned from the wonderful filing cabinet of your memory'.[28] By the same post came a letter from Tavernier, speculating about whether Dirk and he might collaborate on a script about Robert Hamer, the writer and director of *Kind Hearts and Coronets*, who died in 1963 aged fifty-two: 'The idea of playing an idealist who is thwarted by the Studio-Setup and driven to drink and death intrigues me greatly,' replied Dirk. 'I watched it happen to Bob, he was a sweet, brilliant, funny man [...] I saw it happen to Lewis Milestone, and, eventually, to Cukor [...] the destruction of an idealist has always fascinated me.'[29] It was another of those attractive ideas which came to nothing, but Tavernier's enthusiasm, coupled with the wisdom of Dirk's literary agent, gave him a needed lift. The frog, he told Pat Kavanagh, was 'clambering back to the bank very slowly, but no longer huddled in sludge simpering with misery, rage and, undeniable, frustration of the soul!'[30] Loss and declining powers, both physical and – he thought – mental, had been the principal causes; but at least he could make a joke about the removal, at great expense, of his seven remaining teeth, so that he now boasted 'a full upper set of clackers! My smile is rather shy – but *very* like a row of Chicklets.'[31]

When soon afterwards he returned to the theme of his 'half-life in World's End' article by writing another woebegone, hostess-wounding piece called 'A short walk from Harrods',[32] he underestimated its effect. Most welcome was a congratulatory note from John Osborne, who one wet Sunday at Beel had arrived with his wife Mary Ure, 'sodden as a pair of seals', and handed Dirk the typescript of *Look Back in Anger*; he now commended Dirk for his journalism, which he described as 'terrific, very personal, stylish and with a distinction all its own'.[33] In his reply Dirk admitted that the essay's sub-text was to some extent 'a cry of loneliness and despair', but 'I had hoped that it would have amused people rather than got them so sad that they have offered me caravans on sites from Salcombe (with a view of the bay and resident caretaker on the site ...) to Dunoon. People have offered to read to me, write to me, take me for walks in Kensington Gardens or, are you ready, the Yorkshire Dales (Peaceful, bliss, REAL people. Not grotesques like London ...)'.[34] As so often, the self-portrait was skewed towards self-pity and only partially true. His diary – these days, simply an appointments book – was extraordinarily full for someone who pleaded neglect. And, now that he was settled, there were opportunities which simply did not exist 'on the hill'. Not long after the move to Cadogan Gardens he ran into David Jacobs, while they were both 'getting their rations' at the local supermarket, with the result that Dirk was engaged to present the former's lunchtime radio programme for a week – a hark-back to 'I Play What I Like' in 1955 by, as he himself put it, 'Dirge Bogarde'. More substantial was his 'casting' as the narrator for *The Forsyte Chronicles*, a twenty-three-part radio adaptation of John Galsworthy's novel sequence. The producer, Janet Whitaker, approached Jonathan Altaras with little optimism that Dirk would agree; but, to her delight, he did. It was a meaty piece of work; he could record his material without any of the other members of the cast being present; and he would be paid £200 an episode. Once perched in the studio on a tall stool, he was 'as happy as Larry' for three and a half days. Janet Whitaker detected traces of Dirk's stroke: 'There were certain words he had difficulty with, slurring them slightly as if he was a little drunk – mainly sibilants. He would almost over-enunciate to compensate. But it was hardly noticeable.' His contribution to the series was a key to its success: 'He had that wonderful ironic quality, which was exactly what I wanted for the narration.'[35] The only time Dirk regretted his involvement in this ambitious project was when he attended a press reception with the rest of the cast to launch the series 'at a nightclub in the King's Road'. He went on the proviso that he would have nothing to do with anyone from the tabloid newspapers. 'Protection' was arranged. Janet Whitaker returned from giving an interview to find Dirk trapped on a sofa by the foe. He mouthed 'It's all right' and carried on, but as he left the reception, he said to her that he would never work for the BBC again. The coverage the next day made much of him being broke, lonely and walking with ghosts. 'We were terribly naive,' says Janet Whitaker ruefully. 'In our department we simply had not dealt with anything quite like that before.' Not long afterwards Dirk gave her lunch at the Connaught – 'I'd never been anywhere like it' – and within weeks he was back in the studio, recording for her a slightly cut and 'toned-down' version of the 'A short walk from Harrods' essay, with tinkling ice-cubes and twittering birds to complement his ruminations on being back in Britain. Janet Whitaker summarised the piece as 'a grieving; it is bitchy and funny, but it begins and ends with somebody talking about a grieving process, and it is very poignant indeed'. She was interested in how much Dirk's attitudes had changed since the late 1960s, the *Particular Friendship* period. 'Whether he had mellowed, I don't know, but he was pretty anti-Thatcher, and he seemed to have rejected a lot of things his class was holding on to. I realised that I was glad to know him *now*. I don't think I would have liked the film star of the sixties at all.' Exactly at this time, in a long interview with the novelist Gary Indiana, Dirk was drawn more formally on his political views:

The point is that *then* [1967–70] we had a particularly savage socialist government that was doing all the wrong things, as far as I could see. I'm from a very Conservative family. When I started paying 98 per cent tax on the pound – when the studios were being closed, when American movies could no longer come in because they were being taxed so heavily – I realized it was time to quit. They were giving everything to the famous worker and to the unions. And they were pulling the country to pieces, they really were. But with Mrs Thatcher,* and the overt Conservatism that's happening now in England, the situation is appalling [...] My points of view have altered very radically; I'm much more to the left than I ever would have dreamt possible, but what alarms me is that all the politicians have gone weak and wet. Our reputation for

---

* Margaret Thatcher had resigned in 1990 as Prime Minister and Leader of the Conservative Party.

brutality at football matches is extraordinary, we behave like lions, we've gone mad, all wearing Union Jacks – I don't understand it. And the new rich are much worse than any of the old Conservative families.[36]

Nothing so drear as politics was allowed to intrude for long into either Dirk's conversation or his writing. It was a subject that never enticed his Muse from her lair. Sex, however, and sexual politics were quite another matter; and she had a positive spring in her step when Dirk finally committed himself to finishing 'The Jericho Walls' – or *Jericho*, as it became about halfway through, when he decided that it was 'not at all an intellectual piece, more a thriller!' The background was the Aids epidemic: 'NOT an easy story for my elderly readers!' he admitted to Hélène Bordes. 'They will be very shocked I fear, but AIDS, or SIDA, is still almost un-mentionable in this country and I decided that no one had written a detective story about it, so I would!' He had not tried a first-person novel before: 'A curious way to write. He is not coming out as a very nice hero! Rather a selfish prig. Funny! Perhaps it is MY sub-text!'[37] Set in a lovingly depicted Provençal village – a promised land after 'years of rootlessness' – *Jericho* is the story of William Caldicott, a writer of books 'that people leave behind on airplanes', whose marriage has collapsed and who sets out to discover the fate of his estranged younger brother James, a free spirit, who, it transpires, has paid heavily for enjoying 'too much happiness'. There is jealousy; there is hatred; indeed there is a strong echo of *Postillion*: 'My resentment started from the moment that I had, at the age of – what? – twelve, thereabouts, first seen Elpie coming towards me carrying this raw, crumpled creature, fists flailing, mouth wide in toothless fury, silent, wobbling head supported by her hand.'[38] The tale is effectively a belated rite of passage, a completing of the 'crossword puzzle of my life', for William, who discovers as much about himself as he does about his brother. James was, it turns out, as 'Gay as a carousel' and the relationship which produced a Down's Syndrome child called Thomas had been 'a piece of romantic tosh'. James, says one of the characters, 'went against his true nature. He was playing the wrong part in the wrong play.'[39] Above all, the book is steeped in melancholy; Dirk writes of 'l'heure verte' – that time in a summer evening which the French call 'entre le chien et le loup'. But he was too good a writer to allow a one-note story, so he enthusiastically injected scenes of bondage, degradation and 'the glory of sado-masochism'. One of his loyal readers had told him that she and her husband read alternate chapters of his books aloud to each other in bed. 'I'll show 'em!' Dirk said to a friend.

Viking Penguin paid Dirk £80,000 – what some might call 'a quantum leap' – for *Jericho*, which he delivered in February 1991. Six days later Nicholas Shakespeare took me, as his deputy, to have lunch with Dirk at the Connaught. There was a purpose which, although unstated, was perfectly obvious to Dirk: Shakespeare had decided to stand down as literary editor at *The Telegraph*. For the past two years, as part of a hare-brained scheme to create a 'seven-day newspaper', his job had entailed running books pages for the *Daily* and the *Sunday Telegraph*; Dirk's reviews had appeared in both. Now Shakespeare, his English Plank, wanted the time and space to write novels of his own and an official Life of his friend, the late Bruce Chatwin. On his departure three months later the two newspapers reverted to independent coverage of books, and as Nicholas left he handed me a jewel-encrusted baton of regular reviewers to occupy the pages of *The Daily Telegraph*, which Dirk – regardless of how far he might have drifted to the left and regardless of the historical family tie to *The Times* – had come to know as 'my paper'. A large constituency of its readers felt the same way about him, and waited avidly for the next of his firecrackers.

Dirk was seventy – the 'finished product', as the graphologist Renata Propper puts it.[40] In her analysis, he was still 'wrestling with life', having achieved a certain inner detachment that gave his personality character and calibre. He was assertive and self-assured, with authority and a 'somewhat cool superior attitude'; he was 'well aware of his position of fame, *demanding* the tribute as well as *needing* the applause'. While able to display great charm and a sometimes biting cynical wit, he could at times – like most strong individualists – be difficult, irritable and contentious. He never suffered fools gladly. He maintained a reserve, letting only a selected few become close. At times he still reacted strongly to his environment, not always in firm control of his moods or temper – and a certain tendency for feeling depressed. The effeminacy she detected in his adolescent hand, the defeatedness at forty, had gone, and in its place was a sovereign mature personality; but there was still a trace of the 'high-strung balancing act between his sharp intelligence and a more unruly emotional base'. He had failed to solve all his complexities, unlike William in *Jericho*, who had finished 'the crossword puzzle of his life'. Nevertheless his ability to see issues from more than one angle meant that even now he was still 'broadening his horizons'. The seventy-year-old Dirk was 'very much alive, though not always at peace'.

In August 1991, with controversy still bubbling because of his part in the euthanasia debate, Dirk reviewed a batch of four books about the Holocaust. Its heading, taken from a line in his notice, was 'How could such hatred exist?' We must be reminded of the past, he wrote, because the conditions which kept 'all the good Germans [...] trapped by fear' could occur again, here in Britain:

> The Nazis appealed to, and collected, all the yobbos and lager-louts of their day and gave them boots, badges and imposing caps to wear, which gave them a towering superiority [...] Not here? You think? But we have them all ready-made: the Union Jack-underpants fraternity who wreck Spanish bars, Channel ferries, railway carriages, football stadiums. Drunk with beer and rage, mindless, stuffed with false National Pride, they rampage everywhere. And who stops them? Who dares interfere with a rape? Or a street mugging? We dare not. *You can die that way.* So, too, in the Germany of 1934–45.

Why the Jews? he asked. 'No one can give me an answer, and these dreadful (that is, terrifying) books do not help me to come to terms with the attempted slaughter of a whole race.' A month later he was compelled back into print because of the astonishing response to his rhetorical questions. Letters arrived from all over Britain, from Europe, even from Australia. They were mainly in his support, but some were 'abusive, ugly, worrying' – and unsigned; they were first-hand evidence. 'The hatred still exists. And even in the kindest letters there lurks a sad feeling of worry and anxiety. A Jew is not to be trusted. I am counselled to read my Old Testament. To read the Psalms. To understand that the Jews were responsible for the crucifixion of Christ.'[41] For Dirk, the gratifying aspect of the correspondence was that much of it came from the anxious – not abusive – young. At the time the review appeared, he had already agreed to visit Tonbridge School and to talk to the boys about 'The Story of My Life' or 'How To Write' or some such topic, but after this remarkable tapping of the public consciousness he asked his host, the school's head of history, Anthony Seldon, whether the subject should be 'The Holocaust? Euthanasia? Or just Judy Garland and Ava Gardner?' They agreed that Dirk should give over at least part of the time to the Holocaust; his audience would be boys aged between fifteen and eighteen, plus a few members of staff whom it might be hard to keep away. Dirk hoped no offence would be taken if he declined a leisurely lunch in the senior common room: 'I am really not a bit good at the social scene, the job, that is to say talking to the boys, is far more important than glasses of sherry and uneasy chatter [. . .] After years and years of living in a sort of goldfish-bowl I prefer to be left to do the job with the young.'[42] Dr Seldon has never forgotten the afternoon of 11 September 1991:

He arrived with his driver. He was very self-contained, he didn't want to be engaged. He just sat outside in the back of the car, in front of the school, with a thermos and a sandwich. Of all the many speakers we had in the four years that I was at Tonbridge, he stands out; the only one who approached him was Leonard Cheshire. Bogarde had narrated the documentary about Oskar Schindler, but said he had never spoken before on the Holocaust in public. It was an astonishing talk – one of those occasions in your life when you are aware that you are listening to something utterly extraordinary, the like of which you will not hear again. He spoke about enlisting in the Army, about his father in the First World War, and about how he happened to be in the area of Bergen-Belsen on that day, and what it was like to go in. It was an outpouring of *liquid emotion*. And afterwards he just clammed up, he didn't want to speak to anybody, and went home.[43]

For Anthony Seldon it was the most moving talk he had ever heard; when he went through to teach the boys afterwards, they were 'still shell-shocked'. There was no question of a fee, Dirk had stipulated; 'talking to the young is fee enough'.[44] Some months later, he spoke again on the subject, this time to the Board of Deputies of British Jews, at a memorial meeting to mark the forty-ninth anniversary of the uprising in the Warsaw Ghetto. 'Craven with fear at saying the wrong thing, I tried not to be influenced by the hate-mail I had received. When we had parked the car, even the policeman was bloody. "What are you doing with this lot?" he asked. I realized I must stop this meddling, so I pulled in my horns and went back to the typewriter.'[45] Not quite: he fulfilled a final commitment to the pupils of the King's School at Rochester, warning its head of history, Edward Towne, that at Tonbridge 'it had been a bit of a battering' for the boys, who 'had never even heard of the Holocaust!'; 'I am delighted to report that some of the younger boys blubbed. This is not as unkind as it sounds; it merely proved that somewhere a nerve had been touched.'[46] The Roffensians, as the Rochester pupils are known, were just as harrowed, and never more so than when Dirk described seeing an inmate of Belsen recognisable as a girl 'because she had breasts – but only just. They were like spaniel's ears.' That day in Germany, he said, he lost any faith he might have had; of God there was no sign: 'God was invented by man for those who lose faith in living. I believe in another force – the force that helps plants to grow.'[47]

The teenagers who listened spellbound in Rochester will not have known it, but the green and white ribbon Dirk wore in the button-hole of his immaculate grey suit denoted a promotion; Jack Lang, the long-serving French Minister of Culture, had elevated him from a Chevalier to a Commandeur dans l'Ordre des Arts et des Lettres. They were, however, in no doubt about his new-found status in Britain. He was now Sir Dirk Bogarde. The State recognition which he once feared had been jeopardised by his portrayal of 'Boy' Browning, was finally his. The Earl of Gowrie, Margaret Thatcher's Arts Minister from 1983 to 1985, had originally recommended Dirk for a knighthood, without success. 'Being a cheeky fellow,' Grey Gowrie recalls, 'I asked her why he had been turned down. She said, "Because he's a tax exile." I said, "Nonsense. He's simply living abroad with his other half. Look at the way the only English popular matinée idol, adored by all the Tory ladies, has made the transition into a great movie actor." She said, "OK" and put it back into the machine.'[48] The machine ground slowly. In 1991 the critic Alexander Walker found himself at a dinner with Margaret Thatcher's successor John Major and his wife, and Bryan and Nanette Forbes. Dirk's name cropped up in the conversation, and Norma Major asked what he was doing these days. Walker said that Dirk was back in England, but had had a stroke and was unlikely to make any more films. Whereupon the Majors began to reminisce fondly about their cinema-going in south London during the fifties and to express their sorrow at Dirk's plight. Bryan Forbes recalls Norma Major saying to her husband: 'Can't you do something to cheer him up?' In November Dirk received a letter saying that the Prime Minister had it in mind to recommend to the Queen that a knighthood was deserved. Dirk demurred. In *Cleared for Take-Off* he describes ticking the box for a refusal and receiving a 'reprimand' from 'a very pleasant Scots lady somewhere in No. 10' who said he had until Monday to make up his mind.[49] He told his brother Gareth he had 'tried, very hard, to get out of it' and passed 'a pretty bloody weekend. No one to talk to. One is forbidden to even speak of it . . . to wife, husband, parent . . . anyone. And then I finally thought, the hell with it. There is only one other Knight of the Cinema and thats Chaplin. So I said yes.'

Dirk was pronounced one of twenty-nine Knights Bachelor in the 1992 New Year Honours List, alongside the astronomer Martin Rees, the Director-General of the BBC Michael Checkland, the cricketer Colin Cowdrey, the Chairman of Marks and Spencer Richard Greenbury, the heart surgeon Magdi Yacoub and the writer Peter Quennell, Glur Dyson Taylor's former husband. The citation in the *London Gazette*, which gave his real name incorrectly as Dirk Niven van den Bogaerde, read simply 'actor'; his eight books had counted for nothing in these rarefied circles.[50] The ceremony took place on 13 February at Buckingham Palace, where, watched by Elizabeth in a supremely dashing feathered hat, he was dubbed by the Queen to the strains of 'Who Wants to Be a Millionaire?' The dignity of the occasion was somewhat marred immediately afterwards, when they tried to evade the photographers by using a side exit. A flat battery stranded them in the Palace courtyard, where Ron Jones, one of his two trusty regular drivers, had to resort to jump-leads before he could take them to the sanctuary of the Connaught; it made a good story over lunch with Gareth, Lucilla and the Bowlbys. Dirk confided to Gareth that he felt their father would have been 'amused' by the honour: 'He made me promise, faithfully, that I would never accept a political award, or purchase one, or one for a charitable business. I promised. And I dont think that I have broken the promise because this was offered for my service to the Cinema and also, which is rather nice, for being a good ambassador for my country while abroad!' If only Tony had been alive to see it . . . apart from anything else he would certainly have prevented Dirk from signing himself 'Sir Dirk Bogarde'. Someone must have dropped a hint, because he asked Daphne Fielding whether he should be using his 'handle' when he inscribed books. She replied that their buyers probably wanted him to do so, but, really, he should not. It was too late; the solecism is preserved on countless title pages, letters, postcards and advertisements for charity. Even Dennis Rendell, his chum from Mr Thompson's 'crammer' in Hampstead, received a card, saying 'a "K" was *not* what I had in mind in those days at all!'[51], and signed, just as incorrectly as in this more formal piece of correspondence:

Yours sincerely,

Dirk Bogarde.

This was a period which for Dirk combined prominence and activity to a degree that he had not known since the late fifties. He made spasmodic appearances on radio and television, talking not only about the cinema but also about Europe, Britain and, above all, euthanasia. Readings at the Imperial War Museum and elsewhere, and donations of his drawings, attracted valuable attention to various good causes. Janet Whitaker asked him if he would like to do a radio play, thinking he would choose something like a Shaw. Not a bit of it: Pinter, please. 'He doesn't take the easy route, this guy,' thought the producer. 'Here he is in his seventies and he wants to do a bloody Pinter.'[52] The result was a brilliant treatment of *No Man's Land* – with Dirk and Michael Hordern in the roles created by Gielgud and Ralph Richardson – of which the critic Gillian Reynolds wrote: 'It was an evening when the arithmetic of ordinary life became the algebra of universal human experience.' Dirk, she said, was 'shy and sly, slimy sometimes, infinitely wise at the close'.[53] None of those adjectives sprang to mind at the close of 'Dirk Bogarde: By Myself', a two-part interview which went out on Channel Four just after the knighthood was announced. Filmed over two days in the summer of 1991 by Lucida, an independent production company, it was true to its title: Dirk was shown talking for the best part of two hours about his life and work, without any intervention – only clips from some of the movies. He laid down the rules so that, as he told his brother, 'I would be doing a sort of A. J. P. Taylor lecture. Did you ever see him? Historian, splendid, never used a script or referred to a note. It IS possible ... and because you are in complete control you know there wont be a left-fielder suddenly, like Parkinson, Wogan, (I refuse to even read his letters!) or poor old Russel Harty and the rest.' In fact it *was* an interview, but the producer Chris Rodley asked his questions, out of camera-shot, in such a way that the five hours of material could be cut to a monologue.

The programme was a summation, if not a valediction. Rodley and the director, Paul Joyce, who had worked with Dirk before, on a documentary about the European cinema, always considered Dirk 'one of the greats' and, says, Joyce, 'we thought he should be celebrated at the point where he was winding down'.[54] It particularly appealed to Dirk that such an extensive profile should be made on celluloid, not videotape. 'He said to us, "This is my final appearance on film",' remembers Paul Joyce. 'For "appearance", read "performance". And that's why we swallowed his terms.' It was an unprecedented appeal to Dirk's vanity. There were few revelations, apart from his killing-off Bob Thomson and his attempted adoption of Jon Whiteley, although he caused a *frisson* by admitting that the cinema is largely about 'sexual excitement' and that 'the whole thing is fake but then that's what sex is'. The two programmes represent a distillation of Dirk's spoken autobiography and, as such, are entertaining, arch, occasionally malicious and inevitably misleading. Paul Joyce's intention was 'to give him a last opportunity, in sympathetic hands, to be as truthful with himself as he could be in a public arena where he had great support and love and, at the top level, a very sophisticated following. My ultimate sadness is that he rejected that opportunity –

not that he didn't spill the beans, or "come out"; but that finally he was not true to himself.' Joyce and Rodley had hoped to use two snapshots – one of Dirk taken by Tony; the second of Tony taken by Dirk, when they were evidently sitting side by side – which would have linked them silently and inextricably. No chance. And in its fashion, his refusal was symptomatic of Paul Joyce's conclusion about Dirk, that 'there was no solid foundation to his life – everything he built was on shifting sand'.

The programme was received in some quarters as a fascinating insight; in some, as a colossal ego-trip; in others, as both. Helena Bonham Carter says:

I thought he didn't come out in the best of lights. He was very vain, rather narcissistic and waspish. I thought, 'That isn't the real you.' I suppose he was entitled to a bit of self-aggrandisement about his own ability in film. After years of being famous, for self-preservation you erect this public edifice which allows your private self to be safe. I think he came to believe in the public one. He showed a fundamental lack of self-acceptance, which seemed to me to be rather sad in someone who had reached seventy. So much about him was 'I couldn't give a damn'. But you could see he minded still.[55]

Vain, narcissistic, waspish – he was all of those, but, to those who knew him well, only on occasion and usually in a context. On television, however, he tended to leave exactly the negative impression that Helena Bonham Carter describes. Sally Betts had dealt with Dirk since 1975, most often when he was at his most vulnerable, delivering new, unpolished work that sometimes even Tony had not seen. She would watch his interviews and say to the screen: 'You're not the Dirk I know.'[56] John Gielgud, writing to the director and author James Roose-Evans a few weeks after the two programmes were broadcast, observed: 'I think Dirk Bogarde's interviews are quite unworthy of him'.[57] In 1985, following an appearance on *The Michael Aspel Show*, Jack Jones wrote, saying some good and sensible friends had described Dirk as 'arrogant', and adding: 'The very best I've seen you was when you talked to the National Film people three or four years ago;* urbane, friendly and with every ounce of your old charm, which seems somehow to have decelerated into acerbity of a kind, which you of all people should know is picked up by cameras un-blinkingly and un-profitably so far as the projection of your much loved self is concerned.' This longest-serving and most uncompromising of his critics did not see the final, two-hour interview. Jack had died in October 1990. It is safe to say Dirk was spared another 'bad press' from his old friend.

'By myself' now became Dirk's watchword. He had, in *Jericho*, a new book to 'flog'. Perhaps there was a way to avoid the 'absolute disgrace' of sitting at a table

---

* The 1983 National Film Theatre Lecture, broadcast later by the BBC.

beside a jangling till and to give a little more than a scribble and a couple of polite words to people who had shown 'the good manners and interest to queue for miles through Software, Records and Lampshades'. On that first evening with Sue MacGregor at the National Theatre, and again a year later, he had found when it came to the time for questions from the floor that 'the audience began to take me over, and I began to take them into my confidence. It was an amazing experience. Quite new to me.'[58] He enjoyed the stimulus of direct, unmediated contact. However delightful and well-informed his 'monitor', maybe there was no need to have one. Maybe he could do it all by himself, in theatres outside as well as inside London, with just a friendly 'minder' backstage to ensure that he turned up at the right place at the right time, that the supply of books was under control, and that not too many Barmy of Bromley or Crazed of Croydon slipped through the net. In March 1992 Dirk went tentatively 'on the road', first to Edinburgh, then to the National, to Bristol and to Manchester. He took with him a briefcase containing a few 'props': mainly books marked up for extracts, but also the odd scrap of paper bearing some preposterous bureaucratic nonsense, a witticism or a news story. 'I'm going to read some stuff to you,' he announced when the ovation at the Olivier died down. 'The best is mine, at the end.'[59] And so he did, with pieces from Hilaire Belloc; Ronald Blythe's moving collection of Second World War letters, *Private Words*; and the passage in *Jericho* about the twilight hour 'between the dog and the wolf'. He told of a flustered young man struggling with black bag and car keys in a London street who said to him: 'I know you hate this sort of thing, I'm terribly sorry, but it's all because of you that I became a bloody doctor in the first place.' And he read out a fax from New York to Jonathan Altaras which stated: 'Madonna is currently working on a book of photographs with Steven Meisel. The book is essentially a collection of their interpretation of erotica. Both Steven and Madonna have expressed interest in using Dirk Bogard in these photographs [. . .] Unfortunately I cannot give you more details about the content of these photographs but, if Mr Bogard is interested, Madonna or Steven would be happy to call him to discuss the project in depth.' Gales of laughter – and, subsequently, tabloid headlines – greeted this disclosure. 'What is this?' wondered Dirk. 'At seventy-one? *Necrophilia?*'

After a while he invited the audience to ask any question they liked. Most were predictable, but he found fresh ways to answer them. Was it acting or writing that gave him more satisfaction? Writing – 'People say it's a very solitary life. It's really bunk, that. It *isn't* a solitary life at all. You've got to be *alone* to write, but you make so many friends. Look at you all! [. . .] No, writing is wonderful . . . it gives me much more pleasure. Far less money. But more satisfaction. Anyway, it's not quite such hard work. It's seven-to-one.' Asked when he was going to run for Parliament, he said: 'Are we not beset with enough problems? My job is an entertainer, that's all. I'm not partisan.' Do you have any desire to write a film script? 'If you knew, Sir, how *bloody* the people who make the films are, you wouldn't write a script. You wouldn't write them a fortune cookie.' Do you have a piano, and if so do you ever play Liszt? 'I'd *shoot* bloody Liszt!' – and he told of his encounter with the two French concert pianists who were living on the first floor of his block, with twin grands on which they practised their scales from 'when the sun comes up to night-time'. 'Now, twelve and a half hours of brrrring-punnnng drives me nuts. I wouldn't mind Rachmaninov or Schubert, but ... I lost my temper, and ran screaming down four storeys and beat on their door. Shrieking. Beating. I've never done that in my life before. Not even in the war. I don't think I've done it since I was pottytrained.' One of the Labèque Sisters – for it was they – came to the door.

'Cessez!', said Dirk. 'You've got to stop!'
'M'sieu,' she said, 'nous sommes artistes.'
'*I'm* a blank-blank-blanking artist!' he replied. 'I'm trying to write a book up there!'

Eventually honour was satisfied when the Sisters – who, according to Mrs Hayden the housekeeper, were known as 'Thunder and Lightning' – agreed to place foam rubber under the keys.

There were more serious moments, too, during his exchanges with the audience. Somebody enquired what was the most important quality that had helped in Dirk's acting career: 'If I tell you, it's going to sound really, really so pompous. Truth. Being honest. That's all.' Another wanted to know about his poetry: 'I had my first poem published, without nepotism, in *The Times Literary Supplement* when I was nineteen,' Dirk replied, adding, bizarrely: 'I wrote it after I had actually fired in anger at a man and killed him in the war. I've never written poetry since. The war, you see, had a very strange effect on young people, young men – as it did in the Gulf War. You suddenly found that you wanted to write like hell and get things out of your system.' Finally, when he was asked: 'Do you enjoy performing to flog your books?', Dirk replied: 'I love doing *this*. This is *great*. I was two hours on the stage in Edinburgh on Wednesday night. It was the happiest two hours I've spent for *years*. I just love to be asked to talk about *me*.' Afterwards the queue snaked through the foyers as he signed copies of *Jericho* and his other books. Everyone had had their money's worth; and Dirk had discovered the ideal way to do his 'flogging'. He had also invented a new kind of theatre, reminiscent of Dickens's public readings in the mid-nineteenth century, but loosely structured, informal, confidential; with the added value – and, for Dirk, the charge, the danger even – of the 'Q and A'. Three months later it was put to use again, this time not for his own benefit as an author. Dirk had bumped into a woman who had just lost her husband to leukaemia and was raising money for an oncology research unit at St Bartholomew's Hospital in Homerton. He remembered one of his maternal cousins, who died of the disease at the age of three; he remembered Kay Kendall wearing a mink coat in a July heatwave, and saying 'I think I've got cancer and they won't tell me.' He agreed to try to help. So, one Sunday night the billing at the Theatre Royal, Haymarket read: 'Dirk Bogarde: "By Myself" '. The format was the same as before: readings and anecdotes, then questions. It was a huge success – so much so that the impresario Duncan Weldon wanted to book Dirk for a season at that most elegant of theatres.

Jonathan Altaras, who had organised the event, remembers that negotiations had reached an advanced stage, when Dirk suddenly said: 'I'm not going to do it. I think it's vulgar to talk about oneself.' Which was not an especially convincing excuse. More probable was his reluctance to be tied to a theatrical run, however short; the feeling of being trapped; how much better were the one-night stands in different towns. None the less the Haymarket experience had shown how effectively Dirk's love for – and terror of – performance could be deployed, not just to shift piles of books. There was a moment that evening when he was nonplussed. A man stood up in the audience and said that his wife had just suffered a stroke; did Dirk have any advice on how best to cope? He dealt with the question as robustly and wisely as he could; but was bewildered to find himself so publicly in the role of counsellor to people in distress. It was a far cry from being the Idol of the Odeons. 'I am making use of my life in the only way I can,' he had written to Penelope Mortimer, 'that is by helping people one way or another without being soppy and pious. I am about the most irreverent fellow you could meet. But I *do* love people, and they seem to quite like me. It's comforting.' He had come to terms with catastrophe 'and tucked it all away very neatly into the compost of my life'. He was, he said, 'as content as a clam'.[60]

Twenty-six

'*DO* remember it is *not* what we really did'

'I have, to my astonishment, managed to pull myself together a lot since leaving "home" and coming here,' Dirk wrote to Elizabeth in 1994. 'I NEVER thought I'd ever have another career; or that it would be successful. It was something that never *remotely* came into my mind. I just knew that If I Didn't Do Something For Myself I'd very quickly perish. Just sit about and get pissed. People do.' This late flowering had everything to do with his being both wanted and *needed*. The calls of his chosen charities were never too burdensome. Gareth's three sons and his daughter Alice found in their uncle a generous sage – never more so than when Rupert's wife Jacquie vanished from the house they had converted near Perpignan.* Thomas Forwood was equipped with the requisite gear for student life on the south coast, such as an Apple Mac computer. Official godchildren were treated with thought and care. For the last three years life had become ordered, productive and rewarding. He had even been moved to say 'I LOVE going out now' – not to dinner parties, of course, but 'in the streets', where 'I love people liking me, asking me about … oh, Euthanasia … the Holocaust … or my books.'[1] He had his network of small shops in Cale Street; and there were Partridges the grocers and John Sandoe the booksellers, both within a few minutes' walk even at his slowed pace, and both of which he would eulogise in print. The post office was only a little further away, and the surgery within easy reach. It was not wholly unlike Châteauneuf and Pré du Lac, with familiar, friendly, non-intrusive faces. People from his other worlds spotted Dirk pottering about Chelsea. Alec Guinness noted in his diary for 23 June 1995: 'Bumped into Dirk Bogarde in Fry's splendid vegetable shop in Cale Street. He was fingering oddly shaped tomatoes with a knowledgeable air. He rejected them and cast a dark eye over some frivolous greenery. He finally settled for a big, shiny, yellow pepper. I was envious of his concentrated marketing skill.'[2] Those who saw him looking haunted and somewhat dishevelled were mistaken in feeling pity for him, for he was in a sense recreating for himself a village life,

---

* Jacquie Van den Bogaerde's disappearance is the subject of *Daybreak into Darkness: A True Story of Happiness and Heartbreak* by Rupert Bogarde (Macmillan, 2002).

with its own special rules about social barriers and anonymity. And he was cautious; understandably so, because an Essex woman, severely troubled by the Moon and given to writing as many as seven letters a day care of Dirk's agent, had tracked him down; and, to judge by her correspondence over the past decade, was capable of anything in her unrequited state. He did not like to be taken unawares, as when David Jacobs introduced him outside the Europa supermarket to Martha Gellhorn, that doughty war correspondent, who lived nearby. 'You know Martha Gellhorn, don't you,' said Jacobs. 'No,' replied Dirk, and walked away. David Jacobs had read Dirk's essays about returning to London and how he had learned, like Bardot, to say 'no'; but this was carrying things a trifle far: 'Martha Gellhorn couldn't believe it.' Nor could David Jacobs, who, after all, had given Dirk a few enjoyable days behind a BBC microphone.[3] Patricia Losey recalls a similar incident in John Sandoe's bookshop. Shyness, preoccupation, awkwardness in a situation not under his control – they are possible reasons for Dirk's rudeness, but inadequate as excuses. If Tony had been alive, and certainly if Tony had been with him, he would have behaved differently.

So the clam was not entirely content. Maybe it was jealousy. Ever since Elizabeth can remember, the most powerful emotion in her elder brother was that corrosive monster – inflamed by seeing others receiving more attention, or happy as a family, or muscling in on his own sphere of activity, or simply blessed with social poise. His relationship with Elizabeth had not been without its edge, and indeed its silences. Her husband, George, had died shortly before Tony and in equally distressing circumstances. She now became a regular guest at Cadogan Gardens for a 'spoil', and for some of the excellent cooking which he had taught himself – remarkable when one thinks how foreign an oven was to him until his mid-sixties and Tony's emergency operation forced him to try; less so when one remembers that Dirk was a perfectionist. Brother and sister came closer than they had been since the Lullington days. She was, he wrote to her, 'the only one I really have with whome I can share the incredible delights, worries, fears, happiness and intimacy of childhood'. Some of those delights, however, he was ready to share again with his public. Since 1979 Dirk had toyed, on and off, with the idea of complementing the 'Summer' section of *Postillion* by writing a full-length book about 'the Cottage-Great-Meadow thing'. He had been encouraged by the reaction from children whose teachers had used 'Summer' as an aid, so initially he thought a new volume might be aimed at the young, 'but it would not be about talking hedgehogs or dancing mice'.[4] As we have seen, the title he had in mind was 'Lally' – or 'Lallie' according to his spelling of the day – and indeed the splendid Lally had helped him with her reminiscences at an early stage of the writing. By the time Dirk began to work finally with the typescript at the end of 1991, he had settled instead on *Great Meadow*. It was 'an evocation' – the idyll seen through the eyes of Dirk from the age of nine to thirteen. 'I reckon I'll make a bit of loot from it,' wrote the seventy-year-old Dirk, 'because it is so yucky and full of "nostalgia" and Virol and paraffin lamps and all that to-do. We'll see. I think the Blue-Rinses will heave with horror at "Jericho" ... all that bondage ... so this will get me back onto an even keel.' He expected it to sell to 'all those women who write to me on letter paper covered with bunnies and squirrels and hairbells and hedgehogs in gingham. Oh God.'[5] He was right about the 'loot': Viking Penguin paid him £85,000, and earmarked the new book for Total Exposure, in which Dirk would of course participate by taking to the road again with his 'show', concentrating this time on the south and the Midlands, including the home of the Royal Shakespeare Company at Stratford, two more appearances at the National and one at the Chichester Festival Theatre. 'I think I'll need help from On High to get through this tour,' he wrote to Penelope Mortimer: '[...] Some old queen in the street this morning squealed "Seven pounds fifty at Chichester! You'll make a fortune, dear!".'[6]

Great Meadow was received favourably by most critics. John Mortimer said that he recognised and remembered so much of the country childhood described by Dirk that he found it hard to judge with a reviewer's proper detachment. He praised its 'gentle charm', but found 'a faint flavour of Christopher Robin in some of this determinedly boyish prose' and felt Dirk might have been wiser to write 'as though remembering a childhood instead of having a remembered child speak to us'.[7] Diana Mosley said that children want a story, or jokes, so *Great Meadow* was 'for adults only'. She found it 'restful, undemanding and a nice change. No four-letter words, no sex, a minimum of violence.'[8] Ronald Blythe, whose *Akenfield* Dirk had chosen for his second stint as a castaway on *Desert Island Discs*, returned the compliment by saying how impressively Dirk had retrieved 'his child-voice and youthful limitations' in paying homage to 'his four happiest years'.[9] The most hostile note was struck in, of all publications, the magazine *Sussex Life*, where Eithne Farry said that the word 'evocation' made the reader want to be able to smell the grass beneath the young Dirk's feet: 'But what you actually get is an account by a reject member of the Famous Five who kept white mice instead of discovering smugglers along the coast [...] You would not be inclined to wander in the Great Meadow of his memory again because it evokes nothing but boredom, and really you wish you had stayed at home in the first place.'[10] The book carried ten of Dirk's own drawings and a jacket illustration from a 1934–5 painting by Ulric of Windover Hill; there was a glossary to explain such archaisms as 'M.Y.O.B', 'Pip, Squeak and Wilfred', the 'R.101', and the 'Emperor of Abyssinia'. Above all its dedication was to Lally 'and to the memory of my parents'. Dirk sent Lally an early copy, with a postcard which read:

Dearest Lally,
This is 'your' book. I do hope you will like it – *DO* remember it is *not* what we really did – it's just remembering the happy days we had with you at the

Cottage – Thank you for such a wonderful, happy, childhood which you gave
Lu and me – we have *never* forgotten it. This is the proof. With love
    Dirk xxxx

The next four years assumed a curious and generally satisfying symmetry. No
sooner had Dirk completed a book than he was on to another, a novel alternating
with a further volume of memoirs. Some months into the writing he would go
on tour again to flog the one he had last completed. It was, in truth, something
of a phenomenon as his *oeuvre* expanded and as the audiences filled every seat in
every house he 'played'. If the theatre was within sensible striking distance of
London he would travel in a Satchells car driven by either Bob Pearson or Ron
Jones, and usually he was 'minded' by Clare Harington, the feisty head of
publicity at Viking, whom he had affectionately christened 'Hell Cat'. Occasionally his editor, Fanny Blake, went too. Thus, some of the Team became the
Road Crew. There was little ceremony. He would arrive in good time, but not
so early that he had to kick his heels or be subjected to too much official glad-
handing. Once he had done his 'show' and signed every proffered book, it was
straight to the car, and a picnic en route from his own provisions: smoked salmon
sandwiches; beer and whisky for him; champagne for his 'minder'. They would,
Clare Harington recalled, speed back to London gossiping and giggling. These
were good days: Dirk and his public connecting in a different kind of 'love affair
without carnality'. After appearing at Chester he wrote that it had been 'fun: two
hours on stage, two hours signing. Lots of jolly chat, lots of books sold, kindness
spilling like sunlight.'[11] Charlotte Rampling remembers Dirk saying that of all
he had done in his working life, these 'shows' gave him the most pleasure. 'I can't
tell you what it is like when I *feel* these people, feel their warmth, their appreciation and their love,' he told her. 'I've never felt so loved than in those moments.
And at last I'm able to feel and accept that love.' Dirk was, she says, 'a supreme
connector' and this new, third career 'gave him the opportunity to really connect
live, right into people's souls. They would ask a question, he would answer – it
was like a huge one-to-one. And they were inspired because he was an orator –
a very rare breed – and because he was so generous with his ideas and his
thoughts. In the end it was the only thing he loved doing.'[12]

Of the books he flogged during this period there is no doubt about the most
important. Just as *An Orderly Man* had at its core the deaths of Ulric and
Margaret, the falling of the two 'tent-poles', so in *A Short Walk from Harrods*
Dirk described the collapse of the tent itself and the erosion of a supporting
central pillar; or, in his own metaphor, the dissolution of a carefully constructed
sandcastle, beginning when the first wave – 'a touch of Parkinson's' – lapped
against its base. The first, scene-setting chapter was almost word for word the
baleful piece that had appeared in *The Independent on Sunday*, with its final line
'How the hell did I get here?' Then Dirk wafted the reader to Clermont –
disguised as 'Le Pigeonnier' – and with his trademark direct language took the

story up to the end of the Tavernier film. Joanna Trollope wrote that 'the book moves from being a charming – if intriguingly shadowed – account of finding a Lost Eden, to being an exquisite and painful portrait of the slow, miserable business of disintegration.'[13] Although *Postillion* has its own historical significance in Dirk's creative life, *A Short Walk from Harrods* is a more significant work. You feel that more layers of the onion have been stripped away than ever before. As Sheridan Morley pointed out, the earlier volumes of memoirs 'dealt in a curious kind of literary half-truth from which all inconvenient reality had been deleted, rather as though the novels of Somerset Maugham were to have been run through a shredding machine in the publicity offices of the J. Arthur Rank Organisation'. Only now had Tony taken centre-stage: 'in dying, Forwood comes to life for the first time in Bogarde's pages'. Even so Morley found Dirk's book characteristically infuriating and heart-rending by turns: 'The sound here is once again of closet doors being cautiously half-opened and then slammed in our faces just as we were about to poke about inside, but the old wizard knows enough about his loyal readership to understand that it is precisely the mystery that sells his books.'[14] Jonathan Cecil in *The Spectator* was less exasperated, feeling that 'this excellent book is partly an attempt to exorcise pain' by a 'complex, witty and observant artist to whom sorrow has brought a new and impressive dignity'.[15] By far the most wounding 'notice' came from Dirk's nephew Rupert Van den Bogaerde, who told him bluntly that it was 'a work of self-pity', an opinion delivered just after Dirk had written to Hélène Bordes that 'it has moved everyone who has read it to tears! but, I think, I have managed to write truthfully and without any kind of sentiment or self-pity'. When he sent his first Plank a copy of the book, which included an account of how the second came into his life, he wrote: 'I have a feeling that both you and Nicholas Shakespeare were sent to me by God. How else?'[16]

Dirk had met Hélène Bordes by now. They had tea together at the Lancaster in 1990 when he flew to Paris for the promotion of *Daddy Nostalgie*. No spell was broken, as he had feared would happen if he and Dorothy Gordon saw each other; Dirk and the Professor, as Madame Bordes had become, continued their affectionate correspondence exactly as before. However, he would never meet another sophisticated French recipient of his later letters, Dominique Lambilliotte, a former publisher living in Paris, because his two visits to France that year – the first, for an ecstatically received screening of the Tavernier film at Cannes – were his last. The book trade in Holland, Belgium and Italy all played host to him in 1993, but, as he noted the following year, as far as France was concerned, 'alas! [. . .] I am not required there'.[17] In the Low Countries, Dirk was very much 'required'. When he went with Clare Harington to Antwerp and Brussels, he excited interest by mentioning during a television interview that the Van den Bogaerdes had roots in Izegem. He seemed curious to know more of the family's story, so a translator deputed to look after him, Nadine Malfait, offered to seek out whatever information she could. A few weeks later a packet arrived from the Town Hall at Izegem, containing not only various relevant documents and an indication that red-carpet treatment would be on offer if he set foot in the municipality, but also a letter from his cousin Philippe at Château Wolvenhof, saying he would be more than welcome there too. Dirk sat on these for a while, eventually spending much of New Year's Eve 1993 manufacturing excuses not to become involved any further. He wrote to Christiaan De Forche at the Town Hall that grandfather Aimé's 'connections with the present family are so remote that I feel it wise to simply keep the "lid on the box", as we say, and we all feel, my brother and sister, that to intrude after all these years would be unwise and unkind'.[18] Elizabeth and Gareth felt nothing of the sort; Dirk had not consulted them. To Philippe Van den Bogaerde he said that Aimé 'seems to me to have been only a distant relative of you all and had no connection at all with "Wolvenhof" ... to try at my advanced age of seventy-three to interrupt your lives after so long and from so far away seems to me un-necessary and unkind [...] I honestly think we should all let it rest!' It was, he added, 'perhaps unwise of me to speak so freely on TV? But my father, Ulric, was intensely proud of his roots in Izegem and encouraged that pride in me, his eldest son.'[19] Undeterred, De Forche tried again, to be told, 'perhaps one day, in the summer, I might just come across and slip into the town very quietly. No fuss and bother ... it would be very pleasant just to feel the earth of my ancestors once again.'[20] Of course he had no intention of doing any such thing, and when in the winter De Forche wrote to say that he and Philippe Van den Bogaerde were planning an imminent visit to London and hoped they might see him, Dirk contrived a letter signed by 'S. Betts. Secretary' which stated that he was 'presently abroad for some weeks'. And that, as far as he was concerned, was that. De Forche received no reply to two subsequent approaches, and although Dirk remained in friendly contact with Nadine Malfait – he attached her surname to a walk-on figure in *Cleared for Take-Off* – he never breathed a word to his brother about the warm gestures from across the North Sea.

Other invitations Dirk accepted more readily. Although he hated such occasions, whether or not as guest of honour, he agreed to attend a BAFTA tribute to John Gielgud, and – for a moment anyway – regretted doing so. The latter wrote to Alec Guinness the next day: 'I hear Dirk and John Mills are long-time enemies who were somewhat dismayed at their close – or brief – encounter. How lucky that Johnnie couldn't see him.'[21] At about the same time Sussex University, of which Richard Attenborough was Pro-Chancellor, asked Dirk to accept an honorary doctorate of letters, not only because of his distinction as an actor but also as 'a citizen of Sussex, not least in recognition of your recent books'. For the second time it meant cap and gown and a good deal of formality, and as the ceremony approached, its implications evidently began to trouble him. A tetchy letter to Lord Attenborough survives, in which Dirk tells him he can be assured 'that whatever personal difference of opinion rests with you and me it will not affect the Ceremony or the Supper. We are both adults, civilised, and understand

Good Behaviour.' He asked for any citation to be kept 'un-effusive and modestly short'. 'When I was promoted to "Commandeur" des arts et des lettres by J. Lang in 1990 it just meant a medal round the neck, a swift peck on each cheek and a parchment role! Would this business could be so simple!'[22] The conferment went off successfully, with Dirk again having to speak on behalf of all the graduands, and reworking his speech from St Andrews. It was the three 'A's – Astonishment, Audacity, Awareness – which had enabled him to overcome, to some extent, his lack of proper education, and he advised the students, who were 'so much better-off than I', to hold on to those qualities:

> The French writer Colette has said that to be astonished is one of the surest ways of not growing old. Too quickly. If that is the case, and she is right, then I am just about to leave the foetus-stage. And you, sitting here before me, ready to *slide* down the razor-blade of life, take note of what I say. Every time I confront my work I grow more and more uncertain about being able to continue with it. I find reassurance only in the fears themselves. In self doubt. The artist, writer, actor, musician, scientist or doctor who loses self doubt, who gives way, as he grows older, to sudden bursts of euphoria or prolixity, who has quietly become smug and self-satisfied, must seriously think of putting aside his pen, scalpel, brush, test-tube or whatever, and start to lower his curtain. His show will shortly be over.

A few days later Dirk's own astonishment was scarcely confined when he stood in front of the Glyndebourne Chorus and the London Philharmonic Orchestra, providing the narration for a series of concert performances of *The Merry Widow*. He had last seen Franz Lehár's operetta as a twenty-three-year-old captain in Eindhoven when, soon after Arnhem, ENSA staged a production starring Madge Elliott and Cyril Ritchard: 'Because of Madge and Cyril, because of *The Merry Widow* and its frothy nonsense which they and their gallant company brought to us in the darkest of winters in the saddest of places, I swear that hundreds of us took heart and survived.'[23] This time, without the need to wear a greatcoat in the relative comfort of concert halls in Birmingham and London, he was on the platform to hear it sung in the original German by Thomas Hampson and Felicity Lott, and to interject with an ironic commentary by Tom Stoppard, who had elevated the minor role of Njegus, an official at the Pontevedrian Embassy, into something worth Dirk's effort, viz., 'Women in Paris then were only good for two things and the other was discovering radium.' 'I am still pretty unsure what the story is all about,' Dirk confessed in the concert programme. '[...] But it really doesn't matter a fig. The joy is in the music.' His narration on the subsequent recording was decreed 'suave and mocking'.[24] At least the Labèque Sisters had not put him off classical music for good during their brief stay in Cadogan Gardens. 'One magical Sunday,' Dirk wrote to Anne Robinson – the columnist and, more recently, television quiz dominatrix – 'a giant crane arrived and swung the wretched pianos away. We in the building were ill with relief.'²⁵ The ladies were now practising their scales in Paris.

Deservedly, *A Short Walk from Harrods* sold more copies in hardback than any of his other volumes of memoirs, and fell only narrowly short of *A Gentle Occupation*. By the time it was published, Dirk had almost completed the next novel, a sequel to *Jericho*, in which the protagonist, William Caldicott, takes his ten-year-old son Giles properly into his life. Too busy 'flogging the books', he had been 'a bloody awful father', and now, as a contrite late developer, intends to do his best to make up for his past failings. Part of the problem has always been that 'I dreaded possession of any kind'. Again the setting of *A Period of Adjustment* is Provençal France; again the atmosphere is alive with fiddling frogs, chittering cicadas, scissoring crickets and bickering streams; again there is a scene to stifle pillow-talk – on this occasion a 'male-rape' by a terrifying creature from Louisiana, Lulu de Terrehaute, who reduces the unsuspecting William to a frazzle. 'Very important to have fantasies,' he says; and, as so often in the novels, the authorial voice is unmistakable.²⁶ In his review John Sessions wrote: 'Giles keeps trying to bring a smile to the proceedings, but Dirk, or rather, William, is too fond of hunching his weary shoulders against the catastrophes which scream down from the azure heavens like Stukas.'²⁷ David Holloway, that early champion of Dirk's writing, found that he cared more for the characters than he had for those in *Jericho* and was impressed by the rhapsodic tone, but: 'I cannot think why Sir Dirk found it necessary to essay pornography. If it were to boost the novel's chances of reaching the bestseller list, it was a misguided endeavour. The rest of the book would have taken it there perfectly comfortably.'²⁸ Dirk told Daphne Fielding he introduced the scene because he feared that his hero was 'becoming very dull and unattractive'. He added: 'I have dipped my fingers into violent sex. I'm amazed that I even knew how … golly whizz … '.²⁹

Some felt that Dirk indulged in a far greater pornography with his next and final volume of autobiography. *Cleared for Take-Off* was an accomplished reheating of old material, for which Dirk juxtaposed people, places and events. Aisling Foster compared it to a game of Monopoly, 'offering fresh aspects of familiar territory with every tour of the board', with nothing occurring in isolation and with irony written into every scene. It was 'fascinating, maddening and a pleasure to read'.³⁰ Nicholas Mosley, the author of *Accident*, confessed to having read none of Dirk's previous books and found *Cleared for Take-Off* 'affecting and strangely beautiful'.³¹ For Keith Baxter, however, it seemed to be 'driven by the twin-engines of the author's narcissism and bitterness' – an author who 'never expresses any kind of Faith in the goodness of life, is apparently bereft of Hope and devoid of the least hint of Charity'.³² Baxter had a point. One of the chapters was devoted to Capucine, who in March 1990, at the age of sixty-seven, had fallen from her eighth-floor flat in Lausanne: 'Fastidious to the very end, and secretive, she had apparently fed her cats, locked the flat, climbed to the roof and, typically of her, to avoid any distress to others, jumped out over the back of the block and landed sprawled among the dustbins. A slight figure, beautifully groomed and dressed for a lazy stroll round the lake in the afternoon sunshine. She wasn't discovered apparently until later, when the flies had started on her lips.'[33] The gratuitous cruelty of that last sentence is all the worse because it is totally untrue. Capucine was discovered on the lawn beneath her flat within moments of falling; the ambulance men even tried to give her the kiss of life. In an earlier chapter, as we have seen, Dirk depicted Chris Greaves's death as a suicide. Now he tampered needlessly and distressingly with the final moments of another friend, one who was once to him both beautiful and beloved. 'How could such hatred exist?' demanded Dirk, in a different context. We might ask the same.

'I'm so wonderfully happy that I know I'll get clobbered,' Dirk wrote to Penelope Mortimer when life 'By Myself' had taken its turn so dramatically for the better.[34] His books were automatic bestsellers and his advances were edging towards the £100,000 mark; his shows – sometimes he called them 'concerts' – were always packed; his reviews could have a significant effect on the sales of otherwise unnoticed titles; the weight he lent to various campaigns, charitable and other-wise, was gratifyingly publicised and appreciated; the family was more tightly knit than it had been since his childhood. Naturally, there were clouds, as he lost close friends and colleagues; but he could pay his tribute in print: both Theo 'Thumper' Cowan and Kathleen Tynan were celebrated in obituaries. At the memorial service to John Osborne, with whom he had lately begun a cor-respondence magnificent in its political incorrectness, Dirk read from Jeremy Taylor's *Holy Dying*: 'The devils rage and gnash their teeth . . .'. And then he himself began to have health problems.

When he first arrived at the medical practice in Sloane Street in 1982 he was already on pills to control his blood pressure. He was smoking at least forty cigarettes a day, and admitted to having four Guinnesses at lunchtime and a third of a bottle of whisky at night. In the late eighties, when Tony's situation was hopeless, the Guinness consumption was down and the whisky up. Peter Wheeler recalls that he had 'bad asthma and bronchitis – his breathing and lung capacity got less and less, so exertion winded him very quickly. He always had a bad chest and wheezed a lot, and as he approached seventy it became slightly more difficult to control. Because of the smoking the arteries in his legs had narrowed: it was the same with his heart and his head. He generally had bad arteries all over the place.'[35] In 1994 an attack of shingles led to Dirk's heart becoming, as he put it, 'unadjusted'; and he became depressed enough for Peter Wheeler to put him on a course of 'happy pills'. Nevertheless the show went on – literally – and although he announced on the stage of the Richmond Theatre in November that he was 'packing it in', and there were occasions in the meantime when he felt 'as weak as a cobweb', he returned to the National a year later. 'It was just magical,' he wrote to Elizabeth the next day, 'cheers and yells

[...] nothing will ever match last night!' At that point, says Peter Wheeler, 'he was down to about a hundred yards before he had to stop walking, and by 1996 he was struggling a bit. His leg began to be painful. He couldn't get back from Partridges without stopping.' Added to his physical worries was the stress caused by the departure of his editor, Fanny Blake, made redundant at the turn of the year. 'I dived into a black hole of depression,' he told Hélène Bordes; '[...] first I loose the farm, my home, then my Manager of fifty years, and just as I start to TRY again in this wretched city I loose Fanny! I'm a bit old at 75 to keep on fighting back ... but I do hate wandering about with a limp, my leg is still bad and always will be! and doing nothing. Ah me.'[36] He pulled himself together enough to deliver a sixth novel to Viking Penguin, called – as it had been for some sixteen years – *Closing Ranks*. In July, his publishers gave Dirk a party to mark the total sale of a million copies of his books under their three imprints. He was presented with an inscribed pillbox, and said: 'I shall keep my suicide pills in it.'

Dirk went into the King Edward VII Hospital on 18 September 1996, for an angioplasty to dilate the blood vessels and arteries. 'I had rather encouraged him to do it,' recalls Peter Wheeler, 'to keep him alive.' He was still in the recovery room after the operation when he had a pulmonary embolism. 'I thought he was going to die there and then,' says his doctor, 'but he survived resuscitation.' Dirk had lost the use of his left side, his speech was impaired, and his independence had gone for ever. In the dark days that followed, faced with the prospect of spending the rest of his life in a wheelchair, he said to a cluster of his consultants: 'I want euthanasia.' But in fact he was not ready to leave the party. Nor were a lot of other people – principally his nephew Brock, who on that occasion gave him a stern 'talking-to' – going to allow him to do so.

For thirteen weeks Dirk stayed at the hospital, under the name of George Clark, his great-uncle; the elder brother of Aimé's wife, Grace. It says much for the discretion of the staff that not a word leaked to the newspapers until after about a month Brock decided the time was right to let the Press Association know his uncle was recovering from a stroke. In that time the Team had rallied and, true enough, Dirk was making progress psychologically and, within obvious limitations, physically. Physiotherapy was nothing new to him: Susan Pink had already become a fixture in his life. However, this was at another level of intensity, with Dirk far less able to respond on his visits to the gymnasium, or torture-chamber. Back on the third-floor ward, the effort of all concerned was to try to make it as far as possible business as usual. The final copy-editing of *Closing Ranks* was carried out in room sixty-six. His annual contribution to *The Daily Telegraph*'s 'books of the year' coverage was dictated to its editor sitting at the end of the bed. Correspondence was handled by Brock and Gabrielle Crawford, a photographer whom Dirk had met through her closest friend, Jane Birkin. A copy of Sheridan Morley's *Rank Outsider* arrived; back went a card saying 'Could have been worse, I suppose' – praise indeed, considering Dirk's history with books about him by anyone other than himself. Peter Wheeler brought another of his patients, the Princess of Wales, to see him one day when she came to the hospital for an X-ray: 'She didn't know what to expect. I think she was upset to see what had happened to him, but he was very gracious, and she was very pleasant.' From then on a colour photograph of the Princess which Brock snipped from a magazine remained affixed to the wall behind Dirk's head, and he would talk of Diana coming 'to pay homage'. Despite his terrible disability, he had not lost the strength in his right arm, built up by years of work on the land, rather than by Rank's dumb-bells. I remember him reaching one morning for the triangular hoist that dangled above his head, then flexing his biceps and saying: 'Steve Reeves!'

Dirk was discharged on 19 December and returned to Cadogan Gardens, where Brock and his wife Kim had supervised the few basic alterations needed for someone who was unlikely ever to manage without a wheelchair. A new kind of life began: one of almost total dependency, which for Dirk, the free spirit, was the hardest blow. Here was a proud, capable man, reduced to vulnerability, and he did not want those who had known him in his prime to find him like this. He was abrupt with family and friends alike, banishing some for good. It was hurtful, but explicable: he did not wish them to see him – in Jane Birkin's word – *diminished*. On the other hand there was a nucleus of friends, advisers and other professionals who were still welcome – some, just as morale-boosters, like Nicholas Bowlby, the producer Robert Fox and Simon Hopkinson, the chef at Bibendum who would bring him a 'take-away' of unusual quality; others, like the Team from Viking Penguin, who could also give him a feeling, however illusory, of purpose, of being involved still in work. Fanny Blake, now with the Orion group of publishers, had suggested an anthology of poetry and prose which he might compile over the next year – a sound idea, given the range and quality of his own library, and his precise recall of exactly where on the shelves each of the books could be found. A contract was drawn up and an advance of £30,000 paid; but it proved too much of an undertaking. As with so many stroke victims, Dirk went through a period of profound depression. 'I would meet all sorts of people who had gone round to cheer him up,' says Peter Wheeler, 'but no one could lift him out of that. I put him on Prozac and he became very thin, which was strange – it was the first time I'd ever known anyone lose weight on Prozac. I think all that was achieved was to keep his mood fairly flat, and he did lose a considerable amount of weight as a complication of therapy. This all returned, as did his mood, once he had stopped the pills.'

The much abandoned *Closing Ranks* finally saw the light of day about four months after Dirk left hospital. Dedicated to 'Peter Wheeler MB, MRCP. Without whom . . .', it was a spritely satire set on an estate in Sussex, with a cast arranged one by one, like tins on the Clermont flowerpot, ready for dead-eye-Dirk and his hunting gun. There is a nurse with an inescapable resemblance to the 'Hennessy' who felt aggrieved by *Postillion*; an arrogant brother with treacherous charm who 'harboured a deep resentment which quietly throbbed away like the start of an abscess'; a sister-in-law who is often 'as pissed as a fiddler's bitch'; and, alas, a biographer who comes to an extraordinarily nasty end in the now customary bout of sado-masochistic activity. Deep in the background to the story is the repatriation of the Cossacks in 1945 – a dreadful, serious business – and at least one reviewer pointed out that Dirk had miscalculated badly in putting a trite story involving cocaine, transvestism and thongs on to the surface of an authentic tragedy. Certainly it would have been sad if his literary career was to end with a shallow novel. The anthology had proved impossible, but perhaps another kind of collection could be made to work; one that required almost no input from the author. He had over the years contributed to newspapers and magazines enough essays, reviews, obituaries and even letters to the editor to constitute a sizeable book. Pat Kavanagh liked the proposal, and so did Tony Lacey at Dirk's usual publishers, Viking Penguin, who agreed to pay as an advance the same sum that had to be returned to Orion. *For the Time Being* was published in the summer of 1998, and contained a substantial introduction, dictated by Dirk, which told the story of his operation, his stroke, the bad times in its immediate aftermath, and his frightened return home. On publication day, a small group of those involved gathered in Dirk's drawing-room, where, casually but impeccably dressed, he presided in his wheelchair. The news had just come through that the book would be at number one in the bestsellers the following Sunday. Even Dirk enjoyed a flute of champagne that evening.

There was more to toast: he was becoming stronger. With a glass of wine at lunchtime and a Guinness or two in the evening, he was relieved to find his weight back to something like normal. The physiotherapy was not so bad, nor was his first experience of being turned once a week into 'a minor porcupine' by acupuncture. He began to think that he might even be regaining some feeling in his left leg. In a modest way he had resumed his reviewing: a biography of Gerald and Sara Murphy, 'inventors of the Riviera', made his critical juices flow again. He chose Erich Maria Remarque's *All Quiet on the Western Front* as his 'Book of the Century', saying that 'no one has better explained the fate of the ordinary man engaged uncomprehendingly in the viciousness, uselessness and utter waste of war'.[37] He even agreed to talk to the BBC's urbane John Dunn, a long-time champion of his writing; but Dirk's voice was not at its best, strained by nerves, and when he broke down while speaking of the war the interview was abandoned. The one hateful prospect was having to leave the flat, which happened very seldom – and then only for him to return briefly to hospital, or to go to the dentist. It was not so much the going, or the being away from his cocoon; what filled him with dread was being stared at. A news story in *The Sunday Times* stated that he was a virtual recluse, in increasingly poor health and suffering from depression, who had difficulty talking and had little contact with the outside world.[38] To which Dirk replied the following weekend in robust terms. 'All balls,' he wrote. 'I am not a recluse. I just don't go out [...] I am vain, and don't want to be seen being wheeled around in the streets. I am not depressed. There were difficult patches early on, but in fact I am extremely cheerful and bright. I am very comfortable in my flat, surrounded by great piles of books. I am in constant touch with my friends either by telephone or when they visit me. Some have said I'm an inspiration.'[39] The article had been printed under the heading 'Bogarde's living will reopens euthanasia debate', and made much of the fact that he had signed an advance directive. That was some ten years ago, wrote Dirk: 'Anyone can do it, for ten quid, by approaching the Voluntary Euthanasia Society [...] I've been advising people to do so for years'. His health was improving and he was 'a little stronger'. And as for an alleged quote by Sir Ludovic Kennedy – 'He may not be able to speak very well any more, but he can understand what is going on' – Dirk riposted: 'He makes me sound like a demented orangutan. I have a very bad sinus, so the quality of my speech depends on the pollen count. It's as simple as that.' The original story had ended, said Dirk, 'with a load of stuff about my career. It is odd to read your own obituary.'

Of course it was a confined life, partly by his own choice, but he was indeed often 'cheerful and bright', and his visitors would say that they themselves usually felt better for seeing him. By the time the paperback of his collected journalism went to the printers he was able to write in a new foreword: '*If* I can get the messages down to my toes, there is, I'm assured, every possibility that I could at least be able to shuffle about. Nothing tremendous, you understand. It takes time. But I'll settle for a shuffle. That'll do.'[40] And when I telephoned Dirk one Friday evening in May to make the arrangement for our usual 11 o'clock meeting* on the Sunday, he sounded in fine form. I did not know it then, but he had just said *au revoir* – 'goodbye' was not in his vocabulary – to Lauren Bacall, Tony's 'force of life', who had been to tea. There was another review to write for 'my paper'. Gabrielle Crawford was to take some photographs of him. The flat was a blaze of colour from the blooms sent round each weekend as a gift from the nearby florists, Pulbrook and Gould. Things were indeed looking up.

Through all of this – the dreadful lows, the occasional emergency, the slow but sure progress – Dirk's own, constant 'force of life' was Sheila MacLean; the nurse who early in 1997 had arrived at Cadogan Gardens for just a few weeks, with her policy of not becoming 'involved', and who soon had his measure, as he had hers. Neither she nor Dirk knew of the coincidence, but she had once worked in the Glasgow hospital where, many years earlier, his maternal grandfather, Forrest Niven, died. She was, without question, the most significant person to have walked into the grandson's life since that October day in 1940 at the Amersham Playhouse when a tall Army officer took his seat at a performance

---

* Not 10.59, not 11.01, but eleven: Dirk was famously obsessive over punctuality. He had been known to keep visitors trapped in the lift outside his door while he whistled about the flat, reinforcing the fact that they were late.

of an inconsequential piece called *Grief Goes Over.* For now she had become the door-keeper at the very end of Dirk's corridor.

A character in *Closing Ranks* says: 'One is never prepared for death, even if you expect it.'[41] However, thanks in the main to Sheila MacLean, at midday on Saturday, 8 May 1999, Dirk *was* prepared. As he passed through, Sheila quietly shut the door behind him. The Draft of One was on his way. As content, now, as a clam.

Epilogue

'I have always been as green as a frog'

Dirk laid down in typically straightforward terms what was to happen, and not to happen, after his death. His body was to be cremated privately, without any form of ceremony. There was to be no memorial service, nor flowers, music, 'or any kind of religious or theatrical event of any kind held for me'. His nephew Brock made a call to Dirk's driver, Bob Pearson, saying, 'We have one last job to do.' On Thursday, 13 May the two men travelled north-west across London to St Marylebone Crematorium, just three miles from the nursing home where Margaret Van den Bogaerde had given birth seventy-eight years before: Dirk, or rather Derek, had come full circle. A hearse arrived, and his coffin was borne inside on the shoulders of six young bearers from Leverton and Sons, the funeral directors. Brock walked behind them, while Bob waited with the car. The only other people in the chapel were the undertaker and the man in charge of the crematorium. The coffin was placed on the conveyor belt, the six bearers formed a semicircle round it, and bowed. 'We had a few moments' reflection,' Brock recalls. 'I said a few words to myself. And off he went. As Dirk would say, it was all over in the time it takes to strike a match.'

Also in his will Dirk stated that 'I wish my ashes to be scattered on French soil in Provence if that is possible.' For about three weeks his mortal remains sat in the sun-filled drawing-room of the flat, while Brock and his wife Kim made arrangements to go to Nice. As their baggage was searched at the airport on their way out of England, Brock was asked what he had in the unusually shaped container. 'The ashes of my dead uncle,' he replied. 'That'll be fine, Sir.' The Van den Bogaerdes stayed at the Colombe d'Or: nowhere else could possibly be contemplated as Dirk's final caravanserai. But Brock was troubled about where best to honour that last wish. Should he and Kim climb to the parapets of Gourdon, 1,600 feet above the River Loup and dominating Châteauneuf itself, with the awesome panorama that Dirk and Tony would so proudly introduce to their guests? Somewhere around St Paul, perhaps, which they had known for longer still? Or at Clermont – on the terraces at the front of the house, or even up on Titty Brown Hill, as they had named the property's most suitable spot for sunbathing? Brock did not want to approach the owners, the de Pauws, until he was absolutely sure he was doing the right thing by his uncle. He hired an expensive car, and drove to Pré du Lac, the village closest to Châteauneuf, because it had a bar. He and Kim sat outside. 'We put Dirk on the table with our drinks, and sat there for half an hour, working out what was best.' Eventually they decided to go to the house, where they found the path blocked by a gate far more substantial than in Dirk's and Tony's day. Still reluctant to commit himself, Brock considered clambering over the wall, but wisely thought better of it; dogs of more ferocious intent than Labo were known to patrol the property. Instead he pressed the intercom to the house, and found Christine de Pauw at home, full of welcome. They talked on the main terrace outside the Long Room, and after an hour or so Brock 'owned up' about the true reason for his visit. His hostess was enchanted and honoured. Of course, this was where Dirk belonged. And so the ashes were scattered, swirling in the light breeze among the olive trees, on the path, near the two cypresses that Dirk had christened Brock and Kimbo, and, above all, onto the water of his treasured Pond – now more formal, but where fish still swam that he had known. Dirk had come Home.

Over the years there had been a moving correspondence between the de Pauws and Dirk, who constantly expressed his joy that the 'magic house' was being cherished. For a while he could even bring himself to look at photographs of the inevitable changes as a large family made it their own; changes, some of which he gallantly described as 'all the things I promised myself that I would one day do when I had enough money!' Eventually, however, he had to ask the couple to send no more pictures: 'Every time I see Clermont it breaks my heart.' For him the place was too full of *fantômes*. One letter, from August 1991, cast a particular spell over the de Pauws. Dirk told them of his deep gratitude for enriching Clermont with their love and care, adding:

> If one still night, when the moon is high, you think that you see a shadow moving among the olives just below the little terrace, or sitting under the big olive over the pond, say 'Bon Soir!' It will be me.

'Just forget me,' he had said, but little notice was taken. 'On the day Dirk died, all Italy wept,' his agent Olga Horstig-Primuz told Brock. In France they mourned the departure of an 'immense acteur', 'jeune premier, gentleman et dandy', and 'étoile précieuse'. They praised him for his taste and refinement. They likened him to Dorian Gray, and dubbed him 'the prince of ambiguity'. In England – not synonymous with Home, of course – his first career was neatly pinned down by the critic Philip French, who wrote in *The Observer* on the morning after Dirk's death that he had been 'both the most exotically cosmopolitan and the most quintessentially English actor this country has produced'.[1] Clive Fisher the next day in *The Independent* declared that Dirk 'was a major figure because, wherever they were made, his finest films are all somehow about him [...] By the time he renounced acting for writing his numerous renditions of acquiescers, outsiders, self-doubters and repressors of secrets constituted a poetic enquiry into the dramas of pragmatic dishonesty and subterranean emotion and had made Bogarde emblematic, a man who might have been born to play exiles from happiness.' Of Dirk the writer, Fisher said that the autobiographies which had won a reputation for self-revelation were, in fact, camouflage and the 'excursions into the more revealing medium of fiction (inspired by experience) were smooth; but although the slickness of his novels is occasionally animated by accounts of female domination, male narcissism and male prostitution, their author's true pleasures remained classified'.[2] Sheridan Morley in *The Spectator* bracketed Dirk with James Mason as England's greatest screen actor and described him in other respects as 'impossible'.[3] Many of the obituarists, Morley included, commented with varying degrees of indignation on Dirk's failure to admit the truth about himself. Philip Hensher spoke for the more sympathetic: 'What Bogarde did, and did with all the bravery one can reasonably expect, was present gay men with versions of their lives and their desires; not necessarily realistic versions, but fantasies through which they could explore what they actually wanted. He was, certainly, a bit of a missing link. But we couldn't have done without him.'[4]

It was left to the house bard at *Private Eye*, E. J. Thribb, to attempt a pulling-together of various strands:

> So. Farewell
> Then.
> Sir Dirk
> Bogarde.
>
> Actor and
> *Private Eye*
> Shareholder.
>
> Yes, you helped
> The magazine
> Out in the
> Sixties.
>
> Keith says that
> Was your
> Finest hour.
>
> Apart from
> *Doctor In The*
> *House.*
> Obviously.[5]

In the last four years of his life Dirk's stake in the satirical organ had begun to yield an annual dividend, varying between about £100 and £300 – at maximum barely enough to cover two days' nursing care. It was by this time his only shareholding, and any idea that he had died a rich man was dispelled early in 2000 with the publication of his will: his estate was valued at £779,544.33 net of tax, well over half of which was tied up in the flat. His principal beneficiary was Brock, whom he had for some years described to friends as his 'heir'; it was tidier that way. Indeed the brief document carrying Dirk's final wishes – witnessed by Janet Whitaker and a sound engineer while Dirk was recording *Death in Venice* for release as an audiocassette – was entirely appropriate as the last testament of an Orderly Man. Apart from Elizabeth, who was to receive a modest financial legacy for life, he named only one other beneficiary: Anton Troxler, the adviser in Geneva who ran Labofilms and who with his wife had become a greatly trusted friend to both Dirk and Tony, especially during the miserable months in Paris when Elisabeth Troxler did much to cheer them up. Her husband was left two limited-edition works by Picasso – a 1967 lithograph, 'Intérieur rouge', and a ceramic owl, 'Madolita' – 'in the hope that it will remind him of our happy years together at Clermont'. The phrasing was curious; the double gift, an indication of how significant a role the financier had played in reassuring the ultra-cautious Dirk that he would be able to continue a relatively comfortable life *and* to pay whatever medical expenses might arise. That reassurance was tested sorely for two and a half years, and not found wanting.

One more name was added to the will at a later date: that of Sheila MacLean. In 1998 Dirk asked for a codicil to be drawn up, bequeathing her £5,000 'in recognition of the help she has given me'.

Go to the tiny Church of the Good Shepherd at Lullington, and you will of course find no gravestone bearing the name of Derek Niven Van den Bogaerde. Inside the door, however, is a book which has to be replaced every two or three years, so great is the volume of visitors from Mexico, Croatia, South Korea, New Zealand, Thailand, the Czech Republic, America, South Africa . . . The majority, naturally, do not know of any connection between this ecclesiastical oddity in its pastoral setting and a famous actor and author; but a good few do. 'Thanks for the direction Dirk,' reads one entry. Another, 'Here's to you, Dirk, and your sister Elizabeth and your Nanny, "Lally".' A third, 'Always think of dear old Dirk as a boy having a whale of a time in this beautiful countryside.' A fourth, 'Thank you Dirk, God Bless You & may you sleep peacefully in HIS "Great Meadow".' And a fifth, 'In memory of Dirk Bogarde – we won't drink the bottles of poison!' More than fifty such messages were left in the book during the year following his death, and they continue, albeit in a trickle, to this day: 'Once again in Dirk Bogarde's footsteps,' wrote a recent pilgrim. These tributes show how precious was the connection Dirk made with his public; and how, through his books more effectively than through his films, a legendarily private man entered into the lives of others. He did so more consciously, in sustained correspondence not only with the people of a certain prominence whom we have met in this story, but also with – for example – a student called Tina Tallitt who wrote to Dirk from Lancashire and profited over several years from his robust encouragement; likewise with Susan Owens, a mother of five in Cheshire for whom Dirk became her 'still small voice of calm' as she nursed her husband through six awful years following a stroke. He was not going to be forgotten in those quarters.

His instruction was disobeyed in other, more overt ways. Homage was paid at the annual film festival in Dinard, and a retrospective held, gratifyingly, at the Lincoln Center in New York. The David Tindle painting was one of four which went on temporary loan from the National Portrait Gallery to Number 10 Downing Street, replacing those of two naval commanders, a general and a geographer on the walls of the image-conscious Prime Minister's entertaining-rooms. In 2002 the choreographer Matthew Bourne offered an oblique tribute to Dirk's finest performance by creating for the National Theatre *Play Without Words*, a brilliant stylised ballet based largely on *The Servant*, in which at times no fewer than three 'Barretts' could be found simultaneously oiling their way around the stage, corrupting everyone in sight. Martin Amis's 2003 novel *Yellow Dog* included an American porn-film actor called Dork Bogarde,[6] and in Maggie Gee's 2002 study of racial hatred, *The White Family*, the murderous younger son is called Dirk because 'May had loved Dirk Bogarde with swooning intensity; his sideways smile, his dark deer's eyes, the narrow elegance of his body, and though he had mysteriously changed, become old and angry and homosexual, she still felt she had let him down, giving his name to someone who despised it.'[7] A teddy-bear which had once belonged to Dirk was auctioned in aid of the special-needs school at Chailey Heritage, near the family's old home. There was activity on the Internet, as Dirk-watchers assessed his accomplishments and compared their notes, the more sensible grouping together as the Dirk Bogarde Brigade.[8] By the spring of 2004, a request for his name under the Google search engine yielded some 72,500 mentions, about half as many as for Alec Guinness; but then, Dirk never had an Obi-Wan Kenobi among his credits.

Incensed by a comment about Dirk in a newspaper, John Fraser determined to set the record straight regarding the relationship with Tony. He sold from his memoirs-in-waiting a passage, which he had written several years earlier, about a visit in the sixties to Nore, where, on a walk round its gardens, he confided in Dirk about his own homosexual love life and asked outright about that of his host. 'Dirk smiled enigmatically. "We've been together a long time," he said. "Now, we're like brothers." ' Fraser described how he pressed him further and was led up to the house's extensive attic, where on a plinth stood a gleaming Harley Davidson, facing a gigantic picture on the wall of Dirk in *The Singer Not the Song*. The account of how Dirk achieved a form of ecstasy during ten minutes of 'bedlam' astride his mean machine sent the staff at a Sunday tabloid newspaper into almost as great a frenzy – much to the subsequent dismay of Dirk's family and friends.[9] John Fraser now regrets the 'lip-smacking' treatment his essay was given: nothing improper took place that evening. He wanted only to 'come clean' about the love that Dirk and Tony had for each other and to illustrate the harmless, if somewhat noisy, way in which a celibate and 'huge narcissist' sought gratification.[10] It seemed as if the advice allegedly given by the director Jack Lee before Dirk donned his leathers* for *Once a Jolly Swagman* – to take the motorcycle home and make love to it – had been followed to an extent, if not to the letter.

Less controversial was a two-part *Arena* documentary screened by the BBC on Boxing Day in 2001, inspired by and based around the home movies shot on Tony's Bell and Howell camera during that brief period at the end of the fifties and into the early sixties when he and Dirk could afford the luxury of shooting on sixteen-millimetre film. On rare occasions they would project the footage at Clermont, but on their return to England they handed the twelve cans to Brock, who had them transferred onto safety stock. 'Dirk didn't want to watch them again,' says Brock. 'It would have been awful for him.' 'The Private Dirk Bogarde' was remarkable not merely for the quality of those early images and for the portrait they gave of a languid, stylish, carefree existence in beautiful, empty places; but also for the insight it offered into Dirk's character through the voices of those who had never spoken about him in public before – notably, the family. The BAFTA Award-winning programme was directed by Adam Low and narrated by Dirk's second Plank, Nicholas Shakespeare, who, in articles published as precursors to the broadcast, gave the fullest alternative account so far of Dirk's life. What that story revealed, Shakespeare wrote, 'is crucial to an understanding of his achievement. Only by mining the tension that existed between his public image and excessively private life did Bogarde mature into the serious actor – and later, author – of his ambition.'[11] And so the audience heard Gareth Van den Bogaerde describe his brother as 'a great one for pulling the wings off flies all his life'; Elizabeth recalling how in Dirk's playlets she usually ended up being robbed and murdered, and how she became 'useful' as a kind of chaperone; her son Mark telling how as Dirk waited for cigarettes at a shop in Crowborough a woman stuck a pin in his side, drew it out to find it tipped with blood and said: 'Good God, he's real!' Familiar voices, too, were heard – but talking of an unfamiliar subject. Among them was Gore Vidal, who said of the one-time 'heartthrob of all England' that 'Dirk was dark'. He called the union with Tony *un mariage blanc* and said he had known many of those, adding 'if you're wise, you do not have sex with friends'. Another remark from the patrician American writer, and cut from the finished broadcast, was just as telling. Asked why he liked Dirk, Vidal replied: 'He made me laugh. That's the minimum, isn't it?'

---

* The white leathers were acquired by the former world speedway champion Barry Briggs.

And then there was Lally. By now in her nineties, and with a razor-sharp recall, she spoke to Low and Shakespeare of the happy, uncomplicated days at Twickenham and Lullington; of the troubled, benign Ulric; and of the various currents within the family. Her affection for all the Van den Bogaerdes remained undimmed. She talked, too, of the frogs Dirk would find near the cottage, and how he would sit and have long chats with them. 'You know, to him they weren't an animal,' she said. 'They were a person. And he would think up all sorts of little stories about what they did and what they were going to do.'[12]

Dirk had a flair for the original metaphor and simile, but throughout his own account of his life, written and spoken, certain imagery recurs time and again: the 'wall of protection'; the shell; the corridor; and the frog – camouflage expert extraordinary. Dirk was, as we have seen, an all-round master of the craft, both officially as an interpreter and unofficially as a practitioner. Mimicry can be a form of camouflage, a pretence which disguises or distracts attention from the mimic's own persona. Dirk's inhabiting of another character for the camera was one, obvious, form of mimicry; some of the lives he lived were another. In one of his 'concerts' during the nineties, he told his audience that he had only ever let them know what he had *wanted* them to know and that he had never lied to them in anything he had written: 'I've never been a very good liar. I have evaded. That's quite useful. "Evasion" and "lying" are two very different words.'[13] His technique was second to none, because at some risk he made himself, like the frog, such a hypnotically fascinating subject for the observer. By being at once so private and at the same time so available to the public through his auto-biographies, his many interviews and, latterly, his public appearances, he practised deception in an extraordinarily accomplished, even dangerous way.

The dark, inscrutable eyes, skill at concealment, and stillness make the frog seem enigmatic, even slightly threatening; its capacity to spring out of reach when approached too near, makes it tantalisingly elusive. There is an exceptional study of Dirk by Jane Bown, that most sensitive of portrait photographers, which shows him with his eyes wide and protuberant – unquestionably frog-like; it does not flatter, but it has a truth; and when he helped to choose the illustrations in his collection of journalism, *For the Time Being*, he did not hesitate over its inclusion. He used to joke about age giving him an increasing resemblance to a turtle; perhaps the lines and, of course, the shell persuaded him so. Yet it was with the frog that he had the greater empathy, even a likeness. It is not too hard to imagine him immaculately dressed in one of his Nancarrow and Temple suits, his Hermès tie and his handmade shoes, skipping like Jeremy Fisher from leaf to leaf on some celestial lily-pond – perhaps, though, with Barrett's furled umbrella in one hand and his pork-pie hat in the other.

The frog and the toad turn up frequently in Dirk's life and in his writings: 'The bull-frogs were croaking by the swimming-pool'; 'the frogs began to agree among themselves'; there are several variants on 'I have always been as green as a frog'. His 1949 broadcast to the BBC Far Eastern Service highlighted 'the croaking of the frogs in the swamps' which he recalled from his time in Java. In an unusual portrait photograph taken during the filming of *The Wind Cannot Read*, Dirk lounges in a jet-black kimono adorned with a brooch in the shape of a frog leaping towards his left shoulder. The Diary records that in January 1966 Tony bought him a china frog from a shop or a stall on the Left Bank of the Seine. Agnes Zwickl remembers how on one occasion as he left for work Dirk forgot his frog; after dropping him at Pinewood Tony made the journey home and back again to the studio in order to reunite them. The pond at Clermont teemed with frogs, bred from the spawn which Dirk smuggled back from Britain in his spongebag. And as for the toads: 'They arrived in the second year as one pair. Locked together in ugly rapture, struggling valiantly up the steep hill. After some days of violent and uncontrolled waltzing together, the hen toad industriously laid her eggs, ropes of glossy black pearls strung and looped among the pondweed. In May I had two million tadpoles bustling through the water. I was enraptured.'[14] Then again: 'Fat, heavy with promise, golden eyes blazing, [the toad] lumbered slowly up the path on a route which she obviously knew from years before and from animal instinct. She was on her way to her destiny, and her destiny lay in the little stream which bickered and whispered through the boulders beyond the little orchard. Toads, I knew, always return to the place where they were born.'[15] A large black toad sat regally on the Biedermeier secretaire in the drawing-room at Cadogan Gardens, near a mug inscribed with the words 'A frog he would a-wooing go.'

It is precisely because of their mystery – a mingling of charm and threat – that these amphibians held Dirk in their thrall. The frog received the kiss from a pitying princess that turned him into a handsome prince; it was the toad that Shakespeare had in mind when Othello speaks of preferring to 'live upon the vapour of a dungeon,/Than keep a corner in the thing I love/For others' uses'. Some species of frog shed their skin regularly, and perhaps it is not too far-fetched to see just such a transformation in the way that Dirk divested himself of the trappings of stardom in the late sixties to become first agriculturalist and then author. By the end, as we learned from Sheila MacLean, he had undergone a further metamorphosis, ridding himself of pretence and unnecessary baggage to revert to a state of complete simplicity. Like the actor peeling away the layers of the onion, he had more or less discarded all but the bulb at his own heart. For the first time since early childhood and in the most difficult of circumstances, he finally managed to feel *bien dans sa peau*.

It seems only right in this context to confess that the account of Dirk's cremation with which this Epilogue begins is incomplete: there was another silent witness. On the altar Brock had placed a palm-sized glass frog, with a baby clinging to its leg, which for years had been Dirk's companion – probably a successor to the one made of china that he and Tony had found in Paris in the sixties. Just as a piglet accompanied Tony, so the frog lived beside Dirk's bed and travelled with him always; it was there in room sixty-six during those long months at the King Edward VII Hospital, its coating so worn that the glass was almost translucent. When, therefore, Brock returned to Clermont in the summer of 2001 with the *Arena* team he took with him the frog and at the end of the filming handed it to Christine de Pauw, saying that as the object most precious to Dirk it belonged in the *place* that was most precious to him.

Shortly afterwards Brock received an e-mail from Christine, saying how touched she was that he had left with her 'the symbol of Dirk's great attachment to Clermont'. However, she thought he should know that since its arrival a number of unfortunate events had befallen the family. First, their daughter Emilie's beloved horse, Fonceur, died. She went to Brussels to choose another, and on the way to the vet for the customary examination, Fonceur's successor was injured in his horse-box. Next, Christine squashed a toad while shutting the front door. Then the dogs became unwell, and spent an entire week being sick all over the place. Christine and Alain had a furious row and for a fortnight afterwards addressed not a single word to each other; things had never been quite the same between them since. Then all the clocks in the house stopped. When Christine went to feed the fish in the pond, they took no notice of her or their provisions. Clermont was subjected to an unprecedented plague of flies and hornets. And finally Christine, who had never before lost any of her belongings, began to notice that items were disappearing, including one of her rings. At first she thought that the frog was sad, sitting alone on the top of a cupboard, so she put it on her bedside table. In the morning and evening she would stroke it and talk to it, but from that night onwards she herself tossed and turned, and cried herself to a fitful sleep. At 4 o'clock every morning she would wake in a panic.

Eventually, at dawn on 17 July 2001, Christine de Pauw decided that the frog must be missing England and Dirk's family. She wrapped it carefully and took it to the post, where the woman behind the counter accidentally crushed Christine's fingers in the turnstile as she handed over the cardboard box in which the frog was to be despatched. Finally he was on his way back to Britain. From that day, life at Clermont reverted to normal. Christine de Pauw and her husband were reconciled and, as she put it, 'le soleil est revenu'.

The frog now resides peacefully in the countryside *chez* Brock Van den Bogaerde and his family, not all that far from Lullington. And it is a safe bet that when calm was restored at Clermont a shadowy figure, flitting among the olive trees and the cypresses nearest to the Pond, will have smiled his sardonic smile and said: 'So that was all right.'

Acknowledgements

I t started, as these things do, with lunch. Some months after Dirk's death Ion Trewin, editor-in-chief of Weidenfeld & Nicolson, remembered an appreciation I had written of Dirk, and we talked idly about whether or not an official biography might be sanctioned. I thought there was no chance: it was too soon; those who had respected Dirk's privacy in his lifetime would be reluctant to talk; above all, the family would not yet, if ever, give their consent. The tenacious Trewin was not put off, and I was asked to submit a proposal for consideration by the Van den Bogaerde family; by Dirk's literary agent, Pat Kavanagh; and by the publishers. Almost a year went by, during which discussions took place that I knew nothing about, and writers were considered who actually had biographies to their credit. Eventually I was invited to tackle the book – a prospect at once enthralling and utterly daunting. For others, I knew, it was a high-risk commission, and throughout this quest I have been driven by a determination not to let them, or for that matter Dirk, down. Where I have failed, the responsibility is entirely mine, because every one of the names that follow has contributed willingly and generously to the research – some, by allowing continuous access to their own memory and to documents; one or two, with just a remark; most, with something between those extremes.

There are four people without whom the book would have been an impossibility: Brock Van den Bogaerde, Dirk's nephew; G. Laurence Harbottle, Dirk's solicitor and his co-executor with Brock; Dirk's sister, Elizabeth; and his brother, Gareth. All have been remarkable in their helpfulness, hospitality, openness and friendship. Other members of the immediate family – Lucilla, Kim, Rupert, Ulric and Alice Van den Bogaerde, and Mark and Judy Goodings – have followed in the same tradition. I owe a particular debt to their cousins, Forrest and Eva McClellan, and Jean Gulliver; and on the Belgian side, to Michel and Régine van der Haert. Gareth Forwood has played an indispensable part both directly and by introducing me to other members of the Forwood family. And a singular place in this roll of respectful thanks must be reserved for the redoubtable Lally, otherwise Ellen Holt, honorary Van den Bogaerde.

Apart from their vital roles in enabling the project to happen, Laurence Harbottle and Pat Kavanagh made available extensive files. For piloting me through these, and for much else, I am grateful to Kathy Beilby at Harbottle and Lewis, and to Carol MacArthur at Peters Fraser and Dunlop. Many other firms, schools, organisations and institutions were visited or contacted, and are listed here. Some of the guardians of precious material saw more of me than they might have wished – principally Dr Howard Gotlieb, Sean Noel and J. C. Johnson of the Mugar Memorial Library at the University of Boston; Janet Moat and Claire Thomas at Special Collections in the British Film Institute; David Sharp and the staff at the BFI National Library; Michael Bott and Verity Andrews at the Reading University Library; Christopher Sheppard and Sara Land of the Brotherton Library at Leeds University; Jacqueline Kavanagh and Jeff Walden at the BBC Written Archives Centre in Caversham Park; Christine McGilly and Jackie Clark at the Mitchell Library in Glasgow; Alexandra Erskine, Nick Alexander and Gerald Hill at the *Daily Telegraph* Library; Eamon Dyas and Nicholas Mays at the News International Archive; Barbara Hall and Christine Kruger of the Margaret Herrick Library at the Academy of Motion Picture Arts and Sciences in Beverly Hills; and Caroline Sisneros of the Louis B. Mayer Library at the American Film Institute in Hollywood.

Many of those listed below kindly made available letters and cards from Dirk's prolific correspondence. Some private collections stood out, and for allowing me to draw on these I am particularly grateful to Nicholas and Rosalind Bowlby, Hélène Bordes, Lady (Molly) Daubeny, Carol Gordon, Patricia Losey, Ivor Powell, Charles Lind, John Beech, Ann Skinner, Bertrand Tavernier, Dominique Lambilliotte and the late Helen Osborne. In this respect, too, Dirk's family has been lavish.

By supplying the *Arena* team in 2001 with Dirk's and Tony's home movies, and so generating the documentary on 'The Private Dirk Bogarde', Brock Van den Bogaerde initiated another precious resource; I am much indebted to Adam Low and Jane Bywaters of the BBC for giving me a sight of their unique raw material. For reasons explained elsewhere in this book, the programme's narrator, Nicholas Shakespeare, belongs in the 'without whom ...' category.

Those who submitted to interview, either in the flesh or by telephone, are identified below in bold type. Not everyone who spoke 'on the record' is mentioned in the book's text, but absentees should know that their contribution helped me to understand the climate and the mores, as well as the specific circumstances in which they were witnesses to part of Dirk's story. I am as grateful to them as I am to those who are quoted at length. There are also some individuals, unnamed in either the text or the source notes, who came forward with offers to supply material from their own papers and their own research; here, my special thanks go to Sir David Williams and to Josie Whibley, whose 'archive' spared me many hours of commuting and poring over microfilm.

Finally, the hefty object you have in your hands would not be anything like as handsome without the skills and application of the Team at Orion: George Sharp, Natasha Webber, Richard Hussey, Erin Hussey, Helen Ewing and Iram Allam. It was diligently read in typescript and proof by Linden Lawson and Ilsa Yardley respectively, and indexed by Douglas Matthews. To all of them, to Ion

Trewin's assistant editor, Anna Hervé, to Ion himself for entrusting me with this privilege, and to everyone named above and below, my sincerest thanks.

Judith Aller, **Jonathan Altaras**, Amersham Public Library, **Ken Annakin**, Jean Archer, Philippa, Lady Astor, **Dame Eileen Atkins**, **Lord and Lady Attenborough**, Brian Attwood (Editor, *The Stage*), Andreas and Carola Augustin, **Lauren Bacall**, BACUP, Paul Bailey, **Roy Ward Baker**, Tracey Baldwin (*Woman*), Dr Helen Bamber, **Frith Banbury**, Michael Barber, Jason Barnes, Julian Barnes, Tony Barry, **Brian Baxter**, Neville Beale, Rahul Bedi, Betty Beesley and Enid Foster (the Garrick Club), **Laurie Bellew**, John Best, **Sally Betts**, Major Rick Bevan, E. S. Bigwood, the late Edward Bishop, **Kitty Black**, Boaty Boatwright, Renée Bonetto, **Helena Bonham Carter**, **Nicholas and Rosalind Bowlby**, Lady (Perina) Braybrooke, Len Bridge (Secretary, Coastal Forces Veterans Association), Bristol University Library, British Library (Catherine Johnson and Dr Richard Price), Roberta Britton, **Faith Brook**, Natasha Brook, **Christian Browning**, BT Archives (David Hay and Raymond Martin), Buckinghamshire County Library (Bill Torrins), Paulene and **Mark Burns**, Fr Andrew Cain, **James Cairncross**, Camden Local Studies and Archives Centre (Malcolm Holmes, Richard Knight, Aidan Flood), the late Judy Campbell, John Cannon, Rosamund Carter, Cavendish Philatelic Auctions, Chesham Public Library, Daphne and David Cleghorn, Peter Cochrane, Richard Cohen, Bridget Coleman-Leckey, Ed Condon (HarperCollins), Dr Barrington Cooper, Major John Corrigan, Nadia Costes, Linda Courtney, Dorothy Cowan, Gerry Cox, Lt.-Col. (Retd) J. B. (John) Cross, Crowborough Public Library (Martine Lane), Douglas and Robert Dalrymple, Mark Daniel, **Lady (Molly) Daubeny**, **Terence Davies**, Dana Dean, Doreen Dean (BAFTA), **Christiaan De Forche**, Marie-Christine de Jabrun (*Bibliothèque du Film*, BIFI), **Jean de Leon Mason**, Clémentine Deliss (Chelsea College of Art and Design), **John Denison**, Alain and **Christine de Pauw**, Rico and Mieke de Schepper, **Mary Dodd**, Peter Donaldson, Kevin Douglas (Headmaster, University College School, Junior Branch), George Eastop (Allan Glen's), East Sussex Record Office (Elizabeth Hughes and staff), **Anne Edwards** and Stephen Citron, Roy Edwards (Editor, *Health & Strength*), James Elliott (Editor, *Classic and Sports Car*), Richard Ellis (Amersham Auction Rooms), Dorothy Ellsworth, David English (Bunbury Cricket Club), **E. W. Espenhahn**, Dr Robin Essame, Primrose Feuchtwanger, the late **Søren Fischer**, **Bryan Forbes**, Maureen Fortey (Decca), **Philip Forwood**, Joan Foster, **James Fox**, the Revd Frank Fox-Wilson, **John Fraser**, FremantleMedia (Len Whitcher and Massimo);

Marguerite Galbe, Ann Garrould, Baptiste and Maria Garthoff, Diana Gates, William L. Gates (King Leo of Redonda), **Sarah Gibb**, **Bee Gilbert**, Lewis Gilbert, Nicholas Goldwyn, Michael Gough, the Earl of Gowrie, Sue Grantley, Damian Gray and Becky Etheridge (Knight Frank), **John Greaves**, Michael Greaves, Stacey Greenfield, Marion Greenwood (BBC), Lt.-Col. (Retd) H. C. S. Gregory, *Guardian* Library (Helen Martin, Jackie Drennan), Guildhall Library, Philip and **Jean Gulliver**, **Alec Gunn and Bay White**, Mrs J. A. Gunter, **Sir Peter Hall**, Tony Hall (*Liverpool Daily Post & Echo*), **Willis Hall**, Carolyn Hammond (Chiswick Public Library), **George Hance**, Jane Harker, Rebecca and the late John Harrison, **Frank Hauser**, **Patricia Heald**, Odeth Higgins (*London Gazette*), the late Dame Thora Hird, Philip Hoare, Margaret Hodsman, Simon Hopkinson, Joanna Horder, **Derek Horne**, Olga Horstig-Primuz, Dr Tom Houston, James Howard, Geoffrey Hudson (Coastal Forces Historian), **Lt.-Col. (Retd) Bryan Hunt**, Julian Hunt (Buckinghamshire County Library), Mark Hurst, the Lord Hutchinson QC, Angela Huth, Anne Hylands, Sue Hyman, Peggy Hyne, Imperial War Museum (Dr Christopher Dowling, Roderick Suddaby and Diana Condell), **Bruna Isoardi**, **Glenda Jackson MP**, **David Jacobs**, Alan and Rhonda Janes, Michael and Ann Jenkin, **Humphrey Jenkins**, Ray Jenkins (Carlton International Media Ltd), **Glynis Johns**, Boris Johnson, Richard Johnson, Christopher Jolly, **Cynthia Jolly**, Paul Jolly, Derek Jones, J. D. F.

Jones, **June Jones**, **Paul Joyce** and Toby Fernside (Lucida Productions), Julie Kavanagh, John Keay, Spencer Kendal, **Nigel Kingscote**, Sue Korman, **Tony Lacey**, **Sue Lawley**, Barbara Leaming, Derek Leask, Donald and Barbara Lee, Sir Patrick Leigh Fermor, Brian Liddy (National Museum of Photography, Film & TV), the late Jean Lion, Marion and **William Lockie**, Peter Longman (Theatres Trust), **Léon Loschetter**, **Patricia Losey**, **Cornel Lucas**, Janine McDermott, **Geraldine McEwan**, **Ian McGregor**, Sue MacGregor, David McKail, John Mackay, Angus MacKechnie (Royal National Theatre), Sean Mackenzie, **Sheila MacLean**, Deborah McVea (*TLS* Centenary Archive), Nadine Malfait, Richard Mangan (Mander and Mitchenson Theatre Collection), Karel Margry, Harry Marsh, John Marshall (Old Rugbeians), Hugh Massingberd, Christopher Matheson, **Jill ('Maude') Melford**, Joe Mendoza, Christine Michel, John Miller, **Sir John Mills**, Michael Mockford and Brian Dew (Medmenham Club), **John Moffatt**, the late **Tanya Moiseiwitsch**, **Billie More**, **Sheridan Morley**, **Nicholas Mosley**, **Joan Mulcaster**, **Barbara Murray**, Professor James Murray, Shingiro Nakayama, the National Archives, National Army Museum, Ronald Neame, George Newkey-Burden, Professor Ian Nish, Robert Noel (Lancaster Herald, the College of Arms), Brian Nolan and the Old Roffensian Society (King's School, Rochester), Philip Norman, **Nancy Olson**, Jamie O'Neill, Andrew Orgill (Royal Military Academy, Sandhurst), Sylvia Ormond, Brian D. Osborne (Neil Munro Society), Andrew and Janet Owens, **Anthony Page**, Thérèse Papo, Matthew Parris, Mark and Nick Paterson (Woodcote House, Windlesham), Ruth Pawley and Sue Richardson (BBC Audiobooks), Sebastian Peake, Dornie Pearce, **Barbara Peerless**, Clare Peñate, Gérard Perron (Atmosphère), David Phillips, Madeleine Phillips, **Jane Powell**, Stan Procter, **Renata Propper**, the late **Denis Quilley**;

  Charlotte Rampling, **Frederic Raphael**, Pru Rawlings, Louise Ray and Gavin Clarke (Royal National Theatre Archive), Piers Paul Read, Bernard Redshaw (Editor, *The Wire*), Dr Norman Reid (University of St Andrews), Amanda and **Simon Relph**, **Brigadier (Retd) Dennis Rendell**, Stella Richards, Sheila Rickards (Uckfield and District Preservation Society), Alasdair Riley, Dr Sebastian Ritchie (Air Historical Branch, MoD), **Caryl Roberts**, Hilary Roberts (Imperial War Museum), Captain Trevor Rowbotham RN (Coastal Forces Heritage Trust), **Peter Rogers**, Major John Rogerson (Queen's Royal Surrey Regimental Association), François Roux, Royal Institute of British Architects, Bryan Samain, Sir Sydney Samuelson, James Sanders, **Amanda Saunders**, **Arnold Schulkes**, Paul Scofield, Janette Scott, Dr Anthony Seldon, Olivia Seligman, the late **Nerine Selwood**, Victor Selwyn (Salamander Oasis Trust), Margaret Shepherd, Dinah Sheridan, Barbara Siek (Dirk Bogarde Brigade), **Jean Simmons**, **Sir Donald and Lady Sinden**, **Ann Skinner**, Audrey Skinner, Jonathan Smith (Tonbridge School), Pamela Smith, *Spotlight*, **Marcel Stellman**, **Juliet Stevenson**, Jeremy Stocker, **Geoffrey Stone**, **Norman Stone**, Alan Strachan, Shaun Sutton, Matthew Sweet, **Sylvia Syms**, **Bertrand Tavernier**, Dennis Taylor (George Formby Society), Graham Temple (Nancarrow and Temple), Theatre Museum, Jeremy Thomas, Joy Thomas, **Bob Thomson**, **Jean Thomson**, Julia Thorogood, Peter Tipthorp, Edward Towne (King's School, Rochester), **John Troke**, **Anton Troxler**, University of London Library (Ali Burdon), the late **Sir Peter Ustinov**, Lt.-Col. (Retd) Peter Valder (Royal Corps of Signals), **Michel and Régine van der Haert**, Henk van Gelder, Hetty van Winsen, Hugo Vickers, Victoria and Albert Museum Archive, Voluntary Euthanasia Society, the late **Alexander Walker**, **Bernard Walsh**, Kay Walsh, James Walton, Elizabeth Ward (Chelsea College of Art and Design), **David Warner**, Joan Waters, Dorothy Watson, Ian Watson (*Glasgow Herald*), Charles Weaver, Barbara Webber (Amersham Society), Pierre Weiss, Westminster Central Reference Library, Westminster City Archives, **Dr Peter Wheeler**, **Janet Whitaker**, **Leonard White**, Tony White (Editor, *Bucks Examiner*), Christine and **Dr Jon Whiteley**, the late **Christopher Whittaker**, Marek Jaros (Wiener Library), Jeremy Wilson, Kathleen Withersby, **Susan Wooldridge**, Vivienne

Wordley (Foyle's), Joanna Wormald, Graeme Wright, Yale University (Nancy Lyon and David Stern), **Michael and Pat York**, Dorothy and **John Young**, Zoological Society of London, **Agnes Zwickl**.

Sources

The manuscripts, typescripts and letters that Dirk did not destroy are held either by his estate or by Dr Howard Gotlieb's Department of Special Collections in the Mugar Memorial Library at the University of Boston, where they form the Dirk Bogarde Collection – identified below as DBC. The sole further repository of significant material owned by him is Special Collections at the British Film Institute, to which he gave his bound scripts in 1970; they account for about half the films he had made by that time, and conclude with *Accident*. Under the same roof is the Joseph Losey Collection, which has proved of great value here, in part because it contains a small but important set of Dirk's letters. Otherwise, the most substantial holdings of his correspondence not in private hands are to be found at the Universities of Reading and Leeds. As part of its Random House archive the Library at Reading has the Chatto & Windus papers, among them Dirk's early letters to John Charlton and Norah Smallwood; most of his later correspondence with his first publisher is preserved in the Brotherton Library at Leeds, where she received her honorary doctorate. A few letters from Dirk to Tom Stoppard and to Julian Barnes are among their own archives at the Harry Ransom Humanities Research Center at the University of Texas in Austin, abbreviated here to HRHRC, which also holds two unfinished essays by Dorothy Gordon. Dirk's letters to Penelope Mortimer were returned to him in his lifetime and are among his papers in Boston.

While every effort has been made to trace copyright holders, if any have inadvertently been overlooked, the publishers will be pleased to acknowledge them in any future editions of this work.

WORKS BY DIRK BOGARDE

The Books
A Postillion Struck by Lightning (Chatto & Windus, 1977)

Snakes and Ladders (Chatto & Windus, 1978)

A Gentle Occupation (Chatto & Windus, 1980)

Voices in the Garden (Chatto & Windus, 1981)

An Orderly Man (Chatto & Windus, 1983)

West of Sunset (Allen Lane, 1984)

Backcloth (Viking, 1986)

A Particular Friendship (Viking, 1989)

Jericho (Viking, 1992)

Great Meadow (Viking, 1992)

A Short Walk from Harrods (Viking, 1993)

A Period of Adjustment (Viking, 1994)

Cleared for Take-Off (Viking, 1995)

Closing Ranks (Viking, 1997)

For the Time Being: Collected Journalism (Viking, 1998)

The first five titles were reprinted by Triad/Panther and later by Penguin, which became Dirk's paperback publisher on the acquisition of *West of Sunset*. The first four books of memoirs were issued in a single volume as *Dirk Bogarde: The Complete Autobiography* by Methuen in 1988. Extracts from *A Short Walk from Harrods* and *Cleared for Take-Off* were published separately in the Penguin 60s series as *From Le Pigeonnier* (1995) and *Coming of Age* (1996) respectively.

All Dirk's books were recorded on audiocassette, many of them narrated by the author. They were issued variously, and at varying length, by Chivers, Isis, Penguin, the BBC and WEA. Reed Audio released his readings of Thomas Mann's *Death in Venice* (1995) and Michael Jenkins's *A House in Flanders* (1996).

The Poetry

'Steel Cathedrals' has been included in at least three anthologies: *The Terrible Rain: The War Poets 1939–1945* (Methuen, 1966), edited by Brian Gardner; and *Poems of the Second World War* (1985), which was later incorporated into *The Voice of War: Poems of the Second World War* (Michael Joseph/the Salamander Oasis Trust, 1995), edited by Victor Selwyn.

The Discs

Lyrics for Lovers (LK 4373) was released, alas, by Decca in October 1960 and again in December 1981 (MOR 531). Dirk narrated *Alice in Wonderland*, with a cast including Frankie Howerd, Tommy Cooper, Beryl Reid and Bruce Forsyth, on a 1965 EMI double album (MFP 1267/8). In 1980 an EP entitled *Dirk Bogarde reads 'Coventry' Verse* (ZELEPS288) was issued by the Church authorities to help boost employment in that city; it included 'Steel Cathedrals', in which he substituted Coventry for his original Shrewsbury. His narration for the Glyndebourne concert staging of *The Merry Widow* can be heard on a double CD (EMI 5 55152 2).

INTRODUCTION (pp. 5–19)

1 Interview with author.

2 David Caute, *Joseph Losey: A Revenge on Life*, Faber & Faber, 1994.

3 'Dirk Bogarde: Above the Title' (Yorkshire Television), 14/9/86.

4 'Alec Guinness: a Secret Man' (*Arena*, BBC2), 29/12/03.

5 Ibid.

6 Margaret Hinxman and Susan d'Arcy, *The Films of Dirk Bogarde*, Literary Services & Production, 1974.

7 Robert Tanitch, *Dirk Bogarde: The Complete Career Illustrated*, Ebury Press, 1988.

8 *Dirk Bogarde: Rank Outsider*, Bloomsbury, 1996; updated 1999.

9 DB to Norah Smallwood, 4/8/77.

10 'Dirk Bogarde: Above the Title', op. cit.

11 *The Times*, 6/9/86.

12 Penelope Middelboe, *Edith Olivier: From her Journals 1924–48*, Weidenfeld & Nicolson, 1989, p. 290.

13 *A Song at Twilight* from *Suite in Three Keys* by Noël Coward, Heinemann, 1966.

14 John Fraser, *Close Up: An Actor's Tales*, Oberon, 2004; extracted in the *Mail on Sunday*, 27/2/2000.

15 *The Spectator*, 8/11/03.

16 Letter to author, 1/8/03, passim.

17 Bryan Forbes, *A Divided Life*, Heinemann, 1992, p. 257.

18 *A Song at Twilight*, op. cit.

19 *The Spectator*, 4/7/98.

20 Interview with author.

21 *The Telegraph Magazine*, 6/12/03.

22 Richard Chamberlain, *Shattered Love: A Memoir*, ReganBooks, 2003, p. 20.

23 *Daily Sketch*, 28/2/61.

24 Interview with author.

25 J. D. F. Jones, *Storyteller: The Many Lives of Laurens van der Post*, John Murray, 2001, p. 1.

26 *The Sunday Telegraph*, 30/11/03.

27 Interview with author.

28 *The Daily Telegraph*, 23/5/87.

29 'Six Men', 13/4/86; cited in Simon Heffer, *Like the Roman: The Life of Enoch Powell*, Weidenfeld & Nicolson, 1998, p. 901.

30 Chamberlain, op. cit., p. 241.

31 DB to Penelope Mortimer, 29/10/88.

32 Notes for *A Postillion Struck by Lightning* (Dirk Bogarde Collection, Boston University).

33 Richard Mangan (ed.), *Gielgud's Letters*, Weidenfeld & Nicolson, 2004.

34 Morley, op. cit., p. 30.

35 'The Critic as Artist', from *Intentions*, 1891.

36 'Still Cliff' (BBC1), 6/12/03.

37 Interview with author.

38 Michael Gough to author, 14/8/01.

39 *The Daily Telegraph*, 23/5/92.

CHAPTER ONE (pp. 23–39)

1 Jean-Marie Lermyte and Christiaan De Forche, *Izegem: Beeld voor Beeld*, Stadsbestuur Izegem, 2002.

2 Ludovic Halévy, tr. by Aimé Van den Bogaerde and Robert A. Newill, *A Marriage of Love*, Rookes Bros, Stamford; Simpkin, Marshall, 1885.

3 East Sussex Record Office, ESC/214/25/4.

4 East Sussex Record Office, ESC/214/7/2.

5 *A Postillion Struck by Lightning*, pp. 142–5.

6 East Sussex Record Office, ESC/214/25/4.

7 Times Newspapers Limited, Management File, 5/10/1914.

8 Ibid., 22/3/1915.

9 Ibid., 29/12/1920.

10 *The Times* House Journal, July/August 1957.

11 Times Newspapers Limited, Management File, 2/2/1953.

12 *The Times* House Journal, June 1957.

13 Times Newspapers Limited, WRM/2.

14 *The Times* House Journal, June 1937.

15 'The Picture Man', in George Darby (ed.), *The Times – Past – Present – Future*, Times Newspapers, 1984.

16 Ibid.

17 *The Scotsman*, 24/8/1865.

18 Robert S. Wicks and Roland H. Harrison, *Buried Cities, Forgotten Gods: William Niven's Life of Discovery and Revolution in Mexico and the American Southwest*, Texas Technical University Press, 1999; *The Houston Press*, 13/3/1930.

19 *The Chiel*, 1/12/1883.

20 Ibid., 22/12/1883.

21 *The Stage*, 20/2/1885.

22 *Scottish Athletic Journal*, 11/5/1886.

23 *North British Daily Mail*, 2/12/1887.

24 *Glasgow Herald*, 14/12/1888.

25 *Glasgow Evening News*, 14/12/1888.

26 National Library of Scotland, MS26925.

27 *Daily Record and Mail*, 31/10/29.

28 Neil Munro, *The Brave Days: A Chronicle from the North*, Porpoise Press, 1931, p. 142.

29 J. F. McClellan, *Some of My Aunts and Uncles*, privately published, 1992.

30 *Glasgow Evening News*, 5/1/32.

31 *Glasgow Herald*, 5/1/32.

CHAPTER TWO (pp. 40–63)

1 Anthony Armstrong, 'The Art of J. H. Dowd', *Strand Magazine*, September 1937.

2 *Backcloth*, p. 12.

3 Ibid.

4 Ibid., p. 17.

5 Anthony Beckles Willson, *Strawberry Hill: A History of the Neighbourhood*, Strawberry Hill Residents Association, 1991.

6 E. A. Morris and T. H. R. Cashmore, *Church Street, Twickenham*, Borough of Twickenham Local History Society, 1999.

7 *Backcloth*, p. 27.

8 Ibid., p. 24.

9 Ibid., p. 23.

10 Ibid., p. 24.

11 Ibid., p. 25.

12 Interview with author.

13 Ibid.

14 Ibid.

15 *Backcloth*, p. 38.

16 *Postillion*, p. 45.

17 Ibid., p. 45.

18 Correspondence (1977) lent anonymously to author.

19 Mark Daniel, 'Return to Bogarde Country', *The Lady*, 11/9/86.

20 'Windover Hill', in *Places: An Anthology of Britain* chosen by Ronald Blythe, OUP, 1981.

21 Ibid.

22 *Backcloth*, p. 44.

23 *Postillion*, p. 11.

24 Ibid., p. 126.

25 Ibid., p. 127.

26 Ibid., p. 150.

27 *Backcloth*, p. 51.

28 Interview with author.

29 *Postillion*, p. 124.

30 H. J. K. Usher and others, *An Angel without Wings: The History of University College School 1830–1980*, University College School, 1981.

31 Telephone interview with author.

32 Telephone interview with author.

33 Interview with author.

34 Telephone interview with author.

35 Interview with author.

36 Telephone interview with author.

37 Interview with author.

38 *Postillion*, p. 129.

39 Ibid., p. 190.

40 McClellan, op. cit.

41 Interview with author.

42 Ibid.

43 *Backcloth*, p. 66.

44 Edwin Muir, *Scottish Journey*, Heinemann/Gollancz, 1935, p. 115.

45 *Postillion*, p. 153.

46 Ibid.

47 Joseph A. Rae (ed.), *The History of Allan*

Glen's School 1853–1953, privately published, 1953.

48 *Scottish Daily Express*, 14/3/35.
49 Et seq., interview with author.
50 *A Particular Friendship*, p. 23.
51 Rae (ed.), op. cit.
52 *Postillion*, p. 170.
53 Et seq., *Postillion*, p. 175.

54 Jessie and Willie Ure, *Bishopbriggs: The Golden Years*, Strathkelvin District Libraries & Museums, 1987.
55 *Postillion*, p. 161.
56 Et seq., interview with author.
57 *Postillion*, p. 189.
58 Harry Marsh to author, 3/3/02.

CHAPTER THREE (pp. 64–84)

1 *Backcloth*, p. 57.
2 *A Short Walk from Harrods*, p. 200.
3 *Backcloth*, p. 58.
4 *Cleared for Take-Off*, p. 193.
5 *Postillion*, p. 146.
6 *Backcloth*, p. 59.
7 *Postillion*, p. 130.
8 *A Short Walk from Harrods*, p. 3.
9 Richard Edmonds, *Chelsea: From the Five Fields to the World's End*, Phene Press, 1956.
10 Et seq, interview with author.
11 *Postillion*, p. 196.
12 Ibid., p. 197.
13 Ibid., p. 198.
14 *Backcloth*, p. 61.
15 Interview with author.
16 *Postillion*, pp. 202–3.
17 *Sussex Express & County Herald*, 2/12/38.
18 Et seq., DB to Nerine Selwood, 4/12/82.
19 *Magazine of the Chelsea Polytechnic*, Summer 1938.
20 *Sussex Express & County Herald*, 13/1/39.
21 Ibid., 21/4/39.
22 *Postillion*, p. 204.
23 DB to Nerine Selwood, 4/12/82.
24 DB to Nerine Selwood, 18/3/77.
25 Et seq., *Postillion*, p. 198.
26 Interview with author.
27 DB to Sheila Rickards, 9/8/94.
28 *Postillion*, p. 206.
29 Ibid., p. 207.
30 *Backcloth*, p. 75.
31 *Postillion*, p. 207.
32 DB to Sheila Rickards, 9/8/94.
33 Ibid.

34 *Postillion*, p. 208.
35 Ibid., p. 209.
36 Margot Cameron to UVdB., 16/8/39.
37 Joan Mant, *Otherwise a Barn: Twelve Years of Theatre in Shere, Surrey*, Hazeltree Publishing, 1999.
38 Interview with author.
39 Christopher Warwick, *The Universal Ustinov*, Sidgwick & Jackson, 1990.
40 Conversation with author.
41 Tom Kealy to Jympson Harman, 21/12/47 (British Film Institute).
42 Kenneth Barrow, *On Q: Jack and Beatie de Leon and the Q Theatre*, The de Leon Memorial Fund, 1992, pp. 108–11.
43 Interview with author.
44 Barrow, op. cit.
45 *The Independent*, 19/2/91.
46 Barrow, op. cit.
47 *Postillion*, p. 215.
48 Barrow, op. cit.
49 *Postillion*, p. 219.
50 *Brentford & Chiswick Times*, 9/2/40.
51 *The Stage*, 21/3/40.
52 Barrow, op. cit.
53 *Postillion*, p. 221.
54 Souvenir programme, Playhouse, Amersham, 1946.
55 *Postillion*, p. 222.
56 Ibid.
57 *Bucks Examiner*, 28/6/40.
58 *The Stage*, 29/8/40.
59 *Postillion*, p. 226.
60 Letter to author, 28/11/03.
61 Ted Morgan, *Somerset Maugham*, Cape, 1980, p. 280.
62 *Bucks Examiner*, 11/10/40.

63 *Postillion*, p. 223.
64 *Backcloth*, pp. 73–4.
65 Interview with author.

66 *Bucks Examiner*, 15/11/40.
67 Ibid., 29/11/40.
68 Ibid., 20/12/40.

CHAPTER FOUR (pp. 85–105)

1 *Postillion*, p. 232.
2 Sam Heppner, '*Cockie*', Leslie Frewin, 1969.
3 Ibid.
4 *Postillion*, p. 231.
5 Ibid., p. 232.
6 Ibid., p. 234.
7 Warwick, op. cit., p. 67.
8 *Postillion*, p. 241.
9 Et seq., Warwick, op. cit.
10 Et seq., interview with author.
11 Peter Ustinov, *Dear Me*, Heinemann, 1977; Penguin, 1978, p. 128.
12 James Cairncross to DB, 8/8/77.
13 Conversation with author.
14 Interview with author.
15 *Postillion*, p. 240.
16 *The Times*, 24/12/63.
17 *Postillion*, p. 244.
18 *Ibid.*, p. 245.
19 *Snakes and Ladders*, p. 9.
20 Ibid.
21 Ibid., p. 38.
22 Ibid., p. 39.
23 Ibid., p. 41.
24 Ibid., p. 42.
25 Ibid., p. 43.
26 Letter to author.
27 Interview with author.
28 Et seq., Stan Procter, *A Quiet Little Boy Goes to War*, privately published, 1997.
29 Conversation with author.
30 *Cleared for Take-Off*, p. 24.
31 Interview with author.
32 *Snakes and Ladders*, p. 47.
33 Correspondence with author.
34 *Snakes and Ladders*, p. 60.
35 *Evidence in Camera*, vol. II, No. 7; August 1944 (HQ Air Command South East Asia).
36 Constance Babington Smith, *Evidence in Camera: The Story of Photographic Intelligence in World War II*, Chatto & Windus, 1958, p. 13.
37 *Snakes and Ladders*, p. 60.
38 *Chambers Biographical Dictionary*, Chambers, 5th edn, 1990.
39 Sarah Churchill, *Keep on Dancing: An Autobiography*, Weidenfeld & Nicolson, 1981, pp. 61–4.
40 DB to Julie Kavanagh, 15/2/90.
41 Ibid.

CHAPTER FIVE (pp. 106–26)

1 *Cleared for Take-Off*, p. 27.
2 Ibid., p. 26.
3 Et seq., private collection.
4 *Cleared for Take-Off*, pp. 28–9.
5 Major-General Richard Rohmer, *Patton's Gap: Mustangs over Normandy*, Stoddart Publishing, 2nd edn, 1998, p. 7.
6 Ibid., p. 89.
7 *Backcloth*, p. 105.
8 Rohmer, op. cit., p. 138.
9 Ibid., p. 140.
10 DB to Richard Rohmer, 16/9/80.
11 *FLAP*, 39 (RCAF) Wing, January 1945.
12 *Cleared for Take-Off*, p. 1.
13 Lieutenant-General Sir Brian Horrocks, *A Full Life*, Fontana edn, 1962, p. 179.
14 *Cleared for Take-Off*, pp. 8–9.
15 Telephone conversation with author.
16 Et seq., *FLAP*, op. cit.
17 Major A. H. R. Baker and Major B. Rust, *A Short History of the 50th Northumbrian Division*, Northumbrian Division, 1966.
18 National Archives, WO 171/515.
19 Interview with author.

20 *Snakes and Ladders*, pp. 47–8.
21 Interview with author.
22 Interview with author, passim.
23 Interview with author.
24 'A Night to Remember', *The Sunday Telegraph*, 12/1/92.
25 *Snakes and Ladders*, p. 63.
26 Ibid., p. 56.
27 *A Short Walk from Harrods*, p. 108.
28 *Backcloth*, p. 113.
29 *An Orderly Man*, p. 161.
30 *Cleared for Take-Off*, p. 20.
31 DB to Graeme Wright, 20/9/91.
32 *The Daily Telegraph*, 26/11/88.
33 *Snakes and Ladders*, p. 56.
34 Conversation with author.
35 Interview with author.
36 *Backcloth*, p. 114.
37 *The Times*, 22/5/45.
38 *Cleared for Take-Off*, p. 36.
39 *The Cornishman*, 20/11/86.
40 Text of funeral address (26/10/90), shown to author.

CHAPTER SIX (pp. 127–49)

1 Interview with author, passim.
2 Babington Smith, op. cit., p. 85.
3 Ibid., p. 118.
4 *Snakes and Ladders*, pp. 110–11.
5 Ibid., p. 110.
6 *Backcloth*, p. 117.
7 Ibid.
8 *Snakes and Ladders*, p. 113.
9 *Backcloth*, p. 118.
10 *Cleared for Take-Off*, p. 111.
11 Ibid., pp. 118–19.
12 *Snakes and Ladders*, p. 115.
13 National Archives, AIR 26/488.
14 *Snakes and Ladders*, p. 115.
15 *Backcloth*, p. 118.
16 *Amrita Bazar Patrika*, 21/11/45.
17 Lieutenant-Colonel Bryan Hunt papers, Imperial War Museum, 88/8/1.
18 Lieutenant-Colonel A. J. F. Doulton, *The Fighting Cock: Being the History of the 23rd Indian Division 1942–1947*, Gale & Polden, Aldershot, 1951, p. 243.
19 National Archives, WO 172/7021.
20 Lieutenant-Colonel A. J. F. Doulton papers, National Army Museum 1999–11–2–4.
21 Doulton, *The Fighting Cock*, p. 229.
22 Ibid., p. 210.
23 Major-General Douglas Hawthorn file, IWM 7907–27–3.
24 *Backcloth*, pp. 139–40.
25 *The Fighting Cock*, 23/10/45.
26 Doulton, *The Fighting Cock*, p. 291.
27 *The Fighting Cock*, 10/12/45.
28 Ibid., 18/12/45.
29 *Backcloth*, p. 137.
30 *The Fighting Cock*, 29/12/45.
31 Doulton papers.
32 *The Fighting Cock*, 15/1/46.
33 Doulton papers.
34 Ibid.
35 Interview with author, passim.
36 Et seq., conversations with author.
37 *Backcloth*, p. 158.
38 Et seq., conversation with author.
39 Ian Nish (ed.), *Indonesian Experience: The Role of Japan and Britain, 1943–1948*, LSE, 1979.
40 *Backcloth*, p. 166.
41 *The Fighting Cock*, 4/7/46.
42 *Backcloth*, p. 173.
43 *The Fighting Cock*, 8/7/46.
44 Bryan Hunt papers.
45 *Backcloth*, p. 170.
46 Ibid., pp. 172–3.
47 *The Fighting Cock*, 25/7/46.
48 DB to E. S. Bigwood, 28/2/96.
49 'I Speak for Myself', 13/8/49 (BBC Written Archives).
50 *Cleared for Take-Off*, pp. 36–8.
51 Caryl Roberts, interview with author.
52 Jolly family archive.
53 *Cleared for Take-Off*, pp. 39–40.
54 Conversation with author.
55 *Evening Express*, Liverpool, 5/9/46.

CHAPTER SEVEN (pp. 153–72)

1 *The Fighting Cock*, 9/10/46.
2 *Snakes and Ladders*, p. 49.
3 *An Orderly Man*, p. 34.
4 *Scrapbook* (23rd Indian Division, privately published).
5 Ibid.
6 Ibid.
7 Ibid.
8 Interview with author, passim.
9 *The Tatler*, October 1943.
10 Interview with author.
11 Ken Annakin, *So You Wanna Be a Director?*, Tomahawk Press, 2001, p. 37.
12 *Postillion*, p. 222.
13 Et seq., *Snakes and Ladders*, pp. 73–4.
14 Et seq., Peter Daubeny, *My World of Theatre*, Cape, 1971, p. 87.
15 *Snakes and Ladders*, p. 78.
16 Interview with author.
17 Frederick Joachim to DB, 1/12/78.
18 *Snakes and Ladders*, p. 81.
19 Internal memo 8/1/47 (BBC Written Archives).
20 DB to Mrs M. C. Burch, 8/1/47 (BBC Written Archives).
21 'Reluctant Star', 15/2/56 (BBC Written Archives).
22 Et seq., Kenneth More, *Happy Go Lucky*, Robert Hale, 1959, p. 96.
23 *The Observer*, 2/3/47.
24 *The Times*, 27/2/47; *Daily Express*, 26/2/47.
25 *Cavalcade*, 8/3/47.
26 *News Chronicle*, 27/2/47.
27 Et seq., Daubeny, op. cit., p. 88.
28 *Snakes and Ladders*, p. 103.
29 *Evening News*, 9/4/47.
30 *Star*, 9/4/47.
31 *Evening Standard*, 11/4/47.
32 *Snakes and Ladders*, p. 104.
33 Et seq., Joe Mendoza to author, 22/1/02.
34 *Snakes and Ladders*, p. 103.
35 *Daily Express*, 8/4/47.
36 Henry Kendall to DB, 10/4/47.
37 J. Arthur Rank files (Carlton International Media).
38 *Snakes and Ladders*, p. 105.
39 DB to Philip Hoare, 1/12/91.
40 *West London Times*, 21/3/47.
41 Undated cutting, *Woman's Own*, 1947.
42 Interview with author.
43 Geoffrey Macnab, *J. Arthur Rank and the British Film Industry*, Routledge, 1993, p. 104.
44 J. Arthur Rank files (Carlton International Media).
45 *To-day's Cinema*, 26/5/52.
46 Ian Dalrymple to DB, 25/5/47.
47 Internal memo, 12/5/47 (BBC Written Archives).
48 Robert Barr to DB, 23/7/47 (BBC Written Archives).
49 Ian Dalrymple to DB, 18/7/47.
50 Et seq., *Snakes and Ladders*, p. 119.
51 Bryan Samain, personal diary of, 28/9/85.
52 Interview with author.
53 Mrs J. A. Gunter to author, 21/5/03.
54 Interview with author.
55 Et seq., interview with author.
56 *Sketch*, 15/10/47.
57 *Kinematograph Weekly*, 18/12/47.

CHAPTER EIGHT (pp. 173–92)

1 'The Alien Corn' script (BFI Special Collections).
2 DB to Pat Kavanagh, 25/4/85.
3 Muriel Box diary, 30/11/47 (BFI Special Collections).
4 *Snakes and Ladders*, p. 124.
5 Letter to author, 4/2/02.
6 *Snakes and Ladders*, loc. cit.
7 *Daily Mirror*, undated cutting.
8 *Evening Standard*, 1/10/48.
9 Ian Dalrymple to DB, 3/10/48.
10 Unsourced cutting, 1948.
11 *Theatre World*, November 1948.
12 Unsourced cutting, 1948.

13 Interview with author.

14 Brian McFarlane, *An Autobiography of British Cinema: as told by the filmmakers and actors who made it*, Methuen, 1997, pp. 68–9.

15 Donald Sinden, *A Touch of the Memoirs*, Hodder & Stoghton, 1982, p. 191.

16 Et seq., *For the Time Being*, p. 92.

17 Macnab, op. cit., p. 1.

18 J. Arthur Rank speech, Pinewood Studios 21st Anniversary lunch, 30/9/57 (George Blackler Collection, BFI).

19 Gareth Owen with Brian Burford, *The Pinewood Story: The Authorised History of the World's Most Famous Film Studio*, Reynolds & Hearn, 2000, pp. 9–17.

20 Et seq., Sinden, op. cit., p. 190.

21 Interview with author.

22 *Snakes and Ladders*, p. 82.

23 Brian McFarlane (ed.), *The Encyclopedia of British Film*, BFI, 2003.

24 Simon Heffer to author, 24/2/03.

25 '. . . a good reputation for British Films'; speech by Sir Stafford Cripps, 16/1/47 (George Blackler Collection, BFI).

26 *Boys in Brown* script (BFI Special Collections).

27 Et seq., *The Blue Lamp* script (BFI Special Collections).

28 McFarlane, op. cit., p. 68.

29 *The Times*, 20/1/50.

30 Simon Heffer to author, 24/2/03.

31 *The Blue Lamp* script.

32 Andy Medhurst, 'Dirk Bogarde', in Charles Barr (ed.), *All Our Yesterdays: 90 Years of British Cinema*, BFI Publishing, 1986, p. 348.

33 *Snakes and Ladders*, pp. 129–30.

34 Jessie Matthews to DB, 2/1/49.

35 *Picturegoer Film Annual*, 1951–2.

36 *Woman's Own*, undated cutting.

37 *The Daily Telegraph*, 17/3/48.

38 Interview with author.

39 Interview with author.

40 *Snakes and Ladders*, p. 141.

41 *Illustrated*, 27/12/52.

42 'I Speak for Myself', (BBC Far Eastern Service), 13/8/49.

43 *Picturegoer*, 25/2/50.

44 *Daily Mail*, 25/1/50.

45 *The Times*, 25/1/50.

46 Letter to author, 2002.

47 Miscellaneous press reports 31/5/50 and 1/6/50.

48 *Snakes and Ladders*, pp. 140–41.

49 Eve Golden with Kim Kendall, *The Brief, Madcap Life of Kay Kendall*, University of Kentucky, 2002, p. 51.

50 Interview with author.

51 Kitty Black, *Upper Circle: A Theatrical Chronicle*, Methuen, 1984.

52 Interview with author, passim.

53 Interview with author.

54 Interview with author.

55 *Cleared for Take-Off*, p. 46.

56 Interview with author.

CHAPTER NINE (pp. 193–210)

1 Interview with author.

2 Interview with author, passim.

3 *Snakes and Ladders*, p. 134.

4 Val Guest, *So You Want to Be in Pictures*, Reynolds & Hearn, 2001, p. 116.

5 Graham Payn and Sheridan Morley (eds), *The Noël Coward Diaries*, Weidenfeld & Nicolson, 1982, p. 188.

6 Et seq., DB to Philip Hoare, 1/12/91.

7 *Snakes and Ladders*, p. 135.

8 Ibid.

9 Letter to author, 1/7/03.

10 Bryan Forbes, *Notes for a Life*, Collins, 1974.

11 Et seq., interview with author.

12 Letter to author, loc. cit.

13 Lewis Milestone Collection, Academy of Motion Picture Arts and Sciences, LA.

14 DB to Paul Stephenson, 9/9/52 (BBC Written Archives).

15 *Health and Strength*, 27/11/52.

16 Ibid., 22/1/53.

17 *Evening Standard*, 5/9/53.

18 *The Daily Telegraph*, 31/12/53.

19 *Daily Mirror*, 4/12/53.

20 Susan Wooldridge, interview with author.

21 *Evening News*, 10/6/53.

22 *Snakes and Ladders*, p. 137.

23 *Evening News*, loc. cit.

24 Sheridan Morley, *John G: The Authorised Biography of John Gielgud*, Hodder & Stoughton, 2001, p. 243.

25 Hugh David, *On Queer Street: A Social History of British Homosexuality 1895–1995*, HarperCollins, 1997, p. 163.

26 Graham Robb, *Strangers: Homosexual Love in the Nineteenth Century*, Picador, 2003, p. 274.

27 David, op. cit., p. 164.

28 *Turning Points: The Memoirs of Lord Wolfenden*, Bodley Head, 1976, p. 131.

29 David, op. cit., p. 163.

30 Morley, *John G.*, loc. cit.

31 Ibid., pp. 245–7.

32 Interview with author.

33 Michael York, *Travelling Player: An Autobiography*, Headline, 1991, p. 122.

34 Michel Ciment, *Conversations with Losey*, Methuen, 1985, p. 135.

35 Ibid., p. 140.

36 Ibid., p. 138.

37 DB to Patricia Losey, 22/6/84.

38 *Snakes and Ladders*, p. 224.

39 *The Sleeping Tiger* script (BFI Special Collections).

40 DB to Joe and Patricia Losey, 10/2/74.

41 Ciment, op. cit., p. 120.

42 *Los Angeles Times*, 11/2/54.

43 *Daily Sketch*, 12/2/54.

44 *Picturegoer*, 17/4/54.

45 Interview with author.

46 Interview with author.

47 *Snakes and Ladders*, p. 139.

48 Interview with author, passim.

49 *Arena* interview transcript (BBC), 2001.

50 Betty E. Box, *Lifting the Lid: The Autobiography of Film Producer, Betty Box, OBE*, Book Guild, 2000, p. 99.

51 *Bucks Examiner*, 16/1/53.

52 *Snakes and Ladders*, p. 148.

53 *Bucks Examiner*, 24/9/54.

54 *Snakes and Ladders*, loc. cit.

55 Interview with author, passim.

56 *Manchester Guardian*, 29/12/55.

57 *Arena*, op. cit.

58 Hoare, op. cit., p. 393.

59 Joan Collins, *Second Act*, Boxtree, 1996, p. 49.

60 'Non! Non! Non!', *The Daily Telegraph*, 13/8/94.

61 Interview with author, passim.

62 *Picturegoer*, 19/3/55.

63 Box, op. cit., p. 106.

64 'Non! Non! Non!', op. cit.

65 *Initiales B.B.: Mémoires*, Grasset, 1996.

66 'Non! Non! Non!', op. cit.

67 Ibid.

68 DB to Joan Mulcaster, 3/9/94.

CHAPTER TEN (pp. 211–32)

1 DB to John Davis (draft), 31/12/55.

2 Interview with author.

3 *Cast a Dark Shadow* script (BFI Special Collections).

4 Michael Bell to DB, 13/4/55 (BBC Written Archives).

5 *Radio Times* for 15/2/56.

6 Peter Hall, *Making an Exhibition of Myself*, Sinclair-Stevenson, 1993, p. 81.

7 Interview with author, passim.

8 DB to Sylvia and Kathleen Withersby, 27/8/55.

9 *Glasgow Herald*, 11/10/55.

10 *Snakes and Ladders*, p. 168.

11 Conversation with author, passim.

12 *Sunday Express*, 13/11/55.

13 *Plays and Players*, December 1955.

14 *Picturegoer*, 17/12/55.

15 Payn and Morley (eds), op. cit., p. 209.

16 Interview with author.

17 Et seq., 'Reluctant Star'.

18 *Radio Times* for 15/2/56.

19 A. J. Cronin, *The Spanish Gardener*, Gollancz, 1950, p. 103.

20 Stephen Bourne, *Brief Encounters: Lesbians and Gays in British Cinema 1930–1971*, Cassell, 1996, p. 124.
21 *The Spanish Gardener* script (BFI Special Collections).
22 McFarlane, op. cit., p. 69.
23 Interview and correspondence with author.
24 Conversation with author.
25 Et seq., Michael Powell, *Million-Dollar Movie: The Second Volume of His Life in Movies*, Heinemann, 1992, p. 363.
26 AF to Laurence Harbottle, 22/7/56.
27 Mark Amory (ed.), *The Letters of Ann Fleming*, Collins Harvill, 1985.
28 Patrick Leigh Fermor to author, 14/3/01, passim.
29 Michael Powell to DB, 20/11/56 (DBC Boston).
30 DB to James Howard, October 1990.
31 Powell, op. cit., p. 500.
32 Ibid., pp. 384–5.
33 Et seq., *Doctor at Large* script (BFI Special Collections).
34 Unsourced cutting.
35 Et seq., *Films and Filming*, January 1957.
36 *Snakes and Ladders*, p. 151.
37 Et seq., telephone interview with author.
38 *Snakes and Ladders*, p. 161.
39 Ibid., p. 164.
40 Alan Jay Lerner, *The Street Where I Live: The Story of My Fair Lady, Gigi and Camelot*, Hodder & Stoughton, 1978, Coronet edn, 1980, pp. 57–8.
41 *A Particular Friendship*, p. 106.
42 *Evening Standard*, 19/1/57.
43 *Snakes and Ladders*, p. 154.
44 AF to Laurence Harbottle, 20/3/57.
45 Telephone interview with author, passim.
46 *Bucks Examiner*, 14/6/57 and 28/6/57.
47 DB to Betty Box, 20/6/57.
48 Box, op. cit., p. 168.
49 *The Times*, 5/2/58.
50 *Snakes and Ladders*, p. 170.
51 Morley, *John G.*, p. 95.
52 John Gielgud to DB, 22/6/57 (DBC, Boston).
53 *Sunday Express*, 29/12/57.

CHAPTER ELEVEN (pp. 233–51)

1 John Davis to DB, 12/12/57 (DBC, Boston).
2 John Davis to DB, 4/12/57 (DBC, Boston).
3 Interview with author, passim.
4 *Snakes and Ladders*, p. 154.
5 'Dirk Bogarde – By Myself' (Lucida Productions, 1992).
6 Box, op. cit., p. 184.
7 R. J. Minney, *'Puffin' Asquith: A Biography of the Hon Anthony Asquith, Aesthete, Aristocrat, Prime Minister's Son and Film Maker*, Leslie Frewin, 1973, pp. 132–3.
8 Geoffrey Wansell, *Terence Rattigan: A Biography*, Fourth Estate, 1995, p. 267.
9 Piers Paul Read, *Alec Guinness: The Authorised Biography*, Simon & Schuster, 2003, p. 323.
10 Et seq., Minney, op. cit., p. 174.
11 Adrian Turner, *The Making of David Lean's Lawrence of Arabia*, Dragon's World, 1994, pp. 35–6.
12 *Snakes and Ladders*, p. 171.
13 Minney, loc. cit.
14 Jeremy Wilson, *Lawrence of Arabia: The Authorised Biography of T. E. Lawrence*, Heinemann, 1989, p. 1.
15 Minney, loc. cit.
16 Wansell, op. cit., p. 300.
17 Wilson, op. cit., p. 669.
18 T. E. Lawrence to Sir Evelyn Wrench, 1/4/35, cited in Malcolm Brown (ed.), *The Letters of T. E. Lawrence*, Dent, 1988.
19 *Daily Mail*, 29/4/58.
20 *Bucks Examiner*, 2/5/58.
21 *The Times* and *The Daily Telegraph*, 29/5/58.
22 Interview with author.
23 Minney, op. cit., p. 179.
24 *The Sunday Times*, 26/4/59.
25 *Photoplay*, June 1958.
26 Letter to author, 19/10/01.

27 Interview with author, *passim*.
28 *Daily Express*, 23/9/58.
29 *Manchester Guardian*, 24/9/58.
30 *The Observer*, 28/9/58.
31 Interview with author.
32 DB to Sylvia and Kathleen Withersby, October 1958.
33 Cornel Lucas, interview with author.
34 *Daily Express*, 20/9/58.
35 *Picturegoer*, 3/1/59.
36 Olive Dodds to DB (DBC, Boston).
37 *Daily Mail*, 6/12/58.
38 *The Daily Telegraph*, 27/12/58.
39 McFarlane, op. cit., p. 68.
40 *News of the World*, 8/11/59.
41 *Picturegoer*, 18/4/59.
42 Interview with author.
43 *Song Without End* script (BFI Special Collections).
44 DB to Judith Aller, 29/11/82.
45 *The Los Angeles Times*, 2/6/59.
46 *Snakes and Ladders*, p. 182.
47 *Cleared for Take-Off*, p. 151.
48 *Snakes and Ladders*, p. 182.
49 Ibid.
50 Patrick McGilligan, *George Cukor: A Double Life*, St Martin's Press, 1991.
51 AF to Laurence Harbottle, 26/6/59.
52 *The Los Angeles Times*, 31/8/59.
53 AF to Laurence Harbottle, August 1959.
54 Sheridan Morley, *Gladys Cooper: A Biography*, Heinemann, 1979, p. 249.
55 Golden and Kendall, op. cit., p. 153.
56 AF to Laurence Harbottle, 4/9/59.
57 *Snakes and Ladders*, p. 186.
58 *New York Mirror*, 18/10/59.
59 *Sunday Express*, 1/11/59.
60 *Motion Picture Herald*, 9/1/60.

CHAPTER TWELVE (pp. 252–69)

1 *An Orderly Man*, p. 204.
2 Nunnally Johnson to George Mercader, 7/10/59 (Nunnally Johnson Collection, Boston University).
3 AF to Laurence Harbottle, 2/11/59.
4 *An Orderly Man*, loc. cit.
5 Dorris Johnson and Ellen Leventhal (eds), *The Letters of Nunnally Johnson*, Knopf, 1981, p. 180.
6 *An Orderly Man*, loc. cit.
7 *Cleared for Take-Off*, p. 155.
8 AF to Laurence Harbottle, 31/12/59.
9 Annakin, op. cit., p. 83.
10 Interview with author.
11 Roy Ward Baker, *The Director's Cut*, Reynolds & Hearn, 2000, p. 110.
12 Interview with author.
13 Et seq., Ward Baker, op. cit., p. 111.
14 John Mills, *Up in the Clouds, Gentlemen Please*, Orion, revised edn, 2001, p. 415.
15 Et seq., interview with author.
16 *The Singer Not the Song* script (BFI Special Collections).
17 Bourne, op. cit., p. 152.
18 Interview with author, *passim*.
19 *The Times*, 6/1/61.
20 *Evening Standard*, 3/1/61.
21 *Paris-presse*, 17/2/62.
22 John Player Lecture, 8/11/70 (BFI).
23 DB to Roy Ward Baker, 8/5/67.
24 *The Independent*, 7/2/03.
25 *Picturegoer*, 29/8/59.
26 DB to John Davis, May 1960 (DBC, Boston).
27 AF to Laurence Harbottle, 5/5/60.
28 Frederick Joachim to DB, 28/6/60 (DBC, Boston).
29 Frederick Joachim to AF, 11/7/60.
30 AF to Frederick Joachim, 12/7/60.
31 *New York Herald Tribune*, 7/8/60.
32 *The Daily Telegraph*, 6/8/60.
33 *Newsweek*, 15/8/60.
34 *The New Yorker*, 20/8/60.
35 *Variety*, 22/6/60.
36 *Snakes and Ladders*, p. 194.
37 Et seq., *Daily Mail*, 26/8/60.
38 Brad Steiger, *Judy Garland*, Ace Star, 1969, p. 110.
39 Paul Bailey, *Three Queer Lives: An Alternative Biography of Fred Barnes, Naomi Jacob and Arthur Marshall*, Hamish Hamilton, 2001, p. 18.

40 Ibid., p. 19.
41 Interview with author.
42 David Shipman, *Judy Garland: The Secret Life of an American Legend*, Hyperion, 1993, p. 379.
43 Nikolaus Pevsner and Elizabeth Williamson, *The Buildings of England: Buckinghamshire*, Penguin, 1960; 1994, p. 178.
44 *Daily Herald*, 23/9/60.
45 *Vanity Fair*, November 2000.
46 Interview with author.
47 *Lyrics for Lovers* sleeve notes (Decca Records, 1960).
48 Interview with author.
49 *Lyrics for Lovers*, loc. cit.
50 Interview with author.
51 AF to Frederick Joachim, 27/3/60.

52 *Daily Herald*, 20/10/60.
53 Ibid., 30/12/60.
54 DB to Clifford Castle, 11/2/67.
55 Internal memo, Decca Record Company, 4/10/81.
56 Telephone interview with author.
57 Interview with author and letter, 29/7/03.
58 John Trevelyan to Michael Relph, 18/5/60 and to Janet Green, 1/7/60 (Janet Green Archive, BFI Special Collections, JG/10/6).
59 Michael Relph to Janet Green and John McCormick, 22/8/60 (Janet Green Archive, op. cit.).
60 DB to Dominique Lambilliotte, 3/9/96.
61 Michael Relph to Janet Green and John McCormick, 2/1/61 (Janet Green Archive, op. cit.).

CHAPTER THIRTEEN (pp. 270–88)

1 *Victim* script (BFI Special Collections).
2 *Films and Filming*, May 1961.
3 John Player Lecture, National Film Theatre, 8/11/70 (BFI).
4 Ibid.
5 Et seq., interview with author.
6 Interview with author.
7 Et seq., Alexander Walker personal diary.
8 Ibid.
9 Interview with author.
10 Interview with author.
11 Alexander Walker diary.
12 Payn and Morley (eds), op. cit., p. 472 (11/6/61).
13 *Snakes and Ladders*, p. 207.
14 Interview with author.
15 J. M. Keith to Laurence Harbottle, 2/4/59.
16 Renata Propper to author, 27/9/03; telephone conversation, 6/10/03.
17 Kenneth Williams, *Just Williams: An Autobiography*, Dent, 1985, p. 63.
18 *Daily Sketch*, 5/10/55.
19 Wynne Godley, 'Saving Masud Khan', *London Review of Books*, 22/2/01.
20 *Snakes and Ladders*, p. 209.

21 Alec Guinness to Merula Guinness, 22/8/61, cited in Read, op. cit., p. 350.
22 *Arena*, op. cit.
23 *The Sunday Times*, 3/9/61.
24 DB to Dilys Powell, 9/9/61.
25 *Evening News*, 31/8/61.
26 *Evening Standard*, 31/8/61.
27 Alexander Walker diary.
28 Letter to *The Guardian*, 7/7/97.
29 Interview with author.
30 National Film Theatre programme, January 1991.
31 Bourne, op. cit., p. 155.
32 Charles Barr (ed.), *All Our Yesterdays: 90 Years of British Cinema*, BFI Publishing, 1986, p. 352.
33 Russell Davies (ed.), *The Kenneth Williams Diaries*, HarperCollins, 1993, p. 175.
34 *Variety*, 9/11/61.
35 Pauline Kael, *I Lost It at the Movies: Film Writings 1954–1965*, Little Brown/Atlantic Monthly Press, 1965, pp. 202–3.
36 Lord Arran to DB, 5/6/68.
37 'Dirk Bogarde in Conversation: Filmed Interview', *Victim* DVD (Carlton International Media).
38 John Player Lecture, op. cit.

39 'Dirk Bogarde in Conversation', op. cit.
40 DB/Sir Laurence Olivier correspondence 11/9/61–7/10/61 (DBC, Boston).
41 *Snakes and Ladders*, p. 169.
42 Interview with author.
43 *Daily Mail*, 4/4/62.
44 Marie-Jaqueline Lancaster (ed.), *Brian Howard: Portrait of a Failure*, Anthony Blond, 1968.
45 DB to Jean Lion, 29/3/80.
46 Ibid.
47 Ronald Neame with Barbara Roisman Cooper, *Straight from the Horse's Mouth*, Scarecrow Press, 2003, p. 178.
48 Ronald Neame – oral history (Academy

Foundation/AMPAS, LA).
49 National Film Theatre talk, 19/10/03.
50 'Somebody's Daughter, Somebody's Son', BBC TV, 23/2/04.
51 Conversation with author.
52 Ronald Neame – oral history.
53 *Snakes and Ladders*, p. 328.
54 Ronald Neame – oral history, and Neame and Roisman Cooper, op. cit., pp. 187–8.
55 *Snakes and Ladders*, p. 220.
56 Neame and Roisman Cooper, op. cit., p. 192.
57 'Somebody's Daughter, Somebody's Son', op. cit.

CHAPTER FOURTEEN (pp. 289–309)

1 DB to Jean Lion, 29/3/80.
2 Interview with author.
3 Miranda Carter, *Anthony Blunt: His Lives*, Macmillan, 2001, p. 322.
4 *The Guardian*, 28/11/02.
5 Joseph Losey to DB, 21/3/60 (Joseph Losey Collection, BFI Special Collections).
6 Caute, op. cit., p. 1.
7 Et seq., Robin Maugham, *Escape from the Shadows*, Hodder & Stoughton, 1972, pp. 9, 177–9.
8 Stephen Mitchell to Joseph Losey, 11/6/56 (Joseph Losey Collection, BFI).
9 Ciment, op. cit., p. 224.
10 *Snakes and Ladders*, p. 229.
11 Michael Billington, *The Life and Work of Harold Pinter*, Faber & Faber, 1996, p. 150.
12 *Snakes and Ladders*, p. 235.
13 James Fox, *Comeback: An Actor's Direction*, Hodder & Stoughton, 1983, p. 10.
14 Ibid., p. 57.
15 Ibid., p. 58.
16 *Isis*, 1/2/64.
17 *Snakes and Ladders*, p. 230.
18 Interview with author, passim.
19 *Arena*, op. cit.
20 *Snakes and Ladders*, p. 234.
21 DB to Joseph Losey, 14/4/74.

22 *Isis*, op. cit.
23 James Fox interview with author; Ciment, op. cit., p. 168.
24 Fred Harris to Joseph Losey, 3/7/63 (Joseph Losey Collection, BFI).
25 Joseph Losey to Leslie Grade, 3/5/63 (Joseph Losey Collection, BFI).
26 *Sunday Express*, 17/11/63.
27 *The Sunday Times*, 17/11/63.
28 *The Daily Telegraph*, 15/11/63.
29 *Sunday Citizen*, 17/11/63.
30 Sarah Miles, *Serves Me Right*, Macmillan, 1994, pp. 85–6.
31 *Cinémonde*, 15/10/63.
32 *Isis*, op. cit.
33 Ibid.
34 Box, op. cit., p. 230.
35 *Sunday Express*, 8/3/64.
36 *Daily Express*, 6/9/63.
37 Interview with author.
38 *The Daily Telegraph*, 3/1/64.
39 *Films and Filming*, November 1963.
40 Lerner, op. cit., p. 150.
41 Interviews with author.
42 *The New York Times*, 15/3/64.
43 AF to Laurence Harbottle, 4/3/64.
44 Ciment, op. cit., p. 245.
45 *King and Country* script (BFI Special Collections).
46 Ibid.

47 Ciment, op. cit., p. 248.
48 Tom Courtenay, *Dear Tom: Letters from Home*, Doubleday, 2000, p. 131.
49 *Liverpool Echo*, 14/7/67.
50 *Snakes and Ladders*, p. 242.
51 Box, op. cit., p. 242.
52 Interview with author.
53 Laurence Harbottle to J. A. D. Fox, 2/6/64.
54 *Sun*, 23/9/64.
55 *Desert Island Discs*, transmitted 28/9/64 (BBC Written Archives).
56 'Frankly Speaking', recorded 23/9/64; transmitted as 'It Takes All Sorts',

16/2/65 (BBC Written Archives).
57 John Schlesinger archive (BFI Special Collections).
58 Douglas Brown, 'Britain's Dolce Vita', *The Sunday Telegraph*, 16/6/63.
59 *Evening Standard*, 2/11/62.
60 Frederic Raphael, *Personal Terms: The 1950s and 1960s*, Carcanet, 2001, pp. 116, 118.
61 DB to John Schlesinger, 14/12/64 (BFI Special Collections).
62 DB to Ann Skinner, 31/7/77.
63 Et seq., interview with author.

CHAPTER FIFTEEN (pp. 310–26)

1 DB to Hedda Hopper, 20/1/65 (Hedda Hopper papers, AMPAS).
2 *Evening Standard*, 4/5/65.
3 Et seq., Ingrid Bergman and Alan Burgess, *Ingrid Bergman: My Story*, Sphere, 1981, pp. 442–4.
4 'Frankly Speaking', op. cit.
5 *Modesty Blaise* continuity notes, May 1965 (Joseph Losey Collection, BFI).
6 Evan Jones to Joseph Losey, July 1965 (Joseph Losey Collection, BFI).
7 DB to Joseph Losey, 22/7/65 (Joseph Losey Collection, BFI).
8 Interview with author.
9 Raphael, op. cit., p. 136.
10 Joseph Losey to Darryl Zanuck, 4/4/66 (Joseph Losey Collection, BFI).
11 Monica Vitti to Darryl Zanuck, 18/3/66.
12 Interview with author.
13 *Sunday Express*, 22/8/65.
14 DB to Editor, *Sunday Express*, 24/8/65.
15 Joseph Losey to DB, 2/11/65 (DBC, Boston).
16 *The Observer*, 19/9/65.
17 *New York Post*, 4/8/65.
18 *New York Herald Tribune*, 4/8/65.
19 *Mail on Sunday*, 22/2/04.
20 *A Particular Friendship*, p. 2.
21 Harold Pinter, Introduction to *Collected Screenplays One*, Faber & Faber, 2000).
22 Ciment, op. cit., p. 261.
23 DB to Dilys Powell, 16/2/67.

24 Michael York, *Travelling Player: An Autobiography*, Headline, 1991, p. 122; interview with author.
25 York, op. cit., p. 123.
26 Ibid., p. 124.
27 Ibid., p. 377.
28 Nicholas Mosley, *Efforts at Truth*, Secker & Warburg, 1994, pp. 164–9.
29 Interview with author, passim.
30 Ciment, op. cit., p. 271.
31 Caute, op. cit., p. 185.
32 Ibid., p. 184.
33 DB to Joseph Losey, 10/9/66 (Joseph Losey Collection, BFI).
34 AF to Joseph Losey, 11/9/66 (Joseph Losey Collection, BFI).
35 DB to Dilys Powell, 16/2/67.
36 *A Particular Friendship*, p. 21.
37 Delphine Seyrig to Joseph Losey, August 1966 (Joseph Losey Collection, BFI).
38 Joseph Losey to Arnold Schulkes 9/9/66 (Joseph Losey Collection, BFI).
39 AF to Laurence Harbottle, 26/4/66.
40 *Variety*, 14/12/66.
41 Janie Hampton (ed.), *Joyce & Ginnie: The Letters of Joyce Grenfell & Virginia Graham*, Hodder & Stoughton, 1997, p. 382.
42 *The New York Times*, 23/3/67.
43 DB to Dilys Powell, 13/5/67.
44 *Snakes and Ladders*, p. 248.
45 *Newsday*, 25/1/68.
46 Interview with author.

CHAPTER SIXTEEN (pp. 327–46)

1 Edward Thompson to DB, 16/12/63.
2 DB to Edward Thompson, 4/1/64.
3 Edward Thompson to DB, 10/1/64.
4 DB to Edward Thompson, 18/1/64.
5 Malcolm Yorke, *Mervyn Peake: My Eyes Mint Gold – a Life*, John Murray, 2000, pp. 317–18.
6 *Saturday Review of Literature*, 14/8/48.
7 Carol Gordon to DB, 3/7/72.
8 *An Orderly Man*, p. 95.
9 Ibid., p. 96.
10 Ibid., p. 103.
11 Ibid., p. 96.
12 Et seq., ibid., p. 100.
13 DB to Joseph Losey, 26/8/67.
14 DB to Joseph Losey, 18/9/67.
15 DB to Joseph Losey, 30/7/67; 12/8/67 (Patricia Losey); Joseph Losey to DB 5/8/67; 27/9/67 (Joseph Losey Collection, BFI).
16 DB to Joseph Losey, 18/9/67; 4/10/67 (Patricia Losey).
17 *A Particular Friendship*, p. 76.
18 Charles Camplin, *John Frankenheimer: A Conversation*, Directors Guild of America/Riverwood Press, 1995.
19 John Player Lecture, 8/11/70 (BFI).
20 Interview with author.
21 Et seq., Bee Gilbert interview with author.
22 *A Particular Friendship*, p. 89.
23 *The Guardian*, 18/8/79.
24 *A Particular Friendship*, pp. 79–80.
25 AF to John Don Fox, 16/3/68.
26 *A Particular Friendship*, p. 113.
27 AF to John Don Fox, 3/5/68.
28 *A Particular Friendship*, p. 139.
29 Ibid., p. 126.
30 DB to Dilys Powell, 28/7/68.
31 AF to Laurence Harbottle, 24/8/68.
32 Interview with author.
33 DB to Dilys Powell, 12/10/68.
34 Interview with author.
35 Interview with author.
36 AF to Joseph Losey, 15/1/69 (Joseph Losey Collection, BFI).
37 Ibid.
38 Interview with author.

CHAPTER SEVENTEEN (pp. 347–63)

1 Interview with author.
2 DB to Joseph Losey, 22/3/69 (Joseph Losey Collection, BFI).
3 DB to Joseph Losey, 26/7/69 (Patricia Losey).
4 DB to Joseph Losey, 12/8/69 (Patricia Losey).
5 Ibid.
6 *Los Angeles Herald-Examiner*, 17/8/69.
7 DB to Joseph Losey, 12/8/69 (Patricia Losey).
8 'Judy: Impressions of Garland' (BBC), 24/12/72.
9 *A Particular Friendship*, pp. 187–90.
10 Gilbert Adair, *The Real Tadzio: Thomas Mann's 'Death in Venice' and the Boy Who Inspired It*, Short Books, 2001, pp. 12–14; 17; 93.
11 Thomas Mann, cited by Joseph O'Leary in *The Times Literary Supplement*, 29/11/02.
12 Laurence Schifano, *Luchino Visconti: The Flames of Passion*, Collins, 1990, pp. 136–7.
13 Ibid., pp. 375–6.
14 DB to the Bowlbys, 22/7/82.
15 Read, op. cit., p. 376.
16 AF to Laurence Harbottle, 3/9/69.
17 AF to Laurence Harbottle, 28/9/69.
18 *An Orderly Man*, p. 3.
19 Ibid., p. 4.
20 Interview with author.
21 DB to Joseph Losey, 15/2/70 (Joseph Losey Collection, BFI).
22 DB to Joseph Losey, 6/3/70 (Joseph Losey Collection, BFI).
23 DB to Joseph Losey, 18/4/70; 11/6/70 (Joseph Losey Collection, BFI).

24 *The Sunday Telegraph*, 22/2/70.
25 Et seq., DB to Joseph Losey, 6/3/70 (Joseph Losey Collection, BFI).
26 DB to Joseph Losey, 15/2/70 (Joseph Losey Collection, BFI).
27 Caute, op. cit., p. 228.
28 'By Myself', 11/1/92 (Lucida Productions).
29 *Show*, May 1970.
30 AF to Laurence Harbottle, 29/4/70.
31 DB to Dilys Powell, 13/5/70.
32 Ibid.
33 AF to Joseph Losey, 11/6/70 (Joseph

Losey Collection, BFI).
34 Peter Adam, *Not Drowning but Waving: An Autobiography*, André Deutsch, 1995, pp. 281–3.
35 Ibid., p. 282.
36 *Vogue*, December 1970.
37 Ibid.
38 *Mail on Sunday*, 26/10/03.
39 *Vogue*, December 1970.
40 DB to Patricia Losey, 25/9/70.
41 Interview with author, passim.

CHAPTER EIGHTEEN (pp. 364–81)

1 *An Orderly Man*, pp. 19–20.
2 DB to Ann Skinner, 1/9/70.
3 DB to Patricia Losey, 25/9/70.
4 DB to Joseph Losey, 18/4/70 (Joseph Losey Collection, BFI).
5 *An Orderly Man*, pp. 121, 122.
6 DB to Patricia Losey, 25/9/70.
7 'Guinness is good for you', *The Guardian*, 14/8/70.
8 Programme to John Player Lecture, 8/11/70 (BFI).
9 Interview with author.
10 *Mail on Sunday*, 26/10/03.
11 *The Daily Telegraph*, 5/3/71.
12 *The Sunday Times*, 7/3/71.
13 *New York Magazine*, 28/6/71.
14 *The New Yorker*, 26/6/71.
15 *The Observer*, 7/3/71.
16 *Variety*, 7/4/71.
17 John Simon, *Something to Declare: Twelve Years of Films from Abroad*, Clarkson N. Potter, 1983, p. 48.
18 DB to the Loseys, 12/6/71 (Joseph Losey Collection, BFI).
19 John Lahr (ed.), *The Diaries of Kenneth Tynan*, Bloomsbury, 2001, p. 311.
20 Read, op. cit., p. 376.
21 Conversation with author.
22 AF to John Don Fox, 5/7/71.
23 DB to Edward Thompson, 15/4/71.
24 Et seq., DB to Edward Thompson, 20/8/71.
25 Interview with author.

26 DB to Edward Thompson, 16/9/71.
27 Edward Thompson to DB, 3/12/71.
28 DB to Edward Thompson, 16/12/71.
29 Angela Fox, *Slightly Foxed – by my theatrical family*, Collins, 1986; Fontana, 1987, pp. 205–7.
30 DB to Penelope Mortimer, 1/12/71 (DBC, Boston).
31 Penelope Mortimer to DB, 29/11/71.
32 DB to Penelope Mortimer, 1/12/71.
33 DB to Penelope Mortimer, 7/12/71.
34 DB to Penelope Mortimer, 21/5/72.
35 Dorothy Gordon to DB, 28/4/72 (DBC, Boston).
36 *A Particular Friendship*, p. 196.
37 DB to Edward Thompson, 17/6/72.
38 DB to Penelope Mortimer, 7/1/73.
39 DB to Edward Thompson, 17/10/72; 11/11/73.
40 Williams, op. cit., p. 218.
41 DB to Penelope Mortimer, 7/1/73.
42 Ibid.
43 Ibid.
44 *An Orderly Man*, p. 143.
45 Ibid., p. 134.
46 *Ecran*, June 1974.
47 *An Orderly Man*, p. 140.
48 DB to Penelope Mortimer, 7/1/73.
49 Interview with author, passim.
50 *An Orderly Man*, pp. 161–72; 182–94.
51 DB to Ann Skinner, 24/7/73.
52 DB to Penelope Mortimer, 30/9/73.
53 DB to Edward Thompson, 10/8/73.

54 AF to Laurence Harbottle, 30/3/75.
55 *Evening Standard*, 17/1/74.
56 *The Sunday Telegraph*, 20/1/74.
57 *The Sunday Times*, 20/1/74.
58 DB to Dilys Powell, 19/1/74.
59 Pauline Kael, *Reeling*, Atlantic/Little,

Brown, 1976, pp. 342–4.
60 *The New York Times*, 17/11/74.
61 John Goodwin (ed.), *Peter Hall's Diaries: The Story of a Dramatic Battle*, Hamish Hamilton, 1983, p. 155.

CHAPTER NINETEEN (pp. 382–403)

1 John Charlton to DB, 1/11/74.
2 *Bookseller*, 27/10/84.
3 Ibid., 20/10/84.
4 DB to John Charlton, 6/12/74.
5 John Charlton to DB, 12/12/74.
6 DB to Penelope Mortimer, 13/12/74.
7 *An Orderly Man*, p. 199.
8 DB to Penelope Mortimer, 13/12/74.
9 *An Orderly Man*, pp. 173–82.
10 DB to Penelope Mortimer, 4/11/73.
11 *House and Garden*, December/January 1975/1976.
12 *Woman's Weekly*, 21/9/74.
13 *An Orderly Man*, p. 217.
14 *Postillion*, p. 91.
15 *An Orderly Man*, p. 219.
16 John Charlton to Norah Smallwood, 16/9/75.
17 DB to John Charlton, 28/10/75.
18 Interview with author.
19 DB to Penelope Mortimer, 8/10/75.
20 DB to Edward Thompson, 28/12/75.
21 DB to Edward Thompson, 15/1/76.
22 DB to Edward Thompson, 25/1/76.
23 DB to Edward Thompson, 13/3/76.
24 DB to John Charlton, 15/2/76.
25 John Charlton to DB, 6/2/76.
26 DB to Penelope Mortimer, 10/6/75.
27 DB to Penelope Mortimer, 8/10/75.
28 DB to Joseph Losey, 31/3/74 (Joseph Losey Collection, BFI).
29 DB to Joseph Losey, 11/4/74 (Joseph Losey Collection, BFI).
30 *The Daily Telegraph*, 24/11/90.
31 *The Sunday Times*, 28/3/76.
32 *An Orderly Man*, pp. 221; 236–7.
33 *Positif*, January 1977.
34 Ibid.
35 DB to Penelope Mortimer, 14/5/76.
36 Interview with author, passim.
37 DB to Penelope Mortimer, 30/6/76.
38 John Gielgud to DB, January 1977 (DBC, Boston).
39 Richard Mangan (ed.), *Gielgud's Letters*, Weidenfeld & Nicolson, 2004, p. 404.
40 Telephone conversation with author.
41 Et seq., *Sunday News* (NY), 8/8/76.
42 DB to Penelope Mortimer, 30/6/76.
43 Major-General R. E. Urquhart with Wilfred Greatorex, *Arnhem*, Cassell, 1958, p. 4.
44 Cornelius Ryan, *A Bridge Too Far*, Hamish Hamilton, 1974, passim.
45 Brian Urquhart, *A Life in Peace and War*, Harper & Row, 1987, pp. 72–3.
46 Margaret Forster, *Daphne du Maurier*, Chatto & Windus, 1994, pp. 393–4.
47 Oriel Malet (ed.), *Letters from Menabilly: Portrait of a Friendship*, Weidenfeld & Nicolson, 1993, pp. 279–80.
48 Forster, op. cit.
49 *The Sunday Times*, 23/10/77.
50 Iain Johnstone, *The Arnhem Report*, Star, 1977, p. 124.
51 DB to Penelope Mortimer, 18/12/76.
52 Ibid.
53 *The Daily Telegraph*, 24/6/77.
54 *The Times*, 25/6/77; 28/6/77; 7/7/77.
55 Forster, op. cit., p. 398.
56 Interview with author.
57 Interview with author.
58 DB to Dilys Powell, 2/7/77.
59 Interview with author.
60 *The Sunday Times*, 30/10/77.
61 Interview with author.

CHAPTER TWENTY (pp. 404–26)

1 AF to Laurence Harbottle, 7/1/77.
2 DB to John Charlton, 26/4/76.
3 DB to John Charlton, 21/8/76.
4 DB to John Charlton, 8/10/76.
5 DB to John Charlton, 17/10/76.
6 *Postillion*, pp. 113–14.
7 DB to John Charlton, 21/8/76.
8 *An Orderly Man*, pp. 252–3.
9 DB to John Charlton, 8/10/76.
10 Interview with author.
11 DB to Norah Smallwood, 15/3/77.
12 *The Daily Telegraph*, 24/3/77.
13 John Knowler to John Charlton, 27/7/76.
14 *Evening Standard*, 29/3/77.
15 *An Orderly Man*, p. 248.
16 Wallace Steadman Watson, 'The Bitter Tears of RWF', *Sight and Sound*, July 1992.
17 *An Orderly Man*, p. 249.
18 DB to Tom Stoppard, 12/12/76 (Harry Ransom Humanities Research Center, University of Texas).
19 Ibid., 18/12/76.
20 *Omnibus* (BBC1), 27/3/83.
21 Ibid.
22 Ronald Hayman, *Fassbinder: Film Maker*, Weidenfeld & Nicolson, 1984, p. 16.
23 Rainer Werner Fassbinder to DB, 20/6/77 (DBC, Boston).
24 DB to Fassbinder, 24/6/77 (*Sight and Sound*, op. cit.).
25 DB to Tom Stoppard, 8/7/77 (HRHRC, University of Texas).
26 DB to Fassbinder, 24/9/77 (*Sight and Sound*, op. cit.).
27 Tom Stoppard to DB, 10/12/77 (DBC, Boston).
28 DB to Wallace Watson, 2/5/91.
29 Wallace Steadman Watson, *Understanding Rainer Werner Fassbinder:*
Film as Private and Public Art, University of South Carolina Press, 1996, pp. 202–3.
30 *An Orderly Man*, p. 264.
31 DB to Ann Skinner, 14/6/78.
32 *Newsweek*, 12/3/79.
33 DB to Dilys Powell, 24/6/77.
34 DB to Ann Skinner, 23/8/78.
35 DB to Ann Skinner, 21/11/78.
36 DB to Laurence Harbottle, 6/10/77.
37 DB to Ann Skinner, 10/8/79.
38 DB to Norah Smallwood, 27/6/79.
39 DB to Laurence Harbottle, 18/10/77.
40 DB to Laurence Harbottle, 11/12/77.
41 Laurence Harbottle to AF, 27/11/78.
42 *Weekend Telegraph Magazine*, 3/6/79, passim.
43 DB to Norah Smallwood, 28/1/78.
44 *Snakes and Ladders*, pp. 1–2.
45 DB to Norah Smallwood, 23/7/77.
46 DB to Norah Smallwood, 21/10/78.
47 *The Sunday Times*, 15/10/78.
48 *Kaleidoscope*, BBC Radio Four, 13/10/78; *Birmingham Post*, 26/10/78.
49 *The Financial Times*, 4/11/78.
50 *The Observer*, 15/10/78.
51 *Le Monde*, 23/12/77.
52 DB to Norah Smallwood, 28/1/78.
53 John Knowler to DB, 15/8/78.
54 *Postillion*, p. 126.
55 DB to Norah Smallwood, 7/7/79.
56 DB to Norah Smallwood, 22/4/78.
57 DB to Norah Smallwood, 28/4/78.
58 James Lees-Milne, *Through Wood and Dale: Diaries, 1975–1978*, John Murray, 1998, pp. 278–9.
59 DB to Norah Smallwood, 21/3/79.
60 Ibid.
61 Ibid.
62 DB to Norah Smallwood, 20/1/79.
63 DB to Norah Smallwood, 21/3/79.

CHAPTER TWENTY-ONE (pp. 427–45)

1 Author's Note, *A Gentle Occupation*.
2 DB to Norah Smallwood, 27/6/79.
3 DB to John Charlton, 28/6/79.
4 *A Gentle Occupation*, p. 279.
5 DB to Norah Smallwood, 27/6/79.
6 DB to Norah Smallwood and

John Charlton, 10/10/79.

7 *A Gentle Occupation*, p. 77.

8 DB to Norah Smallwood, 21/11/79.

9 *An Orderly Man*, p. 278.

10 Foyle's Luncheon transcript, 19/3/80.

11 *Daily Express*, 20/3/80.

12 *The Sunday Times*, 23/3/80.

13 *Now!*, 21/3/80.

14 *The Daily Telegraph*, 20/3/80.

15 *Cleared for Take-Off*, pp. 167–89.

16 DB to Norah Smallwood, 2/4/80.

17 *An Orderly Man*, p. 283.

18 Interview with author.

19 *Daily News* (NY), 15/7/79.

20 DB to Norah Smallwood, 18/10/79.

21 DB to Norah Smallwood, 6/8/79.

22 DB to Norah Smallwood, 26/12/79.

23 DB to Rosalind Bowlby, 19/9/80.

24 DB to Nerine Selwood, 24/2/81.

25 *Voices in the Garden*, p. 13.

26 DB to John Charlton, 28/6/80.

27 *Voices in the Garden*, pp. 216–17.

28 DB to John Charlton, 14/9/80.

29 *Voices in the Garden*, pp. 183, 187.

30 DB to Nicholas Bowlby, 18/10/80.

31 DB to Norah Smallwood, 31/8/80.

32 DB to Norah Smallwood, 27/12/80.

33 *A Particular Friendship*, p. 2.

34 *The Russell Harty Show* (London Weekend Television), 6/11/75.

35 *The Sunday Times*, 15/10/78.

36 Barry Farrell, *Pat and Roald*, Hutchinson, 1970.

37 Interview with author, passim.

38 *An Orderly Man*, p. 286.

39 *Los Angeles Times*, 30/12/80.

40 Roald Dahl to DB, 9/1/81 (DBC, Boston).

41 DB to the Bowlbys, 1/3/81.

42 *Backcloth*, pp. 183–90; 195–213.

43 DB to Norah Smallwood, 19/1/81.

44 Et seq., DB to the Bowlbys, 1/3/81.

45 *Backcloth*, p. 202.

46 Ibid., p. 208.

47 DB to Norah Smallwood, 7/3/81.

48 DB to Norah Smallwood, 15/3/81.

49 DB to the Bowlbys, 1/3/81.

50 DB to the Bowlbys, 30/3/81.

51 DB to Norah Smallwood, 15/3/81.

52 Telephone interview with author.

53 *Backcloth*, p. 209.

54 Roald Dahl to DB, 9/11/81 (DBC, Boston).

55 DB to Laurence Harbottle, 5/8/83.

56 DB to Norah Smallwood, 29/3/81.

57 *The Sunday Times*, 6/9/81.

58 *The Times*, 10/9/81.

59 DB to Norah Smallwood, 12/9/81.

60 *The New York Times*, 18/10/81.

CHAPTER TWENTY-TWO (pp. 446–64)

1 *The Daily Telegraph*, 10/2/98.

2 DB to Norah Smallwood, 29/9/81.

3 Ibid.

4 *Private Eye*, 20/11/81.

5 DB to Norah Smallwood, 22/11/81.

6 DB to Norah Smallwood, 12/8/79.

7 *An Orderly Man*, pp. 268–70.

8 DB to Rosalind Bowlby, 3/2/82.

9 *A Short Walk from Harrods*, p. 237.

10 James Lees-Milne, *Holy Dread: Diaries, 1982–1984*, John Murray, 2001, p. 36.

11 Margaret Drabble, *Arnold Bennett: A Biography*, Weidenfeld & Nicolson, 1974, p. 151.

12 DB to the Bowlbys, 22/7/82.

13 AF to Rosalind Bowlby, 27/10/82.

14 *Backcloth*, pp. 275–6.

15 *Guardian* Film Lecture, 14/2/83 (BFI).

16 *Backcloth*, p. 275.

17 DB to Norah Smallwood, 14/11/82.

18 DB to Norah Smallwood, 30/6/81.

19 DB to Norah Smallwood, 22/9/82.

20 *West of Sunset*, 'blurb'.

21 Ibid., p. 222.

22 Emlyn Williams to DB, 11/4/83.

23 *Omnibus* (BBC1), 27/3/83.

24 DB to Norah Smallwood, 3/10/82.

25 'Bogarde on his best side', *The Times*, 18/3/83.

26 *Time Out*, 13–19/5/83.

27 DB to Norah Smallwood, 28/5/83.
28 DB to Norah Smallwood, 4/7/83.
29 DB to the Bowlbys, 23/11/83.
30 *Libération*, 1/12/83.
31 DB to Norah Smallwood, 4/7/83.
32 *A Short Walk from Harrods*, p. 144.

33 DB to Norah Smallwood, 15/10/83.
34 *A Short Walk from Harrods*, loc. cit.
35 Goodwin (ed.), op. cit., p. 400.
36 Foyle's Luncheon transcript, 28/3/84.
37 Interview with author.

CHAPTER TWENTY-THREE (pp. 465–84)

1 DB to Dilys Powell, 27/4/84.
2 *Backcloth*, p. 291.
3 DB to Norah Smallwood, 3/6/84.
4 AF to Norah Smallwood, 30/5/84.
5 *Backcloth*, p. 294.
6 AF to Norah Smallwood, 30/5/84.
7 DB to the University of Wisconsin, 17/11/82 (Joseph Losey Collection, BFI).
8 DB to Patricia Losey, 22/6/84.
9 *The Guardian*, 28/6/84.
10 DB to Patricia Losey, 25/9/84.
11 *Backcloth*, p. 304.
12 Ibid., p. 255.
13 *An Orderly Man*, p. 147.
14 DB to Norah Smallwood, 4/7/83.
15 DB to Norah Smallwood, 20/11/83.
16 Adrian Turner, *Robert Bolt: Scenes from Two Lives*, Hutchinson, 1998, p. 439.
17 DB to David Puttnam, 3/12/84.
18 DB to the Bowlbys, 8/11/84.
19 *The Scotsman*, 5/7/85.
20 DB to Hélène Bordes, 9/7/85.
21 Ibid.

22 *Backcloth*, p. 308.
23 DB to Hélène Bordes, 23/10/84.
24 ' "Peuple" et "Pays" dans l'*Autobiography de Dirk Bogarde*', from *Trames: Images du Peuple*, University of Limoges, 1985.
25 DB to Hélène Bordes, 23/2/85.
26 DB to Hélène Bordes, 19/2/85.
27 *An Orderly Man*, p. 97.
28 DB to Hélène Bordes, 11/12/85.
29 Ibid.
30 DB to the Bowlbys, 16/6/82.
31 Graham Greene, *Collected Short Stories*, Penguin, 1986, p. 271.
32 'May We Borrow Your Husband?', shooting script (DBC, Boston).
33 *A Short Walk from Harrods*, p. 155.
34 Ibid., p. 154.
35 DB to Hélène Bordes, 7/4/86.
36 DB to Hélène Bordes, 26/5/86.
37 DB to Hélène Bordes, 17/7/86.
38 *Good Housekeeping*, October 1986.
39 Interview with author, passim.
40 'Dirk Bogarde – Above the Title' (Yorkshire Television), 14/9/86, passim.

CHAPTER TWENTY-FOUR (pp. 485–506)

1 *A Short Walk from Harrods*, p. 168.
2 DB to Hélène Bordes, 18/9/86.
3 *A Short Walk from Harrods*, p. 182.
4 Interviews with author.
5 DB to Hélène Bordes, 13/10/86.
6 Interview with author.
7 DB to the Bowlbys, 31/1/87.
8 Telephone interview with author, passim.
9 Interview with author, passim.
10 DB to Hélène Bordes, 23/4/87.
11 Telephone interview with author.

12 *Sunday Express*, 19/7/87.
13 DB to Hélène Bordes, 2/6/87.
14 DB to Hélène Bordes, 21/8/87.
15 DB to Pat Kavanagh, 6/9/87.
16 *The Sunday Times*, 14/2/88.
17 *Daily Mail*, 22/9/87.
18 Rosalind Bowlby interview with author.
19 *A Short Walk from Harrods*, p. 215.
20 Interview with author; *A Short Walk from Harrods*, pp. 230–1.
21 *A Short Walk from Harrods*, p. 221.

22 *Evening Standard*, 10/5/91.

23 Bonnie Derrick to DB, 3/7/91.

24 *Daily Mail*, 23/12/87.

25 DB to Rosalind Bowlby, 28/1/88.

26 DB to Hélène Bordes, 12/2/88.

27 AF to Laurence Harbottle, 30/3/88.

28 DB to Hélène Bordes, 30/4/88.

29 *A Short Walk from Harrods*, pp. 233–4.

30 Ibid., pp. 235–7.

31 Interview with author.

32 Review of Ludovic Kennedy, *Euthanasia: The Good Death*, Chatto CounterBlasts, 1990; *The Sunday Telegraph*, 22/4/90.

33 *Sunday Express*, 19/7/87.

34 DB to Julian Barnes, 11/6/88 (HRHRC, University of Texas).

35 DB to Hélène Bordes, 21/5/88.

36 *The Daily Telegraph*, 2/10/93, passim.

37 *For the Time Being*, Introduction.

38 *The Daily Telegraph*, 2/4/88.

39 *For the Time Being*, loc. cit.

40 *The Independent*, 19/9/88.

41 Interview with author.

42 Interview with author.

43 *A Short Walk from Harrods*, p. 249.

44 *The Times*, 8/10/88.

45 DB to Hélène Bordes, 18/7/88.

46 *A Short Walk from Harrods*, p. 244.

47 *For the Time Being*, pp. 130–40.

48 DB to Hélène Bordes, 18/8/88.

49 Pat Kavanagh to Anthony Rota, 21/7/88.

50 DB to Laurence Harbottle, 18/8/88.

51 Tanitch, p. 94.

52 Interview with author.

53 Telephone interview with author.

54 'Dirk Bogarde – A Tribute' (Thames Television), 13/10/88.

55 *A Short Walk from Harrods*, p. 237.

56 *Hello!*, 22/10/88.

57 Interview with author, passim.

58 Interview with author.

59 DB to Laurence Harbottle, 8/8/89.

60 *The Daily Telegraph*, 9/9/89.

61 *The Spectator*, 14/10/89.

62 *Literary Review*, October 1989.

63 Interview with author.

CHAPTER TWENTY-FIVE (pp. 507–26)

1 *The Independent on Sunday*, 28/1/90.

2 *The Sunday Telegraph*, 5/5/91; DB typescript (publication untraced).

3 Interview with author, passim.

4 DB to Laurence Harbottle, 10/2/89.

5 Bee Gilbert interview with author.

6 DB to Bertrand Tavernier, 19/7/89.

7 *A Short Walk from Harrods*, pp. 260–1.

8 Odette Laure, *Aimer, rire et chanter*, Flammarion, 1997, p. 262.

9 *The Sunday Telegraph*, 5/5/91.

10 *Interview*, January 1991.

11 *New York*, 29/4/91.

12 *The Independent on Sunday*, 28/1/90.

13 *Positif*, September 1990.

14 Cited in Jean-Claude Raspiengeas, *Bertrand Tavernier*, Flammarion, 2001, p. 375.

15 *New York*, 29/4/91.

16 DB to Bertrand Tavernier, 3/11/89.

17 Letter to author, 27/5/03.

18 *The Sunday Telegraph*, 22/4/90.

19 Telephone interview with author.

20 Foreword to Carolyn Faulder, *A Special Gift: The Story of Dr Vicky Clement-Jones and the Foundation of BACUP*, Michael Joseph, 1991.

21 *The Sunday Telegraph*, 22/4/90.

22 *The Daily Telegraph*, 16/7/91.

23 Richard Eyre, *National Service: Diary of a Decade*, Bloomsbury, 2003, p. 109.

24 Interview with author.

25 *Evening Standard*, 10/5/91.

26 DB to Hélène Bordes, 14/5/90.

27 Ibid.

28 Pat Kavanagh to DB, 17/7/90.

29 DB to Bertrand Tavernier, 18/7/90.

30 DB to Pat Kavanagh, 18/7/90.

31 DB to the Bowlbys, 12/6/90.

32 *The Independent on Sunday*, 30/9/90.

33 John Osborne to DB, 22/10/90 (DBC, Boston).

34 DB to John Osborne, 24/10/90.

35 Interview with author, passim.

36 *Interview,* January 1991.

37 DB to Hélène Bordes, 12/10/90; 22/2/92.

38 *Jericho,* p. 106.

39 Ibid., p. 145.

40 Et seq., letter to author, 27/9/03.

41 *The Daily Telegraph,* 10/8/91; 5/9/91.

42 DB to Anthony Seldon, 2/9/91.

43 Telephone interview with author.

44 DB to Anthony Seldon, 21/6/91.

45 *For the Time Being,* p. 221.

46 DB to Edward Towne, 4/2/92.

47 *Kent Today,* 15/5/92.

48 Telephone conversation with author.

49 *Cleared for Take-Off,* p. 230.

50 *The London Gazette,* 31/12/91.

51 DB to Dennis Rendell, 11/2/92.

52 Interview with author.

53 *The Daily Telegraph,* 25/3/92.

54 Interview with author, passim.

55 Interview with author.

56 Interview with author.

57 Mangan (ed.), op. cit., p. 484.

58 *The Daily Telegraph,* 28/9/93.

59 Olivier Theatre, 20/3/92 (RNT Archive), passim.

60 DB to Penelope Mortimer, 19/9/91.

CHAPTER TWENTY-SIX (pp. 527–40)

1 DB to Penelope Mortimer, 19/9/91.

2 Alec Guinness, *My Name Escapes Me: The Diary of a Retiring Actor,* Hamish Hamilton, 1996, p. 28.

3 Telephone conversation with author.

4 DB to Norah Smallwood, 18/10/79.

5 DB to Penelope Mortimer, 5/2/92, 7/9/92.

6 DB to Penelope Mortimer, 7/9/92.

7 *The Sunday Telegraph,* 27/9/92.

8 *The Daily Telegraph,* 3/10/92.

9 *The Sunday Times,* 11/10/92.

10 *Sussex Life,* October 1992.

11 DB to Penelope Mortimer, 6/10/92.

12 Interview with author.

13 *The Daily Telegraph,* 9/10/93.

14 *The Sunday Times,* 17/10/93.

15 *The Spectator,* 9/10/93.

16 DB to Hélène Bordes, 7/9/93; 10/9/93.

17 DB to Hélène Bordes, 6/1/94.

18 DB to Christiaan De Forche, 31/12/93.

19 DB to Philippe Van den Bogaerde, 31/12/93.

20 DB to Christiaan De Forche, 3/2/94.

21 Mangan (ed.), op. cit., p. 486.

22 DB to Lord Attenborough, 27/6/93.

23 Et seq., 'The Reason Why', programme note for *The Merry Widow,* July 1993.

24 *The Times,* 20/7/93.

25 Ibid., 24/9/94.

26 *A Period of Adjustment,* pp. 74, 125, 172.

27 *Evening Standard,* 19/9/94.

28 *The Daily Telegraph,* 8/10/94.

29 DB to Daphne Fielding, 19/10/93.

30 *The Independent on Sunday,* 29/10/95.

31 *The Daily Telegraph,* 7/10/95.

32 *The Sunday Telegraph,* 8/10/95.

33 *Cleared for Take-Off,* p. 166.

34 DB to Penelope Mortimer, 19/9/91.

35 Interview with author, passim.

36 DB to Hélène Bordes, 23/2/96.

37 *The Daily Telegraph,* 6/3/99.

38 *The Sunday Times,* 31/5/98.

39 Et seq., *The Daily Telegraph,* 6/6/98.

40 *For the Time Being,* Penguin edn, 1999, p. xix.

41 *Closing Ranks,* p. 127.

EPILOGUE (pp. 541–9)

1 *The Observer,* 9/5/99.

2 *The Independent,* 10/5/99.

3 *The Spectator,* 15/5/99.

4 *The Independent,* 10/5/99.

5 *Private Eye,* 14/5/99.

6 Martin Amis, *Yellow Dog,* Cape, 2003.

7 Maggie Gee, *The White Family*, Saqi
   Books, 2002, p. 25.
8 http://groups.yahoo.com/group/
   Dirk_Bogarde_Brigade.
9 *Mail on Sunday*, 27/2/2000.
10 Interview with author.

11 *Radio Times*, 8–14/12/01.
12 'The Private Dirk Bogarde' (BBC2),
    26/12/01.
13 Olivier Theatre, 9/10/95 (RNT Archive).
14 *Weekend Telegraph Magazine*, 3/6/79.
15 *Jericho*, p. 109.

Appendices

CHRONOLOGY

1. Plays

	PLAY	ROLE	THEATRE
1938	*Alf's Button*	Lance-Corporal Greenstock	Derek Hall, Newick
1939	*Babes in the Wood*	Sir Maltravers Goodman	Newick
	Journey's End	Raleigh	Newick
	Mrs Biddlecombe & *the Furriners*	Ernie Saunders	Newick
	Glorious Morning	Leman	Thornburn Playhouse, Uckfield
1940	*Dark Comfort*	Robert Kemp	Newick
	When We Are Married	Fred Dyson	Q
	Little Ladyship	Graves	Q
	Cornelius	Lawrence	Q/Embassy
	Murder by Night-Light	Vojin	Richmond Theatre
	Saloon Bar	Fred	Q
	Grouse in June	Joe Baker	Playhouse, Amersham

(June–Dec.) Twelve further plays with the Playhouse repertory company

	PLAY	ROLE	THEATRE
	Cornelius	Lawrence	Westminster
1941	*Diversion No. 2*	Various	Wyndham's

1941–3 Army productions including *Judgment Day, Rope, Journey's End, The Little Revue*

	PLAY	ROLE	THEATRE
1947	*Power Without Glory*	Cliff	New Lindsey/Fortune
1948	*For Better, For Worse*	Tony	Q
1949	*Foxhole in the Parlor*	Dennis Patterson	New Lindsey
	Sleep on My Shoulder	Simon	Q
1950	*The Shaughraun*	Captain Molineux	Bedford
	Point of Departure	Orpheus	Theatre Royal, Brighton/ Lyric, Hammersmith/Duke of York's
1952	*The Vortex*	Nicky Lancaster	Theatre Royal, Brighton/Lyric, Hammersmith

PLAY	ROLE	THEATRE
1955 *Summertime*	Alberto	Tour/Apollo
1958 *Jezebel*	Marc	Oxford Playhouse/Theatre Royal, Brighton

2. Films

	FILM	ROLE	DIRECTOR
1939	*Come on George!*	Extra	Anthony Kimmins
1947	*Dancing with Crime*	Police radio caller	John Paddy Carstairs
1948	*Esther Waters*	William Latch	Ian Dalrymple & Peter Proud
	Quartet ('The Alien Corn')	George Bland	Harold French
	Once a Jolly Swagman	Bill Fox	Jack Lee
1949	*Dear Mr Prohack*	Charles Prohack	Thornton Freeland
	Boys in Brown	Alfie Rawlings	Montgomery Tully
1950	*The Blue Lamp*	Tom Riley	Basil Dearden
	So Long at the Fair	George Hathaway	Terence Fisher
	The Woman in Question	Robert 'Bob' Baker	Anthony Asquith
1951	*Blackmailed*	Stephen Mundy	Marc Allégret
1952	*Hunted*	Chris Lloyd	Charles Crichton
	Penny Princess	Tony Craig	Val Guest
	The Gentle Gunman	Matt Sullivan	Basil Dearden
1953	*Appointment in London*	Wg/Cdr Tim Mason	Philip Leacock
	Desperate Moment	Simon van Halder	Compton Bennett
1954	*They Who Dare*	Lt David Graham	Lewis Milestone
	Doctor in the House	Simon Sparrow	Ralph Thomas
	The Sleeping Tiger	Frank Clements	Joseph Losey
	For Better, For Worse	Tony	J. Lee Thompson
	The Sea Shall Not Have Them	Flt Sgt Mackay	Lewis Gilbert
1955	*Simba*	Alan Howard	Brian Desmond Hurst
	Doctor at Sea	Dr Simon Sparrow	Ralph Thomas
	Cast a Dark Shadow	Edward Bare	Lewis Gilbert
1956	*The Spanish Gardener*	José Santero	Philip Leacock
1957	*Ill Met by Moonlight*	Major Patrick Leigh Fermor	Michael Powell
	Doctor at Large	Dr Simon Sparrow	Ralph Thomas
	Campbell's Kingdom	Bruce Campbell	Ralph Thomas

* Because the definition of 'release' is blurred, the year given is that of the first UK national press screening.

	FILM	ROLE	DIRECTOR
1958	*A Tale of Two Cities*	Sydney Carton	Ralph Thomas
	The Wind Cannot Read	Flt Lt Michael Quinn	Ralph Thomas
1959	*The Doctor's Dilemma*	Louis Dubedat	Anthony Asquith
	Libel	Sir Mark Loddon/Frank Welney/Number Fifteen	Anthony Asquith
1960	*Song Without End*	Franz Liszt	Charles Vidor and George Cukor
1961	*The Singer Not the Song*	Anacleto Comachi	Roy Ward Baker
	The Angel Wore Red (*La sposa bella*)	Arturo Carrera	Nunnally Johnson
	Victim	Melville Farr	Basil Dearden
1962	*HMS Defiant*	Lt Scott-Padget	Lewis Gilbert
	The Password Is Courage	Sgt-Major Charles Coward	Andrew L. Stone
	We Joined the Navy	Dr Simon Sparrow (cameo)	Wendy Toye
1963	*The Mind Benders*	Dr Henry Longman	Basil Dearden
	I Could Go On Singing	David Donne	Ronald Neame
	Doctor in Distress	Dr Simon Sparrow	Ralph Thomas
	The Servant	Barrett	Joseph Losey
1964	*Hot Enough for June*	Nicolas Whistler	Ralph Thomas
	King and Country	Captain Hargreaves	Joseph Losey
1965	*The High Bright Sun*	Major McGuire	Ralph Thomas
	Darling	Robert Gold	John Schlesinger
1966	*Modesty Blaise*	Gabriel	Joseph Losey
1967	*Accident*	Stephen	Joseph Losey
	Our Mother's House	Charlie Hook	Jack Clayton
1968	*Sebastian*	Sebastian	David Greene
1969	*Oh! What a Lovely War*	Stephen	Richard Attenborough
	Justine	Pursewarden	Joseph Strick and George Cukor
	The Fixer	Bibikov	John Frankenheimer
1970	*The Damned* (*La caduta degli dei*)	Friedrich Bruckmann	Luchino Visconti
1971	*Death in Venice* (*Morte a Venezia*)	Gustav von Aschenbach	Luchino Visconti
1974	*The Serpent*	Philip Boyle	Henri Verneuil
	The Night Porter (*Il portiere di notte*)	Max	Liliana Cavani
1975	*Permission to Kill*	Alan Curtis	Cyril Frankel

	FILM	ROLE	DIRECTOR
1977	*A Bridge Too Far*	Lt-Gen. Frederick Browning	Richard Attenborough
1978	*Providence*	Claud Langham	Alain Resnais
	Despair	Hermann Hermann	Rainer Werner Fassbinder
1991	*These Foolish Things* (*Daddy Nostalgie*)	Daddy	Bertrand Tavernier

Dirk also narrated two documentaries for cinema release: *Exile* (1965) and *Return to Lochaber* (1968).

3. Television

*	TITLE	ROLE	BROADCASTER
1947	*Rope*	Charles Granillo	BBC
	Power Without Glory	Cliff	BBC
	The Case of Helvig Delbo	Jan	BBC
1964	*Little Moon of Alban*	Lt Kenneth Boyd	NBC
1965	*The Epic That Never Was*	Narrator	BBC
1966	*Blithe Spirit*	Charles Condomine	NBC
1973	*Upon This Rock*	Reader (as Bonnie Prince Charlie)	NBC
1981	*The Patricia Neal Story*	Roald Dahl	CBS
1983	*Schindler*	Narrator	Thames
1985	*Le plus grand musée* (Louvre documentary)	Co-presenter	TFI
1986	*May We Borrow Your Husband?* (also screenplay)	William	Yorkshire
1988	*The Vision*	James Marriner	BBC

A Franco-British production of *Voices in the Garden*, scripted by Lee Langley and directed by Pierre Boutron, was screened by the BBC in 1993.

---

* Date of first known transmission in the UK or the country of production.

DIRK'S *DESERT ISLAND DISCS*

28 September 1964 with Roy Plomley

1. Liszt's Consolation in D flat played by Jorge Bolet
2. Oscar Straus's 'C'est la saison d'amour' from *Les trois valses*, sung by Yvonne Printemps
3. Liszt's Piano Concerto No. 1 in E flat and 'Hungarian Fantasy', played by Jorge Bolet with the Los Angeles Philharmonic Orchestra (Stoloff)
4. Gordon Jenkins's 'The Worst Kind of Man', sung by Judy Garland, from LP *The Letter*
5. 'Vilja' from Lehár's *The Merry Widow*, sung by Elisabeth Schwarzkopf with the Philharmonia Orchestra (Matacic)
6. Beethoven's Symphony No. 5 in C minor, played by the Columbia Symphony Orchestra (Walter)
7. 'Hello Dolly' from Jerry Herman's *Hello Dolly*, sung by Carol Channing
8. 'I've Grown Accustomed to Her Face' from Lerner and Loewe's *My Fair Lady*, sung by Rex Harrison – but not broadcast, because Dirk and Plomley ran out of time

Outright choice: the Beethoven
Book: *The Swiss Family Robinson* by Johann David Wyss
Luxury object: 'Conversation Piece', John Singer Sargent's painting of the Sitwells

31 December 1989 with Sue Lawley

1. Finale of Act Two of Puccini's *Tosca*, sung by Maria Callas and Tito Gobbi
2. 'La fileuse', played by Yvonne Arnaud with string orchestra conducted by Sir John Barbirolli, from LP *Glorious John*
3. Third movement of Franck's Symphony in D minor, played by the Berlin Philharmonic Orchestra (Giulini)
4. 'Je t'aime', from LP *Les triomphes d'Yvonne Printemps*
5. Fourth movement of Mahler's Fifth Symphony, played by the New York Philharmonic Orchestra (Bernstein)
6. Liszt's Piano Concerto No. 1 in E flat, played by Lazar Berman with the Vienna Symphony Orchestra (Giulini)
7. Richard Strauss's *Der Rosenkavalier*, played by the Vienna Philharmonic Orchestra (Maazel)
8. 'New York, New York', played by the Boston Pops Orchestra (Williams)

Outright choice: the Mahler (theme music to *Death in Venice*)
Book: *Akenfield* by Ronald Blythe
Luxury object: A distillery

WHAT THEY SAID ABOUT DIRK...

'Dirk fought the system and he carries scars, but I would say that he has won.' – Joseph Losey

'His Life was all made up, you know.' – John Gielgud

'He was a rascal.' – Sheila MacLean

'He was curious, like a cat.' – Patricia Losey

'I always thought he would go into comedy, dressing up as somebody quite different from what he was.' – Lally

'... a great believer in long distance and remote devotion.' – Penelope Mortimer

'I both disliked and loved him. There were times when I could cheerfully have throttled him.' – Barbara Murray

'He was there be be chastised.' – Frank Hauser

'He was most at one with himself after lunch. He would get out his wheelbarrow, and put on his gardening gear. You would hear him whistling away' – Gareth Forwood

'I was in awe of him because I was very new to the game, but I realised what a wonderful actor he was. It was all to do with the simplicity of his work. No tricks, no gimmicks. It wasn't acting, it was being. You see it all in the eyes.' – Jean Simmons

'He had to use his wit, and his very alert and very astute brain, to combat anyone who had had a formal education.' – Nerine Selwood

'He was really out of his century. I would have put him in the sixteenth, not even the seventeenth. Or maybe he would have been part of the Spanish Inquisition: he would have done well there!' – Glynis Johns

'He flaunted his ability to conceal his inferiority.' – Bill Lockie

'Dirk had a lot of guilt in him and he carried it around like a sort of knapsack. And yet, when you pinned it down, there was nothing really for him to feel guilty about at all.' – Sheridan Morley

'Dirk was an elusive butterfly.' – Denis Quilley

'Dirk was very like J. M. Barrie: he had a passion for young beauty, be it male or female.' – Bee Gilbert

'Introspection on screen was his speciality.' – Gore Vidal

'... he had a very good quiet style altogether and was, or so it seemed, utterly unspoiled and unstagey and genuine'. – Patrick Leigh Fermor

'He was full of umbrage and dudgeon.' – John Fraser

'Dirk's life was full of broken seams.' – Judith Aller

'All Dirk's absences added up to a presence on the screen.' – Frederic Raphael

'He wanted to be around people who were challenging.' – Adam Low

'He had to have a secret garden. It's something to do with our business.' – Sheila Attenborough

'You felt protective towards him even if you did not know him personally.' – Cheryl Young

'He was a soul in incredible torment, though his books helped enormously.' – Charlotte Rampling

'He was profoundly romantic. He had a sincere belief in the best of human nature.' – Glenda Jackson

'I think Dirk always felt in some way slightly deracinated: he was an Englishman but yet he wasn't.' – Alexander Walker

'He was one of the most gracious and charming people you could meet, but I always felt there was profound unhappiness inside him. Whether that was entirely due to his personal situation or whether it was something that was part of his restless spirit, I don't know.' – Peter Hall

'I never believed more than one sentence of what Dirk wrote.' – Glynis Johns

'He knew the quality of stillness.' – Bryan Forbes

(On Dirk's screen clinches) 'He had that wonderful ability to appear on the point of vomiting – extreme nausea manfully repressed.' – Nick Mason

'He liked to unsettle you.' – Tony Lacey

'He was a romantic and he lived with dreams.' – Cornel Lucas

'He liked to see people, but he also liked them to *go*.' – Søren Fischer

'He tried to be an ordinary man: he never repulsed people by his intellectual superiority. He was very attentive to the most intimate desires of people whom he liked.' – Léon Loschetter

'He always admired anybody who did their job well, whatever that job was.' – Amanda Saunders

'I think he was very AC/DC when he was young. It's such a shame: he would have made a wonderful husband.' – Kitty Black

'There are many people with a public and a private face. Dirk had more public faces than most.' – Dr Barrington Cooper

'Dirk had a very vivid, very dazzling personality; he was gifted with intelligence and imagination and sensitivity in his work.' – Paul Scofield

'If it was all an act, it was a great act, carried off with enormous thespian skill. But at what cost?' – Michael York

'He played roles that were the complete opposite of his character.' – Anton Troxler

'He knew far more about gardening than most of the people queuing at Chelsea Flower Show.' – Philippa, Lady Astor

'He was in love with beauty, and loved to be surrounded by beautiful things.' – Sylvia Syms

'He did evolve and grow. Some people just stop.' – Helena Bonham Carter

'He didn't take to Safeway's at all. Not one bit.' – Jill ('Maude') Melford

'In Dirk was all the world.' – Hélène Bordes

... AND ABOUT DIRK AND TONY

'It was a marriage like few are.' – Mary Dodd

'I felt Dirk touched happiness sometimes: Tony was where the happiness came from.' – Charlotte Rampling

'They were happy together and they shared it with their friends.' – Glynis Johns

'My father subjugated his own ego.' – Gareth Forwood

'There was a respect for the other's space, and that sounds like a very perfect marriage to me.' – Faith Brook

A RECIPE FROM DIRK

Chicken Clermont
(Perhaps *poulet* would sound better?)

WHAT YOU NEED

One deep, oven-proof, lidded, casserole
One plump chicken. Preferably NOT
battery.
Four firm leeks
Four firm endive (chicory)
A good fat spray of tarragon and thyme

Dessert spoon brown sugar
Half-pint white wine
One lemon
Three cloves garlic
Two tablespoons olive oil
Salt/pepper

WHAT YOU DO

Un-truss chicken. Stuff with halved lemon and halved garlics.

Cut leeks and endive into two-inch pieces. Make a bed on casserole bottom. Spread herbs liberally, and sugar. Salt and pepper them.

Set chicken, stuffed with lemon and garlic bits, on top. Pour wine all around. Sprinkle the olive oil all over the bird. Cover pan and bake in oven (400°F or 200°C. Gas 6.) *undisturbed* for 45 mins.

Remove lid and cook on another 15 mins, or until the bird is golden brown and cooked through. Add a titch of water to the sauce *if* it has evaporated fully. You should have a decent sauce at the end of the cooking. And that is that! Remove, carve and enjoy!

Good with guinea fowl too . . . better almost. Tarragon is best. And don't be mingy with the herbs. Serve with plain boiled taters.

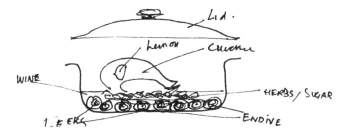

Author's note: Dirk taught himself to cook using Elizabeth David's *French Provincial Cooking.*

Index

Writings by Dirk Bogarde (DB) appear under title; works by others under author's name

Abeles, Arthur, 296
Academy of Motion Picture Arts and Sciences, 310–11
Accident (film), 14, 17, 294, 317–22, 323, 331
'Achilles Affair, The' (proposed film), 299, 340
Achilleus (liner), 208–9
Acropole (French publishing house), 460
Ad Lib Club, 304–5, 307
Adair, Gilbert, 351
Adam, Peter, 359–60
Adam's Farm, Sussex, 317, 325, 329–30, 337, 339–41, 344, 346
Adderley, John, 229
Adler, Buddy, 260
Adrian, Max, 82, 305
Adventures of Harry Dickson, The (film), 318
Agate, James, 82, 156
Aimée, Anouk, 189, 344
Aitken, Matt, 262n
Aitken, Sir Max, 339
Albery, Bronson, 79
Alexandra, Princess, 339, 418
Alfriston, Sussex, 46, 65
All Quiet on the Western Front (film), 198; *see also* Remarque, Erich Maria
Allan Glen's School, Glasgow, 56–7, 61–3
Allen Lane/Penguin Press, 455, 462
Allen, Captain Sydney, 112, 116–17, 120
Allen, Woody, 416
Aller, Judith, 246
Aller, Victor, 246–8
Allied Central Interpretation Unit, 103
Allied Film Makers, 268
Alpar, Gitta, 86–7
Alta (French publishing house), 423
Altaras, Jonathan, 472–3, 515, 524, 526
Altman, Robert, 442
Amersham Film Society, 230
Amersham Playhouse, 81–4, 88
Amis, Martin: *Yellow Dog*, 545
Anderson, Michael, 292
Anderson, Robert, 437
Andresen, Björn, 356, 361, 367
Andrews, Eamonn, 212

Angel, Danny, 286
Angel Wore Red, The (film; earlier 'The Fair Bride'), 252–3, 255
Annakin, Ken, 157, 179, 193, 254
Anne, Princess Royal, 367, 502–3
Anne of the Thousand Days (film), 356
Another Country (film), 467
Anouilh, Jean: *Jezebel* (play), 241; *Point of Departure* (earlier *Eurydice*), 190–2, 216
Antwerp, 531
Appointment in London (film), 195–6, 198
Arena: 'The Private Dirk Bogarde' (TV programme), 546
Ark Royal, HMS, 102
Arnaud, Yvonne, 63
Arnhem, battle of 'Operation Market-Garden', 396–402
Arnold, Eve, 315, 344
Arran, Arthur Archibald Gore, 8th Earl of ('Boofy'), 282, 318
Asher, Jane, 304
Ashmore, Peter, 190
Asquith, Anthony ('Puffin'), 188, 226, 236–8, 240, 311
Assassination of Trotsky, The (film), 369, 371
Astor, Philippa, Lady, 264
'At Santa Monica' (DB; poem), 371
Atkins, Dame Eileen, 489–90, 496
Attenborough, Charlotte, 481
Attenborough, Richard, Baron: and DB's fantasism, 5; in film *Dancing with Crime*, 166; with Rank, 179; plays in *Boys in Brown*, 180; co-founds Allied Film Makers, 268; and *A Bridge Too Far*, 295–8, 402; and *Gandhi* film, 311; films *Oh! What a Lovely War*, 346; and Clermont, 365, 395, 476, 480; DB blames for *A Bridge Too Far*, 401–2; entertains DB in Paris, 488; awards DB British Film Institute Fellowship, 492; and BAFTA's offer of award to DB, 502; and Sussex University's award of honorary doctorate to DB, 532
Attenborough, Sheila, Lady *see* Sim, Sheila
Aubert, Jean-Pierre, 379, 432
Auden, W.H., 433
Axford, Thomas, 48
Aylmer, Felix, 240

Babes in the Wood (pantomime), 69–71
Babington Smith, Constance, 103, 128–9
Bacall, Lauren, 4, 300–1, 495, 539
Bachardy, Don, 455
Backcloth (DB): frontispiece and illustrations, 40, 132; on Belsen, 122; on life in Batavia, 139; and DB's views on end of Empire, 140; on California, 439–40; on DB's *Guardian* Film Lecture, 454; on Cannes Film Festival awards, 467; on Nora Smallwood's health decline, 469; writing, 475, 477, 483; publication, 480, 486–7; on hermit-crab syndrome, 484; success, 487; paperback edition, 491
BACUP (cancer charity), 502, 512
Baddeley, Hermione, 241, 257
Bahamas, 332, 335
Bailey, Paul, 261
Baird, Teddy, 237
Baker, George, 301
Baker, Roy Ward, 254–5, 257–8
Baker, Stanley, 179, 229, 250, 320–1
Balchin, Nigel, 255
Baldock, Stuart, 458–9, 482
Baldwin, James, 369
Ballhaus, Michael, 415
Bamber, Helen, 123
Bandol, France, 508–9
Barber, Lynn, 491, 497
Bardot, Brigitte, 208–10, 222, 298
Barker, Felix, 379
Barker, Frank Granville, 214
Barker, Ronald, 213
Barnes, Julian, 497–8
Barr, Robert, 169
Barrault, Jean-Louis, 191
Barrett, Jane, 166
Batavia, 134–40, 146
Bates, Alan, 18, 308, 331, 333, 437–8
Batsford Gallery, London, 124–5, 143
Baxter, Brian, 261, 366–7
Baxter, Keith, 368, 534
Bay, John, 394
Baylis, Lilian, 77
Beaton, Sir Cecil, 8
Beatty, Robert, 188
Beaumont, Hugh ('Binkie'): power and influence, 10; and Kitty Black, 190; rejects Maugham's *The Servant*, 292
Beaverbrook, William Maxwell Aitken, 1st Baron, 280
Bedford Theatre, Camden Town, 187–8
Beel House: DB buys and occupies, 205–6, 210, 220; protective mound built ('bastion'), 239–40; redecorated, 241; DB's growing disenchantment with, 249–50; DB sells, 253, 261
Beer, Patricia: *The Postillion Was Struck by Lightning*, 423
Bell, Michael, 213
Bell, Rosalind *see* Bowlby, Rosalind
Bellew, Sir George, 316

Bellew, Laurie, 216
Bells Are Ringing (stage musical), 225
Belsen, 121–3, 483, 519–20
Bendrose Film Productions Ltd, 217, 241, 304; wound up, 378
Bendrose House, Buckinghamshire, 85, 186–90, 194, 197
Bennett, Arnold: *Buried Alive*, 451; *Dear Mr Prohack*, 185
Bennett, S.E. Holland, 162
Benois, Nadia, 78
Bentham, Trevor, 11
Berenson, Marisa, 363
Berger, Helmut, 343, 391, 422
Bergman, Ingrid, 312, 315, 345; death, 469
Beriosova, Svetlana, 278
Bernstein, Walter, 248
Besch, Joseph, 352
Betjeman, Sir John, 81
Betti, Ugo: *Summertime*, 213, 217
Betts, Sally, 388, 420, 425, 523
Bilbow, Tony, 453
Billington, Michael, 292
Billington, Norman ('Harold Quigley'), 188, 295
Billington, Rachel, 445
Billy Liar (film), 265
Birchens Spring *see* Drummers Yard
Birkin, David, 509
Birkin, Jane, 508–10, 536–7
Bismarck (German battleship), 129
Bissett, Jacqueline, 472
Biziou, Peter, 467
Black, Kitty, 190–1, 243, 304
Black Knight, The (film), 357
Black, Rivka, 72
Black, Vivienne, 160–1
Blake, Fanny, 471, 480, 530, 536–7
Blond, Anthony, 304
Bloom, Claire, 370
Blue Lamp, The (film), 181–2
Blunt, Anthony, 290
Blythe, Ronald, 529; *Akenfield*, 512
Board of Deputies of British Jews, 520
Boatwright, Alice Lee ('Boaty'), 301
Bogaerde, family Van den, 24–5, 531
Bogaerde, Aimé Van den (Amatus; DB's grandfather): life and career, 25–8; death, 29; reappearance, 50; urges DB to observe, 65, 103; burial, 69; and family history, 532
Bogaerde, Alice Van den (Gareth's daughter), 13, 527
Bogaerde, Brock Van den (DB's nephew): and DB's friends, 15; examines DB's clothes, 18; meets Fassbinder with DB, 414; stays with DB at Clermont, 417; persuades DB to film 'May We Borrow Your Husband?', 480; and DB's party at the Lancaster, 488; and DB's late medical problems, 536–7; and DB's funeral arrangements, 541–2, 548–9; benefits under DB's will, 544; and Tony's home movies, 546

Bogaerde, Elizabeth Van den (DB's sister) *see* Goodings, (Margaret) Elizabeth

Bogaerde, Emil Van den, 24; death, 31

Bogaerde, Gareth Van den (DB's brother): on DB's apprehensions, 17; finds grandfather's burial place, 25; writes on grandfather Aimé, 26–7; birth, 49, 53; DB hurts as child, 65; and DB's call-up into Army, 91; admires Jack Jones, 101–2; and US soldiers in war, 106–7; meets DB on return from Far East, 153; plays film part as youth, 173; lodges with DB in Chester Row, 184–5; on DB at Bendrose House, 189; in Rome, 253; career, 276–7; dyslexia, 276; relations with DB, 276–7, 332, 487; marriage collapse, 315; informs DB of father's death, 374; rejects DB's proposal to act as guardian to Brock, 417; and Elizabeth's looking after mother, 431; at mother's funeral, 432; helps DB move from Clermont, 487; and DB's paralysis of leg, 493; and DB's knighthood, 521; children, 527; and family roots in Izegem, 532; on DB's propensity to cruelty, 546

Bogaerde, Grace Lizzie (*née* Clark; DB's grandmother), 26–8

Bogaerde, Jacqueline Van den (Rupert's wife), 479, 494–5, 527

Bogaerde, Joseph Van den (ancestor), 24

Bogaerde, Jules Van den (DB's great-grandfather), 25

Bogaerde, Julianus Van den, 25

Bogaerde, Julie Van den (DB's great-grandmother), 25

Bogaerde, Kim Van den (Brock's wife), 537, 541–2

Bogaerde, Lucilla Van den (Gareth's wife), 374, 387, 496

Bogaerde, Margaret Van den (*née* Niven; DB's mother): and birth of DB, 23–4, 541; and Aimé, 28–9; background and career, 34–5, 37–8; and husband's work at *The Times*, 34; birth, 35; courtship and marriage, 38–9; appearance, 40; pregnancy and birth of Elizabeth, 40–1; character and manner, 44, 124; and birth of Gareth, 49; and DB's schooling, 51, 56; relations with DB, 54, 58–60, 276, 366; on DB's amateur acting, 72; performs on stage with DB, 76; dismisses DB's engagement to Anne Deans, 83; wartime activities, 91, 100, 106–7; DB describes to Dorothy Fells, 145; trip to Costa Brava with DB, 217, 219; trips to France with DB, 230, 299; helps move into Nore, 285; in Rome, 253; in St Moritz with DB, 316; in USA with DB, 323; stays at Clermont, 365–6; fractures shoulder, 374; and husband's death, 374; in nursing home, 384; depicted in *A Postillion Struck by Lightning*, 408; death, 431; portrayed in *An Orderly Man*, 447, 456, 530

Bogaerde, Philippe Van den (DB's cousin), 532

Bogaerde, Rupert Van den (Gareth's son), 479, 487, 494, 495, 527, 531; *Daybreak into Darkness*, 527

Bogaerde, Thérèse Van den (DB's great-great grandmother), 24

Bogaerde, Ulric Gontron Jules Van den (DB's father): and DB's birth, 23–4; birth, 27; relations with father, 28–9; character and career, 29–33, 39, 66, 406; war service, 30–2, 42; courtship and marriage, 38–9; and father-in-law's death, 38; and manner, 44, 124; and motor car, 44–5; nerves, 44; in Lullington, 45, 48–9; and DB's schooling, 53, 56, 64; relations with DB, 54, 276, 365, 374; house in Chailey, Sussex, 65–6; urges DB to be observant, 65, 103; and DB's career, 66, 69, 154; helps DB in early stage career, 77, 79; on DB's call-up into Army, 91; wartime activities, 100, 106–7; letter from DB on victory in Europe, 123; trip to Costa Brava with DB, 217, 219; retires from *Times*, 230; trips to France with DB, 230, 299; pencil portrait of DB shown at Royal Academy, 231; joint exhibition of paintings with DB, 241; in Rome, 253; helps move into Nore, 285; nightmare, 302; in St Moritz with DB, 316; in USA with DB, 323; stays at Clermont, 365; death, 374, 530; depicted in *A Postillion Struck by Lightning*, 408

Bogaerde, Valerius Julius Emilius Van den (Valère; Aimé's cousin), 24–6

Bogarde, Sir Dirk: death, 1–2, 540; Sheila MacLean nurses in later years, 2–4, 539; writings, 5–7; correspondence and papers, 7–8; Diary (with Tony), 8, 91–2, 159, 201, 252, 262, 277, 316, 339, 341, 374, 385, 391, 398, 424, 441, 452, 454, 455, 478, 489, 548; sexuality, 9–13, 61, 201, 272, 490; claims to have fathered child, 13; relations with Tony Forwood, 13–14, 18, 102, 188, 200–1, 206, 229, 294, 335, 474, 484, 491, 511, 545–6; effect of war service on, 16; reputation, 17; appearance, 18–19, 179–80, 231, 234, 264; interest in nature, 18, 47–6, 65–6; birth, 23; baptised Derek Niven Van den Bogaerde, 24; genealogy, 24–5; meets grandfather Aimé, 28; jealousy of sister, 42; schooling, 42, 50–3, 56–63; Lally (Ellen Searle) supervises, 43; childhood in Sussex, 45–8; spelling and punctuation, 46n, 61; dislikes sports and games, 51, 321; junior and amateur theatricals, 51–2, 69–73; in Glasgow as youth, 54–63; relations with parents, 54, 365–6; dress, 57, 60, 171, 255, 438–9, 547; interest in cinema, 59–60; self-reliance and solitude, 64–5; cruel behaviour, 65, 185, 546; attends Chelsea School of Art, 67–8; describes losing virginity, 68; poetry, 75–6, 90–1, 93–4, 97, 371, 525; early play writing, 76–7, 93, 120; auditioned at Old Vic Dramatic School, 77–8; decides on stage career, 77; early stage and film appearances, 78–9, 166–7, 173–6, 181–2, 193–4; first professional appearances, 80–4; announces engagement to Anne Deans, 83; in *Diversion No. 2* (revue), 88–9; meets Tony Forwood, 88; called up into Army (Signals), 90–2; watercolours and sketches, 90, 110, 124; officer training and commission, 95–6; Army career, 96–8, 102, 125; relations with Jack Jones, 100–1, 106, 125–6; works in interpretation of aerial photographs, 103–5, 110–12; with invasion forces

Bogarde, Sir Dirk—*cont*

in France and N.W. Europe, 108–22; promoted Acting Captain, 116; acquires dog in war, 119–20; religious attitudes, 122, 496–7, 520; drawings exhibited at Batsford Gallery (1945), 124–5; posted to India, 127–8; draws cartoons, 128; and Eve Holiday, 130–2, 170, 184–6; claims to have run over soldiers in India, 131; transferred to Indonesia, 133–9; writes for newspaper *The Fighting Cock*, 135–7, 139–41; corresponds with Dorothy Fells, 141–6; leaves Java, 146–7; return to England and demobilisation, 149, 153–4; writings on leaving Army, 154–5; meets Dorothy Fells in London, 155–6; resumes relations with Tony Forwood after war, 158–9; adopts name Dirk Bogarde, 161; first TV appearances, 161–2; success in *Power Without Glory*, 162–5, 216; interviewed for *West London Times*, 167; film contract with Rank, 168–9, 176–8, 186, 194, 217, 231, 258–9; questions own identity, 170; interest in publicity and image, 171–2; radio broadcasts, 173, 187, 196, 212, 305, 515–16, 522; describes ideal woman, 183–4; occupies Bendrose House with Tony Forwood, 186–90, 197; returns to stage, 187–8; acting nerves, 190–1, 214–15; short stories, 196; pet animals, 197–8, 205–6, 289, 335, 346, 347–8, 353, 385, 426, 436, 486; popularity rating as film star, 198, 207, 228, 232, 244, 250, 300; works with Losey, 201–2, 290–3, 295–8, 312–13, 318–23; film breakthrough in *Doctor in the House*, 203–5; buys Beel House, 205; adopts squire life-style, 206; avoids right profile shots, 212, 234, 305–6; musical taste, 212, 511; stage performance in *Summertime*, 213–15; hepatitis, 214; outspoken comments, 215–16; radio profile of, 216–17; sets up film company, 217; attitude to Jon Whiteley, 219–20; on film stardom, 223; on allure to women, 226; considers living abroad, 227, 244, 253, 258; proposes rationing film parts, 227, 241; attitude to women, 228–9, 260, 313, 325–6; stand-in, 229–30; swearing, 229, 234; accent, 234; learns cinema and camera technique, 234, 320; sprains ankle in India, 235; protests at girls' school next to Beel property, 239; acts with Hermione Baddeley in *Jezebel*, 241–2; invests in production company, 241, 277, 332, 335, 379; joint exhibition of paintings with father, 241; philanthropy and charitable work, 241; pleurisy and double pneumonia, 242–3; plays Franz Liszt for Columbia film, 244–8, 502; travels to and works in Hollywood, 245–6, 248–9; studies piano-playing under Aller, 246–8; on Gawsworth honours list, 250–1; art collecting, 253, 315–17, 335, 340, 386, 492, 501; differences with John Mills, 255–6; performance in *The Singer Not the Song* criticised, 256–7; reception in New York, 260; lectures at National Film Theatre, 261, 366–7; sells Beel and buys Birchens Spring, 261–2; makes record of love lyrics, 263–4, 446; house guests and entertaining, 264–7; and *Victim*, 267–73, 279–82; ends Rank contract, 273; handwriting analysed,

274–5, 518; family attachments, 275–6; supposed aversion therapy for homosexuality, 278; declines Olivier's Chichester offer, 282–3; buys and sells Hale Court, 283; buys Nore, 284; wins Variety Club Award, 284, 301; domestic staff problems, 289, 304, 325, 332; as company director, 290; praised for *The Servant*, 297; tax anxieties, 298, 300, 332; whistling, 298, 417, 539n; broadcasts *Desert Island Discs*, 305, 511–12; liver trouble, 311, 315–16; sells Nore, 312, 315; smoking, 315, 368, 535; buys Adam's Farm, 317; political attitudes, 318, 436, 516–17; courted by publishers, 327–8, 369–70, 382–3, 386–7; corresponds with Dorothy Webster Gordon, 330–1, 336–7, 372–3, 504; registers company in Bahamas, 332; makes commercial, 337–8; leaves England, 346; home in Italy, 347–8; on Judy Garland's death, 349–50; buys house in France, 353–5, 362; non UK residence recognised, 353; life at Clermont, France, 364–5, 378, 385–6, 404, 417–18, 460, 478; acting appraised, 366; dental problems, 368; father's death, 374; drinking, 377, 485, 491, 535; financial management, 378; compulsive letter-writing, 385; attacked for portrayal of Frederick Browning, 400–3; disagreement with Attenborough, 401–3; reception, 408; appeals to younger generation, 416–17, 432; unsolicited letters and attention from fans, 418–19, 465, 528; at book signings, 421, 429, 460, 463, 487, 506, 530; novel-writing, 424–5, 433, 454, 482–3, 514; attends literary luncheons, 429, 462–3; presents 1980 Palme d'Or at Cannes, 432; ill-health at Clermont, 435; considers moving to Switzerland or USA, 437; fear of Russian occupation, 437; travels on Concorde, 439; sixtieth birthday, 441–2; literary earnings, 444, 454, 517, 529; on act of writing, 448; press features on, 457–8; awarded French honours, 460, 520, 533; commentates on French TV documentary, 461; as president of Cannes Film Festival 1984 jury, 461–2, 465–8; on Losey's death, 468–9; honorary doctorates at St Andrews and Sussex, 471, 474–5, 532–3; shooting, 476–7; claims aversion to baths, 480; portrait of, 482; sells and leaves Clermont, 486–7; French-speaking, 488; buys house in Dukes Lane, Kensington, 491–2, 493; puts on weight, 491, 501; awarded British Film Institute Fellowship, 492; suffers paralysis of leg, 493–4; and Tony's death, 496–8; supports euthanasia, 497, 512–13, 522, 527, 539; book reviewing, 498–9, 518, 538; bitterness after Tony's death, 499–500; buys lease on Cadogan Gardens flat, 500–1; sells literary papers, 501; misbehaves at BAFTA ceremony, 502–3; reads at National Theatre, 503–4; financial stringency, 507; broadcasts for charities, 512; gives master-classes in acting, 513–14; at seventy, 518; on Holocaust, 518–20; speaks to schools, 519–20; knighthood, 520–1; theatre readings and talks, 524–6, 530, 535; sense of purpose in later life, 527; learns to cook, 528; narrates for production of *The Merry*

Widow, 533; medical problems and stroke, 535–7; punctuality, 539n; cremated and ashes scattered in France, 541; obituary tributes, 542–3; will and estate, 544; posthumous reputation, 545–7; motorcycle thrill, 546; and frogs and toads, 547–8
Bogart, Humphrey, 15
Bolet, Jorge, 246, 502
Bolt, Robert, 238, 451, 473
Boluda, Eduardo and Antonia, 335, 339, 344, 347, 353, 355, 365
Bonham Carter, Helena, 11, 489–90, 523
Boom! (film), 332, 356
Boot, Charles, 179
Bordes, Hélène: writes to DB, 471, 475–6; DB's correspondence with, 476, 478–9, 482, 491, 495, 501; and DB's reaction to Tony's death, 498; and DB's views on AIDS, 517; and DB's *A Short Walk from Harrods*, 531; meets DB, 531; and DB's depression in old age, 536
Boston University: Mugar Memorial Library, 7
Boucicault, Dion: *The Shaughraun*, 187
Boulting Brothers, 311
Bourne, Matthew: *Play Without Words* (ballet), 545
Bourne, Stephen, 218, 257, 281
Boursier-Mougenot, Jean-Pierre, 353, 355
Bowers, Lieut.-Colonel P.L., 95
Bowlby, Nicholas: marriage to Rosalind, 433n; DB's attachment to, 434; and DB's *Voices in the Garden*, 435; on DB's 60th birthday, 441; and Tony's 'The Last Summer', 448; stays with DB, 459–60; *West of Sunset* dedicated to, 471; and DB's honorary doctorate, 474; helps Tony run house, 483; with DB at BFI award, 492; visits DB in decline, 537
Bowlby, Rosalind (*earlier* Bell): DB meets, 405; at Chatto party for booksellers, 407; and launch of *Postillion*, 421; marriage, 433n; and title of *Voices in the Garden*, 433; DB's attachment to, 434; on DB's 60th birthday, 441; Tony writes 'The Last Summer' for, 448; DB seeks advice from, 449; pregnancy, 450; recommends agent to DB, 455; stays with DB, 459–60; leaves Chatto and works as freelance, 462; and Norah Smallwood's death, 470; *West of Sunset* dedicated to, 471; and DB's honorary doctorate from St Andrews, 474; 'minds' DB in Scotland, 474; persuades DB to see Russell Harty for last interview, 483; present at DB's meeting with Lynn Barber, 491; with DB at BFI award, 492; comforts DB after Tony's death, 496
Bowles, Peter, 400
Bowood Productions, 284, 378
Box, Betty: and *Doctor* films, 203–4, 208; and Bardot's view of DB, 209; and Sinden's hair bleach, 212; DB returns to film with, 227, 299; and DB's part in *A Tale of Two Cities*, 230; and *The Wind Cannot Read*, 233, 235; DB seeks to break from, 235; visits Drummers Yard, 274; buys Drummers Yard, 283; and *The High Bright Sun*, 303
Box, Sydney, 165–6, 203, 291
Boxer, Mark, 410

Boyd, William, 444
Boys in Brown (film), 180, 182, 186, 227
Brabourne, John Ulick Knatchbull, 7th Baron, 302
Braden, Bernard, 304
Bramley, E., 230
Brand, Mrs (toyshop owner), 41
Brando, Marlon, 203, 254, 257
Bream, Julian, 339
Bridge on the River Kwai, The (film), 237–8
Bridge Too Far, A (film), 395–402, 404
Briggs, Barry, 546n
Brighton, 28; DB acts in, 242–3
Brighton Rock (film), 179
British Academy of Film and Television Arts: makes best actor award to DB, 301, 317; gives Tribute Award to DB, 502; tribute to Gielgud, 532
British Board of Film Censors, 267
British Film Academy *see* British Academy of Film and Television Arts
British Film Institute, 367; awards Fellowship to DB, 492; *see also* National Film Theatre
Broken Journey (film), 166
Brook, Faith, 186
Brook, Natasha, 488
Brook, Peter, 190
Brooks, Elsie, 66
Browne, Coral, 455
Browning, Christian, 400
Browning, Daphne, Lady *see* du Maurier, Daphne
Browning, Lieut.-General Sir Frederick ('Boy'), 395–402, 437, 520
Brunner, Hugo, 447
Brussels: liberated (1944), 114; DB visits to promote book, 531
Bryan, John, 218–19
Brynner, Yul, 374
Buchanan, Sir Colin, 239–40
Buchanan, Jack, 232
Buchman, Harold, 201
Buckingham Palace, 339, 521
Budapest, 333–5
Budberg, Baroness Moura, 290, 300, 349, 455–6
Bullough, Donald, 474
Burch, Mrs M.C., 161
Burgess, Guy, 199
Burgess Hill, Sussex, 100
'Buried Alive' (proposed TV film), 451–2, 454
Burke, Alfred, 370
Burns, Mark, 361–2
Burstyn, Ellen, 392–3
Burton, Lambert, 340
Burton, Richard, 254, 257, 259, 311, 319, 332, 356, 371, 472
Burton, Sybil, 301, 304–5, 324, 336

Cabrol, Dr Gilles, 452, 477–9
Cadogan Gardens, London, 500
Café de Paris, London: bombed, 90
Caffe, Nino, 253

Caine, Derek Hall, 87, 235
Caine, Sir Michael, 324
Cairncross, James, 89, 370
Cal (film), 466
Callil, Carmen, 447, 450
Campbell, John, 262
Campbell, Judy, 508–9
Campbell, Patrick, 369
Campbell's Kingdom (film), 227, 234, 240
'Canary Cage, The' (DB), 330–1
Cannes Film Festival: Losey wins Palme d'Or, 268; DB presents prize at, 432; DB serves as president of 1984 jury, 461, 465–8
Capri, 304
Captain Boycott (film), 155
Captain Horatio Hornblower RN (film), 188
Captain's Table, The (film), 237
Capucine (born Germaine Lefebvre), 13, 247–50, 253, 261, 264–6, 278, 348, 417, 490; death, 534–5
Cardiff, 489–90
Carey, John, 421–2
Carey, Joyce, 274
Carlyle, Thomas, 18
Caron, Leslie, 224, 240
Carr, Sir Raymond, 320
Carson, Johnny, 301, 335
Carson, Peter, 505
Carstairs, John Paddy, 166
Carter, Miranda, 290
Carthage, SS, 127
Case of Helvig Delbo, The (TV play), 169
Casey, R.G., 129
Cass, Henry, 82
Cassavetes, John, 13, 203, 307
Casson, Sir Lewis, 454
Cast a Dark Shadow (film), 212, 279
Castle, Barbara, Baroness, 419
Castle, Clifford, 264
Catania, Sicily, 252
Catterick Camp, Yorkshire, 92
Caute, David, 6, 291, 296, 302, 321, 357
Cavani, Liliana, 374–8, 380, 390, 447
Cecil, Lord David, 8
Cecil, Jonathan, 531
Chakiris, George, 303
Chamberlain, Neville, 75
Chamberlain, Richard, 12
Channing, Carol, 301
Chapman, Mrs (schoolteacher), 42
Chariots of Fire (film), 450–1
Charles, Prince of Wales, 209
Charlton, John: invites DB to write book, 382–3, 506; visits DB in France, 386; as DB's editor, 387–90, 404–7, 434, 448–9; and DB's book titles, 423, 427, 433; and DB's fictional sex-scene, 435; relations with DB deteriorate, 450; and *Time Out* article on DB, 458
Chartoff, Robert, 310
Chatto & Windus: publish DB, 13, 387, 390, 404,

410, 421, 423, 433–4, 448–50, 456; invite DB to write, 382–4; payments to DB, 389, 423; DV visits office of, 405–6; editorial and managerial changes, 447, 450, 470
Chatwin, Bruce, 518
Chelsea: DB's life in, 527
Chelsea Polytechnic, 67, 69, 71, 407
Cheshire, Group Captain Leonard, VC, 519
Chester Row, 170–1, 184, 186
Chevalier, Maurice, 224
Chichester Festival Theatre, 282–3
Chiel, The (Glasgow journal), 35
Christie, Julie, 306–8, 316–18, 338, 348
Christopher, Jordan, 324, 336
Church, Esmé, 77
Church of the Good Shepherd, Lullington, 45–6, 544
Churchill, Sarah, 104
Cimino, Michael, 482
Cinémonde, 298
Clark, Petula, 161
Clarke, T.E.B., 181
Clayton, Jack, 323, 325, 371
Clayton, Sussex (Hillside Cottage), 100–1, 126, 153
Cleared for Take-Off (DB): on Jack Jones, 101; on military advance in Europe, 114; on Belsen, 122; and Hugh Jolly in Singapore, 148; and DB's near-nervous breakdown, 191; on Capucine's arrival in Rome, 253; and offer of knighthood, 520; on Capucine's death, 534–5; reception, 534
Cleary, Eustace and Sylvia, 101
Clegg, Christine, 67, 69–70
Clement-Jones, Dr Vicky, 512
Clermont *see* Haut Clermont, Le
Cliburn, Van, 244
Clift, Montgomery, 13, 186, 194, 252, 257
Closing Ranks (DB; novel), 536–7, 539
Coates, Austin, 133
Cochran, Sir Charles Blake ('Cockie'), 86
Cogan, Alma, 304
Colette, 533; *Gigi*, 224
Colleano, Bonar, 207
Collier, John: *Witch's Money*, 291
Collins, Joan, 208
Colman, Ronald, 230
Columbia (film corporation), 246, 248
Come on George! (film), 78
Connaught Enterprises (company), 332, 335, 365, 379
Connaught Hotel, London, 241, 346, 387, 442, 450, 457, 463, 477–8, 487–8, 515
Connaught Productions Limited, 332
Connery, Sean, 398
Conti, Tom, 432
Cooke, Alistair, 212
Cooper, Lady Diana, 434
Cooper, Gladys, 249
Coote, Sir Colin, 94
Cordeaux, Captain E.C., 99
Cortina d'Ampezzo, 227–9

Costello, Elvis, 263

Costigan, James: *Little Moon of Alban*, 300–1

Costin, Captain Kenneth, 112

Courtenay, Sir Tom, 18, 229, 302–3, 368

'Covenant with Death' (proposed film), 302, 482

Cowan, Theo ('Thumper'), 178–9, 216, 315, 386, 469, 535

Coward, Sir Noël: sexuality, 11; compliments cast of *Power Without Glory*, 164–5; advice to DB, 165, 167, 198, 422; on DB and Michael Redgrave, 208; on Johnnie Ray, 215; lives abroad, 244; visits DB at Drummers Yard, 274; plays in *Boom!*, 332–3; knighthood, 402; *Blithe Spirit*, 323; *Peace in Our Time*, 167; *A Song at Twilight*, 6, 10; *The Vortex*, 194–5, 242

Cox, Derek, 68, 71

Cox, Heather, 68, 71, 73

Cox, Lionel, 68–71, 73–5, 83, 100, 102

Cox, Nerine, 68–9, 71–3, 75, 83, 91, 102, 112, 186, 189

Cox, Winifred, 68

Coyte, Derek, 178

Craig, H.A.L., 352

Craig, Michael, 229

Craig, Wendy, 298

Crane, Stephen: *Hotel de Dream*, 291

Crawford, Gabrielle, 535, 539

Crawford, Michael, 304

Crichton, Charles, 193

Cripps, Sir Stafford, 180

Crist, Judith, 367

Croft, Peggy, 330

Croft-Cooke, Rupert, 199

Cronin, A.J.: *The Spanish Gardener*, 218–19

Cross, Beverley, 373

Cross of Iron (film), 395

Cruel Sea, The (film), 195

Crutchley, Rosalie, 280

Cukor, George, 225, 248–9, 253, 260, 344, 349, 502, 515; death, 469

Curtain Up (Army show), 139

Curtiz, Michael, 203

Cusack, Cyril, 376, 473n

Czechoslovakia: Soviets invade, 341

D-Day (June 1944): preparations for, 106–8; landings, 109

Daddy Nostalgie (*These Foolish Things*; film), 508–12, 531

Dahl, Roald, 437–8, 440, 442–3

Dahl, Tessa, 438, 440

Daily Express, 457, 463

Daily Herald, 264

Daily Mirror, 198, 458, 463

Daily Telegraph, The, 498–9, 518, 536

Dalrymple, Ian, 169–70, 173, 175, 234

Damned, The (film), 337–8, 340–3, 345, 348–9, 350–2, 360, 365, 371, 391, 442

Dancing with Crime (film), 166

Danesfield, Buckinghamshire, 104

Daniel, Mark, 47

Daniell, Lieut.-Colonel Bob, 121

Danjoux, Henri and Marie, 378, 462

d'Arcy, Susan: book on DB (with Margaret Hinxman), 7, 391

Darjeeling, 132

Darling (film), 13, 306–9, 311, 314, 316, 324

Darling, Lieut.-Colonel R.R.A., 94

Darlington, W.A., 184; *Alf's Button*, 69–70

Dassin, Jules, 203, 250

Daubeny, Molly, Lady, 499–500, 503, 506

Daubeny, Sir Peter, 159, 164–7, 172, 184, 499

David, Hugh, 199–200

David Jacobs Show, 264

Davies, Terence, 280–1

Daviot, Gordon *see* Mackintosh, Elizabeth

Davis, Allan, 160

Davis, Bette, 324, 371–2, 492

Davis, John: position at Rank, 179; qualities and character, 179; antagonism to homosexuals, 201; letter from DB on roles at Rank, 211, 216, 218; belief in DB, 221; opens distribution operation in USA, 222; visits DB at Beel, 226–7; differences with DB, 227, 235, 244; gives celebration lunch for DB, 231; proposes revised ending for *The Wind Cannot Read*, 233; and DB's hopes of playing T.E. Lawrence, 237; recommends DB to John Stafford, 254; and DB's Rank contract, 258–9, 272; on possible closure of Pinewood Studios, 299

Dawson, Beatrice ('Bumble'), 231, 264, 332

Dawson, Geoffrey, 34

Day, Frances, 184, 250

Dean, Basil, 80

Dean, James, 216

Deans, Anne, 82–4, 88, 91, 102

Dearden, Basil: works on *Come on George!*, 78; at Q Theatre, 80; and *The Blue Lamp*, 181–2; and script for *The Gentle Gunman*, 194; buys Beel from DB, 261; killed, 262n; and *Victim*, 267–8, 271, 280; visits Drummers Yard, 267; and *The Mind Benders*, 285

Death in Venice (film), 351–2, 355, 357–63, 365–8, 443, 450

Decca record company, 263–4

de Grey, Roger, 70

de Havilland, Olivia, 245, 456

de Leon, Beatrice, 79–82, 158, 176, 184, 276

de Leon, Herbert, 160

de Leon, Jack, 79, 81, 176, 184

Delf, Harry: *The Family Upstairs*, 82–3

Delon, Alain, 318, 349

Demongeot, Mylène, 256, 299

Dempsey, General Sir Miles, 112

Denby, David, 509–10

de Niro, Robert, 473

Denison, John, 96–7, 101, 103, 119

Denison, Michael, 157, 172, 250

Derrick, Bonnie, 494

Desert Island Discs (radio programme), 305, 511–12
Despair (film), 410–16, 425, 507
Desperate Moment (film), 196
Diaghilev, Serge, 33
Diamond, Jean, 273
Diana, Princess of Wales, 537
Dickson, Dorothy, 88, 90
Dieppe Raid (August 1942), 100
Dietrich, Marlene, 172
Dillon, Carmen, 231
Dimanche à la campagne, Un (film), 167
Dimbleby, Richard: visits Belsen, 122
Dinard: film festival, 545
Diplock, Ronnie ('Reg Fluke'), 48, 405
Dirk Bogarde: The Complete Autobiography, 501n
'Dirk Bogarde – By Myself' (TV interview), 220,
    522–3
Diversion No. 2 (revue), 88–90, 216
Doctor at Large (film), 222–3, 227
Doctor at Sea (film), 208–10, 222, 234
Doctor in Distress (film), 299
Doctor in the House (film), 203–5, 207, 222, 240
Doctor's Dilemma, The (film), 240, 245
Dodd, Mary (*née* Forwood), 90, 186, 189, 194, 276
Dodds, Olive, 166, 186, 216, 237, 239, 244, 264
Doillon, Jacques, 509
Donat, Robert, 81
Donen, Stanley, 11, 466
Door, The (TV play), 293
Doorne, Henry Van, 26
Dors, Diana, 250
Douglas, Lord Alfred, 199–200
Douglas, Robert, 159
Doulton, Lieut.-Colonel A.J.F., 134, 137, 139
Dowd, J.H., 40
Drummers Yard, near Beaconsfield (*formerly* Birchens
    Spring), 262–3, 265–7, 273–4, 283
Duke of York's Theatre, 190
du Maurier, Daphne (Lady Browning), 396–7, 399,
    400–2, 438
Dunkirk evacuation (1940), 83
Dunn, John, 538
Durgnat, Raymond, 321
Durrell, Lawrence, 344–5; *The Alexandria Quartet*,
    338
Dyson, Hugo, 307

Eardley, Joan, 315
East, David, 126
Easton, George, 501
Edison, Thomas, 35
Edney, Alan, 272
Edwards, Robert Gordon, 374–5
Egyptian, The (film), 203
Elizabeth II, Queen (*earlier* Princess), 159, 339, 367
Ellacott, Joan, 210
Elliott, Denholm, 198, 206, 508
Elliott, Madge, 120, 533
Ellis, Vivian, 429

Espenhahn, Major E.W. (Ted), 119
Essame, Brigadier Hubert, 96–7, 103, 118, 137, 174
Essame, Peter, 103
Essame, Robin, 96
Esther Waters (film), 173, 175, 184, 234, 240, 276
euthanasia, 122, 497, 512–13, 522, 539
Evans, Dame Edith, 88, 90, 335, 350, 369
Evans, Olwen, 198
Evening Standard, 379
Ewing, Peter, 102, 453–4
Exile (film), 311
Eyre, Sir Richard, 513

'Fair Bride, The' (film) *see Angel Wore Red, The*
Faithfull, Marianne, 294
Far from the Madding Crowd (film), 318
Farewell to Arms, A (film), 228
Farjeon, Herbert, 88–90
Farrar, David, 178
Farrell, Barry: *Pat and Roald*, 437
Farrow, Mia, 376
Farry, Eithne, 529
Fassbinder, Rainer Werner, 410–16, 447, 469
Feldman, Charles, 247, 249–50, 253, 260
Fellini, Federico, 352
Fellowes, Julian (Julian Kitchener-Fellowes), 489
Fells, Dorothy, 141–6, 155–6, 337
Fermor, Sir Patrick Leigh, 220–2, 224, 437
Ferréol, Andréa, 414–15
Ferrer, José, 203, 352
Ferrer, Mel, 253
Feuchtwanger, Primrose (*née* Essame), 103
Ffrangcon Davies, Gwen, 213
Fielding, Daphne, 221, 264, 284, 285, 317, 434, 505,
    521, 534
Fielding, Xan, 221, 285, 317
Fields, Gracie, 304
Fighting Cock, The (Army newspaper), 135–7, 139–41,
    330–1
Films and Filming, 223, 271, 300
Finch, Peter, 191, 254, 277
Finney, Albert, 18, 344
Firbank, Ann, 264
Fischer, Søren, 261, 366–7
Fisher, Clive, 542–3
Fisher, Mr and Mrs (of Adam's Farm), 344, 346
Fitzgibbon, Constantine, 78
Fixer, The (film), 331–5, 340
Fletching, Sussex, 241
Florian (gardener), 206, 220
Fluke, Reg, 405
Foggia, Italy, 303
Fonda, Henry, 17, 374
For Better, For Worse (play), 176, (film), 211
For the Time Being (DB): illustrations, 109; published,
    538
Forbes, Bryan: on Rattigan, 10; on filming of
    Appointment in London, 195; co-founds Allied Film
    Makers, 268; makes *The L-Shaped Room*, 293; and

proposed film of *Barbouze*, 301; and *The Whisperers*, 355; visits DB at Clermont, 402; and DB's knighthood, 520

Forbes, Meriel, 350

Forbes, Nanette (Nanette Newman), 402, 520

Forche, Christiaan De, 532

Ford, Anna, 462

Ford, Glenn, 259

Foreman, Carl, 201

Formby, George, 78

Forster, Margaret, 397–8

Forster, Peter, 410

Forsyte Chronicles, The (radio adaptation), 515

Forsyth, Major A.F.J., 94–5

Fortune Theatre, 164, 166

Forwood family, 85, 205

Forwood, Anthony (Ernest Lytton Langton Forwood): keeps joint Diary, 8, 91–2, 159, 201, 252, 262, 277, 316, 339, 341, 374, 385, 391, 398, 424, 441, 452, 454, 478, 489; in DB's writings, 9; death, 9, 496–7, 499; relations with DB, 13–14, 18, 102, 188, 200–1, 207, 239, 294, 335, 474, 484, 491, 511, 545–6; birth and background, 85–8; acting career, 86, 158, 184–6, 188; meets DB, 88; military service, 88, 156; marriage and child with Glynis Johns, 156–8; as theatrical impresario, 156; resumes relations with DB after war, 158–9; friendship with Daubeny, 164; secures first film part for DB, 166; divorce from Glynis Johns, 184; moves into Chester Row house, 184–5; at Bendrose House with DB, 186–90; film parts, 193–5; gives up film career, 201; Agnes Zwickl on, 207; and filming of *Doctor at Sea*, 209; on success of *Summertime*, 213; forms film company with DB, 217; trip to Spain with DB, 217, 219; visits USA with DB, 224–6, 245–6, 310, 323, 345, 439, 440; and DB's rationing film-making, 227; in *The Wind Cannot Read*, 235; nurses DB with double pneumonia, 242; writes to Harbottle from film locations, 248–9; in Rome, 253; on DB in *Song Without End*, 260; moves to Birchens Spring, 262; life at Drummers Yard, 265; and DB's part in *Victim*, 271; moves into Nore, 285; domestic staff problems, 289, 304, 325; and *The Servant*, 294; in Italy with DB, 299, 303, 313–15; and DB's black periods, 311; picture collection, 317; takes morning Guinness, 320; thanks Losey for gift of book, 322; on Barbra Streisand, 324; and DB's tax problems, 332; in Hungary, 332–4; and plans to live abroad, 338–9; on filming of *The Damned*, 341–3; leaves England to live in Italy, 346–8; life in France, 353–5, 362, 376, 378, 385, 404; in Venice with DB during filming, 358–60; gives up smoking, 368; approves DB's writing book, 370; on DB being taken seriously, 370; damages fingers, 374; cooking, 385, 479, 494; and filming of *Providence*, 392–4; on DB in *A Bridge Too Far*, 398; and attacks on DB for portrayal of Frederick Browning, 401; in DB's *A Postillion Struck by Lightning*, 406; and filming of *Despair*, 412–13, 416; in *Snakes and Ladders*, 421;

and death of pet dogs, 426, 486; in 'William Hickey' column, 429; calcified foot, 435; pension, 444; *An Orderly Man* dedicated to, 448; writing, 448–9; and father's death and funeral, 449, 469; ill-health, 449–50, 452, 462–3, 465, 469, 472, 477–9, 486, 489, 491, 493, 495; surgical operations, 452–4, 457, 477–8; on DB's declining publicity, 462; at Cannes 1984 Film Festival, 466, 468; on Norah Smallwood's death, 470; and *The Mission*, 473; treated for Parkinson's disease, 481–2; returns to England for treatment, 487–8; Helena Bonham Carter on, 490–1; life in Queen Anne House, Kensington, 491, 493–6; portrayed in *A Short Walk from Harrods*, 531; 'The Last Summer', 87, 448

Forwood, Edith (*née* Westing; Tony's mother; 'Esmé'), 85–6

Forwood, Ernest, 84, 87

Forwood, Gareth: born, 157; Christmas 1956 entertainment, 225; at Drummers Yard Christmas, 264; helps move into Nore, 285; in France, 289; in Venice, 299; acting career, 316; visits DB and Tony in Italy, 349; visits father at Christmas, 494; and father's death, 496

Forwood, Gwen (Tony's aunt), 497

Forwood, Jane *see* Powell, Jane

Forwood, Leslie Langton (Tony's father), 85–6, 449, 469

Forwood, Mary *see* Dodd, Mary

Forwood, Thomas, 501, 527

Fosse, Bob, 432

Foster (Adam's Farm houseman), 325

Foster, Aisling, 534

Foster Grant sunglasses, 337

Four Horsemen of the Apocalypse, The (film), 259

Fowles, John, 18

Fox, Angela, 355

Fox, James (William), 159, 293–5, 297, 400

Fox, John Don, 311, 338

Fox, Robert, 537

Fox, Robin, 292, 317, 355, 360; death, 371

Foyle, Christina: Literary Luncheons, 429, 457, 462–3

France: DB films in, 220–1; DB considers buying house in, 227, 253, 353; DB visits, 227, 230, 289, 299; DB buys house in, 353–4, 362; awards honours to DB, 460, 520, 533; DB at home in, 460; *see also* Haut Clermont, Le

Frank, Elizabeth, 164

Frankenheimer, John, 333

Fraser, John, 9, 545–6

French, Harold, 174

French, Philip, 542

Fröhlich, Gustav, 86

Frost, Sir David, 462

Frost, Lieut.-Colonel John, 400

Fry, Christopher, 312

Fuller, Miss (schoolteacher), 51

Fyfe, David Maxwell *see* Kilmuir, Viscount

Gabor, Eva, 301
Gainsbourg, Serge, 509
Galbe, Marguerite, 487
Gandhi (film), 311
Gandhi, Indira, 235
Garbo, Greta, 225
Gardner, Ava, 19, 250, 252, 261, 384, 490
Garland, Judy, 225, 227, 261, 272–4, 284–8; death, 349–50
Garrick Club, 406
Garson, Greer, 202
Garthoff, Bert, 137
Gary, Paula J., 372
Gawsworth, John, 128, 250
Gee, Maggie: *The White Family*, 545
Geeves, Val, 330
Gellhorn, Martha, 528
Genevieve (film), 222
Gentle Gunman, The (film), 194–5, 255n
Gentle Occupation, A (DB): 'Harri' in, 139; on life in Batavia, 140; plot and characters, 427–8; title, 427; publication, 428; reception, 430–1; sales, 433, 444, 534; discreet sex content, 434
Gibbs, Patrick, 297, 367, 399
Gibson, Chloë, 162–4, 185, 216
Gielgud, Sir John: and blackmail, 18; in Coward's *The Vortex*, 194; arrested for soliciting, 199–200; proposes film of *Richard of Bordeaux*, 231–2; in *Sebastian*, 326; gives address at Vivien Leigh's memorial service, 332; declines *Death in Venice*, 352; writes book, 369; plays in *Providence*, 392–5; and Tavernier film offer, 508; on DB's TV interview, 523; BAFTA tribute to, 532
Gielgud, Val, 169
Gigi (film), 224, 227, 453
Gilbert, Bridget ('Bee'; 'Snowflake'), 334–5, 507–8
Gilbert, Lewis, 207, 212, 278–9
Giscard d'Estaing, Valéry, 460
Glasgow: DB attends school in, 54–63, 408–10
Glen, Allan, 56; *see also* Allan Glen's School
Glendinning, Victoria, 430
Gloag, Julian, 323
Glover, Stephen, 430
Go-Between, The (film), 368
Godfrey, Cecil, 39
Godley, Wynne, 278
Godwin-Austen, Robert, 284, 284–5
Goethe, J.W. von, 351
Goetz, William, 247
Golden, Eve, 189
Golders Green, 44–5
Goldman, James: *The Lion in Winter*, 232
Goldman, William, 395, 397–9
Goldschmidt, Frédéric de, 466
Goldsmith, John, 383
Goodings, (Margaret) Elizabeth Marie (*née* Van den Bogaerde; DB's sister; 'Lu'): birth, 41; DB's jealousy of, 42, 528; punished by father, 45; childhood in Sussex, 47, 65–6, 389; and DB's

absence in Glasgow, 57–8; performs in amateur theatre, 70–1, 76; wartime activities, 91; and John Nelson, 103; serves in WRNS, 106, 113; correspondence with DB on active service, 112, 114, 116–22; romantic expectations, 112; marriage, 220; DB invites on Continental holidays, 276, 331, 333, 384–5; and DB's urge for country living, 283; takes over DB's pets, 346; visits DB in Italy, 348; and father's death, 374; responsibility for mother in decline, 384–5, 431; correspondence and relations with DB in later life, 385, 528; and DB's writing, 388–9; DB describes *Providence* to, 392; and DB's part in *A Bridge Too Far*, 395, 399; and *A Postillion Struck by Lightning*, 406–8; *Snakes and Ladders* dedicated to, 421; and mother's funeral, 432; on Norah Smallwood, 447; and Tony's convalescence from cancer operation, 454; looks after Clermont, 462; helps DB move from Clermont, 487; helps DB in Cadogan Gardens flat, 501; and DB's sense of purpose in later life, 527; and family roots in Izegem, 532; legacy from DB, 544; posthumous account of DB, 546
Goodings, George (Elizabeth's husband), 220, 276, 283, 315, 421, 431–2, 454, 462; death, 501, 528
Goodings, Mark (Elizabeth's son), 289, 417, 546
Gordimer, Nadine: *July's People*, 444
Gordon, Carol, 329–30, 504
Gordon, Dorothy Webster ('Mrs X'): letters published (as *A Particular Friendship*), 8, 504; correspondence with DB, 328–31, 336–8, 372, 446, 470, 506; death, 372; letters returned to DB, 373, 504; DB considers publishing correspondence, 424–5, 433, 498, 501; described in *An Orderly Man*, 448
Gordon, Edward Blair, 328–9
Gordon, Richard (Dr Gordon Ostlere), 204–5
Gordon, Ruth, 324
Gorky, Maxim, 290
Gottlieb, Bob, 435, 456
Gough, Colonel Frederick, 400
Gough, Michael, 19, 159, 187
Gowrie, Alexander Patrick Greysteil Hore-Ruthven, 2nd Earl of, 520
Grade, Leslie, 292, 296
Graham, Sheilah, 249
Graham, Virginia, 325
Granada Television, 451
Granger, Stewart, 155, 177–9, 268
Grant, Cary, 13, 194
Graves, Robert: *I, Claudius*, 312
Gray, Dulcie, 157, 250
Great Meadow (DB), 45, 528–9
Greaves, Flight Lieutenant Christopher: war service with DB, 107, 110, 112–13, 115, 120, 124; death, 125, 535; peacetime career, 125; shares London flat with brother, 170–1
Greaves, John, 125, 170–1
Greaves, Margaret, 125
Green, Guy, 268

Green, Janet, 212, 267–8, 270
Green, Maurice, 33
Greene, Graham, 237, 432; 'May We Borrow Your Husband?', 477, 480–1
Grenfell, Joyce, 88–9
Griffiths, Trevor: *Comedians* (play), 380
Grimley, P.A., 56
Grunwald, Anatole de, 236–7, 240, 245
Guardian, The (earlier *Manchester Guardian*): praises DB's acting in *Jezebel*, 242; Film Lecture series, 453; obituary of Losey, 469
Guerin, Ann, 358
Guest, Val, 194
Guildhall School of Music and Drama, 514
Guinness, Sir Alec: established before war, 1; elusiveness, 6–7; reputation, 17; popularity rating, 198, 244, 250; film parts, 237; plays T.E. Lawrence in Rattigan's *Ross*, 238; in Rome, 253; acts with DB in *HMS Defiant*, 278–9; in *Tunes of Glory*, 285; declines *Death in Venice*, 352, 368; Losey suggests film part for, 432; ignores press, 457; meets DB in Chelsea, 527; letter from Gielgud on DB's animosity towards John Mills, 532
Guinness, Merula, Lady, 279
Gulliver, Jean (DB's cousin), 62–3
Guthrie, Sir Tyrone, 77, 282
Gwynn, Michael, 213
Gwynne, Lieut.-Colonel R.V., 48

Hackett, General Sir John, 399
Hackman, Gene, 398
Haert, Michel van der, 24
Hakim, André, 196
Hale Court, Withyham, Uckfield, 283
Halévy, Ludovic: *A Marriage of Love*, 26
Hall, Sir Peter, 213–14, 380, 463–4, 503
Hall, Willis, 265–6
Hamer, Robert, 515
Hamilton, Patrick: *Rope*, 161–2
Hamlin, Angela, 2–3
Hampson, Thomas, 533
Hanbury-Sparrow, Lieut.-Colonel Alan, 230
Hanff, Helene: *84 Charing Cross Road*, 505
Harbottle, Laurence: on DB's sexuality, 9–10; on Tony Forwood, 14; in Hasker Street, 168; as Director of Bendrose, 217; on DB's enjoying *Ill Met By Moonlight*, 221; defends DB's bastion at Beel, 239–40; and DB's proposals for living abroad, 244; Tony writes to from Vienna and Hollywood, 248–9; and DB's Rank contract, 259; and DB's pop recording, 263; and DB's extravagance, 274; and DB's favourable reception in USA, 301; and DB's investment in *Private Eye*, 304; and DB's unpaid fee for *Darling*, 324; and filming of *The Damned*, 341; visits DB in Italy, 349; and DB's settling abroad, 353, 379; and DB/Tony's life at Clermont, 404; letter from DB on Brock at Clermont, 417; and DB's unsolicited correspondents, 418; and Mrs Rolls's case against DB, 424; and payment for *Death*

in Venice, 443; advises against suing *Time Out*, 458; letter from Tony on typing inadequacies, 495; and slight on DB in Tanitch's *Dirk Bogarde*, 502; and DB's reference to Lord Christopher Thynne, 505; and DB's financial worries, 507
Harding, Gilbert, 194
Harington, Clare, 530–1
Harmony in an Uproar (satire), 328
'Harri' (half-Indonesian girl), 139, 146
Harris, Elizabeth, 359
Harris, Fred, 296
Harris, John, 307
Harris, Julie, 264, 301
Harris, Miss (schoolteacher), 42
Harris, Rosemary, 324
Harrison, John, 329
Harrison, Noel, 265
Harrison, Sir Rex: DB and Tony stay with on Long Island, 224, 421; in *My Fair Lady*, 224–5, 241; DB admires, 226, 305; visits DB at Beel, 241; and death of Kay Kendall, 249; record of song, 305; wins New York film award, 310–11; in Venice, 359
Harrison, Sara, 265
Harrison, Stephen, 162
Hart to Hart (TV series), 443
Hartley, L.P.: *The Go-Between*, 10
Harty, Russell: interviews DB, 6, 379–80, 382–3, 407, 436, 471, 480, 483–5, 498–9, 504; death, 499n
Harvey, Anthony, 437, 442
Harvey, Laurence, 307, 325
Hasker Street, 167–8
Hatfield, Angela ('Angelica Chesterfield'), 47, 68, 112
Hathaway, Henry, 286
Hauser, Frank, 241–3
Haut Clermont, Le (La Treille), Châteauneuf de Grasse: DB buys and occupies with Tony, 178, 353–5, 362, 364–5, 368, 385–6, 404, 417–19, 478; The Pond and wild life, 419–20; struck by lightning, 444; DB puts up for sale and withdraws, 458–9; DB puts on market again, 482; DB sells, 486–7; DB's ashes scattered at, 542; de Pauws' misfortunes at, 549
Hawkins, Jack, 179, 198, 211, 268
Hawthorn, Major-General Douglas, 134–5, 137, 139–40
Hawthorne, Nigel, 11
Hayden, Phyllis, 500, 525
Hayman, Ronald, 412
Hayward, Susan, 250
Heald, Patricia, 382
Heald, Tim, 430
Health and Strength, 196–7
Heath, Sir Edward, 436
Heatherden Hall, Iver Heath, Buckinghamshire, 179
Heffer, Simon, 180–1
Heinemann (publishers), 383–4, 389; *see also* Thompson, Edward
Hello!, 503
Hennessey, Nurse *see* Rolls, Mary Elizabeth

Henrey, Robert: *The Siege of London*, 148

Hensher, Philip, 9, 543

Hepburn, Audrey, 224, 253

Herbert, A.P.: *Home and Beauty* (revue), 86

'Hickey, William' (newspaper diarist), 429

Hickman, Arthur, 34

Higgins, John, 448

High Bright Sun, The (film), 303, 322

Hilda (servant), 325, 332

Hiley, Jennifer (*née* Lake), 51

Hiller, Arthur, 318

Hillier, Mr and Mrs (housekeepers), 289

Hinxman, Margaret, 273, 356, 366, 379; book on DB
   (with Susan d'Arcy), 7, 391

Hippodrome, London: bombed, 90

Hird, Dame Thora, 159, 174

Hirschhorn, Clive, 314–15

HMS Defiant (film), 273, 278

Hoare, Philip, 167, 194

Hodge, Merton: *Grief Goes Over* (melodrama), 85,
   88

Hodges, Mike, 451–2

Hodgkinson, Leading Aircraftman, 131

Hodson, James Lansdale, 301

Hofsess, John, 513

Holbrook, Elisabeth, 174

Holbrook, Owen, 174

Holiday, Edna Flavelle ('Eve'; 'Nan Baildon'): in India
   with DB, 128–33; in DB's house in Chester Row,
   170, 184–5; rejoins Air Force, 186

Holland: DB serves in during war, 115–16, 118–21, 123;
   DB's *A Gentle Occupation* published in, 429–30;
   DB visits to promote book, 531

Holland, Mary, 305

Holloway, David, 408, 534

Hollywood: disfavours DB, 12–13, 300; interest in
   DB, 202–3; DB's offers from, 244–5; DB in, 246,
   248–9; DB eulogises, 250; Glenda Jackson on, 440

Holm, Ian, 334–5

Holt, Ellen ('Lally') *see* Searle, Ellen

Holt, Rinehart (US publishers), 406–7, 423, 433

homosexuality: and discretion, 9–12; in 1950s Britain,
   199–201; in films, 267–8; depicted in *Victim*, 270–
   2, 280–2

Hope, Vida, 90–1, 93, 102

Hopkins, Antony, 328

Hopkinson, Simon, 537

Hopper, Hedda, 203, 310

Horder, Joanna, 89

Horne, Kenneth: *The Good Young Man* (comedy),
   83–4

Horrocks, Lieut.-General Sir Brian, 114

Horst (photographer), 351

Horstig-Primuz, Olga, 208, 385, 461, 542

Hot Enough for June (film), 299–300

House and Garden, 385

House Un-American Activities Committee (USA),
   201

Houston, Donald, 204

Howard, Brian, 284–5

Howard, Irene, 253, 264, 315, 349, 385; death, 469

Howard, Trevor, 366

Howe, James Wong, 248

Hudson, Hugh, 450–1

Hudson, Rock, 13, 203, 228, 317, 455

Hughes-Hallett, Lucy, 483, 485

Humphries Film Laboratories, 296

Hungary, 332–5

Hunt, Lieut.-Colonel Bryan, 139, 146

Hunt, John (*later* Baron), 33

Hunt, Jonathan, 493

Hunted (film), 193, 201, 219

Hunter, Gordon, 63

Hunter, N.C.: *Grouse in June*, 82

Huppert, Isabelle, 466

Hurst, Brian Desmond, 211–12

Huston, John, 467

Hutchinson, Lawrence, 132

Hutton, Michael Clayton: *Power Without Glory*, 162–
   6, 169, 171, 216; *Sleep on My Shoulder*, 186

Huxley, Aldous, 77

Hyde-White, Wilfred, 188

I Am a Camera (film), 453

I, Claudius (failed film), 312

I Could Go On Singing (film; earlier 'The Lonely
   Stage'), 285–8, 350, 367

'I Play What I Like' (radio show), 212–13

Ill Met By Moonlight (film), 220–2

'Impressions in the Sand' (DB; article), 492

'In the Secret State' (proposed TV play), 472

Independent, The (newspaper), 499

Independent on Sunday, The, 530

India: DB posted to, 127–33; DB films in, 235, 237

Indiana, Gary, 516

Indonesia, 133–41, 146; *see also* Java

Innes, Hammond, 227

Innocente, L', 391

Irons, Jeremy, 451, 473n

Irvin, John, 311

Isherwood, Christopher, 453, 455; *Mr Norris Changes
   Trains*, 146

Isis (magazine), 295

Isoardi, Bruna, 378, 487

Isoardi, Marc, 378, 419, 486, 487

Isoardi, Marie-Christine, 441, 462, 479

Isoardi, Thierry, 462, 479

'It Takes All Sorts' (radio broadcast), 306

Italy: DB visits, 250, 299, 303, 313–15; DB and Tony
   live in, 347–8

Izegem (Belgium), 24–5, 40, 114–15, 392, 531–2

Jack, Ian, 437

Jackson, Glenda, 437–40, 442–3, 451–2, 477

Jacob, Naomi, 250

Jacobs, David, 446, 515, 528

Jagger, Sir Mick, 294–5, 452n

Jaipur, Maharajah and Maharani of, 235, 241
Jamaica, 336
Janni, Joseph, 307, 318, 325
Japan: surrenders (1945), 130
Jarre, Jean-Michel, 461
Java, 133–41, 146–7; in DB's *A Gentle Occupation*, 427–30
Jeans, Isabel, 195
Jenner, Caryl, 81
Jericho (DB), 483, 498, 514, 517–18, 523, 529, 534
Jerrold, Mary, 159
Joachim, Frederick: as DB's agent, 160–1, 168–9, 207; DB terminates association, 259, 273; and DB's recording of pop lyrics, 264
Jodl, General Alfred, 123
Joffé, Roland, 472–3
John XXIII, Pope, 350
John, Sir Elton, 417–18, 433, 452
John Player Lectures, 366–7
Johns, Glynis: and DB's sexuality, 19; marriage and child with Tony Forwood, 156–8; career, 157–8; divorce from Forwood, 184; on DB's selfish behaviour, 185; at Bendrose House, 187; on DB as friend, 189; film career, 193; and DB's relations with Forwood, 200–1; at Beel House, 206; at Christmas celebrations with Kay Kendall, 225; in Rome, 253; worry over son's upbringing, 256; and proposed film of *I Am a Camera*, 453
Johns, Mervyn, 156
Johnson, Hewlett, Dean of Canterbury, 286
Johnson, Lyndon Baines, 324
Johnson, Nunnally, 252, 315
Johnson, Richard, 187
Jolly, Caryl, 147
Jolly, Cynthia, 191
Jolly, Geraldine, 148, 191
Jolly, Hugh: in Singapore with DB, 147–8, 161, 171, 235; death, 191; as doctor in London, 191
Jones, Evan, 301–2, 313
Jones, George, 98–9, 125
Jones, Hugh, 98–9
Jones, J.D.F., 13
Jones, Jennifer, 228
Jones, John Francis (Jack): background, 98–100; relations with DB, 100–1, 106, 125–6; yacht designing, 100–1, 126, 155; in Normandy invasion, 109; wartime letters from DB, 119–20, 133; DB drawing reserved for, 124; surgical operations, 125; letters and stories from DB in Indonesia and Singapore, 136–7, 140, 148; and DB's stay in Suffolk, 155–6; DB meets in London, 171; destroys early letters from DB, 201, 454; on DB's *A Gentle Occupation*, 430–1; praises DB's *An Orderly Man*, 456; on DB's TV appearance, 523; death, 523
Jones, June, 100
Jones, Ron, 521, 530
Jourdan, Louis, 224, 453
Jowett, P.H., 69
Joyce, Eileen, 174
Joyce, Paul, 522–3
Justine (film), 338, 343–5, 349

Kael, Pauline, 281, 380, 392
Kaufman, Hank, 341
Kavanagh, Patricia, 455, 471, 497, 499, 501, 514–15, 538
Kaye, Danny, 224, 508
Kealy, T.J. (Tom), 79
Kearley, Charles, 317
Keegan, Nurse, 243
Keen, Geoffrey, 210
Kelly, Orry, 253
Kendall, Henry, 166
Kendall, Kay: visits DB at homes, 109, 187, 205–6, 241; DB visits on Long Island, 224; diagnosed with myeloid leukemia, 225, 525–6; Cukor directs, 248; death, 249; friendship with Gareth, 277; in *Snakes and Ladders*, 421
Keneally, Thomas: *Schindler's Ark*, 461
Kennaway, James, 285
Kennedy, Sir Ludovic, 497, 539; *Counterblast*, 513
Kennedy, Robert, 339
Kennedy, Rose, 339
Kennerley, Mitchell, 329
Kerr, Evelyn S., 184
Keys, Nelson, 86
Khan, Masud, 278
Kid Rodelo (film), 242
Kidnappers, The (film), 218
Killing Fields, The (film), 472
Kilmuir, David Maxwell Fyfe, Viscount (*later* Earl) of, 199–200, 226
Kilmuir, Sylvia, Viscountess (Rex Harrison's sister), 226
Kilroy-Silk, Robert, 262n
Kimmins, Anthony, 78
Kind Hearts and Coronets (film), 515
King and Country (film), 301–3, 310
King's School, Rochester, 520
Kingscote, Nigel, 106
Kingston, Jamaica, 336
Klimov, Elem, 492
Knight, Mrs (cook/housekeeper), 304, 307
Knights of the Round Table (film), 201
Knopf, Alfred (US publishers), 433, 435
Knowler, John, 408, 423
Knox, Alexander, 321
Korda, Sir Alexander, 156, 186, 236, 290, 312
Kreipe, General Heinrich, 220
Kroll, Jack, 416
Kurosawa, Akira, 432

L-Shaped Room, The (film), 293
Labaro, Italy, 347
Labèque, Katia and Marielle, 525, 533
Labofilms, 379, 432–3, 492, 544
Labouchère, Henry, 200
Lacey, Tony, 471, 505, 514, 538

Ladbroke Grove, London, 315–16
Ladd, Alan, 357
Lake, Dr Bernard ('Bunny'), 50–3
'Lally' *see* Searle, Ellen
Lambilliotte, Dominique, 531
Lancaster, Burt, 352
Lancaster Hotel, London, 488, 508
Landa, Alfredo, 466
Lang, Charles, 248
Lang, Fritz, 218
Lang, Jack, 460, 520, 533
Langtry, Lillie, 500
Lantz, Robert, 311
Last Tango in Paris (film), 379
Latimer, Sally, 81
Laura (film), 472
Laure, Odette, 508–10
Lawley, Sue, 511–12
Lawrence of Arabia (film), 236–8, 268
Lawrence, Thomas Edward, 227, 236–9
Leacock, Philip, 195, 218
Lean, Sir David, 237–8
Le Bret, Robert Favre, 461–2
Lee, Barbara, 139, 148
Lee, Christopher, 172
Lee, Donald, 139
Lee, Jack, 174, 546
Lees-Milne, James, 425, 450
Lehár, Franz: *The Merry Widow*, 533
Leigh, Vivien: and Laurence Olivier, 157; lives at
    Tickerage Mill, 262; death, 331
Leigh-Hunt, Barbara, 503
Leighton, Margaret, 157, 172, 188, 225
Lejeune, C.A., 217
Leon, Anne, 205, 241
Lerner, Alan Jay, 224, 226, 246, 300, 301, 324
Les Girls (musical film), 225, 248
Lessing, Doris, 19
Levine, Joseph, 324–5, 396
Lewis, Jeremy: *Kindred Spirits*, 405n
Libel (film), 245
Liberace, 11
Lichfield, Patrick Anson, 5th Earl of, 344, 359, 378
Lichtenberg, Georg, 420n
Lieberson, Sandy, 472
Lieven, Albert, 188
Lillie, Beatrice, 88
Lindop, Audrey Erskine, 254
Linnett, Michael, 449, 491
Linton, David, 129
Liszt, Franz, 244–6, 254, 511, 525
Littell, Robert: *The October Circle*, 451
Little Revue, 90, 98
Livingstone, David, 35
Lloyd, Frederick, 169
Lockie, Dr William: at school in Glasgow with DB,
    57–61; DB introduces to Yvonne Arnaud, 63; loses
    contact with DB, 64; and DB's title *A Postillion
    Struck by Lightning*, 387

Lockwood, Margaret, 212
Loewe, Fritz, 224
Logan, Josh, 241
Logan, Saxon, 456
Lollobrigida, Gina, 318
London Management (agency), 273, 455
'Lonely Stage, The' *see I Could Go On Singing*
Longest Day, The (film), 284
Lonsdale, Frederick: *But for the Grace of God* (play),
    158–9
Loren, Sophia, 248
Los Angeles, 344–5, 439–40, 456
Los Angeles Herald-Examiner, 349
Los Angeles Times, 248
Loschetter, Clair, 353, 355, 450, 455
Loschetter, Léon, 354–5, 362, 419, 432, 487
Losey, Joseph: background and exile from USA, 201;
    first works with DB, 201–2; makes *The Servant*
    with DB, 290–3, 295–8; films *King and Country*,
    301–2; and *Modesty Blaise*, 312–13, 319; films
    Accident, 318–23; correspondence with DB, 331–3,
    348, 353; and Vivien Leigh's memorial service, 331;
    makes *Boom!*, 332, 356; presents from and to DB,
    332–3; DB's estimate of, 346, 511; and DB's
    purchase of house in France, 355; differences with
    DB over remarks in interview, 356–7, 365; awarded
    Palme d'Or for *The Go-Between*, 368; films *The
    Assassination of Trotsky*, 369; hopes to work with
    DB again, 391; writes foreword to Hinxman-d'Arcy
    book on DB, 391; resumes contact with DB, 432;
    and Glenda Jackson, 438; on Cannes Film Festival
    awards, 466, 468; death, 468–9; honorary
    doctorate at Wisconsin, 468; Tavernier and, 507
Losey, Patricia, 6, 261, 313, 333, 364, 468–9, 528
Lott, Dame Felicity, 533
Low, Adam, 546–7
Löwitsch, Klaus, 414
Lowndes, William, 205
Lowry, Malcolm: *Under the Volcano*, 371
Lowry, Suzanne, 16
Lucas, Cornel, 171, 182, 231, 243
Lucas, Susan (*née* Travers), 243
Ludwig (film), 391
Luft, Lorna, 287–8
Luft, Sid, 225, 261, 286
Lullington, Sussex: Bogaerde family holidays in, 45–
    50, 404; visitors to church, 544
Lumb, Major C.E., 95
Lunghi, Cherie, 473
Lynn, Ralph: *Is Your Honeymoon Really Necessary?*
    (farce), 160
Lynn, (Dame) Vera, 101
Lyric Theatre, Hammersmith, 190, 195, 241
Lyrics for Lovers (DB's record), 263–4, 446

McCallum, John, 157
McClellan, Forrest, 54–5, 62, 409
McClellan, Hester (*née* Niven; DB's aunt), 35, 62–3,
    102, 409

McClellan, John, 62
McClellan, Nickie, 62
McCormick, John, 267, 270
McDermott, Hugh, 159
MacDonald, Richard, 296
McDowall, Roddy, 249, 301, 455
McEwan, Geraldine, 213–14
McGilligan, Patrick, 248
McGregor, Ian, 51
MacGregor, Sue, 506, 524
McKell, Robert, 59–60
McKellen, Sir Ian, 11–12
McKenna, Virginia, 212
Mackintosh, Charles Rennie, 56
Mackintosh, Elizabeth ('Gordon Daviot'; 'Josephine
    Tey'), 231
MacLaine, Shirley, 455
MacLean, Alistair, 244
Maclean, Donald, 199
MacLean, Sheila: at DB's death, 1–2, 4; nurses DB,
    2–4, 539–40, 548; in DB's will, 544
Macmillan, Harold (1st Earl of Stockton), 318
MacNaughton, Alan, 280
Macowan, Norman: *Glorious Morning* (play), 73, 76
MacQuitty, William, 205
Madonna, 524
'Magic Flame, A' *see Song Without End*
Maharis, George, 307
Mahler, Gustav, 351–2, 355, 367, 512
Mahoney, Bob, 480
Major, John, 520
Major, Dame Norma, 520
Makins, Major P.V., 95
Malamud, Bernard, 331
Malet, Oriel, 398
Malfait, Nadine, 531, 532
Mallaby, Brigadier A.W.S., 134
Man for All Seasons, A (film), 317
Manchester Guardian see *Guardian, The*
Mann, Thomas: *Death in Venice*, 351–2; *The Magic
    Mountain*, 391
March, Elspeth, 262, 264
Margaret, Princess, 159, 319
Markham, David, 161–2
Marks, Alfred, 311
Marsh, Harry, 63
Martin, Frank, 501
Martin, Professor Pierre, 481, 491
Martinez, M., 465
Martinez, Madame (French daily help), 378, 465
Mary, Queen of George V, 190
Mason, James, 178, 180, 182, 268, 366, 543
Mason, Richard, 233
Massie, Paul, 245
Mastroianni, Marcello, 415
Matlock, 103
Matthew, Brian, 217
Matthews, A.E., 159
Matthews, Jessie, 182

Maude *see* Melford, Jill
Maugham, Robin: *The Servant*, 291–2
Maugham, W. Somerset: visits set of 'A Magic Flame'
    in Vienna, 248; *The Painted Veil* (play), 82; *Quartet*
    (adapted by R.C. Sherriff), 173–4, 182
Mauretania (liner), 224
Maxibules (play), 304
'May We Borrow Your Husband?' (TV play), 477,
    480, 483
Mayer, Peter, 471
Mayflower Pictures (company), 195
Medhurst, Andy, 182, 281
Medmenham, Buckinghamshire, 104, 129
Medwin, Michael, 180
Meisel, Steven, 524
Melford, Jill ('Maude'; 'Swiss Army Knife'), 290, 299–
    300, 448, 463, 489, 493
Melly, George, 367
Mendoza, Joe, 165–6
Mengers, Sue, 317–18
Menuhin, Yehudi, Baron, 226
Mercer, David, 392, 394
Merchant, Vivien, 321
Merman, Ethel, 324
Merrick, David, 241
Mészáros, Márta, 460
Metro-Goldwyn-Mayer (MGM), 245, 252–3
Michael Aspel Show, The (television programme), 523
Michel, Christine, 487
Miles, Bernard (Baron), 81
Miles, Sarah, 293, 297
Milestone, Lewis ('Milly'), 198–9, 224, 515
Milland, Ray, 227
Millar, Stuart, 286
Miller, Arthur: *All My Sons*, 185
Miller, Gilbert, 225
Miller, Sir Jonathan, 17
Mills, Sir John, 180, 194, 255–6, 258, 285, 403, 532
Milnthorpe, Chailey, Sussex, 65–6, 100
Mind Benders, The (film), 288, 298, 320
Minnelli, Vincente, 259
Minney, R.J., 236
Miracle, The (film), 241
Mirales, Vicente and Manolita, 289
Mirren, Dame Helen, 466
Mishcon de Reya (solicitors), 505
Mission, The (film), 473
Mitchell, Stephen, 292
Mitchell, Yvonne, 250, 353
Mitford, Nancy, 429
Mitterrand, François, 460
Moby Dick (play), 276
Modesty Blaise (film), 312–15, 319, 325
Moffatt, John, 191
Moiseiwitsch, Tanya, 79
Monarch of Bermuda (liner), 148–9
Monsarrat, Nicholas, 195
Monsey, Derek, 250, 273
Montagu of Beaulieu, Edward, 3rd Baron, 199

Montand, Yves, 345
Montgomery, Field Marshal Bernard Law, 1st
    Viscount, 110, 115, 123, 396–7, 400
Month in the Country, A (play), 312
Moonfleet (film), 218
Moore, George: *Esther Waters*, 169, 173
Moore, Henry, 67, 407
Moore, Kieron, 172
Moore, Sir Roger, 241
Moore Street, Chelsea, 489–90
Moorhouse, Geoffrey, 366
Morahan, Christopher, 472
More, Kenneth, 163, 165, 179, 204, 216, 250, 254, 277,
    286, 447; *More or Less*, 422
Morgan, Michèle, 460
Morley, Robert, 240
Morley, Sheridan: DB denies homosexuality to, 13;
    on DB's relations with Tony Forwood, 18;
    biography of John Gielgud, 199, 232; on
    homosexuality in Britain, 199–200; DB describes
    Gladys Cooper to, 249; and DB's *Snakes and
    Ladders*, 422; on DB's *A Short Walk from Harrods*,
    531; article on death of DB, 543; *Dirk Bogarde:
    Rank Outsider*, 7, 536
Morricone, Ennio, 466
Mortimer, Sir John, 471, 529
Mortimer, Penelope: and DB's film roles, 371;
    friendship and correspondence with DB, 372, 385,
    390, 395; DB asks about Chatto's standing, 383;
    and portrayal of Lally in *Postillion*, 388; and DB's
    portrayal of 'Boy' Browning, 398; and DB's busy
    schedule, 519; and DB's efforts to help others, 526;
    DB admits to being happy, 535
Mosley, Diana, Lady, 529
Mosley, Leonard, 166
Mosley, Nicholas, 318, 320–1, 534
Mosley, Sir Oswald, 429
Motion Picture Association of America: Production
    Code, 267, 281
Motion Picture Herald, 198, 232, 244, 250, 300
Motley Films: DB buys, 241, 277; DB's assets
    transferred to, 379
Mountbatten, Louis, 1st Earl, 400
Mugar Memorial Library, Boston, 501
Muir, Edwin: *Scottish Journey*, 55
Munro, Neil, 35–6
Murdoch, Dame Iris, 382
Murphy, Gerald and Sara, 538
Murray, Barbara, 180n, 227–9, 265, 276, 503
Murray, Sarah (DB's aunt; 'Sadie'), 54–5, 58–9, 62,
    102, 189, 390, 408–10
Murray, Stephen, 82
Murray, William (DB's uncle), 54–6, 58–9, 62, 189,
    409–10
Music Lovers, The (film), 437
My Fair Lady (stage musical), 224–5, 241

Nabokov, Vladimir, 475; *Despair*, 410–11, 415
Naplo (film), 467

Nassau, Bahamas: DB registers company in, 332, 335
National Enquirer, 310
National Film Theatre: DB lectures at, 261, 366–7,
    453–4, 457, 506, 523, 535
National Theatre: DB reads at, 503–4, 506: DB gives
    master-classes at, 513
Neal, Patricia (Mrs Roald Dahl), 437–8, 440, 442–3
Neame, Ronald, 78, 285–8
Negresco, Hôtel, Nice, 227, 480–1
Nelson, John, 102, 154
Nesbitt, Cathleen, 225
Nettlefold (studio), 202
New Lindsey Theatre Club, Notting Hill, 162, 164–
    5, 184, 185
New Musical Express, 446
New York: DB retrospective at Lincoln Center, 245;
    DB in, 260, 300–1, 310, 323–4, 335–6, 439
New York Herald Tribune, 260
New York Times, 349, 380
New Yorker, The, 367
Newick Amateur Dramatic Society (Sussex), 70–1,
    74, 76
Newill, Robert A., 26
Newman, Nanette *see* Forbes, Nanette
News of the World, 245
Nice-Matin (newspaper), 368
Nichols, Dandy, 163
Nicholson, Ben, 340, 386, 492–3
Nicholson, John, 444
Nicholson, Louise (Mrs Nicholas Wapshott), 457
Nicholson, William, 489
Night and the City (film), 203
Night of the Generals, The (film), 317–18
Night Porter, The (film), 374–80, 396, 432, 436
Night to Remember, A (film), 254
Niven family, 62, 408–9
Niven, David, 180, 383, 447
Niven, Forrest (DB's maternal grandfather):
    background and career, 35–8; death, 38, 62, 539;
    DB given watercolour by, 192
Niven, Hester (DB's aunt) *see* McClellan, Hester
Niven, Hilda, 409
Niven, James, 35
Niven, Jane (*née* Nelson; DB's maternal
    grandmother), 35, 41, 62
Niven, Neil Munro (DB's uncle), 36, 409
Niven, Sarah (DB's aunt), 35
Niven, William, 34–5, 35, 54
No Love for Johnnie (film), 272, 315
Nore, Godalming, 284–5, 289, 298, 300, 304, 311, 315
Normandy: invasion and battle (1944), 108–13
Northcliffe, Alfred Harmsworth, Viscount, 29–30,
    32
Novello, Ivor: *We Proudly Present*, 184
Noyelle, Gérard, 26–8
Noyes, Revd H.E., 24
Nutt, Arthur, 45
Nutt, George and Edith (*née* Clark), 27, 39
Nutt, Kathleen, 40

Oakes, Philip, 305–6
Oba, Sadao, 140
O'Brian, Patrick, 14
Oh! What a Lovely War (film), 346, 349
O'Hagan, Colo, 508
Old Vic: auditions DB, 77
Olivier, Edith, 8–9, 14
Olivier, Laurence, Baron: in *Journey's End*, 71; and Vivien Leigh, 157; and founding of Chichester Festival Theatre, 282; in *Bunny Lake is Missing*, 311; at Vivien Leigh's memorial service, 332; makes commercial, 337–8; supposed homosexual affairs, 454
Olson, Nancy, 224, 300
Omnibus (TV programme), 454, 456
Once a Jolly Swagman (film), 174–5, 546
One That Got Away, The (film), 254
O'Neal, Ryan, 398
O'Neill, Jamie, 483
Oradour-sur-Glane, 393
Orderly Man, An (DB): on Belsen, 122, 461; on life at Clermont, 364; on DB's relations with parents, 365, 384, 408, 431, 456, 477, 530; on *The Night Porter*, 377; on relations with publishers, 384; describes Chatto office, 405; on film *Despair*, 415; writing, 433, 447; on Glenda Jackson, 438; publication, 447, 449, 453–4; dedicated to Tony, 448; Tony criticises early chapters, 449; editing, 450; promoted, 452; publisher's advance, 455; reception, 456; on friendship, 476
Ormond, Sylvia (*née* Greaves), 171
Orr, James, 400
Osborne, John: *Look Back in Anger*, 231, 515; *Epitaph for George Dillon*, 265, 273; congratulates DB on journalism, 515; memorial service, 535
Osbourne, Ozzy, 262n
Otherwise Club, Shere, Surrey, 78
O'Toole, Peter, 311, 508
Our Man in Havana (film), 237
Our Mother's House (film), 323, 325, 331, 335, 337, 391
Owens, Susan, 545
Oxford Playhouse, 241–3
Oxley, David, 220

Page, Anthony, 442
Palmer, Lilli, 2, 317
Paris: liberated (1944), 113–14; *see also* France
Paris, Texas (film), 467
Parker, Cecil, 187
Parker, Dorothy, 306, 501
Parris, Matthew, 11
Parry, Lusia, 102, 158, 469
Parsons, Ian, 382
Particular Friendship, A (DB): 'Mrs X' in, 8; on Rex Harrison, 226; on Jean Kennedy Smith's visit, 339; on Soviet invasion of Czechoslovakia, 341; on filming in St Peter's, Rome, 350; on publication of DB's letters, 373; writing, 425; publication, 504, 505–6

Partridges (Chelsea grocers), 527
Pasadena, 439
Passavant, Elise, 76–7
Password Is Courage, The (film), 283, 285
Paterson, Mark, 154
Patricia Neal Story, The, 437–43, 455
Pauw, Alain and Christine de, 486–7, 541–2, 549
Pavlova, Anna, 33
Payne, David, 451
Peake, Sir Charles, 209
Peake, Mervyn and Maeve (Gilmore), 328
Pearson, Bob, 492, 530, 541
Pebble Mill at One (TV programme), 462
Peck, Gregory, 17, 189, 508
Peckinpah, Sam, 395
Peeping Tom (film), 222
Peerless, Barbara, 498
Penelope (film), 318
Pennington, Mary, 205
Penny Princess (film), 194
Penrose, Sir Roland, 339
Peppard, George, 301, 317
Period of Adjustment, A (DB), 534
Perkins, Anthony, 13
Permission to Kill, 384, 386, 388
Peters, A.D. (literary agents), 455
Petit, Marushka, 138, 140
Pevsner, Sir Nikolaus, 262
Philadelphia Story, The (film), 350
Philip, Prince, Duke of Edinburgh, 87, 400
Philipe, Gérard, 191, 243
Phillips, Madeleine, 115
Photoplay, 240
Picturegoer, 203, 215, 244–5
Pidgeon, Walter, 202
Pigott-Smith, Tim, 503
Pike, Jeffrey, 432
Pink, Susan, 495, 536
Pinter, Harold, 291–3, 295, 309, 317–19, 321, 371, 391; *No Man's Land* (play), 522
Platen, August von, 351
Players' Theatre, London, 90
Plomley, Roy, 305, 511
Plumb, Blossom, 393
Plummer, Christopher, 301
Plunket, Patrick, 7th Baron, 339
Plus grand musée, Le (TV documentary), 461
Poetry Review, The, 97, 128
Poitier, Sidney, 324
Pook, Maureen, 163, 165
Pope, Alexander, 41
Porter, Robert, 29–31
Post, Sir Laurens van der, 13–14, 133
Postillion Struck by Lightning, A (DB): on life in Sussex, 45, 48, 408, 528; Bill Lockie in, 58; on experiences in Glasgow, 61–2; on Paul Scofield, 82; writing, 387–90, 404; illustrations, 404–6; published, 406–7; DB's family in, 408–9; reception and success, 408, 410, 412, 421–3; on Scottish

Postillion Struck by Lightning, A—cont
  experiences, 408–9; French translation, 422–3;
  sales, 444
Poteau, Dr, 435, 449
Potter, Dennis, 432
Powell, Anthony, 499
Powell, Dilys: praises DB in *The Doctor's Dilemma*,
  240; reviews *Victim*, 279; praises *The Servant*, 297;
  letters from DB, 319, 322, 330, 340, 358, 416; reviews
  Death in Venice, 367; and private screening of *The
  Night Porter*, 379; and DB in *A Bridge Too Far*, 401;
  and DB's accepting presidency of Cannes Film
  Festival jury, 465
Powell, Enoch, 16
Powell, Jane (*née* Forwood), 189–90
Powell, Michael, 220–2
Powell, Robert, 502–3
Power, Tyrone, 306
Preminger, Otto, 311, 362
Pressburger, Emeric, 220
Price, Dennis, 179, 271
Price, James, 328
Priestley, J.B.: Gawsworth honours, 250; DB reviewed
  together with, 408; *Cornelius* (play), 80, 82; *When
  We Are Married* (play), 80
Priggen, Norman ('Spike'), 293
Private Eye, 304, 447, 544–5
Procter, Stan, 97, 101
Production Facilities (Films) Limited, 168
Propper, Renata, 274, 518
Proust, Marcel, 351, 391
Providence (film), 392–5, 412
Prowler, The (film), 201–2
Purdom, Edmund, 203
Puttnam, David, Baron, 450–1, 472–3, 482, 488

Q Theatre, Kew, 79–80, 82, 176, 184–6, 276
Quantrill, Jimmy, 995
Quebec Films, 277
Queen Anne House, Kensington, 491–6, 501
Queen Elizabeth (liner), 245, 323
Queen Mary (liner), 226
Queen's Royal Regiment, 95–6, 105
Quennell, Sir Peter, 290, 521
Quiet American, The (film), 472
Quilley, Denis, 160
Quinn, Anthony, 311

Rabal, Francisco, 466
Rampling, Charlotte: DB meets, 340; in *The Damned*,
  342–3, 442; DB's paternalism towards, 343, 442,
  509; in *The Night Porter*, 376–80; on DB's drinking,
  377; lunches with DB at Connaught, 452; DB
  dedicates book to, 461; and *The Quiet American*,
  472; meets DB and Tony in Paris, 488; and DB's
  tours, 530
Rank, J. Arthur, Baron, 178–9
Rank Organisation: DB works for, 168–9, 176, 178–
  81, 186, 194, 217, 231, 244, 258–9; lack of success in

USA, 222; difficulties, 233; abandons *Lawrence of
  Arabia*, 237–8; and DB's Hollywood offer, 244;
  declines to release DB, 259–60; ends contract with
  DB, 272–3
Raphael, Frederic: on DB's uncertainties, 13; on
  Belsen, 123; scripts *Darling*, 307–9, 316–17; on
  DB's attitude to Monica Vitti, 313; on DB's social
  life in London, 500
Rapper, Irving, 241
RAPWI (Repatriation of Allied Prisoners of War and
  Internees), 133, 137
Rattigan, Sir Terence, 10–11, 225, 236–7; *Ross* (play),
  238; *Who Is Sylvia?*, 276
Rave (magazine), 446
Raven, Simon, 430
Ray, Cyril, 399
Ray, Johnnie, 215
Ray, Satyajit, 467
Rayner, Prebble, 39
Rayner, Richard, 457–8
Read, Piers Paul, 352, 368
Read, Thomas, 31
Redford, Robert, 301, 396
Redgrave, Sir Michael, 180, 207–8, 226, 312, 369
Redgrave, Vanessa, 318
Redonda (island), 250
Reed, Rex, 395
Rees-Mogg, William, Baron, 34
Reeves, Steve, 197
Relph, Michael, 181, 267–9, 271, 285
'Reluctant Star' (radio profile of DB), 216–17
Remarque, Erich Maria: *All Quiet on the Western
  Front*, 538
Remick, Lee, 311, 489
Rendell, Brigadier Dennis, 50–2, 521
Rendell, Ruth, Baroness, 471
Renoir, Jean, 335
Resnais, Alain, 319, 335, 359, 365, 392, 394–5
Reunion Theatre Association, 159, 175
Reynolds, Gillian, 522
Reynolds, Jim, 407
Rhys, Jennifer, 506
Richard of Bordeaux (proposed film), 231
Richard, Sir Cliff, 18–19, 292, 300, 462
Richard, Kenneth Dalton Kennedy, 339–40
Richards, Keith, 452n
Richardson, Sir Ralph, 350
Richler, Mordecai, 299
Riddell, Squadron Leader Peter, 129
Riley, Alasdair, 386
Ritchard, Cyril, 120, 533
Robards, Jason, Jr, 260
Roberts, Rachel, 324
Robertson Justice, James, 193, 204, 216, 293, 299
Robinson, Anne, 533
Rocco and His Brothers (film), 349
Rodley, Chris, 522–3
Rogers, Eric, 263
Rogers, Ginger, 202

Rogers, Peter, 208–9, 274, 283, 303
Rohmer, (Major-General) Richard, 109–12
Rolls, Mary Elizabeth (*née* Hennessey), 423–4, 537
Roman Catholic National League of Decency, 182
Romantic Englishwoman, The (film), 438
Rome, 250, 253, 338–41, 350
Roose-Evans, James, 523
Rosay, Françoise, 174, 182
Rosoman, Leonard, 386, 492, 501
Rota, Anthony, 501
Rourke, Mickey, 482
Routh, Jonathan, 265
Roux, Yvonne, 481–2, 488
Rowland, Toby, 213
Rubinstein, Richard, 51
Rumbold, Richard, 352
Russell Harty Show, The (TV programme), 379, 471
Russell, Ken, 437
Ryan, Cornelius, 396–7
Ryan, Kathleen, 173

St Andrews University: awards honorary doctorate to
    DB, 471, 474–5
St John, Earl: disagreements with DB, 179, 409;
    position at Rank, 179; on DB in *Penny Princess*, 194;
    and *Doctor in the House*, 203; on *Ill Met by
    Moonlight*, 221; dines at Beel, 227; on *Saturday
    Night and Sunday Morning*, 231; and abandonment
    of *Lawrence of Arabia*, 237; on DB's ranking, 250;
    and *The Singer Not the Song*, 254–5, 257, 259; and
    Victim, 268, 272, 282; DB proposes ending Rank
    contract, 272
St Moritz, 316
St Mungo (newspaper), 37
Saint-Denis, Michel, 89
'Saki' (H.H. Munro), 503–4
Salmon, William, 45
Sanda, Dominique, 376
Sandoe, John (Chelsea bookshop), 527–8
Santoro, Elise, 329
Santos inocentes, Los (film), 466
Sapphire (film), 267
Sarigny, Peter de, 211–12
Sassard, Jacqueline, 321–2
Sassoon, Siegfried, 8
Saunders, Amanda, 503–4, 506
Saunders, Sir Peter, 79
Schell, Maximilian, 307
Schiele, Egon, 386
Schifano, Laurence, 351
Schiller, Larry, 438, 442–3, 455
Schindler, Oskar, 461
Schlesinger, John, 307–8, 324, 337, 455, 500
Schneider, Romy, 376
Schulkes, Arnold, 229–30, 303, 307, 323, 326, 344,
    346–7, 474, 480
Scofield, Joy, 499
Scofield, Paul, 82, 255, 257, 319, 499, 508
Scott, Paul: *The Raj Quartet*, 472

Sea Shall Not Have Them, The (film), 207–8, 379
Searle, Ellen (*later* Holt; 'Lally'): as live-in nanny for
    DB's family, 43–4; country life in Sussex, 46, 48;
    and DB's schooling, 51, 53; on DB's relations with
    father, 54; DB's attachment to, 66; on Ulric's
    nightmare, 302; in DB's book, 388–90, 406, 408;
    and DB's title *A Postillion Struck by Lightning*, 397;
    Princess Alexandra on, 418; on Mrs Rolls, 424; and
    DB's mother's funeral, 432; DB dedicates *Great
    Meadow* to, 529; in Lullington church visitors'
    book, 544; describes DB and family, 547
Searle, George, 43, 245
Searle, Jane, 43
Sebastian (film), 325–6, 328
Secret Ceremony (film), 356
Seldon, Anthony, 519
Seligman, Olivia, 512
Sellers, Peter, 304, 311
Selznick, David O., 228
Semprun, Jorge, 466
Sendelhofer, Willi and Greta, 250, 262
Serafini, Luigi and Aigle, 284, 289
Serpent, The (film), 373–4, 391
Servant, The (film), 291–8, 300–1, 310, 327, 443; ballet
    version (*Play Without Words*), 545
Sessions, John, 534
Sexual Offences Act (1967), 282
Seymer, Lieut.-Colonel V.H., 95
Seyrig, Delphine, 321, 323
Shakespeare, Nicholas: DB denies homosexuality to,
    13; as literary editor of *Daily Telegraph*, 498–9, 501;
    lunches at Connaught with DB, 517; leaves *Daily
    Telegraph*, 518; writes life of Bruce Chatwin, 518;
    relations with DB, 531; account of DB's life, 546–7
Sharif, Omar, 318
Shaw, George Bernard, 240, 290
Shelley, Elsa: *Foxhole in the Parlor* (play), 185
Shepperton Studios, 299
Sher, Sir Antony, 501
Sheridan, Dinah, 195, 201
Sherriff, R.C.: adapts Maugham stories as *Quartet*,
    173–4; *Journey's End*, 70–1, 73, 102
Shiner, Ronald, 198
Short Cut, The (film), 250
Short Walk from Harrods, A (DB): self-revelation in,
    9, 530; on Belsen, 122; on life at Queen Anne
    House, 495; writing, 515–16; reception, 530–1; sales,
    534
Shulman, Milton, 232
Sicilian, The (film), 482
Sicily, 250, 252
Siegel, Sol, 259
Signoret, Simone, 339, 345, 369, 391, 481
Sillitoe, Alan: *Saturday Night and Sunday Morning*,
    231
Sim, Alastair, 198, 240
Sim, Sheila (Lady Attenborough), 5, 166, 346, 365,
    401–3, 449
Simba (film), 211

Simmons, Charles, 50

Simmons, Jean, 177, 187, 189, 203, 261

Simon, John, 367

Sinatra, Frank, 194

Sinden, Sir Donald: on Frederick Joachim, 161; on
    Cowan, 178; on John Davis, 179; on Gielgud's
    conviction for soliciting, 200; in *Doctor in the
    House*, 204–5; in *Simba*, 211–12; on DB's put-down
    comment, 215; on DB's camp behaviour, 257

Singapore, 147–8

Singer Not the Song, The (film), 253–9, 280, 400, 507,
    545

Sitwell, (Sir) Sacheverell: Life of Liszt, 248

Skene, Tony, 165

Sketch (magazine), 172

Skinner, Ann, 307–8, 314, 364, 377, 385, 415–16, 418

Skouras, Spyros, 259

Sleeping Tiger, The (film), 201, 203, 206, 292

Smaggasgale, C.E.F. ('Smaggie'), 51, 53

Smallwood, Norah: publishes DB, 7, 387, 389, 404–
    7, 420, 424, 433, 448, 449, 476; character and
    qualities, 382–3; sees DB's interview with Russell
    Harty, 382; letters from DB, 418, 421, 431–2, 436,
    439, 441, 444, 447, 455; and DB's indiscretions in
    naming characters in books, 424; and DB's
    proposed novel, 425; and DB's *A Gentle
    Occupation*, 428–9; retirement, 434, 470; attacked
    in *Private Eye*, 447; sciatica, 449; and DB's
    California novel, 456; DB complains to about
    English newspapers, 457; and DB's cancelled sale
    of Clermont, 459; and DB as president of jury at
    Cannes Film Festival, 467; health decline and
    death, 469–70, 472, 475; DB's attachment to, 470;
    and DB's doctorate at St Andrews, 474; on
    snobbery, 483

Smith, Alexis, 202, 264

Smith, Constance Babington, 103, 128–9

Smith, Dodie: *Call It a Day*, 82

Smith, Jean Kennedy, 324, 339

Snakes and Ladders (DB): writing, 7, 405; and DB's
    wartime duty as aerial photographic interpreter,
    112; on Eve Holiday, 131–2; and DB's post-Army
    career, 154; on DB's audition for Reunion Theatre
    Association, 159–60; on DB's adopting name, 161;
    on Noël Coward, 165; on success of *Summertime*,
    213; on Bob Thomson, 234; on turning down
    Chichester Festival Theatre offer, 283; on Garland
    tantrum, 287; on Barrett in *The Servant*, 295; on
    Fishers, 346; on filming of *Death in Venice*, 360;
    publication and reception, 420–3, 437; sales, 444

Snowdon, Antony Armstrong-Jones, 1st Earl of, 319

So Long at the Fair (film), 177, 183, 203

Soames, Mary, Lady, 291

Sondheim, Stephen, 324

Song Without End (film; earlier 'A Magic Flame'), 244,
    247, 259–60, 291, 344, 454, 456, 502

Spain: DB visits, 217–19, 257, 278–9, 282

Spanish Gardener, The (film), 217–19

Spender, Michael, 129

Spiegel, Sam, 237–8, 318–19

Spoleto, 345

Spurling, Hilary, 422, 499

Spurling, John, 499

Stafford, John, 254

Stamp, Terence, 313

Standing, John, 290, 299

Steel, Anthony, 179

Steel, James, 56, 61, 63

Steele, Tommy and Ann, 304

Steiger, Brad, 261

Stellman, Marcel, 263

Stevenson, Juliet, 513

Steward, Ernest, 235

Stewart, Hugh, 169

Steyn, Mark, 446

Stock, Nigel, 214

Stone, Geoffrey, 119

Stone, Norman, 489–90

Stoppard, Sir Tom, 410–11, 413, 415, 533

Storey, David: *Flight into Camden*, 291; 388

Storrs, Sir Ronald, 236

Story of Robin Hood and His Merrie Men, The (Disney
    film), 193

Strachan, Alan, 6

Strawberry Hill, 41

Strayton, Fred, 325

Streisand, Barbra, 324

Stribling, Melissa, 261–2, 267

Strick, Joseph, 344, 349

Striplings, The (film), 304

Stritch, Elaine, 394–5

Stuart, Campbell, 32

Suckling, Pilot Officer Michael ('Babe'), 129

Sun (newspaper), 304

Sunday Express, 250

Sunday Times, The, 538

Surrey, University of, 514

Sussex Life, 529

Sussex, University of: awards honorary doctorate to
    DB, 532–3

Sutherland, Graham, 67

Sutherland, Kathleen, 67, 407

Sweet, Matthew, 258

Switzerland, 244, 258, 437

Syms, Sylvia, 270–4, 281

Tale of Two Cities, A (film), 10, 230–1, 234–5, 240, 280

Tallitt, Tina, 545

Tamiroff, Akim, 198

Tani, Yoko, 235

Tanitch, Robert: *Dirk Bogarde: The Complete Career
    Illustrated*, 7, 502

Tavernier, Bertrand, 467, 507–11, 514–15, 531

Taylor, A.J.P., 522

Taylor, Dame Elizabeth, 189, 210, 332, 468

Taylor, Joyce Dyson ('Glur'), 290, 352, 356, 385, 406

Tender is the Night (film), 260

Tennant, Stephen, 8

Tennent, H.M.: power and influence, 10, 190; Tony Forwood scouts for, 88

Tey, Josephine *see* Mackintosh, Elizabeth

Thal *see* van Thal

Thatcher, Margaret, Baroness, 436, 484, 516, 520

Theatre Royal, Haymarket, 526

These Foolish Things see Daddy Nostalgie

They Who Dare (film), 198–9

Thomas, Denis, 170

Thomas, Joan, 78

Thomas, Ralph: and *Doctor* films, 203–4, 208–9, 234; works with Betty Box, 227, 299; and DB's part in *A Tale of Two Cities*, 230; and *The Wind Cannot Read*, 233; and *The Singer Not the Song*, 255; and *Victim*, 272–3; and *The High Bright Sun*, 303

Thompson, Bernard, 50, 52

Thompson, David, 489

Thompson, Edward, 327–8, 369–70, 373, 378, 384, 389, 506

Thompson, Ethel, 50

Thomson, Bob (H.A.R.), 233–5, 257, 272, 306, 522

Thomson, Jean (*née* Winterbottom), 67, 69, 387

Thorburn, Elissa, 73–4, 76, 78

Thorndike, Dame Sybil, 200, 454

'Thribb, E.J.', 543

Thynne, Lord Christopher, 505

Tickerage Mill, Uckfield, Sussex, 262

Time magazine, 281

Time Out, 457–8, 463

Times, The: Ulric works for, 29–34, 66, 406; Ulric retires from, 230; on DB's performance in *A Tale of Two Cities*, 231; criticism of DB's 'Boy' Browning portrayal, 401; interview with DB, 457

Tindle, David, 18, 482, 545

Tipthorp, Peter, 241

To Dorothy, a Son (farce), 276

Tobruk (film), 317

Todd, Ann, 293

Todd, Sir Ian, 454, 463

Todd, Richard, 179, 193

Tolstoy, Count Nikolai, 14

Tonbridge School, 519

Towne, Edward, 520

Toye, Wendy, 376

Tracy, Spencer, 17, 356, 358, 366

Treille, La *see* Haut Clermont, Le

Trevelyan, John, 267

Trevor, Elleston, 244

Triad (paperback publishers), 406–7, 422

Troke, John, 203, 262

Trollope, Joanna, 531

Trouble in Store (film), 222

Troxler, Anton (Tony), 379, 432, 482, 544

Troxler, Elisabeth, 544

Truman, Harry S., 130

Tully, Montgomery, 181

Tunes of Glory (film), 285

Tunisia, 343–4

Turing, Alan, 200

Turman, Larry, 286

Turner, Adrian, 237

Twentieth Century-Fox, 259, 338, 345

Twickenham, 41–4

Tynan, Kathleen, 344, 359–61, 368, 455–6, 495; death, 535

Tynan, Kenneth, 242, 316, 352, 368, 383, 456

Uckfield, Sussex, 73–4, 262

Under the Volcano (film), 411, 467

United States of America: unenthusiastic about Rank films, 222; DB visits with Tony, 224–6, 245–6, 260; DB's TV plays in, 300–1; *The Night Porter* condemned in, 379–80; DB's books published in, 423, 433, 435; *see also* Hollywood; New York

University College Hospital, 204

University College School, 50–3

'Upon This Rock' (NBC documentary), 350

Ure, Mary, 515

Urquhart, Major Brian, 396–7

Urquhart, Major-General Roy, 399

Ustinov, Sir Peter: on autobiography, 15–16; in Otherwise Club, 78; in *Diversion No.2*, 88–90; firewatching in war, 90

Vadim, Roger, 210

Van den Bogaerde *see* Bogaerde

van Thal, Dennis, 273, 317, 323, 472

van Thal, Herbert, 388

Variety, 281, 325, 367

Variety Club of Great Britain: gives Actor of the Year award to DB, 284, 301

Varley, Beatrice, 163

Vaughan, Helen, 325

VE Day (8 May 1945), 123

Venice, 209, 299–300, 351, 355, 358–61

Verneuil, Henri, 373

Vickers, Hugo, 505

Victim (film; earlier 'Boy Barrett'), 267–8, 270–2, 278–82, 284, 292, 320, 391

Victory (Army weekly), 128

Vidal, Gore, 546

Vidor, Charles, 244, 248, 260

Vienna, 247–8, 333

Viking Penguin, 456, 480, 501, 505, 517, 529, 536, 538

Villa Berti, Labaro, Italy, 347

Villiers, Lieut.-Commander Alan, 100

Visconti, Luchino: directs DB, 337–8, 340–2, 348–52, 355–62, 367–8; DB admires as 'The Emperor', 346, 510–11; stroke and death, 391, 447, 470; note thanking DB for visiting, 470; *see also Death in Venice*

Vision, The (TV film), 11, 493

Vitti, Monica, 313, 511

Vogue, 416

Voices in the Garden (DB), 433–5, 444–5, 447, 455; French publication, 460

Voight, Jon, 415

Vollmer, Jurgen, 406
Voltaire, François Marie Arouet, 463
Voluntary Euthanasia Society, 513, 539

Wagner, Robert, 443
Waldringfield, Suffolk, 98–9, 125, 155
Walker, Alexander, 272, 273–4, 279, 379, 422, 520
Walker, Kenneth, 281
Wallis, Hal, 357
Wallis, Minna, 246
Walsh, Bernard: finds homes for DB, 262, 283, 284, 300, 304, 311–12, 315, 317, 340–1, 346, 491, 500; and DB's reaction to Tony's death, 496, 498
Walsh, Raoul, 188
Wanamaker, Zoë, 503
Wapshott, Nicholas, 457
Ward, George Courtney, 206, 231, 264
Warhurst, Bill, 112–13
Warner Brothers, 241, 296–7, 350, 358
Warner, David, 333–4, 393–5, 398
Warner, Jack, 182
Waterhouse, Keith, 265–6
Waterman, 'Split' (speedway rider), 174
Watkyn, Arthur: For Better, For Worse (play), 176; film version, 211
Watling, Jack, 207
Watson, Gwendoline, 170
Watson, Wallace Steadman, 411, 415
Watts, Peter, 169
Waugh, Evelyn, 284; Scoop, 5
Wayne, John, 247
We Joined the Navy (farce), 286, 376
Webb, Clifton, 472
Weeks, Annie and Kate, 23–4
Weldon, Duncan, 526
Welles, Orson, 276–7, 301, 350
Wells, H.G., 290
Wenders, Wim, 467
Wesley, Mary, 505
Wessex Films, 169
West, Morris: The Shoes of the Fisherman, 335
West, Dame Rebecca, 250
West of Sunset (DB; novel), 362, 456, 462–3, 471–2
Westerby, Robert, 198
What Ever Happened to Baby Jane? (film), 371
Wheeler, Dr Peter, 2, 493, 535–7
Whisperers, The (film), 335
Whistler, Rex, 8, 14
Whitaker, Janet, 515–16, 522, 544
White, Leonard, 190–2
Whitehall, Richard, 300
Whitehead, Captain C.P., 95
Whitehorn, Katharine, 474
Whiteley, Christine, 219–20
Whiteley, Jon, 193–4, 218–20, 235, 522
Whiteley, Marsali, 219–20
Whitman, Stuart, 299
Whitman, Walt, 175
Widmark, Richard, 203, 254–5

Wightman, William, 74, 78, 81, 83, 102, 130, 406
Wilde, Cornel, 244, 246
Wilde, Oscar: sexuality, 11; on Judases, 18–19; trials, 199; films on, 267; statue, 317
Wilder, Billy, 367
Wilding, Kay see Young, Kay
Wilding, Michael, 86, 156, 203, 207
Wilding, Susan, 324–5
Williams, Alan: Barbouze, 301
Williams, Emlyn, 456; Night Must Fall (play), 75, 456
Williams, Kenneth, 272, 276
Williams, Tennessee: The Milk Train Doesn't Stop Here Anymore, 332
Williamson, H.S., 77
Wilson, A.E., 175
Wilson, Harold (later Baron), 172, 318, 332, 419, 436
Wilson, Jeremy, 238
Wilson, Max, 312, 315
Wind Cannot Read, The (film), 9, 231, 233, 235, 237, 240, 548
Windlesham, Surrey, 154
Winkler, Irwin, 310
Winner, Michael, 416
Winsen, Hetty van, 139
Winsor, Kathleen: Forever Amber, 146
Wintour, Charles, 280
Wisdom, Sir Norman, 222, 250
Wiseman, Thomas, 226, 273, 297, 299; The Romantic Englishwoman, 391, 410
Withers, Googie, 157, 187
Withersby, Sylvia and Kathleen, 213, 216, 242–3
Wogan, Terry, 462
Wolfenden, Sir John (later Baron), 200; Report, 267, 281, 318
Wollheim, Richard, 97
Wolvenhof, Château see Izegem
Woman (magazine), 274
Woman in Question, The (film), 188, 233, 236
Woman's Own, 167, 171
Wood, Christopher, 316, 335, 386
Wood, Natalie, 318, 324, 443
Woodward, Joanne, 246
Wooldridge, John, 195
Wooldridge, Susan, 198
Woolf, Virginia, 405
Wooll, Edward, 245
Woolley, Geoffrey, 34, 237
World of Suzie Wong, The (film), 241
Wrigley, Peter, 493, 512

'X, Mrs' see Gordon, Dorothy Webster

York, Michael, 14–15, 201, 319–21, 344–5
York, Patricia, 14, 344–5
York, Susannah, 326, 346
Yorke, Malcolm, 328
Young, B.A., 422
Young, John, 127–8, 130–1, 133

Young, Kay (Kay Wilding), 86, 189–90, 246, 301
Yvonne Arnaud Theatre, Guildford, 312

Zanuck, Darryl, 203, 259–60, 284, 313
Zapata, Emil, 35

Zeffirelli, Franco, 319, 352
Zetterling, Mai, 190–1, 196
Zinnemann, Fred, 317
Zwickl, Agnes, 206, 220, 242, 250, 548
Zwickl, Hans, 206, 220, 250, 273, 284